# James Burnham
## AND THE STRUGGLE
## FOR THE WORLD

# James Burnham

## AND THE STRUGGLE
## FOR THE WORLD

## *A Life*

## Daniel Kelly

ISI BOOKS
*Wilmington, Delaware*
2002

Cataloging-in-Publication Data

Kelly, Daniel
    James Burnham and the struggle for the world : a life /
    Daniel Kelly. — 1st ed. — Wilmington, Del. : ISI Books, 2002.

    p.  ; cm.

    ISBN 1-882926-76-5
    1. Burnham, James, 1905-1987. 2. Journalists—United States—Biography. 3. Anti-communist movements—United States—Biography. 4. Conservatism—United States—Biography. 5. Biographies. I. Title.

PN4874 .B844 K45 2002    2001097017
070.92 dc21         CIP

Printed in Canada

Published in the United States by:
ISI Books
P.O. Box 4431
Wilmington, Delaware
www.isibooks.org

*To my wife, Wendy Anne*

# Contents

Foreword by Richard Brookhiser     ix

Chronology     xiii

Preface     xix

Chapter 1 ◆ Student     1

Chapter 2 ◆ Teacher     21

Chapter 3 ◆ Bolshevik     41

Chapter 4 ◆ Deviationist     63

Chapter 5 ◆ Prophet     91

Chapter 6 ◆ Strategist     115

Chapter 7 ◆ Warrior     149

Chapter 8 ◆ Casualty     183

Chapter 9 ◆ Mentor     211

Chapter 10 ◆ Die-Hard     239

Chapter 11 ◆ Pathologist     269

Chapter 12 ◆ Protester     297

Chapter 13 ◆ Moralist     325

Chapter 14 ◆ Coming to Rest     355

Notes     373

Index     435

# Foreword

I N AUGUST 1991 I was in Cairo, so I read the most important news story of my life in the *International Herald Tribune,* whose headline on the fateful morning was: COMMUNISM'S COLLAPSE. History still produces problems and horrors, but the world changed for the better in that summer week when Boris Yeltsin confronted Mikhail Gorbachev—two communists struggling out of their cocoons, but at crucially different rates—and Yeltsin, the more revolutionary, prevailed.

James Burnham had died in 1987; his professional life had ended, after a massive stroke, nine years earlier. Probably only his former colleagues at *National Review* connected him with the moment. But if the fall of communism was chiefly the work of Ronald Reagan—and it was—and if the road to Reagan's election had been prepared by the postwar American conservative movement—and it had—then Burnham, a key figure in that movement, deserved a share of the credit.

That is one reason for reading Daniel Kelly's keen and thorough book. Another is to follow the arc of a twentieth-century mind. Burnham passed through three phases. The first was ideological. In the early thirties, as Kelly relates, Burnham, a well-born young professor at New York University, where he specialized in aesthetics and philosophy, caught the communist virus (Trotskyite strain). Suddenly his life became interesting. He corresponded with Trotsky himself on matters of *weltpolitik*—how degenerate a worker's state was the Soviet Union?—while scheming in the tiny world of New York hard-left grouplets. As he dreamed of the future and stacked the deck of the present, Burnham continued to teach his courses, to host black-tie dinners at his Sutton Place apartment, and to spend his vacation playing high-stakes *chemin de fer* at French casinos. Such anomalies are amusing, but since communism is a wicked doctrine, this part of the story is cautionary.

Burnham emerged from his dogmatic slumbers into a phase of anti-ideology. In the first flush of liberation, he expressed his newfound freedom with a rather ideological rigor and zest. His most famous book, *The Managerial Revolution,* breathes this atmosphere. The real revolution, the ex-revolutionary explained, was a worldwide putsch of bureaucrats and organizers, who would divide the planet into superpowers whose contentions masked their similarity. Readers eagerly consumed Burnham's tale of their impending enslavement. *The Machiavellians,* perhaps Burnham's best book, dug deeper into the analysis of modern social forces and offered a wan measure of hope. Clear-eyed analysts of politics such as Machiavelli (and Burnham) could see that all ideologies were shams concealing the ambitions of the men who advanced them. But in the circulation of elites, bits of freedom occasionally fall, like table scraps, to the rest of us. If we studied the world and our rulers without illusion, we would be better able to seize our opportunities.

As time passed, these anti-ideological views of Burnham's, never abandoned, mellowed somewhat. All ideologies, it turned out, were not equally oppressive. The people who split Trotsky's head were bidding to rule the entire world, not just their portion of it. Only the United States, and a few heroic Europeans— Burnham admired the postwar Charles de Gaulle—stood in their way. So Burnham began a struggle—his column in *National Review,* begun in 1955, was first called "The Third World War," then "The Protracted Conflict"—against communism.

But coexisting with his second phase was a third, fostered by the demands of journalism but also generated by an aspect of his intelligence, which was as real as his fascination with systems. This third phase might be called "observant." To me, the greatest merit of Kelly's book is the fine eye it shows for the myriad perceptions of this phase. Burnham is not just sitting at Machiavelli's elbow, watching the big boys; anything might catch his attention. The interstates, he wrote after driving them, were an engineering achievement comparable to the medieval cathedrals, though unlike the cathedrals, they were boring and inhuman; strip malls were their "all-too-human . . . dialectical opposite." The Woodstock rock festival in 1969 was more than dirty, copulating teenagers: it was "a mass ritual and mystery, a surge out of the deep and hidden springs of the spirit." From nudity to spandex: "Americans," Burnham wrote of the hippies' parents, are "the fattest people on earth." Their avoirdupois "exuded, cascaded, ballooned, quivered, undulated in blobs and globules." Burnham studied behavior as well as appearances, formulating a collection of gnomic sayings that became known around the *National Review* office as "Burnham's Laws." "Just as good, isn't," said one; "You cannot invest in retrospect," warned another. Nothing could be further from Trotsky, who might have profited from the eighth law—"Every member must pay his dues"—and its application to a band of visionary gangsters.

Frequently, Burnham returned to one observation: the steadiness of the country on which he had once hoped to lay revolutionary hands. "Inventions multiply, American goods, aircraft and citizens range the earth and the moon, roads and cities spread over the land, gasoline is in the pumps. . . . The country shrugs off the fires of the arsonists, the crime of the cities and the riots of the youth as a great ship shrugs off the waves." That almost sounds like Ronald Reagan; the attitude is surely Reaganesque. Reagan's confidence in America's strength, like Burnham's, is one of the reasons, maybe the main reason, America buried communism.

As these quotations show, when Burnham was in his journalistic groove he wrote very well—always clearly, often powerfully, never flashily. When one of his sharper editorials entangled *National Review* in a lawsuit, Burnham, in the witness box, told the plaintiff's lawyer that he had written his assault in "fifteen or twenty minutes." How long did you take to revise it, the lawyer asked. "I don't need to revise," Burnham said.

I was fortunate enough to have my prose revised by James Burnham during the two years when, as a summer intern and an associate, I overlapped with him at *National Review.* My senior colleagues, all good editors, each worked in his own way. William F. Buckley Jr. delighted in adding the kicker closing. James Burnham would grasp the thrust of the argument (deep arguments I made at 22) and make it, with the minimum necessary adjustments, clear, carefully trimming any globules. The book you are about to begin will allow you, if you did not have my luck, to have an experience of James Burnham.

— *Richard Brookhiser*

# Chronology

1905     James Burnham, the first of his parents' three sons, is born in Chicago on November 22.

1914     Moves to the Chicago lakeshore suburb of Kenilworth.

1921     Is enrolled at the Canterbury School, a private Catholic boarding school in New Milford, Connecticut, from which he graduates at the head of his class.

1923     Matriculates at Princeton, where he majors in English.

1927     Graduates from Princeton as his class's top scholar. Enters Balliol College, Oxford, where he studies English literature and medieval philosophy, and where he gives up his religious beliefs. Makes plans with his professor of philosophy at Princeton, Philip E. Wheelwright, to launch a literary-philosophical journal, to be called the *Symposium*.

1929     Joins the philosophy department at New York University's Washington Square College, where Wheelwright is philosophy chairman. Gains a reputation as a specialist in aesthetics.

1930     Publishes the first issue of the *Symposium*.

1931     With Wheelwright, co-authors a primer on philosophical method, *Introduction to Philosophical Analysis.*

1932     Becomes engaged to Martha Dodd, daughter of historian William E. Dodd, but for undisclosed reasons the engagement is soon broken off. Horrified by the Depression, fears for the survival of Western civilization. Is increasingly drawn to politics. Moves toward Marxism under the influence of NYU colleague Sidney Hook. Publishes star-struck review of Leon Trotsky's *History of the Russian Revolution.*

1933    Comes close to joining the Communist Party, but in the end is put off by its position on the "Negro Question" (the Communist position calls for an autonomous black republic in the Deep South). Instead, encouraged by Hook, joins the fledgling American Workers Party (AWP).

1934    Marries Marcia Lightner of St. Paul, Minnesota. The *Symposium* folds. Works for a merger between the AWP and a tiny American Trotskyist organization called the Communist League of America. Becomes a Trotskyist when the merger goes through. Joins Max Shachtman as co-editor of the *New International,* a Trotskyist theoretical journal.

1935    Backs a proposed "French Turn," a plan for Trotskyists to enroll in the Socialist Party, break it up by worsening its factionalism, and then snare its more radical members for Trotskyism.

1936    The Burnhams' first child, Marcie, is born. The Trotsykists carry out the "French Turn."

1937    Buys an eighteenth-century farmhouse in Kent, Connecticut. In a debate with Trotsky, denies that the Soviet Union is a true "workers' state."

1938    Plays a leading role in the Trotskyists' new party, the Socialist Workers Party (SWP), holding a seat on its political committee and contributing a regular column to its newspaper, the *Socialist Appeal,* while continuing to co-edit the *New International.*

1939    When war breaks out in Europe, condemns the Soviet invasion of Poland as pure imperialism, and rejects Trotsky's claim that good revolutionaries must "unconditionally" defend the USSR. The issue forces the SWP toward a split. The Burnhams' second child, James Bernard, is born.

1940    Is expelled from the SWP by the pro-Trotsky majority. Joins a new party of Trotskyist schismatics, but resigns almost at once, explaining that he has lost his faith in socialism.

1941    Publishes *The Managerial Revolution,* which becomes a bestseller.

1943    Publishes *The Machiavellians*. The Burnhams' third child, John Lightner, is born.

1944    Writes a paper for the Office of Strategic Services (OSS) on Soviet postwar political and territorial ambitions.

1945    Publishes "Lenin's Heir" in *Partisan Review*, where he sits on the editorial advisory board.

1947    Publishes *The Struggle for the World*, which grows out of his 1944 OSS paper. Enthusiastically endorses the Truman Doctrine. Meets and is deeply impressed by Jerzy Giedroyc and Józef Czapski, who in Paris put out the free Polish journal *Kultura*.

1948    Testifies before a House Committee on Un-American Activities subcommittee on a bill requiring communists to register with the attorney general's office. Meets Arthur Koestler, who becomes one of his collaborators in anticommunist political activity. Meets André Malraux, with whom he co-authors *The Case for De Gaulle*. Takes his family on a sweeping car tour of the United States, and comes home buoyed by Middle America's willingness to resist communism.

1949    Becomes an eager advocate of "political warfare," believing it to be the best Cold War strategy for America. Leaves NYU to serve as an undercover consultant to the Office of Policy Coordination (OPC), the U.S. government's new covert action arm, soon to be integrated into the CIA. The Burnhams move to Washington.

1950    Publishes *The Coming Defeat of Communism*. Helps to establish the Congress for Cultural Freedom (CCF), which is largely a CIA venture.

1951    Goes to India, Japan, and other Asian countries to help launch CCF affiliates. Joins the executive board of the CCF's American affiliate, the American Committee for Cultural Freedom (ACCF). Is named a trustee of the Free Europe University in Exile, in which the CIA has a major hand. Tries unsuccessfully to enlist mobster Frank Costello in an operation to nab communist spies. Works with the Senate Subcommittee on Internal Security during its investigation of the Institute for Pacific Relations.

1952  Supports Dwight D. Eisenhower against anti-interventionist Ohio sena-
      tor Robert A. Taft for the Republican presidential nomination.

1953  Publishes *Containment or Liberation?* Gives up his CIA consultancy, prob-
      ably under pressure from the agency. The Burnhams settle permanently
      in Kent. Writes introductions for *What Europe Thinks of America,* a col-
      lection of essays by some of his European friends, and *The Secret War for
      the A-Bomb,* by Medford Evans, which warns of espionage at U.S. atomic
      energy facilities. Resigns from the editorial advisory board of *Partisan
      Review* at the request of the editors.

1954  Publishes *The Web of Subversion.* Takes his family on a five-month trip to
      Europe. Resigns from the American Committee for Cultural Freedom,
      which he thinks wishy-washy on the issue of domestic communism.
      Accepts an invitation from William F. Buckley Jr. to help edit a conser-
      vative weekly magazine Buckley hopes to found.

1955  Reluctantly agrees to testify as an expert witness for the Justice
      Department at a hearing on whether his old Trotskyist comrade Max
      Shachtman should be allowed a passport. The first issue of Buckley's
      magazine, *National Review* (NR), appears. Serves *NR* as a senior editor
      and columnist on foreign affairs.

1956  After the failure of the Hungarian revolt against Soviet domination, pro-
      poses as a way of ending Moscow's satellite empire the mutual with-
      drawal of NATO and Soviet forces from central and eastern Europe and
      the reunification, neutralization, and disarmament of Germany. The pro-
      posal triggers protests at *NR*.

1957  Is named to act as Buckley's stand-in at *NR* when Buckley is absent from
      the magazine.

1958  Becomes de facto chief editor of the *National Review Bulletin,* a newsletter-
      style publication that comes out alternate weeks after *NR* goes biweekly.

1959  Publishes *Congress and the American Tradition.* Delivers a series of lectures
      at the Carnegie Institute of Technology which are critical of liberalism.
      These lectures provide the core of his next book, *Suicide of the West: An
      Essay on the Meaning and Destiny of Liberalism.*

1960    Prefers New York's governor, Nelson A. Rockefeller, to Vice President Richard M. Nixon for the GOP presidential nomination. At the invitation of the Republican National Convention's Rules Committee chairman, sends the committee a systematic outline of ideas for a Republican foreign policy.

1962    Suffers bitter disillusionment with France's president, Charles de Gaulle, who surrenders French Algeria to native nationalist rebels. Urges that *NR* publicly oppose the right-wing sectarian John Birch Society.

1963    Condemns the U.S.–Soviet nuclear test ban treaty. Leads a six-session seminar at Princeton that carries forward his criticism of what he calls "the liberal syndrome."

1964    Publishes *Suicide of the West.*

1965    An *NR* editorial he had written in 1962 attacking pro-Soviet apologist Linus Pauling and others leads his targets to sue *NR*. The plaintiffs lose at trial.

1966    Lectures on American foreign policy at the South African Institute of International Affairs at South Africa's Witwatersrand University, then tours the country.

1967    Publishes *The War We Are In: The Last Decade and the Next,* a collection of his *NR* columns on the Cold War and American foreign policy.

1971    Is one of a group of prominent conservatives who announce that they are "suspending" their support (the phrase is Burnham's) for the Nixon administration in order to underline their disapproval of the liberal tilt of its domestic measures and détente-oriented foreign policy. Soon after, condemns Nixon's economic policies, which include wage and price controls.

1972    Opposes the U.S.–Soviet SALT and ABM treaties, and says that détente is usually a euphemism for appeasement.

1973    Voices skepticism regarding Nixon's Vietnam cease-fire agreement. Denounces administration attempts at a Watergate cover-up.

1974    Helps draft a statement for Republican-Conservative senator James L.

Buckley of New York calling on Nixon to resign. Visits Yugsolavia, his only trip to a communist-ruled country.

1975    Decries the Helsinki accords as a give-away to Moscow. In an introduction to a reissue of *Suicide of the West* expresses a more pessimistic view of the West's future than he had in the original. Retinal problems weaken his eyesight.

1976    Prefers Ronald Reagan to incumbent Gerald R. Ford for the GOP presidential nomination. Tells Buckley he plans to begin a semi-retirement.

1977    Criticizes President Jimmy Carter's foreign policy, but thinks the policy also has redeeming features.

1978    In January, while flying home from a debate at the University of South Carolina, suddenly loses much of his eyesight, and is diagnosed as likely soon to go blind. In November suffers a massive stroke. Makes a good recovery, but cannot retrieve his short-term memory, and so must give up work entirely. After the stroke, his eyesight mysteriously ceases to deteriorate.

1980    Receives a lavish tribute from Buckley at *NR's* twenty-fifth anniversary dinner, which he is able to attend.

1982    Suffers a heart attack, but recovers. Marcia dies suddenly of a pneumonia-like viral infection.

1983    Is awarded the Presidential Medal of Freedom by Ronald Reagan at a White House ceremony. Receives the Richard M. Weaver Award for Scholarly Letters from the Ingersoll Foundation.

1987    Tests reveal that he is suffering from inoperable cancer of the kidneys and lungs. Returns to the Church and receives last rites. Dies at home in Kent on July 28. Funeral service is held at the local Catholic Church. Is buried in the town graveyard next to Marcia.

# *Preface*

WHEN I WAS IN college in the late 1950s my father used to pass on to me issues of a new conservative political magazine to which he subscribed. The magazine was called *National Review*, and it was in its pages that I first encountered James Burnham. A senior editor and the magazine's columnist on foreign affairs, Burnham struck a responsive chord in me from the start. One reason for this was his somber-toned realism, his unfailing awareness of the tragic vein running through human life. He seemed to see the world as it actually was rather than through the distorting lens of traditional American optimism (characterized by the faith that in the end all tears can be dried). Another reason was his prose. Carefully nuanced and vividly concrete, it always did justice to the world's anomalies and contradictions. Still another was his avoidance of a moral approach to all issues. Unlike many of his *NR* colleagues, he did not treat every political question as if it posed a choice between good and evil. Nor, to my delight, did he ever bow to the liberal etiquette that governed so much political discussion in the 1950s and after. The living embodiment of what would later come to be known as political incorrectness, he never hesitated to say things it was considered in bad taste to say, despite their being true.

In other ways, too, Burnham was a singular thinker. For example, he sometimes grouped Adam Smith with Karl Marx as an "ideologue" (i.e., one whose ideas sprang more from emotional preferences than from historical experience), he called for U.S. recognition of Communist China at a time when conservatives heatedly opposed such a step, and he urged Washington to transfer sovereignty over the Panama Canal to the Panamanian government, a position that unfailingly raised conservative hackles. Furthermore, he had once been a trusted adviser to Leon Trotsky, had taught aesthetics (of all things) at New York University, and knew well the thought not only of such conservative intellectual stalwarts as Edmund Burke, but also the writings of Machiavelli and the twentieth-century "Machiavellian" theorists Vilfredo Pareto, Roberto Michels, and Gaetano Mosca. In addition, he had once had close ties with the modernist and originally Marxist *Partisan Review,* flagship of the cultural avant-garde. Even more surprising—and this summed up his peculiarity in a nutshell—he admired the work of Picasso, an artist most conservatives detested. At the early *National Review,* then, Burnham seemed an odd man out, someone who had wandered in from another world. Many years later, with my curiosity about him as strong as ever, I decided to make him the subject of a biography.

As I studied Burnham through his writings and letters and through the recollections of people who had known him, it became clear that he did not limit his signature phrase, "the struggle for the world"—the title of his 1947 book—to the Cold War alone. For although he applied the phrase only to the Western-Soviet conflict, which he usually viewed as the paramount conflict of his time, he first signaled a climactic, global struggle in his Trotskyist writings, which dwelt on a worldwide contest between "workers" and "bosses." In 1940, when he gave up Marxism, he replaced the Marxist class war with a new form of world struggle, one pitting old-fashioned capitalists and socialists against a rising elite of "managers." From the 1950s on, he paid increasing attention to Third World hostility to the West, which he thought might engender still another kind of world struggle (and in the late 1950s he flirted briefly with a variant of this idea: a conflict between the West and an awakened Asia). At first he tied Western–Third World clashes to the Cold War, warning that the USSR was seeking to marshal the Third World against the West. But by the 1970s he could envisage a Western–Third World conflict as an autonomous collision, one in which communism played no important part. And from the 1930s to the 1970s, he also pointed to a far-flung duel between ideologues and realists, the former fostering centralizing tyranny and social dissolution, the latter, personal freedom and social order. In short, the theme of a "struggle for the world," whether between communists and anticommunists or some other set of antagonists, formed an enduring leitmotif of Burnham's thinking. Hence my use of the phrase in the title of this book.

◆   ◆   ◆   ◆

Burnham's name was once well known to the educated public. Catapulted to intellectual stardom by his book *The Managerial Revolution* (1941), he retained that status for approximately fifteen years. But in the 1950s his star began to dim as his hard-line anticommunism and "anti-anti-McCarthyism" led to his expulsion from the ranks of America's celebrity pundits, a cohort largely liberal and anti-McCarthy. In the late 1960s his one-time prominence was all but extinguished, and aside from an occasional *New York Times* op-ed piece, he confined himself to articles and columns for *National Review*. In 1978 his professional life ceased completely when a stroke left him permanently deprived of his short-term memory. At the time of his death in 1987, his name still resonated for an aging group on the Right. But younger conservatives who recognized the name often knew little more of him than that he had written some famous books, including trenchant volumes on the Cold War, and had once been a lofty personage at *National Review*.

People who today remember Burnham sometimes picture him as an apocalyptic prophet—and one whose predictions not seldom failed to materialize. It is true that he was wont to don the prophet's mantle, often with indifferent results (though frequently his forecasts stumbled more in their secondary detail than in their primary thrust). But Burnham's flair lay not in prophecy but in synthesis, in spotting connections and patterns that others missed, and uniting them into broader, more significant wholes. Thus, fusing the separate insights of other observers, he became the first to construct a comprehensive theory concerning the trend toward ever-greater private and public sector bureaucratic rule, and to plumb the ramifications of this trend. He was also the first to offer a detailed account of modern American liberalism that gave attention not only to that worldview's political axioms, sociological dimensions, and psychological sources, but to its historical origins and present functional meaning as well. Most important, he was the first to provide an all-embracing study of the Cold War that brought together an exploration of its causes and current progress, an assessment of the strengths and weaknesses (political, cultural, economic, strategic, geopolitical, psychological, etc.) of its major adversaries, and a grand strategy for achieving Western victory. To have tackled any one of these huge subjects in the able way that Burnham did would have sufficed to make him noteworthy. To have tackled all three (and more) makes him one of his era's most remarkable political intelligences—and a thinker who should not be allowed to sink into oblivion.

◆　◆　◆　◆

Many people helped me to write this book, among them Daniel Bell, June Boissonas, Linda Bridges, Frances Bronson, Richard Brookhiser, Joseph Bryant III, Priscilla L. Buckley, William F. Buckley Jr., James B. Burnham, John L. Burnham, Mary Effie Burnham, Mrs. Philip Burnham, Nelson R. Burr, Emma Cohn, Edward T. Cone, John Patrick Diggins, Lev E. Dobriansky, Tessa DiNicola, Ernest Erber, Joseph Frank, Norman Fruman, Warren G. Fugitt, Emanuel Geltman, John L. Gillis Jr., L.P. Gillis, Albert Glotzer, Clement Greenberg, George F. Greiner, M.D., Suzanne Gillis Hamm, Jeffrey Hart, Karl Hess, Irving Howe, Norman Jacobs, John Jones, George F. Kennan, Russell Kirk, Lincoln Kirstein, Henry Kissinger, Irving Kristol, Katherine Lightner, Nancy Macdonald, Jean Paul Mandler, Morris A. Mayers, J. P. McFadden, Thomas Molnar, Alex W. Olsen, Irving Panken, Cleo Paturis, William Phillips, Joseph L. Rauh Jr., Alan Reynolds, William F. Rickenbacker, William A. Rusher, Donald Seldin, M.D., Yetta Shactman, Edward Shils, Oscar Shoenfeld, Kevin J. Smant, Charles Sternberg, Ralph de Toledano, Diana Trilling, Gus Tyler, Jeanne Wacker, David Wigdor, Jane Wilmerding, Lucius Wilmerding, and Curtin Winsor. Unfortunately, not all are still alive; nonetheless, I want to thank them all again for their assistance.

I also want to thank Jeremy Beer, Patricia Bozell, and Jeffrey O. Nelson of ISI Books, as well as Christopher B. Briggs, until recently senior editor at ISI Books and now executive director of Aid to the Church in Russia, for the able job they did with a daunting manuscript.

Among the many people to whom I am indebted, the most important is my wife, Wendy Anne Korbel Kelly, who was always on hand with a patient ear, a critical eye, and unflagging encouragement. It is not hyperbole to say that in a real sense this book is the result of her work as well as mine.

I received help as well from many institutions. My thanks go first to the Research Institute of the City University of New York for covering some of my research costs. Thanks are also due to the Beinecke Rare Book and Manuscript Library, Yale University; the British Library; Butler Library, Columbia University; the Canterbury School; the Library of Congress; Eaton's Ranch, Wolf, Wyoming; the Federal Bureau of Investigation; the Hoover Institution on War, Revolution and Peace; Houghton Library, Harvard University; the Ingersoll Foundation; the Kenilworth Historical Society; Lilly Library, Indiana University; Mugar Library,

Boston University; New Trier Township High School; the New York Public Library; the New York University Archives, Bobst Library, New York University; Regenstein Library, the University of Chicago; Seeley G. Mudd Manuscript Library, Princeton University; Sterling Memorial Library, Yale University; Tamiment Library; Van Pelt Library, the University of Pennsylvania; and the York College Library.

The judgments the book renders and the conclusions it reaches are my own, as are any errors it contains.

*Daniel Kelly*
*New York City*
*August 2001*

# Chapter 1

# Student

T HE 1880S, YEARS OF collapsing grain prices, brought financial ruin to farmers around the world. Among the victims were Harry and Fanny Burnham of Yaxley, near Peterborough, England, who, after a futile struggle to wring a living out of the soil, gave up in the mid-1880s and moved to Canada. There, they may have intended to raise horses.[1] But if so, they did not get very far with their plan, for they soon moved again, this time to St. Paul, Minnesota, where they finally settled. What kind of work they took up in St. Paul is not known. But it seems to have paid better than farming.

Of the Burnhams' three sons and three daughters, one, Claude, born in Yaxley in 1882,[2] became a striking success in the classic American mold. While a schoolboy in St. Paul, Claude landed a job delivering newspapers at the head office of railroad tycoon James J. Hill's Great Northern line, and at fourteen was hired by the line as an office boy. In love with railroads, and born with a head for figures, he began studying the economics of railroad traffic in the Far East, and within a few years was an expert in the field.

As luck would have it, Hill, too, took a keen interest in the Far Eastern side of the business. Impressed by Claude's dedication, in 1902 he transferred the eager office boy to a job in the foreign traffic department of another Hill line, the Chicago-based Chicago, Burlington and Quincy. In 1904 Claude was named the Burlington's foreign traffic agent and in 1910 its vice president in charge of traffic (which probably made him the country's youngest railroad vice president). In 1917 he moved up once again, this time to the post of executive vice president of the line. A year later, when America's involvement in World War I led to a federal takeover of the railroads, he was made federal manager of the Burlington and of the Quincy, Ohio and Kansas City line as well. Still in his thirties, he had joined the country's business elite.

Meanwhile, Claude's private life also flourished. In 1904 he married. His bride, Mary Mae Gillis,[3] also owed her presence in America to rural hardship in Britain, though her immigrant ancestor, Finley Gillis, a crofter from the Scottish Highlands, had crossed the ocean decades before the Burnhams. Landing at Canada's Prince Edward Island in 1803, Gillis labored for eleven years as the indentured servant of a farmer, saved whatever money he earned, and was eventually able to buy a farm of his own. Later in the century, his descendant James Gillis migrated, like the Burnhams, to Minnesota. There he settled in Stillwater, joined the police force, and with his wife, Bridget, an Irish immigrant, raised six children, the same number as the Burnhams. One of this brood was Mary Mae.

Born in Stillwater in 1880, Mary Mae Gillis grew up to be a strong-willed woman whose sometimes imperious manner earned her the nickname "Bloody Mary." A photograph of her taken at the turn of the century shows a handsome girl with an oval face, a high forehead, and eyes that aim a deadpan look at the camera. While a student in Minneapolis at the University of Minnesota she met Claude. Tall and dark, combining good looks with good humor, he so dazzled her that, despite his being a Protestant and she a rigorous Catholic, she did not discourage his suit. "She probably considered herself very lucky to have landed him," said one of her relatives. "She was simply besotted with him"—and would remain so for the rest of her life.

After their marriage, the young couple at first lived in Chicago, and it was there, on November 22, 1905, that their first child, James, was born. Two more children followed: David, in March 1907, and Philip, in July 1910. But with a trio of boys to raise, the Burnhams may have found city life too confining, for in 1914 they moved to the recently built northern suburb of Kenilworth, a well-heeled "village" on the shore of Lake Michigan that sported large houses, maple- and elm-shaded streets whose names were taken from the works of Sir Walter Scott, and a rail link to the city.[4] The house they bought stood on Roslyn Road, a five-minute walk from the lake. It was a three-story, twelve-room, brick and timber

structure, with a lawn in front, a garage in back, and broa
woodwork within. One frequent visitor thought the house
feel" and an atmosphere reminiscent of a library.[5]

The Burnhams seem to have fitted comfortably into the Ke
of early twentieth-century, upper-middle-class suburban life. Gol
lake provided recreation; a chauffeur, a cook, and a maid helped e
of daily existence; and a country club furnished the pleasures of
the fit was not perfect. The North Shore suburbs were Re͵ᴜᴏɪican and
Protestant, while Claude Burnham, though qualifying on the score of religion,
was a loyal Democrat (as a teenager he had become well known in St. Paul for
his soapbox oratory),[6] and Mary Mae was a Catholic at a time when Catholicism—a religion of working-class immigrants like her parents—fell short of full
social acceptability. Thus, though not markedly at variance with their neighbors,
the Burnhams were not quite "regular," either. Their departures from the norm
do not seem to have caused them any trouble. But decades later, James Burnham,
who was raised in his mother's faith, wrote that he had always thought of himself
as "non-national," partly because of religion.[7]

◆　◆　◆　◆

James Burnham—"Jim," as he was called—took after his mother. He had the
same light coloring and cast of feature and the same matter-of-fact attitude
toward the world. His life in Kenilworth was typical for a boy of that place and
time. He went to school, played tennis, read, swam in Lake Michigan, and took
piano lessons. On the Fourth of July he attended the local parade, and would later
remember the "carriages and cars elaborately decorated with flags and bunting;
bicycles covered with red, white, and blue ribbons; the smaller children dressed as
Uncle Sam, Minute Men, drum-and-fife boys," readings of the Declaration of
Independence, and oratory "full of flag-waving phrases, talk about the Father of
his Country and patriot blood." When evening came his father would set off railroad flares, "with their special kind of red and green glowing light," on the lawn.
Then the day would end with a trip to the lake shore to let loose paper balloons
filled with air heated by burning wood shavings.[8]

In one way, however, Jim's life deviated from the norm. Like many boys, he
loved railroads, but unlike most, he also had a father high up in the railroad

ness, and so could boast of adventures that others could only dream of. From the time he was five, he traveled far and wide over the vast American railroad network,[9] eating in dining cars, sleeping in Pullmans (until his father acquired a private car), riding in locomotives, and perhaps trying on the engineer's cap and sending off a blast or two from the steam whistle, as cities and villages, mountains, prairies, and forests went racing by. Though in the distant future he would have to give up railroads (whose passenger service was by that time disappearing) for automobiles, drives around the country—long treks covering thousands of miles—would always provide one of his major pleasures.

Among Jim's favorite destinations was Eaton's Ranch,[10] near Sheridan, Wyoming, one of the new dude ranches that had begun to crop up in the recently tamed West and a frequent Burnham vacation spot. Spread over several thousand acres along the slopes of the Bighorn Range, the ranch offered guests an array of "western" pastimes, including trail-riding through stands of cottonwood and pine up into the nearby mountains. To Jim, an enthusiastic horseman, hardly anything could top a stay at Eaton's.

In September 1918, two months short of his thirteenth birthday, Jim entered New Trier Township High School in neighboring Winnetka (Kenilworth had no high school of its own). There he embarked on a college preparatory program: English and math, Latin and French, and ancient and American history. In the summer of 1921, he added typing, a skill he would use for the next six decades. He was one of New Trier's best students, running up an impressive number of A's; his few B's came mostly in "physical training."[11] When not busy with schoolwork, he read, polished his tennis game, and, a member of the school radio club, tinkered with his crystal set.

In his second year at New Trier, the school literary magazine, *New Trier Echoes,* ran what is probably James Burnham's first published work. This one-page story, "Cam's Camouflage,"[12] tells of a burglar who slips into a seemingly rich family's house one Christmas Eve, only to discover that the family has lost its wealth. So moved is the thief that instead of stealing, he disguises himself in a Santa Claus outfit lying at hand, and passes out presents. The story's O. Henry-ish irony may make it sound like a typical piece of high school fiction. But it is raised above that level by a verbal fluency and a narrative skill far exceeding those usually displayed by fourteen-year-old authors.

◆ ◆ ◆ ◆

Jim did not graduate from New Trier, for after his third year there his parents transferred him to the Canterbury School in New Milford, Connecticut. Founded in 1915 by a group of ambitious Catholic laymen, Canterbury was intended to solve a problem such people faced. Though enrolling their sons in Catholic secondary schools for the religious education these schools provided, they hoped to send them on to Ivy League colleges for the social prestige the latter bestowed. But this ambition was fiercely resisted by the priests in charge of the Catholic secondary schools, who frowned on the Ivy League as Protestant, if not downright pagan, and often refused to supply the recommendations and transcripts necessary for college admission. Hence, the creation of Canterbury: since the school was Catholic, it taught religion, but since it was lay-controlled, students could apply, say, to Yale.[13] Why the Burnhams decided to move their sons to Canterbury is not known, but a desire for a Catholic education plus the prospect of the Ivy League may well have prompted the choice.

So it was that in September 1921 fifteen-year-old Jim, with his fourteen-year-old brother David in tow (Philip, eleven, was still too young) set out for rustic New Milford, at whose north end, atop a steep hill overlooking the town green, sat the school. Still rather new in 1921, Canterbury had only sixty students, who trooped in noisy bands from classroom to library, refectory to dormitory, playing field to chapel, and on Friday evenings to movies (Harold Lloyd comedies were the favorite fare) brought up the hill from the humdrum world below.

Jim entered Canterbury as a fifth-form boy, the equivalent of a high school junior. From the start one of the school's top students, in his first year he earned the highest grades in his form and the second highest in the school, and in his second year the highest in both. He also rolled up the best scores any Canterbury student had ever achieved on the math and English tests that were the forerunners of today's SATs. Only in French, in which his grades never rose above the mid-80s, was his performance merely average.[14]

True to the boarding-school ethos, Canterbury kept its boys busy outdoors as well as in. Tall and slim, Jim played second-string end on the football team. When the school launched an intramural hockey league of four teams, he was named, appropriately enough, captain of the Owls, who rarely won. But he came into his own on the tennis court, taking second place in the 1922 Senior Tournament.

Jim also exercised another old talent at Canterbury. In November 1922, at the behest of the headmaster, Nelson Hume, this alumnus of the New Trier radio club was entrusted with the highly responsible task of tuning in the broadcast of the Yale-Princeton game on the school's new "radio receiving apparatus"—so reported the school paper, the *Tabard*.

At the beginning of his second term, Jim entered the competition for a position on the *Tabard*. But he either failed, or as seems more likely, dropped out of the running, for his name never appeared on the masthead. It may be that he preferred the school literary magazine, the *Quill* (renamed the *Canterbury Quarterly* in his senior year), which offered more scope for a student who wanted to write. But Jim not only published many pieces in the magazine; as a senior, he also served as its business manager, the first of many magazine posts he would hold over the next half-century.

Markedly diverse in kind and tone, Jim's school writings offer a comprehensive look at the mind of the young James Burnham. The earliest, "Riding a Morning Roundup,"[15] is a third-person account of a horse roundup at a Wyoming dude ranch. Obviously based on Eaton's Ranch, the piece offers no opinions but only a vivid and detailed description of the roundup. Quite different is a review Jim wrote for the *Quill* of the explorer Vilhjalmur Stefansson's book *The Friendly Arctic*. Called "A New View of the Arctic,"[16] the review discusses polar exploration and delights in Stefansson's correction of common misconceptions about the Far North. It also approves a remark of Stefansson's that when explorers encounter Arctic hardships, "the well-bred men of the better class [as Jim puts it] easily adapt themselves to any conditions such as these, while the common workers of the expedition are always the first to complain of them." This stuffy linking of social status and moral fortitude, at the time a commonplace in adventure fiction for boys, has no echo in Jim's other writings then or later. But in its disapproval of people who cannot endure adversity, it foreshadows the adult James Burnham, who felt scorn for those unable to face the world's hard truths.

Jim appears in still another guise in two history essays that are probably his first published pieces of political analysis. One of these, "Unusual Politicians,"[17] hails eighteenth-century Britain's Whigs and especially Charles Edward Fox, whom Jim celebrates as "an outstanding example of a really great politician . . . in spite of his follies" because he possessed the virtue (a cardinal virtue in the adult James

Burnham's eyes) of grounding his political positions in "realities." The other, "Two Men, Two Ideas, and Washington,"[18] won a gold medal as Canterbury's best history essay of 1923. Mainly a look at the differences between Hamilton and Jefferson, the essay argues that both men were essential to the infant American republic because each served as a brake on the other's excesses. Without a counterweight, Jim wrote, Jefferson's ideas "might easily have resulted in anarchy" and Hamilton's "in suppression of liberty." Washington brought stability, he went on, but it was Lincoln who "expressed the idea we should strive for, the correct combination of governmental theories: America resolves that 'government of the people, by the people, and for the people shall not perish from the earth.'"[18]

In addition, Jim supplied the *Quill* with fiction. Almost all his stories are romantic fantasies, and in mood and tone so distant from his essays that they appear to be the work of a different person. For example, the brief "John's Dreamy Voyage"[19] tells of a boy "in the land of imagination" who sails through the universe "in a fairy ship" until he sees "on a throne the Queen of the Star— his Queen of all Stars—" with an empty throne beside her. Here the story ends, suggesting that the author has fallen prey to a mammoth crush.

Two more stories, both resting on the romantic cliché of the rebel who has withdrawn from society, reveal yet another side of Jim's imagination. The first, "The Lens of Lost Ages,"[20] concerns a self-described "exile from humanity," who is "rejected by my fellow human beings," and lives alone in a forest "where so-called civilization could no longer have its effect on my study and my research." Yet something keeps drawing the exile away from "silent study and serious thought" to nearby hills on a quest he cannot explain. One day, a wraith-like figure leads him to a half-ruined hut in the hills. Inside, he finds a mysterious lens through which he can see the hills as they looked in prehistoric times when fierce beasts roamed and fought on their wooded slopes. "And I lived thereafter in the long lost hut," the exile ends his story, "and I dwelt in peace and contentment."

The second story, "The Stars and the Rushing Waters,"[21] is about another, but happier, solitary rebel. Much admired by those who meet him, but puzzling to them, this person leads a life of monastic simplicity, spending his nights walking along the bank of a great river. Only once does he disclose anything about himself. He had originally intended to become a lawyer, he says, but noting that lawyers "never had a restful hour in which they might sit still and think," and knowing that he "had to think," he had given up the idea of practicing law, left his native land, and come to the great river. One day the thinker disappears. Yet the river valley's inhabitants know that he has not gone away, but become "a real part of the clear shining stars and the endlessly rushing waters."

Both stories have heroes who turn their backs on a world hostile or indifferent to thought to lead lives wholly given up to thinking. Jim's attraction to this theme may mean no more than that he was young. But perhaps he sensed that he, too, someone who "had to think," might someday find himself an outsider, unable and unwilling to fall in with mainstream views.

A final story, "The Green, Green Hills,"[22] has to do with a child who leads an idyllic life in the country with his mother and grandfather. Every afternoon, the child goes for a walk in the woods with the grandfather, and as they walk asks questions: why do birds sing, and stars shine? Why are the hills green? "That, oh little child, only they . . . and the years . . . can tell you," the grandfather answers. "Then one day, the old man died," reads the story's last line, "and the woman wept, and the child wondered greatly." With its fable-like diction and melancholy tone, the story strikes a mannered note. But it also expresses a sense of the world that would surface again and again in the work of the adult James Burnham: that the world is full of mystery and pain, that nothing in life is ever secure, that death comes even in Arcadia.

Jim made writing itself the subject of his final school essay, his entry in the 1923 Headmaster's Essay Contest. America stood "on the verge of an age of writing that [might] far surpass the age of Elizabeth," he announced in reply to the question, "Do Present Conditions in America Stimulate the Production of Literature?" The source of the new era was World War I, which "changed life in every way . . . revivified existence . . . [and lent] new impetus to everything." America now offered a host of subjects—"flappers and philosophers, reformers and bootleggers, politicians and socialists"—that would inevitably inspire writing. But in addition, "the divine spark of literary fire" had set some of America's youth ablaze. These young people "scorn easy worldly success, and live to write," Jim declared. "They wish to write, and they will write." Jim's essay won the contest, netting him the prize of twenty-five dollars.[23]

A picture taken of Jim for the *Tabard*'s graduation issue shows an even-featured, poker-faced seventeen-year-old with a high, broad forehead and prominent ears. But it does not convey the psychological complexity of its subject, who, to judge by his writings, could alternate without missing a beat between the roles of self-confident analyst, romantic fantasist, mournful fabulist, down-to-earth reporter, and enthusiastic prophet of an American literary golden age.

Jim graduated from Canterbury in June 1923. Most of his classmates had hoped for admission to Yale, but Jim, in an early instance of his lifelong tendency to go his own way, had decided on Princeton, and it was at Princeton that he would spend the next four years.

◆  ◆  ◆  ◆

Princeton, New Jersey, was in the 1920s a quiet town of some five thousand people surrounded by farmland and cow pastures. Today's suburban landscape, industrial parks, and nearby interstate highway still lay in the distant future. Trolley cars swayed over tracks crossing open fields to the state capital, Trenton, and the Pennsylvania railroad stopped at Princeton Junction before heading on to Philadelphia or New York. Princeton was "remote from the practical and utilitarian world," remembered one of Jim's classmates, and at times Princeton Junction could even seem "rather lonesome."[24]

Dominating the town was the university that bore its name, an institution that in the 1920s showed a double face. Seen from one side, it suggested a seat of higher learning at which dedicated students embraced the life of the mind and scholars engaged in passionate debate, especially at the Divinity School, where fundamentalists and modernists thrust and parried in endless combat. Seen from the other, it looked more like a postadolescent playground amid whose ivy-draped towers the "high-hat" sons of wealthy parents made merry in a four-year revel. This was the Princeton whose public image owed much to the fiction of alumnus F. Scott Fitzgerald, the Princeton not of laboratories and libraries, but of raccoon coats, visiting flappers, and bacchanalian football weekends.

Both images contained a measure of truth. People devoted to learning found Princeton congenial, for the faculty, led by President John Grier Hibben, took education seriously. In 1923, the year Jim matriculated, the college adopted a "Four Course Plan" to toughen the undergraduate curriculum. The plan reduced the programs of juniors and seniors from five courses to four to achieve a more thorough coverage of subjects, assigned heavier reading lists to students in their major courses, and called for detailed discussion of readings by groups of three to six students guided by faculty "preceptors," which could be demanding.

Moreover, a Presbyterian moral sensibility, a legacy of Princeton's past, still lingered on campus. Sunday chapel was compulsory, and the deans did not treat student hijinks lightly. When a classmate of Jim's, the future novelist William M. Spackman, proposed in the student literary review, the *Nassau Literary Magazine,* of which he had just been elected chairman, that the Divinity School be turned into a brothel to give toiling professors a place to recover from their labors, the administration was not amused. Suppressing the article, it summarily fired Spackman from the *Lit,* and agreed not to expel him only after he had consented to psychiatric treatment at his own expense.[25]

Yet many students took less interest in their courses than in the extracurricular side of college life: eating clubs, sports, parties. As for academic matters, they sought an undemanding "gentleman's education."[26]

In some ways Jim's life at Princeton fit the usual student pattern. As a freshman, he wore the black cap and necktie required of all first-year students. As a sophomore, he took part in the annual "bicker" (the quest for admission to the eating clubs around which student social life revolved), and was accepted at Tower (whose standing was respectable, though not exalted). He joined the Radio Club and then drifted out of it. He also joined the Law Club, which held monthly smokers at which members could "meet personally the leaders of the American legal profession."[27] But he soon lost interest in the law too. In addition, he joined the Catholic Club, a tiny group on a campus overwhelmingly Presbyterian and Episcopalian, and by the evidence of yearbook listings remained in this club until graduation.

Jim kept up his tennis at Princeton, and he added golf, which he ultimately came to prefer. He also took up boxing, probably to meet the college's physical education requirement, and turned out to be a powerhouse in the ring.[28] Bridge afforded him a more peaceful pursuit, and he often sat at the card table until the small hours of the morning. In his senior year he owned a car and took friends on jaunts around the adjacent region. One one occasion they drove to Bethlehem, Pennsylvania, for a Bach festival. On another the destination was Sommerville, New Jersey, for the trial of a cousin of a friend of Jim's who stood accused of murdering her clergyman husband and a member of the church's choir, with whom she suspected her husband of having an affair. But when Jim's party arrived at the courthouse, they found the line for seats so long that they went off to play golf instead.[29]

Like many of his classmates, Jim took little interest in politics. As a senior, he described himself as a member of the "third party," an expression used by students to convey their contempt for Republicans and Democrats alike—and, by implication, for politics as such.[30]

◆ ◆ ◆ ◆

Despite his many nonacademic involvements, Jim was one of his class's most serious students. In his first and second years, he signed up for courses in a mostly prescribed group of subjects: Latin, French, mathematics, physics, geology, and his major, English. As a sophomore, he added an elective in philosophy (not one of Princeton's more popular subjects), and eventually took all four of the philosophy courses the college offered. In his third year he moved on to the "Four Course Plan," which in his case called for two English courses per term as a junior and three per term as a senior, as well as the preceptorial discussions the plan required. He also took up ancient Greek, and by the end of his senior year, had read long portions of the *Iliad* and the *Odyssey* in the original language. Ironically, though he would one day gain fame as a writer on politics, he never took a course in history or political science.[31]

Among Jim's teachers, two in particular made a strong impression on him. One was an instructor in English named F. Cudworth Flint. A graduate of Reed College in Oregon and a Rhodes Scholar at Oxford who would one day head the English department at Dartmouth, Flint came to Princeton in 1923 at the age of twenty-seven. He was soon a hit with students, partly because of his cutting wit and enormous collection of dirty limericks, but also because of his learning and his flair as a teacher. He pursued the study of literature with passion, and by example encouraged Jim to do the same.

The other, and stronger, influence on Jim was Philip E. Wheelwright, the teacher under whom he studied philosophy. The son of a New Jersey stockbroker, and only four years older than Jim, Wheelwright himself had gone to Princeton, earning a B.A. in 1921 and a Ph.D. in 1924. He then taught for a year at his alma mater (at which time Jim became his student) before joining the philosophy department at New York University's Washington Square College. Though he did not subscribe to any particular school of philosophy, Wheelwright leaned toward the empiricism and common-sense logic of Aristotle. This penchant Jim came to share (if he had not already espoused Aristotelian philosophy, which he would have encountered in the Thomist theology he had learned at Canterbury).[32]

Jim also carried on his education outside the classroom. On top of his course assignments, he read voraciously on his own, later citing *War and Peace* and the early volumes of Proust's *Remembrance of Things Past* "as perhaps [the] chief literary experiences" of his years at Princeton. At the same time, he became a devotee of T. S. Eliot (whom Wheelwright, too, read with fervor), championing not only Eliot's poetry, but also his views on social and cultural issues.[33]

Besides reading, Jim wrote at Princeton, and as at Canterbury, did so in markedly divergent veins. Despite his often rarified intellectual interests, he published many pieces in the college humor magazine, the *Princeton Tiger,* where he had a seat on the editorial board. A photograph of the *Tiger* board in the 1926 yearbook shows him wearing the poker face he usually put on for cameras, the suit with vest that campus fashion decreed, and slicked-back hair parted precisely down the middle. The *Tiger,* aiming at a tone of breezy sophistication, filled its pages with jokes, comic sketches, humorous poems, cartoons, and "Tigerisms" (e.g., "Helen of Troy was the first woman on record to go to Paris to complete her education"),[34] and Jim's writing, running to comic verse and ironic humor, stuck closely to the formula. His "Little Sister's Letter to Santy,"[35] for example, is a flapper's letter to Santa Claus listing the presents she wants for Christmas: a "good cocktail mixer," a monogrammed silver flask, a case of gin "(not bootleg)," a pearl-handled thirty-two caliber revolver, and "a first edition of Freud."

But quite out of tune with the *Tiger* spirit was his last contribution (or at least the last that can be identified as his work), a piece called "As Tiny Tim Remarked."[36] Here, too, the subject is Christmas. The piece starts out as a conventional poke at the commercial hoopla surrounding the holiday ("an institution invented by the department stores, working in conjunction with the Salvation Army"). But it ends on a note of weariness shading into disgust: "A man with a sense of humor enjoys Christmas. It is so pathetic." It is as if a college humorist has somehow turned into the bitter finder of the lens of lost ages.

Jim also wrote for the *Nassau Literary Magazine,* a review whose contents generally consisted of sober fiction and poetry, book reviews, essays, and comment on Princeton and world affairs. Unlike his brother David, who followed him to Princeton in 1925 and went on to become the *Lit's* chairman, Jim did not sit on the magazine's editorial board. But he did publish two stories in the *Lit,* pieces utterly unlike the ones that appeared in the *Tiger.*

The first, "Through a Glass Darkly,"[37] concerns a farmer who marries for the sole purpose of begetting an heir. He does not love his wife. But when she dies giving birth to a son, he is uneasy, and finds it strange that the baby has survived when the mother has not. The farmer seems lost in the world, which the story depicts as a bleak and mournful place. The narration is utterly deadpan, and has a modernist flavor in that its transitions are unsignaled and abrupt.

In the second story, "Anchor,"[38] a man remembers his last day with his grandfather. They had gone sailing, and the grandfather had overtaxed himself. Upon returning home the grandfather, like the one in "The Green, Green Hills," had suddenly died. Once again an anchor has suddenly vanished, and once again the reader feels a sense of the mystery, melancholy, and insecurity pervading the world. Jim's acute awareness of the somber aspects of human existence may have stemmed from a young man's desire to seem sophisticated. But it may also have stemmed from something native to his temperament: a consciousness of tragedy and of its ubiquity and ineluctability that brought him closer to Augustine than to his preferred theologian-philosopher, Thomas Aquinas.

◆ ◆ ◆ ◆

Though no extrovert, Jim made close friends at Princeton, some of whom would remain his friends for life. One of these was Lucius Wilmerding, a New Yorker who would teach English at Columbia for a time before publishing a scholarly study of the Electoral College, a biography of James Madison, and other works. A second was Bernard Heyl, like Jim a member of Tower, who would one day head the department of art at Wellesley. Others were Franklin Gary, a fellow English major who would return to Princeton to teach, and William Spackman, who, once released from the woodshed, went back to writing. The most rambunctious of the lot was a Virginian and fellow *Tiger* writer named Joseph Bryan III. A naval officer in World War II, Bryan, the *Princeton Alumni Magazine* was to report in 1944, had captured an atoll from the Japanese and run up a Confederate battle flag to mark his conquest. He had also instructed the atoll's inhabitants in certain American regional customs, thanks to which "some Yankees who later landed on the beach were a bit confused, to put it mildly, when they were greeted by luscious South Sea maidens with that same Rebel yell that put the fear of God into their grandparents."[39] After the war, Bryan turned his hand to a variety of endeavors, from writing a biography of Pacific Fleet Admiral Chester W. Nimitz to helping launch the covert operations branch of the CIA.

Still, for all his campus successes, Jim sometimes seemed a bit out of place at Princeton. The compelling interest in ideas that bound him to his friends (several of whom, like him, became teachers) set him apart from the mass of his fellow undergraduates, among whom his absorption in matters intellectual found little echo. Thus, few students, if any, besides Jim took every philosophy course Princeton offered, and most took none at all. In Jim, by contrast, the appetite for debating ideas amounted to a passion. For the sheer pleasure of arguing, he would even defend positions he did not hold. In one instance, replying to a friend's claim that Picasso and other modern painters were "historically degenerate," he strenuously defended the moderns, only to admit later that he had agreed with his adversary all along. (He also confessed that he could not help liking modern art anyway.) The anomalous side of his presence at Princeton is summed up in a persistent petty frustration he faced: high among the subjects he loved to debate was Catholic theology, but since not even his friends took the slightest interest in this field, he hardly ever had a chance to do so.[40]

Jim's visibility on campus was magnified by his mordant manner. Naturally reserved and probably harboring a shy streak, he wore a cool, ironic mask that, joined to a dry wit and an intelligence that some thought arrogant, made his intellectually less self-assured classmates feel uneasy. Some of them were even a little afraid of him, one recalled, worried that if they should say something foolish "he would not be slow to let them know it."[41] His personality seems to have resembled that of his hero T. S. Eliot during the poet's student days at Oxford. The philosopher Brand Blanshard, who once accompanied the young Eliot on a holiday ramble in Dorset, found him "reserved, shy, economical of speech, [and] rather frostily formal of manner."[42]

At Princeton, as at Canterbury, Jim graduated as his class's top scholar. Thus he was named its Latin salutatorian, and so had to deliver a quasi-humorous speech of greeting in Latin at commencement. (This brief address was supplied by the college, which had little faith in the Latin ability even of its salutatorians.) Jim also won several academic awards, the most important of which was the Wanamaker Prize, given to the junior who had written the best exam and thesis in British philosophy. "Without any question the finest brain I have encountered in all my years at Princeton," Dean R. K. Root said of Jim to Joe Bryan years later.[43] Jim's parents, who came to graduation in their private railroad car, must have found the moment splendid.

What now awaited Jim was more schooling. He had not yet decided on a career, reported the senior classbook, the *Nassau Herald,* and in the immediate future intended to enroll at Balliol College, Oxford, to study literature.[44] Why he wanted to do so the *Herald* did not say, but it is easy to see how the ancient university, radiating English social and cultural prestige, would appeal to a twenty-one-year-old Princetonian with literary interests, a generous father, and no particular plans. Besides, his preceptor, F. Cudworth Flint, had studied at Oxford, and his friends Lucius Wilmerding and Franklin Gary, as well as several others in his class, were Oxford-bound, so enrolling at Oxford may have struck him as his natural next step.

◆　◆　◆　◆

Oxford's pace in the twenties was even more sedate than Princeton's. Telephones, for instance, were not yet widely used. Instead, recalled the novelist and Oxonian (Hertford College) Evelyn Waugh, college messengers delivered notes on crested cards. As for traffic, Waugh added, "clergymen on bicycles were, with the cattle coming to market, the only hazards."[45]

Of Oxford's many colleges, Balliol, founded in the thirteenth century, was one of the oldest and most celebrated. In appearance, however, it was one of the least impressive. The college "stood out for bleakness," said the novelist Anthony Powell, a Balliol man, and its architecture could only be considered "dismal."[46] Some 250 students lived at Balliol in the 1920s, in quarters that have been described as "drab" and "dingy." Most of the college still made do with Victorian plumbing, and each morning "scouts" had to bring in hot water for shaving and carry out chamber pots.[47] Nor did students enjoy the comforts of central heating, instead spending winter evenings huddled over fires in their hearths.

Like its plumbing, Balliol's rules of conduct harked back to Victorian times, especially when it came to contacts with women. A student who intended to stay out overnight—a serious infraction of college rules—would ask a friend to rumple his bed and use his chamber pot to cover up his absence.[48]

But these hardships were far outweighed by the college's renown. Balliol's legendary Victorian master, the classicist Benjamin Jowett, had tried to form a student body joining the aristocracy of birth with that of talent. Whether he
succeeded is open to debate, but H. H. Asquith, a Jowett student who went on to
become prime minister, felt that an "effortless superiority" was the distinguishing
mark of the Balliol man.[49] By the 1920s, the college had acquired a reputation
for "arrogant brilliance," Powell wrote, and although its "great days" were over, "a
certain puissance still clung to the name."[50]

Jim spent two years at Balliol. As his chief subject he chose English literature,
which at Oxford required that he study Anglo-Saxon. This he did under J. R. R.
Tolkien, future author of *The Hobbit* and *The Lord of the Rings*. He also took up
medieval philosophy with a brilliant English priest, Martin D'Arcy, who headed
the Jesuit house at Oxford, Campion Hall. ("Blue chin and fine, slippery mind,"
Evelyn Waugh summed up Father D'Arcy, who had a hand in Waugh's conversion to Catholicism, and is reputed to have served as a model for his fictional
cleric, the worldly Father Rothschild.)[51] Studying under Father D'Arcy allowed
Jim finally to debate theology. But it did nothing to preserve his attachment to
religion, for at Oxford, without explanation or any sign of inner turmoil, he left
the Church.[52]

Jim had no trouble adjusting to his new life. "Oxford so far has been like a '27
class reunion," he told a Princeton friend. "In many ways it is scarcely any change
at all. The general atmosphere and the attitude are most extraordinarily alike. With
due allowance for lack of central heating, inadequate arrangement for baths, etc.,
and no napkins for meals, Baliol [*sic*] isn't so bad. I must confess that, in spite of
[F. Cudworth] Flint, the movies and story books, I haven't found signs of any
greater culture or intellectual life than were floating around Old Nassau, but there
is the same pleasant round—golf, bridge, movies, drinking, etc., with tea occupy-
ing a much more considerable place in the scheme of things than [at Prince-
ton]."[53]

"It's not a third so different from Princeton as the story books tell us, Oxford
isn't," he reported to Charlotte Eckhart, a Kenilworth neighbor, "especially with
ten of my own class here, and eighteen other Princeton men besides. Of course
the town is bigger than Princeton, and the buildings are older, and it rains more,
and there's no central heating, but people *do* just about the same things: drink and
play cards and go to the movies (they're 'flicks' in England) and talk nonsense and

study a little and drink."

But Oxford also offered pastimes unknown at Princeton. "Last week," he continued, "they had the races known familiarly as 'Toggers,' in which the boats of all the colleges line up one behind the other, and chase each other for a mile and a half. If you can bump the college ahead, you advance one place in the line. When they bump, moreover, they sure do bump—I saw one boat smashed to pieces, and then lots of them turn over." When, after six days, the racing came to an end "Balliol, neatly enough, was head of the river . . . and held a celebration that night that wouldn't be believed in an American college. But *that,* of course, I can't go into." Still, he acknowledged, Oxford also had its flaws. "The undergraduettes are without doubt the most discouraging things in Oxford. They wear funny gowns and much funnier caps, and clutter up all the lectures, writing furious notes and looking dreadfully serious. I tell you, moreover, in all veracity, that there's not a good looking pair of legs in England. . . . If you ever feel discouraged, come to Oxford and feed your conceit."[54]

Holiday breaks at Oxford gave Jim a chance to travel. On one trip, he went to Scotland to play golf at St. Andrews, the birthplace of the game. The Christmas holiday of 1927 found him in Paris staying near the Luxemburg Gardens. During the 1928 spring break he went to Florence. "I'm going to try to learn Florence the same way I learned Paris, with a stop at Cannes on the way down," he told Charlotte Eckhart. "There're no apartments in Florence to be rented for such a short time, but I'm going to stay in an Italian family . . . and wander around to Siena and Volterra and places the weekends."[55] The following spring he returned to Florence, where he spent much of April. In July 1929, with his work at Oxford completed, he went to Rome and then joined his friends Bernard Heyl and Curt Winsor in Bayreuth for the Wagner Festival. *Die Götterdämmerung*'s last act, he decided, was nothing less than "cosmic."[56]

Jim sometimes ran into trouble during his travels. In his first year of flying, probably 1927 or 1928, he was involved in three airplane mishaps, one of them a forced landing in France because of engine failure.[57] But each time he emerged unscathed and ready to take off again. Always fascinated by new technology, the former crystal radio set builder (and future Apollo space program enthusiast) would not give up air travel simply because planes might crash.

Only one dark moment intruded upon Jim's Oxford idyll. In June 1928, after six months in bed with a heart ailment, Claude Burnham died of pneumonia. He had just turned forty-seven. Shortly before his death he formally entered the Catholic Church, just about the time Jim left it.[58]

◆   ◆   ◆   ◆

At Oxford, Jim made long-range plans for the future. He had kept in touch with his Princeton philosophy professor, Philip Wheelwright, now chairman of the small philosophy department at NYU's Washington Square College, and by 1928, if not before, the two had decided to publish a magazine. It would be a "quarterly journal for critical discussion," Jim told the English novelist Sidney Schiff (who wrote under the name Stephen Hudson). Each issue would contain articles on literature and other subjects, but also a symposium on a topic of "contemporary intellectual interest." The journal, unsurprisingly, would be called the *Symposium*.[59]

While Jim pursued his studies at Balliol, Wheelwright went to work getting the *Symposium* going. Besides seeking out the needed money, much of which he eventually obtained from Washington Square College's wealthy dean, James Munn,[60] he solicited articles for the magazine's first issue. With the help of a short, peppery, twenty-four-year-old philosophy instructor named Sidney Hook, who was just beginning a decades-long career at NYU, he was able to line up pieces from two of Hook's former teachers, John Dewey of Columbia University, then one of the leading American philosophers, and Morris Raphael Cohen, a philosophy professor at Hook's undergraduate alma mater, City College. (To get his help, Hook later claimed, Wheelwright dangled a *Symposium* editorship before him, but although Hook delivered, Wheelwright did not.)[61] Jim, too, tried to recruit a contributor, offering Schiff seventy-five dollars for a lead article on "the form of the modern novel." But Schiff turned the offer down, pleading that he was a novelist, not a critic.[62]

As plans for the *Symposium* went forward, Wheelwright also arranged for Jim to join the NYU faculty. At first he got Jim a job in the most logical place, the English department.[63] But when the position fell through, he turned to his own bailiwick, philosophy, and found a post for Jim there. This shift of fields was possible in those days, especially for someone with Jim's advantages. Besides being bright and able, he was more than casually interested in philosophy, and by this time sufficiently versed in the subject to teach it. These qualifications, along with his degrees from Princeton and Oxford and Wheelwright's backing, were all the credentials he needed at a time when academic specialization was less narrow than it is today and a Ph.D. not yet a professional requirement. Thus, when asked what he planned to do after leaving Oxford, Jim told Lucius Wilmerding's fiancée that he would coedit the *Symposium* and teach.[64]

Midway through 1929, Jim took his final examination at Oxford. He received a second, signifying a good but not stellar performance, and so obtained another B.A. In 1933 Oxford granted him a master's degree to boot, not for any further study, but, as John Jones, the present dean of Balliol, has explained, because of "the mere passage of time . . . all in line with immemorial mysterious Oxford custom."[65] For most of the preceding twenty years Jim had been a student. For the next twenty he would be (among many other things) a teacher.

# Chapter 2

# Teacher

TOWARD THE END OF AUGUST 1929, James Burnham, twenty-three years old and with no experience as a teacher, sailed from England to New York to take up his new profession. The university that awaited him bore little resemblance to Princeton or Oxford. Without a campus, housed in what looked like a row of undistinguished office buildings just to the east of Greenwich Village's Washington Square Park, and enrolling a subway-commuting student body, NYU's liberal arts school, Washington Square College, exuded a gritty, urban aura not usually associated with American colleges.

Burnham began at NYU as an instructor, the lowest full-time faculty rank, at a salary of $2,300 a year, and with the customary weekly teaching load of twelve class hours.[1] Three of the four courses he taught were sections of the philosophy department's basic offerings: "Introduction to Philosophy" and "Introduction to Ethics." The fourth, thanks to Wheelwright, was an advanced, elective course, "The Philosophy of Criticism," which came closer to Burnham's primary field of study.

Wheelwright was helpful to Burnham in other ways as well, putting him up until Burnham could find an apartment of his own. Soon, however, Burnham needed assistance of a different kind. Only weeks after his arrival, the stock market crashed and the country started its slide into depression. In 1930, as the slump deepened, NYU began to feel the pinch, and before long rumor had it that the faculty would soon be trimmed. Untenured and his department's junior man, Burnham was in a perilous position, which shows in a group photograph of the philosophy faculty taken for the 1930 edition of the college yearbook, the *Album*. Sitting with a solemn Wheelwright, an impassive Hook, and another member of the department, Rudolf Kagey, he has shed the deadpan expression he usually wore for cameras for an anxious one, and seems to be wringing his hands and squirming in his seat.

Wheelwright soon launched a campaign to save his friend's job. To begin with, he inflated the length of time Burnham had worked at the college. Thus, on the basis of information that only he, as department chairman, could have supplied, the 1930 *Album* identified Burnham as a faculty member who, along with Hook, had spent the 1928–1929 academic year "in absentia." In the case of Hook, who had spent that year in Germany on a Guggenheim Fellowship, the statement was accurate. But in the case of Burnham, whom the yearbook described as having "returned" to the college after a year's leave for work on the *Symposium,* it was misleading, for in coming to NYU, Burnham was not "returning." But it did give Burnham seniority equal to Hook's.[2]

As the danger of cutbacks grew, Wheelwright redoubled his efforts. In 1931 he persuaded Dean Munn, backer of the *Symposium* and the Wheelwright regime at the philosophy department, to institute a department of comparative literature, which Burnham would head, and to raise the new chairman (who could not remain a humble instructor) to the rank of assistant professor. Thus, in the 1931–1932 college bulletin Burnham appears as the chairman—and sole member—of the comparative literature department. But Wheelwright's success proved brief, for Homer Watt, chairman of the English department and of greater weight at NYU than Wheelwright, regarded the new department as a threat and demanded that it be abolished. Pressured by Watt, Munn reversed his position, and after a year the department of comparative literature vanished.[3]

Unwilling to rely solely on his comparative literature gambit, Wheelwright launched a second maneuver on Burnham's behalf in 1931. Scheduled to spend the fall of that year in Europe, he got Munn to agree that during his absence, Burnham, who had just been named chairman of the comparative literature department, should also handle the routine chores of the philosophy department.[4] In effect, Burnham now held two chairmanships. Though he was far from happy about the extra work this entailed, he seems to have performed well enough, for in 1932 Munn approved yet another proposal from Wheelwright, now back in New York, that Wheelwright resign as philosophy chairman in favor of Burnham. So it was that in the fall of 1932 Burnham formally became chairman of the philosophy department, though from behind the scenes Wheelwright still called the tune.[5]

While Burnham went along with Wheelwright's schemes, he was embarrassed by them. He was especially upset by rumors that—given his closeness to Wheelwright, their rooming together for a time, their common bachelor status, and Wheelwright's blatant championing of his cause—he and Wheelwright were lovers. This is unlikely. On the evidence, Burnham was wholly heterosexual, and people who knew him at the time regard the imputation as absurd. Wheelwright, on the other hand, though he would one day marry and become a father, may conceivably have felt a sexual attraction to Burnham, though if he did, nothing in the record suggests that he tried to act on it. Still, the rumor disturbed Burnham, and may have encouraged his eventual drift away from his patron.[6]

Like his comparative literature maneuver, Wheelwright's transfer of the philosophy chairmanship to Burnham did not succeed for long. In 1933 Dean Munn, under whose aegis the Wheelwright-Burnham team had flourished, left NYU for a deanship at Harvard. His successor, Rufus Smith, thoroughly disliked Wheelwright, who, joined by Burnham, sometimes made fun of him behind his back, going so far as to imitate his lisping speech.[7] In 1934 Smith put Hook, who had stayed out of a departmental feud pitting the Wheelwright-Burnham duo against an anti-Wheelwright faction, in Burnham's place as chairman. Unable to bear the thought of serving under Hook, Wheelwright left the college and in time found a job at Dartmouth. Burnham, meanwhile, managed to escape the fiscal ax and stayed on at NYU. But for whatever reason, he would not be promoted to the next academic rank, associate professor, until 1946.

◆ ◆ ◆ ◆

Despite the distractions posed by Wheelwright's maneuvers, the *Symposium*'s editorship, and (soon) political involvements, Burnham paid great attention to his teaching. Unwilling to confine himself to a narrow specialty, he tended to locate his advanced courses in an ambiguous zone between philosophy and literature. His first regular electives were "Aquinas and Dante" (inspired, perhaps, by the views of T. S. Eliot, who regarded these two as the supreme heroes of Western culture)[8] and "Thought and Literature of the Renaissance," which he introduced in 1931 and 1932. In 1934 and 1935 he first offered "Principles of Aesthetics" and "Problems of Aesthetics," which would cause him to be classified chiefly as an aesthetician.

Starting in the fall of 1934, while continuing to teach at Washington Square College he also taught regularly at NYU's graduate school, offering more demanding versions of his undergraduate electives. In addition, he conducted Oxford-style tutorials with graduate students, meeting weekly with individual students to analyze philosophical writings such as passages from Aquinas's *Summa Theologica*. In the 1940s, though still teaching his old standbys, he set off in new directions, giving courses such as "Philosophies of Power" (which dealt with political theory), "Philosophy and Modern Science," and "Modern Irrationalism" (whose focus on Dostoyevsky and Kafka, among others, allowed him to keep straddling the line between philosophy and literature).

Along with his electives, he continued his introductory courses. Students who enrolled in these, he believed, were looking for answers to "'fundamental questions'" such as "God, Freedom, Immortality, Universe, Reality, Creation, and the like." He described his job as helping them to clear up their intellectual confusion by showing them how to think critically, clarify problems, and recognize the difference between "significant statement and nonsense," so that they would come to realize that the "fundamental questions" were not "genuine questions at all, but requests for emotional satisfaction." The iconoclasm in this process disturbed some students, he noted. But others (the best, he thought) became aware that they were "reaching daylight from a land of mists."[9]

Hook regarded Burnham as a splendid teacher and "really remarkable in aesthetics,"[10] though their teaching styles differed greatly. A practitioner of the Socratic method, Hook turned his classes into dialectical duels, firing questions at his students, then demolishing their answers and spurring them on to further thought. Burnham, in contrast, gave lectures.[11] His presentations were informal in that he did not read from notes. But they were also highly organized and polished, with an obvious beginning, middle, and end, and never sacrificing substance for rhetorical flourishes. At times he would underline a point with a slight, enigmatic smile; at other moments, his fingertips pressed together to form an arch, he would take a question, whereupon a brief discussion might ensue, or he might allow himself a moment of dry wit. But soon he would resume his lecture. Sometimes he would say something his students found provocative, for example, that newspaper reviews had to be read with skepticism since their primary purpose was to sell theater tickets, books, and so on. But he always did so in a quiet, matter-of-fact way, never dropping the low-keyed manner former students remember as "cool." To Joseph Frank, a Burnham student in the 1930s and later a biographer of Dostoyevsky, Burnham seemed "very sophisticated, very serious, and very intense."[12]

In an aesthetics class, Burnham might lead his students through a poem by W. H. Auden, Wallace Stevens, or T. S. Eliot. (Conservatively dressed and reserved in manner, he himself seemed to his student Emma Cohn like a character from an Eliot poem.) On one occasion he brought a *Partisan Review* galley sheet of one of Eliot's *Four Quartets* to class to give his students brand-new work to analyze. One of his standard exercises was to have students compare superior with mediocre art: a sonnet of John Donne's with a piece of greeting card verse, André Derain's "Model Resting" with the cover of a romance magazine. Or he would take a class to an exhibit at the Metropolitan Museum of Art, or to the Squibb Building, which he would have students compare, on the basis of the aesthetic principles it embodied, with an adjacent bank. He would also ask for comments on well-known essays in aesthetics, such as Tolstoy's *What Is Art?* or articles by the critic Herbert Read. Sometimes he would call upon students to invent their own assignments—visits to 57th Street galleries (for exhibits of works by Picasso, Klee, and other modern painters), to movies (one choice was *The Brothers Karamazov*), to concerts—and keep notes on their reactions to what they saw or heard. He would then review their notebooks, writing concise comments in a small, neat hand.[13]

Burnham's students did not resent his reserve or his hard grading. Most came to like him, and some to hold him in awe. One day in the mid-1930s, when Burnham casually remarked that no one could consider himself educated who had not read Russell and Whitehead's *Principia Mathematica,* one student, Oscar Shoenfeld, who found Burnham "mesmerizing," raced to the library in search of the indispensable volume, only to discover that its long stretches of complex logical notation put it utterly beyond his reach. It was a hard blow for Shoenfeld, who now had to face the certainty of never being educated. (Decades later, a wiser Shoenfeld voiced the suspicion that Burnham himself had never really digested the work.)[15] But if Burnham could seem aloof, he could also show kindness to his students. On one occasion, he gave some extra tickets for an early New York performance of Benjamin Britten's opera *Peter Grimes* to his student Jeanne Wacker and one of her classmates, sensing that for them the opera would be a special treat.[16]

But Burnham's attraction rested on more than the quality of his teaching. With his English shoes and tweeds, cultivated diction, and what his student Norman Jacobs called his "Oxonian bearing," he also appealed "mightily as a type to us Jewish lads for whom his demeanor was so different from [the Brooklyn-tenement-bred] Hook's."[17] In Burnham's class, students felt they were entering a world of higher culture and social status, which dazzled them. They would have been surprised to learn that this Gentile aristocrat-intellectual was the son of a hard-working, self-made immigrant from a background not unlike their own.

◆ ◆ ◆ ◆

Burnham's workload at NYU was always heavy. On top of the twelve hours a week he spent teaching, he had to prepare his lectures, grade papers and exams, hold office hours, attend faculty committee meetings, and serve as faculty advisor to the Poetry Club. But despite his crammed schedule, in 1930 he and Wheelwright signed a contract to coauthor a philosophy textbook and deliver the finished manuscript to the publisher by July 1, 1931. "Circumstances" forced him to take on the work, he told Sidney Schiff, suggesting that he may have run into financial problems, or felt that to protect his job he needed to shore up his academic credentials. Though working on the book under pressure, he managed to squeeze out enough time in the summer of 1930 for what he called "some irregular traveling in the West."[18] But early in 1931, overwork felled him, laying him up for two weeks with a case of shingles. By mid-May 1931, with the manuscript due in six weeks, he and Wheelwright were far behind schedule, and once the spring term was over, they had to spend almost every waking moment getting the job done. In the end they met the deadline. But Burnham gained little respite, for the next day Wheelwright sailed for Europe, leaving his worn-out coauthor, who was now also slated to take charge of the philosophy department, to deal with galley sheets and other prepublication chores. To make things worse, Burnham also had to superintend his family's Depression-menaced finances, a duty requiring his daily attention.[19]

*Introduction to Philosophical Analysis,* as the book was called, sought to familiarize students with the nature of philosophical inquiry. The first of its two parts, "Method," explained the process of formal reasoning, while the second, "Problems," applied the rules laid out in the first to such "realms of discourse" as aesthetics and ethics.[20] Since the book was a primer, it was not widely reviewed, but those who did review it thought well of it. Hook described it as "first rate."[21]

But despite the praise, Burnham never took on such a project—an "academic" work—again. Indeed, the idea of a career in philosophy now repelled him. "I have a more than occasional dismay at the imperious demands of my profession," he confided to Schiff in a letter about the book. "Though I do not regret what philosophical training I have been so far able to acquire, I cannot look forward without horror to the sterility of academic philosophical discussion as an enduring prospect."[22] He nonetheless remained at NYU for many years to come, and by no means unhappily.[23]

◆　◆　◆　◆

On top of everything else, Burnham was busy coediting the *Symposium.* Despite his lack of experience, he tackled the job with his usual air of self-confidence. Hard-headed and matter-of-fact, he supplied an invaluable complement to Wheelwright, who was bright and articulate but also unbusinesslike, fretful, and absent-minded. (Leaving the office one day, Wheelwright mistook his secretary's hat, a wide-brimmed panama with velvet streamers down the back, for his own, and wore it all the way home before he noticed his error.)[24]

For a brief moment in the fall of 1929, just as Burnham and Wheelwright were preparing the first issue, it looked as if the *Symposium* might not come out, at least not as the two had originally envisaged it. A recent Harvard graduate, Lincoln Kirstein, later to head the American Ballet Theater, was in 1929 the editor of a small literary magazine called *Hound & Horn,* which in certain respects had anticipated the *Symposium.* In October 1929 Kirstein suggested to Burnham and Wheelwright that the two journals merge. The *Symposium* editors, still worried about money, unhappily accepted, and Burnham and *Hound & Horn*'s editors were soon corresponding about articles and poetry they might publish. But at the end of November, Burnham and Wheelwright called the merger off, suspecting that the *Hound & Horn* group wanted only to eliminate a possible competitor. (Burnham and Kirstein stayed in touch, however, and three years later were still discussing ideas for literary projects.)[25]

In January 1930 the first issue of the *Symposium* was published. Within its sober grey covers appeared the promised pieces by John Dewey and Morris Raphael Cohen, both of whom pondered philosophical issues; articles by the French writer Ramon Fernandez and the critic David Garnett; and book reviews by two members of the NYU philosophy department, Laurence Buermeyer and Rudolf Kagey, and a young professor of English at Columbia, Lionel Trilling.

The issue also had the look of a showcase for Burnham's Princeton friends. For along with a column called "Comment," which he and Wheelwright coauthored, it contained articles by Burnham's classmate Franklin Gary, his former preceptor, F. Cudworth Flint, and Burnham himself, who reviewed a new book by the critic I. A. Richards. Buermeyer, too, having taught philosophy at Princeton in the 1920s, with Burnham as a student, can be included in this group.

Future issues maintained this Princeton tilt. Gary and Flint continued to contribute articles, while the second issue contained a piece by William Spackman, and the third a review of Gide's *Immoralist* by a more recent graduate, Burnham's brother David. When David Burnham published his first novel, *This Our Exile* (a chapter of which the magazine ran as a story), the *Symposium* gave the job of reviewing it to Wheelwright, who awarded it a passing grade. But within a year or so, such fledgling critics (and non-Princetonians) as F. W. Dupee, Dwight Macdonald, and Harold Rosenberg entered its pages. By 1932, the magazine was offering its readers less an echo of the *Lit* than an anticipation of *Partisan Review.*

Burnham viewed the *Symposium* with anything but complacency. The first issue, he wrote to Schiff, did not quite reflect his and Wheelwright's original plan, though the second, more "symposial" in content, had come closer.[26] More serious was the problem of finding able critics. Especially in the United States, he lamented, critics "willing to think and write carefully" seemed in short supply. "I feel more as I read and hear more that Americans, for whatever reason, simply cannot analyze their own ideas," he elaborated. "The daily appearing studies of the economic depression provide quite as illuminating examples as the superficialities of the literary reviewers. This may, though, be quite natural to the Age of the Cinema. I find it rather breathtaking (and not at all unpleasant) to witness the magnificent technique, the perfect directing, the lovely sets and the exquisite acting that Broadway gives a play the literary and intellectual content of which could scarcely satisfy a kindergarten."[27]

He was also troubled by what he called the *Symposium*'s "pedantry" and "highbrowism." He and Wheelwright were at grips with the problem, he told Schiff, "and not, I know, successfully." He constantly ran into such faults in his own writing, he confessed, and often failed to overcome them. "I wrote the whole thing first in as 'plain speaking' a manner as I could," he said of a forthcoming article he had just finished. "I went over it carefully and it seemed cheap. I then wrote it as meticulously as I could, and it seemed a quibble, with the main issue obscured by technicalities. As it stands now . . . I am afraid it varies between the two, in a manner that will be generally unsatisfying."[28]

Burnham criticized his writing too severely. If "highbrowism" means a preoccupation with the more recondite aspects of thought and culture, then his pieces were indeed "highbrow." Yet highbrow concerns are the reason such articles are written. He was on more solid ground in worrying about his style. Sometimes his tone turned haughty, and this may partly have been what he had in mind when he wrote to Schiff. He was also guilty, even if rarely, of stylistic pretentiousness— for example, the use of a plural verb with a collective noun,[29] which could give his prose an affected, Angloid ring. Still, whether natural in style or forced, his pieces were always honest, proceeding from a deep-seated moral and intellectual seriousness that came through in everything he wrote.

But what is most striking about Burnham's *Symposium* pieces is not their "highbrowism" or "pedantry," but their tone of unanswerable finality. Burnham wrote with unwavering self-assurance and an occasional hint of weariness, as if tired of always having to set other people straight. Though still only in his midtwenties, he was never intimidated by the greater reputation of the writers he discussed, and did not hesitate to issue corrections. "Works of art . . . often force me to a probably not unhealthy humility," he wrote to Schiff, "[but] this is an attitude I never carry over into my criticism."[30]

As a critic, Burnham followed his philosophical bent, writing more about "meaning" and the aesthetic principles on which criticism should be based than about the formal properties of works he was reviewing. In one article, "Progress and Tradition," he advanced a view close to the "reader response" theory in fashion four decades later, arguing that paintings and literary works did not possess fixed meaning, since with the passage of time both their context and those who

read or looked at them changed. The original *Divine Comedy,* for example, had
been "irretrievably lost," he contended, and "only a sentimentalist" could think
otherwise. The poem's words now "symbolize[d] a different context of meanings," making it "a different poem" from the one Dante had written.[31] Nor, he
maintained—strangely for someone soon to head a department of comparative
literature—could literary works be validly compared. Comparison was "almost
always futile," since it compelled critics to disregard "the uniqueness" that distinguished every true work of art.[32] As a modernist, he stressed the importance of
"form, of 'the medium,'" of works of art, which he feared could "easily be under-
emphasized." But as an admirer of Aquinas, he also took a neomedieval position
on aesthetic issues, rejecting the idea of art for art's sake and any idea of divorcing art from moral meaning. Such a separation, he warned, would "only make art
barren and idle."[33]

The literary genre that most interested him was the novel, and not only
because of the aesthetic problems it posed—for example, whether "naturalism"
and "art" were compatible, or why a work of fiction impressed readers as "realistic." "I hope someday to write what would probably be called a novel," he told
Schiff. "Ten years ago I thought that I should begin when I left college; but not
long after that I realized that I should not know enough, either about literature
and ideas, or about human beings, or about myself. Now, before beginning, I wish
to be as clear and sure as there is any reasonable possibility I can be."[34] As things
turned out, Burnham wrote many books, but never a novel, which is probably
just as well. With a talent more for critical analysis than for storytelling, and a temperament inclined to emotional reticence, had he tried to portray emotion, he
would probably not have surpassed his school fiction.

Now and then, Burnham took up purely philosophical topics. Here, as in his
literary criticism, he targeted what he saw as intellectual confusion. Thus, in
commenting on James Kaye's *The Dynamic Universe,* an account of the extrasci-
entific philosophizing of some well-known scientists of the day, he scornfully
pronounced the quasireligious reflections of these thinkers, ungrounded in
quantifiable evidence, to be nonsense. Always an empiricist, he now seemed to
lean toward the logical-positivist version of empiricism, rejecting as meaningless
any position not based on "hard" (i.e., measurable) fact.[35]

A literary semiportrait of Burnham at the turn of the 1930s appears in his
brother David's novel *This Our Exile.* Published in 1931, and drawn from the life

of the Burnham family at the time of Claude Burnham's fatal illness, the novel concerns the Eatons of Kenilworth, Illinois: the father, a banker, who dies of heart disease; the mother, who is convulsed by her husband's death; and their three sons, Jackie (Philip Burnham), a frightened teenager, Jim (David Burnham), a student at Princeton and the novel's narrator, and Frederic (James Burnham).

Fred Eaton, a Yale man who has recently completed two postgraduate years at Cambridge, lives in Paris, where he and a friend have founded a literary review. He has recently married, but his wife has left him, unable to put up with his chilly and caustic personality. Fred is brilliant, highly serious about his writing, and a glutton for work, but also compulsively dry and ironic and always ready to let loose a withering epigram. He scorns romantic love as "an insult to the intellect, an abnegation of progress and civilization," and with relentless iconoclasm declares his preference for honesty over tact, common sense over emotion, and purely rational conduct over social convention. Yet one of the novel's more perceptive characters sees that beneath his cold exterior he is deeply emotional, more so even than his mercurial mother. In the end, Fred achieves a kind of redemption. He retains his mordancy, but drops his pose of sophistication, and begins to leaven his irony with melancholy. "In a million years man has been able to evolve but one constant," he tells his brother Jim, "and that is loneliness."[36]

Fred's life has many obvious parallels with Burnham's, and resemblances of personality abound. Like Fred, Burnham was by nature an ironist, tried to view the world with emotional detachment, enjoyed playing the iconoclast, and harbored feelings more intense than he liked to reveal. But unlike Fred he did not try to hide his earnest streak, or fail to own up when he thought he had done something wrong.[37]

The question of likeness takes on added interest from the fact that Burnham collaborated in the creation of his fictional alter ego. In the spring of 1930 he worked with David on the novel, going through the manuscript line by line.[38] Whether he took advantage of the chance this editing gave to make Fred less— or more—like himself is impossible to say. But it is not hard to imagine that the twenty-five-year-old Burnham, unyielding champion of serious art, was willing to draw an unflattering portrait of himself in the hope of a better novel.

◆ ◆ ◆ ◆

Despite his heavy work schedule, Burnham kept up ties with his college friends. On Sunday mornings he would drop in on Lucius Wilmerding, recently married and living in New York, with whom he would work on solutions to mathematical puzzles. He wanted to be married himself, he confided to Wilmerding's wife, Jane, who later remembered him as "eager" to find a bride.[39]

By early 1932 it looked as if his wish would soon be granted, for he became engaged that winter to a lively brunette named Martha Dodd, the twenty-three-year-old daughter of University of Chicago historian (and later U.S. ambassador to Nazi Germany) William E. Dodd. Like Burnham, Martha had literary interests. She wrote short stories and had worked as assistant literary editor at the *Chicago Tribune*. She made a plausible mate for Burnham, but before the two had been engaged for very long, something went awry. "I must answer your kindness in congratulating me on my engagement to Martha Dodd by telling you that our engagement has not proved in all respects successful, and that our marriage has been indefinitely at least postponed," Burnham wrote opaquely to Schiff in May 1932. "There has been no quarrel; but the imminent prospect of marriage, for reasons that I think neither of us fully understands, convinced us both that marriage itself, now at least, would be unwise."[40] To a question from Schiff about his idea of married life, Burnham answered, "I am not, in this, with my generation; I look upon marriage as a serious and permanent undertaking. There are not many values that in this present world, I find I can accept. Among those that I can, I believe highest and most important—along with what I may call the integration of my own self, which I place in a sense first—the relations with the few other persons toward whom I have or may yet have friendship and love. And of these, if I marry, I hope that the chief may be in my relations with my wife."[41] The engagement was never resumed.

(In view of later events, the relationship was ironic. In the early 1950s, Burnham was a well-known, hard-line anticommunist, while Martha Dodd, now married to a rich leftist named Alfred K. Stern, had long supported the Communist Party, of which she was probably a member. In 1953, with the Justice Department on their heels, the Sterns fled to Mexico. In 1957, having been indicted in absentia as Soviet spies, they moved on to Prague, where Martha lived until her death in 1990. At the time of the Sterns' bolt behind the Iron Curtain, the conservative journal *National Review,* at which Burnham was a senior editor, printed a brief, unsigned paragraph noting their flight. The author of the paragraph was James Burnham.)[42]

◆ ◆ ◆ ◆

During his earliest years at NYU, Burnham showed little interest in politics. His work at the *Symposium* showed that his consuming passions were literature and philosophy, and a prediction in 1931 that he would soon become a political writer and activist would have been ludicrous. The closest he came to a political position was a cultural outlook he had imbibed from his intellectual beacon, T. S. Eliot,[43] which Eliot, in turn, had taken from the French writer and journalist Charles Maurras, editor of the nationalist newspaper *L'Action Français* and leader of a monarchist movement of the same name.[44] A militant opponent of France's democratic and anticlerical Third Republic, Maurras stood for royalism against republicanism in politics, classicism against romanticism in the arts, and, though an atheist, Catholicism, seeing in the Church (which he thought had instilled the "Roman" principles of authority, hierarchy, and discipline in a once "romantic" early Christianity) a bulwark of order in the decaying modern world.[45] "Classique, catholique, monarchique," the *Nouvelle Revue Française* summed up Maurras's outlook. Eliot, a reader of Maurras, had borrowed this formula, calling himself in his 1928 essay collection, *For Lancelot Andrews,* "classicist in literature, royalist in politics, and Anglo-Catholic in religion."[46] Through Eliot's version of the formula, the Maurrasian creed had made its way to Burnham.

What appealed to Burnham about this outlook was neither its royalism nor its classicism, but its stress on the Church as a cultural bastion and social stabilizer.[47] Since this logically pointed to conservatism in politics, the Burnham of 1930, had he not been politically apathetic, might have been classified as a conservative of a clerical-traditionalist stripe.

Burnham's apathy did not survive the Depression. Alarmed by the economic slump and the threat of social breakdown, he, like many intellectuals who had once looked askance at politics, now moved toward political involvement. Marxism, however, which made numerous converts among intellectuals in the 1930s, at first left him cold. In their *Introduction to Philosophical Analysis,* he and Wheelwright scoffed at "the dogmatic nonsense of reductive materialism," and cited economic determinism as an example of fallacious logic. In the April 1931 *Symposium,* Burnham went on to denounce "dogmatic materialism [as] perhaps the most degrading ideology that has ever been imposed on a large section of mankind."[48] And though agreeing with the Marxists that the old social order had failed, he spurned an alternative that seemed to devalue the individual person. Thus, he roundly endorsed a January 1931 *Symposium* article by Ramon Fernandez, who argued that "for the intelligent man the defense of the individual ... [was] not merely a duty but an ineluctable necessity."[49] "I found an unusual excitement in the fact that [Fernandez's] defense of the individual was based on grounds so firmly intellectual as emotional," he wrote to Schiff. True, the social order was bankrupt, but like Fernandez, he could see "no escape from moral defeatism except through a clear recognition of the primacy of personal values."[50]

It was in 1932, the year the economy hit bottom, that Burnham first wrote about politics at any length. In a "Comment" appearing in the April issue of the *Symposium,* he took up what he called "the two great problems of our day: economic disruption and war," which he declared to be "plainly and imminently" endangering Western civilization. But the column was not entirely political, for its subject was less depression and war and the threat they posed to Western civilization than certain confusions of "meaning" that the column blamed for muddling discussion of these problems.[51] Still, the piece can be called Burnham's first effort as a political writer.

As Burnham's interest in politics waxed, his hostility to Marxism waned. The Depression certainly underlay this change of feeling, but a more proximate cause was the influence of Sidney Hook, at the time a Marxist and close to the Communist Party. In July 1931 the *Symposium* published a long article by Hook, "Towards the Understanding of Karl Marx," that rejected the "Orthodox" conception of Marxism as a dogmatic "science of social development" with roots in Hegel's dialectical logic, and portrayed it instead as a pragmatic philosophy that used the empirical method to gain insight into social dynamics. Hook's view of Marxism seems to have aroused a not-unfriendly curiosity in Burnham. Hook at least thought so, and urged his colleague to pursue his budding interest.[52]

The first public sign that Burnham was warming to Marxism was his review in the July 1932 *Symposium* of the first volume of Leon Trotsky's *History of the Russian Revolution.* (It was also his first review of a political book.) With unusual enthusiasm, he praised the former Bolshevik leader as a writer and historian, and attributed the book's brilliance to Trotsky's use of "dialectical materialism" as his mode of analysis, by which he seems to have meant Trotsky's explanation of the Russian Revolution as the result of an interplay between human intention and impersonal, historical forces. But he found the book exciting for a further reason, he said. It prompted the question whether in America social upheaval would not also lead to communism.[53]

With this review began Burnham's fateful encounter with Trotsky, a major architect of the Russian Revolution, first foreign minister of the newborn Soviet state, founder of the Red Army, and loser in a fierce power struggle with his rival, Joseph Stalin, that had already caused his expulsion from the USSR and would climax in his death at the hands of a Stalinist assassin. Trotsky would shape Burnham's life to the end of the 1930s and his thinking, in some ways, for much longer.

Curiously, the beginning of the relationship was marked by an episode that foreshadowed its stormy ending eight years later. In his review, Burnham mentioned having heard that Trotsky had deliberately omitted important information from the book and misdated several significant quotations in order to strengthen the case he was building against Stalin. Reading the review, which an American follower had brought to him at his current refuge, the island of Prinkipo, off Istanbul, Trotsky was happy enough with Burnham's praise of his work. But he bristled at the reference to his having monkeyed with the documentary record. The reviewer must *"name clearly and exactly what 'important quotations' I erroneously dated and what I consciously omitted,"* he sternly demanded in a letter to the *Symposium*. Trotsky had misread him, Burnham replied. The charges had merely been noted, not endorsed.[54] This seems to have mollified Trotsky. But Trotsky now wanted to learn more about his reviewer. "I remember very well how great an impression your article in the *Symposium* produced upon me at Prinkipo," he later wrote to Burnham, "and with what insistence I asked [the American radical] Max Eastman about you in order to clarify for myself the possibility of further [*sic*] collaboration with you."[55]

By the time his review appeared, Burnham had left New York to spend the summer with his family at St. Jean de Luz, a fashionable French resort town on the Biscay coast near Biarritz. There, he devoted himself to chemin de fer, playing in a daredevil fashion and often winning. (Similar recklessness at a casino in Deauville later that summer brought him a reprimand from the manager: *"Monsieur,* you have a responsibility to the people betting on you. Here, you are not permitted to take such risks.")[56] But as usual, he could not escape work. For one thing, NYU had just cut two philosophy professors and parceled their courses out among the remaining faculty; for the survivors this meant more preparation. For another, he came to the aid of his brother David, whose publisher had turned down his second novel, *Wedding Song.* Burnham understood why, calling the book, a tale of American expatriates in Venice, "somehow wrong, . . . somehow *perverse.*" But, believing it could be salvaged, he worked with David to revise it, until David was felled by sunstroke.[57]

When not otherwise occupied, Burnham pored over the writings of Marx and Engels (an ironic choice of authors for an opulent, bourgeois holiday) hoping to understand better the world economic crisis.[58] How much this reading influenced him is hard to say. But his anxiety about the future continued to mount. The historian and biographer Matthew Josephson, who met him in 1932, at first regarded him as "a shy young mental prodigy of the type we tend to label 'frosty intellectual.'" But as Burnham began to talk about Marx, Lenin, and Trotsky, Josephson noted, a change came over him. He seemed lost in a vision of "vast blood baths that would attend the overthrow of our society."[59]

Since his review of Trotsky's history, Burnham had been finding virtues in Marxism, but he still questioned the Marxist worldview. Thus, in a *Symposium* article of January 1933 called "Marxism and Esthetics," he voiced his ambivalence about the Marxist philosophy of art. The "extreme Marxist" interpretation of art as a product of society's economic structure could not furnish a basis for discriminating between better and worse, he pointed out. Moreover, the Marxist insistence that art enlist in the cause of revolution risked subordinating aesthetic values to politics. Yet he was also hostile to "the bourgeois individualist (the 'liberal') cry for [artistic] freedom," which he decried as "almost always a cover for irresponsibility and lack of direction and in the end, unconsciously, for reactionary class privilege." But Marxism could "never be merely rejected," he concluded. "There is so much in Marxism that is true and good that if we do not accept it we must find a position that will include its true and its good." He nevertheless ended the article on an anti-Marxist note. "Because I believe that Marxism is, in the last analysis, false," he wrote, "false in this sense—inhuman and offering an order of values not acceptable to man nor in keeping with man's nature—I do not rest my hopes for art in any esthetics it can give birth to."[60]

In March 1933, soon after the appearance of "Marxism and Esthetics," Burnham read Hook's just published *Towards the Understanding of Karl Marx: A Revolutionary Interpretation,* a book-length version of Hook's 1931 *Symposium* article. Marxism should be viewed not as a body of dogma, the book argued, but as a mode of analysis and as "naturalistic, historical, and empirical throughout."[61] More open to Marxist ideas than he had been in 1931, Burnham found Hook's pragmatist-instrumentalist reading of Marxism persuasive, and now adopted an outlook more Marxist than not.

Burnham's position by March 1933 is seen in an editorial statement that he and Wheelwright (with Burnham probably the main author) published in the *Symposium*'s spring issue. Called "Thirteen Propositions," the statement was a reply to complaints from readers that the magazine was deliberately avoiding politics. Denying this, the editors waded in, condemning "capitalism," and endorsing violence to replace it with socialism, which they pronounced indispensable if "western civilization" were to be saved. (They seemed not to notice that the civilization they wanted to save was, in a Marxist sense, a "bourgeois" one.) To succeed, they went on, the revolution would have to be led by "a militant and organized party." The Communist Party, however, did not fill the bill, because its sectarianism, utopianism, and rigid adherence to Soviet positions made no sense in an American context. For example, its answer to the "Negro problem," "self-determination for the Black Belt," wrongly viewed the Deep South, with its large black population, as the equivalent of an ethnic minority region in the USSR. The party was also disqualified for leadership in the United States by its "barbaric" ideas about morality, literature, art, religion, and human nature. What the country needed was a revolutionary party that would reject totalitarianism, keep its hands off culture, and make the establishment of a socialist economy its only aim.[62]

Though he now viewed the world from a more or less Marxist standpoint, Burnham was still respectful of other opinions. Thus, in the October 1933 *Symposium* (the magazine's last issue, as it turned out), he wrote with excitement about a new book called *The Modern Corporation and Private Property,* the work of two Columbia University law professors, Adolf A. Berle and Gardiner Means. American business had undergone a sweeping, though mostly unnoticed, structural transformation, the book argued. The diffusion of ownership in modern corporations through shareholding had separated formal property rights from actual control, making "managers," not legal owners, the true masters of the corporate world. "This dissolution of the atom of property" was undermining the base on which the economy had hitherto rested, opening the way for a new system that would eventually become as "all-embracing" as feudalism had once been.[63]

In Burnham's eyes, the book's well-argued case that a kind of managers' revolution was taking place made it one of the most important works of social analysis in years. All the same, loyal to his newly acquired Marxism, he felt obliged to qualify his praise. "Marxian analysis alone" he asserted, could unravel the mystery of social development. Hence, the non-Marxist *Modern Corporation and Private Property,* while very good, fell short of the highest level. (The review also showed how far Burnham had moved to the left. The Roosevelt administration, he wrote in an echo of the communist line on the New Deal, was merely "Fascism without shirts.")[64]

Until the summer of 1933 Burnham's Marxism was, as he later put it, only "theoretical."[65] But that summer, traveling through the industrial Midwest, he saw "at first hand," in his words, "the class struggle, the starvation and the terror in act . . . among Detroit auto workers, in the steel mills, in the Illinois coal districts." He came home in shock. He was now convinced, Lucius Wilmerding remembers, that "the real world was the world of strikes, organizing, and labor violence."[66]

He had changed his views "considerably" since the previous spring, Burnham announced in the *Symposium.* He no longer agreed with everything he had written in "Thirteen Propositions," or at least now would "state many things differently." In particular, he felt more sympathy for the Communist Party. He still believed his criticism of communism to be "substantially correct," but having just witnessed the difficulties communists faced, he now thought criticism should try to help the party. The country's options had narrowed to three: communism, fascism, "or complete breakdown." He chose communism, and his choice was "unequivocal."[67]

All the same, he confessed, he retained some doubts about communism. He was not prepared to sacrifice intellect to militancy, and wanted to honor reason along with justice. Thus, he rejected the "delusion" that revolution would bring utopia. Because need was limited "only by the imagination," no society could live by the precept "to each according to his needs." Nevertheless, despite its failings, communism offered the "only hope" of saving the West.[68]

Having gone this far, he would have to go further, he decided. Logic and duty demanded that he act on his beliefs, that he work for the establishment of a communist society. But to do so he would have to enlist in a solidly organized collective effort, for neither correct ideas alone nor individual action would bring success. Hence, he must consider joining the Communist Party, which possessed the needed discipline and cohesion. What counted most about the party, he told Hook, was its "effective centralized structure," since without such a means of advancing them, ideas were only "talk."[69] Hook attributed the party's allure for Burnham to the same "organizational absolutism" that Burnham simultaneously admired in the Catholic Church.[70]

Moving toward party membership, Burnham agreed in the fall of 1933 to act as "educational advisor" to the NYU branch of the Young Communist League, some of whose members had signed up for his courses. These students then arranged for him to discuss the communist program with the party's general secretary, Earl Browder, who wanted to make him party leader at NYU. Meeting with Browder, Burnham accepted almost the entire program. But on a single matter—"self-determination for the Black Belt"—he balked, still finding the idea absurd. Browder, not wanting to scare off his prey, did not pressure him, but readily agreed to give him time to think.[71]

Soon after, Burnham reviewed a biography of Lenin for the communist literary monthly, the *New Masses.* This was further proof of his closeness to the party, which reserved such work for members and trusted fellow travelers. The review was everything the party could have hoped for. Extolling the founder of the Soviet state as "the chief historical figure of our time, and probably the chief political leader of all time," Burnham also lavished praise on dialectical materialism as the only theory capable of explaining "the relation of the . . . leader to history.[72]

But by the time the review appeared, Burnham's flirtation with the Communist Party had ended. Aside from his inability to swallow "self-determination for the Black Belt"—proof of the party's subordination to the USSR—he listened to Hook, who, deciding that the party was "insufficiently Marxist both in its slogans and in its practices," which leaned heavily toward authoritarianism, had broken with communism, and was urging Burnham to do the same. Within a short time, Hook won Burnham over. But as Hook himself well knew, his success owed less to his talent for persuasion than to the launching late in 1933 of a new revolutionary socialist party that he had helped to organize: the American Workers Party (AWP).[73]

# Chapter 3

# Bolshevik

T HE AMERICAN WORKERS PARTY (AWP) was founded by a group of militant labor leaders—among them, Gerry Allard of the Illinois Progressive Mine Workers' Union, J. B. S. Hardman of the Amalgamated Clothing Workers Union, and Louis F. Budenz—aided by leftist but anticommunist intellectuals such as Sidney Hook. At the head of the party stood A. J. Muste, a Dutch-born former clergyman who, under the shock of World War I, had turned pacifist and given up his ministry for labor organizing. After winning his spurs in the bitter Lawrence, Massachusetts, textile workers' strike of 1919, Muste had founded the Brookwood Labor College in Katonah, New York, to train professional labor leaders. At first, the college enjoyed the support of the mainstream labor movement. But in 1928 the American Federation of Labor (AFL) turned hostile to Muste, accusing him of organizing pro-Soviet demonstrations and attacking religion, and a few years later had him removed from Brookwood's board of directors. Meanwhile, in 1929, Muste launched a new venture, the Conference for Progressive Labor Action (CPLA), whose aims were to unionize mass production workers, fight union corruption, and establish a political party akin to Britain's Labour Party.[1]

With the onset of the Depression, Muste moved sharply to the left. Dropping the model of a moderate, British-style workers party, he now called for an American radical party that, unlike the merely reformist U.S. Socialist Party, would fight for full-scale social revolution, and unlike the U.S. Communist Party, which was genuinely revolutionary but obedient to Moscow, be "rooted in American soil" and concerned with "American conditions and problems." To this end he founded the AWP.[2]

Hook, who was on the AWP's organizing committee and busy dissuading Burnham from joining the Communists, cited the AWP as a better alternative. Burnham was ready to bite. But what landed him was meeting another member of the organizing committee, Gerry Allard, charismatic labor leader and editor of the newspaper *Fighting Miner.* Burnham was dazzled by Allard, whose commitment to revolution was equalled only by his hostility to the Communist Party, and who seemed the living embodiment of working class militancy.[3]

The AWP was formally established by the Committee for Progressive Labor Action in November 1933 at a convention in the grimy factory town of Pittsburgh. Muste was named party chairman, Hardman vice chairman, and Budenz executive secretary. The party platform's foreign affairs plank was written by Burnham, who borrowed heavily from Lenin. Should the capitalists start a war, this provision declared, the AWP would act to turn the conflict into a workers' revolt against the war makers. Similarly, if the USSR came under capitalist attack, the AWP would come to its defense by joining with the workers to overthrow the U.S. government. But Burnham also criticized the Soviet policy of "socialism in one country," charging it with abandoning the principle of "proletarian internationalism" and the goal of world revolution.[4]

The AWP began with a discouragingly modest base. Only about a thousand people paid dues to the new party, and a thousand more extended their moral support.[5] But if this tiny phalanx of left-wing militants garrisoned in a shabby office on Manhattan's East 19th Street could not boast of its size, it could point with pride to its zeal and an explosion of hectic activity. Brimming with energy, Burnham threw himself into the bustle, writing, traveling, and organizing, and handling Muste's correspondence when the chairman went to Ohio to help lead a strike. Moreover, with Hook, he did much to set the party's ideological tone, hewing to a strict Marxist line in everything but aesthetics.[6]

Showing the same earnestness as he had in editing the *Symposium,* he worked hard to bring the AWP message to the world. Thus, after losing a bet to Lucius Wilmerding, he refused to pay Wilmerding in cash, but instead gave him a subscription to the AWP's newspaper, *Labor Action.*[7]

Burnham's most visible AWP activity was a column he wrote for *Labor Action.* Debuting in March 1934, and called "Their Government," the column concentrated on "exposing" the New Deal, which it portrayed in conventional Marxist fashion as a capitalist bail-out operation poorly concealed behind a phony show of sympathy for the laboring masses. Franklin D. Roosevelt was probably the smartest politician ever to sit in the White House, Burnham wrote. Never before had a president so successfully feigned concern for the common man. Yet FDR was in fact working for big business, the banks, the rich, and the munitions makers. He was even arming for war "to protect and increase" capitalist profits and to win new opportunities for capitalism. Both major parties were run by the industrialists and the bankers, Burnham charged, and differed only in their tactics for maintaining the "capitalist dictatorship." Holding elections under capitalism was like permitting prisoners every few years to elect their warden: one warden might be a bit more easy-going than another, but whoever won, prison life would remain largely the same. True democratic government would consist of "political councils based on workers in the shops and fields and mines [and] responsible to the workers," i.e., soviets. The workers would make real rather than illusory gains only when they seized everything owed them.[8]

The appearance of "Their Government" completed a key transition in Burnham's life. The nonpolitical critic had turned into a political activist and columnist. This change was accompanied by a change in his writing style. Since his new readers might not have had much education, he worked himself free of his "pedantry" and "highbrowism" and developed a sharper, more direct style and a knack for punch lines. His writing eschewed erudition and grew in energy and impact.

❖ ❖ ❖ ❖

Burnham also continued to teach a full load of courses. Divided between two wholly separate callings, his life took on a schizophrenic quality. Aquinas, Dante, the Renaissance, and aesthetics remained his daily fare in the classroom. But when he rolled a sheet of paper into his typewriter, it was to expose the falseness of New Deal social policy or the crooked capitalist system. Only once, in 1934, did his classroom and political lives overlap, when he gave a course called "The Philosophies of Communism and Fascism." His students found it hard to relate the classroom Burnham to the radical Burnham. One student, his image of Burnham entirely shaped by an aesthetics class, was amazed to come upon his reserved and seemingly nonpolitical professor haranguing a crowd of demonstrators from the steps of the Arts and Sciences Building.[9]

But despite his Marxism, Burnham could still praise non–Marxist writers, especially when their ideas appealed to his Augustinian sensibility. Foremost among these was the theologian Reinhold Niebuhr, whose doubts about the possibility of social progress he readily echoed. Niebuhr took his view of man from Machiavelli, Burnham noted in a 1934 review of Niebuhr's book *Reflections on the End of an Era*. Niebuhr knew that human nature, "with its dark springs," ruled out any chance that social justice would triumph in history, and in his grasp of the human condition so far surpassed most social critics that he was "always worth reading."[10] The belief that tragedy always had and always would cast a pall over human existence had long been a basic component of Burnham's own worldview. Ironically, this belief did not sit well with Marxism, which prophesied the salvation of man through revolution.

When Burnham embarked on the path of political activism, he gave up editing his literary quarterly. Early in 1934, after its twelfth issue had come out, the *Symposium* ceased publication. The ostensible reason was lack of money, Dean Munn's move to Harvard having dried up its funding. Burnham and Wheelwright could, of course, have looked for money elsewhere, but they did not. Burnham may have decided that his duty now lay in working for revolution. Wheelwright, whose interests had not changed, might have tried to save the magazine had his old relationship with Burnham remained intact. But Burnham was no longer the man he had been four years earlier. Not only had he fallen head-over-heels for Marxism, he was also spending more time with Hook, who had taken Wheelwright's place as the main influence on his thinking. This opened up a gap between Wheelwright and Burnham, one which widened in March 1934 when Burnham married (a step Hook thought might have caused the gap to begin with).[11] When Hook was appointed chairman of the philosophy department, Wheelwright decided it was time to leave. And so he walked away, allowing the journal to expire.

◆   ◆   ◆   ◆

Burnham's bride was Marcia Lightner, twenty-two at the time, and the oldest of the three daughters of Frank and Helen Lightner of St. Paul, Minnesota.[12] Frank Lightner had grown up in Detroit and graduated from the University of Michigan. Going into the dry goods business, he had risen to become an executive at the St. Paul firm of Strong and Warner. In St. Paul he met his wife, Helen Dean, who came from a local family. The Deans were Presbyterians, and the Lightner children were raised as such. An Episcopalian (his father was a priest), Frank Lightner nevertheless sometimes escorted his family to church on Sunday, protecting his orthodoxy by dozing off during the sermon. As this suggests, Presbyterian spirituality does not seem to have influenced his behavior, for when Prohibition was enacted, he installed a roomy liquor cache, accessible through a trap door, under the living-room floor of his big house on Grand Avenue. Though enjoying good health all his life, he died before his daughters had grown up, succumbing to pneumonia in April 1928 at the age of fifty-nine.

Tall, blond, and high-spirited, Marcia was sixteen when her father died, and a junior at the Masters School, a boarding school for girls in Dobbs Ferry, New York. Upon graduating a year later, she persuaded her mother—left with money by her husband but in anguish over his death—to take the family to Paris for an extended stay. In September 1929 Mrs. Lightner and her three girls sailed for France, where they boarded at the home of a French family in Auteuil, just outside Paris. While her younger sisters went to the American School in Auteuil, Marcia studied painting at an atelier in the Place des Vosges. She also developed a liking for nightclubs, and once attended a performance by Josephine Baker, then in the first flush of her celebrity. But the Lightners did not stagnate. In February 1930 Mrs. Lightner took Marcia to London to see a much-publicized art exhibit, and the following summer the whole family went touring. Not until autumn did they head back to St. Paul.

Marcia had many interests, music—she played the piano well—and painting among them, but at this point no real plans. The thought of college held little appeal, but neither did she want to vegetate in St. Paul. Headstrong and, as her sister Katherine put it, liking to do "flamboyant things," in September 1933, at the age of twenty-one, she moved to New York, and there, despite the Depression, landed a job as a kitchenware "demonstrator" in Stern's department store.

Soon afterward, Marcia met James Burnham, probably through Burnham's Princeton friend Dean Clark, who happened to be her first cousin. Jim and

Marcia's lives had many parallels. Both were midwesterners with close ties to St. Paul. Both were the oldest of three children of the same sex, had gone east to boarding school, and had lost their fathers in 1928 to pneumonia. Both played the piano, loved good music, and had a strong interest in painting. Both were tall and slim, took pains with their dress, and projected an aura of quiet elegance. (Jim showed great interest in Marcia's wardrobe. Years later, friends remember, he liked to talk with her about her clothes, asking, for example, why she had chosen to wear one dress rather than another on a given occasion.)[13] Though in temperament they diverged sharply, she animated and expressive, he cool and reserved, each seemed to delight in the other's distinguishing traits, he in her spontaneity, and she in his intelligence and range of knowledge. True, she disliked his political views, but not enough to drop him. After knowing each other a mere two or three months they decided to marry.

Marcia broke the news to her family in December 1933 when she returned to St. Paul for Christmas. Her mother was far from pleased. "Much fuss about Marcia and this Jim Burnham," Marcia's sister Katherine wrote in her diary. Outwardly, Mrs. Lightner opposed the marriage on the ground that Marcia was not yet ready. Inwardly, she may have feared the loss of a daughter who had been a key source of emotional support since her husband's death. On New Year's Eve she fell ill and had to be hospitalized, perhaps partly because of this new worry.[14]

But there was no stopping the determined Marcia. By mid-February she had completed her wedding arrangements. Mrs. Lightner had meanwhile thrown in the towel. On March 31, 1934, during NYU's spring break, Jim and Marcia were married in the Lightners' living room, a Presbyterian minister officiating. Notably absent was Burnham's mother, even though at the time she was visiting in St. Paul. She too disapproved of the marriage—possibly, a cousin speculates, because, like Mrs. Lightner, she disliked losing her child, but perhaps also because she opposed the Protestant service.[15] (Though she herself had married a Protestant, the wedding seems to have been performed by a Catholic priest, and the groom had promised that their children would be raised as Catholics.)

Right after the wedding the newlyweds dashed back to New York, since Jim's teaching schedule left no time for a honeymoon. Their first apartment was in Greenwich Village several blocks west of Washington Square. Along with the usual furnishings was an upright piano, on which they played duets, often Schubert pieces. Though their courtship had been brief, their marriage proved long and solid. After breaking up with Martha Dodd, Jim had told Sidney Schiff that of the various relationships he would form in the course of his life he hoped that the one with his wife would be the most important,[16] and so it was.

◆   ◆   ◆   ◆

In the year of his marriage, Burnham became involved in another relationship that marked him for life. For in 1934 he helped to negotiate a merger between the AWP and the Communist League of America (CLA), which led to his becoming a top lieutenant of Leon Trotsky.

At the head of the CLA stood James Patrick Cannon, in 1934 a man in his mid-forties whose blunt features, stocky build, and florid complexion made him look more like a New York police sergeant than a Bolshevik revolutionary. Raised in a Kansas farming community by Irish-American, fiercely socialist parents, he had in his youth joined both the syndicalist Industrial Workers of the World (IWW), for which he had worked at the dangerous job of itinerant organizer, and the Socialist Party (SP), enlisting in its radical wing. But under the spell of the Russian Revolution, and impatient with the Socialist Party's gradualism, he had resigned in 1919 and helped to found the SP's more militant communist rival. As a Communist Party leader, he had gone to Moscow in 1928 to serve on the program committee of the Sixth Congress of the Communist International (Comintern), the Soviet-run world organization of communist parties, and there his life-long Trotskyism had begun.

Leon Trotsky, in 1928, seemed a man in ruin. He had been stripped of all his state and party posts, even of his party membership, and banished to Alma Ata, the remote and primitive capital of Soviet Kazakhstan. But followers somehow smuggled his criticisms of the Comintern draft program into the Congress, criticisms that amounted to an indictment of Communist Party general secretary, Joseph Stalin. Cannon, who studied the criticisms, was at once won over. "It was as clear as daylight," he said, "that Marxist truth was on the side of Trotsky."[17]

Back in New York, Cannon publicized Trotsky's anti-Stalin views. Almost at once he was joined by a handful of like-minded militants, foremost among them a party comrade named Max Shachtman. Born in Russia in 1904, and brought to the United States as a baby, Shachtman had grown up in the Bronx in relative comfort. As a teenager, he had joined the Communist Party, and after a year at

City College had dropped out to work as a full-time revolutionary.[18] In superficial ways, he and Cannon stood poles apart. While Cannon could be ponderous, Shachtman had the nimble, rapid-fire wit of a Borscht Belt spritzer. Cannon loved "organizational" work, Shachtman found it tedious. But the two were as one in their commitment to the Bolshevik cause, whose truest spokesman since Lenin's death, they agreed, was Trotsky.

Angered by the Trotskyism of the Cannon group, in October 1928 the Communist Party expelled it. Undaunted, the Trotskyists at once started publishing a newspaper, the *Militant,* and laying the groundwork for a political organization. In May 1929 delegates representing a grand total of about a hundred Trotskyists nationwide met in Chicago to launch the "Communist League of America, Left Opposition of the Communist Party," a name meant to identify the CLA not as a new party in competition with the Communist Party, but as an opposition caucus within the party. That way, said Cannon, it would be easier to win new members from among the Stalinists, a tactic he was counting on to build up his tiny band.[19]

The ultimate aim of the CLA, Cannon wryly declared, was "to take power in the United States." But its means were virtually nil. Close to flat broke, not until its second year could it scrape together enough money to rent seedy quarters on Manhattan's Third Avenue. The appearance of the *Militant* was always in doubt, for the paper was printed on a second-hand linotype machine that broke down often.[20] Matching the party's poverty was the personal poverty of many of its members. One, an immigrant house painter from Denmark named Arne Swabeck, had so little money that one day at the office he fainted from hunger.[21]

To make things worse, the CLA failed to draw recruits from the Communist Party or any other source. "We had no friends, no sympathizers, no periphery around our movement," Cannon later wrote. "We were utterly isolated, forced in upon ourselves." Trotskyism languished in obscurity, "an isolated handful against the world."[22] Now and then, shrouded in Celtic melancholy, Cannon would vanish—to drown his sorrows in drink, his comrades suspected—and not show up again for weeks.[23]

Cannon nevertheless regarded himself as a natural leader. "Max," he would tell Shachtman, "you either got it or you ain't got it," and many of his comrades agreed that he indeed had it. Not least among his talents was a gift for rousing oratory.[24] His booming jeremiads against capitalists and Stalinists could bring audiences to their feet. But unlike many in the movement, he was no intellectual. He had had little schooling, and was not much of a reader (though he did like light verse, and enjoyed reciting poetry). His lack of aptitude for dialectical fencing made him self-conscious, and to save face, he played ʻ.e bluff man of action who, while respecting "the serious intellectual," disdained chattering theorizers.[25]

As far as Cannon was concerned, there was no need to theorize. Trotsky had already done so, and the proper work of his followers was to serve as "the Old Man's" messengers.[26] Trotsky charged that the Russian Revolution had been "betrayed." A greedy and power-hungry bureaucracy, the product of Russia's social and cultural backwardness and the economic collapse brought on by the Russian civil war, had seized control, and was waxing fat in a poverty-stricken society. Stalin had risen to power as the bureaucracy's champion, and now, though seemingly a dictator, was really its front man.

Ultimately, Trotsky asserted, the revolution's decay stemmed from its failure to take root outside the USSR, for without the aid of more advanced economies Russia could do little to further its own development. The solution lay in rejecting Stalin's policy of "socialism in one country" and returning to Lenin's policy of world revolution. Still, true Marxist-Leninists need not despair over the USSR, since the Soviet regime, despite its perversion, had built a collectivist economy, thus laying the basis for socialism. Accordingly, the USSR, though "deformed," remained a workers' state. The revolution had been "betrayed by the ruling stratum," "but not yet overthrown."[27]

These pronouncements of Trotsky's Cannon took as gospel. As far as he was concerned, they were all the theory he needed. They were all the theory that *any* good Bolshevik needed.

◆   ◆   ◆   ◆

In exile since 1929, Trotsky strove to pry the communist movement out of Stalin's grip and make it again the spearhead of world revolution. At first he hoped to do this by leaving his disciples in the world's communist parties as "opposition" factions that might one day take those parties over. Hence, the original self-conception of Cannon's CLA. But in 1933, having failed to make headway, he decided that the Stalinists had grown too rotten to be reinvigorated, and that his

followers must therefore form parties of their own, along with a new international body to compete with the Comintern. He also now thought that instead
of seeking to recruit new members from the communist parties, Trotskyists
should focus their efforts on socialist parties, whose more radical members they
might be able to attract. If successful, they could increase their own numbers,
while simultaneously destroying the cohesion of their reformist rivals.[28]

This new tactic was first attempted in France, where in 1934 the hundred or
so members of a French Trotskyist group called the Communist League of France
carried out a "turn" into the French Socialist Party, hoping to win its militants to
their banner.[29] Taking his cue from the "French turn," Cannon decided to launch
a similar maneuver in the United States. As his target he picked the fledgling
AWP, which he derided as "a political menagerie which had within it every type
of political species . . . from proletarian revolutionists to reactionary scoundrels
and fakers."[30] In January 1934 he went into action, inviting "the Musteites" to
meet with the CLA to discuss a merger.

The AWP gave the invitation a mixed reception. Wary of the Trotskyists,
whom they considered totalitarians, J. B. S. Hardman and Louis Budenz opposed
a merger. Muste was not sure.[31] Hook had doubts at first, but then turned in
favor, hoping for "a strong and active anti-Stalinist force on the left."[32] Burnham
supported a merger from the start. Already a Trotsky enthusiast, he had written to
the Old Man (as Trotskyists called their leader) just before the *Symposium*'s
demise, inviting him to contribute an article to the journal. Joining forces with
serious revolutionary Marxists, he believed, would foster a needed hardening of
the AWP. "Fundamentally," he told Hook, "there is the question of whether or
not the AWP is going to be a revolutionary party or a confused bunch of labor
agitators, reformists, good fellows, etc." Therefore steps should be taken to promote a merger: "joint membership meetings; joint meetings of the national committees every two weeks; . . . exchange of writers in the respective organs;
inter-party bulletins. . . ."[33]

But for all his zeal, Burnham did a poor job of defending his cause. Too
confident of the power of pure logic, he ignored the emotional aspects of the art
of persuasion. His audiences seem to have found him condescending. Every time
Burnham spoke on behalf of a merger, said Hook, "we lost support because of his
unpersuasive—though very logical—presentation." Muste's friends jeered at
Burnham for having no contact with real workers. Hardman, in particular, dis-

liked him and accused him of being dogmatic and inflexible. Burnham, equally combative, fought back, attacking Hardman as a "non-revolutionist" and demanding, though to no avail, that he be dropped from the committee named to hold talks with the CLA.[34]

Weighed down by the burdens of teaching and politics, Burnham longed to escape. In the summer of 1934, he succeeded at least part of the time by renting a house in New Milford, not far from Canterbury. He spent three days a week in the city, he wrote to Hook, "and the other four in the country reading Aristotle and Aquinas, and getting sunshine. Their close, golden reasoning is a relief to the spirit after many [AWP] meetings I remember, and the sunshine is certainly fine for the body."[35]

That autumn, the merger talks went into high gear, with Burnham and Hook the AWP's most avid negotiators.[36] In November 1934, after almost a year of bargaining, the AWP finally agreed to merge. Not only had the Trotskyists yielded on certain points of doctrine. Under the leadership of Cannon's truck-driver friend Vincent Dunne, Trotskyist boss of the Teamsters' Minneapolis local, they had also led a long and violent strike in Minneapolis, thus proving that they, too, were genuinely serious about the labor movement, not simply about the Trotsky-Stalin conflict. Moreover, the AWP had not made nearly the splash that Muste had hoped for. A merger, he came to think, might revive his flagging venture.[37] Meanwhile, Trotsky had approved the concessions Cannon had made.

On December 1 and 2, 1934, delegates of the AWP and the CLA met at the Stuyvesant Casino in downtown Manhattan to seal the bargain. The party that emerged was dubbed the Workers Party of the United States (WPUS). Cannon was given the post of national chairman, and remained editor of the *Militant,* now renamed the *New Militant,* while Muste was named national secretary.[38] Hardman and Budenz, unreconciled to the merger, broke with Muste and went their separate ways. More surprising was a decision by Hook not to stay active (on the excuse that he needed time for writing). Burnham, viewed by Hook as the person most eager for the merger,[39] joined Shachtman as coeditor of the *New International,* a monthly "theoretical" journal Shachtman had started a few months earlier. There, Burnham wrote under the name "John West," chosen, he once said, to express his hope that "a new Western renaissance" lay ahead.[40]

The merger turned into a conquest for the Trotskyists, who, far more aggressive than their Musteite partners, quickly took over the WPUS. "In one operation," crowed Cannon, "we cleared a centrist obstacle from the path and enlarged our own forces." Or as Hook succinctly put it, "The Trotskyists swallowed the AWP."[41] Not surprisingly, Muste began to regret the merger. Burnham did not. Captivated by the drive and toughness of his new comrades, and feeling no nostalgia for the AWP, he went over to Cannon.

◆ ◆ ◆ ◆

Burnham labored mightily for the Trotskyist cause, making his typewriter his major weapon in the struggle not only as coeditor of the *New International,* but also as a contributor to the *New Militant.* As a writer, he stood somewhat apart from the Trotskyist mainstream, favoring a nonrhetorical style over bombast and analysis over denunciation, although he did not always succeed in avoiding Marxist jargon. He continued to make the New Deal his primary target,[42] but he also trained his guns on Stalinism, calling it a policy of tyranny at home and collaboration with the "imperialist" powers abroad in order to consolidate the dominance of the Soviet bureaucracy. The USSR was nevertheless still a workers' state, he affirmed, echoing Trotsky, and hence a country all Marxist-Leninists had to defend—not, of course, by supporting Stalin, but by seeking the victory of genuine Bolshevism both in the USSR and around the world.[43]

Burnham also wrote about Marxism, the theory that lay behind his political analysis. He took great pride in what he saw as its hard-headed view of the world in contrast to philosophies rooted in "dreams and illusions." When an erstwhile quasi-Trotskyist, the veteran radical Max Eastman, argued in the *New International* that Marx, despite his aim of doing away with "philosophy" (i.e., subjective imagining dressed up as objective truth) in favor of "science," had simply produced another "philosophy," Burnham peremptorily called Eastman on the carpet. What Marx had wanted to do away with, he retorted, was philosophy that reasoned deductively from abstract premises. It was through rigorously empirical inquiry that Marx had arrived at his understanding of history and his belief that his thought was "scientific."[44] Burnham showed equal impatience with Marxists who treated what he considered an experimental philosophy as a kind of holy writ. Genuine Marxism, he asserted, was characterized "not by exhaustiveness of scholarship, not by skill in quoting and counter-quoting or by abstract 'logical' consistency," but by "cogency of concrete analyses, the accuracy of specific predictions, and . . . the practical success of strategy and action."[45]

Besides serving as a mainstay of the party press, Burnham carried on a voluminous correspondence with fellow party members, commenting at length on current party doings, on doctrine and tactics, on forecasts of ultimate triumph or tragedy, depending on which faction in which intraparty conflict came out on top. The amount of time and energy he poured into these letters and his absorption in the trivia they contained suggest that he had lost his sense of measure, and was hovering on the brink of a full-blown sectarian neurosis. His behavior in June 1935 illustrates his state of mind.

With a grueling college year just ended and a chance to relax at hand, he and Marcia drove to North Carolina to visit an aunt of Marcia's, and planned to go next to St. Paul and Kenilworth for more vacationing and visiting. But when an emergency meeting of the WPUS's National Committee, of which he was a member, was suddenly called for the following week, he raced hundreds of miles back to New York, despite his exhaustion convinced that he "would have to be there." His health (and Marcia's) fared poorly in this atmosphere of chronic urgency. His physical condition had been "lamentably bad . . . during the past six months," he wrote that summer to Hook, whom he counseled, given his own "unpleasant experience," to get in a "real vacation" before the fall term began. Hook did what he could to ease the pressure on Burnham by giving him a convenient teaching schedule, but this was not enough to do much good.[46]

Still, Burnham did not succumb to the party completely. When Cannon, in the summer of 1935, urged him to drop "the two-for-a-nickel business of instructing college students" and come to work for the party full-time, he turned down the proposal. He did not think it wise to commit himself totally to a cause that might not come to fruition in his lifetime, he explained to an incredulous Cannon. He even accused the WPUS of failing to understand practical politics. Absorbed in ideology and believing that they would ultimately triumph, Trotskyists, he warned, were doing too little to publicize their views.[47] Even true ideas did not triumph automatically.

◆　◆　◆　◆

Like the AWP before it, the WPUS entered the world with great expectations, sure that it would draw a mass following to its cause. Thanks to donations from veteran Muste supporters, the party was able to rent an office in what Cannon called "a grand palace" at Fifth Avenue and 15th Street, hire a secretary, and install a switchboard. For Trotskyist alumni of the Third Avenue days, it was like living in a dream. But before long the happy dreamers were rudely awakened. Again few recruits showed up, and soon the money ran out, whereupon the secretary left, the switchboard shut down, and the party was evicted. Now an office was found more in keeping with Trotskyist tradition: a loft in a dingy building on East 11th Street. For a while the new headquarters had a telephone, but the service proved too expensive and had to be cancelled.[48]

But far from despairing, the ambitious Trotskyists embarked on a new project. Having splintered the AWP and enticed its more radical members into their ranks, they set out to execute a "French turn" into the Socialist Party. Some twenty thousand strong in 1935, the SP was deeply divided over how to respond to the New Deal, and so made inviting prey. To Cannon, it seemed a "centrist mishmash," a "headless, helpless party." If the Trotskyists joined the SP for a while, they might be able to capture its left wing and its youth division, the Young People's Socialist League (YPSL), and take the converts with them when they left.[49]

Whether to attempt a French turn first became an issue for formal WPUS debate in June 1935. Against Cannon, with whom Burnham enthusiastically sided,[50] stood Muste and his friends from the AWP. For eight days the debate raged. Muste aimed the brunt of his attack at Burnham. He "used all the Hardman stuff," Burnham told Hook, "'Professor,' 'Cannon stooge,' 'Thomist,' 'Teacher lecturing,' etc." Burnham fired back, impressing his listeners by quoting from Shakespeare and the Bible without having to rummage through *Bartlett's Familiar Quotations*. The debate ended with the issue unresolved. But Burnham was so exhausted that he now considered a vacation medically necessary.[51]

In the months that followed, Burnham fought tirelessly for the French turn. "We are not concerned over the *names* of things," he argued in the *Workers Party Internal Bulletin,* a mimeographed sheet for intraparty debate. The WPUS had value only as a means of advancing the revolution, and could be "altered, merged, modified, repaired, or discarded" whenever a better means came along. Those who disagreed, he added in Lenin-like tones, should be purged.[52]

In March 1936 the WPUS voted in favor of the French turn. But the Socialist "Old Guard," the moderates who controlled the party's New York branch, would not permit Trotskyists to join. Then in May the moderates broke with the SP majority and formed a party of their own, the American Labor Party (ALP). With the way now clear, the Trotskyists rushed into action, starting talks with the Socialists on the terms under which the latter would admit them. "It was a difficult and sticky job," Cannon wrote, "very disagreeable. But that did not deter us. A Trotskyist will do anything for [his] party, even . . . crawl on his belly in the mud." When the talks bogged down, Hook stepped in, inviting Cannon and the Socialist leader, Norman Thomas, to his apartment for further negotiating. Thomas, a centrist, did not think much of Cannon, who returned his dislike. But with the aid of Hook, the two leaders reached agreement. The Trotskyists could join the Socialist Party, Thomas stipulated, only as individuals, not as a unit. They must swear not to organize as a faction within the party and must shut down the *New International* and the *New Militant*. Cannon solemnly accepted, and in June 1936, as one Trotskyist, the poet Harry Roskolenko, put it, "We simply danced like Bolshevik ballerinas into their pink-hued china shop."[53]

Once entry had been achieved, Cannon, ill from over-exertion and heavy drinking, went off to California to recover. The remaining Musteites, who had long since had their fill of Trotskyism, resigned. Muste himself, who was in a position to know, described the French turn as "a fake union" (as did Burnham, who later called it "one hundred percent phony"), and turned his back on the Trotskyists. On a trip to Europe later in 1936, he paid a call on Trotsky himself, perhaps hoping to unravel the mystery of the Old Man's charisma. But soon after, on a visit to Paris, he had a vision, the content of which he did not reveal, in the church of St. Sulpice and thereupon washed his hands of revolutionary politics.[54] Burnham thought this decision reflected a failure typical of idealist intellectuals faced with practical political demands. "You know as well as I do that politics has certain rough but more or less objective laws, and that intellectuals, who tend to Platonism [i.e., to a belief in unchanging abstractions] and moralism about politics, tend to get tangled up in those laws," he once remarked to Hook. "Cf. Muste as a perfect example."[55]

"Virtuosos of ideology," the Trotskyists made a brilliant addition to the Socialist Party, recalled the literary critic Irving Howe, then a YPSL member. But their notion of themselves as "the vanguard of tomorrow's vanguard made it all but impossible for them to fuse with any other group." Genuine fusion, however, had never been their aim.[56] With Cannon absent, Shachtman, Burnham, and the impoverished house painter Arne Swabeck took charge of the movement's key New York chapter, intending to maintain it covertly as a disciplined unit despite Cannon's pledge to Thomas. The Trotskyists also found a replacement for the journals they had had to give up, a newspaper called the *Socialist Appeal*. An authorized Socialist Party publication, it was "legal" under the Cannon-Thomas pact but it belonged to a Chicago labor lawyer and independent Trotskyist, Albert Goldman, who quietly agreed to put it at the disposal of Cannon.[57] Thus armed, and calling themselves the Socialist Party's "Appeal Caucus," the Trotskyists took up their work of conversion and demolition.

◆   ◆   ◆   ◆

During the French turn period, Burnham, now thirty years old, consolidated his newfound status as a Trotskyist leader. To begin with, he became one of the Old Man's chief advisers. His first important exercise of this function was prompted by the work of the American Committee for the Defense of Leon Trotsky (a group of 120, mostly prominent, American intellectual and literary figures, among them the critic Edmund Wilson, the novelist James T. Farrell, and Reinhold Niebuhr) to vindicate Trotsky against the Soviet regime's charges of treason. In March 1937 the committee set up a Commission of Inquiry, in theory to hear and evaluate the testimony of Trotsky and others but in fact to impugn the charges and mount a counterattack on Stalin. Both the Defense Committee and the Commission of Inquiry were chaired by John Dewey, whose prestige and reputation for honesty were meant to give the proceedings an aura of impartiality.

Trotsky, now living just outside Mexico City as a guest of the painter Diego Rivera, was delighted with this large-scale propaganda campaign on his behalf. But he felt uneasy about John Dewey, fearing that the philosopher, who was nearing eighty, might doze off during the proceedings, or worse, as a reputed friend of the USSR, exculpate Stalin. In a letter to Trotsky on strategy, Burnham blithely waved away these worries. Dewey was just the right man for the job, he declared with finality. In the same authoritative tone, he went on to address the problem of the inquiry's staging. Trotsky should drop a rumored plan to hold the hearings informally at Rivera's villa, he advised. Rather, to emphasize its gravity, the inquiry should be conducted in a public hall before a large audience of invited reporters and guests. Moreover, Trotsky's suggestion that "three or five solid, honest workers" should be seated on the commission ought to be scrubbed, since everything had to be done "in a thoroughly dignified way."[58] Trotsky did not follow Burnham's advice in all respects, but when the hearings opened Dewey presided, and there was no sign of any "solid, honest workers."

Burnham also served as a lobbyist for the Trotsky Defense Committee. In October 1936 he went with Shachtman to solicit Norman Thomas's blessing for the committee, and he often spoke around New York on its behalf. How persuasive he was is uncertain, for he had apparently not yet shed his previous podium style. "Burnham gives speeches as if we were his students," the quasi-Trotskyist writer James T. Farrell complained.[59]

Burnham also stood out as a writer for the movement. An editor at the *Socialist Appeal,* he more than ever directed his fire at the Stalin regime. "We [bureaucrats]," he summed up its essence, "have altogether abandoned the international revolution; we have given up the class struggle; we are liquidating the revolution inside the Soviet Union; we are interested only in the maintenance of our power and privileges."[60] Stalin's "popular front" strategy of collaborating with noncommunists in a joint defense against fascism had the same aim, he wrote. With a new war coming, Stalin was signaling prospective allies, imperialist Britain and France, that in exchange for formal alliances with the USSR the Kremlin would help them to stifle the rebelliousness of their workers.[61]

A similar purpose motivated Stalin's terror, he argued. The Soviet boss knew that the bureaucracy's betrayal of the revolution would provoke opposition, and was determined to crush all potential resistance before the approaching war had begun. The defendants in the Moscow trials were innocent. Their false confessions had been wrung out of them by "the psychological terror of months of GPU isolation, preceded by 10 years of capitulation; threats and promises concerning relatives; faint hope for personal salvation; confrontations with co-confessions . . . , all of which combine to complete moral disintegration."[62]

The correct revolutionary response to war and terror was not pacifism, he added, for that "subtle and dangerous enemy" could "suffocate" the campaign for peace and freedom in a fog of sentimentality. The right response was what it had always been—ever-mounting class struggle and the fight for world revolution.[63]

Hoping to deepen Trotskyist influence among Marxists of different dispensations, in late 1936 Burnham joined with Hook and others to found the *Marxist*

*Quarterly,* a journal for Marxist scholarship in politics, philosophy, literature, art, and economics. The quarterly would avoid doctrinal exegesis, its maiden issue announced, and in an ecumenical spirit base its editorial judgments on "evidence and truth" rather than party loyalty. It would also try to break the old Marxist habit of ignoring the United States and stress "American history, conditions and problems" (an aim of Burnham's since his AWP days). But quarreling among the editors over the Moscow trials broke out and after its third issue the journal closed up shop.[64]

Burnham was willing to contribute more than words to the movement. Physically tougher than his academic appearance suggested and a trained boxer, he was also ready to use his fists if needed. Left-wing politics in the thirties was anything but sedate. On one occasion when he was slated to speak at an anti-Nazi demonstration outside Madison Square Garden, it seemed as if fighting would surely break out. Burnham arrived on schedule, and gave his speech, ready to shift from words to blows, but the threat blew over.[65]

At Washington Square College Burnham served as the official movement leader. Though never bringing politics into class, he took his movement duties with the utmost seriousness, speaking at rallies, publicizing meetings, and doing whatever else he could to advance the cause. He was assisted by Oscar Shoenfeld (the student in despair over Russell and Whitehead's *Principia Mathematica),* who headed—and, according to Shoenfeld, was much of the time the only member of—the NYU branch of the Spartacus Youth League, the Trotskyist youth organization. Burnham and Shoenfeld got on well. Shoenfeld, who with comradely informality called Burnham "Jim," found him unfailingly amiable, but not given to intimacy. (As Hook said of Burnham in the 1930s: "[he was] outwardly polite—that's the way he'd been brought up"—but with "no great warmth" and "internally quite hard.")[66] Yet Burnham once intervened decisively in Shoenfeld's life. When the communist student leader at NYU volunteered to fight in the Spanish Civil War, Shoenfeld felt he, too, must do so. As Trotskyist student leader, he could not let his Stalinist rival outdo him. But when he told Burnham of his plans, he met with an adamantly negative reaction. If Shoenfeld went to Spain, Burnham warned, the Stalinists, tipped off by their American comrades, would be waiting for him and would kill him. But honor demanded that he go, Shoenfeld insisted. Hour after hour the two debated, until at last, unable to match Burnham's skill at argument, Shoenfeld gave in. "James Burnham saved my life," he later said.[67]

◆　◆　◆　◆

As the Trotskyists prepared for the French turn, Burnham's life took a major turn of its own. In March 1936 Marcia gave birth to their first child, a girl, who was named after her mother and nicknamed Marcie.

Marcie's arrival may have prompted the Burnhams to look for a house outside the city, a retreat for the summer months and college holidays. Returning to Connecticut in the summer of 1937, they soon found a colonial farmhouse in the Housatonic river town of Kent, eighty miles north of New York and in the middle of what Burnham once described as "a rather primitive area of the north-west Connecticut hills."[68] Kent had changed little since the Civil War. Its thousand or so inhabitants earned a meager living as their ancestors had, by farming, growing tobacco, and raising cattle. A somnolent town buried deep in the state's poorest county, Kent was hardly viewed as chic (though it later became so). But its backwater existence made it an alluring haven from urban life.

The farmhouse, a white, clapboard structure built in about 1760, was set against a gently rising hillside flanked by forests. Though not large, it was divided into three floors connected by steep, narrow staircases, and contained eight small and medium-sized rooms. Near the house stood a ramshackle barn that served as a garage—and in time would give the Burnhams extra storage space: in the 1990s, old reading notes of Burnham's could still be found scattered on the barn floor. Beyond the driveway ran a brook that fed a small pond, and on several sides at varying distances lay woodland. Other houses stood nearby, but none close enough to be obtrusive. The property's greatest asset was its atmosphere of peaceful solitude, an atmosphere that struck both Burnhams as idyllic.

The Burnhams did some interior remodeling over the years, and added flower beds and two paved terraces outside. Still, the house retained much of its original flavor. Furnishings and decor were simple and even a trifle spartan (though not rustic). Given the Burnhams' otherwise urbane tastes, some visitors found the spare atmosphere surprising, one going so far as to call it "strangely primitive." But the Burnhams thought their bucolic retreat enchanting—all you had to do was mention Kent, a friend recalled, and they would start raving—and spent as much time there as Burnham's New York commitments would allow.[69]

◆　◆　◆　◆

Meanwhile, the French turn was running into trouble. As the price of their admission to the Socialist Party, the Trotskyists had promised not to form a faction or publish a newspaper, but once admitted they quickly broke both pledges. The *Socialist Appeal* maneuver enabled them "legally" to circumvent the newspaper ban, while informal links—including the bulky letters on ideology and tactics they were addicted to sending each other—allowed them to continue functioning as a unit. In late 1936 they moved toward a more formal mode of organization, using as a cover a Socialist Party body called the Revolutionary Socialist Educational Society, the creation of a New York party leader and non-Trotskyist named Herbert Zam. Soon the Trotskyists came to occupy a key place in the society—Burnham and Shachtman, for example, gained seats on its board of directors—and set out to make it a vehicle for their ends.

Such signs of bad faith made moderate Socialists angry. One of the latter, Jack Altman, the executive secretary of the party's New York branch and an opponent of admitting the Trotskyists to the SP, early in 1937 brought charges of misconduct against Burnham, who at a meeting of the society had laced into its moderate wing with immoderate vigor. Altman may also have been reacting against the party program proposed by the *Socialist Appeal* in December 1936, which denounced the party's pacifism and adherence to the Stalin-inspired popular front and demanded that the party become revolutionary "in the full sense."[70]

Altman's attack on Burnham failed, but it caused the now nervous Trotskyists to pick up the pace of their recruitment. Thus, they asked the Revolutionary Education Society's board to call a national meeting of the Socialist left wing, planning to use the meeting to tighten their ties with party militants. When the society refused, they acted on their own, announcing an "Appeal Institute," to be held in Chicago on the weekend of February 20, 1936, and open to "any and all left wingers in the party." At the institute, the announcement went on, the problems of the Left and the party would be thrashed out, in order to achieve "complete cooperation" between the party's left-wing groups—i.e., unification of the left around the Trotskyists—at the annual Socialist convention scheduled to meet in New York the following month.[71]

One hundred fifty delegates attended the Appeal Institute. Prominent among them was Burnham, who not only sat on the resolutions committee, but addressed a plenary session, calling upon all real leftists to break with the moderates and join the Trotskyist world organization, the "Fourth International."

Burnham was also elected to a new "National Action Committee," intended as a permanent caucus through which the Trotskyists hoped to further left-wing unification.[72] Often in the spotlight at the institute, he came home with his leadership status solidly confirmed.

As the Socialist Party convention drew near, the moderates geared up to purge the party of Trotskyism. Cannon, fearing that the French turn's days were numbered, but wanting to hang on for a while longer, opted for a tactical retreat. Rushing back from California, he begged Thomas not to expel his comrades, and agreed to Thomas's price for staying the ax: a resolution to be passed by the convention banning from the party all factional publications, including the *Socialist Appeal,* the resolution's intended target. But once having agreed, the slippery Cannon devised a way to escape the resolution's full impact: "a system of multi-copied personal letters," as he put it, that would carry on the Trotskyist paper's unifying function.[73]

In the end, Cannon's labors proved unnecessary. Trotsky decided that the French turn had outlived its usefulness. In April 1937 he told Albert Glotzer, a young Chicagoan who had served as one of his gun-toting Prinkipo bodyguards, that since the trend of world events demanded a "revolutionary policy," the time for the Trotskyists to break with the Socialists had come. In a letter of June 15 to Cannon, Shachtman, Burnham, and a "Comrade Weber," he made this decision official, naming November 7, 1937, the twentieth anniversary of the Bolshevik Revolution, as the date by which the break was to be completed.[74]

Cannon, for whom Trotsky's every word was law, at once assented. Shachtman, after brief hesitation, also fell into line. But Burnham, believing that the French turn had not yet exhausted its potential, disagreed. "A year in this Party is certainly enough to make most comrades awfully sick of it," he wrote to Glotzer. "But I believe that we still have some business to do within the framework of the Socialist Party."[75]

"Our job was and remains to rally the maximum number of the active militants in the [Socialist] party around [Trotskyism]," Burnham wrote to Cannon on June 15. "We must leave the road open for taking over the party. We have nothing to lose by this; and a possibility (even though a small one) for great gain." The current tactic should be to use the moderates' willingness to continue popular front collaboration with the Stalinists as a basis for attacking the Socialist center and building a bigger caucus on the Left. This effort would be more likely to succeed, he added, if Cannon paid some attention to matters of "tone." The Trotskyist recruitment drive was not aided by Cannon's denunciation of those who fell short of total agreement with him as "scoundrels, bloodhounds, sons of bitches, shysters, miserable, and contemptible." Collaboration should depend on a common outlook on serious issues, not on whether a potential ally spelled "Bolshevik" with a large or small "B," or only backed the workers of Barcelona instead of backing them "passionately."[76]

Burnham also took his case directly to Trotsky. More time was needed to win over Socialists "inclined toward us but not yet solidly won," he advised the Old Man. Moreover, there remained "a small off-chance" of gaining control of the party. If, however, the Trotskyists had to break with the Socialists, then "in leaving the party we must smash it thoroughly. This we cannot do by merely diving off. A dive leaves the spring board unscathed." But Trotsky's mind was made up. "The decisive steps must be taken in the next months," he wrote back, "even at the risk that some sympathizers will remain in the S.P. The best of them will come to us later."[77]

His arguments having failed, Burnham loyally joined in preparing the break. In late July the Trotskyist high command met in New York to give official endorsement to Trotsky's new line, and went on provocatively to resurrect the *Socialist Appeal*. The central committee of the Socialist Party's New York branch at once struck back, expelling fifty-four Trotskyists on August 9. In September the Socialist national executive committee suspended all party members linked to the *Socialist Appeal,* decreeing that the suspension would become permanent for those who had not left the paper by October 1 and petitioned for re-admission to the party.[78] But the Trotskyists did not seek re-admission. Their work was done.

The French turn proved to be a modest success for the Trotskyists. If they failed to put the Socialist Party out of business, they did carry off several hundred of its more radical members and perhaps a majority of the YPSL ("enchanted captives heading straight into the hermetic box of a left-wing sect," in the words of Irving Howe, himself one of the captives).[79] With these converts in hand, they at once got to work on their next project: the founding of a party all their own.

# Chapter 4

# Deviationist

BURNHAM'S DISAGREEMENT WITH TROTSKY over the French turn concerned only a passing tactical problem. But as preparations for the new Trotskyist party moved forward, the two found themselves at odds over a more serious issue, and this time a doctrinal one: the political nature of the USSR, or in Trotskyist parlance, "the Russian question."

The issue was first raised by one of the movement's senior members, a twenty-seven-year-old New Yorker named Joseph Friedman (usually called by his party alias, "Joe Carter"). Briefly a Communist student leader at City College, Carter had been expelled from the party in 1928 for Trotskyist heresy. Finding his way to Cannon, he had helped to launch the CLA, and now managed the movement's East 12th Street bookstore. A Bolshevik zealot, Carter devoutly read a few pages of Lenin every day, as a fervent puritan might daily read his Bible. But he also read other socialist writers, among them the German theorist Rudolf Hilferding. It was probably under Hilferding's influence that he decided, perhaps in 1936, that the USSR was no longer a workers' state, not even (as Trotsky said) a "degenerated" one, but a state whose defining characteristic was "bureaucratic collectivism."[1]

In the fall of 1937, Carter won Burnham to his theory. ("One day, I tried to relate [Trotsky's] formulas to reality," Burnham later wrote. "On such scrutiny it did not take long for the formulas to evaporate.")[2] To call the USSR "a workers' state in the traditional sense given to that term by Marxism" was no longer possible, the two argued in the November 1937 issue of the movement debate sheet, the *Internal Bulletin*. Rather, the USSR had become the property of its bureaucracy and other elites. But Carter and Burnham did not reject orthodoxy completely. Since the Soviet state had taken the genuinely socialist step of expropriating the capitalists, they conceded, workers still had a duty to defend it.[3]

From his Mexican stronghold, Trotsky promptly riposted. The USSR was indeed a genuine workers' state despite the decay that had set in under Stalin, he insisted in the *Internal Bulletin*'s next issue. A nationalized economy and central planning sufficed to make it so. Carter and Burnham had gone astray in their analysis because they had failed to take "an objective dialectical approach to the question."[4]

But the two dissenters would not yield. In a rejoinder to Trotsky called "From Formula to Reality," Burnham, proceeding on empirical grounds, maintained that the Soviet regime could best be understood as a tool of "the privileged strata of Soviet society"—the bureaucracy, the intellectuals, the GPU, and the Red Army, among others—which should be viewed as a new bourgeoisie seeking to consolidate its power. Hence, the claim that workers had a duty to defend the USSR, though justified by the surviving "progressive" features of Soviet life, had to be qualified. It would hold good if the USSR were attacked by imperialist powers, but not if the USSR were the aggressor. Moreover, he reminded his readers, Bolshevism aimed at far more than a nationalized economy. Nationalization was merely a means of attaining the higher end of a free and egalitarian society. If Trotskyists, confusing means and ends, lost sight of this truth, the movement would lose its rationale, and Stalinism, which had already completed the work of nationalization, would be "the better choice."[5]

Carter couched his answer to Trotsky in similar terms, but, more than Burnham, fixed his attention on the Soviet economic directorate. This stratum ("managers of trusts, foremen in factories, highly skilled technicians, etc.") had evolved into a new class, he contended, whose interests and ambitions were merging with those of the bureaucrats. Managerial power now defined the Soviet state.[6]

Trotsky reiterated that revolutionaries had a duty to defend the USSR, an unconditional duty.[7] But if his stance was adamant, his tone was mild, perhaps partly because the dissenters, despite their reservations, still endorsed "defensism," partly because the issue was only theoretical, and partly because he did not want a split in the movement just as his new party was being formed. After his second response, he suspended the debate, assigning its settlement to the party's founding convention.

The skirmish over the Russian question led Burnham to raise a second issue in late 1937: the "organization question," or problem of dictatorial leadership in the movement. Among those to whom he complained was his student Norman Jacobs, a former Musteite who, suspecting Trotskyism of totalitarian leanings, had dropped out of the AWP when it merged with the CLA. "My background permitted [Burnham] to sound off freely in discussions during [tutorial sessions] ostensibly devoted to Aquinas," Jacobs remembered. "I used to wonder how he could still remain a leader of one of the principal factions of the American Trotskyite movement and be agreeing with my criticisms." Burnham also raised the issue with Cannon and Shachtman. He had a hunch, he told them, that if they ever came to head an American Soviet government, they would be "just as ruthless as Stalin."[8]

The resolution on party organization that Cannon and Shachtman drafted for the founding convention increased Burnham's uneasiness. Based on the Leninist principle of "democratic centralism," it put its stress on "centralism" and the need for strong leadership and discipline, warning that the party could not operate like "a discussion club."[9] Seeing an omen of dictatorial rule, Burnham, again working with Carter, drafted a counter-resolution shifting the stress from "centralism" to "democratic," and calling for the distribution of party functions among "a far greater number of members than ha[d] been the case in the past." The party should also be open to a wide range of opinions, the two added, including the Carter-Burnham view of the USSR.[10]

Burnham also took his worries directly to Trotsky. In the past, he wrote the Old Man, Trotskyists had never made opinion a condition of party membership, but had welcomed all comers willing to do party work and accept party discipline. Now, however, Cannon seemed to want to impose a narrow doctrinal conformity and to expel people for purely intellectual differences. He himself opposed intellectual straitjackets. He did not demand that a party mirror "exactly and in every respect" his own views, but choose the party whose ideas came closest to his own and that was "genuinely serious" about its goals, and he expected that "in the course of our common work [the members would] mutually influence each other."

In his reply, Trotsky sought to allay Burnham's anxiety. Party rules would be "elaborated, corrected, and improved" over the years, he promised. His own main concern was the Russian question, since disagreement on that issue could, in the near future, push the party into "total breakdown."

Trotsky also wished to keep Burnham in the movement, and thought that a meeting between them might help. He had been delighted to learn of Burnham's adhesion to the Fourth International, he added in his letter on the organization question. "I follow with the greatest possible interest your writings in the party press and I should like very much to meet you sometime personally. Don't you believe it would be possible?"[11]

Burnham's answer has disappeared, but he and Trotsky were never to meet. Trotsky, however, need not have worried about losing his prize recruit, for Burnham was far too committed to the movement to think about leaving. Indeed, at Cannon's request, and despite his own awareness that an official party credo might encourage the very dogmatism he feared, he even agreed to draw up a "Declaration of Principles" for the founding convention.[12]

On December 31, 1937, delegates from Trotskyist and left-wing socialist groups around the country convened in Chicago to launch the new party: "The Socialist Workers Party (SWP), American Section of the Fourth International." Though the delegates approved the Declaration of Principles Burnham had drafted, they roundly defeated the Carter-Burnham resolution on the Russian question, 89 to 4. Burnham and Carter then loyally accepted a majority resolution affirming Trotsky's position, including "unconditional defense" of the USSR. Those who would not submit were at once ejected. At Cannon's behest, Burnham officially proclaimed the expulsion of these diehards.[13] In addition, he agreed to serve with Cannon and Shachtman in the SWP's three-man National Secretariat and to sit on its Political Committee, or Polcom (the equivalent of the Soviet Communist Politburo), which acted as the party's day-to-day ruling body. Moreover, as the *New International* prepared to resume publication, he returned to his old post of coeditor. He had not only proved his allegiance to the SWP, he had also emerged as one of its supreme commanders.

◆　◆　◆　◆

In outward form a political party, in inner substance the SWP was much like a religious sect.[14] At the center of the party stood the cult figure of the Old Man, with his distinctive goatee and great shock of unruly hair. To his followers, Trotsky seemed a hero-martyr who had helped Lenin to lead a world-saving revolution, only to be robbed of his rightful place as Lenin's heir by the usurping Stalin, and forced to eat the bitter bread of exile. Yet not all was lost, Trotsky's followers believed, for the tragic victim still possessed his sacred knowledge, the gnosis of the Marxist dialectic, through which, one day, the evil Stalin would be laid low and mankind redeemed. Both an intellectual (political theorist and strategist, master polemicist, writer on literature and culture, historian) and a man of action (chairman of the Petrograd Soviet, architect of the Bolshevik revolution, creator of the Red Army), Trotsky radiated charisma for his disciples.

These disciples, an ardent band of zealots, put their Trotskyist faith at the center of their lives. Many lived entirely for and through the movement. To the New Yorkers among them, SWP headquarters, now on University Place near Washington Square College, marked the epicenter of a cosmos whose center was Trotsky's Mexican villa. Steeled against the surrounding fallen world, the party provided its members with a total community, furnishing not only a cause that gave meaning to existence, but also a social life and often even their spouses.[15] In a story called "The Renegade," about a fictional party closely modeled on the SWP, the novelist James T. Farrell described the New York Trotskyist milieu: "The life and activity of the Party was largely internal. Party members saw one another constantly, and when they were together they talked and bragged about the Party and Party life." The party's leader, a self-important windbag named Patrick A. Nolan, proclaims "Bolshevik hardness" to be the party's motto and signal virtue. The typical party member sees himself "as one of a small and almost unknown band that was scorned and opposed on all sides, but which would nonetheless someday change the entire history of the world." "Our leaders," declares one, "are the advance guard of humanity." Another says, "Stalin is more afraid of us than of any other force in the world."[16]

When not busy trying to spread their gospel, organizing protest rallies, executing "turns" and other tactical operations against leftist rivals, savaging Stalinists and liberals, publishing the *New International* and the *Socialist Appeal,* and otherwise toiling for the cause, the Trotskyist faithful came together to relax. At "socials" they danced, gossiped, argued, flirted, and gathered around an upright

piano to sing labor songs. Socials often featured Cannon pursuing a favorite pas-
time: entertaining the comrades by giving a poetry recital.

To raise money, the SWP sometimes held more elaborate festivities. One
event, a 1938 "Harvest Masquerade," boasted a "swing band, competitions, enter-
tainment, prizes for the best costumes," and as "master of ceremonies" the
irrepressible Shachtman. Another had as its high point a "modern dance" performed by Mary McCarthy, then debuting as a drama critic, and the writer
Eleanor Clark. Decades later, one former SWP member fondly remembered that
the "delectable" Mary McCarthy had sat on his lap.[17]

◆   ◆   ◆   ◆

Burnham, however, rarely took part in Trotskyist high life. What he sought in the
SWP was not an all-embracing community but an instrument to revolutionize
society. Aside from a few exceptional instances—an appearance at a fundraiser, for
example, or dinner with the Shachtmans—his social life remained entirely outside the movement. His friends found his Trotskyism mystifying. ("Of all people!"
was the common reaction.) His Princeton friend Curtin Winsor beseeched him
to give up the SWP. Lucius Wilmerding stopped talking with him about politics.
Sidney Schiff was also bewildered, and asked David Burnham whether he could
explain his brother's odd behavior.[18]

Still, despite his perplexing Trotskyism, Burnham remained in many ways the
man he had always been: earnest, a firm empiricist (at least in intent, for like other
Marxists, he tended to argue as much from ideological premises as from observation, his position on the Russian question notwithstanding), and a tireless worker.
And now as before, he edited a high-brow journal, albeit one devoted to politics
rather than culture. Nor had the tone of his writing changed: if less academic than
his literary criticism for the *Symposium,* his political articles for the *New
International* breathed the same total self-assurance. He also still paid close attention to practical matters, insisting on the importance of careful organization, for
example, which he considered indispensable to the effective diffusion of ideas.

Finally, the Augustinian streak in his temperament—the sense that the world
was shot through with evil and sadness, and that much that was wrong could be
traced to human nature—shaded his view of life as much as ever. One reflection
of this was his dislike of political optimists (the reformist left, liberals, progres-

sives), who, he believed, lacked the stomach to face up to reality and so took refuge in consoling myths about the world and man. (This aspect of his personality was perhaps what led Hook to describe him as "inwardly quite hard.") His aversion to "sentimentalists" rang out in the scathing tone in which he wrote about them. Thus, reviewing the political scientist Louis Hacker's *My America, 1928–1938,* a liberal reformist meditation on the 1930s, he did not simply criticize Hacker's ideas, but assaulted the book as an expression of "muddled, wishy-washy and indeed Philistine democratism."[19]

Nor did he have any use for middle-of-the-roaders. "Of all the forms of politics," he wrote elsewhere, "'centrism' is the lowest. Centrism in politics is the equivalent of hypocrisy in personal morality."[20] This "realism" and "tough-mindedness" played no small part in his gravitation to Trotskyism, for the movement loved to picture itself as hard-boiled.[21] But if realism and tough-mindedness helped convert him to Trotskyism, his critical bent and need for autonomy acted as counterweights, keeping him from ever embracing the movement completely.

An equally powerful counterweight was Marcia Burnham, who gave Trotskyism as wide a berth as possible. Though she had dinner now and then with the Shachtmans and drinks at least once with the movement journalist Dwight Macdonald and his wife, Nancy, nothing short of a gun to her head could have persuaded her to spend an evening listening to Cannon recite poetry. Oscar Shoenfeld had a clearer impression of the almost invisible Mrs. Burnham than most party members, but only because he had once caught a fleeting glimpse of her—a tall, slim blond in a silk dress, he recalled—as he passed by the door of Burnham's NYU office.[22]

By affording her husband a life apart from Trotskyism, Marcia weakened the magnetic pull of the SWP. So, too, did Burnham's classes at NYU, which drew him away from politics into philosophy. Yet the siren call of the movement never abated. When the SWP was on the point of being launched, Cannon again pressed him to work full-time for the party. Other comrades echoed the leader. At the SWP's founding convention, one delegate, an old trucker, said to him during a break in the debate on the Russian question, "Now, Jimmy, just come in with us full-time and we'll vote for any resolutions you want to write."[23]

As before, Burnham held out against the pressure. Yet his resistance troubled him, and in January 1938 he asked Cannon and Shachtman to discuss his problem with him. According to Cannon, when the three met, Burnham agreed that

Cannon might be right in tracing the differences between them to the "contradictions between [Burnham's] personal life" and his "responsibilities" as a "revolutionary leader." But he was not yet ready to resolve these contradictions, he said. Could he be temporarily released from party duties to have time to ponder the matter? Cannon and Shachtman acceded, hoping (as Cannon wrote Trotsky) to "save Burnham for the revolution."[24] But Burnham continued to hold back. "Try as we would," Shachtman remembered, "—directly, by indirection, by pressure, by suggestion, by cajolery, by every device we could think of—we could never induce him to come to work in the party office. . . . It was obvious—and as I became increasingly more intimate with him, increasingly obvious—that he was torn. There were clearly times when he was on the verge of throwing it all up— namely, his job at the university—and perhaps other personal involvements and coming to work for the party, and that he felt this urge very strongly and very sincerely."[25]

But in the end, Burnham stayed put. To his comrades this probably came as no surprise. "All of us—and this went for Cannon and myself in particular—felt that although he was with us and with us thoroughly, he was not, so to say, of us," Shachtman later commented. "[Burnham] does not really feel himself to be one of us," Cannon told Trotsky. "Party work, for him, is not a vocation but an avocation."[26] Shachtman yielded with good grace to Burnham's decision. But Cannon, already exasperated by Burnham's ideological deviations, seems to have felt a deepening hostility toward him.

Cannon and Shachtman blamed Burnham's behavior on his "bourgeois" background. "His social environment is entirely different," Cannon observed. To Shachtman, Burnham's very presence in the SWP seemed "accidental."[27] And indeed, Burnham resembled no one's idea of a Trotskyist. Polite, reserved, conservatively dressed, he projected the image not of a Bolshevik revolutionary, but of a partner in a Wall Street law firm. ("He wore hundred dollar suits," noted a fascinated Harry Roskolenko. "He went to the theater, too.") At the time of the AWP-CLA merger, William Randolph Hearst's *New York American* had accused Hook and Burnham of leading a party "even more radical than the Communists," and demanded that NYU fire them. But the university would not do so—partly, thought Hook, because the administration simply could not see in Burnham, to all appearances "a pillar of the right-thinking establishment," a menace to the social order.[28]

Burnham's private life dramatized his distance from the movement. Trotskyists tended toward a hand-to-mouth existence. In late 1934 the Burnhams moved from the Village to firmly haute-bourgeois Sutton Place. One evening, Shachtman appeared at Burnham's door with some *New International* galley sheets that needed reviewing, only to find Burnham in formal dress (Burnham was the only Trotskyist to own a tuxedo, Shoenfeld felt sure), hosting a dinner party. Leaving the table, Burnham took his fellow Bolshevik to another room where they gave the galley sheets the required going-over, after which Shachtman sped off, and Burnham, a task on behalf of the world revolution completed, returned to his guests.[29] On another occasion, Trotsky's secretary, a Frenchman named Jean van Heijenoort, was visiting New York and received a dinner invitation from the Burnhams. Arriving at their apartment, he was surprised to find awaiting him an elegantly set, candle-lit table.[30] The sight would not have given pause to a Stalinist: in the 1930s well-off people sometimes found Stalinism chic. ("The revolutionary barricades had become everybody's jungle gym," the critic Diana Trilling once said of the thirties.)[31] But in the down-at-the-heels world of American Trotskyism, the Burnham household was unique.

If Burnham's fellow Trotskyists, like his college friends, were puzzled by his presence in the movement, many were glad to have him with them. For one thing, his character earned him their approval. He quickly acquired a reputation for "impartiality" and "fairness," Shachtman remembered, while Albert Glotzer recalled that party members found him "honest and straight-forward." For another, the comrades were struck by his intelligence and skill at debate. For still another, he was, as one of them put it, "fresh." Having come to the Left in his late twenties rather than, as they had, in his teens, or even earlier, he was free of the conventional Marxist mindset and party clichés. Moreover, he usually wrote about the American rather than the Soviet scene, thus bringing needed breadth to the Trotskyist focus. To Shoenfeld, he seemed the very model of the radical intellectual. That he had none of the left's tub-thumping style and was "in touch with America" only heightened his appeal in Shoenfeld's eyes. Farrell, too, noted Burnham's familiarity with the American scene, calling him the one SWP member who "made consistently good analyses of American political events, American business in relation to what is happening here, and to what is going on in the major political parties etc."[32]

The comrades also agreed that Burnham had no great knack for public speak-

ing. Still, he was now a reasonably competent orator. His speeches might be short
on "razzle–dazzle," recalled Shachtman's wife Yetta, but they were long on content. Moreover, by the later 1930s he had shed the didactic tone that had alienated his early audiences, and so no longer faced the hostility he had once
provoked. Yet his restrained and concise podium style could also work against
him. Thus, during one intraparty debate, he spoke for a mere two hours,
prompting some of those present, used to endless tirades on such occasions, to
doubt his seriousness. But such doubts were rare. "His participation in the party
may have been part-time, but his interest in the party was full-time," Shachtman
once commented, and because the great value of his contribution was universally
recognized, "no one ever dreamed of questioning the appropriateness of his position as a party leader."[33]

Yet if the comrades admired Burnham, his reserve, superior social status, and
full life outside the movement made some of them uneasy. Irving Howe thought
him "haughty in manner and speech, . . . logical, gifted, terribly dry." Manny
Geltman, a Trotskyist of the first hour, called him "not cool, [but] cold!"
Burnham's ability to "sit through an endless faction fight on the hottest day or
night, in a room with little air, and never open his shirt collar or loosen his tie"
caused Geltman to marvel. Yetta Shachtman, who described Burnham as "impressive," found his reserve intimidating. "Not that he was snobbish," she said, "but
you didn't just go up to him." Glotzer, another Burnham admirer, echoed Mrs.
Shachtman. Burnham "wasn't cold," Glotzer told an interviewer, but he "held
himself in such a way that people didn't come up and slap his back."[34]

The writer James T. Farrell saw Burnham in a different light. "Burnham is a
nice guy, but prissy and ministerial, and his face looks it," he noted in his diary.
"He is doing penance for his Symposium past, and tends to overpoliticize everything." Burnham served as the basis for a character in Farrell's novel *Sam Holman,*
set in the radical New York of the 1930s. Typically, when NYU philosophy professor and militant Trotskyist "Betram Jackson," a "tall brown-haired fellow about
thirty" with "a soft, almost mushy, face," goes to a party, he heads for a corner and
spends the evening debating Hegel's logic.[35]

Burnham was saddened that he made some comrades uneasy. To become more
approachable, he tried to make his bearing less forbidding. Sometimes he
attempted a matey manner, dropping his polite, "bourgeois" mode of speech in
favor of what he seems to have viewed as proletarian earthiness. But seldom suc-

cessfully, for his deep-seated sense of propriety would trip him up. "When Jim says 'fucking,' he blushes," Shachtman chuckled.[36]

With Cannon, to whom he had early taken a dislike (he described the Trotskyist leader to Hook in 1935 as "lazy, arrogant, impatient, and a drunkard"), Burnham's relations were often strained. During one SWP debate, the two almost came to blows when Burnham, opposing Cannon on the point at issue, remarked, "Everyone knows Jim likes to drink. . . ." As Cannon balled his fists and seemed about to charge, Burnham added, ". . . milk."[37] But between Burnham and Shachtman a friendship developed, the only personal relationship Burnham ever formed in the SWP. It was Burnham who gave Shachtman his first lesson in modern art. At Burnham's apartment one day, seeing a painting that Yetta Shachtman thinks may have been a Mondrian, Shachtman was surprised that the painting was considered special. "I could have done that myself," he protested. Whereupon Burnham, assuming his role of professor of aesthetics, pointed out the qualities that made the work important. "What I would like to do is to sep-arate Shachtman from Cannon," Burnham confided to Hook. "Shachtman, in spite of obvious deficiencies, seems to me the only one of the old CLA who has creative political ideas."[38]

◆　◆　◆　◆

All the while, Burnham continued to work hard for the movement. In the *Socialist Appeal* (for which he resumed his *Labor Action* column, "Their Government") and the *New International* he fired salvo after salvo at the New Deal, portraying it as a proto-fascist plot to save a moribund capitalism from extinction. But he now focused his attention on what he alleged to be Roosevelt's drive toward war, which he accused the president of "deliberately and consciously" seeking as the ultimate means of forestalling a capitalist collapse. The New Deal, he wrote, had become "the War Deal." Its domestic goal was "a total-itarian military dictatorship" that would last as long as American "imperialism" continued. Abetted by his liberal and communist allies (Stalin, a "social imperial-ist," was backing American war plans in hopes of achieving a U.S.–Soviet alliance), Roosevelt was trying to persuade the workers that the main enemy was Hitler, when in fact it was "the boss at home, and the bosses' government." Naturally, the U.S. imperialists—led by "the Sixty Families," the high command of the plutocracy that ruled the United States—were trying to conceal their war plans behind slogans about making the world safe for democracy. But their true aim was "to make the world safe for profits."[39]

There was only one way to keep America out of war, Burnham argued. This was neither collective security, which was really just a ploy to guard the loot Britain and France had bagged in World War I, nor isolationism, which had to fail because the Sixty Families would force the United States into war. Nor could anything be expected of liberal pacifists, who were simply diverting anti-war sentiment from the true causes of war—capitalism and imperialism—into channels harmless to the warmongers. No, the only way to stop wars was to overthrow the imperialists who started them.[40]

Burnham also lectured on behalf of the movement. In the fall of 1938, he, Shachtman, and Cannon taught a course at the SWP's "Marxist School" called "The Bridge to Revolutionary Action," which met Tuesdays from 8:45 to 10:15 P.M. at party headquarters. The following spring, the Marxist School offered another course, "Problems of American Politics," with Burnham again teaching. In the fall of 1939 he returned to the Marxist School's podium, now in tandem with Dwight Macdonald, for a six-lecture series entitled "The War Deal in Action."[41]

Burnham pitched in further by serving the movement as a strategist. Though acknowledging that the party's primary business was world revolution, he thought it crucial that Trotskyists also be involved in more modest undertakings, and so willingly took up tactical issues of the most limited scope. Thus, in 1939 he wrote at some length to an SWP leader in Chicago on an upcoming municipal election. "Isn't it possible for us to run some kind of candidate *on the ballot* in the Chicago election?" he asked, unhappy with a plan to mount a write-in candidacy. "Couldn't the Chicago organization pick an office and a district of the city where it would be possible for us to do whatever you have to do to get an SWP name and label on the ballot? . . . Experience shows that a write-in campaign doesn't mean a damn. . . ."[42]

Meanwhile, Burnham still had to meet a heavy teaching schedule at NYU, including all the extra chores teaching requires. Not surprisingly, he continued to come down often with minor illnesses. "Another session of sinus and heavy cold infection left me just enough energy to get through to the end of summer school," he reported to Hook, "and the doctor has ordered me to be sure to get into good general condition if I don't want to be in bad shape all next winter."[43]

◆ ◆ ◆ ◆

When Burnham shut down the *Symposium* and took up politics, he did not stop writing literary criticism. Nor did he give up his earlier critical standards for Bolshevik standards, which viewed art through the prism of politics, replacing aesthetic criteria of judgment with political criteria. Hence, he treated the crudely politicized fiction of the 1930s with severity. "For the novel . . . as in the case of all art, classes of any sort are abstractions," but "art is above all concrete," he warned "proletarian" authors in a review of Albert Halper's novel, *The Foundry,* a typical specimen of 1930s "socially conscious" fiction. "If proletarian novelists want to learn how to make classes and the class struggle the subject matter of their novels, let them go not to the *New Masses* and the John Reed Club [a communist-sponsored writers organization] magazines but to Balzac and James and Proust." The best revolutionary novels that he knew, he wrote in 1935, were Ignazio Silone's *Fontamara* and André Malraux's *Man's Fate,* both of which presented "a revolutionary view of the world and of men so integrally fused into the structure of the novels that the primitive antagonisms and oppositions—propaganda versus art, class versus individuals, and so on—do not raise problems." Novelists must learn that "'social significance' is not a decoration to be purchased from a political warehouse and tacked on to a novel," he asserted in a *New International* review of Hemingway's *To Have and Have Not.* "It must—as *Man's Fate* or *When the Looms Are Silent* or *Fontamara* teach (or, for that matter, all great novels)—be simply the organic relevance of the novel both internally and to its own time." He found Silone (an Italian communist who had broken with the Communist Party at the turn of the thirties) especially appealing, calling his *Bread and Wine* "an admirable and moving novel."[44]

A major source of present-day literary mediocrity, he charged, was Stalinism, which condemned its adherents to "the stultification of intelligence and sensibility." Stalin himself wrote in an "indescribably tedious style," which was "perhaps not the least among [his] sins." In a review of James T. Farrell's *A Note on Literary Criticism* for the Socialist Party's *American Socialist Monthly,* he congratulated Farrell for rejecting the Soviet dogma that literature must serve politics, declaring that it was not "the business of a 'party line' to dictate plot and sentence structure." (All the same, he himself, according to Farrell, later called Farrell's book incomplete for failing to show how the literary faults of communism stemmed from the Stalinist policy of "Socialism in One Country.")[45]

In 1938 Burnham found a new vehicle for his criticism, a magazine called *Partisan Review.* This journal, which had first come out in 1934, was the brainchild of two young Marxist critics, Philip Rahv and William Phillips, who had persuaded Joseph Freeman, editor of the Communist Party literary journal the *New Masses,* that the party needed a more genuinely literary magazine. Agreeing, Freeman had given the two money to publish *Partisan Review,* for which the communist-run John Reed Clubs served as sponsor. But before long, the party had begun to treat *Partisan Review* as it did the *New Masses*—ordering it to subordinate literary standards to political needs. Rahv and Phillips had rebelled against the party dictate and in 1936 *Partisan Review* had folded. But the next year its editors found new money, and *Partisan Review* was reborn, this time as "a Marxist literary monthly" favoring modernism in the arts and the anti-Stalinist Left in politics.[46]

The Trotskyists at once took a lively interest in the new *Partisan Review* as a potential asset for the movement. In view of certain communist enmity, Burnham proposed to Rahv and Phillips that they commit the magazine to Trotskyism in return for his "cooperation." They refused. But they did give Burnham a seat on *PR*'s editorial advisory board.[47] Burnham also sent information on *PR* contributors to Trotsky, who followed the magazine's fortunes with an eagle eye. Mary McCarthy, *PR*'s drama critic, Burnham described as "a handsome, black-haired Irish girl, of some wit and shrewdness" and "apparently a kind of literary 'career woman,'" who sees anti-Stalinist left intellectualism as a good current racket" and *Partisan Review* as a handy "stepping stone." His SWP comrade Dwight Macdonald, who had enlisted as one of the magazine's editors, he summed up as "a most delightful and dynamic and rather hare-brained person." But Macdonald was "not a consistent political thinker," he warned, "and I don't think he ever will be."[48] Trotsky found these reports encouraging enough to ask *PR* to publish an essay of his on the ties between the natural and social sciences. Nothing came of his request, but the magazine did eventually run another Trotsky piece, "Art and Politics."[49]

But more important to Burnham than *Partisan Review* was the *New International.* He wanted this journal to "become the real center for intellectual life in this country," he told Hook. He hoped to make people think that "they must buy it if they want to know what is going on," and so was "very anxious" to publish "'discussion' articles outside of and even against 'Trotskyism.'" This aim however, led his thoughts back to *Partisan Review*. Putting the *New International* at the center of the country's intellectual life would be easier, he calculated, if the two magazines could merge, a step that would yield "a large and fully rounded monthly" and just possibly "a weekly."[50] But he never pursued a merger, perhaps doubting that Rahv and Phillips, who resisted being classified as Trotskyists, would ever agree to one. Instead, while toiling to bring luster to the *New International,* he also began writing criticism for *Partisan Review,* adhering to his usual exigent standards. One author who suffered his stern appraisal, the literary critic William Troy, complained to Farrell that "Burnham was too logical about criticism."[51]

◆　◆　◆　◆

Though a fervent Trotskyist, Burnham nevertheless persisted in his ideological straying. Irritated with conventional readings of Marx, in 1938 he proposed to Hook that they coauthor "a short snappy book to be called 'Toward the Revision of Karl Marx,'" if only to refute the widely held, but now to his mind mistaken, idea that dialectical logic was basic to Marxist thought. Since untestable, dialectics had to be meaningless, he wrote in *Partisan Review* (though years before he himself had signaled dialectical thinking as the key to Lenin's success in 1917 and Trotsky's brilliance as an historian). Its true importance lay in its function as a metaphor: anti-Marxists attacked it as a way of attacking Marxist politics, while Marxists defended it as a symbol of the revolutionary cause. But dialectical philosophy had by this time outlived its usefulness. It now existed solely as a "vestigial remnant" that, like the appendix, was not only useless, but also "liable to dangerous infections." What was needed, therefore, was an intellectual appendectomy and a correct understanding of Marxism, which was not primarily a body of abstract theory, but "the science and art of social revolution."[52]

Burnham further revealed the idiosyncratic bent of his Trotskyism in another brush with Max Eastman, who in March 1938 published a piece in *Harper's* citing Soviet life and the findings of modern science as reasons to question the compatibility of socialism and personal freedom and the validity of the socialist philosophy per se. Outraged at such effrontery, Trotsky wanted to see Eastman "mercilessly" refuted, and turned to Burnham to do the job (in hopes of yoking him more tightly to the movement, Burnham later speculated). Burnham agreed, and accused Eastman of advancing an overly abstract, nonhistorical, and therefore meaningless idea of freedom—but hinted that the charge of abstractness could also be brought against his fellow Trotskyists. ("I assume you noticed that my critique was in one respect rather against closer friends than Eastman," he remarked to Hook.) In a second article, a reply to Eastman's counter-rebuttal, he stuck to his maverick course, claiming that he could never make a final political commitment. "I am for my part always ready to examine any program," he wrote, "and to accept it if I find it better than the one I hold."[53]

Burnham was also bothered by what he called "the general problem of Bolshevism." "If it is the case that without the revolution civilization perishes; and that only under the leadership of the Bolsheviks can the revolution succeed; but that the present ideology and practice of Bolshevism carries the seeds of totalitarianism; (all three of which premises seem most plausible); then what to do for a longer term perspective than month by month?" he mused in 1938. Later that year, commenting on a draft article of Hook's, he confessed himself "much troubled in my reflections on the nature of democracy, and its relations to Russia, to socialism, and to what is worthwhile in general." The usual democratic claim was that "government should 'represent the will of the majority.' But, for example, the majority of what? Of the nation as it just happens to be now? Or some subdivision of it? Down to what? A town, a ward, a block?" What should be done if socialism were established in the United States, "but Iowa, Kentucky, and Queens didn't want it? Or suppose with U.S. socialism, a socialist revolution having in the first instance minority support began in Canada. What would be your orders to the U.S. Red Army?"[54]

But if Burnham's commitment to Trotskyism was cooling he gave no sign of it in his day-to-day activity. In January 1939 he again showed his dedication in a long *New International* article he wrote with Shachtman (but of which he was probably the principal author). Called "Intellectuals in Retreat," the article denounced Hook, Eastman, and other former radicals for pulling back from the revolutionary cause and demanding an "'intellectual freedom'" that was really freedom from "responsibility." The "'philosophical discussion'" the defectors claimed to want was really only "a smokescreen" to hide their real goal, the article warned. For behind their Left-sounding "'formal,' avowed or alleged program" lurked "an 'actual,' politically decisive program" that could be inferred from the stands they took on specific issues—a program of reformist liberalism. Yet reformism, however well concealed, would fail, the authors declared, striking the hard-boiled pose Trotskyists loved to affect. For politics was not a "polite parlor game" but "the struggle for power, and a very brutal struggle" to boot. The world could be saved only by revolution.[55]

"Intellectuals in Retreat" triggered a strong response. Burnham was becoming "unspeakable [*sic*] self-righteous," acting as if he were "giving out certificates to people certifying that they [were] or [were not] Marxists and revolutionaries," Rahv complained to Farrell. Hook, the major villain of the article, was furious. "Sidney and Jim Burnham had a run in here [at Farrell's apartment]," Farrell wrote in his diary, "and I believe there is something brewing there which must have burst in personal acrimonies." The critic William Troy saw the article as the latest example of a pattern he thought visible in Burnham's life. Burnham "inclines to be strongly influenced in an intellectual sense by people, and then to turn from them drastically," he commented to Farrell. "At Oxford . . . it was Father D'Arcy. Then Wheelwright. Then Hook." But for the Trotskyists, especially the SWP's younger members, the article's resounding affirmation of the revolutionary faith and no-holds-barred condemnation of the apostates had the galvanizing impact of a fiery revivalist sermon. Decades later, elderly SWP alumni still vividly remembered how it had braced them.[56]

Did Burnham, however unconsciously, write "Intellectuals in Retreat" to bolster his own revolutionary faith? Was he beginning to feel doubts and seeking to exorcise them? There is no way of telling. But given his differences with Trotsky and his tendency to agree with the very Sidney Hook the article attacked, this may quite possibly have been the case.

◆　　◆　　◆　　◆

Within the SWP, Burnham continued to clash with Cannon. Just before the party's 1939 national convention, he put a resolution before the Polcom aimed at moderating Cannon's dictatorial brand of leadership. Cannon parried the thrust. But he was mettled by Burnham's attempt to curb his power.[57]

In contrast, Burnham remained on excellent terms with Trotsky, and continued to furnish the Old Man with help and advice. Knowing that Trotsky needed money, he worked out a deal in 1939 with his Princeton classmate Noel Busch,

now a senior editor at *Life,* under which Trotsky would sell the magazine a character sketch of Stalin and a piece on Lenin's death, illustrated with photographs
of the author by the news photographer Margaret Bourke-White. (The articles
were never written.) That same year, Burnham had a hand in dissuading Trotsky
from appearing before the House Committee on Un–American Activities, which
was planning legislation to outlaw the Communist Party. Trotsky had been eager
to testify in order to publicize Stalin's terror.[58]

Yet between Burnham and Trotsky a chasm was about to open. On August 23,
1939, Germany and the USSR signed a nonaggression pact that included secret
protocols providing for the partition between them of Poland and the tiny Baltic
states. For the SWP the Russian question was back with a vengeance and not as
a theoretical problem, as in 1937, but as a practical issue, immediate and pressing.

It was Burnham who first resurrected the Russian question, launching what
Cannon would call "the most voluminous party discussion in the history of
mankind."[59] On September 3, two days after the Germans invaded Poland, and
the day France and Britain declared war on Germany, Burnham asked for an
emergency meeting of the National Committee, the SWP's highest authority
short of a national convention, to review the party's position on the USSR; a
meeting was scheduled for the end of the month. Two days later, he contended
at a Polcom meeting that the USSR, which he denied could be called a workers' state "in any sense whatever," would soon attack Poland, not to defend the
collectivized Soviet economy, but for purely "imperialist" reasons. The SWP
commitment to "unconditional defense" of the USSR, he went on, should therefore be scrapped. (As for Poland, "the endless crimes of the Polish landlords,
industrialists, politicians, and generals against democracy" made that country also
unworthy of SWP support.)[60] On September 18, the day after Soviet forces
crossed the Polish frontier, he moved that the Polcom condemn the USSR for
waging "a war of imperialist conquest." Opposed by Cannon, the motion was
defeated. But Shachtman came over to Burnham, and at the September 30
National Committee meeting, made a motion of his own upholding the anti-
Soviet view. Once again, Cannon prevailed, but this time by a mere three votes.[61]

Now Trotsky himself waded into the fray. In a *New International* article called
"The U.S.S.R. in War," he levelled his usual charges at Stalin, but reaffirmed
unconditional defense of the USSR on the ground that Soviet socialism had to
be preserved. The same principle, he went on, justified the Soviet invasion of

Poland, for the USSR, however base its motives, would abolish private property in Poland, thereby advancing the world interests of socialism. Moreover, he added in a follow-up article a month later, because the term "imperialism" denoted "the expansionist policy of finance capitalism," the USSR, by definition, could not be imperialist.[62] But Burnham and Shachtman would not yield to semantic obfuscation. The war was a contest between "rival imperialisms for a new division of the world," they retorted. The sole issue was, "Who is going to get the major share of the swag?"[63]

By late 1939, Cannon's anxiety about the Burnham-Shachtman group, now probably a majority in the SWP's New York branch, had become acute. In a letter to a fellow Trotsky loyalist, Joseph Hanson, he diagnosed the source of the trouble as "the unfavorable social composition" of the New York branch, where real workers were outnumbered by "petty-bourgeois intellectuals."[64] When Burnham asked that the dissidents be guaranteed access to the party press, Cannon, backed by a Polcom majority, refused. Burnham wanted the SWP to be "a perpetual talking shop," he huffed.

But Cannon's victory prompted new complaints about a "one man party."[65] Trotsky, hoping to head off a split, and worried that the ham-handed Cannon might seek unity through "organizational methods," i.e., the expulsion of the minority, called for "discussion." Cannon, as always, did his master's bidding. The *Internal Bulletin* would henceforth have two editors, he decreed, one from each faction, and a commission consisting of two members of each faction would be set up to look into complaints. In addition, Burnham and Shachtman would still edit the *New International* (over which Shachtman had legal control anyway). But, as in the past, Cannon did not keep his word. Thus, another dissident, Dwight Macdonald, who had, as he put it, "no trouble getting printed in *Fortune, Harper's, the Nation,* [and] the *New Yorker,*" had his submissions to the *Internal Bulletin* "monotonously rejected."[66] When Burnham continued to call for an equal voice in the party press, Cannon exploded. This "demagogic demand for 'freedom of the press' represents a petty-bourgeois, anarchistic revolt against revolutionary centralism," he stormed.[67]

The Soviet attack on Finland in November 1939 poured more fuel on the fire. For the Cannon faction, the attack marked a new advance by socialism, even if, as Trotsky put it, by "bureaucratic methods." The SWP dissidents condemned the attack. But they were also hostile to "bourgeois" Finland, and put a resolution before the Polcom calling on both Soviet and Finnish workers to revolt. Burnham formally adhered to this "third camp" position, claiming that the work-ers alone were entitled to the support of socialists.[68] But his true feelings may have been different. In mid-December, during a debate on Finland that Cannon described as "hard and bitter," Burnham shed his usual detached manner, and in furious tones voiced the hope that the Red Army would be defeated. (Years later, he claimed that he had sided with Finland, and Poland, all along. Though this was not his public stance in 1939, the anger that possessed him during the December debate lends the claim credibility.)[69]

A few days later Burnham fired off a new polemic, "The War and Bureaucratic Conservatism," which accused the Cannon faction of turning Stalinist, that is, putting the interests of the SWP bureaucracy before all else. But he exempted Trotsky from this charge. ("Trotsky matches his organization to his policy which he arrives at in principled fashion," he told Farrell.) Then he fell into heresy, remarking that history's "best run revolution with the best collective leadership" was the American Revolution. Coming from a Trotskyist, for whom the supreme revolution should have been the communist seizure of power in Russia in 1917, such a statement was appalling. "In the organizational sense," Farrell concluded, Burnham was no Bolshevik.[70]

Trotsky did not reciprocate Burnham's generosity. In a scathing article called "A Petty-Bourgeois Opposition in the Socialist Workers Party," which Burnham loyally ran in the New International, the Old Man sternly called the deviationist Burnham to order, arguing as he had in 1937 that the root of Burnham's errors lay in his failure to think dialectically. Stung by word that Burnham had reacted to this scolding with a shrug and a dismissive "I stopped arguing about religion long ago," Trotsky raced back to his typewriter, and loosed a second blast, "An Open Letter to Comrade Burnham," which charged that while Burnham, the intellectual leader of the opposition, might be highly educated, he showed no more understanding of politics than "a witch-doctor." Burnham's defects, Trotsky now joined Cannon in claiming, stemmed from his bourgeois background. The party wanted only those bourgeois who had cast away "their social past, and . . . come over decisively to the standpoint of the proletariat."[71]

As the battle raged on, Trotsky grew increasingly bitter. Burnham was one of his prize catches, and he had worked hard to tie him tightly to the movement. But now the brilliant young man had gone too far. He had turned traitor, and with his scornful quip about dialectics, a condescending traitor at that. To Trotsky, Burnham was a rebellious son who had compounded injury with insult and refused to repent.

In contrast to Trotsky, Burnham never lost his composure. He replied to Trotsky's tirades in an even tone that sometimes hinted at sadness. Trotsky's writing style could mesmerize him, he confessed in his reply to the Old Man's attacks, an essay called "Science and Style." He had found the prose of Trotsky's *History of the Russian Revolution* "wonderful." But now he realized that Trotsky saw "persuasive rhetoric as logical demonstration, a brilliant *metaphor* as argument"; in Trotsky's eyes dialectical thinking was itself "a *device of style*." Nor was this Trotsky's only flaw. By invoking the authority of Hegel, "that century dead archmuddler of human thought," in his defense of dialectics, while ignoring such modern works on logic as Russell and Whitehead's *Principia Mathematica* and C. I. Lewis's *Survey of Symbolic Logic,* Trotsky also revealed that he was intellectually out of date. But the key problem was not whether dialectical logic was valid, but a practical matter—and a most urgent one: *"the strategic orientation of our movement during the first phase of the second world war"*—and on this issue Trotsky's position amounted to a defense of Stalinism *"as the lesser evil."*

Burnham ended the piece by lamenting the conduct of the majority faction. "I judge a political struggle *morally* as well as politically," he wrote. "Socialism is a moral ideal, which reflective men choose deliberately, by a moral act. Cold and sober scientific analysis convinces me that this ideal dictates an appropriate morality which must govern the struggle for it. Just as we say that the white man cannot be free while the black is enslaved, so a social order based upon truth and freedom and loyal cooperation cannot be won by those who in their relations with each other base their methods of action on lies and disloyalty and slander."[72] Though Burnham does not seem to have realized it, these words were his swan song as a Trotskyist.

"Science and Style" enraged Trotsky supporters. The truth, snapped Cannon's friend Joseph Hanson, was that Burnham did not have a scientific view at all, "but just the brain-sickness of a petty-bourgeois moralist." An indignant reader in Kansas protested: "There is only one adjective I know that completely describes ['Science and Style'] . . . NASTY. While reading and reflecting upon it, a picture persisted upon intruding—a picture of a decayed aristocrat, groomed to perfection in purple and fine linen, perfumed and lolling on silken cushions—and expounding in the exquisite finished diction of classical erudition his contempt for, his cruel hatred of the 'rabble.'" Cannon agreed, writing to Trotsky that "in impudence and disdain and *class hatred* of the [SWP's] proletarian majority," the article exceeded all Burnham's previous factional writings. Trotsky issued a cooler condemnation, dismissing Burnham's views (as Burnham had just dismissed his) as intellectually outmoded. "Burnhamism," he commented, was "only a belated reproduction of pre-Marxian petty-bourgeois socialism."[73]

All the while, the rift in the party continued to deepen, and by early 1940 the SWP leadership had decided to hold an emergency national convention to resolve it. But several weeks before the convention, Cannon went to Burnham and Shachtman with an alternative solution: that they carry out a "cold split," i.e., a peaceful breakup of the party, with a proportional division of party property between the factions. The dissident leaders refused. Cannon, Shachtman speculated, hoped to bolster his power as leader of the SWP by getting rid of the rebels.[74]

While reviling the entire opposition faction as "liberal philistines," "renegades," "stinkers," and "traitors" out to ruin "the only revolutionary movement in the whole world," Cannon saved his choicest abuse for Burnham, to his mind a social and intellectual snob who not only had the temerity to criticize Trotsky, but also refused to work for the party full-time. It was Burnham's "conscious design," Cannon charged in a letter to the party membership, to "bring about the maximum possible disruption of our movement before taking his formal departure."[75]

Burnham, meanwhile, growing weary of the struggle, began to withdraw from it. He attended a national meeting of the opposition in Cleveland in February 1940, but played so inconspicuous a role that another participant, Albert Glotzer, later wondered whether he had really been there. (It may be significant that he registered in Cleveland as "James Bunham," a name much closer to his own than was his party alias, "Kelvin.") Nor was he now much in evidence in New York.[76]

Shachtman found Burnham "very badly disenchanted" by Trotsky's behavior, especially the Old Man's blind support of Cannon. And on top of his disillusionment with Trotsky, Burnham now seemed uncertain about the value of the movement and even of socialism. After confiding his doubts to Shachtman, and going through the pros and cons of staying in the movement, he would decide to stay, only to take up the issue all over again a few days later. "It was a running effort on my part, and I suppose to a certain extent on his part, to keep him in,"

Shachtman recalled.[77]

After seven months of increasingly furious debate, the factional struggle finally reached its climax. At the SWP emergency national convention, held in New York in April 1940, the Cannon wing carried the day, passing by a vote of 55 to 34 resolutions endorsing Trotsky's dicta on the USSR and its role in the war, and refusing the minority's demand for a newspaper of its own. A week later, the National Committee banned oppositionists from holding party posts until they had accepted the majority position. In practice, this meant the expulsion of Burnham, Shachtman, and others who would not recant.[78] Cannon showed no graciousness in victory. The SWP could not be led by "dilettants [sic] whose real interests and real lives are in another world," he later wrote. Otherwise put, those who preferred Sutton Place dinner parties to SWP socials (and their own opinions to Cannon's) need not apply.[79]

In the months following the split, Trotsky reapeatedly voiced his disappointment with Burnham, the "educated witch-doctor," "strutting petty-bourgeois pedant," and "intellectual snob." But he also paid a kind of tribute to the black sheep's talents. Burnham "can write," he admitted, "and has some formal skill in thinking, not deep, but adroit. He can accept your idea, develop it, write a fine article about it—and then forget it. . . . However, so long as we can use such people, well and good. Mussolini at one time was also 'good stuff'!"[80]

Burnham did not reply, but dumped his correspondence with Trotsky into his apartment incinerator. In the future he would speak of the Old Man critically, but never vituperatively. Indeed, years later, his emotional wounds having long since healed, he gave the writer Charles Lam Markmann the impression that he still viewed his first political mentor with great respect.[81]

◆ ◆ ◆ ◆

With the SWP irrevocably fractured, the expelled minority at once set about forming a new party, the Workers Party (WP), to preserve a pure Bolshevism purged of Trotsky's errors. At first, Burnham took part in this effort. He spoke at the new party's inaugural public meeting—"and spoke very well," Shachtman remembered—and was slated to report to the founding convention on the party constitution.[82] But on the eve of the convention, he suddenly resigned from the WP. A review of his beliefs, he explained in his letter of resignation, had convinced him that he could no longer accept Marxism, whose ideas modern historians, economists, and anthropologists had shown to be false. Nor could he accept the Leninist idea of a party, which seemed to him "incompatible with genuine scientific method and genuine democracy." He should have left the movement earlier, he confessed, but had held back out of "a sense of moral obligation" to people with whom he had worked and whose thinking he had influenced. He still admired socialism as a moral ideal, and thought it would be "a good thing" if it were achieved. But he did not think it would be achieved, for mounting evidence had persuaded him that what history now held in store was "a new form of exploitive society," which he called "'managerial society.'"[83]

Burnham's abrupt resignation stunned party members, though perhaps not Shachtman. "The news came like a blow to the head," recalled one WP member, Irving Panken. The most common response, said another, Albert Glotzer, was not anger, but disappointment and sadness. Some comrades, however, did react angrily, not because Burnham had changed his politics, said member Irving Howe, but because he had "led them into the split, and then left them in the lurch," never so much as hinting that he had lost his faith in Marxism. "It was like the feeling you get from a bad divorce," Howe noted half a century later. According to Hook, Dwight Macdonald, who idolized Burnham, felt betrayed.[84]

Perhaps uneasy about the suddenness of his exit, Burnham tried to soften its impact. To minimize embarrassment to the WP, he would keep his resignation secret for as long as the party wanted, he told Shachtman. In addition, he was willing to write a column for the newspaper the WP was planning. Shachtman, who knew when the game was over, did not take him up on these offers. Burnham was also ready to help in another way. Soon after his departure, Glotzer, lacking the money to print an issue of the *New International,* appealed to the paper's former coeditor for assistance. In reply, Burnham sent him twenty dollars. It was his last service to the movement.[85]

In a letter of 1976 to the British political analyst Brian Crozier, Burnham furnished his own explanation of how he had come to embrace and then reject Trotskyism. Claiming never to have swallowed "dialectical materialism, or, more generally, the ideological side of Marxism," he described his participation in the movement as basically "pragmatic, resting on a simple syllogism." Convinced by the Depression and Hitler's coming to power that capitalism was collapsing and no longer capable of sustaining an "acceptable" society, "I assumed . . . that socialism was the only alternative. And perhaps partly by accident, I tied up with the Trotskyists with the notion that a 'new revolutionary party' was the way to achieve socialism." But as time passed he had come to see that the USSR "was neither a workers state nor a capitalist one" and that all forms of revolutionary Marxism had to turn totalitarian. And so he had said goodbye to Trotskyism, leaving the movement as coolly as he had joined it. "I never had the sort of 'commitment' to Bolshevism . . . usual among those who have active, leading roles in a Bolshevik organization," he told Frazier. "More exactly, my commitment was rational and pragmatic, not spiritual. That is why I did not go through the usual emotional and spiritual turmoil that, in most cases, marks the break with Bolshevism. God had not failed, so far as I was concerned. I had been mistaken, and when I came to realize the extent of my mistakes, it was time to say goodbye."[86]

As this letter implies, Burnham liked to picture himself as able to rise above emotion, view the world with analytical detachment, draw rational conclusions from his observations, and then take appropriate action. "Cold and sober scientific analysis" had led him to join the movement, he explained, and when experience proved that he had made a mistake he had left. Yet there are reasons (for example, his stunned reaction to industrial violence in the Midwest in 1933 and his agonizing with Shachtman in 1940) to question his account, to think that his embrace of socialism had originated at least as much in emotional upset as in dispassionate analysis, and that his departure from the movement was less the result of cool deliberation than an abrupt climax to months of nervous strain. "Midway this way of life we're bound upon, I woke to find myself in a dark wood, where the right road was wholly lost and gone," begins Dante's *Inferno,* the first part of what Burnham once called "the most wonderful poem ever written."[87] Teaching the *Inferno* regularly at NYU, he knew it well. When he woke to find himself in his own dark wood, Trotskyism, did Dante's words ever cross his mind?

◆　◆　◆　◆

It is tempting to write off Burnham's Trotskyist phase as wasted time, a six-year detour into the sterile world of left-wing sects. But this judgment would be wrong. True, Burnham's Trotskyist writings, purveying a conventional Marxist-Leninist view of the world, do not show his intellectual powers to best advantage.

Also true, he spent much of his time in the movement caught up in barren factional squabbling. But in important ways the involvement prepared him for what would be his real career. It was because of Trotskyism that he shifted his focus from literature to politics, began to read and ponder political theory, discovered his flair for political analysis and commentary, and became engrossed in the USSR and communism. Trotskyism, in short, was Burnham's school of politics. At first glance, the Bolshevik James Burnham who edited the *New International* might seem poles apart from the conservative James Burnham who edited *National Review.* Yet in reality they were much alike.

No one was more aware of Burnham's debt to Trotsky than Burnham himself. Many former leftists "were taught our first lessons by Trotsky," he wrote several years after his break with the movement. "This primary instruction has influenced not only our subsequently reached opinions but, more enduringly, the categories and presuppositions through which we try to understand political events."[88] He had learned, for example, that economics exercises a powerful sway over politics. This idea helped to shape his book *The Managerial Revolution* (published in 1941 when his outlook was still heavily influenced by Marxism), and although it would eventually figure much less prominently in his thinking, it still continued to surface from time to time. Thus, in the draft of an article probably written in the 1960s, he asserted, "When there is not enough to go around, one part of the population will take all it needs and wants, and enforce social and political arrangements to make sure the others can't horn in." And again: "When used broadly," Marxist analysis was valid, he told the historian John P. Diggins in 1971. Five years later he wrote to Brian Crozier, "I still think there are elements of truth in the Leninist theory of the State, in some aspects of the economics, and some insights of the economic theory of history."[89]

Trotskyism, Burnham believed, had also immunized him against ideology as such. "Having come to know something of the gigantic ideology of Bolshevism," he wrote a generation after leaving the movement, "I knew that I was not going to be able to settle for the pigmy ideologies of Liberalism, social democracy, refurbished laissez-faire or the inverted, cut-rate Bolshevism called 'fascism.'"[90]

Burnham thought Trotskyism had marked him in another way as well. "In spite of my present rejection of Communism," he told the French writer André Malraux (another thirties leftist who had moved to the Right) in 1947, "... I nevertheless feel that *the experience of Communism* may have been a necessary phase in the moral development of our generation. Two men today who seem outwardly to agree completely in their views will continue to sense an age between them if one has, and one has not, lived *through* Communism."[91]

Burnham did not seem to find his Trotskyist past embarrassing. In later times he sometimes alluded to his movement years, and always in a matter-of-fact tone. Yet on one occasion, his usual aplomb deserted him. In the late 1960s, when a young *National Review* staffer with whom he was chatting happened to mention his distant Trotskyist period, the only reply he could muster was a blush.[92]

# Chapter 5

# Prophet

I F BURNHAM FOUND BREAKING with Trotskyism more painful than he would later admit, once he had left he showed no regret. His life outside the movement had never ceased, and it eased any pang of loss he may have felt. To begin with, he had his family, now larger thanks to the arrival of a son, James Bernard, in October 1939 (and soon of a third child, John Lightner, in November 1943). He had his house in Kent, a retreat that never failed to cheer him. And he had friends from his pre-Trotsky days, among them the Wilmerdings (who found him easier to get along with after the break),[1] Bernard Heyl (along with the rest of his Princeton crew), and Sidney Hook, with whom he was back on good terms after the chill caused by "Intellectuals in Retreat." Then too he had his teaching, which, despite his complaints, often brought him pleasure. A candid photograph in the 1941 college yearbook shows him beaming with joviality—a mood cameras seldom caught—as he chats with some faculty colleagues.

Finally, nonacademic projects absorbed the energy he had once poured into the SWP. For a time, he thought about trying to revive the *Symposium*.[2] But instead he tightened his connection with *Partisan Review*. Signs that *PR* was giving up its Marxism encouraged him, as did the resignation in 1943 of a key *PR* editor, Dwight Macdonald, who had tried to gain control of the magazine and failed. Burnham liked Macdonald, but thought him politically witless. He was looking forward to "the deDwighted PR with hope and good wishes," he wrote to Phillips and Rahv.[3]

Meanwhile, he was swept up in a new undertaking. In his letter of resignation from the Workers Party, he had predicted that the future would belong not to socialism, but to a novel kind of "exploitative society," which he had labeled "managerial society."[4] Now he was writing a book about the rise of the managers, a phenomenon he called "the managerial revolution."

◆　◆　◆　◆

As Burnham readily acknowledged, the idea behind the book was by no means his alone. "It would be my judgment that my . . . thinking and writing in the '40s rose fairly naturally out of the historical intellectual environment, and that I was making explicit—crystallizing—existing implicit ideas rather than stating novelities," he once wrote to an inquirer curious about the book's genesis.[5]

And indeed, for decades students of politics had been observing modern society's technocratic tendency and speculating about what it might portend. The Polish socialist Waclaw Machajski, for example, in his book of 1904, *The Intellectual Worker,* had argued that a workers' revolution might culminate in the rule of a hereditary class of intellectuals—"managers and engineers"—who would tyrannize over the masses just as their capitalist predecessors had.[6] In 1939 a broadly similar idea was put forward by a book called *La Bureaucratisation du monde,* the work of a certain "Bruno R.," later revealed to be an Italian quondam Trotskyist named Bruno Rizzi. Pondering Trotsky's charge that the USSR had fallen into the clutches of a tyrannical bureaucracy, Rizzi had come to see the USSR, Nazi Germany, and Fascist Italy as different versions of a phenomenon he called "bureaucratic collectivism," a form of government in which bureaucrats, having gained control of the means of production, wielded totalitarian power. In support of his theory, Rizzi cited ideas expounded by the American Trotskyists "B" and "C" (i.e., Burnham and Carter, the second of whom had coined the phrase "bureaucratic collectivism") in their 1937 debate with Trotsky on the Russian question.[7]

It was not, however, in Machajski and Rizzi (whom he had not read in 1940)[8] but in Trotsky's polemics against Stalin that Burnham first encountered leftist theorizing on managerial rule. Stalinism and fascism, though resting on different social bases, were "symmetrical phenomena," the Old Man had written in *The*

*Revolution Betrayed.* "In many of their features they show a deadly similarity."[9] Burnham would advance approximately the same proposition, though his idea stemmed not only from Trotsky but from Joseph Carter.

According to Burnham, his theory was also influenced by two non-Trotskyist works. One was the sociologist Thorstein Veblen's *The Engineers and the Price System* (1921), which contended that a sharp divergence of interests was opening up in the American economy between the owners of industry, most of whom played little if any part in the productive process, and the "managers," who were the real producers. The growing ambition and group consciousness of these technicians would probably not push them as far as revolution, Veblen believed, but if a revolution did take place, the ruling "Soviet" it would create would take the form of a committee of managers.[10]

The other source Burnham drew on was Berle and Means's *The Modern Corporation and Private Property,* a book he had reviewed enthusiastically in the *Symposium.* In the modern corporate world, this work argued, real power had shifted from formal owners to "managers." As a result, old-fashioned capitalism was giving way to a manager-dominated economic system that in time would come to be "as all-embracing as the feudal system." "No more potentially important book than this, in its or any allied field, has been published in this country for many years," Burnham had declared in his review. He apparently still thought so, for he made the book's argument a cornerstone of his theory.[11]

Certain other writers may also have influenced his thinking. One was Thurman W. Arnold, Yale Law School professor and Justice Department trustbuster, whose *The Folklore of Capitalism,* published in 1937, contrasted the traditional image of U.S. business and politics with what Arnold believed to be their true reality. Burnham had judged the book trivial in *Partisan Review.* But Arnold's description of capitalism as irreversibly in decline and his signaling of a "new class" consisting of "engineers, minor executives, salesmen, and social workers— all engaged in actually running the country's temporal affairs"—conveyed a picture that in some respects resembled Burnham's.[12]

Another influence may have been a much discussed book of 1936, Lawrence Dennis's *The Coming American Fascism.* A Harvard man turned Depression-era visionary, Dennis wrote with Burnham-like scorn of "soft-thinking liberal leaders," diagnosed the market economy as in its death throes, and announced a social transition so vast that it would equal in magnitude the transition from feudalism to capitalism. In Dennis's view, the government of the future, foreshadowed by the New Deal, would be "fascist," i.e., an authoritarian system of technocrats who would replace the obsolete free market with central planning. Years later, Burnham recalled, "I cannot judge whether [*The Coming American Fascism*] had any direct influence on my views but I thought it (and still think it) a provocative and (certainly for its time) a rather impressive book, and it was doubtless part of the general intellectual atmosphere in which changes in my own ideas occurred."[13]

Further influences may have included the so-called "Machiavellian" political theorists, Gaetano Mosca, Vilfredo Pareto, and Robert Michels, whose insistence on a strictly empirical social science Burnham applauded, and whose belief in the inevitability of oligarchy he found persuasive. He had begun reading the three in the late 1930s, as his managerial theory was first taking shape.[14] A few years later he would write a book about them.

Yet if Burnham's theory emerged as a fusion of the ideas of others, it also possessed originality. For by bringing together insights from quite different thinkers about bureaucracy, the modern business world, and the rise of technocratic elites, it was able to show one of the twentieth-century's major trends in a new light. Its novelty, then, lay not in its components, but in the broad explanatory synthesis that Burnham made of them.[15]

◆    ◆    ◆    ◆

Written in the cataclysmic year 1940, *The Managerial Revolution: What Is Happening in the World* offered a key to the underlying meaning of contemporary history. Mankind was in the midst of an epochal revolution, the book announced. Just as in the late Middle Ages an exhausted feudal society had crumbled before the advance of a youthful capitalism, so now an obsolete capitalist society was crumbling in turn. A new elite of "managers" (the planners and administrators, organizers and technicians who controlled industry), obeying the "historical law" that "all social or economic groups of any size strive to improve their relative position with respect to power and privilege in society," was replacing the hitherto dominant capitalists as the ruling class. This supplanting of capitalism by managerialism would bring a radical transformation of the economy. Collectivism and central planning would replace private ownership and the free market.

But the managers would go beyond the economic realm to transform political, social, and cultural life as well. An "unlimited" state, "a fused political-economic apparatus" of corporate managers, government bureaucrats, and the military, would come into being, supported by ideologies placing authority and discipline above freedom and private initiative. Probably, this totalitarian system would prove temporary, a phase of the transition to mature managerial rule. But it would be a long, long time before real democracy appeared again, and "drastic convulsions" would occur before it did.[16]

Worldwide in scope, the managerial revolution had already made great strides. Stalin's USSR ("the nation most advanced toward managerial structure")[17] and Hitler's Germany were not opposites in essence, but merely two variations on a single, managerial theme. The United States, too, was fated to a managerial future, which, even now, could be discerned in the centralizing and bureaucratic New Deal. "The New Deal is not Stalinism and Nazism," Burnham granted. "It is not even a direct American analogue of them. . . . But no candid observer, friend or enemy of the New Deal, can deny that in terms of economic, social, political, and ideological changes from traditional capitalism, the New Deal moves in the same *direction* as Stalinism and Nazism." Accordingly, the future would not resemble the past. For example, the election of 1940 might be the last the United States would ever hold.[18]

With its drive to rationalize and integrate all productive forces, managerialism logically called for a single world-state. But since any effort toward that end would run into "insuperable" problems (administrative and technical difficulties; the impossibility of adequate policing; ethnic, cultural, and climatic differences), a world-state could not be achieved in the foreseeable future. More probably, a small group of "super-states" would emerge and partition the globe between them (though some historic nations, while eliminated "in *fact*," might survive "in *form*"). These superstates would probably number three: the United States, Germany, and Japan, though "not necessarily . . . as we know them today." The first would take charge of the Western hemisphere, and act as "receiver" for a bankrupt British Empire, while the second and third would command blocs based on Europe and East Asia, respectively. Russia, too backward to build a durable bloc of its own, would split in two, its western half gravitating to the European bloc and its eastern half to the Asian. Once they had consolidated their strategic bases, the superstates would clash, but since each would be too strong to

be conquered, their wars would result in the rounding off of their world partition. The conflict now raging in Europe was but a prelude to the coming superstate struggle, since its real point was to decide whether Britain, champion of the
moribund capitalist past, or Germany, herald of the dawning managerial future,
would build the European superstate. But with Germany's stunning victory over
capitalist France, the outcome seemed clear. Germany—the future—would
win.[19]

Many people would view the coming age as tragic. But they would be wrong.
For while the future would differ greatly from the past, "if we choose to accept
it—and most will accept it, whether or not they choose—there will be some satisfaction in doing so in terms of realities, not illusions."[20] What was more, "tragic"
had no meaning in this context: "Tragedy and comedy occur only *within* the
human situation. There is no background against which to judge the human situation as a whole. It is merely what it happens to be."[21]

As its ending suggests, almost as striking as the book's message was its air of
emotional detachment. Burnham's deadpan tone was intended to stress that his
aim was, as he asserted, purely analytical. Readers who believed he was advocating managerial rule were mistaken, he insisted. Indeed, his "personal interests,
material as well as moral, and [his] hopes" stood in conflict with his conclusions.
His purpose was simply to illuminate what was happening in the world. The
book's epigraph emphasized this aim. A passage from a letter of Machiavelli in
which that pioneer of dispassionate political analysis denies favoring the wickedness reported in his book *The Prince,* it read in part: "If any man will read over
my book . . . with impartiality and ordinary charity, he will easily perceive that it
is not my intention to recommend that government or those men there
described. . . ."[22]

But Burnham's detached tone had another source as well. Convinced that an
iron age was about to dawn, he seems to have viewed loss of heart at this grim
prospect as a weakness. The right response, he implied, was not to seek refuge
from the truth in wishful thinking, but to acknowledge reality and face it with
stoic imperturbability. His detachment, then, also stemmed from a penchant of
temperament, the same insistence on an unsentimental view of life that had
inspired the bleak stories he had written as a student, his high regard for
Reinhold Niebuhr, and his enthusiasm for Bolshevik "hardness."

❖    ❖    ❖    ❖

When Burnham set out to find a publisher a dozen houses turned him down. Lewis Corey, who read the manuscript for Knopf, and Max Nomad, who did so for Vanguard, even accused him of stealing his ideas from them. Deeply discouraged, he came close to consigning the book to the wastebasket. But then Hook stepped in and persuaded his own publisher, Richard Fleming of the John Day Co., to take a chance on it.

Fleming doubted that he would sell a thousand copies of *The Managerial Revolution,*[23] but to his astonishment the book turned into a runaway success. *Fortune* pronounced it "by all odds the most debated book published so far this year." *Time* chose it as one of the six top books of 1941 (along with Arthur Koestler's *Darkness at Noon* and Rebecca West's *Black Lamb and Grey Falcon*). Every ambitious junior executive had a copy concealed in his desk, people joked. In the United States and Britain more than 100,000 copies were sold in the early 1940s (British sales would have been still bigger had it not been for wartime paper rationing), and a later, paperback edition did even better. After the war, translations came out in Spanish, Italian, French, German, Greek, Polish, Russian, Ukrainian, Swedish, Hindi, Arabic, Hebrew, Chinese, and Japanese.[24]

Reviewers, on the other hand, gave the book a mixed reception. Ralph Thompson of the *New York Times* called it "acute and closely reasoned and, once its major premise is granted, extraordinarily cogent and impressive." But "I stall at the premise," he added, "and wouldn't grant it to someone who knows twice as much as Mr. Burnham." The literary critic Malcolm Cowley, writing in the *New Republic,* thought Burnham had come up with "a new and plausible explanation of what is happening in the world." Yet like many reviewers, he found the book's emotional detachment upsetting. Burnham was as anti-Nazi as anyone, Cowley told his readers, "but objectively the burden of his book would seem to be that some sort of Nazism is going to triumph . . . , and that we might as well make up our minds to surrender." Louis Hacker, in the Sunday book section of the *New York Herald Tribune,* took Cowley's complaint a step further. Despite Burnham's protests to the contrary, his outlook was "totalitarian" and defeatist, Hacker charged. The book seemed to be telling opponents of dictatorship that they "might as well curl up and die." Lewis Corey, who had rejected the book for Knopf, echoed this view in the *Nation.* Burnham had yet to shed the "determinist

absolutism" of his Trotskyist days, wrote Corey, and at bottom was offering "a program of submission to a totalitarian doom against which man can do nothing."
What the book really expressed was "the Olympian defeatism of a doctrinaire
radical gone sour." The historian Golo Mann, a refugee from Hitler, agreed.
Writing in the magazine *Decision,* he accused Burnham of succumbing to "a traditional German vice," that of excusing evil as "the inevitable outcome of historical logic." Disappointed idealism lay at the root of the problem, he concluded,
but not that alone. For Burnham had once been a Trotskyist, and there had "never
been a political movement so absolutely lacking in human love, so cursed with
scientific pretension, arrogance and cruelty as Trotskyism."[25]

Other reviewers also took note of the book's partly Marxist origins. Peter
Drucker, in the *Saturday Review of Literature,* predicted that Burnham's work
would "probably become the Bible of the next generation of neo-Marxists."
Some believed Marxism had caused Burnham to get things backward. Thus, the
sociologists Hans Gerth and C. Wright Mills argued in *Ethics* that in Hitler's
Germany power belonged not to managers but to politicians. "The crucial fact in
Germany concerning [managers] in their relation to power," the two wrote, "is
that their very indispensability and scarcity value for a war economy insures their
loss of income and personal freedom."[26]

Burnham's theory found no favor at all with his former comrades. *Partisan
Review*'s critic, Dwight Macdonald, joined the reviewers who equated managerial
rule with fascism, and complained that Burnham's determinism aided the fascist
cause by making the struggle against fascism seem futile. Albert Glotzer, in the
*New International,* accused its former coeditor of producing "a justification for fascism and all forms of totalitarianism." As an "apostate," Burnham was suffering
pangs of guilt, Glotzer claimed, and to "salve his conscience" was trying to prove
socialism impossible. Joseph Hanson, a Trotsky partisan during the SWP faction
fight, contended in the party's new journal, *Fourth International,* that the "petty
bourgeois snob" Burnham had stolen his managerial theory from Bruno R. In
"Intellectuals in Retreat," Hanson reminded his readers, Burnham had warned
that intellectuals who deserted the revolutionary movement for Stalinism or
imperialism would degenerate in mind and character, since such ties could "breed
only maggots." Now, Hanson exulted, one such maggot had composed "his own
epitaph."[27]

The most fascinated critic was the British socialist George Orwell, who found

*The Managerial Revolution* simultaneously magnetic and repellent. Though Burnham pretended to be impartial, Orwell commented in the British left-wing newspaper the *Tribune,* in reality he hoped for a German victory over Britain and a totalitarian future. The true source of Burnham's theory was his "belief in the invincibility of the German army," but the certainty that Germany would now lose the war (Orwell was writing in 1944) had "already blown [the theory] to pieces."[28] Upset by these accusations, Burnham protested to the *Tribune.* Far from hating Britain, he declared, he rated her "political achievements more highly than those of any other nation." Nor had he ever regarded the German army as invincible. (The truth of this denial is debatable, given the book's clear expectation—from the vantage point of early 1941—of a German victory.) As for totalitarianism, he hated it, seeing in it the enemy "of human well-being and of those human ideals of freedom, truth, love, and beauty which for me constitute the justification of human existence." The prime example of totalitarianism, the Stalin regime, seemed to him "the worst [government] so far known in history."[29]

Unconvinced, Orwell returned to the charge. In a long essay of 1946 called "Second Thoughts on James Burnham," he claimed that a "power instinct" lay at the root of Burnham's thinking. The managerial theory reflected a "power worship" widespread among intellectuals, who wanted to replace egalitarian socialism with a hierarchical kind under which the intellectual could "at last get his hands on the whip." Moreover, the book sounded "a note of unmistakable relish over the cruelty and wickedness of the processes that are being discussed." (What Orwell really heard was Burnham's pleasure in puncturing his former comrades' eschatological expectations.) For while Burnham claimed to be dealing in facts rather than in preferences, he was clearly "fascinated by the spectacle of power." In his prophesying, meanwhile, he erred in believing that whatever was happening in the present would go on happening. Thus, he assumed the recent trend toward oligarchy to be "irresistible, rather as a rabbit fascinated by a boa constrictor might assume that a boa constrictor [was] the strongest thing in the world."[30]

Yet for all his objections to *The Managerial Revolution,* Orwell was spellbound by Burnham's nightmare vision of a world divided among three perpetually warring totalitarian superstates, and when he wrote his novel *1984,* he took its totalitarian, tripolar-world setting from Burnham. In fact, *The Managerial Revolution* itself appears in *1984.* It is *The Theory and Practice of Oligarchic Collectivism,* the major work of the Trotsky-like Emmanuel Goldstein, whom the people of the Stalinoid superstate of Oceania ("Big Brother is watching you") are daily summoned to hate.[31]

*The Managerial Revolution* also provoked a strong response from the reading public. H. G. Wells, author of *The Shape of Things to Come,* among many other books, warned Burnham against forecasting the future too confidently. If the managers could not persuade people to submit to them, he argued, then the managers would be destroyed. The poet Delmore Schwartz, a former student of Burnham's, wondered how the managerial elite, lacking property and inheritance rights, would perpetuate itself. It "would have to choose the stars of each June's graduating class," he decided, but he could not imagine any "human or social motivation which would keep this going, especially in the economy of plenty, which a country like ours would surely provide." Running into Burnham on a visit to New York, Schwartz put this question to his old teacher. Burnham, he thought, seemed unable to supply an answer.

Burnham's detachment was criticized not only by reviewers but by casual readers, among them the master of Balliol, A. D. Lindsay. It was unfortunate, Lindsay wrote to his former charge, that the book's attitude seemed morally questionable. "It is to me a sign of the terrible isolation which has come over the American universities," he elaborated, "that you seem to suppose it is your business just to look on as a scientist at the inevitable," while withholding all moral judgment. The financier Bernard Baruch reacted more positively. He had not read the book, but only the *Time* review, he confessed in a letter to Burnham. Still, his own experience with government bureaucrats had convinced him that Burnham was on to something big.[32]

Burnham received letters from less prominent readers as well. One of these called *The Managerial Revolution* "the keenest analysis of social and economic evolution since *Das Kapital*." Another thanked Burnham for his "contribution for human progress." Still another savored the book as "very admirable and cruel," while a fourth urged the author to seek salvation in the Baha'i faith. A widow writing from Philadelphia asked Burnham to handle her investments. The dean of boys at New Trier Township High School, not sharing A. D. Lindsay's misgivings, wrote to congratulate the one-time New Trier student on his great success. If at least one reader thought the book naïve ("You claim that bureaucracy is not more inefficient than private business except where capitalists interfere. My dear boy, have you ever worked in a govt. bureau as I have done?"), another found it utterly gripping. "I cannot begin to express in words how much I enjoyed every page," gushed this enthusiast, "so much so that on reaching the end I am left with the ardent desire to begin at the beginning and read it again and again." Before long, groups ranging from merchant's associations to women's clubs were flooding Burnham with invitations to address them. And the deluge of mail continued for years, for once World War II had ended, letters poured in from abroad.[33]

*The Managerial Revolution* brought Burnham more than mail and royalties. It also earned him a high place among the country's public affairs pundits, the corps of intellectuals from whom the media routinely sought comment on current issues.[34]

The great success of *The Managerial Revolution* can be attributed mostly to characteristics it shares with other best-sellers that have purported to reveal the deeper meaning of some important trend. To begin with, at a time of global crisis, the book seemed to hold the key to current history. As *Time's* review put it: "[Burnham's] slyly casual sub-title [*What Is Happening in the World*] promises to tell [readers] something they want desperately to know."[35] In addition, though the ingredients of the theory were, as Burnham noted, already "in the air," a factor that bolstered the theory's credibility, these same ingredients, when fused into a sweeping explanatory hypothesis, paradoxically added the contrary appeal of novelty. Further, the theory seemed to touch on a favorite topic of the time, the widely discussed issue of the "decline of the West" (which had gripped Burnham since the Depression and perhaps since his reading at Princeton of T. S. Eliot; whether he had read Spengler is uncertain), and to view it from a fresh angle. Then, too, the book contained a raft of predictions that, if dubiously "scientific," were certainly sensational and by no means implausible. Finally, the theory was cogently set forth, couched in brisk, lucid prose, and packaged in a volume whose moderate length, 250 pages, did not intimidate.

But a further factor may have been at work. Burnham had set out on a project that he defined as "scientific," analyzing and explaining certain things that were "happening in the world." But he had ended up writing not only that book, but also an epic drama of social destiny. What had started as "science" had turned into a work of art.

◆   ◆   ◆   ◆

Soon after Burnham published the book, he began to soften its message. At one of the public affairs symposia to which he was invited to discuss his theory, he spoke of the future's "possibilities of freedom," arguing that although the market economy was headed for extinction, democracy did not need private property and free enterprise to survive. When accused of wanting a managerial dictatorship, he would not only deny the charge, but also maintain that people were free to choose their future. The book's aim, he would say, was only to make his readers "more clearly aware of the general trends within society" so that they could make history "the servant of [their] . . . ideals, instead of . . . becoming the helpless victims of history."[36]

But in arguing that people had the power to choose their future—and not merely to discover it—he came close to repudiating one of *The Managerial Revolution*'s central tenets. In the book he had stressed historical inevitability, and now he was asserting the existence of free will. Trying to strike a balance between the two principles, he began to describe historical trends not as inexorable, but as tendencies that, while powerful, could at least to some degree be shaped by conscious choice. Though he never took up the freedom/determinism problem at any length, this nuanced position would henceforth be his standpoint.[37]

Over the years, Burnham continued to revise his theory. In 1943 he wrote that he had not given the military a large enough place in the managerial elite, and now thought that soldiers would form "a considerable section" of the future ruling class. In 1960, in an introduction to a reprint of the book, he reaffirmed his belief that a managerial form of society was emerging, but called his original statement "too rigid and doctrinaire." He would now not portray the future as inevitably totalitarian, but would allow "many degrees of relative freedom and justice, ranging from unrestricted tyranny to a measure of constitutional liberty under the rule of law. . . ." While it remained true that the managers in charge of "the great power aggregates" (large-scale industry, government bureaucracies, the mass labor unions, the armed force) had become "the dominant class" in the world's developed societies, he added, this did not mean that "all other class relations [had been] wholly supplanted by the managerial equations." But for all its shortcomings, he thought the book still useful, remarking that "even the crudities and errors of this rather impressionist first attempt [could] be instructive, and provocative of fresh inquiry."[38] A decade later, speaking with the historian John P. Diggins, he voiced a further criticism: that when he had written the book, he had not realized the importance of the "pure politician," the "manipulator" whose power rested on political talent, not technical expertise.[39]

Today, *The Managerial Revolution* reads like a Depression-era period piece. Heavily freighted with what its author, in 1972, called "remnants of Marxism,"[40] the book espouses economic determinism; regards social classes, economically defined, as the main actors in history; confidently predicts the imminent collapse of capitalism; takes for granted the superiority of central planning; foresees a future in which "bourgeois democracy" has no place; regards ideas and values as by-products of class interest; and rests on a conventional Marxist view of history—until the twentieth century, when the revolution against capitalism transfers power not to the workers but to the managers.

Yet much of the book's picture of the future has held up. If a new elite of managers has not achieved a monopoly of power, in many countries in recent decades credentialed specialists have gained a commanding position in both the public and private sectors, and links between such persons in government, the military, industry, finance, and the universities have multiplied and tightened. At the same time, within government, executive departments, commissions, boards, and agencies of all sorts, often invested with semi-authoritarian powers, have become familiar features. And if several totalitarian regimes have recently collapsed, and the free market has come back into fashion, technocrats still rule many roosts, while elected lawmakers, in theory legally empowered to curb bureaucracy, in practice often seem unable to do so.

At first glance, Burnham's forecasts regarding the world distribution of power may look less successful. After all, Germany and Japan ended up losing World War II, while the USSR, far from cracking in two, rose to superpower status. Nor, despite the postwar era's Soviet-Chinese-American hostility (and occasional fighting), did the globe turn into an arena in which three superstates engaged in endless combat. So much for Burnham the prophet, one might conclude. But in the economic sphere, the world has indeed moved toward a tripolar structure, and one corresponding to Burnham's. The United States commands the world's largest economy, and through the North American Free Trade Agreement (NAFTA) is pursuing the economic integration of the Western hemisphere; a European bloc, the European Union (EU), has arisen, with Germany, not Britain, as its economic powerhouse; and Japan has become Asia's top industrial power and the world's remaining economic giant. The USSR, meanwhile, has broken up, even if not in the way Burnham expected.

Thus, if many of Burnham's individual forecasts missed their mark, his general depiction of the future has been more successful, correctly predicting the directions in which power would flow.[41] And his analysis has proved to be pioneering. For it was Burnham who coined the expression "managerial revolution," introduced the idea to the general public, defined the revolution's essential nature and characteristics, and created the conceptual framework (corporate-bureaucratic tyranny vs. individual freedom) in which it would be discussed.

◆　◆　◆　◆

Nine months after the publication of *The Managerial Revolution,* the United States formally entered World War II. Thirty-six years old, married, and the father of two, Burnham held a 2A draft classification, which meant in effect an exemption from military service.[42] An opponent of U.S. involvement in the war in his Trotskyist days, he had remained one after his break with the movement (and had taken to praising German music and Japanese gardening to needle interventionist friends). But after Pearl Harbor, he did a complete about-face and called for an all-out war effort. At NYU faculty meetings, he resolutely defended the "morale" courses in philosophy, history, and government that formed the core of a new, "pre-military" curriculum. Axis victories proved the value of such courses, he maintained. Students had to "be given the basis for an intelligent faith in Democracy; [had to] know what they were fighting for if they [were] to be good soldiers."[43]

During the war, Burnham's NYU workload grew heavier. As younger teachers left for the armed forces, their older colleagues filled the resulting gaps. For Burnham this meant adding math to his course list. He also did some teaching outside NYU. Thanks to an invitation probably inspired by his book, in 1942 he began a six-year stint as a lecturer on economics and politics at the "Graduate School of Banking," a lecture series offered annually at Rutgers University by the American Banking Association.[44] In addition, he still gave some time to his prepolitical interests. His friend Bernard Heyl, in a book of 1945 on aesthetic analysis, cited conversations with Burnham as having helped him to illuminate his subject.[45]

In 1941 the Burnhams moved to an apartment at the corner of East 73rd

Street and Lexington Avenue, and there they lived for the next eight years. Setting up his typewriter (which Marcia dubbed "the bread and butter machine")[46] in the foyer near the entrance to the living room, Burnham continued to turn out articles, book reviews, and lectures. But he also spent time reflecting on his political beliefs—"to review the mistakes" he had made in the 1930s, he later told the columnist Mary McGrory.[47] His instructor in what he called his political "re-education," a Virgil to lead his Dante out of the dark wood of ideology, was Machiavelli, whose influence on him he had made evident in *The Managerial Revolution*. But other Virgils, writers whose work he had come to know more recently, also helped. These were Robert Michels, Vilfredo Pareto, and Gaetano Mosca, often referred to as "Machiavellians" because of their intellectual kinship with the author of *The Prince,* and the syndicalist philosopher Georges Sorel, not a member of the Machiavellian group, but in some ways close to it.

Though they did not form a school, the Machiavellians had a good deal in common. Michels (1876–1936), a political scientist of German and French ancestry, had derived from his experience in the German socialist movement the thesis of his best-known work, *Political Parties: A Study of the Oligarchic Tendencies of Modern Democracy* (1915). Democracy understood as majority rule could never be attained, the book argued, because mass organizations, for reasons inherent in their structure, inevitably concentrated power in the hands of the few. This pattern Michels called "the iron law of oligarchy." "It is organization," he wrote, "which gives birth to the dominion of the elected over the electors, of the mandatories over the mandators, of the delegates over the delegators. Who says organization says Oligarchy." Doctrinaire democrats thus pursued their dreams in vain.[48]

Pareto (1848–1923), a civil engineer who gave up engineering to study economics and politics, and who taught at the University of Lausanne, agreed with Michels on the inevitability of minority rule. But he theorized on a much broader scale, laying out in his vast and diffuse *Trattato di sociologia generale* (published in English in 1935 as *The Mind and Society*), an all-embracing theory of human behavior. Using graphs, quasi-mathematical notation, and a terminology of his own, and claiming to adhere strictly to what he called the "logico-experimental" method (i.e., empiricism), Pareto, in ironic and sometimes haughty prose, explained human behavior as the product not primarily of conscious choice, but of "residues" (constant or only very slowly changing psychic tendencies, much

like instincts), which are expressed and made to seem rational through "deriva-
tions" (ideas and other transient cultural forms).[49]

Mosca (1858–1941), a Sicilian, was both a theorist and an active politician. By
temperament part Whig and part Stoic, he had little faith in the political judgment of the average man, doubted the possibility of substantial social progress, and
made intellectual freedom its highest value. This last, he contended in his major
work, *The Ruling Class,* could best be attained not through law, but through the
checks that competing interests imposed on one another, for history had demonstrated that "freedom to think, to observe, to judge men and things serenely and
dispassionately, has been possible . . . only in those societies in which numbers of
different religious and political currents have been struggling for dominion."

Like his fellow Machiavellians, Mosca aimed at achieving a "science" of politics, a physics of political behavior. And like the other Machiavellians, he espoused
a pessimistic brand of realism. History, he argued, showed the hopes of progressive ideologues to be utopian fantasies. No society could be based "exclusively
upon the sentiment of justice," and no matter what kind of constitution a society adopted, power would forever rest with "organized minorities," which always
possessed "the means . . . to impose their supremacy on the multitudes." Only by
acknowledging this reality would it be possible to achieve a society favorable to
freedom.[50]

The French thinker Georges Sorel (1847–1922) resembled Pareto (with
whom he corresponded) in having started out as an engineer and then changed
careers—in Sorel's case to become a social theorist with ties to the revolutionary
labor movement known as syndicalism. In his *Reflections on Violence* (1908), he
assigned to "myth"—belief rooted in emotion rather than in reason, and able to
rouse the masses to collective action—the crucial role in forming mass movements, and so discounted reason as a significant factor in politics.[51]

What linked the Machiavellians was, first, their belief in the possibility of a
"science" of society. History, they argued, offered a vast fund of factual data,
which, when correlated, would reveal the "laws" governing political and social
behavior. (This was one of several beliefs they shared with Marx.) Second, they
agreed on the overwhelming importance of the nonrational in politics. In
Michels's view, power in political parties owed far more to forces inherent in their
structure than to conscious intent. For Pareto and Sorel, political opinions originated less in rational thought than in "residues" and "myths." For Mosca, all rul-

ing classes governed under a "political formula" (i.e., a nonrational belief, such as the divine right of kings or the sovereignty of the people) that was intended to justify their power.[52]

Third, all believed in the inevitability of minority rule, and so denied the possibility of democracy as usually defined. For Pareto, minority rule could certainly not be eliminated by revolution, which merely replaced the old elite with a new one, thus bringing about a "circulation of elites." Michels agreed. "The majority of human beings," he wrote, "must be content to constitute the pedestal of an oligarchy."[53] Nor, given what history taught about human nature, did they think that class warfare would ever cease. "Human beings have a natural tendency toward struggle," observed Mosca, and since humans were social animals, this tendency would often take the form of social conflict.[54]

Finally—and in sharp contrast to Marx, who took a hugely optimistic view of man's future prospects—all were firmly anti-utopian. Indeed, extolling "the melancholy realistic attitude" of the Book of Ecclesiastes, Mosca declared that the author of that scriptural text showed "a refinement of moral sense, and . . . a lucid perception of realities which only a long period of civilization makes possible, and then only in a few men of lofty minds and noble hearts."[55]

◆　◆　◆　◆

Burnham first read the Machiavellians in the late 1930s, at the urging of Hook, who wanted to expose him to intelligent criticism of Marx. But, still a determined Marxist at the time, he did not find them appealing.[56] Later, on the rebound from Marxism—though not from the "scientific" realism he had once attributed to Marx—he read them again, and this time with enthusiasm. Since discovering the Machiavellians, he told Charles Lam Markmann in 1972, he had not been significantly influenced by any other political theorists or changed his "general point of view" in any basic way. Because of them, he said on another occasion, he had come to understand "more thoroughly" something he had long known intuitively: "that only by renouncing all ideology can we begin to see the world and man."[57]

He could not say what had drawn him to the Machiavellians, Burnham once told an interviewer.[58] Yet the reason seems obvious. Not only did they offer a supposedly empirical science of society that struck him as markedly superior to that of Marx, but in a political atmosphere misty with wish-based ideology, they also appeared to be defenders of hard-headed realism. For someone like Burnham, disenchanted with Marxism, but not with the ideal of a severely empirical science of society, and eager for tough-minded analysis, the attraction of these thinkers must have been overwhelming.

While regarding Pareto as "perhaps the most brilliant" of the group, and calling Michels's dissection of mass organization "profound," Burnham was most taken with Mosca.[59] Though he never explained why, he may have been responding to Mosca's stoic stance, which resembled his own, and to Mosca's tendency to affirm traditional political wisdom. Thus, thinkers from Polybius to Montesquieu and Madison had already, in one way or another, put forward Mosca's idea that only power, not formal law or high ideals, could restrain power. Moreover, Mosca seemed devoted above all to the defense of freedom, to Burnham an invaluable—and now endangered—good.

Burnham's effort to "re-educate" himself politically,[60] along with his concern about the "managerial" trend in government, led him to write a new book, *The Machiavellians: Defenders of Freedom,* which came out in 1943. Mainly an account of "Machiavellian" political thought, this work also explained his method of political analysis, added new forecasts to those of *The Managerial Revolution,* and warned of trends he saw in American political life that he believed inimical to constitutional rule and personal freedom.

Though *The Machiavellians* enthusiastically endorsed the ideas of these men, it bestowed its highest praise on Machiavelli himself—for Burnham, not the wicked counselor of betrayal and murder for political ends, but the father of the analytical study of political power, the originator of an empirical theory of politics, the first modern political scientist. "We may burn an occasional Bruno, imprison a Galileo, denounce a Darwin, exile an Einstein," Burnham declaimed in words taken from the rhetorical conventions of liberalism. "But time, we imagine, restores judgment, and a new generation recognizes the brave captains of the mind who have dared to advance through the dark barriers of ignorance, superstition, and illusion. Machiavelli was so plainly one of these. His weapons, his methods—the methods of truth and science—he shared with Galileo and Darwin and Einstein; and he fought in a field of much greater concern to mankind. He tried to tell us not about stars or atoms, but about ourselves and our common life."[61]

To bring out Machiavelli's specific virtues, Burnham returned to the distinction between "real" and "formal" meanings he had drawn in his Trotskyist essay "Intellectuals in Retreat." Using Dante (whose poetry he loved, but whose politics he scorned) as a foil for Machiavelli, he analyzed the poet's *De Monarchia,* a plea for universal monarchy under the Holy Roman Emperor, and summed the work up as a mixture of wishful thinking and bad faith inspired by Dante's hope of resurrecting his defeated political faction. Dante's argument bore no relation to historical reality, he argued, but was an example of "politics as wish," whose formal and real meanings sharply diverged. Machiavelli, to the contrary, writing in the spirit of scientific inquiry, and openly stating his aims, made a "moral ideal" of fidelity to truth and reality. Moreover, since his writings harbored no ulterior motives, their real and formal meanings were the same.[62]

Equally forthright, Burnham maintained, were the modern Machiavellians, who also followed Machiavelli in grounding their arguments exclusively in historical evidence. This had enabled them to formulate a genuine science of politics, one that not only described the world as it really was, but that also provided a practical political benefit. Only by banishing daydreams and facing reality could man make whatever progress the human condition allowed.[63] Hence, a choice had to be made: Machiavellian realism (facts, empiricism, honesty) or "idealism" (illusions, ideology, sentimentality).

Burnham also intended *The Machiavellians* to sound a warning. The world was moving toward plebiscitarian dictatorship, he wrote, an all-encompassing, leader-based, bureaucratic form of government that in theory derived its legitimacy from the will of the people. This "democratic totalitarianism" or "Bonapartism," the kind of government favored by the rising managerial elite, did away with the freedoms traditionally associated with democracy. But because it rested its claims on a democratic sanction in an age when democratic formulas had become sacrosanct and universal, arousing opposition to it could be especially difficult. Bonapartism had reached maturity in the USSR, Nazi Germany, and Fascist Italy. Now it was taking root in the United States, with the Roosevelt administration as its vehicle and Vice President Henry A. Wallace as its "major prophet." Burnham remained deeply hostile toward Roosevelt after breaking with Trotsky, though he now viewed the president as a front man for the managerial class rather than for the plutocratic "sixty families."[64]

The global crisis, Burnham went on, helped to fuel the Bonapartist trend, and crisis conditions would continue. Once the war had ended, the world economy would fall into severe depression, and the United States and other countries would repudiate their public debt. In addition, if the peace treaties restored a Europe of many independent countries, the postwar settlement would soon collapse. Meanwhile, the Pacific war promised to go on indefinitely. Finally, the Roosevelt administration might seek to stay in power for yet another term, in which case it would "have to curtail political liberty further."[65]

Yet like *The Managerial Revolution,* which had held out the hope that managerial government would in time mellow enough to allow a measure of freedom, *The Machiavellians* saw reason for hope in the long run. "During the monstrous wars and revolutions of our time, there has already begun on a vast scale a purge of the ranks of the ruling class," ran the book's cryptic ending. "That purge, and the recruitment of new leaders which accompanies it, may be expected to continue until they bring about a change in the present course. Though the change will never lead to the perfect society of our dreams, we may hope that it will permit human beings at least that minimum of moral dignity which alone can justify the strange accident of man's existence."[66]

◆    ◆    ◆    ◆

Lacking *The Managerial Revolution*'s historical sweep and oracular bravura, and sometimes resembling a textbook, *The Machiavellians* did not attract large numbers of readers. But of those who did read the book, many thanked Burnham for helping them to understand the "real" world.[67] Reviewers, on the other hand, because of Burnham's celebrity status, were numerous, but they rarely joined the chorus of approval. John MacCormac, in the Sunday *New York Times,* and Louis Hacker, in the Sunday *New York Herald Tribune,* delivered negative verdicts. Another unhappy reviewer—ironically, Reinhold Niebuhr—accused Burnham in the *Nation* of descending into "an abyss of cynicism," and, pointing to the Machiavellian view of human nature, asked why readers should not "discount anything [Burnham] has to say about the operation of political forces, on the ground that his conclusions are nothing else than dishonest pretensions which hide the power impulses of the social scientist." Malcolm Cowley, in the *New Republic,* applied Burnham's distinction between formal and real meanings to the book, and decided that its real meaning, indirectly conveyed in its warning against

Bonapartism, was that the true danger was democracy.[68]

Here and there a favorable review appeared. The *Atlantic Monthly* called *The Machiavellians* "a work of high quality," and compared its author's "keen and cutting" mind to a scalpel. But reviewers who praised the book often thought it could have been better. Philip Wheelwright, in the *Kenyon Review,* called *The Machiavellians* "a generally trenchant book," but one that exaggerated the degree to which the study of politics could be scientific, and that for all its claim to detachment was in fact "partisan and tendentious." Had Burnham achieved "a more careful objectivity of method, statement, and tone," Wheelwright concluded, he might have come up with "a first-rate book"—in sum, a B-minus from Professor Wheelwright to his former student.[69]

One of the more discerning reviews came from the *New York Times*'s weekday critic, John Chamberlain. Struck by what he saw as the poor fit between Burnham the advocate of a value-free social science and Burnham the champion of freedom, Chamberlain was reminded of Francis Thompson's poem "The Hound of Heaven," whose would-be atheist narrator futilely struggles to escape a pursuing God. Burnham "runs away to Renaissance Florence," Chamberlain commented, "but Thomas Jefferson is right behind him. He hides himself among French Syndicalists, but James Madison plucks him by the sleeve. He hobnobs with modern Italian 'Machiavellians' . . . , but John Taylor and Henry George pop up from under the cafe tables." What did Burnham's theory of freedom as the byproduct of conflict between rival social forces amount to in the end but "our old friend out of the pages of 'The Federalist,' the system of checks and balances"? "A Machiavellian? Tush, tush," Chamberlain smiled. At heart, Burnham was "just an old-fashioned American liberal" who would fight to prevent slavery of the managerial or any other kind.[70]

In an introduction to a new edition of *The Machiavellians* published twenty years later, Burnham offered his own criticisms. He had been grateful to the Machiavellians for helping him to slip the bonds of ideology, he wrote, and so had perhaps given them "rather more than their due." In addition, some of what he had written now struck him "as a little callow," although possibly it was "just as well not to lose too many illusions too early." But in any case, the book provided a fair and accurate introduction to its subject, and so still had value.[71] In time, Burnham came to see *The Machiavellians* as his most important book, because it was there, he said, that he had first set forth the analytical principles that guided his thinking about politics.[72]

In some ways, *The Machiavellians,* with its hard-boiled view of the realities that underlay politics, reads like a sequel to *The Managerial Revolution*. It also recalls the earlier book in its wavering position on free will. This was a graver problem in the second book because, going beyond pure analysis, *The Machiavellians* sought to rally its readers to the defense of freedom, a goal that implicitly ascribed to them the power to choose and the possibility of acting efficaciously on their choice. Yet on the whole the book granted little scope to free will. "*The general pattern of social development,*" Burnham wrote, was "determined by technological change and by other factors quite beyond the likelihood of human control," and the power of free will was "confined within very narrow limits."[73] Pulled one way by his feelings, which demanded a broad measure of freedom, and another by his intellect, which drew him to deterministic social science, Burnham again solved the problem as he had in *The Managerial Revolution*: by stating that impersonal social forces, though very powerful, held less than absolutely total sway, so that an awareness of them and of the limits they imposed on free will could improve people's chances of exercising their freedom effectively.[74]

In some ways, however, *The Machiavellians* diverged from *The Managerial Revolution*. For one thing, it emphasized the power of the irrational element— "myth," "residue," "political formula"—in politics. For another, while repeatedly stressing the importance of "scientific" fact, it also looked at its subject from a moral standpoint, not simply analyzing and describing political phenomena, as *The Managerial Revolution* had done, but subjecting these phenomena to moral judgment. For example, though noting that it would be "absurd to call [oligarchy] good or bad; it is simply the way things are," Burnham wrote elsewhere in the book, "Granted that there are always rulers and ruled, then we may judge that the societies of some ruling classes are good, or more good, just, or less unjust, than others." And when discussing "Bonapartism," he by no means confined himself to detached analysis, but explicitly voiced strong moral disapproval. Similarly, he had a moral reason for believing in freedom. Freedom was "necessary" not only for such practical benefits as progress in scientific knowledge and "an advanced level of civilization," he wrote, but for "individual self-development," which was a "great and significant" good.[75]

◆    ◆    ◆    ◆

*The Managerial Revolution* and *The Machiavellians* confirmed that Burnham's concerns had shifted substantially during the preceding decade. The phase of his intellectual life that had begun in his student years and persisted alongside his Trotskyism was over. To be sure, the transformation was not completely clear-cut. Some people still thought of him as primarily a literary intellectual, his Trotskyist interlude and two recent books notwithstanding. Thus, rumor at NYU in the mid-forties had him working on a "definitive" study not of a political topic, but of aesthetics.[76] Moreover, as if to thicken the ambiguity surrounding him, he continued to turn out articles like those he had once written for the *Symposium;* for example, critical pieces on Allen Tate's criteria for the evaluation of poetry, James T. Farrell's literary aesthetic, and fiction by Albert Camus, Simone de Beauvoir, and Franz Kafka.[77] Nevertheless, because of *The Managerial Revolution* and *The Machiavellians,* by the mid-forties most people who knew of him probably associated him with political analysis rather than literary and aesthetic criticism.

But he had yet to acquire his most familiar public identity: hard-line anticommunist. He was soon to do so, however. For the mushrooming growth of Soviet power in the final stages of World War II led him to shift his attention from managerial rule and Machiavellian political thought to the ambitions of the USSR, a power he had long denounced as a totalitarian police state, and one he now also viewed as a waxing global menace.

# Chapter 6

# Strategist

B Y 1943, REMEMBERS THE economist Lev E. Dobriansky, then teaching at NYU and a regular luncheon companion of Burnham and Hook, Burnham had fixed his attention on the USSR, which, with Nazi Germany clearly on the ropes, he believed to be the greatest threat to Western freedom.[1] His hostility to the USSR went back to his Trotskyist days. But it now grew sharper, as he began to fear (contrary to his prediction in *The Managerial Revolution*) that Stalin's nightmare state would soon swallow up its western neighbors and possibly the rest of the European continent as well. Americans, he worried, had not grasped the threat posed by this communist empire, which Washington touted as "our great democratic ally." It was high time they did.[2]

Hence, Burnham became an active participant in anticommunist causes. In February 1942, he joined the editors of *Partisan Review* and more than two hundred other, mostly left-leaning, anticommunist intellectuals (among them John Dewey, Reinhold Niebuhr, Norman Thomas, and a reactivated A. J. Muste) in sending a letter to the president of Mexico protesting the "reign of terror" Mexican communists were alleged to be conducting against Trotskyists and other anti-Stalinist refugees in that country. The following year, he took part in a campaign launched by Dwight Macdonald against the movie *Mission to Moscow*, a pro-Stalin whitewash based on the memoirs of Joseph E. Davies, recently U.S. ambassador to the Kremlin.

By 1944, he had made publicizing the Soviet threat a major activity. He summed up the threat in his reply to the question, "Is Russia Aiming at the Postwar Domination of Europe?" in a radio debate of February 1944 with bridge expert and World Federationist Ely Cuthbertson. Yes, he said, Moscow did indeed seek this end, and if it succeeded, calamity would ensue. World economic conflict would worsen. Europe would fall prey to a new totalitarianism not unlike Hitler's. The balance of power would be so badly upset that "a gigantic new war" would break out. And Roosevelt's Four Freedoms would become modern history's "bitterest joke."[3]

Two articles Burnham published in 1944 added detail to his reading of Soviet aims and stressed the role of the world's communist parties in Soviet strategy. "The sixth period of official communism is now in flower," he declared in "The Sixth Turn of the Communist Screw." In this period (he labeled it the "Teheran period," after the Roosevelt-Churchill-Stalin summit the previous autumn), the Soviet managerial elite, using the international communist movement as a "hardened, fully trained, absolutely reliable and remarkably flexible tool," planned to turn victory over Germany into "*de facto*" control of Europe. Indirectly, by triggering mutinies in British-led Greek military units in Egypt, for example, the USSR had already launched a war against the West, the sole obstacle to the expansion of its power. Further hostile actions could be expected.[4]

Stalin was also using captive German officers for Soviet expansion, the second article, "Stalin and the Junkers," asserted. Through the Free German National Committee, a Soviet-created body made up of war prisoners representing elements in the German officer corps and of delegates of the refugee German Communist Party, he was laying the groundwork for future Soviet control of Germany, which he hoped to make the outer bulwark of his "Eurasian fortress." On the outcome of his plan would depend the fate not only of Europe, but of Eurasia, "and, perhaps, of the world."[5]

Because Stalin had become a key figure in world politics, Burnham warned in a 1945 article called "Lenin's Heir," it was crucial to realize that he was neither the "cipher" of Trotskyist myth, nor FDR's "genial Uncle Joe," but a clever and grasping pragmatist who had never donned the shackles of ideology. He stood in stark contrast to the doctrinaire ideologue Trotsky, "a Platonic communist" for whom revolution had been "a Form, subsisting in an independent, non-historical realm of Being." When that realm had chanced to coincide with the "histor-

ical world of Becoming," as in Russia in 1917, Trotsky had seemed a "great historical figure." But when Being and Becoming, abstract ideas and empirical realities, had diverged again, he had ceased to be effective. Hence Stalin, not Trotsky,
was Lenin's true heir. Trotsky had only been Lenin's "temporarily adopted son,
left unremembered in the legal will."[6]

The real meaning of Soviet-based communism could be discovered not by
reading the movement's formal program, Burnham went on, but by observing the
policies Moscow followed. Thus examined, communism was revealed to be at
base "a conspiratorial movement for the conquest of a monopoly of power in the
era of capitalist disintegration." The movement had already made impressive
headway toward this end. "Starting from the magnetic core of the Eurasian heartland," Burnham noted, the Soviet power,

> like the One of Neo-Platonism overflowing in the descending
> series of the emanative progression, flows outward, west into
> Europe, south into the Near East, east into China, already lap-
> ping the shores of the Atlantic, the Yellow and China Seas, the
> Mediterranean, and the Persian Gulf. As the undifferentiated
> One, in its progression, descends through the stages of Mind,
> Soul, and Matter, and then through its fatal Return back to
> itself, so does the Soviet power, emanating from the integrally
> totalitarian center, proceed outward by Absorption (the Baltics,
> Bessarabia, Bukovina, East Poland), Domination (Finland, the
> Balkans, Mongolia, North China, and tomorrow Germany),
> Orienting Influence (Italy, France, Turkey, Iran, central and
> South China . . . ), until it is dissipated in . . . the outer material
> sphere, beyond the Eurasian boundaries, of momentary
> Appeasement and Infiltration (England, the United States).

Facing the truth about the USSR could be "very unpleasant," Burnham conceded. But there was no other choice.[7]

"Lenin's Heir" contained in a nutshell the view of the USSR's world aims and
strategy that would shape Burnham's arguments in the decades-long Cold War
debate soon to begin. But the article's immediate result was to feed his reputation for power worship. To drive home his point that Stalin was not a genuine

ally or, as Trotskyists contended, a mere figurehead of the Soviet bureaucracy but a dangerous enemy—and also, Burnham later confessed, to "épater les Trotskyistes"—he had included a partly tongue-in-cheek description of the Soviet leader, calling him the heir of "the tradition of the most spectacular of the Tsars, of the Great Kings of the Medes and Persians, of the Khanate of the Golden Horde, of the banquet we assign to the gods of the Heroic Ages in tribute to the insight that insolence and indifference and brutality on such a scale remove beings from the human level."[8] But this "put-on," as he called it, backfired, for it drew more attention than the alarm he had wanted to sound. Burnham's intellectual career could be viewed as an endless search "for a Father, for authority, from Thomas Aquinas to Trotsky to Pareto to Hitler to Stalin," claimed a tone-deaf Dwight Macdonald (who may have been miffed at seeing himself referred to in the article as "one of the sentimental dilettantes of revolution"). Mesmerized by Stalin, what Burnham really wanted to do was yield to him. "'Beat me, daddy, eight to the bar,'" expressed Burnham's wish. Orwell voiced a similar reaction. Burnham's treatment of Stalin might carry "a tinge of irony," he acknowledged, yet it seemed that Burnham also felt "a sort of fascinated admiration" for the tyrant. To Burnham, "'greatness'" seemed "inextricably mixed up with the idea of cruelty and dishonesty." "Lenin's Heir" offered "a rhapsody . . . on the strength, cunning, and cruelty of Stalin" that "probably" signified approval, even if of "a rather horrified kind." (Burnham blamed Orwell's criticisms on MacDonald. The "Orwell business has become something of an international plague as far as I am concerned," he wrote some years later to the Indian politician and diplomat Minoo Masani, and could be traced to Macdonald's misreading of "Lenin's Heir.")[9]

Seeing in Soviet communism a system of limitless, soul-crushing despotism, Burnham hated it. Even so, he understood its appeal, especially for intellectuals. It was precisely because communism was "*a perversion of the good,* of close to the best," that it was "more horrifying and more seductive than any other social movement of our time," he wrote in a 1947 article on the political troubles of the Soviet film director Sergei Eisenstein. Communism's moral attractions explained why it could "never be definitively unmasked, why the task of refuting, exposing and combating it must be daily renewed." Its "chains for the human spirit" had been "twisted from the most splendid of man's feelings and hopes—his cry for justice, his sense of brotherhood, his longing for freedom." Further, in assigning artists a social duty, communists affirmed an important truth. Art, as Plato knew, had a social function: that of "forming the souls of the citizens of the Republic." Outside the communist sphere, great artists, isolated from and unintelligible to society, proved that the principle of art for art's sake could not give art "an adequate human basis." But even as communists upheld this truth they corrupted it, enslaving artists to the totalitarian state.[10]

In these statements Burnham also implied that such values as justice and freedom were absolute rather than relative. But on this he was not consistent, for he sometimes adopted a relativist position. In 1944, even as he affirmed his belief in "freedom, truth, love, and beauty" in his protest against Orwell's criticism of *The Managerial Revolution,* he also published a review of the historian Charles Beard's *The Republic,* in which he rebuked Beard for talking about values as if they were "permanent" and "eternal," i.e., absolute rather than culture-bound.[11] Possibly, the tension between his emotions and his intellect evident in his wavering on the determinism-freedom problem also led to his shifting view of the nature of values, his emotions pushing him toward absolutism, his intellect toward relativism.

◆ ◆ ◆ ◆

Burnham's remark of 1972 that no one had influenced him significantly since the Machiavellians was not wholly true. In the mid-1940s, as his anxiety about the Soviet-communist threat mounted, he turned for broader perspective on the problem to two thinkers whose work he had come to know more recently: the British historian (and Balliol man) Arnold Toynbee, then at the peak of his fame, and Toynbee's fellow Briton, the geopolitical analyst Halford Mackinder, who during the war years seized the attention of foreign-affairs specialists at such places as the Institute for Advanced Studies at Princeton and Yale's Institute for International Studies.[12] Though their specialties differed, Toynbee and Mackinder were in one respect quite similar. Both speculated on a grand scale and held out interpretive keys to vast and complex matters, Toynbee purporting to have extracted from the endless detail of history the "laws" he thought ruled universal historical development, and Mackinder plumbing the globe's material structure to determine the relationship of world geography to power. Moreover, though both set forth their thoughts in restrained and formal language, both could write prose that hummed with muted drama. One recent browser in Toynbee described his writings as "rousing boys' stuff," which, besides much else, it sometimes is.[13] In short, the two were theorists of the kind Burnham loved, and both were to have a lasting impact on his thinking.

In *A Study of History* (whose first six volumes had come out by the mid-1940s),[14] Toynbee examined the twenty-one civilizations (seven of which, including the West, still existed) that he thought had developed in the course of history, and argued on grounds he insisted were empirical that all had moved, or were moving, through the same "law"-governed sequence of stages from genesis to disintegration. At some point in their historical trajectory, all but the West (whose turn might now be coming) had suffered a period of breakdown, a "Time of Trouble," and then regained stability through the intervention of a geographi-cally peripheral and culturally primitive power that had restored order by impos-ing a "Universal State." Thus rough-hewn Rome had brought peace to the culturally superior but chronically strife-torn Hellenistic world. Toynbee's theory of civilizational breakdown and recovery made a strong impression on Burnham, who would use it to diagnose and prescribe for the crisis-ridden West.

A student of the geographical basis of military power, Mackinder first expounded his ideas at length in a work of 1919, *Democratic Ideals and Reality: A Study in the Politics of Reconstruction.* Here he identified the primary terrestrial fea-tures of world geography as the "Heartland" (the great plain, broken only by the Urals, that stretched from eastern Europe to Mongolia, and that was invulnerable to sea power) and the "Coastlands" (chiefly western Europe, China, and India, with their extensive exposure to the open sea). Heartland and Coastlands together, along with Africa, formed a still larger unit, the "World-Island." In rela-tion to this "joint continent," the Americas resembled offshore islands facing a dominant land mass. The crucial weight in the world balance of power, Mackinder argued, was now the Heartland, for the transportation revolution embodied in the railroad, automobile, and airplane made it possible for the first time in history to mobilize the peoples and resources of this "citadel of the World-Island." Accordingly, if the Heartland were "under a single sway" that also possessed "invincible sea-power," that state would have world empire, "the ulti-mate threat to the world's liberty," within reach. The key to control of the Heartland was control of Eastern Europe. "Who rules Eastern Europe commands the Heartland," Mackinder summarized. "Who rules the Heartland commands the World-Island: Who rules the World-Island commands the World."[15]

During World War II Mackinder elaborated on this thesis. In an article called "The Round World and the Winning of the Peace," he stressed the danger that would follow if Germany gained control of the Heartland. But he also signaled the power potential of the USSR. If the latter defeated Germany, he wrote, it would "rank as the greatest land Power on the globe." It would also enjoy "the strategically strongest defensive position," for the Heartland was not only "the greatest natural fortress on earth," but for the first time could be "manned by a garrison sufficient both in number and quality."[16]

Mackinder's 1919 answer to the threat of a Heartland-based adversary had been a counterweight in the guise of a British Empire remodeled into a world league of democracies. But by the 1940s he had come to envisage the North Atlantic countries as the basis of his democratic league.[17] Though he did not say so, an Atlantic league could also serve to check the USSR.

Burnham first revealed his debt to Toynbee and Mackinder in a paper he wrote in 1944 that he could not then publish (though parts of it appeared in some of his articles of the time). This was a study of Soviet aims he produced at the request of the Office of Strategic Services (OSS), wartime forerunner of the Central Intelligence Agency (CIA). In 1947, however, he published the paper in full as the first section of a book he had written on Soviet ambitions. He called the book *The Struggle for the World*.[18]

If any single book of Burnham's can be described as "apocalyptical," this, surely, is the one. Gripped by his old fear that the West faced imminent destruction, Burnham now saw the source of the danger not in economic collapse, as he had in the 1930s, but in Soviet-communist aggression and subversion. "I must say that my reason is absolutely convinced," he wrote to Hook while working on the book. "Either Western Civilization is going to be—quite quickly—literally destroyed; or communism will conquer the world (which would also mean, in a somewhat different sense, the destruction of Western Civilization). . . . And it more than ever seems to me that the issue is going to be decided fairly soon."

With time so short, the tocsin had to be sounded. Yet for him to be assuming that task struck Burnham as anomalous. In the past, he had at times functioned in settings in which he looked out of place, but he had never seemed to feel any sense of incongruity. Now, however, he found himself in what he called "schizoid conflict." "All my life I have thought of myself as non-national," he confessed to Hook. "Catholicism, art, knowledge, Marxism—they have been much of my life, and I have always conceived of them as supranational, as simply human. And however I understand this new book, the opinions of others—which I no doubt should not think of—will regard me in it as nationalist, not to say chauvinist, imperialist, fascist, and so on."[19]

◆   ◆   ◆   ◆

"The Third World War began in April, 1944," read *The Struggle for the World*'s first sentence, the opening shots fired by mutinous Greek soldiers and sailors stationed in Alexandria under British command. The mutiny was triggered by the military arm of a Greek political coalition led by the Greek Communist Party, a member of the Soviet-directed world communist movement. Correctly understood, the mutiny amounted to a preliminary skirmish between communism and the West (in this instance represented by the British Empire) in a new world war that was begining before the old one had ended.[20]

With the world now "sharply and decisively" divided between communists and noncommunists—not just on the international plane, but within each non-communist country—this new conflict, Burnham argued, could not be avoided. What made the conflict inevitable was the atom bomb, which complicated beyond measure the problem of the balance of power. For now, the United States alone possessed this terrible weapon. But the USSR would have it soon, and when it did, each of the two powers would come under irresistible pressure to launch a pre-emptive strike against the other, reasoning that if it did not land the first, and possibly terminal, blow, the other would. Hence, the end of civilization lay in sight. Fear of retaliation, "the entire history of war and society" showed, would not deter attack. The one alternative was "monopoly control" of atomic weapons, which only the United States and the USSR could hope to attain. Since the winner in this race would also achieve world empire in the sense of "world dominating" political influence, the conflict would be a struggle for survival. Both countries might be destroyed in the course of the contest—"but one of them must be."[21] (This view of the future differed substantially from the one he had offered in *The Managerial Revolution,* Burnham noted. The reasons for the change were the emergence of not three but only two superstates from World War II and the invention of the atom bomb. But the managerial revolution remained "the world revolution of our time," he added, and the kind of superstate conflict he had forecast in 1941 might "still in the end" take place.)[22]

Communism made a formidable enemy, Burnham continued. A global conspiracy aiming at worldwide rule, the movement possessed a "monolithic structure," "steel discipline," the "cement of terror," a "rigid and total ideology," and a following committed to the cause as "'dedicated'" men. The communist had "no life apart from his organization and his rigidly systematic set of ideas. Everything that he does, everything that he has, family, job, money, belief, friends, talents, life, everything is subordinated to his communism. He is not a communist just on election day or at Party headquarters. He is a communist always. He eats, reads, makes love, thinks, goes to parties, changes residences, laughs, insults, always as a communist." What inspired such a life was a single passion, from which nothing, "neither wife nor child nor friend, neither beauty nor love nor pleasure nor knowledge cherished for its own sake," could distract him. That passion, reduced to essentials, was the "will to power."[23]

Nor was communism mere camouflage for traditional Russian imperialism, he went on. True, communists gave their loyalty to the USSR, but what they saw there was "not a 'national fatherland'" but "the 'fortress of the world revolution.'" They supported Russian expansion because it meant communist expansion.[24]

The victory of communism would mean the destruction of all the ideals the West held sacred, among them "the absolute value of the single human person" and "personal freedom and dignity," as well as certain values the West shared with other cultures. Communist victory would also doom the West's ideal of objective truth and refusal to identify might with right, for communism defined truth and right as whatever aided communist ambitions. Further, communism robbed the individual of "his conscience, his honor," and forced him to "lie and grovel, cheat and inform and betray" at the behest of his masters. The threat of this moral abyss, not fear of a lower living standard, was what made resistance to communism urgent. "What . . . is our moral ballot: For or Against?" Burnham asked, adding that some who realized what was at stake would rather see mankind perish than communism win.[25]

And win it might, for since 1939 the USSR had made striking progress toward its goal. Moving out from "'the inner Heartland' of the 'World Island,'" it had annexed several neighboring countries, and forced puppet regimes on others. Now its main target for puppet status was Germany, since control of Germany would enable Moscow to dominate Europe and complete the western salient of its Eurasian stronghold. Beyond this the USSR aimed at "orienting influence" in western Europe, the Middle East, and Latin America, while in Britain and the British Commonwealth its policy was one of "infiltration and demoralization."[26]

But the United States topped the list of countries marked for subversion. Partly by sapping the American will to resist, and partly by means of a "very extensive" apparatus trained for "direct action—espionage, sabotage, stimulation of riots and revolts, etc.," the communists hoped to cripple the United States before the present, low-intensity conflict had turned into all-out war. Areas marked for infiltration included communications, intelligence, the media, shipping, technology, and science, especially the crucial field of nuclear physics, where communist efforts had already enjoyed success. The communists were also working to turn Americans against one another by sharpening social, racial, religious, and economic divisions. The outbreak of full-scale war between the United States and the USSR could find the United States "so internally weakened, divided, and demoralized, that it [would] be unable even to make a good showing in the struggle."[27]

The USSR enjoyed several major assets: control of the Heartland, key to control of Eurasia, which, Burnham knew from Mackinder, geopolitically "encircle[d] America, overwhelm[ed] it"; a gigantic reserve of manpower and natural resources; a world organization that included an "incomparable" intelligence division and "the greatest propaganda office ever known or conceived"; a potent myth that embodied "the great dream of a Kingdom of Heaven on Earth," and whose appeal increased as traditional religion and the hold of liberal-democratic myths weakened; and perhaps its biggest asset, the extraordinary political skills of Soviet leaders.

True enough, the USSR also suffered from serious problems: a primitive economy and a rudimentary level of culture, which, together with the backwardness of Soviet technology, lowered the quality of the communist giant's armed forces. Nevertheless, it remained a daunting foe—not least because of the inadequacy of Western leaders, who, in contrast to their Soviet enemies, "grope[d] and fumble[d]" and refused to face reality.[28]

One response to the Soviet threat, Burnham suggested, might be a Western "defensive policy." If the United States chose this course, it would have to recognize that the West and communism were truly at war, and make an "open bid" for "world political leadership." To begin with, such a policy would require a worldwide propaganda campaign defining the basic issue between the West and communism as freedom versus "totalitarian slavery." In addition, the United States would have to make victory, not peace, its supreme aim; disregard such principles as "the equality of nations" and noninterference in the internal affairs of other countries; let the world know that it would bestow its favors exclusively on its friends; and make clear that it was willing to use force to uphold its interests. Above all, it would have to assume the task of defending the World Island's Coastlands and Japan (a potential U.S. offshore "outpost") to prevent the Soviets from mastering the whole of Eurasia. Once it had taken these steps, it could then bend its efforts toward overthrowing communist rule in countries outside the USSR's 1940 borders, and so turn communism's "expansive advance into a demoralizing retreat."[29]

A defensive policy would not suffice, however. The enemy had to be toppled, not simply held at bay, and for that an "offensive policy" was necessary. First, an "American empire" exercising "decisive world control" (i.e., not direct rule, but irresistible influence) would have to be established, so that politically the non-communist world would act as one. The chief step to this end, a step that would "instantaneously transform the whole of world politics," would be the formation by the United States, Britain, and the British Dominions of a full-fledged political union, complete with common citizenship—though "forceps" might have to be used to achieve its birth. Next, the Continental European nations not under communist rule would have to join in a "European Federation." If these countries balked, once again pressure would have to be applied, though a promise of economic aid might bring them around. Then would come the alliance of the Anglo-American combine and the European Federation, the form in which the West, now deep in its "Time of Trouble," would become a Toynbeean "Universal State," with the United States in the role of the peripheral, semibarbarian, unifying power. But the offensive policy would not stop at the West's frontiers, for political and economic concessions might induce non-Western nations to act with the West against communism. British India, for example, could be granted a status like that of the Philippines: independence on the condition that its government adopt an anticommunist policy.

Once the U.S.-led anticommunist bloc had been assembled, the time would have come to strike at the communist sphere. The means would be economic and political, however, not military, and would aim first at freeing Soviet satellites from communist rule. But the offensive policy would also cross the USSR's 1939 border to liberate the Soviet peoples and "pre-eminently" the Russian people, communism's first victims. It would be useful, Burnham added, to give the offensive policy—the only policy able to defend freedom, defeat communism, and ensure the U.S. atomic monopoly on which the future depended—a name. A good choice would be "the policy of democratic world order."[30]

The offensive policy would also include action against communism at home. Since communists and "ingrained communist sympathizers" were at war with the United States, the party and its "activities and propaganda" would have to be made illegal, and communists removed from the U.S. government and armed forces. "Any individual right or freedom is properly extended only to those who accept the fundamental rules of democracy," Burnham asserted, foreseeing liberal objections to the proposed ban. "How . . . could any society survive which deliberately nursed its own avowed and irreconcilable assassin, and freely exposed its heart to his knife?"[31]

While "certainly grandiose," the offensive policy was not unrealistic, Burnham argued. For one thing, it assumed that people would act as they always had, i.e., largely out of self-interest. For another, it took heed of the existing balance of power. But most of all, it would "really solve" the problem behind the world crisis, and "nothing less than this" could be viewed as realistic. Since the world could not live with communism, there was "no other way" but to destroy it, and only an offensive policy could do so.[32]

But although Burnham cast the United States as the West's "deputy" in the great world struggle, he doubted its ability to fill the role successfully. Expressing a view long common among American intellectuals, he described the United States as a business-obsessed and culturally stunted society, endowed with an extraordinary talent for industrial production, but "socially, politically and culturally" ill-equipped to act as champion of Western civilization. Having originated as a "colonial offshoot" of Europe, and in the nineteenth century having fixed its mind on economic development, this "gawky adolescent" of a country had "no art of its own, no music, no literature, no great philosophy or religion, none of those signs of an inner and deeper wisdom." Hence, it now suffered from "cultural lag" and a parochial mindset that raised questions about its ability to exercise global power. "Who," Burnham asked, "listening a few hours to the American radio, could repress a shudder if he thought the price of survival would be the

Americanization of the world?"[33]

American inadequacy showed most strikingly in the country's political culture, which oscillated between the "abstract, empty, sentimental rhetoric of democratic idealism" made the American norm by Jefferson and "ward-heeling,
hotel-and-saloon, spoils system, machine practices." How could the United States
lead the West to victory over communism when it viewed politics as a matter of
"quashed parking tickets, building contracts, and soft jobs in the local court
house"? Nor did the schools provide encouragement, for they taught no world
political history, military history, geopolitics, or global economics.[34] Not surprisingly, therefore, the United States appeared incompetent in foreign policy, usually
mixing "abstract moral sentiment with short-term selfish interests, both projected
without any reference to world political facts."[35] President Truman was said to be
shifting to a tougher line toward Moscow, but this seemed to be mostly
"rhetorical"—"a kind of seasoning added to the mush of appeasement."[36]

In short, though the United States had the means to defeat communism, it
would probably do little toward that end. Its policy would waver between toughness, appeasement, calls for a United Nations-based world government, and isolationism. Such a policy would invite disaster. True, the United States disposed of
enormous power, but power without a sound policy to guide it always proved
"sterile." Hence, when war came (here Burnham brilliantly foretold the U.S.
experience in Vietnam), the United States would lose, since in the absence of an
intelligent policy,

> its dreadful material strength would appear to the peoples as the
> unrelieved brutality of a murderer. . . . Americans themselves
> would be sickened and conscience-ridden by what would seem
> to them a senseless slaughter, never-ending, leading nowhere.
> The military leadership would be disoriented by the inability of
> their plans based on technical superiority to effect a decision.
> The failure to conceive the struggle politically would have
> given the communists the choice of weapons. From the stand-
> point of the United States, the entire world would have turned
> into an ambush and a desert. In the long night, nerves would
> finally crack, the sentries would fire their last shots wildly into
> the darkness, and it would all be over.[37]

All-out war between the United States and the USSR was "very probable," the
book's final chapter repeated. It would most likely break out within the next four
or five years (i.e., once the Soviets had built enough atom bombs), though maybe
even "before these sentences are published." Since the United States lacked the
qualities needed for the mission thrust upon it, "the darkness of great tragedy"
might soon bring the country's "short, bright history" to an end. Yet if it made
sense to predict American failure, Burnham concluded in an oblique last appeal
for his offensive policy, that was "only a measure of how great the triumph could
be."[38]

◆    ◆    ◆    ◆

In many ways, *The Struggle for the World* was vintage Burnham: Augustinian in its
keen awareness of the world's imperfection (solutions to political problems could
never be more than "temporary and partial");[39] provocative in outlook; often syl-
logistic in its manner of argument; assertively "realistic" in its view of human
nature ("Men . . . and nations will continue to act politically as they have always
acted, primarily, though not quite exclusively, from self-interest");[40] professorial
in its shifts of tone between the didactic and the ironic; scornful of liberal idealism; deeply imbued with a vision of lowering disaster; and endowed with a special intensity through its calmly analytical treatment of a hair-raising subject.
"Whew! What a book!" Orville Prescott of the *New York Times* ended his
review.[41]

In one respect, however, the book struck a new note for Burnham—its
assignment of decisive importance to will. Some of his postpublication glosses on
*The Managerial Revolution* and his protest against Bonapartism in *The
Machiavellians* had implied that will counted for much in politics. But *The Struggle
for the World* explicitly made will the indispensable requirement for success. Still,
Burnham also reminded his readers of the limits on will. "Meaningful political
choice," he warned, was "narrowly limited by the structure of social facts, by the
concrete situation within which the choice must be made." Hence, "the most,
surely, that we can propose to ourselves is to alter by a degree or two . . . the direction or rate of [history's] advance."[42]

The tonal (not intellectual) inconsistency of its view of will was not the sole
reason for the book's vulnerability. Thus, though Burnham claimed to be build-

ing his case on empirical grounds, he sometimes seemed deaf to the demands of empirical reason. His assumption that if two countries possessed atomic weapons, each would be forced toward a pre-emptive attack on the other, rested more on abstract logic than on historical evidence. So, too, did his belief (which experience was to belie) that "fear of retaliation" would not deter atomic attack.[43]

In addition, the book exaggerated the strength of the enemy. Burnham's communists are so unfailingly competent that they seem closer to creatures of fantasy than to the actual flesh-and-blood, fallible beings at Moscow's command. It is as if Burnham had meant his rendering of these paragons to be less a true mirror of reality than a foil against which to show up the "mushy" progressives he so scorned. For in their ruthless realism and resoluteness, his communists are the polar opposite of his appeasement-minded liberals, who, when faced with "two extreme and seemingly opposed views . . . customarily [feel] . . . that the truth must lie in a compromise halfway between them," and so evade "the grim duty of facing the flat truth, and recognizing that on most matters all views except one are simply false."[44] Further, in his portrayal of communism, he came close to committing the sin of platonic "essentialism" with which he had taxed Beard, Eastman, and Trotsky, among others. For he wrote of communism as if it were an immutable "form" standing above the flux of history.

But the most obvious weakness of *The Struggle for the World* lay in the contrast between what it predicted and what actually happened. For from the 1940s to the 1980s, a still "gawky adolescent" United States persisted in a "policy of vacillation" toward the USSR, sometimes opposing the Soviets by force of arms, sometimes seeking a settlement with the Kremlin, and sometimes pursuing both courses simultaneously. But despite these vagaries and the Soviet acquisition of a gigantic nuclear arsenal, the two powers did not end up in Burnham's all-out war, but stood locked for decades in a nuclear standoff. If at times fighting did break out between them (as in Korea and Vietnam), it never exceeded the bounds of conventional warfare, nor did their armies ever clash directly. And in the end, the USSR went down to defeat, laid low not by a Western "offensive policy," but by structural flaws that rotted the Soviet system (some of which Burnham had noted in *The Struggle for the World*).

Nevertheless, if the world of 1947 is viewed without the benefit of hindsight, Burnham's worries begin to sound more reasonable. A united, Moscow-led world communist movement did exist in 1947, and had vaulted to a level of power and influence that only a few years before would scarcely have seemed possible. The communist tide, moreover, continued to rise. Communists had seized power in most of eastern Europe, showed impressive strength in France and Italy, and were well on their way to taking over China. Furthermore, the movement's full-time agents, if not its rank-and-file, acted with impressive skill and dedication, and if they did not always perform on the lofty level Burnham claimed for them, they nonetheless scored successes with alarming frequency.

At the same time, the USSR had shed the military incompetence it had shown as recently as 1941. In 1947 incontestably a great power, with massive ground forces stationed in the center of Europe, it seemed easily capable of over-running a demoralized continent that had barely begun to recover from World War II. Nor was Burnham's alarm about Soviet spying and subversion "paranoid." By 1947 evidence abounded that the USSR relied heavily on such methods, and that evidence has recently been supplemented and confirmed by the Soviet archives.[45]

In other words, if Burnham exaggerated when he wrote that "all of world politics" now revolved around "the struggle for power between Soviet-based communism and the United States," he had plausible reasons for this claim. But his highly colored picture of the Soviet-communist threat can also be attributed to his habit of writing provocatively and to his way of defining a problem (or, in his words, seizing "the key to the situation"), i.e., stripping away all nuance to expose its essence. He knew full well the danger this practice entailed, admitting that it "simplifie[d] or "even over-simplifie[d]" reality. But, he added, unless the key were seized, no adequate understanding of world politics could be attained. As for the "Third World War" policy he proposed, given his far from outlandish picture of world politics, in broad outline it made sense.[46]

◆    ◆    ◆    ◆

The most "dramatic" moment for publishing *The Struggle for the World* had passed, Burnham lamented to Hook in the summer of 1946 while still working on the manuscript.[47] But as things turned out, the timing could not have been better. In March 1947, less than a week before the book was due to appear, President Truman convoked a joint session of Congress to request aid for Greece, which had fallen into a communist-triggered civil war, and Turkey, target of menacing Soviet territorial demands. "It must be the policy of the United States," Truman told Congress, "to support free peoples who are resisting attempted subjugation by armed minorities or by outside pressures."[48] The "Truman doctrine," as this initiative came to be called, marked a major turning point in U.S. foreign policy: the abandonment of nonintervention abroad in time of peace for the role of world sentinel against Soviet expansion. Burnham strongly approved, calling Truman's decision "100 per cent correct." If it meant we were "getting over our illusions about the Communists," he said, "then it is the most important step in the history of our foreign policy."[49]

The coincidence of the book's appearance on the heels of the Truman speech brought it a rich harvest of publicity. Some opponents of the new Truman policy detected a sinister link between book and speech. "There is reason to fear it more than a coincidence that the Truman doctrine was announced and the Burnham book published in the same week," darkly observed the liberal *Christian Century.* Truman's program "*is* the Burnham program transferred from paper to action," and its consequence could well be another war.[50] The book also aroused the ire of isolationists in Congress. One such critic, Lawrence H. Smith of Wisconsin, went so far as to denounce it as "a veritable *Mein Kampf.*" Communists, unsurprisingly, also heaped abuse on Burnham. The French communist writer Pierre Courtade published a novel called *Jimmy,* whose title character, an "American imperialist" named "Jimmy Slaughter," was allegedly based on Burnham. According to a Burnham student of the time, the party had NYU members enroll in Burnham's courses, the better to keep this enemy under watch.[51]

He hoped debate over the book "would not get lost in fake arguments about [his] being a warmonger," Burnham told an interviewer.[52] But he hoped in vain. Burnham's ideas would lead "to a new war," protested the *Christian Century,* "to global tyranny, with ourselves the tyrants; to destruction, with humanity rising against us as we rose against Hitler, and for the same good reason." Lewis Corey, in the *Antioch Review,* accused the book of giving "aid-and-comfort to the people and policies that may bring a Russian-American war," just as *The Managerial Revolution* had given "aid-and-comfort to the totalitarian elites." Liberal columnist Max Lerner agreed, calling Burnham "the new hero of the war-with-Russia forces," while the isolationist historian Harry Elmer Barnes denounced the book as "a blueprint for war, more gratuitous and provocative than anything which, to my knowledge, ever emanated from the Comintern or from . . . the Nazis."[53]

Whether hostile to the book or not, some reviewers taxed it with treating the communist problem too reductively. Thus Orville Prescott and James Reston, in the daily and Sunday *New York Times* (the latter featured the book on the book review's front page), found Burnham's argument logical, but also, in Reston's words, "too neat and simple." Waldemar Gurian shared this opinion, arguing in a *Commonweal* review that although the book had merit, it sinned on the score of "apocalyptical oversimplification." The Harvard historian Arthur Schlesinger Jr. voiced a similar opinion. In a review for the *Nation,* he called the book "an able presentation of an allowable viewpoint" and superior to "the confused and messy arguments of the appeasers," but found Burnham's conception of communism too narrowly focused. Burnham had described only "the maximum Communist position," Schlesinger went on. He did not see that there could also be "a minimum position" to which the USSR could be held by the right American policy.[54]

Another who saw merit in the book, but also exaggeration and oversimplification, was a veteran Burnham watcher, George Orwell. Burnham addressed "real issues," and demonstrated "intellectual courage" in defending an unfashionable point of view, Orwell conceded, and if the danger were as grave as he thought it was, his policy "would probably be the right one." But he had once again committed his "besetting sin" of overstating his case. Communists were not the "huge secret army of fanatical warriors" he made them out to be, and if Stalin really did control such a force in every country, resistance would be futile. Burnham's error stemmed from his fascination with "power" and "'realism,'" which led him to overvalue the importance of "sheer force." Moreover, he was "too fond of apocalyptical visions": he believed that "everything must happen suddenly and completely, and that the choice must be all or nothing, glory or bust." But history proceeded in a messy fashion, moving along lines less logical than "muddled."[55]

There is no way of determining overall reader response to the book, but those who read *Life*'s condensed version and reported their feelings by writing to the magazine often reacted, whether for or against, with vehemence. One pro-Burnham enthusiast saluted *Life* as "the reincarnation of the winged Pegasus" for having published the piece, and hailed Burnham, the steed's "erect, tense, alert, eager" rider, as "the reincarnated spirit of Paul Revere." Hostile readers, on the other hand, often echoed Congressman Smith, likening Burnham to Hitler and the book to *Mein Kampf.* No poll was taken of *Life*'s entire readership, but the magazine's count of the letters it received revealed that for every reader who sided with Burnham, two denounced him for writing what one called "a vicious and evil work."[56] What Burnham thought of such judgments he did not record, but they may well have confirmed him in his doubts about the American public.

◆ ◆ ◆ ◆

The effort of writing *The Struggle for the World* left Burnham eager for a respite from political analysis. "Is there a review of something quite different—a novel or a myth or a criticism" that would interest *Partisan Review*? he asked William Phillips once he had completed the book.[57] But when he did take a break, it was short, for this was all he thought the struggle against communism would allow. "I spent last evening listening to a Polish woman who had been arrested by the Soviet occupation, and sent to prison and concentration camp until 1942," he told Alfred Kohlberg, an importer of Chinese textiles and a fellow "hard" anti-communist. "What the communists do is, I think, simply beyond the possibility of American comprehension."[58] But if Americans were to be brought to a true understanding of communism, then their political education would have to be relentlessly pursued.

Burnham's efforts to educate the public through magazines ranged from *Partisan Review* and another journal of the anticommunist Left, the *New Leader,* to the mass circulation *Reader's Digest,* all of which published articles by him on Soviet and communist policy.[59] In addition, hoping to reach a politically crucial audience, he joined Kohlberg in a plan to send a copy of *The Struggle for the World* to every member of Congress, ghost-writing Kohlberg's cover letter urging the lawmakers to read the book. He also appeared on public affairs radio programs, such as "Town Meeting of the Air" and "The People's Platform" and on the new medium of tele-vision, appearing on "Author Meets the Critics" as defending critic for *Seeds of Treason,* a book on the Hiss-Chambers case by *Newsweek* reporter Ralph de Toledano and labor journalist Victor Lasky. He found another opportunity at his Princeton class's twentieth reunion. The main speaker at an alumni forum on world affairs, he outlined the argument he had made in *The Struggle for the World,* and shocked some in the audience by wondering whether, given the likelihood of a nuclear war, a thirtieth class reunion would ever be held.[60]

He also took advantage of invitations from colleges and political affairs associations to expound his thesis. One such group was the World Affairs Council, whose treasurer, his Princeton friend Curt Winsor, arranged a debate for him with a well-known Soviet apologist on whether the USSR posed a threat to the United States. Several times in the early 1950s he spoke at sessions of Harvard's Defense Studies Program, a forum organized by Harvard political science professor Henry Kissinger. Moreover, for about a decade following the publication of *The Struggle for the World,* he regularly addressed audiences at the School for Advanced International Studies, the National War College, the Army War College, the Air War College, and the Naval Institute.[61]

◆   ◆   ◆   ◆

In December 1947, with NYU on its winter break, Burnham went to Europe for the first time since 1932, for "travel and observation," he said.[62] While in Paris, he made some new friends, people who touched him deeply, and whose example helped move him toward his life's next major turn. These were Polish refugees gathered around Jerzy Giedroyc, editor in prewar Poland of a political and literary monthly called *Kultura,* which Giedroyc revived in Paris in 1947 as a journal hostile to Soviet imperialism, friendly to European federalism, and looking to the United States as the only feasible leader of world anticommunism.

Among the Poles, no one made a stronger impression on Burnham than Giedroyc's chief colleague, Józef Czapski. Fifty-one in 1947, tall, and with a wild mop of hair, Czapski was by calling a painter, writer, and art critic. But he was also a man of action who had fought the Russians in the Polish–Soviet war of 1919–20 and the Germans in 1939. Imprisoned in the USSR during Stalin's alliance with Hitler, he had been released after the German invasion of the USSR and had gone to London to work for the Polish government in exile. There he had served on the commission that investigated what turned out to be the Soviet massacre in the Katyn Forest of thousands of Polish officers in 1940. In 1945, rather than return to Poland, now in the grip of Stalin, he had moved to Paris, where he divided his time between painting and putting out *Kultura.*[63]

Burnham reacted to Czapski with the same excitement he had felt about Gerry Allard, the miners' union leader who had helped to found the AWP. As Allard had personified to him homegrown American revolutionary socialism, so

Czapski personified militant eastern European resistance to communism. In the years to come he and Czapski would work closely together. It was because of Czapski, for instance, that Burnham became involved in one of his pet undertakings of this period: a project to establish in western Europe a university for eastern European refugees from communism that would serve both as a conventional institution of higher learning and as a resource for anticommunist liberation movements.[64]

Back home in January 1948, Burnham found yet another forum for publicizing his message. This was a subcommittee of the House Committee on Un-American Activities that in February 1948 held hearings on a bill introduced by GOP committee members Richard M. Nixon of California and Karl E. Mundt of South Dakota requiring communist groups to register with the attorney general, and making it a crime to conspire against the U.S. government on behalf of a foreign dictatorship. Testifying at the hearings as an expert witness on communism, Burnham told the subcommittee that although the Communist Party would, in the end, probably have to be outlawed, he did not think this step should be taken at once. The public would first have to be enlightened about the Communist Party—which was not a conventional political party at all, but an instrument of Soviet policy—so that it would understand why the ban was needed and not react with sympathy for the party. The bill offered "a good experimental approach," he commented. But "scrupulous care" would have to be taken to avoid lumping "genuine Communists together with socialists, liberals, honest progressives," and other "legitimate" social critics and reformers. For not only did this false linkage always benefit communism, but fighting communism would be pointless unless "a reasonable amount of decency and democracy" were preserved.[65] (The Nixon-Mundt bill later passed in the House, but failed in the Senate.)

Several weeks later, Burnham made a new friend, the political writer and novelist Arthur Koestler. A few months older than Burnham, the short, dark Koestler had grown up in Budapest. After embarking on a career in journalism, he had become a communist, and in the 1930s had spent time in the USSR. After imprisonment by the Nationalists in Spain, where he had gone to cover the civil war, and internment by the French on the eve of the German invasion of 1940, he had managed during the fall of France to make his way to England. By this time, under the impact of the Nazi-Soviet nonaggression agreement, he had bro-

ken with communism. In England he wrote his novel *Darkness at Noon,* in which
he explained the realities of Soviet life and the psychology of the communist
faithful through the experience of the book's protagonist, the Old Bolshevik
Rubashov, who falls victim to Stalin's terror. A 1941 bestseller (like *The Managerial
Revolution,* a book Koestler praised), *Darkness at Noon* won its author not only
fame and fortune but also an influential voice among anticommunist intellectuals.

Coming to the United States in March 1948 for a tour on behalf of the
International Rescue and Relief Committee, Koestler spent his first evening in
New York at a *Partisan Review* party, where he was introduced to Burnham.
Though the extroverted, saturnine Koestler and the reserved, proper Burnham
were worlds apart in personality, they hit it off at once. In the days that followed,
Koestler saw a good deal of the Burnhams, meeting them for lunch, going to
their apartment for drinks, and driving down to Princeton with them to visit the
Institute for Advanced Studies. When it came time for Koestler to return to
England, Burnham took him to the airport, the two companionably passing a
bottle of bourbon back and forth on the way.[66]

Midway through Koestler's stay in the United States, Burnham took advantage
of NYU's spring recess to return to Paris, this time for talks with André Malraux
that were to be published in *Partisan Review* as "The Double Crisis: A Dialogue"
and as a book, *The Case for De Gaulle.* For sheer glamor, Malraux's career surpassed even Koestler's. Writer, shady traveler in Indochina in the 1920s, left-wing
activist who flew for the Loyalist air force in the Spanish Civil War (the basis of
his novel *L'Espoir,* which Burnham considered his best), resistance fighter in
wartime France, and above all, indefatigable self-mythicizer, this romantic figure,
moved by anti-Stalinism and war-inspired patriotism, now served as "delegate for
propaganda" in the Gaullist party of the day, the militantly anticommunist Rally
of the French People (RPF). How Burnham and Malraux first met is not known,
but when they did, they quickly became friends. (In the early 1950s they were to
talk of trading sons for a year or so to give the boys the benefits of a cosmopolitan upbringing.)[67]

In their talks of 1948, which took place only weeks after the communist coup
in Czechoslovakia, Burnham reaffirmed his belief in a world-transforming "long-
term crisis," the managerial revolution. But "superimposed" on this crisis "like a
wind-driven wave added to the deeper ground swell," he went on, there existed

the "shorter but still more acute crisis" triggered by the invention of atomic and bacteriological weapons and the struggle between the USSR and the United States to decide which would head "a world political order." Western leaders, he said, seemed unable to understand communism or realize that western Europe could not be rebuilt until its communists had been "reduced to impotence." Particularly muddled was the European "Third Force" outlook, which considered itself anticommunist yet believed that in a democracy communism could not be suppressed. Unhappily, the United States, the only country capable of leading the world's anticommunists, was also governed by men of Third Force tendency, who still trusted "that a general and workable agreement with the Soviet Union (that is to say, with Stalinism, for an agreement with a non-Stalinist Russia would be easy enough) [could] be gained by the methods of a shrewd horse trader." But such thinking was pitifully wrong, as was clear to people such as Malraux and himself, who had "lived *through* Communism." Malraux appeared to agree, though untypically he said relatively little.[68]

◆　◆　◆　◆

By the spring of 1948, a year after the publication of *The Struggle for the World,* the Truman administration seemed to be adopting some of the book's recommendations, at least in approximate form. The CIA had been established, a security program to rid the federal government of communists instituted, and an anticommunist propaganda effort mounted. In addition, the interventionist foreign policy announced by the Truman doctrine was materializing. In May 1947, partly under American pressure, communists were dropped from the Italian and French cabinets, and in April 1948 the United States covertly intervened in Italy's parliamentary election in hopes of keeping the communists from winning. (They didn't.) Washington also gave active support to European unification, and with the Marshall Plan was pursuing that goal, along with nurturing Europe's economic reconstruction. Moreover, a Mackinder-like Atlantic alliance joining the United States, Canada, and most of western Europe under quasi-imperial American leadership was in the offing, and in 1949 would be launched as NATO.

But Burnham did not think these steps sufficient, and criticized Truman's policy as timid, inconsistent, and, most important, lacking a strategic vision. "I am becoming increasingly alarmed at the failure of our government to adopt any

coherent policy whatsoever," he wrote to Kohlberg in May 1948. Washington had
not yet worked out "a political plan." The USSR, he was certain, would have
atom bombs in a year or less, and would then do what the United States was mistakenly not doing, i.e., use the bombs as a way to exert political leverage. It was
hard "not to be discouraged."[69]

Now working on a new book on Cold War policy, and wanting to find out at
first hand what Americans thought about the struggle for the world, Burnham
decided to spend the 1948–1949 academic year on leave and devote the time to
writing and cross-country travel. In late August 1948, he and Marcia piled their
three children (ranging in age from twelve to four), fishing rods, camping gear,
typewriter, and family dog (a Doberman Burnham said he was training "to smell
Stalinists at half a mile") into their station wagon, and set off on a trek west that
would last seven months and cover twenty thousand miles. Often they camped
out along the way, on one occasion on the north shore of Lake Erie, on another
on the banks of the Mississippi. After driving for what seemed to Burnham like
"several million miles across the north-central plains—with the endless fields of
corn and wheat . . . and soybeans and flax; and then the prairies with the white-
faced Herefords around the water holes, and the towns of four or five thousand
inhabitants thirty miles apart," they arrived in mid-September at Montana's
Glacier National Park, which, with summer over, they had almost entirely to
themselves. Camping on the shore of Lake MacDonald, they hiked in the woods
and caught fish in the Flathead River ("very primitive" fish, said Burnham, an
endless fund of random information, after examining the catch), though the children, to their dismay, also had to study spelling, multiplication tables, and
Shakespeare. From Montana the Burnhams headed south to Yellowstone National
Park and then west to Seattle. Reaching the Pacific, they meandered down the
coast across Oregon and into California, and finally turned inland to Arizona,
where at Rex Ranch, in Amado, forty miles south of Tucson, they rented an
adobe house for the winter. America was "an absolutely remarkable country,"
Burnham summed up his impressions in a letter to Hook.[70]

Amado was tiny: a post office, a two-room schoolhouse, and a railroad station
on a branch line, over which a single-car passenger train and a freight train passed
once each day. The two older Burnham children, twelve-year-old Marcie and
nine-year-old Jim, were enrolled at the local school, where a no-nonsense teacher
took their education in hand. The youngest, John, spent his days playing at the

ranch. Though Burnham was busy with his book, he found time to take Marcia roaming on horseback through the surrounding desert, which, as they got to know it, became an enchanted landscape teeming with life. "There are more birds than I have seen anywhere," Burnham wrote to William Phillips, "and as soon as you begin to see the desert it is filled also with animals and insects and all the fabulous flora of cholla and opuntia and saguaro and yucca and palo verde and mesquite and squaw's tea and creosote and stool." And the atmosphere was "wonderfully unpressed."[71]

Burnham was elated by his trip, describing it to Phillips as "in excess of any of our hopes, though these were very high," and to Hook as "a fabulous experience." The reason for his elation, however, was not his discovery of primeval fish in the Flathead River or even the bewitching Arizona desert, but the people he had met along the way. "I have come to feel during the past six months that in this country today, the masses—to use the old Marxian language—are in advance of their leaders," he wrote to Hook from Amado. He had not felt this way at first: the people he and Marcia had met seemed indifferent to politics. "But gradually we began to know people better, to talk to them longer, to drink with them and fish and hunt with them, and so on," and so were able to learn what they really thought. "There is obviously going to be a war with Russia," ran the prevailing opinion. "The Easterners and politicians are just farting around, in their speeches and conferences and writings, with twaddle and double-talk—so why should I waste my time paying any attention to their words; naturally, I (or my son . . . ) will have to do the fighting in the war, which I don't like, but there isn't any way out of it; why in the Hell don't they have the war and get it over with?" Given such feelings, Burnham concluded, it was easy to see why people showed no interest in politics. But he was now convinced that "the great mass of the country would respond . . . very quickly" if given real leadership, for most Americans still had the will to live.[72]

At the beginning of March 1949 the Burnhams left Amado for home. But after only two or three days in New York, Burnham left again, this time for Europe, "to gain information about political, economic, and social conditions" for his new book. On this trip (and most future trips), Marcia went with him, having made it clear that when he traveled abroad she would go too. The trip took the Burnhams to Britain, France, Italy, and occupied Germany, cockpit of the Cold War and now the scene of the Berlin airlift, the huge American and British effort to provision the beleaguered city by air after the Soviets had blocked access to it by land. Unlike his American trip, this one brought Burnham no comfort, for the mood he encountered, especially in France, struck him as listless and demoralized.[73]

Returning home in May, Burnham spent the summer finishing his book, which he called *The Coming Defeat of Communism*. He described the book as "a continuation, more or less, and concretion of *The Struggle for the World*," and said that he had grounded it (as he had *The Machiavellians*) in "the catastrophic point of view."[74] The United States had given up the suicidal policy of appeasing the USSR, the book's first section noted approvingly. The new U.S. policy—"containment," as it had come to be called—aimed at holding the line against further Soviet expansion, calculating that if the USSR could be fenced in, frustration and exhaustion would drain away its expansionist dynamic and put Moscow on the road to normal international behavior. Containment, then, at least recognized that the USSR was an enemy. But this change of outlook was cause for only minimal celebration, for while an improvement on appeasement, it fell far short of what was needed. By nature reactive, it abandoned the initiative to the Soviets, who were thus free to shape the agenda, timing, pace, fields of combat, and "mood" of the struggle for the world. Worse, it aimed not at winning, but only at not losing, and so could achieve merely "negative," not "positive," successes. Since such a policy had to mean defeat for the West in the long run, containment, like appeasement, must be replaced by a better strategy.[75]

The specifics of such a strategy, a variation on the offensive policy laid out in *The Struggle for the World,* made up the bulk of the new book. The Western goal, Burnham repeated, must be to end the Soviet threat, a goal that could be reached only by fully eliminating communist power. Given the unprecedented gravity of the world crisis ("an *extreme situation,*" Burnham called it, using italics), the means employed must also be "novel and extreme." Conventional warfare had to be ruled out, for the death toll would be staggering. So too a preventive attack, despite present U.S. military superiority, for the American public was too "confused" about the Cold War to accept such a step. Instead, the United States should adopt "the only rational alternative" to the military option: "political-subversive" warfare, a strategy that had brought the communists great success.[76]

Huge propaganda campaigns should be mounted that stressed western values, such as "the restraint of power by custom, moral principle, and law" and "the right of men not to be snatched from bed at three in the morning by the agents of an uncontrolled secret police." An effort should be made to break the communist grip on foreign labor unions by funneling U.S. support to anticommunist unions. Aid should be offered to anticommunist leaders, such as Charles de Gaulle, and to bodies hostile to communism, such as the Catholic Church, anarchist workers groups, organizations in the Muslim world friendly to the West (with further backing for a Muslim resistance in the USSR), anticommunist forces in China, and eastern European "refugee-liberation" movements (a "high priority"). An operation to overthrow a vulnerable communist regime—Albania's, for example—should be launched to weaken communism's current momentum and aura of invincibility. A "liberation" university should be set up in western Europe for eastern Europeans who had fled their communist-ruled homelands.

At the same time, to ensure security, information about such projects should not be passed on too freely to European governments, for these had been deeply penetrated by communists and communist sympathizers. But an exception should be made for Britain, which could be relied on "in almost any undertaking, even the most confidential." (Ironically, the Britain Burnham was speaking of was the Britain of Philby, Burgess, McClean, et al., soon to be exposed as Soviet agents.) As for execution, much of the program could be entrusted to existing federal agencies, such as the Departments of State and Defense and the CIA, while private organizations, such as foundations, publishing houses, universities, and labor unions, could also lend a hand. But to plan, direct, and coordinate the policy, a new agency, with its own head, should be established and placed directly under the president.[77]

Burnham admitted that his political-subversive strategy might provoke Moscow to an all-out military response, but thought the risk slight. True, he granted, the USSR might look formidable. It enjoyed the strategic advantage of possessing the Heartland, and could boast superb political leadership and vast armed forces. But this advantage was being eroded by modern technology, and the United States could close the leadership gap if it chose. Moreover, economically and culturally the USSR remained primitive, which could only sap its military strength. And there were signs that the contradiction between communist theory, with its promise of freedom and equality, and communist practice, a system of totalitarian slavery, was pushing some communists toward "a grave theoretical and . . . moral crisis" that would leave them demoralized and thus psychologically ill-equipped for war. A further enemy weakness was the highly centralized and bureaucratic nature of the Soviet state, which possessed "ponderous and crushing strength," but lacked flexibility and resilience, and so would "crack and break from well-directed blows." Meanwhile, Moscow had not yet built up a stock of atom bombs. Nor, as evidenced by Yugoslavia's successful bid for independence from the Soviet Empire, had the USSR firmly subjugated its east-European satellites, whose people cordially loathed their Soviet masters. In fact, if war broke out, the Red Army might well retreat, nervous about the satellites, which lay across its westward lines of communication. And were Stalin and his gang, old men and no daredevils, likely to gamble on conventional warfare when the slower but surer method of political warfare promised to deliver everything they wanted? Finally, history showed that while the USSR saw conciliation as weakness, it backed off when faced with a feisty opponent. All told, then, Soviet military power existed more in appearance than in reality. "We now incline to overestimate the Soviet military potential," Burnham concluded, "even more grossly than we underestimated it in 1940."[78]

Hence, for Americans, political-subversive warfare offered the best way to victory. Not only could it be pursued with the knowledge that if a shooting war broke out in the next few years, the United States would run "no risk of military defeat." It offered the "*only*" means of eliminating communism without mass killing or a nuclear holocaust.[79]

As the final component of his strategy, Burnham outlined "a deal" the United States might offer the USSR—in effect, surrender terms the Soviets would have to accept if they wanted to survive. Under these terms, Moscow would have to give up its foreign ambitions, dissolve the world communist movement, end its propaganda campaigns abroad, withdraw from all areas beyond its 1939 borders, allow the people of these liberated countries governments of their own choosing, open the USSR to normal contact with the outside world, agree to a ban on the manufacture of weapons of mass destruction, and permit international inspection to ensure compliance with the ban. As "a voluntary appendix" to the deal, but not as part of it (for the deal was not a bargain), the United States would refrain from making war on the USSR, permit international control of its own atomic weapons, and offer the Soviets economic aid up to fifty billion dollars.

The Soviet leadership would certainly not accept, Burnham acknowledged. Still, the offer might encourage a split in the ruling elite: those who were upset by the gulf between communist theory and practice and afraid of war might form an internal opposition, thereby paving the way for the fall of the existing regime. To such potential oppositionists the United States should say: "We are ready to settle without war. Here are our demands. Meet them, and you may live."[80]

The alternative to such a strategy, the book concluded, was more containment, "that guarantor of ultimate defeat." Victory demanded new initiatives, imagination, boldness, for history did not "distribute its favors to bashful suitors." But in the end the most crucial factor was will. "Does the United States *choose* to win?" was the paramount question. "Can it make the necessary *decision?* Is it going to have, at the required tension, the *will* to survive?"[81]

◆  ◆  ◆  ◆

In contrast to the mostly gloomy *Struggle for the World, The Coming Defeat of Communism* viewed the West's Cold War prospects with relative optimism. Aglow over the potential of political-subversive warfare, Burnham put aside his usual Augustinian sense of limits and sounded convinced that the strategy would succeed. Indeed, the book's very title seemed to view the West's victory as a foregone conclusion. Hook, worried that the title struck a more confident note than the text warranted and so might encourage complacency, begged Burnham to change it. But Burnham, still buoyed by his cross-country trip, would not budge. "The issue is no longer in doubt," he declared in the book's final pages. "Doubt is vanquished by the act of will which makes the decision. The future becomes servant, not master," is shaped by conscious choice, not blind forces. "The death even of civilizations as a whole is not decreed by any unchallengeable court. Civilizations die, in truth, only by suicide."[82]

The book also voiced Burnham's new attitude toward the United States. To be sure, he again upbraided the country on a number of counts, such as political culture. ("Will our politics improve? I refer to our international politics; our ward-heeling politics are too good already.")[83] And he heaped scorn on American businessmen, to his mind the country's dominant class and one revealing major flaws. Though "a genius" at business, he claimed in a chapter called "The Suicidal Mania of American Business"—which joined the intellectual's disdain for the philistine to the crusader's contempt for the profit-seeker—the typical American businessman was also "drearily prejudiced, emptily pompous, narrowly unper-

ceptive, hopelessly backward-looking, naively credulous." Worse, in the struggle
with communism, he was proving to be a disaster: "too ignorant, too greedy, too
reactionary and, in a certain sense, too cowardly." Businessmen even aided the
communists, though unwittingly, he charged. They were always ready to trade
with the enemy in hopes of making "a few easy dollars," while their "monstrous
incomes and profits" drove resentful and alienated workers into the arms of the
enemy. Their one saving grace was their subjective loyalty. But that was not
enough to absolve them of their sins. (In contrast, Burnham praised organized
labor, mostly because of the anticommunist activism of certain union leaders.)[84]

Still, he no longer described America as "semi-barbaric," but hailed its freedom
and abundance and the ebullient spirit to which that abundance gave rise. "One
afternoon," he wrote almost lyrically in *The Coming Defeat of Communism* of a
moment during his cross-country trip,

> we were driving southwest from Detroit, past the Willow Run
> plant, just as the shift had ended. Out of the wide entrance of
> the plant yards, the cars of the workers—workers, not bosses—
> came rushing by the hundreds, and swinging into the highway.
> Were they more miserable because a great machine, under their
> control, was taking them where they wanted to go, and because
> they were not trudging dustily on foot or swarming into dirty
> trams toward miserable rooms without light or baths? Twenty-
> five miles further on, we turned off into a State Park of trees
> and small hills. We saw ahead, again, many hundreds of cars,
> many of them the same that had come from the plant a little
> earlier, but now stopped. Beyond them were dozens of acres of
> wooded grounds, with tables, benches, stone fireplaces, and
> heavy iron charcoal grills placed on iron posts (mass produced,
> no doubt, by Midland Steel Foundries). It was beginning to
> darken, and the reddened charcoal in the grills gleamed among
> the trees like lamp posts. At the tables, hundreds of families—of
> workers and clerks and stenographers—were finishing their
> steaks and hamburgers and hot dogs, and Cokes and beers.
> Beyond them was a large lake; and there hundreds more were
> swimming, laughing, diving, shouting, and in the deeper water

sweeping or drifting along in canoes, rowboats, and outboards (mass produced by Evinrude). There seemed to be values present there in abundance—of friendship and love—that were something more than "material"; and yet without the material, without those cars and that iron, that processed wood and well-preserved meat and skillfully bottled drink, neither the values nor the people rejoicing in them would have been there.[85]

Indeed, Burnham not only celebrated mainstream America; he seemed eager to identify with it, or at least to distance himself from his usual cultural milieu. "Don't forget that I am not a New Yorker," he wrote to Hook from Amado in the first flush of his enthusiasm. "I am more convinced than ever (though I never really doubted it) that the standard-brand variety of New York intellectual knows nothing, but nothing, about the United States. . . ." He also wrote in this vein in *The Coming Defeat of Communism,* implying that he was in close touch with the American scene and so stood apart from "the often brilliant but ingrown intellectual circles of the northeastern seaboard, which draw their spiritual fuel from Europe and the Soviet Union rather than from America, and whose members have for the most part never seen a factory in Detroit, an oil well in Texas, the vegetables in the Imperial Valley, a grain field in the Big Bend, range land in Wyoming, fruit along the Hood River, ore ships crowding the Sault, copper mines in Utah, the generators at Grand Coulée, steel mills at Gary, logging in Oregon, chemical works at Beaumont, not these or the people who man them."[86]

Hence, if *The Coming Defeat of Communism* was a guide to how to win the Cold War, it also evidenced a change in Burnham's sense of self. Not that his attachment to the United States was wholly new: he had, after all, joined the AWP in hopes of finding a revolutionary socialist party inspired by specifically American radical traditions, and had almost always devoted his Trotskyist newspaper columns to American politics. Still, he had never found mainstream American life congenial, and given his cultural interests, seemed often to feel out of place in his native land. Indeed, even the "nationalist" Burnham of *The Struggle for the World* identified more with "the West" than with the United States. Now, however, hailing what he saw as an America with a "will to live," he made it clear that he wished to join the nation.

◆   ◆   ◆   ◆

Reviewers treated *The Coming Defeat of Communism* much as they had *The Struggle for the World*. Some applauded its view of the Cold War, and eagerly seconded its policy proposals. Others decried the book, charging that it oversimplified complex realities, reasoned too rigidly and narrowly, paid too little heed to the roots of communism's appeal, and preached that ends justified means. Several argued that as a prophet Burnham had a rather spotty record. (To the latter he replied, "My batting average is well up, I'd say. Take Rogers Hornsby. Just because Mr. Hornsby didn't hit 1.000 doesn't make him a lousy hitter.") But most mixed praise and blame. The *Atlantic*'s Charles J. Rolo thought many of Burnham's strategic counsels made "extremely good sense," but found his "fixation on power" difficult to distinguish from "the psychology of the Commissar." *New York Times* columnist Arthur Krock tried to get George F. Kennan, one of the State Department's few Soviet experts and the intellectual father of containment, to review the book. But Kennan demurred, noting that his work made anything he wrote an "official pronouncement."[87]

As before, Burnham also heard directly from readers. William C. Bullitt, first U.S. ambassador to the USSR and a fervent anticommunist, offered a laudatory blurb. The radio commentator H.V. Kaltenborn congratulated Burnham on being "as good as a Communist in your anti-Communist arguments." Another reader sent Burnham a song he had written to accompany the anticommunist struggle. Burnham often answered such letters. To a reader who lamented that "the race for the dollar" had caused people to lose sight of "the higher values in life," and speculated that the United States might have to "go through a real catastrophe" to regain moral clarity, he replied that he, too, often thought a disaster might be needed to straighten the country out. "Life has really been too easy for the United States," he wrote. "Sophocles may have been right in believing that we cannot learn without suffering." Among readers who disapproved of the book was Burnham's former colleague Max Shachtman, who now headed a tiny group of post-Trotskyist radicals called the Independent Socialist League (ISL). Commenting several years later on Burnham's anticommunist writings, Shachtman condemned them for their "amoralism," and declared himself floored by the "urbane detachment" with which his former comrade maintained that in the fight against communism "anything and everything goes."[88]

Eager to publicize his ideas, Burnham again seized every opportunity: book luncheons, interviews, radio forums, and speeches to public affairs clubs. He also worked with Max Eastman to condense *The Struggle for the World* and *The Coming Defeat of Communism* for the *Reader's Digest*. The magazine's editor, Paul Palmer, eventually dropped the project, but individual chapters of the second book, sometimes slightly revised, appeared as articles in several magazines, including the *Digest,* and Eastman completed the condensed version he had been working on.[89]

Burnham hoped that "circles that can count" would read the book, and they did. Burnham's ideas were "the current staples of conversation at Washington salons and dinner tables and in the offices of the Pentagon," noted one newspaper in an article called "Burnham vs. Kennan." The State Department and the CIA also paid attention to the book, a Washington observer recalled, especially after the outbreak of the Korean War in June 1950. By the early 1950s, Burnham's prescriptions had become Cold War orthodoxy for conservatives, and in 1952 the GOP drew heavily on them for its platform's foreign policy plank, which demanded an end to containment and a strategy of "rolling back" communism. But despite this success, Burnham spoke sadly of his heavy political involvement. Politics had become "the most important activity of our time," he told a *New York Times* reporter, "but for me it is the least personally rewarding." His "primary love," he said, was still aesthetics.[90]

Was this true? Perhaps, in the sense that the study of beauty brought him greater satisfaction than did politics. All the same, he did not make his primary love his primary calling. For by the turn of the 1950s, though he still wrote a nonpolitical piece now and then (a review of Malraux's *The Voices of Silence,* for example, which he rated "a work of art, and of the highest order"),[91] he had committed himself totally to pursuing the struggle for the world.

# Chapter 7

# Warrior

W HEN BURNHAM SET OUT on his cross-country car trip, he expected to be back at NYU the following fall, and so wrote to Hook in January 1949 to ask for his usual fall term teaching schedule.[1] But he soon changed his mind, deciding instead to extend his academic leave indefinitely and enlist full-time in the struggle for the world.

The chain of events that led him to take this step began with the 1947 Princeton commencement. Present at his chilling assessment of world affairs was his classmate Joseph Bryan III, the Virginian who had gone to war with Japan flying a Confederate battle flag. A writer when the war broke out, Bryan resumed his old trade once it had ended.[2] But in 1948, partly under the inspiration of Burnham's Princeton speech, he joined the newly founded CIA, where he headed the Political and Psychological Warfare division of the Office of Policy Coordination (OPC), the agency's semi-independent covert action branch.[3]

Founded in 1947, the CIA at first defined its function as the collection and analysis of intelligence. But the success of a covert operation run by an ad hoc CIA group to prevent a communist victory in Italy's 1948 parliamentary election led George F. Kennan, director of the State Department's Policy Planning Staff, to press for the creation of a permanent covert action arm. Hence, in June 1948 the National Security Council (NSC) established the Office of Special Projects, later the Office of Policy Coordination, which was to wage clandestine war on

Soviet communism. The new unit's tactics, the NSC specified, were to include "propaganda; economic warfare; preventive direct action, including sabotage, demolition, and evacuation measures; subversion against hostile states, including assistance to underground resistance movements, guerrilla and refugee liberation groups; and support of indigenous anticommunist elements in threatened countries of the free world."[4]

In form the OPC belonged to the CIA, but not entirely. For while the intelligence agency was made responsible for OPC personnel, office space, and budget, the secretary of state was to name its head, and the Departments of State (in time of peace) and Defense (in time of war) were to oversee its operations. But in substance, the OPC enjoyed a large measure of autonomy, partly because the authority to which it answered was divided, partly because CIA Director Admiral Roscoe Hillenkoetter did not assert his supervisory rights, and partly because its first chief, Frank Wisner, did not submit readily to the direction of others.

Wisner, thirty-nine, came from Laurel, Mississippi. After studying law at the University of Virginia, he had joined a Wall Street law firm. During the war, he had headed OSS stations in Istanbul and Bucharest and at war's end moved briefly to occupied Germany as top aide to U.S. intelligence chief Allen Dulles. Back at his law practice, Wisner missed the excitement of covert action, and when offered the OPC post he jumped at it. He found his new job utterly absorbing, so much so that he often did not bother to cash his paychecks.[5]

With his romantic imagination and limitless energy, Wisner saw the OPC as an elite force vying with the Soviets in a struggle to win the world. His sentiments found a strong echo in his agents, mostly men in their twenties and thirties, often alumni of Ivy League colleges and the OSS, tending to be liberal (pro-New Deal and internationalist) in politics, and resembling college faculty members (which some of them had been).[6]

The resources allotted to this white-shoe war band were at first modest: office space in the Naval Hospital's S Building and then in some ramshackle structures (put up as temporary offices during World War I) beside the Reflecting Pool, a budget of $4.7 million, 302 employees, and seven field stations. But under Wisner's spirited leadership, the OPC burgeoned. Within three years it commanded a budget of $82 million, 2,182 employees (plus some 3,000 contract employees abroad), and forty-seven field stations.[7]

Wisner's covert operations ran the gamut from clandestine political ventures to irregular warfare: attempts to rid newspapers, unions, and student groups abroad of communist influence; plans for "stay-behind" networks equipped with arms, communications gear, and explosives for use behind enemy lines in the event of a Soviet invasion of western Europe; campaigns to harass communist governments by means of internal resistance forces such as the Carpathians-based Ukrainian band that until the early 1950s waged guerrilla war on Soviet rule; and "liberation" offensives by militant émigré groups aimed at destabilizing Soviet puppet regimes.[8]

It is unclear whether Burnham knew anything about the OPC when he wrote *The Coming Defeat of Communism*. But the book's proposals resembled the OPC agenda, while the OPC itself sounded much like Burnham's idea for a "political-subversive" warfare department.

Burnham's keen interest in "polwar" (the bureaucratic abbreviation) led him immediately to accept an invitation he received early in 1949 from Joseph Bryan, who had been back in touch with him at least since 1947 and so may have known of his enthusiasm for this type of strategy. He had just begun a new job, Bryan wrote, one "as remote from any previous experience of mine as would be, say, singing in the Sistine Choir." But not remote from Burnham's experience, he went on, "and I'd like very much to discuss it with you." Would Burnham come to Washington for a talk? "Your speech at our reunion two years ago is partly responsible for my being here," he added, "so I think I have a fair claim on an hour of your time."[9]

Bryan's offer to Burnham was a consultantship with the OPC.[10] The job would require Burnham to reorder his life considerably, but by 1949 he had been teaching for twenty years and may have wanted a change. Moreover, he had been meeting people—Czapski and Malraux, for example—who were involved in day-to-day work against communism, intellectuals who were also men of action, and he perhaps wanted this combination for himself.[11] But probably the key reason was his moral seriousness: he had once feared that the West would fall unless saved by social revolution, and had therefore felt morally obliged to sign up with Trotsky; he now feared it would fall unless communism were defeated, and therefore felt morally obliged to join the OPC.[12]

Hence, in February or March 1949 Burnham applied for "federal employment."[13] On his application form he stated that he was seeking a job in "intelligence," and cited "25 years of study, and direct or indirect experience of modern revolutionary movements, particularly of communism, and of modern politics, especially international" as his qualification. To a question asking for his reasons for wanting to change jobs, he replied, cryptically, "none." Listing his interests as the arts, literature, gardening, and music (but not mentioning philosophy), he went on to rate himself "good" at bridge, "fair" at tennis, riding, and swimming, and "poor" at golf, as a fluent reader and "fair" speaker of French, but with only a "slight" ability to write that language correctly and an equally "slight" ability to speak and read, and no ability to write, Italian.[14]

He worried that upper-level officials in the Truman administration might blackball him for his sharp criticism of administration policy. But in July 1949 he was approved.[15] Meanwhile, NYU renewed his leave for another year, accepting his explanation that the "emergency" facing the United States made it his duty at present to devote himself to government work.[16] At the end of August the Burnham household moved to Washington, and in October Burnham formally began his new career. No longer a professor who also warned of the Soviet danger, he was once again a warrior in a tiny phalanx, now engaged full-time in the struggle for the world.

◆　◆　◆　◆

Burnham kept his work with the OPC a secret. NYU explained that he had gone on leave "to do research," and he himself claimed to be in Washington as a "freelance writer." To maintain his cover, he never visited the temporary buildings beside the Reflecting Pool, where his identity was concealed under the code names "Hamburn" and "Kenneth E. Hambley," but worked at home, using two upstairs rooms as offices, with a secretary to do his typing. He never told his children why the family had moved to Washington, and even years later remained close-mouthed about his job.[17]

In his work with Bryan's OPC unit (a group that included the writer and former *Tiger* chairman Finis Farr, and the future Watergate figure E. Howard Hunt),[18] Burnham concentrated on what he summed up as "the general psychological warfare field." He pointed out people with whom he thought the OPC should be in touch, magazines to which it should subscribe, and articles OPC officers should read. He also served as a political analyst and made policy proposals, for example, on how the OPC could help Soviet ethnic minorities work for the dissolution of the USSR. At the same time, he passed on reports he received from informants abroad. On at least one occasion, he took part in a simulation exercise (a technique the CIA had just begun to use in its efforts to fathom Soviet strategic thinking), playing a participant in a meeting of the Communist Information Bureau, the postwar successor to the Comintern.

His imagination teemed with ideas for propaganda projects, such as mounting an exhibit in Rome in 1950 (to take advantage of the Catholic Jubilee Year, when millions of pilgrims were expected to visit the city) dramatizing communism's persecution of religion; using the anniversary of Lenin's death to draw attention to the grimness of life in the USSR; creating a gallery of repellent Soviet cartoon characters (e.g., "the Commissar," "the MVD agent"); launching a "semantic" campaign to change habitual ways of labeling the USSR and communism—for instance, the classification of communists as on the Left and anticommunists as on the Right, which risked bringing the enemy unconscious sympathy. (Similarly, he urged that Soviet-dominated countries be referred to as "colonies," not "satellites," which was emotionally and factually too mild. "In general," he advised, communism and the USSR should be linked "with all the key retrogressive words: 'reactionary,' 'imperialist,' etc.")[19]

He also handled requests from abroad for money to finance anticommunist publications. Typical was a query from a Dr. Arthur Arzt of Wiesbaden, West Germany, a former socialist and member of the pre-Nazi Reichstag, who wanted 100,000 DM to start an anticommunist magazine. He had shown the request to "a number of friends," Burnham replied, but though interested, they needed detailed answers to questions about the magazine's aims, target audience, likely number of readers, and so forth before their interest "could become more practical." In this instance, the "friends" took almost a year to make up their minds (to the consternation of Arzt, who described the sum he had asked for as "only a flea bite for the Americans"). But then Burnham was able to inform Arzt that his project had been approved to the tune of 5,000 DM a month. Another beneficiary of such help was Giedroyc's *Kultura,* which was put out on a shoestring, and by 1950 was running a $600 monthly deficit. In March 1950 Czapski sent Burnham a list of the magazine's expenses, and two months later got word that *Kultura* would receive a subsidy. At home, on his own initiative, Burnham sought aid for the anticommunist *New Leader,* recommending—apparently in vain—that the OPC take out a thousand subscriptions and have the magazine sent to U.S. embassies and offices abroad.[20]

In addition, he obtained OPC funds for publishing *The Coming Defeat of Communism* abroad in places where commercial publishers could not be found. Eager to bring the book out in Russian translation, he made a payment of 5,000 DM to a Russian émigré publishing house, Possev, which planned to spirit the edition behind the Iron Curtain. The translation appeared in the fall of 1951, but whether it was smuggled into the USSR—and if so, with what effect—the record does not show. When a refugee from communist China wrote to him from New Delhi seeking permission to translate the book into Chinese, Burnham at once consented, adding, "I think that I may be able to interest a number of my friends in providing some financial assistance for the project."[21]

Burnham also championed a more militant brand of polwar. In a paper called "The Development of the Anti-Communist Exile and Resistance Movements," he urged immediate steps to bolster such movements, coordinate their efforts, and, with their help, form resistance groups inside Soviet puppet states. Anticommunist exile centers should be set up in the United States, Western Europe, and North Africa, he advised. They would conduct intelligence research and analysis, and plan "psychological warfare [and] subversive and Resistance operations." Young exiles should be formed into military and paramilitary units. A "Congress of Liberation of the Peoples Now Subject to the Communist Tyranny," with several hundred prominent exiles attending, should meet in a place of high visibility, such as New York, for "propaganda and morale" purposes. Resistance should also be fostered in the USSR, he argued in another paper, and he was ready to counsel Russian émigrés working toward that end.

What was more, he added in a paper called "The Strategy of the Politburo and the Problem of American Counter Strategy," the Soviet ruling class should be made a target. Washington should "*initiate on the most massive scale possible a series of measures in the psychological, economic, political, moral, and subversive fields, both overt and covert, all of which should be organized and oriented to serve the objective of the disintegration of the communist elite.*" Such measures should aim at sowing "doubt, insecurity, demoralization, suspicions, jealousies, quarrels, cross-purges, [and] mental and physical exhaustion" in "the Soviet state power apparatus." Propaganda, bribery, and disinformation should be employed to encourage factionalism, defections, and transfers of allegiance to the United States. The ruin of Soviet morale should also be sought by causing bewilderment in Moscow through apparently irrational U.S. actions, inciting revolt among Soviet labor camp inmates, and projecting total confidence in Western victory.

At the same time, he met with his one-time NYU colleague Lev Dobriansky, now an economist at Georgetown University and liaison between the Ukrainian Congress Committee of America and the Republican National Committee, to help formulate a "rollback" policy toward eastern Europe as the GOP's answer to the Democrats' policy of containment.[22]

Burnham's enthusiasm for polwar brought him close ties with foreign anti-communists. On visits to Washington, such people often stayed with the Burnhams as houseguests, causing *Washington Post* columnist Mary McGrory to describe the Burnham home as "a mecca for iron curtain refugees." Among the visitors were Czapski, who put up at the Burnhams' in the spring of 1950, and the French political scientist Raymond Aron, an incisive critic of the Stalinism then in vogue among French intellectuals. The Burnham children could soon tell French-accented from Polish-accented English, locate Ukraine on a map of Europe, and boast stamp collections that were the envy of their friends.[23]

All the while, Burnham attempted to broaden his circle of Washington acquaintances, meet members of organizations for Americans of eastern European ancestry, introduce people he thought should know one another, form ties with the media, and find publishers for anticommunist books. And somehow he continued to lecture and write.[24] His speech-making did not always go smoothly, however. "Jim went off tonight to speak to the Ukrainian gathering at Carnegie Hall and thereby get himself into some more trouble, I guess," Marcia Burnham wryly told a friend in 1950. She may have been thinking of an earlier speech of Burnham's to a Ukrainian-American audience during which he had unwittingly provoked an uproar by calling for an end to Soviet rule in Ukraine, while seeming to assume that Ukraine would continue to be governed by (a now postcommunist) Russia. At the time, he may not have realized that national-minded Ukrainians and their American cousins opposed not only Soviet but any kind of Russian rule over Ukraine.[25]

Ironically, Burnham's anticommunist projects sometimes ran afoul of the 1950 Internal Security Act, a law sponsored in the Senate by Nevada Democrat Pat McCarran that banned entry into the United States to foreigners who were, or had been, supporters of totalitarian movements. Because engaged anticommunists had often once been communists (as Burnham, a former Trotskyist, had in a sense been), they could not always be sure of obtaining U.S. visas. Sometimes a plea from Burnham to the State Department could get the ban lifted, but this process was often arduous and slow. When the Polish communist diplomat and poet Czeslaw Milosz defected to the West in Paris in February 1951 (taking refuge in Czapski's apartment), Burnham, convinced by a long conversation with Milosz that he was no "enemy agent" in disguise, worked hard to get him the needed visa. Though the visa was finally granted, as late as February 1953 Burnham told Charles Sternberg of the International Rescue Committee, "I am rather in despair about the Milosz case. I have myself spent a very long time on it." In the meantime, he tried to keep up the spirits of Milosz's wife, Janina, who, with the couple's two children, was stranded penniless in Washington. Maybe Senator Joseph McCarthy (who had burst into the headlines in February 1950 by accusing the State Department of being honeycombed with communists) could be used against Senator McCarran, Burnham joked to his young OPC aide, Warren G. Fugitt, narrowing his eyes and flashing a stage Chinaman's fiendish grin.[26]

◆　◆　◆　◆

The Burnhams never got firmly settled in Washington. First living in a house on 47th Street, they moved in March 1950 to one on 33rd Street, a few blocks from the Georgetown University campus, and in July 1951 to another, on Cleveland Avenue, where they lived for the last two years of their stay in the capital. But whatever his Washington address, Burnham kept to the same routine. In the morning, he would closet himself in his study with his work: an article to be drafted, a trip to be arranged, correspondence to be dealt with, a meeting to be scheduled, OPC projects to be pursued. At the end of the workday he would come downstairs to join Marcia and any guests on hand for a drink. At the 33rd Street house, an enormous philodendron lent a dramatic note to the living room, climbing up the wall and spreading across the ceiling. Over the fireplace hung a Chagall showing a satyr chasing a nymph. (Max Eastman, after cocking a critical eye at the painting, pronounced it "good of Marcia, less good of Jim.") Warren Fugitt, who sometimes stayed on for a drink, once described the typical Burnham cocktail hour. The talk centered on politics, with Burnham commenting acidly on the reluctance of politicians to fall afoul of liberal dogma, Eastman "declaiming in front of the fireplace, Aron waiting for us to ask precisely the right question, and Koestler waxing furious" on one thing or another. Fugitt found the relationship between Burnham and Marcia "striking." "It was as if they were newlyweds," he recalled. "They always kissed goodbye, even when he was just going out for lunch." Marcia was "bright, entertaining, full of verve, petillante." She acted as a "rudder" for Burnham, and "softened his sharp edges in social situations."[27]

◆　◆　◆　◆

Burnham did much of his OPC work on the Cold War's "cultural front," where Washington and Moscow vied for the support of writers, artists, and scientists. This competition led to his single most important OPC effort: the creation of the Congress for Cultural Freedom (CCF), a body intended to counter Soviet propaganda among intellectual and cultural figures, and highlight the contrast between communist repression and Western freedom.

Founded in 1950, the congress grew out of two related undertakings. The first was a protest against a March 1949 pro-Soviet propaganda festival called the "Cultural and Scientific Conference for World Peace." Held at New York's Waldorf Astoria Hotel, sponsored by the fellow-traveling National Council for the Arts, Sciences, and Professions, blessed by such left-leaning notables as Charlie Chaplin, Albert Einstein, and Leonard Bernstein, and featuring a host of "progressive" American cultural celebrities and guests from the stellar reaches of the Soviet cultural world, the Waldorf Conference declared as its goal the promotion of "peace and friendship" between the USSR and the United States. But Sidney Hook and other veteran anti-Stalinists saw it as nothing more than a Soviet psychological warfare maneuver designed to advance Moscow's political agenda. Thus, after vainly seeking permission to address the conference (where he planned to skewer the communist idea of "class truth"), Hook brought together a group made up mostly of anti-Stalinist leftists, including Dwight Macdonald, Norman Thomas, Mary McCarthy, and James T. Farrell, at Macdonald's Greenwich Village apartment to plan a protest rally. What the meeting came up with was an "Ad Hoc Committee for Intellectual Freedom," which quickly organized a counterconference, to be held at Freedom House, on West 40th Street, on the final day of the Waldorf affair. Some two hundred people signed up as sponsors of the Hook rally, many of them contributors to *Partisan Review* and the *New Leader.* Money was short, but the group's publicist, a young newsman named Arnold Beichman, persuaded David Dubinsky, head of the International Ladies' Garment Workers Union (ILGWU), to help get the ball rolling with a donation from the union treasury (to which Dubinsky later added a personal loan to Hook).

Mounted at a moment's notice and with meager funding, the rally nonetheless scored a hit, drawing a crowd so big that it spilled out of Freedom House onto 40th Street and across into Bryant Park. Inside Freedom House, a jammed auditorium listened to speeches by Hook, Arthur Schlesinger Jr., Max Eastman, and others decrying the communist destruction of cultural freedom, while the overflow crowd outside heard the speeches over loudspeakers. Afterward, elated by the rally's success, its organizers decided to keep the Ad Hoc Committee in being, and to this end revamped it into a permanent body, Americans for Intellectual Freedom (AIF).[28]

Meanwhile, the second undertaking behind the Congress of Cultural Freedom was materializing, as two Americans living in Berlin also worked to counter communist cultural propaganda. Melvin Lasky, City College radical in the 1930s, OSS officer during the war, and correspondent in Germany after 1945 for *Partisan Review* and the *New Leader,* now edited *Der Monat,* a magazine formally sponsored by the State Department, secretly funded by the CIA, and intended to exert pro-Western influence on German intellectual and cultural life. Lasky's friend Michael Josselson, born in Estonia, had lived in Berlin and Paris and then emigrated to the United States in 1936. Military service and a post with the OSS brought him back to Berlin in 1945, where he worked as a State Department public-affairs officer and as a covert CIA officer dealing with cultural affairs. Like Lasky, Josselson thought it crucial that anticommunist intellectuals resist the Moscow-orchestrated philo-Stalinism and anti-Americanism then rife in European intellectual circles, and he favored some sort of large-scale counteraction.[29]

While visiting New York in March 1949, Josselson attended Hook's Freedom House rally. "We should have something like this in Berlin," he told the composer Nicolas Nabokov, one of the rally's organizers.[30] And indeed, an event loosely resembling the rally was soon to take place abroad. To protest a communist-controlled "World Congress of Partisans for Peace," to be held in Paris in April 1949,

David Rousset, a French socialist and a survivor of Nazi imprisonment who had heard about the Freedom House rally, was planning an "International Day of Resistance to Dictatorship and War," also to meet in Paris, and had invited Hook to attend for the AIF. (Rousset would not invite Burnham, Koestler, or Aron, whom he regarded as "too anti-Communist.") Hook agreed to come, hoping to create an international anticommunist cultural organization, one "independent of all governments."[31]

While in Paris, Hook spoke with Lasky, also at the Rousset rally, who agreed that a world organization of anticommunist intellectuals was needed. The following August, Lasky drew up a plan for an international conference a year hence at which well-known anticommunist intellectuals would gather both to condemn communism's corruption of intellectual life and establish an organization to defend cultural freedom. *Der Monat* would sponsor the gathering, and the CIA, behind the scenes, would foot the bill. Rousset, also involved, thought the conference should be held in Berlin, the most dramatic point of confrontation between Western freedom and Soviet totalitarianism, and Lasky concurred.[32]

In January 1950, in a few lines at the end of a letter on other subjects, Lasky revealed his plan to Burnham. Delighted, Burnham at once joined in preparing the conference as agent for the OPC, which now became the major force behind it. Disbursing funds, obtaining travel documents for prospective delegates, working on a conference agenda, and handling many other such matters, he played such a central, if inconspicuous, role that Hook dubbed him the conference's "éminence grise."[33]

Burnham envisaged the conference as "an 'anti-communist united front'" open to "Socialists and non-Socialists, Right as well as traditional Left, religious and non-religious, etc.," who would all join against the common enemy, with only totalitarians excluded. At the same time, true to his Bolshevik past, he insisted that the gathering be carefully managed to ensure a pro-Western, not neutralist, outlook. "I am taking this Conference very seriously," he told Koestler, who had also become involved. "It is a chance for something really serious, both in itself and in what it could lead to."[34]

In April 1950 preparations for the conference, now called the Congress for Cultural Freedom and scheduled to meet in Berlin in June, took Burnham to Germany. In early May, on his way back to Washington, he stopped off at Verte Rive, Koestler's new home near Paris, where with Koestler and Aron, who was also to take part in the conference, he went over his plans. All agreed that a special effort should be made to get T. S. Eliot to attend, and that to give the congress "emotional appeal" a composer and a poet should be hired to write a "Song of Free Europe," to be performed by an orchestra and choir.[35]

Upon first meeting the soft-spoken, shy-seeming Burnham, Koestler's dark-haired English wife, Mamaine, thought him "very sweet and gentle." She was shocked, then, to hear him say at dinner that if war broke out, the United States could destroy the USSR in a day or so by bombing all its major cities to bits. "He looked quite pleased at the idea," she noted. "K[oestler] and I were horrified." Despite his mild manner, Burnham was apparently "much less scrupulous about means than K, who doesn't look sweet and gentle and isn't." Her revised impression of her guest was soon confirmed. The following evening, when the Koestlers took Burnham to dinner with Pierre Bertaux, chief of France's Sûreté Nationale, the talk again touched on the problem of ends and means. "K was very good on this," she thought, "said, with everything it is a matter of degree, but one can draw arbitrary lines, e.g., I will tell the truth but not the whole truth. Burnham again much less scrupulous than K., said he wouldn't necessarily reject torture in certain cases."[36]

On June 15, ten days before the congress was due to open, Burnham left Washington for Berlin like a nervous expectant father rushing to the hospital early. This time he brought Marcia with him. "Her presence would be desirable and perhaps essential as a cover for my role," he explained to the OPC. "Particularly in view of the fact that I shall present to the Congress what will probably be the key political paper, it is necessary to make certain that the other delegates shall regard me as a private individual."[37]

At last the big moment arrived. On June 25, 1950, in West Berlin's Titania Palace, under the patronage of the philosophers Bertrand Russell, John Dewey, Benedetto Croce, Karl Jaspers, and Jacques Maritain, the Congress for Cultural Freedom held its opening session. First came a moment of silence in memory of people who had given their lives for freedom, then (the "Song of Free Europe" plan had been dropped) a performance by the Berlin Philharmonic of Beethoven's Egmont Overture. The atmosphere was tense. Just as the congress convened, word arrived that communist North Korea had invaded South Korea (triggering a conflict that Burnham would call not "the Korean War," but "the Korean phase of the war"),[38] and rumors circulated that a Red Army advance into western Europe might follow. Since congress delegates, many of them well-known anticommunists, would have been hard put to escape in Soviet-encircled West Berlin, such talk was particularly alarming. A Soviet seizure of the city could land them in a Siberian prison camp.

Numbering more than a hundred, these participants included such prominent figures as the novelist Ignazio Silione, the art critic Herbert Read, the philosopher A. J. Ayer, and the theologian and historian Denis de Rougement. (T. S. Eliot, as it turned out, did not attend.) Besides Burnham, the U.S. contingent included, among others, Hook, Arthur Schlesinger Jr., the playwright Tennessee Williams, the writer Carson McCullers, the actor Robert Montgomery, black newspaperman George Schuyler, and the *New Leader's* editor, Sol Levitas. Politically, most of the delegates came not from the Right, but from the liberal center and the social democratic Left. Over the five days of the congress, they divided their time between panel discussions on issues of cultural freedom and plenary sessions at which speakers addressed more pointedly political questions. Nor were the proceedings allowed, in Burnham's words, to "flop along." Early each morning, Burnham, Hook, Koestler, Lasky, and Irving Brown, "International Representative" of the AFL and pipeline for OPC money to anticommunist European labor unions, met as a *sub rosa* steering committee to plan for the coming day and make sure the congress stayed on course.[39]

Burnham also played a prime public role at the congress. Expecting neutralism (which he defined as the "denunciation on equal terms of American and Soviet barbarism"), allied with pacificism, to be the gathering's "principal political problem," he tackled the problem head on. He knew all too well "the deficiencies of American life and culture," he said in his speech to a plenary session of the delegates. Still, it was necessary to preserve "a minimum sense of proportion": Coca-Cola might be dreadful, but it was "not quite in the same league with [the Soviet labor camp] Kolyma." Nor, he continued, had the atom bomb converted him to pacifism, whose practical result was to sap the West's will to survive. "I am against those bombs . . . designed for the destruction of Paris, London, Brussels, Rome, Stockholm, New York, Chicago, . . . Berlin, and of Western civilization generally," he specified. "But I am . . . *for* those bombs made in Los Alamos, Hanford, and Oak Ridge."[40]

Burnham's speech provoked a scandalized reaction. The idea that someone might approve of atom bombs "horrified some of the soft liners present," recalled his former student Norman Jacobs, in Berlin to cover the conference for the Voice of America. Hook thought the speech inept. "Let's face it," he said, "Jim is right, but his problem is that he doesn't know how to deliver the unpalatable truth in a way that is digestible."[41] But Hook misunderstood Burnham. It was not ignorance of oratorical techniques that explained Burnham's blunt endorsement of U.S. atom bombs, but his insistence on forthrightly stating his convictions, along with his itch to blaspheme against the pieties of the "sentimental" Left. Few things grated on him more than progressives who hid behind the "mush" of "idealism" (and idealism's pretense of moral superiority) to avoid unwelcome truths, and his impulse to outrage such people could exceed his wish to convert them. So he did not regret having caused a scandal. He knew he had aroused "a certain amount of immediate indignation," he remarked to Philip Rahv, but the uproar had not lasted. The protesters, he told Koestler, were only the usual "mush heads."[42]

The Berlin gathering culminated in a reading by Koestler of a "Freedom Manifesto" he had written. "Freedom has seized the offensive!" Koestler cried on finishing.[43] The manifesto was then submitted to the delegates for ratification, which duly followed. The Congress for Cultural Freedom had been successfully launched. The task now was to build on this promising beginning.

Upon leaving Berlin, Burnham went to Stockholm to confer with leaders of Estonian and Latvian exile groups, and then to Paris for further congress business. For two weeks, he met almost daily either in Paris or at Verte Rive with Aron, Koestler, Brown, and Lasky (all, like him, members of the CCF's executive committee chosen in Berlin) to work on a permanent structure for the congress and discuss projects the Berlin delegates had approved, such as Czapski's plan for an "exile university." Believing the congress would need publications to gain influence, Burnham recommended, to general agreement, that the organization's French branch, Les Amis de la Liberté, begin publishing a magazine as soon as possible. (The congress eventually put out several magazines, including *Preuves* in France, *Tempo Presente* in Italy, *Encounter* in Britain, *Quadrant* in Australia, and Lasky's *Monat*.) All the while, the French communist weekly *L'Action,* keeping an eye on the committee's daily comings and goings, charged that a "terrorist militia" was being secretly trained at Verte Rive.[44]

While in Paris, Burnham also spoke at length with Charles de Gaulle, who believed war between the West and the USSR was imminent. Could the West defeat the USSR with "political-psychological-subversive methods?" Burnham asked. "Logically and theoretically," yes, de Gaulle answered, but in practice it would be "impossible," because Western leaders such as Truman and Britain's prime minister Clement Attlee were not capable of mounting and persevering in such a strategy.[45]

In late July the executive committee wrapped up its work. Now free, the Burnhams set off to England and Ireland for a brief holiday, and in early August headed home.

◆　◆　◆　◆

Back in Washington, Burnham resumed his normal routine, but like an anxious parent tending a frail infant, he gave the bulk of his time to nurturing the congress. In November 1950 he went back to Europe for more congress business, this time to Brussels, where the executive committee was to meet to adopt a constitution and continue discussion of projects the congress wished to pursue. Hoping to gain publicity for the congress, he suggested, in vain, that the meeting not be limited to executive committee members, but that Arthur Schlesinger and other prominent CCF adherents be invited. He also urged that the meeting go beyond mere technical matters to broach "real political and ideological" issues. It was perhaps because of this last that the executive committee released a statement denouncing "the pro-Soviet aims of the so-called World Congress of Partisans for Peace," then meeting in Warsaw. In addition, the committee heard a report from Czapski on his exile university plan, and confirmed approval of the plan. It also voted in favor of public debates with the Partisans for Peace, an annual prize for literary or artistic achievement, and a plenary CCF conference in Paris in 1951.[46] Five months after Berlin, the future of the congress remained hopeful.

Still, to secure that future, the congress would have to find what Burnham called "a solid (however small) nucleus of support." The OPC had paid for its Berlin debut, but had not promised any further aid, and AFL funds, handled by Brown, were to continue for only six months. By the fall of 1950, however, thanks to the OPC's increasing interest, the "solid nucleus" appeared to be materializing.[47]

The OPC found the congress more and more to its liking. Many congress members, it noted, leaned to the left, an excellent recommendation for the OPC, which viewed the noncommunist Left (the "NCL" in CIA jargon), with its social democratic outlook, as communism's sole effective opponent. Thomas W. Braden, OSS veteran, fervent liberal, and first head of the OPC's International Organizations division, which was to arrange congress funding, later wrote that in postwar Europe, "socialists, people who called themselves 'left' . . . were the only people who gave a damn about fighting communism."[48] Thus, in the fall of 1950, the OPC began to look for a way to provide the congress with a permanent subsidy. He was going to close out the old CCF bank account, Burnham told Arnold Beichman in October 1950. "A new setup is going to be established, and new financial and banking arrangements will be involved."[49]

But it took time to work out the desired arrangement. In January 1951 Nicolas Nabokov, who now presided over the congress's Paris-based International Secretariat, complained that financial uncertainty was throwing a pall over CCF activity, and he implored Burnham to help achieve "an efficient modus operandi." As late as April 1951, Hook was still trolling for money, but in vain.[50] In the end however, the OPC devised the needed conduit. This was a cover organization called the Fairfield Foundation, incorporated in New York in January 1952, ostensibly to encourage Free World cultural projects and to support groups publicizing the totalitarian threat to the arts, literature, and science. Heading Fairfield's board of directors was Julius Fleishman, a scion of the Cincinnati distilling family, former publisher of the *New Yorker,* and a loyal trooper who obstinately denied any link between the foundation and the CIA.[51]

In early 1951, with the congress up and running, Burnham formally resigned from NYU. Washington Square College Dean Thomas Pollock urged him to stay, promising a further extension of his leave.[52] But Burnham, engrossed in his OPC projects and above all in the work of overseeing the congress, was adamant.

◆　◆　◆　◆

In Burnham's view, the congress needed constant oversight to ensure that it did not drift in a politically undesirable direction or turn purely cultural. To keep close tabs on opinion at the International Secretariat, he seems to have planted an informant at the Paris office. "I have complied with your instructions concerning an inconspicuous activity and a role within our team which you desired to be far from any kind of self-assertion," a certain Louis Dobos–Gibarti, once a high-ranking Comintern agent, wrote to him from Paris in November 1950. "I have perfectly understood your reasons and the situation from which they derived. . . . Thus I hope to have avoided . . . contribut[ing] from my part to a political taint [rumors were already rife that the congress was a CIA operation] which, according to some critics, prevails somehow in the machinery of the Congress." He had also "carefully avoided to mention anything from our contacts and conversations," he reassured Burnham.[53]

Burnham's deepest anxiety was that the congress would fall prey to neutralism. This, he warned the Paris office in January 1951, would subvert the principle on which the congress was based, and reduce it to "another useless centrist mush." When Denis de Rougement suggested inviting the pro-Soviet French writers Jean-Paul Sartre and Simone de Beauvoir and the neutralist German novelist Thomas Mann to take part in a CCF conference, but seemed to have no plan to include well-known anticommunist writers, Burnham feared the worst. The Freedom Manifesto explicitly rejected neutrality between "relative freedom and total unfreedom," he reminded Rougement. He would resign from the committee if the invitations were extended. He was also upset by what he saw as the Paris staff's anti-Gaullist tilt. "Partly by design and partly by inertia," he complained to Nabokov in January 1951, "the leftists, who dominate the staff numerically, are always tending toward the transformation of the [CCF] into simply another clique in their own image. Unless the [CCF] can maintain a united front which bridges the traditional right and left (and in France this means to include Gaullists), its whole point of existence evaporates."[54]

Another who feared that the Congress was turning "soft" was Koestler. His suspicions may have been triggered by the OPC, which, unhappy about his divisive personality, was trying to ease him off-stage. They were probably sharpened, however, by his volatility. ("I had the day before yesterday a kind of nervous crack up," he confided to Burnham in September 1950. In this condition he had resigned from the executive committee, only to change his mind almost at once.) By early 1951 Koestler was blaming Burnham for what he saw as the ruin of the congress. "I believe that you are an important political thinker in our time but a rotten judge of people," he wrote to Burnham in January 1951, claiming there had been "constant friction" between them over CCF personnel. "Ghibarti [*sic*], Bondy [François Bondy, a French journalist and a leading figure in the CCF's French affiliate] and Denis de Rougement were so to speak your inventions. The latter two have now apparently succeeded in undoing all we have tried to do. Unless they immediately retrace their steps I am out of this."

Burnham attempted to calm Koestler down, noting that the congress had "some real accomplishments" to its credit and "promise[d] even more." Yet his own unease continued unabated, and was now made worse by his need to placate the explosive Koestler. His relations with Koestler were "rather stormy," he informed the OPC in a memorandum devoted to plumbing Koestler's psyche. Koestler was "neurotic in the strict pathological sense," and showed evidence of "a manic depressive cycle," "an aggressive compensatory defense mechanism, and at least one specific obsession": a "fixation on 'conspiracy.'" Hence, though he possessed "intellectual and technical abilities of a very high order," and could sometimes, as at Berlin, greatly benefit the anticommunist movement, he could also be "passively negative, or even actively destructive."[55]

For a few weeks in early 1951, Burnham's worries about the CCF found a focus in a staffing change at the Paris office: the replacement of a Gaullist, Daniel Apert, as acting secretary by a socialist, Jacques Enoch, allegedly because of string-pulling by Irving Brown and AFL potentate Jay Lovestone [a former communist leader and now Brown's boss at the anticommunist AFL]. "Replacing Apert by Brown henchman," Burnham protested in a telegram to Paris, "would mean first destroying political united front which is basis and sole justification for Congress second breaking principle link to serious cultural figures in France third reducing Congress to province of Lovestone empire. I would personally have below zero interest in a mushy leftist Lovestone-ite Congress." In a letter to Bondy, he poured out his concerns, emphasizing the necessity of keeping the congress a united front that welcomed Gaullists, and charging that despite the already excessive neutralist current in the CCF, Apert, "by a kind of corridor putsch," had been removed in favor of Enoch. "I have, even, a sense of real tragedy in relation to this present crisis of the Congress," he told Bondy. Burnham misconstrued what had happened, Bondy hastily replied, naming some Gaullists working at the CCF French branch's headquarters. Apert had been replaced not for political reasons, but for poor performance. Rougement seconded Bondy, assuring Burnham that the change carried no "political" implication.[56]

While apparently mollified, Burnham soon fell prey to a new worry. Congress efforts in France were languishing because "publicly distinguished individuals" did not participate in its programs, he wrote to Nabokov in June 1951, and because there was "too much tendency to make the Congress an 'office operation'—and not enough splashing in the open public world." Nabokov, however, had a different explanation for the congress's wallflower status. "Here I think our constant efforts should be directed toward proving to European intellectuals that the Congress for Cultural Freedom is . . . not an American secret service agency," he answered.[57]

But his complaints notwithstanding, Burnham sometimes expressed delight over congress projects. He was especially excited by a plan of Nabokov's for a mammoth arts festival to be held in Paris in 1952 that, it was hoped, would feature the Boston Symphony Orchestra, the National Philharmonic Orchestra of Paris, the first French performance of Alban Berg's *Wozzeck,* a new opera by Igor Stravinsky, the New York City Ballet, Laurence Olivier in a play by T. S. Eliot, an exhibition of famous paintings, and, for a climax, a performance at Notre Dame of Mozart's Mass in C Minor to commemorate the victims of twentieth-century totalitarian oppression. "I altogether share your enthusiasm," he wrote to Nabokov. "If this could be properly done, it alone would assure the world standing of the Congress for ever after." But the festival should also have "an over-all 'angle'" to set it apart from other arts festivals and enable it to play "a major part in the struggle for the world," he added, ever mindful of the CCF's ultimately political purpose. "It seems to me that we should think of it as a kind of concentrated expression of the 'values' of our culture, a confident contrasting display of what [the Soviets] and we have to offer in the arts, music, and literature, and an answer thereby to which side represents the future."

Burnham not only happily endorsed "Masterpieces of the Twentieth Century," as the Nabokov project came to be called; he became involved in preparing its program, negotiating with the Boston Symphony and composer Virgil Thomson over their participation, and arranging for the loan of a Cezanne from the National Gallery.[58] In addition, he advised on the festival's administration and financing, matters he said he was approaching "from the point of view of OPC interests." He was "in a position," he told the OPC, "to arrange the transfer, by methods which are both confidential and secure, of sums of various amounts up to an over-all total of $100,000."[59]

◆　◆　◆　◆

Always ambitious for the causes he championed, Burnham wanted to extend the congress beyond the West. This wish was realized in 1951 when the editors of the Indian anticommunist journal *Thought* and Minoo Masani, a member of India's parliament who had once been jailed by the British as a militant nationalist, but who favored a Cold War alignment with the West, announced plans to establish an Indian branch of the CCF.[60] Wanting to give the new affiliate a well-publicized debut, its founders went on to plan an inaugural conference, which would be held at Bombay in late March 1951 and be paid for with CCF money.

Burnham was delighted. Hailing the Indian branch as of "the very highest importance," since it might weaken neutralist and pro-Soviet influence in India, he not only helped with the planning but also agreed to attend as a guest delegate and speaker. Marcia accompanied him to Bombay. His OPC aide, Warren Fugitt, also went with him, disguised as a reporter for the *New Leader*.[61] Other guest delegates included Rougement, Norman Thomas, Ignazio Silone, the journalist Louis Fischer, the diplomat and historian Salvador de Madariaga, and the poets W. H. Auden and Stephen Spender.

The Bombay conference proceeded without major incident, though not always smoothly. Burnham, in his address, stressed the moral values that united East and West. These two worlds differed culturally in many ways, he observed: their "basic notions of personality and being and the Holy" were not identical, and problems between them would not be eased by pretending otherwise. Nevertheless, they agreed in acknowledging the right of other cultures to exist, whereas the communists sought to destroy "everything that [was] not theirs."[62] But not all the guests treated the conference so seriously. Auden gave what one listener described as an "amiably muddled, slightly drunken speech" that bewildered his hosts. "My nanny always told me that we were put on earth to do good for others," the poet reported. "I've often asked myself, what on earth, then, are the *others* here for?" Moreover, in contrast to the Berlin conference, the audience in Bombay included communists and fellow travelers who peppered the speakers with hostile questions and comments.[63]

While in India, the Burnhams made a side trip to Ceylon so that Burnham could further spread the congress gospel. They then caught a plane for Bangkok, where yet another CCF branch was in the making.[64] From Thailand, they went on to Japan to allow Burnham to take part in the launching of a Japanese CCF affiliate, and after a few days in Tokyo flew back home.

Burnham's satisfaction with the Indian affiliate did not last long. He had the impression that the new Indian CCF, which he called "identical" to the editorial office of *Thought,* was not "functioning at all actively or responsibly," he wrote to Nabokov. Rather, it appeared that "the interests of the Congress were [being] sacrificed to the maintainance [*sic*] or promotion of the magazine."[65]

But if Burnham was unhappy with the editors of *Thought,* the editors, stung by an article he had written for *Partisan Review* upon returning home, were doubly unhappy with him. In form a travel memoir, the article "Parakeets and Parchesi: An Indian Memorandum," amounted to a savaging of India, on whose appalling poverty and squalor it dwelt at length. In India "each sense and every spiritual rampart is systematically attacked," read a typical passage. "The nose is never released by that remarkable smell of the Indian city: compound of heavy flowers, filth, incense smoking from great piles, dried excrement and dust, the rotted corruption of half-burned human entrails, thrown into the river from the funeral *ghats,* uncovered sewers. . . ." All told, India struck visitors as "stark, abject, disease- and dirt-ridden, absolutely and unyieldingly wretched." What a relief, then, to return to the West as embodied in a KLM airliner and its crew. "How clean was each inch of upholstery," Burnham exclaimed, "how rationally arranged each functional gadget! The tall, blond Dutch steward and the brisk, blond, bronzed Dutch stewardess, with their unclouded blue eyes and their well-soaped, unspotted skin and their nurse-clean blouse and shirt, looked as if they had just jumped, intact and fully clothed, out of the forehead of a laundry machine."[66]

These last lines may have struck Indian readers as the ultimate insult. For although Burnham did not attribute the West's greater advancement to race, his mention of blond hair and blue eyes in the same breath as cleanliness, rational order, and efficiency could easily be read as a boast of race-based superiority.

To write in this fashion was clearly to ask for trouble, especially since Burnham did not try to balance his picture by signaling attractive features of Indian life. His failure to do so may have resulted from his Augustinian tendency to dwell on the bleak side of existence, or from his perennial impulse to violate liberal etiquette (writers describing poor non-Western countries should point to their positive as well as negative aspects, and the negative aspects should be viewed with compassion), or perhaps from a belief that in India the negative so heavily outweighed the positive that no balance could be struck. But it may also have stemmed from his dislike of India's prime minister, Jawaharlal Nehru ("that brilliant, devious, self-righteously double-dealing spellbinder, torn by his fused envy and hatred of the West," and conducting a "Soviet-serving policy of neutralism"), whom he may have decided to show up by exposing Indian reality.[67]

Burnham's Indian hosts considered the article outrageous. J. R. D. Tata, the millionaire industrialist with whom the Burnhams had stayed as houseguests in Bombay, wrote to him of the "unfortunate impression" that it had made in India, and pronounced himself "somewhat disappointed because of its exclusive emphasis on unfortunate features of Indian life." *Thought* was more direct. "No country or race is perfect. . . ," its editors riposted. "The ugliness of our present life is not only not ineffaceable but merely incidental to certain facts of history. Those who gloat over it [which Burnham had not done] only betray the ugliness of their own souls." But a well-known American liberal praised the article. "Your brilliant piece," Arthur Schlesinger wrote to Burnham, "expressed all the sentiments which have been rumbling around indistinctly in the back of my mind for the last seventeen years."[68]

◆   ◆   ◆   ◆

By this time, an American branch of the congress had emerged. Hook, in January 1951, had reincorporated his Americans for Intellectual Freedom as the American Committee for Cultural Freedom (ACCF), an "independent affiliate" of the Congress for Cultural Freedom.[69] At the outset, the ACCF was strapped for cash. It obtained short-term financing from the ILGWU, *Time,* and several ACCF members. But a year later, the Fairfield Foundation stepped in with regular contributions, and the money problem eased. The ACCF was now able to set up shop in what a one-time ACCF secretary recalled as "a rather elegant office" in a town house on West 53rd Street, just down the block from the Museum of Modern Art. Burnham, a member of the ACCF's executive board, seems to have arranged for the payments.[70]

Burnham had high hopes for the ACCF, both as a possible counterweight to the influence of Soviet apologists among American intellectuals and as a beacon for the CCF, and with the attention he always paid to the practical side of politics, he looked for ways to better its chances of success. To achieve greater impact, he counseled Hook shortly before the ACCF was incorporated, the organization should have an executive board as inclusive as possible, one that went beyond "the old radical and avante [*sic*] garde circles" to take in "more conventional 'American' types." If the board turned out to be "too much a Partisan Review-New Leader" crowd, the ACCF would not last. His wish was not entirely met, for although people connected with *Partisan Review* and the *New Leader* did not monopolize the executive committee, they still loomed large enough to set its tone. Nonetheless, he continued to show enthusiasm and in the months to come bombarded Hook with proposals for ACCF activities.[71]

Sometimes he came up to New York for executive committee meetings, wanting to speak in person for projects he strongly favored. At the June 1951 meeting, he proposed that the ACCF call upon the CCF to stage a debate in Paris that might appeal to intellectuals, and suggested as a topic the question of whether religion was vital to the West's "struggle for survival." Participants, he said, might include the pro-Soviet Sartre, a Jesuit, a "Naturalist," and persons holding other points of view. At the same meeting, he introduced Czapski, who briefed the committee on his talks with the National Committee for a Free Europe (NCFE)—an ostensibly private, but in fact CIA-funded body that gave aid to Iron Curtain refugees—on his exile university project. At the December 1951 executive committee meeting, he urged that the ACCF at once contact the Japanese novelist Yukio Mishima, soon to visit the United States, since a meeting would afford "a splendid opportunity" to forge ties with the Japanese literary world.[72]

All the while, Burnham worked on other projects. Among these, the one he valued most was the exile university plan, upon which he lavished an abundance of fretful concern. "I hope that you, personally, are going to keep your hand very much in that affair," he wrote to Nabokov soon after his return from Asia. "We must absolutely not let it become bogged down in a timid or conventional approach." In mid-June 1951 he again raised the subject with Nabokov, recommending that the university be linked with the CCF to keep the project from turning "politically sterile." He was "most distressed about the delay in launching the University," he wrote to Czapski in early July when progress seemed to have stalled.[73]

But by midsummer, it looked as if his hopes would be realized. On July 23, 1951, the *New York Times* reported the founding near Strasbourg, France, of the "Free Europe University in Exile," a school that would not grant degrees, but would enable young refugees from behind the Iron Curtain "to prepare for future service" to their homelands once the latter had been liberated. Funding would come from the National Committee for a Free Europe and the Crusade for Freedom (a fundraising organization through which money was funneled to the NCFE's broadcasting department, Radio Free Europe). The university's president would be DeWitt C. Poole (original director of Princeton's Woodrow Wilson School, former OSS officer, former State Department officer, and more recently chairman of the board at Radio Free Europe). Its trustees would be Princeton president Harold Dodds, former U.S. ambassador to Japan Joseph C. Grew, Sidney Hook, Reinhold Niebuhr, Adolf A. Berle, and James Burnham.[74]

Once this stage had been reached, Burnham might have been expected to relax. But now he feared that the "dynamic" institution he had envisaged was turning stodgy. The project's implementation had been "far too timid, official, formal, and bureaucratic," he protested in August 1951 to the school's secretary, Levering Tyson. As things stood, the school risked being "smothered in files and procedures." There had also been too much humoring of "polite French opinion" and too little effort at countering communist attacks. The university's staff, moreover, was too "official and 'respectable.'" It should include "at least a few persons who [were] a little off the standard track or even rather wild"—Czapski, for example, even if some people found him "a little eccentric or Bohemian."[75]

The Free Europe University opened its doors in November 1951. At the outset, it had about a hundred students—Romanians, Bulgarians, Yugoslavs, Lithuanians, Poles, Czechs—most of whom lived at its resident center, the Pourtalès estate overlooking the Rhine at Robertsau, outside Strasbourg. The estate served as a teaching center as well, though many students also took courses at the University of Strasbourg. After attending the inaugural ceremony, Burnham came home somewhat heartened, deciding that despite "problems," the "net indication so far [was] certainly plus." Still, intellectual achievement was not keeping up with organizational achievement, he observed, noting that the school had opened with hot water but no faculty or books.[76]

As time passed, Burnham's anxiety revived. "I regard the University, potentially at least, as a project of absolute first importance," he wrote in January 1952 to fellow trustee Adolf A. Berle. "It will be a tragedy if we throw away such a chance as it offers." And increasingly it seemed to him that the chance was being thrown away. "All the reports I get," he told Berle a few weeks later, "unite in the view that a recent letter [probably from Czapski] put by saying, 'The intellectual and political life of the University is *an absolute vacuum.*'" With Czapski, on the other hand, he adopted an encouraging tone. The university's launching showed that at least something concrete had been achieved, he noted in a letter of February 1952. Still, "like you," he admitted, "I am gravely alarmed at its failure to develop an intellectual and political side."[77]

At the end of February, he sent Tyson, now vice president of the university, a long list of criticisms. One problem with the school, he wrote, was "the apparently systematic neglect" of its "intellectual and ideological side," which seemed to be the result of "deliberate blockage." Worse, in the absence of efforts to inculcate the European federalist ideal in the students, "chauvinistic tendencies" had begun to crop up. Worse still, the students were being taunted by procommunists and neutralists at the University of Strasbourg as "American valets," and, "humiliated or cynical," had taken to calling the Robertsau center "the tragic bordello." Moreover, the choice of instructors and students showed a bias toward "the polite and right wing," toward people without a future in their homelands and of little value in the struggle against communism.[78] Burnham's complaints were not well received. The school's point was not to produce "freedom firebrands," one administrator snapped in reply. But to Burnham, that was precisely the point.[79]

Meanwhile, the school's problems continued to mount. Instructors of the right kind were hard to find. Most students did not speak French well enough to pass courses. And while it had been assumed that students would do the maintenance work at the Pourtalès estate, most spurned such work, disclaiming manual labor.[80]

In the end, the university never came close to meeting Burnham's hopes. Several more lackluster years followed, until in the mid-1950s the administration threw in the towel and downgraded the institution to a summer school. By that time, Burnham had also given up. After 1953 he mentioned the university only rarely, and then, despite his bitter disappointment, in a detached tone that showed no trace of the passion he had once felt for it.[81]

❖  ❖  ❖  ❖

Though Burnham spent most of his time working on his OPC projects, he occasionally resumed his pre–Cold War political theorizing. Still weighing on his mind was the threat of a totalitarian White House, a possibility he had been warning of since his Trotskyist denunciations of Roosevelt. In a lecture called "Democracy,

Oligarchy, and Freedom," which he gave at the Aspen Institute in 1952, he took up a theme he had first broached in *The Machiavellians,* though he now treated it in terms that recalled Tocqueville's in *Democracy in America.* The word "democratic," he observed, was used to denote two forms of government that actually had little or nothing in common. The first, "constitutional government," or "rule by law," was characterized by the existence of "intermediary bodies" (parliaments, political parties, lobbies, etc.) that stood between the individual and the state, and upheld the law and individual rights against "the raw will" of the executive. The second, "Caesarism" (the "Bonapartism" of *The Machiavellians*), was a caricature of democracy in which a "leader" claiming to express "the general will" of the masses wielded unlimited power. The modern world's most typical form of despotism, Caesarism had arisen as "a political phase" of the managerial revolution and always entailed bureaucratic rule, centralization, and the destruction of intermediary bodies. In the United States Caesarism was clearly gaining ground, promoted by liberals who championed the supremacy of the federal government over state governments and the president over Congress. But managerial "social dominance" did not have to mean political tyranny, he concluded. Caesarism could be stymied by means of surviving intermediary bodies, which, though weakened by liberal attack, could nevertheless be preserved by a determined effort.[82]

But the danger of Caesarism seemed less pressing to him than the danger of communism. In the struggle for the world, he still argued, "the best way" to victory was polwar. Yet he wondered if Americans could handle a polwar strategy. The United States possessed potential for polwar, he asserted in notes for a paper of 1953 or 1954 entitled "Can the United States Conduct Effective Political Warfare Against the Soviet Union?" But "social" and "cultural" factors, leading to problems of "knowledge, attitude, will," had rendered the country's elites—"college-educated and leading strata, Govt., business, labor, professions, especially ideologizing professions (teachers, lawyers, writers, mass communicators, preachers)"—"unsuited" to the approach. American leaders knew little about communism, and they did not read. Dwight D. Eisenhower never ventured beyond westerns, whodunits, and one-page memos. Moreover, the United States was "too luxurious, materialistic, day-by-day, unwilling to sacrifice." The elites believed all conflicts could be settled through deals. They were also susceptible to "humanitarian, secular 'liberalism,' full of vague half-ideas: pacifism; sentimental internationalism; do-goodism; 'no preventive war'; anti-colonialism; [and] 'common manism.'" Hence, "in general," they could not play a "responsible world role," having "no emotive-spiritual armor" against communism, and "no sharp weapons . . . in clear and sharp contrast to [their] anti-Nazism." "Spiritually *soft,*" they revealed "an impossible attitude base for effective anti-Sov. polwar." Adding to the problem was the American businessman, who saw in the USSR less an adversary than "a great field for the next stage of American capitalism." The "masses," for their part, showed a much better attitude, but without leadership they could not act.

The blend of ignorance and softness shown by the elites, he concluded, came down to "a defect of will," the "sin against [the] Holy Ghost." The governing class did "not seem to possess a serious will to defeat [the] enemy, to destroy his capacity to harm." Other countries, sensing this defect, hesitated to follow U.S. leadership. If the United States did not overcome its failure of will, it would meet with disaster: either defeat through nonmilitary means or a plunge into a terminal nuclear war.[83]

Burnham took a broader look at Washington's conduct of the Cold War in his third major work on the conflict, a book called *Containment or Liberation?,* published in 1953 and condensed for the *New York Herald Tribune*'s Sunday magazine, *This Week.* Elaborating on ideas first set forth in *The Coming Defeat of Communism,* the new book was the fruit of his reflections on the Truman administration's Cold War policy and of his zeal for polwar. At its core lay a hostile analysis of containment; a detailed argument for his favored alternative, a polwar-based "liberation" strategy; and an explanation of U.S. clumsiness at polwar.

Containment had to fail for many reasons, Burnham argued. To begin with, it required a purely defensive stance. And a country at war, like a boxer in the ring, could not win merely by parrying blows, but had to deliver some blows of its own. Moreover, if the United States aimed merely at blocking further Soviet expansion and did not attack the foundations of Soviet power, the USSR would be able to consolidate the resources and territories now in its grip, making its "complete world victory" certain. Then too, containment envisaged the contest in territorial terms. The enemy, however, was also a supranational ideological movement active in countries still free of Soviet control. But of all containment's defects, "perhaps the crucial" one was its totally negative character: it could never satisfy human "moral and spiritual" demands. The idea that anyone would "willingly suffer, sacrifice, and die" for such a policy was "ridiculous."[84]

Since the "minimum condition" for Western survival was "a considerable breakup" of the Soviet empire, Burnham asserted, an effective strategy could turn neither on repelling a Soviet invasion of western Europe, the essence of containment, nor, as Asia-firsters wanted, on blocking communist advances in the Far East, although both these goals were of critical importance. What was needed was a focus on eastern Europe (the area stretching from the Iron Curtain to the Urals), for there "*the key to the situation*" was to be found. There must be a new stress on the "liberation" of this region.[85]

A liberation policy, Burnham explained, would not involve conventional military action unless circumstances made it desirable. In that case, the geopolitical position of the United States argued for air action: "winged soldiers, air cavalry, able to raid two thousand miles behind the lines tonight and be gone before the defense arrives tomorrow, ready to liberate a Siberian slave labor district this week, spearhead a revolt in the Caucasus the next, and blow up an enemy powerhouse over the weekend." But usually the liberation strategy would mean political warfare (i.e., means "other than those of formal military warfare, insofar as these methods are guided by a strategic objective"), whose scale and tempo would far exceed the current norm. Polwar would stress nonmilitary forms of offensive action such as: propaganda campaigns; agitation, subversion, and sabotage behind the Iron Curtain; aid to people seeking to escape from communist countries; and the mobilization of refugees against the Soviet-backed puppet rulers of their homelands. And the Communist Party of the United States would be outlawed.[86]

There was little likelihood that Moscow would reply with war, Burnham repeated. Not only did the Soviet elites know that the United States had the USSR outgunned; they also knew that their empire contained national and social fissures so deep that military defeat could bring the end of communist rule.[87]

To be sure, he acknowledged, the United States had been waging polwar since the late 1940s, but with little success. Polwar operations had been poorly conceived. U.S. information programs, for example, did not achieve the ends desired, but conveyed, above all, "the passionate wish to be loved." Americans had "not yet learned the tragic lesson that the most powerful cannot be loved—hated, envied, feared, obeyed, respected, even honored perhaps, but not loved."[88]

To wage polwar effectively, he went on, two things were needed: expertise in skills ranging from slogan-coining to the use of high explosives and a "sufficient knowledge and profound rejection of communism." But few in Washington possessed the required skills and attitudes. To the extent that the United States had been fighting communism, it had been "trying to do so without anti-communists." Polwar offices were manned by "stock brokers, academic social scientists, lawyers, investment bankers, members of café or conventional society out for a fling at secret missions and Washington salons, or unattached 'administrators,'"— not people who united the requisite "knowledge and passion."[89] No key policy level job was in the hands of "a hard and informed anti-communist." George F. Kennan, for example, was "unquestionably" anti-Soviet and intellectually anti-communist. Yet nowhere in his writings did one sense "a hatred of communism." Rather, his anticommunism seemed "pale and abstract."[90]

Much of the failure to wage serious war on communism could be traced to the deep vein of pragmatism in American culture, a lack of "feeling for ideology." Also to blame was the "progressive" outlook of a minority of officials, which left them reflexively averse to a hard anticommunist policy.[91]

Given the present mess, it seemed doubtful that the United States had the "temperament, insight and will" necessary for a polwar strategy.[92] But if it did want to win the Cold War, it would have to develop the required qualities of mind and spirit and shed the illusion that in a pinch it could fall back on its atomic arsenal. For as Lenin knew, in the end it was political will, not armaments, that counted. If polwar failed, a resort to atom bombs would come too late.[93]

❖　❖　❖　❖

In contrast to the hopeful *Coming Defeat of Communism, Containment or Liberation?* exuded pessimism (its gloom probably reflecting the frustration Burnham suffered in Washington, as the brighter mood of the earlier work reflected the encouraging signs he had seen on his cross-country trip). Paradoxically, however, the book turned optimistic whenever it took up polwar. Then, the normally dry and detached Burnham, withering critic of sentimental illusions and wishful thinking, abandoned his cool skepticism for boundless confidence.[94] Was it a romantic streak, and not just his belief that there was an alternative to nuclear war, that fueled his enthusiasm?

*Containment or Liberation?* did not fare well with reviewers. Though some critics wrote favorably of certain aspects of the book, few gave it anything like full approval. *Foreign Affairs* commented that Burnham had made "some telling criticisms of inconsistencies in the American position," but had also allowed "his temper at times [to outrun] his argument." The political scientist Robert Strausz-Hupé summed up *Containment or Liberation?* as "a good bad book," one filled with apt criticism of the Truman administration's foreign policy, but suffering from factual errors and "partisan sniping," in which Burnham had been preceded by "better marksmen."[95]

Many reviewers rounded fiercely on Burnham's arguments. With the furor over domestic communism at its peak in 1953, William H. Hessler, writing in the *Reporter,* denounced *Containment or Liberation?* as an intellectual's brief for "the McCarthy-Jenner-Taft [i.e., Republican hard-line] case" that the country had been "sold down the river by Communists in the State Department." As Burnham had expected, hostile critics also charged that a liberation strategy would increase the risk of nuclear war. Burnham denied any danger, Richard Rovere noted in *United Nations World,* but this was the same Burnham who had made "more false prophecies than almost any other prophet of his time."[96]

Casual readers were more varied in their responses. Some decried the book and even questioned Burnham's sanity. "Any man who thinks the U.S. can liberate the world single handed is as crazy as a coot," wrote one irate reader to Burnham. But others applauded it, among them de Gaulle, who sent Burnham a letter of praise. Still others showed an interest that, had Burnham known of it, might especially have pleased him: the Soviet Communist Party's Central Committee, uneasy about the new Eisenhower administration (whose secretary of state, John Foster Dulles, was then loudly sounding the "liberation" theme), directed Georgi Arbatov, future head of Moscow's USA and Canada Institute, to translate the book into Russian, hoping to gain insight from it into American strategic thinking.[97]

Containment's original theorist, George F. Kennan, did not then publicly comment on Burnham's criticisms. But twenty years later, in his memoirs, he wrote of his anxiety in the 1950s about people who "scoffed at the thesis that there might be a gradual mellowing of Soviet power," and seeing little danger of war, "urged that American policy should be one of purely political attack on the various Communist regimes, aimed at their overthrow by a combination of American propaganda and the action of local anti-Communist groups, the outcome being conceived as the 'liberation' of the Soviet peoples. . . ." Had such thinking emanated only from "extremists," Kennan went on, "I might not have viewed it with such alarm; but it had, by this time, made deep inroads on the opinions of people who could not be relegated to that category," for instance, James Burnham, whose "*Containment and Liberation* [*sic*] [was] a well-written and persuasive book aimed largely against myself and the doctrine of containment."[98]

Given the fate that ultimately befell the USSR, Burnham might seem to have lost his debate with Kennan. But it can be plausibly argued that had the United States and its allies taken Burnham's advice, instead of acquiescing in Soviet control of eastern Europe and seeking to normalize Western-Soviet relations, the Soviet collapse might have come much sooner than it did. Burnham, at any rate, thought so. Though counterfactual hypotheses could not be proved, he noted in 1961, he believed that if a policy of the kind he had outlined, at least in the first two books of his Cold War trilogy, had been adopted, communism "might well by now have been sufficiently tamed or defeated."[99]

As this comment, fully reaffirming only the first two books of the trilogy, suggests, Burnham would eventually hesitate before the hardier counsels of *Containment or Liberation?* The loss of the U.S. nuclear monopoly, he later observed, occurring only after the first two books were written, had introduced "complications, and [made] judgment more questionable." He also came to criticize the trilogy as a whole, though from a different angle. His analysis of the communist problem was "obviously correct," he told his son Jim in 1961, but his proposals for solving the problem had not been heeded. That fact pointed to a practical question the books had never raised: whether such proposals had ever stood a chance of being accepted. "If I had been a political leader instead of an intellectual," he went on, "my procedure would have been entirely different. . . . The preoccupying problem would have been political: how to bring about a power equilibrium that would have made the anti-communist policy the policy of the U.S. government. (When Lenin got serious about the revolution . . . he did not write a treatise on capitalism or socialism, but a handbook—*What Is to Be Done?*—on what kind of organization was required, and how to build it.)" Given "the mood of the postwar Western world, the American traditions and ideology, etc.," it had not been "'realistic' to think that the U.S. would adopt a clear-cut long-term 'Machiavellian' strategy and policy such as I was proposing. But to have modified the strategy and policy sufficiently to give them a real chance of adoption almost certainly meant to make them no longer adequate. . . . The dilemma here is the core dilemma of politics, of course. ('Between the idea and the act,' as Eliot puts it, 'falls the shadow.')"[100]

His failure to consider what reality made possible in the postwar years rendered the trilogy "rather academic and sterile," he noted in 1966.

> It was not a question of opening eyes to the truth, and that sort of thing. It was a problem of power. It was unrealistic to suppose that the kind of people who were running the U.S. government and dominating U.S. opinion would pursue a serious and adequate Cold War policy; and there were insufficient cadres of persons who might have replaced them and done so. Moreover, the masses were not prepared for any such change in policy or personnel. A nation cannot learn by being lectured to. In this sort of case, I guess it has to learn by being hurt, hurt badly; and this the U.S. has not been since the Civil War. In a large nation, moreover, when some democratic factors are present, the primary problem for every ruling group must be the domestic problem; their first concern is to keep in the saddle. How could it be otherwise?[101]

His whole approach to the Soviet-communist problem had been wrong, he concluded in a later book, *Suicide of the West*. *The Struggle for the World* was "the first systematic analysis" of the Cold War, but the solution it came up with—a broad, programmatic solution—was "too abstract." If "the opposite of liberal in its content, it was like the typical liberal proposal in conception—'rationalist' in the sense defined by [the British political theorist] Michael Oakeshott." Nor could the solution ever have been put into practice, he added, reverting to his 1947 view of American society. "Americans were, and are, too immature for the undertaking, peculiarly untrained by their historical experience and their ideological preferences to fill the role that would have had to be theirs."[102]

◆　◆　◆　◆

In 1953, *Containment or Liberation?* makes clear, Burnham was convinced that a large-scale U.S. polwar effort would win the Cold War. But the book also reveals his frustration. Much of his chagrin may have been caused by the preferences of CIA Director General Walter Bedell Smith, once Eisenhower's chief of staff and from 1946 to 1949 U.S. ambassador to the USSR, who took up the CIA post in October 1950. A more assertive boss than his predecessor, Admiral Hillenkoetter, and favoring intelligence-gathering over covert action, Smith brought the OPC firmly to heel, and in 1952 combined it with the CIA's intelligence branch. He also set up an OPC project review board, which decided that a third of the OPC's covert operations should be cancelled.[103] Burnham, of course, wanted to step up polwar, not wind it down.

But the 1952 Republican electoral victory gave him hope, for Eisenhower's secretary of state-designate spoke not of containing the USSR, but of rolling it back and freeing the many countries it had taken "captive." Was the liberation strategy about to come into its own?

## Chapter 8

# Casualty

BURNHAM'S USUAL WEAPONS IN the struggle for the world were his OPC projects and his typewriter, but he once tried to add organized crime to his arsenal. One day in 1950 or early 1951, he and *Newsweek* editors Ralph de Toledano and Karl Hess, with whom he often played bridge, saw a newspaper story about a defecting Communist Party courier who told the FBI of carrying large sums of money for party purposes. Why not rob such couriers, and use the loot for anticommunist ends, Toledano, in Hess's recollection, proposed. Burnham and Hess liked the idea. But doubting that they themselves would make competent hold-up men, they decided to appeal to New York mobster Frank Costello, who out of patriotism, they hoped, might supply them with professional help. A few days later, Burnham and Hess went to New York to put their idea to Costello, only to be told by Costello's lawyer, George Wolfe, that whatever the newspapers claimed, his client was really just an ordinary businessman, and so could hardly engage in criminal mischief.[1]

In Toledano's version of the story,[2] he, Burnham, and Hess fell to wondering why high-level Soviet spies in the United States always seemed to escape detection until they were safely out of the country. If communist small fry could be identified by "triangulation," seized, pumped full of sodium pentothal ("truth serum"), and grilled, it might be possible to nab some higher-ups before they could escape. But because the FBI was forbidden to use such methods, they might have to do the job themselves. Such an effort, they calculated, would require a panel truck for transport, a house in Greenwich Village (where odd comings and goings would go unnoticed) for interrogations, and a doctor to inject the truth serum. The bill would come to less than $100,000. Burnham thought he could raise the money, but failed.

Toledano then remembered that New York's Cardinal Spellman had prevailed upon the Sicilian-born Costello to contribute money to the Christian Democrats' campaign against the communists in Italy's 1948 election. Maybe Costello would aid another anticommunist venture. So he, Hess, and Burnham went to New York to sound out George Wolfe. More meetings followed, the last of which was interrupted by three of the "biggest, most sinister-looking goons" he had ever seen, Toledano recalled. "We come ta get da papers," the three growled, but they had obviously come to memorize the visitors' faces. Since Costello had gone so far as to take this precaution, the chances seemed good that he would help. But when Senator Kefauver's committee investigating organized crime held hearings in New York in 1951 and subpoenaed Costello, the mobster broke off contact with Burnham and friends. "James who? Ralph who? Karl who? Frank who?" Wolfe asked when Toledano phoned to confirm what he expected to be the meeting at which the deal would be clinched.

"The project was dead," Toledano later wrote, and Burnham never mentioned it again. What struck Toledano most about the affair was Burnham's "readiness to put his whole career on the line to accomplish an important task." "I believe, though I have no evidence," he added, "that there were other such episodes in his life—little hints in conversation which didn't quite light up a dark corner."[3]

Burnham's anticommunist zeal also led to his involvement in the 1951 investigation by Senator McCarran's Subcommittee on Internal Security to determine whether the Institute of Pacific Relations (IPR), a think tank founded to promote knowledge of the Far East, had abetted the communist seizure of power in China. To Burnham's delight, the inquiry also publicized an array of communist polwar tactics. The hearings would go down "as one of the great public inquiries in history," he wrote to Czapski. The committee's report, which Burnham helped draft, denied that the IPR had plotted to hand China over to the communists, but argued that it had been exploited by communists to aid the Chinese communist drive to power. The IPR had been "the most influential Communist front in this country," Burnham contended, because the great majority of its employees had had no idea that they were working in a front.[4]

Burnham set down his thoughts on the IPR case in an article called "How the IPR Helped Stalin Seize China," which had been commissioned by the liberal anticommunist magazine *Commentary,* but was instead published by the conservative *Freeman* after *Commentary* rejected the finished piece as too hard-line.[5] The IPR had been Moscow's "primary instrument" for keeping the United States from blocking the communist conquest of China, the article charged. IPR communists had skillfully used the organization to foster a pro-communist outlook, and thus mounted "a continuous and resolute conspiracy." While it would be "ridiculous" to claim that the communists had come to power in China because of the IPR, they probably could not have done so without it.

The core of the article, however, concerned the question of why the communist operation—"a political masterpiece"—had succeeded so well. One reason, Burnham claimed, was American ignorance of Pacific affairs. Americans were also "immensely ignorant" of communism. They were, indeed, "such babies in these matters, so immature, naive, and trusting, that most of them [would] not know how to recognize a pro-Soviet policy, organization, or action even when their noses [were] pushed into the middle of it." Still another reason was Western businessmen, who cared only about profits and expected a communist China to become a large-scale purchaser of Western goods. Finally, Americans were deeply influenced by "that jellyfish brand of contemporary liberalism—pious, guilt-ridden, do-goody—which uses the curious dogma of 'some truth on both sides' as its principal sales line," and "always [makes] a great show of 'anti-imperialism.'" "Ignorance, emptiness, ideological mildew, and greed," then, were communism's allies in its manipulation of the IPR. But since there had also been "a continuous and resolute conspiracy," merely to explain what had happened was not enough. Also necessary was moral condemnation, for it was "the occasional duty of a moral man to judge as well as to comprehend."[6]

◆　◆　◆　◆

At the time of the IPR hearings, the storm that had risen in the late 1940s over communist spying and subversion in the United States was approaching its zenith. At the center of the storm stood Wisconsin Republican Senator Joseph R. McCarthy, whose claim in a speech of February 1950 that he had in hand a long list of communists employed by the State Department had thrust him from obscurity into national prominence. Since then, armed by the Senate with investigative powers, McCarthy had gone on to dominate the headlines, mounting sensational searches for communists in federal agencies.

McCarthy's investigations deeply divided the American public. Some saw the senator as a national savior who was exposing communist infiltration of the federal government. Others regarded him as a mixture of good and evil who used nasty means to accomplish valuable ends. Still others, including most liberals and intellectuals, viewed him as a quasi-fascist demagogue, who, through red-baiting, innuendo, smear tactics, and "witch hunts," was seeking to intimidate "progressives" and stifle "dissent." By 1952 feelings about "McCarthyism" had become the key test applied by the anti-McCarthy majority of the intelligentsia to gauge moral and intellectual worthiness. Those who flunked the test were sentenced to ostracism.

Burnham viewed McCarthy with ambivalence. In March 1950, he wrote to Peter Ehlers, *Time*'s Russian expert, "It's hard not to get discouraged when you see a great opportunity to get some important facts on the record neglected through the blundering and worse of a man like McCarthy." Yet he also thought the senator might prove useful, noting in the same letter: "It looks from [McCarthy's] speech today as if he may have enough to prevent Lattimore [Owen Lattimore, a Far Eastern affairs specialist who was already under a political cloud, and whom the IPR hearings would label a communist] from being completely whitewashed by the press."[7]

As time passed, Burnham continued to criticize McCarthy. He bridled when the senator called James A. Wechsler (editor of the *New York Post* and a communist in his youth) before his committee in 1953, and proceeded to label Wechsler's claim to have turned against communism a trick to hide an enduring loyalty to Moscow. "By this kind of reasoning, no one could ever prove his loyalty," Burnham protested. "If you support Communist objectives, you are obviously a Communist; if you attack them, this is a deceptive maneuver, and you are still a Communist." McCarthy's charge must be rejected, for "that way lies madness."[8]

Yet he also criticized opponents of McCarthy. In a letter of 1954 to his friend Christopher Emmet, a fellow member of the ACCF, he spoke at length. "These are matters about which my mind is not altogether made up," he wrote.

But I am at any rate sure that I am an "anti-anti-McCarthyite"
[a play on "anti-anticommunist," i.e., one who did not profess
communism, yet opposed those actively hostile to commu-
nism]. . . . To put it in its simplest terms: I know that the anti-
McCarthy team is not my team. In my opinion those
anti-Communists who consider themselves to be anti-
McCarthyites have fallen into a trap. They have failed so far to
realize that they are, in political reality, in a united front with the
Communists, in the broadest, most imposing united front that
has ever been constructed in this country. As in all united fronts,
only the Communists can benefit from it. . . . It is conceivable,
and indeed unavoidable that I occasionally have the same position on a specific issue as the Communists. And, indeed, I have
had the same position on certain of McCarthy's specific acts,
with which I have disagreed and which I have condemned. But
"anti-McCarthyism" is not a specific issue or act. It is a "tendency," a "movement." I am an anti-Communist, and I cannot
join with Communists in any tendency or any movement, no
matter how innocuous or even proper it may seem from a "formal" point of view. In terms of the old-fashioned rhetoric: I am
on the other side of the barricade.

Politically, Burnham went on, anti-McCarthyism served as "a screen and cover for
the Communists and as a major diversion of anti-Communist efforts." Behind
that screen, communists were finding their way to respectability.[9]

He amplified his view of the McCarthy controversy in a letter to Hook revealing the sheer intensity of his anticommunism. "It does not seem to me obvious
to say, as you did, that McCarthy has been a disaster for anti-Communism," he
wrote.

I would consider it more accurate to say that the liberal
response to McCarthy and to what is called "McCarthyism" is
such a disaster. . . . Most of the charges against McC. seem to me
to be baby-talk. The one that I find serious (though seldom
made) is his "Caesarism"—his leap over the "intermediary insti-

tutions" to direct relation with the masses, and his accompanying denigration of the intermediary institutions. . . . [Caesarism] seems to me justified only if the leadership is extremely, indeed disastrously, bad and if the normal procedures can't get them out (if the system as well as the leadership are [*sic*] disastrously bad, then a full revolutionary solution is called for). I am inclined to think that these two conditions are present. The leadership seems to me literally suicidal. With respect to the world struggle (which is decisive), the entrenched leadership of both parties . . . —at least those sections of it that are in control of the apparatus and that function in the executive branch of the govt.—is virtually the same in ideology and in personal type (a not unimportant point). If so, the threat of the masses has to be brought against them more directly (at least by implication) than can be done by completely normal processes. (Incidentally, on questions of the Soviet Union and Communism I think that the masses have been more correct than the governing elite.) This, McC. has to some extent done, though so far within a very limited framework. For whatever personal reasons, McC. has expressed an attitude of *irreconcilability* toward Communism and Communists. The governing elite does not have such an attitude, and that is precisely why its leadership is suicidal.[10]

This position put Burnham in a bind. If it allowed him to reproach McCarthy for "specific acts," it forbade him to move from these *ad hoc* rebukes to a general condemnation of the senator, lest in doing so he play into the hands of the enemy. In practice, then, his anti-anti-McCarthyism boiled down to a defense of McCarthy against critics of all stripes, firm anticommunists included, with only mild disapproval of the mischief the senator did.

◆   ◆   ◆   ◆

Burnham first bloodied his sword in the McCarthy wars in the debate over the senator that broke out in the ACCF. From the dawn of the McCarthy era, some ACCF members (Arthur Schlesinger, for one) called upon the committee to condemn McCarthy as an unscrupulous demagogue and a menace to civil liberties. Others, such as Max Eastman, believed that communist infiltration and subversion, which they thought McCarthy was bringing to light, posed a far greater threat to freedom than the senator's tactics. Still others, such as William Phillips and *Commentary*'s editor, Elliot Cohen, at first tried to downplay the issue, fearing its disruptive potential for the ACCF.[11] But in vain. By 1952 ACCF meetings were riven by clashes over the issue. The passion McCarthy aroused was such that when anti-McCarthyites and anti-anti-McCarthyites squared off at an ACCF forum held in March 1952 at the Waldorf, Eastman set forth his position so heatedly that some of the liberals, otherwise great defenders of free expression, said he should not have been allowed to speak.[12]

Burnham entered the fray the day after the Waldorf battle, loosing a broadside in the *Washington Post* against the anti-McCarthyite faction. "The impressive thing about these intellectuals is their apparently tireless zeal; and sometimes it seems a bit unfair to let them bear the whole burden of saving civilization," he sarcastically commented, playing the ordinary citizen out of patience with self-important eggheads. "After all, they are so few, and the rest of us are so many! Perhaps it is time that we organized ourselves in Lowbrows for Liberty, or Fatheads for Freedom, or Dimwits for Democracy, or something of that sort."[13]

After the Waldorf fracas, the sociologist Daniel Bell, a frequent contributor to the *New Leader,* and Irving Kristol, then an editor at *Commentary,* tried to heal the breach, introducing at an executive committee meeting in April 1952 a resolution condemning McCarthyism and communism alike. Burnham rejected the resolution as a spurious show of evenhandedness. Rather than condemning all lying for political ends, he charged, it focused heavily on McCarthyism, and thus was divisive. "I am not for McCarthyism," he said. "I don't know what it means. I think it is a good thing that [McCarthy] forced some things out into the open."[14] The resolution ended up in limbo.

Burnham's growing estrangement from the ACCF was further evidenced by the tone of a verbal skirmish he had in October 1952 with a former ally, Schlesinger. The occasion was the 1952 presidential race. Burnham backed Republican nominee Dwight D. Eisenhower, though more by default than positive attraction,[15] for he considered Eisenhower's Democratic rival, Illinois governor Adlai E. Stevenson, impossible. Stevenson, he wrote in the *American Mercury* shortly before the election, belonged "by temperament" among those liberals who had created the ideological atmosphere in which "pro-Communist points of view and individual Communist agents have flourished." These were the people who had "furnished the intellectual props for Yalta, and . . . —without knowing what they did—made smooth the road" over which the communists had marched to victory in China. No one could doubt Stevenson's loyalty, he hastened to add. But given the governor's support for the Soviet spy Alger Hiss, it was impossible to say as much for his knowledge and judgment. For if "it was not a crime to have been a friend" of Hiss, it was "a grievous political sin to refuse to face today what Hiss, and the Hisses, signify."

In the same article, Burnham also fired several shots at Schlesinger, who was Stevenson's research director and a prominent member of Americans for Democratic Action (ADA)—a liberal lobby Burnham disparaged as "a pretentious outfit of nostalgic New Dealers looking for a new depression to save the country from, and specializing in anti-anti-Communism." Not only was Schlesinger an anti-anticommunist, Burnham claimed; his wife was the sister of China historian John K. Fairbank, whom the McCarran Committee had identified as a sometime party member.[16]

Schlesinger was taken aback. "Jim's piece is worse and more vindictive than I could have imagined," he wrote to Hook. "I cannot understand what has got into him; even his prose has become cheap in his current mood." Hook responded with a letter to the *American Mercury* describing Schlesinger as "one of the leading anti-Communists of our generation"—but he sent a copy to Burnham with the message, "If you think it ought not to be published, telephone me." Instead, Burnham fired off a letter of his own to the magazine accusing liberals of adhering to a double standard. "No smear thrown at those whom they classify as the Right produces even a twitch of their nostrils," he wrote. "But say so much as Boo to a brother of the vital left-of-center [a jab at Schlesinger, whose book *The Vital Center* was one of the key texts of liberal anticommunism] and they are apt to bleat like lambs at South Chicago."[17]

Schlesinger, in response to the *American Mercury,* denied that he was soft on communism, recalling that he had written a favorable review of *The Struggle for the World,* for which Burnham had been "grateful enough" at the time, and noting that his wife was Fairbank's sister-in-law, not sister. Unchastened, Burnham riposted in turn, rejecting Schlesinger's protest, but yielding on the question of Mrs. Schlesinger.[18] It was Schlesinger, however, who got in the last lick.

Reviewing *Containment or Liberation?* for the *New Republic* a few months later, he mauled the book as "a careless and hasty job, filled with confusion, contradiction, ignorance, and misrepresentation." It was "an absurd book written by an absurd man."[19]

Burnham and Schlesinger's quarrel augured ill for the ACCF's future. Kristol and other organizers of an ACCF forum on the question "Liberation or Containment?" in which Burnham and Schlesinger were to take part as panelists, feared that the committee might not survive the evening. It did, but splintered; it could not regain its unity. So deep was the rift that Burnham urged the executive committee to stop issuing policy statements on domestic issues in the name of the entire membership. It should confine itself to resolutions against communism and neutralism abroad, he said, subjects on which all members could still agree.[20]

◆  ◆  ◆  ◆

Burnham's anti-anti-McCarthyism also landed him in controversy at the CIA. Outwardly, his Washington career seemed to be thriving. He was now a well-established writer on the Cold War and, behind the scenes, a person of some consequence in the shadowy world of polwar. Many who worked with him thought him brilliant. When the CIA was preparing its 1953 operation to topple Iran's anti-Western premier, Mohammed Mossadegh, Kermit Roosevelt, who ran the CIA's Middle East Division, thought it wise to invite Burnham to participate in the planning. His presence, Roosevelt believed, would give the project "credibility."[21]

But as articles he published in early 1953 indicate, Burnham still found little to praise in U.S. foreign policy, which the change from Truman to Eisenhower did not seem to have improved. Stalin's death (in March 1953) left "a major vulnerability in the Soviet system," he argued. A power struggle would now break out among Stalin's would-be successors, handing Washington a golden opportunity for a grand-scale polwar offensive. "Why don't we free the anti-Communist prisoners in Korea [i.e., Chinese POWs hostile to Mao] tomorrow? Make clear the welcome that we will give a freed Albania? Speed the formation of exile military units? Help Chiang Kai-shek advance his schedule? Bring Moscow up on formal charges of genocide and aggression? Make the captive peoples know that

Stalin's death can be the preface to their freedom? Tell the Soviet subjects that we are with them, and against their Bolshevik tyrants whether they are called Stalin or Malenkov or Jones?" These things and more could be done, he insisted. But would they be?[22]

He did not have to wait long for an answer. The United States was slowly acquiring a political warfare doctrine, he noted in May 1953, but there was no sign yet "of any union between that doctrine and . . . practice."[23] Nor were his hopes for the new administration being met. "For a while, at the end of Truman's administration and the beginning of Eisenhower's the govt. *did* try to follow, in a half-hearted way, a watered down version" of the liberation strategy, he wrote some years later.[24] But Eisenhower was no bold spirit, and Secretary of State John Foster Dulles's actions suggested that for him "roll back" had been a mere campaign slogan. Meanwhile, Dulles's brother Allen, an old polwar fan whom Eisenhower had named to head the CIA, appeared to be having second thoughts about the strategy. Containment remained the order of the day and the non-communist Left the partner of choice. Moreover, Eisenhower's foreign policy appointments, such as career diplomat Charles Bohlen—to Burnham, an establishmentarian conformist—as U.S. envoy to the USSR, were anything but encouraging. Nor did the spread of bureaucracy in the CIA show any sign of abating.[25]

But if Burnham often complained about the CIA, some CIA officers complained with equal frequency about him. A number thought him "too" hard-line, and a few went so far as to label him a "fascist."[26] What especially galled them was his attitude toward McCarthy, which contrasted sharply with the anti-McCarthyism of the agency. ("Those wretched little people," one CIA officer is said to have called McCarthy Committee staffers, scorning them on grounds not only political but social.)[27]

Burnham's anti-anti-McCarthyism took on more ominous significance for the CIA in April 1953, when Allen Dulles received an inquiry from the McCarthy committee concerning CIA spending on foreign newspapers and radio broadcasts. Was the senator about to launch an attack on the agency, CIA people wondered, and if so, would he get inside help, for instance, from Burnham? Wisner issued an order forbidding all further contact with a man who now seemed a threat, and by the end of April Burnham's CIA career was over.[28] "The circumstance that gave a special importance to my continuing on formal leave has ceased to exist," Burnham wrote to NYU's Dean Pollock on May 1, "and we are, in fact, planning to leave Washington altogether in June."[29]

It is not clear whether Burnham left the CIA voluntarily or was pushed out, though the latter seems more likely. Still, given his exasperation with U.S. policy, the push, if there was one, may simply have hastened a departure already in the making. What is certain is that he resigned under a cloud.[30]

◆　◆　◆　◆

Upon leaving Washington, the Burnhams decided not to return to New York, but to live permanently in Kent. When the opportunity arose, they bought more land, extending their property into the adjacent forest. In the early sixties, using beams from an old barn, they built a second house, a one-story structure modeled on the farmhouses they had seen while traveling in Provence. A short walk up a gentle slope from the main house, the "mas" (Provençal for such a building) contained a big living room, a small pullman kitchen, a bedroom, and a bathroom. The Burnhams used the mas as a place for parties and putting up guests. That way, Burnham said, "we don't get in their hair, and they don't get in ours."[31]

Though the farmhouse exuded a homespun aura, Marcia gave it a touch of elegance, adding flowers and a versatile wine cellar. Her masterwork was a living room-study that took up the small ground floor and offered a fireplace, flagstone paving, and comfortable arm chairs. It also contained a windowed alcove, perhaps five feet deep, in which Burnham did his writing. As a desk he used a smoothly finished plank set into one side of the alcove at right angles to the window. Both alcove walls held built-in bookshelves, whose contents included, among other volumes, *The New Oxford Book of English Verse,* eighteenth-century editions of various Shakespeare comedies, a *Petite Larousse* and an Italian dictionary, the *Federalist Papers,* Burke's *Reflections on the Revolution in France,* Tocqueville's *Democracy in America,* Adam Smith's *Wealth of Nations,* the *Ploetz Manual of Universal History,* and a one-volume *Basic Works of Aristotle.* Descending to the living room-study after breakfast, Burnham would work through the morning, stop at midday for a sandwich, and then go back to work. When finished, he would spend some time outdoors. Next would come drinks with Marcia in the living room-study, then the evening news on television, and finally dinner.[32]

The Burnhams went about accompanied by music. Burnham was elated when an aerial he raised on the roof of the house managed to pull in a classical music station from Schenectady, New York. Opera fans, the Burnhams always bought season tickets to the New York Metropolitan. Marcia loved Wagner, above all *Parsifal,* though she was also partial to Mozart and Verdi. Burnham's taste extended far and wide, though he disliked what he called "the dreary symphonies" of Shostakovitch and Prokofiev.[33]

Both Burnhams, family members agree, were "disciplined," never idling.[34] A passionate gardener, Marcia planted masses of flowers at the edge of the lawn skirting the house and the mas, often enlisting her husband's help. Burnham, who enjoyed this kind of work, also did other outdoor chores, chopping wood, pruning trees, removing fallen branches from the woodland paths he liked to walk with his dog, and tapping his sugar maples to make syrup. Indoors, he practiced the art of baking, at which he came to excel. A specialist in breads, he would go through phases, concentrating for a time on French sourdough, suddenly switching to raisin bread, and then just as abruptly to still another kind.[35]

Though Burnham kept trim, he relished a good meal, and as a frequent tablemate put it, "liked to do it all up right," from soup to nuts. If his preferences in cooking ran to French and Italian fare, the range of his tastes was broad. It was rumored, however, that he leaned toward opulent settings. "Last time [Burnham] talked to a hot dog vendor was at a four-star restaurant in Hamburg," one friend joked. "The vendor was in white tie and the hot dog cost $25." Marcia could turn out a first-class meal herself (though she often had her husband do the baking). One guest dined on venison she had dressed and roasted, the meat coming from a deer shot by a neighbor. Another was served a cut from a steer the Burnhams had had butchered. "Did I tell you that our steer (Hyssop) has turned into the best beef, in almost all cuts, that we can remember?" Burnham happily informed a friend.[36]

Marcia did not immerse herself in domesticity, however, but a few years after settling in Kent opened a real estate agency. (Friends said she did so to bring "the right people" to the area.) It was an opportune moment. In the 1960s, the northwest Connecticut real estate market began to boom, and soon hordes of urbanites in search of country retreats—pianist Vladimir Horowitz and novelists Francine du Plessix Gray and Philip Roth, among others—were beating a path to her door.[37]

Still brimming with energy, in the 1970s Marcia began a second business, breeding Norwich terriers. Burnham at the time had a German Shepherd, a brawny creature named Lucy, who made a striking contrast with the almost toy-like terriers. One day a customer who had been admiring Lucy asked him if she were for sale. "Oh, no," said Burnham. "She's an employee here."[38]

◆　◆　◆　◆

Having left the CIA, Burnham could dispose of his time as he wished. Hook, dangling a course on Aristotle as bait, tried to lure him back to NYU. Burnham thought about teaching a one-term course, but in the end told Hook that commuting from Kent would be too tiring.[39] Still he could not live buried in the Connecticut countryside, passively watching the struggle for the world from the sidelines. So he went on with his writing and lecturing. In July 1953, he spoke before Henry Kissinger's International Seminar at Harvard, and that fall he assembled and wrote an introduction to a book of essays by Aron, Czapski, and other European friends called *What Europe Thinks of America*. There he again struck the apocalyptic note he had sounded in *The Struggle for the World,* painting a fearsome picture of the West under future siege by Soviet-led, non-Western countries, and argued that the United States needed a healthy Europe to ensure its own survival.[40]

Meanwhile, his anti-anti-McCarthyism led readers of *Partisan Review* to protest the presence of the "McCarthyite" Burnham on the editorial advisory board, and the editors asked him to resign. In September 1953 he did so. "I do not regard myself as either 'pro-McCarthy' or 'anti-McCarthy,'" he said in his letter of resignation. "I approve many things that McCarthy has done, and certain of his 'methods'; I disapprove some of his actions, and a number of his methods.... But 'McCarthyism' is not McCarthy. I believe 'McCarthyism' to be an invention of the Communist tacticians, who launched it and are exploiting it, exactly as they have done in the case of a dozen of their previous operations in what might be called *diversionary semantics.*"[41]

But even as he ended his long association with *PR,* he found himself in a new uproar, sparked by the introduction he had written to a book called *The Secret War for the A-Bomb.* The author of this work, a former professor of English named Medford Evans, had left academic life in 1945 for a job at the Atomic Energy Commission's installation at Oak Ridge, Tennessee, where in 1951 he was made

"Chief of Training," including security training. But he resigned in 1952, upset that none of his proposals for improving security had been adopted. In the fall of 1953 he published his book, which accused scientists in the U.S. atomic energy program of spying for the USSR and delivering fissionable material to Soviet agents. In his introduction, Burnham roundly endorsed Evans's charges and added a thought of his own. The record showed that "vulnerability" to communism was "especially widespread among the college-educated intellectual 'élite' from which the 'opinion molders,' the writers, editors, preachers, university professors, scientists, and upper government employees are drawn," he asserted. But the most vulnerable of all were physicists, who seemed to have "a peculiar affinity" for communism. Why didn't "prominent physicists like, say, Harold Urey or J. Robert Oppenheimer, tell what they [knew] about what went on in the atomic energy project, about such things as Medford Evans writes about in this book?"[42]

Many liberals reacted to *The Secret War for the A-Bomb* with indignation. Reviewing the book for the *Bulletin of the Atomic Scientists,* the University of Chicago sociologist Edward A. Shils complained that Evans had furnished no proof for his charges, but was simply conveying "delusions of conspiracy." As for the book's introduction, Shils went on, Burnham was peddling "an intellectually and morally irresponsible phantasy" that stood "firmly in a one-hundred-and-fifty-year old tradition of political paranoia and disruption."[43]

The *Bulletin's* editor-in-chief, Eugene Rabinowitch, who had once worked at the Atomic Energy Commission and was currently a member of the ACCF executive committee, went further. Describing the book to ACCF executive director Sol Stein as "pathological and slanderous abracadabra—on the same level of truth with the Protocols of the Wise Men of Zion," he threatened to resign from the committee unless it "disassociate[d] itself from Mr. Burnham." This put the ACCF in a difficult position, Daniel Bell told Hook. "PR, as you know, asked Bunham [*sic*] to resign. . . . It would be fanning the flames for us now to step in and ask Burnham to go; it would only polarize the situation. My approach would be to write to Rabinowitch and tell him, which is true, that Burnham is inactive [as a committee member], that his position has a term turn, and that we don't want to seek purges. . . ."[44]

Told by Stein that Rabinowitch was demanding his scalp, Burnham counterattacked. Rabinowitch seemed to want "a spot of book burning," he replied to Stein. But the real issue for the executive committee should be, "*What accounts for the total boycott of Medford Evans's book by the leading book review media?"* And before issuing "false and presumptively libellous statements concerning Medford Evans, why not bring him into the act? He would seem to be a party in interest."[45]

Four days later the executive committee took up the Rabinowitch ultimatum. Burnham, it seemed, had few supporters. Bell thought him guilty of the "inverted Leninism of looking at the 'objective' consequences" of the actions of the atomic scientists Evans had attacked rather than at the intentions behind those actions. Harvard sociologist David Riesman, writing to Stein about the case, deplored "the kind of hysterical production Mr. Burnham has recently been indulging in." Nathan Glazer, also a sociologist, believed, according to Reisman, that "'though any summary of what [Evans] says makes him look like a madman or a fanatic, he is neither—indeed, he is more sensible than Burnham." At a recent executive committee meeting, Stein told Riesman, the majority had agreed with Glazer's view. Having read the Evans book himself, he went on, he found Rabinowitch's accusations "defensive, rash, unwarranted, and possibly libellous." Still, the committee would "probably give serious consideration to the broader implications of the present controversy: the position of Burnham and his friends in American intellectual life." In the end, the executive committee rejected Rabinowitch's demand for Burnham's excommunication. At the same time, Hook later commented, hardly anyone present had shared the opinions of Burnham.[46]

◆　◆　◆　◆

Never one to back away from a fight, Burnham now published a book of his own on communist spying and subversion. In the summer of 1953, Peter Palmer of *Reader's Digest* proposed that he write a book about the communist penetration of U.S. government agencies. Although he had already contracted with the John Day Co. to author a more general study of communism, Burnham put that project aside in favor of Palmer's. "The idea is to . . . tell a clear and readable story, with a minimum of abstract discussion," he told John Day's Richard J. Walsh. "I have tentatively taken the title *The Web of Treason*. Politically, I hope to show that the basic culprit in this whole business is not this or that American citizen or official, but the conspiracy centered in the Kremlin." Burnham also explained his aim to the McCarran Committee's research director, Ben Mandel. The book offered a "terrific opportunity to communicate the story on a big scale," he said, "and also to present the investigating committees in a new and very favorable light."[47]

Based in large part on testimony given at hearings of the McCarran Committee, the McCarthy Committee, and the House Un-American Activities Committee, Burnham's book served as a supplement to his Cold War trilogy, whose focus it narrowed to Soviet-communist infiltration in Washington. The book's authorship, he intimated, was in a sense dual, for as his acknowledgments indicate, Marcia helped greatly with the task of analyzing and summarizing vast amounts of committee testimony. During the drafting, Burnham dropped the original title—*The Web of Treason*—as too close to Toledano and Lasky's recently published *Seeds of Treason,* and the book came out in 1954 as *The Web of Subversion: Underground Networks in the U.S. Government.*[48]

In the 1930s and 1940s, the book began, "an invisible web" was spun over the federal government. Woven by the Moscow-directed communist movement for the purpose of spying and subversion, the web had by now spread to "nearly every executive department and agency," including the Pentagon and the White House, but also to many congressional committees. He was writing not for the sake of making accusations, Burnham added, probably anticipating charges of McCarthy-style "witch-hunting," but simply to lay out the evidence for the web's existence. He would not impute "legal guilt" to anyone cited as an agent of the web unless that person had been formally convicted in court.[49]

The bulk of the book consisted of summary accounts, taken mostly from the transcripts of congressional investigations, of the careers of a few dozen federal civil servants working in the Treasury Department, the State Department, the White House, the armed forces (which the book claimed had been "heavily penetrated" by the web),[50] and other government agencies who had been identified under oath as communists. Not all who had "collaborated" with the web, including even some who had taken the Fifth Amendment before congressional committees, understood the consequences of their actions, Burnham allowed, and so "were not consciously disloyal, much less outright traitors." Still, they had given aid to the communist cause, however unwittingly, and as long as they refused to testify, continued to aid it.[51]

The web did not always accomplish its aims, he conceded. It had been unable, for example, to block U.S. intervention against the communists in the Greek civil war and in Korea. Moreover, despite its efforts to conceal itself, sections of it had been brought to light and eliminated. All the same, though the United States could "survive even colossal mistakes,"[52] some of its interests had been seriously harmed by the web.

To this day, the web remained difficult to penetrate because of "its sly use of our genuine concern for civil liberties," which it had made into "a protective shield for its own treachery." Moreover, if steps to rend the web had enjoyed some success, several of its strands were still in place and might be expanding. "From the fact that fishermen have caught a good many fish in it, you don't conclude that a lake is empty," Burnham noted, borrowing a metaphor from Medford Evans.[53]

How, then, could surviving web strands be uncovered? To begin with, the law should be made equal to the task. For example, the statute of limitations on the kinds of crimes committed by web agents should be extended, and legal categories such as "political conspiracy" and "subversion" be more clearly defined. In addition, federal courts should admit evidence obtained through wiretaps, Fifth Amendment protections should be interpreted less generously, and witnesses who took the Fifth should be denied government jobs.[54]

At the same time, public awareness of the web had to be increased, a necessity that made congressional investigations "indispensable." In addition, anticommunist feeling had to be fostered, especially since some prominent people appeared to be less hostile to the web than to those who exposed it. Some even thought it obligatory for persons wanting to be identified as liberals to denounce attempts to uncover the web as "witch hunting" and "hysteria," and to revile persons who cooperated with congressional committees as "paid informers," "renegades," "reactionaries," and "stool pigeons." But ultimately, victory over the web would demand "*resolution*": the United States would have to possess "the will to survive and to be free."[55]

◆　◆　◆　◆

With the exception of his *Introduction to Philosophical Analysis, The Web of Subversion* was Burnham's most low-keyed book. Absent were the ironic jabs, apocalyptical forecasts, historical threnodies, and moments of chill detachment that had marked his earlier works. With its subdued, expository treatment of a passion-provoking subject, it was a book hard to accuse of being McCarthy-like.

Many critics reviewed the book favorably. *Newsweek* thought it "impressive," and called Burnham "a balanced, detailed, compelling student of the Red Menace." The *Chicago Tribune* pronounced its message "appalling" but "convincing," and praised Burnham as "an outstanding scholar in the field of subversive trends." The *New York Times* paid it only brief notice, but commented that Burnham had done his work "ably and carefully" and come to "more moderate and reasonable" conclusions than those of some congressional committees. (The *Times* later included the book on a list of twenty-four "outstanding" nonfiction works of 1954.)[56]

But liberal critics mostly disliked the book. Schlesinger, writing in the *Saturday Review,* conceded that there had been Soviet spies in Washington under Democratic administrations, but argued that Burnham had erred in treating all charges of infiltration as equally serious. What was more, the highly partisan Schlesinger claimed, the book left no doubt that if the federal government had a security problem, the fault did not lie exclusively with liberal Democrats, nor the solution with conservative Republicans. Liberal anticommunist Robert Gorham Davis, professor of English at Smith College and in 1954 chairman of the ACCF, reproached Burnham in the *New Leader* for not showing the committment to civil liberties he had shown in *The Machiavellians* and for blowing the domestic communist danger out of proportion. In addition, Burnham failed to see that politically inspired anticommunist exaggeration might hamper efforts to cope with communism "on a world scale." But worst of all, Davis charged, he came "very close" to equating "wrong hypotheses with objective disloyalty."[57]

◆　◆　◆　◆

When the first reviews of *The Web of Subversion* appeared, Burnham was not on hand to read them, for in January 1954, the Burnham family set off on a five-month trip to Europe. Their first stop was Spain, where they rented a small villa in the mountain hamlet of Alcalà de las Gazules, ten miles outside Málaga. Spain had its drawbacks, Burnham noted. Its romance was "linked, perhaps inseparably, to what is from an economic and social standpoint backward and underdeveloped." At the Alcalà villa, "everything mechanical, from doors to plumbing to lamps, cheerfully fail[ed] to work." The only events that began on time were bullfights. "Inefficiency, laziness, bureaucracy, and corruption" were rife. But the country offered sights, such as Seville's Alcazar and Granada's Alhambra, that left him "enraptured." Moreover, thanks to the recent treaty between Washington and Madrid allowing U.S. air bases in Spain, good will toward the United States was growing, "a pleasant and unusual experience" for Americans in an anti-American time.[58]

"I was fascinated by Spain," Burnham told the conservative publisher Henry Regnery, who wanted him to write at length on the country, "and I would like to put my experiences there . . . into a book." But he never did.[59]

When spring came, the Burnhams left Spain and meandered by car through France, Germany, Switzerland, and Italy. Though the route they followed took them to regular tourist stops, they spent much of their time off the beaten track. Often their meals were simple picnics on the road: freshly baked bread, local cheeses and wine—though the Burnham boys happily discovered a cafe in France that served hamburgers. To Burnham's delight, people everywhere received them hospitably. Anti-American feeling seemed confined to intellectuals. But he was upset also to find a casual acceptance of communism. The French did not seem to think it scandalous that as their Indochinese bastion Dienbienphu fell to the Soviet-backed Viet Minh rebels, the Comédie Française, without a qualm, performed in Moscow. "No one is surprised or shocked or alarmed," he lamented, "no one, at any rate, whose voice can be loudly or widely heard. This was the mood, perhaps, in Athens, which, after the harsh times with Sparta and Thebes and Macedon and the marauding legions, transformed itself into a passive museum and pleasure-house for the tourists, bureaucrats, and idlers of all-conquering imperial Rome."[60]

But then in May, while in Italy, Marcia came down with infectious hepatitis, and back in Kent the disease not only drained her strength, but also taxed her emotionally. She "had never really been ill before," Burnham told Eastman, "and it was a grim psychological as well as physical experience." It was not until early 1955 that she recovered completely.[61]

◆　◆　◆　◆

In 1954, the controversy surrounding McCarthy's investigations reached its peak. All the while, tension within the ACCF continued to worsen, causing Burnham ever greater dismay. "It would be good to give more discussion to the problem of disunity among anti-communists and less to McCarthy," he remarked to Hook in July 1954.[62] In September 1954, his hopes for the ACCF finally exhausted, Burnham left the committee. He was resigning, he told its chairman, Robert Gorham Davis, "because of my conviction that over the past year and a half the Committee has developed into a narrow and partisan clique" ("an anti-anti-Communist clique," he specified to Regnery). He should have resigned after the 1952 election, he said in a letter to Eastman, "but I stayed because of certain international connections [i.e., his OPC/CCF ties]. You, George [Schuyler, the newspaperman, who left the ACCF when Burnham did], I and a few others have been doing nothing except disguise the fact that the Committee has become just one more phony anti-anti-Communist front. What is needed is a plain, straightforward Anti-Communist League, just that, without ideological decoration." In another letter to Eastman, he added a word on the fault line running through the ACCF. "It may be that the basis of that Committee was false from the beginning, and that you cannot mix pro-statist and anti-statist persons on any project," he mused. Anti-McCarthyism and support for the New Deal, though they seemed logically unrelated, might actually spring from a common root. "Has it struck you that all the intellectuals who were pro-McCarthy or even merely anti-anti-McCarthy were anti-statist? This is especially interesting because of the fact that no statist problem was directly or overtly involved."[63]

By late 1954, McCarthy's days were numbered. For many Republicans, his usefulness as a stick for beating Democrats had ended, and his investigations now promised to do the GOP more harm than good. Moreover, he had publicly criticized Eisenhower. Hence, in the fall of 1954, the GOP-controlled Senate took steps to censure him, a move that led Burnham and such pro-McCarthy authors and journalists as Eugene Lyons, Frank Hanighen, George Schuyler, Freda Utley, John T. Flynn, and William F. Buckley Jr. to protest in a collective letter to the *New York Times* that censure would benefit only the communist enemy.[64]

But Burnham was also concerned with the broader issue of the legitimacy of congressional inquiry as such. Upset that Congress was considering procedural changes that he feared would hamper future congressional investigations, he drew up a brief defending such probes as both lawful and necessary. "Tribunes of the People," which appeared in the *Freeman* and in condensed form in the *Reader's Digest,* granted that McCarthy and McCarran had committed "excesses" and so had "sometimes deserved" criticism. (There was also a less savory motive for the campaign against the committees, Burnham told Regnery. "Looked at historically," the attacks formed "part of the preparation—foreshadowed by the McCarthy censure—for a really super-Munich," a huge act of appeasement of the USSR.) But despite their excesses, the article went on, the committees made it possible "at last . . . to deal effectively with the subversive conspiracy against our survival as a free nation." And the committees also bolstered freedom in another way. As agents of an independent legislature, they could "challenge without fear of reprisal the immense power of the police, the Army, and the Executive."[65]

In November 1954 the Senate censured McCarthy, and his star quickly dimmed. In April 1957, his health shattered and his drinking out of control, he checked into Bethesda Naval Hospital and there four days later he died. The time had come to plumb the inner meaning of the controversy surrounding him. At the heart of the uproar, Burnham wrote, lay a conflict over national self-definition that pitted the country's liberal elite against the mass of its citizens. In some charismatic way that cannot be explained by his own often inept acts and ignorant words,

> McCarthy became the symbol through which the the basic strata of the citizens expressed their conviction—felt more than reasoned—that Communism and Communists cannot be part of our national community, that they are beyond the boundaries: that, in short, the line must be drawn somewhere. This was really at issue in the whole McCarthy business, not how many card-carrying members were in the State Department or whether Jimmy Wechsler had been, was or might be a fellow-traveler. The issue was philosophical, metaphysical: what kind of community are we? And the Liberals, including the anti-Communist Liberals, were correct in labeling McCarthy the Enemy, and in destroying him. From the Liberal standpoint— secularist, egalitarian, relativist—the line is not drawn. Relativism must be Absolute.[66]

By this time, Burnham himself had become a casualty of the McCarthy wars. Since his days as coeditor of the *Symposium,* he had been a figure of note on the New York intellectual scene. But in the mid-1950s, he was expelled from his old stamping ground. *PR* had sent him off "into the snow for whoring with McCarthy," he joked in a letter of 1954 to Phillips and Rahv.[67] But this quip summed up his larger fate. After the mid-1950s, as the philosopher William Barrett, a colleague of Burnham's at NYU, later noted, though Burnham still occupied "a solid and respected place" among American thinkers, that place was to be found in "a certain conservative sector of American opinion," and "was not the place that his own impressive gifts might have brought him if the intellectual climate in America and especially in its politics, had been different." Philip Rahv put the matter succinctly. "The Liberals now dominate all the cultural channels in this country," he said. "If you break completely with this dominant atmosphere, you're a dead duck. James Burnham has committed suicide."[68]

ACCF member and *PR* contributor Diana Trilling spoke of this anathema. One day in the mid-'50s, she and her husband, the critic Lionel Trilling, ran into the Burnhams in a Madison Avenue shoe store. The two couples chatted amiably for a few minutes, and as they were about to part, Marcia "asked in what I thought was a most wistful voice whether [the Trillings] would be willing to come out to visit them in Connecticut. Her tone and her use of the word 'willing' made me very unhappy for her. They were being ostracized by Burnham's old friends and university associates."[69]

But if Marcia was upset by this fate, the victim himself showed no sign of distress. "I never heard him express the slightest bitterness about [it]," said *National Reviewer* editor Joseph Sobran. "He'd known what he was dealing with—History, on a certain scale—and I don't think he took it personally."[70]

Two decades later, Burnham explained to Brian Crozier, who was puzzled to see that the London Library had no books of Burnham's published after 1953, what he thought was the reason. In the United States, Burnham said,

> the "McCarthy period" saw the rise to cultural predominance
> of "the non-Communist left," which soon became "anti-anti-
> Communist." This formation was a soft target for well directed
> pressures from the Communist world apparatus, and for infiltra-
> tion. There were parallel developments in the cultural-commu-
> nications fields in most other non-Communist nations, in
> particular in Western Europe. In almost all the countries,
> uncompromisingly anti-Communist writers, no matter what

the intellectual and aesthetic level of their work, lost resonance. Genuine dialogue became impossible, because there was a contradiction between certain of the axioms and basic attitudes operating on each side. Since the non-Communist/anti-anti-Communist Left prevailed, and still prevails, writings in which anti-Communism was an element, even a very minor element, seemed irrelevant at best, and, often, eccentric and kooky (as, of course, some of them were).[71]

◆   ◆   ◆   ◆

Where exactly did Burnham now stand on the political spectrum? His anticommunism by itself did not suffice to define his position, for anticommunists could be found on the Left as well as the Right. After the war, he had still considered himself a man of the Left, he told the historian George H. Nash in 1972, though, of course, of the anticommunist Left. Talking with William Barrett in 1948, he had approvingly quoted a remark of Malraux's: "The Communists are not of the Left, and when they attack me, they do not establish me on the Right." He gave Barrett the impression that he wanted to find a new political stance, one beyond the conventional categories of Left and Right (the second of which may have implied for him a cramped and carping attitude toward modernity).[72] Yet in some ways Burnham clearly stood close to conservatism. His abiding Augustinian sense of the world's incurable imperfection, which made liberal optimism and reformism seem sentimental and futile, by itself logically pointed to a conservative political outlook.

In the 1940s the distance between Burnham and conservatism narrowed. To what had once been little more than a general worldview with conservative implications he now added fully formed ideas of conservative stamp, notably the "political science" of the Machiavellians. By 1953 he was identified closely enough with the Right for Russell Kirk, America's leading expositor of Edmund Burke, to ask his publisher, Regnery, to send Burnham a copy of Kirk's just-published book *The Conservative Mind*. What Burnham thought of the book he did not record, but two years later he gave Kirk's new book *A Program for Conservatives* a favorable review (though noting that it sometimes succumbed to "an agrarian sort of crankiness"). Kirk was trying to rescue conservatism, he commented, both from "sterile reactionaries" and from "verbalists who, paying out a few modish conservative phrases, are . . . trying to hitch a ride on the shifting Zeitgeist." Kirk's target was "secular, humanitarian progressivism, the current—paradoxical— variety of centralizing 'liberalism,' as we usually call it."[73]

Somewhat incongruously, for he too was a secular, if not a liberal, thinker, Burnham might now sometimes sound like an upholder of religion. In 1956, reading that paleontologists had unearthed the remains of an apparently human creature who lived ten million years ago but did not reveal any ape-like charac- teristics, he gleefully asked: "What is going to happen to the Progressive Story of Creation if we have no apes in our family tree, and the schools have to go back to the long outmoded doctrine that men are human?"[74] (Still, he seems to have been pleased by the discovery not because it supported the biblical account of man's origins, but because it might jar liberal intellectual complacency.)

But Burnham could also veer toward a quasi-anarchist libertarianism. In a 1955 article called "No Firecrackers Allowed," he waxed nostalgic about the Fourth of July celebrations of his youth and assailed Connecticut's ban on the private possession of fireworks, which he called "symbolic of the erosion of indi- vidual liberties today." From this minor example of government intrusiveness, he went on to decry the "leviathan state's" innumerable curbs on freedom, such as the need for visas and passports for travel; the withholding of Social Security taxes from paychecks; the invasive behavior of the Internal Revenue Service; the fed- eral power to conscript (the draft might be needed for national security, but it was "a long detour from liberty"); the licensing requirements for lawyers, barbers, physicians, pharmacists, dentists, and saloon keepers; the ban on private stills; the obligation to take cover during air raid drills, which coerced people who might rather "take their chances with bombs"; and the inability of employers to hire whomever they wanted and of job-seekers to pursue opportunity freely. Some of these laws might be "for our own good," he conceded, or at least "unavoidable" in a world of "mass industry, swollen population and international tension." Yet they did reduce freedom. But what bothered him most was the public's docile submission to such restrictions. This was libertarianism *à outrance*. Talking about the article years later, a friend of Burnham's said it sounded as if it had been writ- ten by "a kook."[75]

Burnham was not content simply to denounce the state, however; he put his libertarian impulse into action. Determined to frustrate the overweening IRS, he did zestful—and often successful—battle with the tax collectors. He also applauded a proposal that people told by a government agency to identify themselves by some sort of number should misplace a digit in order to derail the system.[76]

Yet if Burnham had become a man of the Right, he stood apart in many ways from garden-variety conservatives. For one thing, he was a literary intellectual, and thus not typical of mid-twentieth-century American conservative thinkers, who ran more to laissez-faire economic theorists and rather prim cultural traditionalists, not to mention hard-line anticommunists. In addition to editing a literary-philosophical quarterly and a leading Marxist theoretical journal, he had served as an advisor to Trotsky; enjoyed a long association with that flagship of cultural modernism, *Partisan Review;* published articles on writers such as Franz Kafka; pondered the fate of the West with Koestler and Malraux; lectured fluently on painters from Giotto to Klee; written admiringly of Picasso (of whom he once said in a Nietzschean turn of phrase, "Supermen are more dangerous than H-bombs") despite the artist's arch-modernism and fellow-traveling; and helped found the largely liberal Congress for Cultural Freedom. Such credentials—cosmopolitan and high-brow—made him only slightly less extraordinary among 1950s conservatives than his candle-lit, black-tie dinners had among 1930s Trotskyists.[77]

Moreover, he wrote scathingly of American business, and seemed much better disposed toward organized labor (or at least union hard-liners on communism). And he did not champion the creed of *laissez-faire,* which he treated as simply another ideology and therefore as rooted at least partly in wishful thinking.[78] In any case, he did not think economic ideas counted for much. "In our day major economic problems are not solved by economic means," he wrote in 1948, sounding more like Georges Sorel than Adam Smith. "The economic measures instituted by Roosevelt when he took office in 1933 did not greatly differ from those of Hoover, and many of them were ridiculous from a narrowly economic point of view. It was the dynamic and integrating myth of Roosevelt and his New Deal that swept the nation out of the depression."[79] Finally, he not only did not express the usual conservative hostility to public ownership, but even defended that symbol of the New Deal and bugbear of the Right, the federally run TVA.[80]

Nor did he oppose social insurance measures. "In a huge, population-swelled, technologized society, is it really *possible* to handle the problems of old age, illness, etc. by individual savings, individual charity, etc.?" he asked in 1957. "I am anti-Communist and anti-Soviet: and since I am 100% both, I guess I am Extreme in that dimension," he summed up his views to Brian Crozier in 1976. "But on social and economic questions . . . I have a general *presumption* in favor of freedom, which I take to mean pluralist democracy in politics and the market in economics, but I don't regard this presumption as an absolute."[81]

But most important, he diverged from typical American conservatives of the 1950s in his intellectual method and assumptions. His thinking was firmly secular, and he arrived at his ideas through induction from observed fact rather than deduction from religious and moral first principles. "James Burnham was a utilitarian, really, . . . a modernist," the traditionalist conservative Russell Kirk once wrote. "I gather you can't accept a Supreme Being or supernatural force: the Christian tradition," the writer F. Reid Buckley once said to Burnham. "NR [the conservative journal *National Review*, at which Burnham by that time was working as an editor] has always been a dichotomy, with Bill [i.e., William F. Buckley Jr., *National Review*'s editor-in-chief and a practicing Catholic] on one side [and] you on the other. . . ."[82] Moreover, he continued to count irrational drives as a primary source of political belief. "Political man, Aristotle or no Aristotle, is seldom a rational animal," he wrote in 1977, still true to Pareto and Sorel. "Confronting a political issue, most of us try to present our point of view with a respectable overlay of rational-sounding rhetoric, but you can still hear the drumbeats throbbing underneath."[83] The drumbeats were certainly audible in his own case: his views often seemed to stem as much from his emotions and temperament as from empirical reasoning, though he explained them as derived from his observation of what was happening in the world. But his acknowledgment of the influence of the irrational found little echo among American conservatives, who disapproved of outlooks they regarded as tainted by "determinism."

Yet if Burnham stood apart from the conservatism of the 1950s, he foreshadowed a brand of conservatism that would appear a generation later. For despite differences on particular issues, his general stance—secular, empirical, modernist, resigned to the welfare state as inevitable in a mass industrial society, emphatic on the need for victory in the struggle for the world—afforded a preview of the neoconservatism of the 1970s.[84]

◆    ◆    ◆    ◆

"In every country of the world," Burnham wrote in *The Coming Defeat of Communism,* "there ought to be at least one newspaper, magazine, and publishing house defending the point of view of the world anti-communist offensive. Where such do not exist they ought to be created." Asked in 1953 by Kevin Corrigan of Regnery Publishing what he believed to be the most pressing anticommunist need of the moment, he answered, "A magazine," preferably one that, like the *New Republic* and the *Nation* in the 1930s, would be read by "opinion-makers all over the country every week."[85]

In the early 1950s, the main conservative journal was the *Freeman,* in which most of Burnham's articles now appeared. But unlike the *New Republic* and the *Nation,* the biweekly *Freeman* rarely reported and commented on immediately current news. Moreover, besides publishing hard-line anticommunists, it also gave much space to writers such as Frank Chodorov and Henry Hazlitt, whose passion was not anticommunism but the free market—in Burnham's view a far less urgent matter. Hence, the *Freeman* was not the kind of journal he had in mind when he spoke with Corrigan. Nor was the more newspaper-like, Washington-oriented *Human Events,* which, while anticommunist and conservative, and concerned with matters of the moment, usually bypassed topics of broader sweep.

Burnham was not alone in wanting a "hard" anticommunist magazine. Max Eastman shared his wish, and proposing that Burnham join him, briefly pondered starting such a journal. Also interested was Henry Regnery. In the spring of 1953 Regnery wrote to Burnham about publishing a magazine that would defend not only hard-line anticommunism, but also a more comprehensive conservative outlook. In addition, Regnery wanted to launch a conservative book club. Burnham approved. "In my own mind, the central problem can perhaps be defined as that of creating a new literate audience," he wrote to Regnery with an eye to the practical business of shaping opinion. "This is a long process and requires many different measures.... [T]he development of a magazine, or rather several related magazines on different planes, seems to me the most important and key task. A book club, even if quite modest to begin with, is also part of what ought to be done. If it can be worked out, I should be glad to join the board of editorial advisers or whatever they would be called." He also agreed with Regnery that such an effort should be more than "simply 'anti-Communist,'" he added, for he thought that something larger than the defeat of communism, as crucial as that was, had to be achieved. Fighting communism, after all, was "only part of the more general problem [i.e., how to end the liberal ascendancy], and it would surely be a mistake to conceive the shift to a new cultural perspective within a narrow anti-Communist frame."[86]

In June 1954 the magazine problem worsened. The *Freeman* was sold to the libertarian Foundation for Economic Education, which would use it to uphold radical laissez-faire economics and an isolationist foreign policy—the latter, to Burnham, a sure "disaster." The *Freeman* would become a magazine "of an abstract kind, with little relation to current affairs," he wrote to Regnery, and since there was nothing to take its place, "a complete vacuum in the active 'public opinion' field [will] now exist." A new conservative, anticommunist journal simply had to be launched, for which reason he was going to talk with some people in New York. They would study the possibility of continuing the *Freeman* under another name. "Right now the organization, audience, and writers exist to keep going, if something is done immediately. Within a few months, this will be dissipated, and one will have to start again from nothing." He would be happy to edit a new magazine himself, he wrote to Hook in August 1954. "[B]ut it takes more than the wish to get one. In fact, it takes a lot of money these days. And as to whether one can do any public thing 'solo' I have grown skeptical. The world seems to be so constructed that it is difficult to have one's own way. And others, most benightedly, seem to have their own notions about how things ought to be done."[87]

But as Burnham worried, a possible solution suddenly came into view. The young conservative journalist William F. Buckley Jr. was seriously thinking about starting a political weekly, Regnery wrote to him on August 3. "I urged him to talk to you about it." Buckley must have acted at once on this advice, for a week later Burnham was able to write back to Regnery, "I have heard from Bill Buckley about the magazine, and am going to talk to him about it tomorrow."[88] Though Burnham did not know it, a new and major stage in his life was about to begin.

# Chapter 9

# Mentor

WILLIAM F. BUCKLEY JR., a boyish-looking twenty-eight-year-old in 1954, was one of ten children. His family roots lay in the South, his mother coming from New Orleans, and his father, a self-made oil tycoon, from Texas. The Buckley children, however, grew up in the Connecticut town of Sharon, ten miles north of Kent, where the family lived in a big, rambling house called "Great Elm." Buckley served in the army in World War II and then moved on to Yale. There, he won a place on the student newspaper, the *Yale Daily News,* where his distinctive prose style, ready wit, skill as a polemicist, and boundless energy eventually brought him the post of chairman. His work at the paper was his apprenticeship in journalism.

Politically, Buckley stood on the Right, but his outlook cut across the usual right-wing categories. As a devout Catholic, he had much in common with the traditionalists. Yet he also shared the small-government, free-market views of the libertarians. Unlike many libertarians, however, he rejected isolationism in favor of an internationalist, anti-Soviet foreign policy. He thus espoused a syncretistic kind of conservatism that would one day help him to become a unifying force on the Right.

Buckley graduated from Yale in June 1950 and married a few weeks later. By that time, the Korean War had broken out. While he approved of U.S. intervention, he also believed that he had satisfied his own military obligation through his

World War II service and thus was justified in trying to escape a second call up. Sympathetic to this wish was a fellow conservative, the political scientist Willmoore Kendall, who had taught Buckley at Yale and become a friend. As an alternative to the military, suggested Kendall, who had CIA connections, Buckley might apply to join the OPC.

And so in the fall of 1950 the two went to Washington. When they arrived, Kendall called Burnham, whom he had known since the late 1930s. Bring Buckley over, said Burnham, wanting to form a firsthand impression of the applicant. Upon arriving at Burnham's Georgetown house, the visitors found a dozen guests on hand listening to some Mozart records Burnham had just bought. Once the music had ended, Kendall introduced Buckley to Burnham, and as the other guests looked on, sang his praises so ardently that Buckley came close to cringing. Burnham then chatted with Buckley for a while, and apparently found him satisfactory, for a few days later Buckley was accepted by the OPC.[1]

Buckley's polwar career did not last long, however. Fluent in Spanish thanks to childhood years spent in Mexico, he was sent to Mexico City to help a Chilean ex-Marxist, Eudocio Ravines, translate his book *The Yenan Way* into English. But he seems to have found the OPC unappealing, for in early 1952, with the translation completed and his wife expecting a baby, he resigned, telling his boss, E. Howard Hunt, that he wanted to try his hand at political journalism.[2] He next worked at the *American Mercury,* then a conservative monthly that had published chapters from Burnham's Cold War books. But when the magazine was sold, he left, suspecting the buyer of intending to convert it to liberalism.[3]

By this time, Buckley's new career had begun to flourish. In the fall of 1951, his first book had come out, a work called *God and Man at Yale,* which accused his alma mater's mostly liberal faculty of collectivist and antireligious bias, and proposed that conservative alumni show their displeasure by denying the university financial support. A best-seller, the book outraged liberals, who denounced it as an attack on academic freedom. But it delighted the Right and made its author a conservative celebrity.

Three years later, Buckley struck again, coauthoring with L. Brent Bozell, a Yale classmate who had been his partner on the college debating team and was now his brother-in-law, a book called *McCarthy and His Enemies.* This work, an assessment from an anti-anti-McCarthyite standpoint of the criticisms aimed at the senator, further darkened Buckley's image in the eyes of liberals. But it confirmed his status as a rising star on the Right.

By now, Buckley had begun to ponder a new project, not another book, but a weekly political journal that would provide news and commentary from a conservative perspective. Such a venture would be difficult to launch. Money would have to be raised, writers enlisted, and a staff assembled. Moreover, Buckley had only modest experience in journalism: his years at the *Yale Daily News* and his brief stint at the *American Mercury*. Nor was the kind of journal he had in mind likely to be welcomed by much of the establishment press, which, under the sway of liberalism, decided which ideas were worthy of discussion, and dismissed opinion outside the acceptable spectrum (bounded on the Left by Stevenson and on the Right by Eisenhower). But Buckley was not timid. Buoyed by a mixture of conviction and combativeness, he relished the thought of playing a conservative David who would battle the liberal Goliath on a weekly schedule.

He did not plan to embark on the venture alone, however. With him was an editor at the *Freeman,* William S. Schlamm, the veteran of an often turbulent career in journalism. As a youth in his native Vienna, the dark-haired, edgy Schlamm had joined the Communist Party, which he had seen as a force fighting for a better world. But he had soon become disabused, and leaving the party in disgust, had since maintained an implacable hostility to communism. Once asked to state his philosophy of life, he answered, "The Ten Commandments and Mozart." But he might also have cited the cause of anticommunism.

Following his break with communism, Schlamm's life became a sequence of uprootings. By the mid-1930s, as a journalist on the Left (where he remained for some years) and as a Jew, he began to find life in Vienna increasingly nerve-wracking. Repeatedly menaced by local Nazis, he finally moved to Prague, but when Czechoslovakia seemed about to fall to Hitler, he moved again, this time to Belgium, carrying poison he planned to take if his plane were forced down over Germany. After a short stay in Belgium, he moved yet again, now to New York, where he wrote for the *New Leader* and then for Henry Luce's *Fortune.* For a while he prospered, but the day dawned when Luce tired of the tightly wound Schlamm, who reacted by moving to the *Freeman.* He would much rather have started a magazine of his own, but he doubted his ability to raise the necessary money.[4]

In 1954 Henry Regnery, then preparing *McCarthy and His Enemies* for publication, hired Schlamm to edit and write an introduction to the book, a job that led to Schlamm's meeting Buckley. He and Buckley, it soon became evident, had much in common. Not only did they think alike politically, but Buckley too wanted to publish a magazine. Since Buckley seemed better placed to raise money, Schlamm suggested that they launch a magazine together. Though the journal they aimed at would nominally belong to Buckley, who would be the publisher, editor-in-chief, and primary shareholder, he himself, Schlamm seems to have thought, would have the real power. For as Buckley's superior in age, experience, and worldly wisdom, he would easily assume the leading role.[5]

But before going forward, Buckley wanted to know whether Burnham (whom he had not seen since Washington) would sign on. "I would have found it very hard to proceed without a commitment from Burnham," he later said. Hence his letter of August 1954 to Burnham, and the talk between them a few days later in Kent.

As things turned out, Burnham proved easy to recruit.[6] Since May he had been stressing the urgency of replacing the *Freeman*. Moreover, with his previous magazine outlets no longer available, a new platform could not have failed to interest him. But above all, he could not ignore a call to duty. Once again, a tiny phalanx was being mustered in a vital cause, and as always, he had no choice but to enlist.

Next came the work of making the magazine a reality. To begin with, it had to have a name. At first Buckley wanted to call it the *National Weekly,* but when that choice was vetoed by the state of New York as being too close to the name of an existing publication, the *National Liquor Weekly,* he decided in favor of *National Review* instead.[7] In addition, money had to be raised, publicity generated, advertising space sold, a staff hired, and subscribers found. Burnham, though he had agreed to join the magazine only as a columnist and senior editor, took on such chores with inexhaustible energy. "There has just got to be a weekly magazine," he told Buckley.[8] A well-produced anticommunist journal (as the historian and one-time *National Review* editor Garry Wills put Burnham's thinking) could "have some real impact on the overall strategic stance of America.... [A] bright voice for the hard line could make even softies shift a decisive inch or two in the right direction."[9]

In the fall of 1954 and on into 1955 Burnham ranged far and wide in search of money, a contribution from Buckley's father having covered only part of the project's cost. "I made a pretty substantial pitch for N.W. [i.e., *National Weekly,* as the magazine was still called at this point] while I was in Dallas," he told Buckley in November 1954. He had also found potential backers in St. Paul and Chicago. "Have you talked to Robert Humphreys at Republican headquarters?" he asked. "That seems to me a very important thing to do." Such efforts, however, could fill him with frustration. "These rich people do seem much to prefer sounding off to writing checks," he groaned. All the same, he never relented. "I want *NATIONAL WEEKLY* to succeed," he declared to Buckley, "and I want to do those things which I best and most relevantly can to make it succeed." But for all their exertions money trickled in slowly. "Have you ever put NW's financial problem to Joe McC [McCarthy]?" he asked Buckley. "If he chooses to do so, I feel sure that he could by a few telephone calls complete the sum. After all, he has been getting a dose of press isolation that fully shows why NW ought to be." Three months later—and without any help from the fading McCarthy—Buckley announced that the needed sum had been collected—125 investors had contributed $290,000, and subscriptions and advertising had brought in $160,000 more.[10]

Burnham also wanted plenty of publicity for the magazine. When Buckley was invited to a meeting of an obscure Florida group called the Orlando Committee, which had sent him a plan for combating "a major aspect of the communist conspiracy," Burnham urged him to attend. "I think it important that you should show yourself," he said. It might also be useful to organize "a Conference Against Appeasement," he added, a gathering the magazine could use as a kick-off event. Further, there should be a publicity campaign run by "a suitable professional public relations outfit." Conservatives had "been much handicapped by a failure to use adequate professional techniques in these matters." But although he plumped hard for "a professional public relations assist," he failed to persuade the frugal Buckley.[11]

Burnham also solicited articles for the magazine. Hoping for pieces from his European friends, he worried that the pay rate Buckley envisaged would be too low. The sociologist Jules Monnerot would probably accept the five-cents-a-word rate Buckley was planning, he guessed, but Malraux and Aron would want more. He also saw possible contributors in old OPC and Princeton friends, and some would one day write for *National Review*. Medford Evans, whom he hoped to enlist as a contributing editor, at first held back, objecting that the magazine would be "'too eastern,' too Ivy League." "Actually, I rather agree with this judgment myself," Burnham commented to fellow Ivy Leaguer Buckley, "and that is precisely why I have been anxious to see NW linked up more with the West."[12] In the end, Evans agreed to come aboard.

Burnham did not limit his recruitment goals to writers. "I want to return to the subject at which I have so frequently hammered: youth," he wrote to Buckley in 1955. "I do believe that a bright young person just out of college ought to be in the office...partly to be a kind of psychological bridge to the campus...." The right person could help to achieve a conservative "entry into the universities," the veteran of the Trotskyist French turn pointed out, "a primary target we all agree."[13]

◆    ◆    ◆    ◆

In the summer of 1955, Burnham's toil for the magazine was interrupted by a ghost from the past. Since the 1939–40 SWP faction fight, his former comrade Max Shachtman had not been faring well. The Workers Party, now called the Independent Socialist League (ISL), had dwindled to a handful of dogged Shachtman loyalists. Though nothing could have been farther from the ISL's mind than revolution-making, the group still theoretically adhered to Bolshevism, for which reason it had been placed on the attorney general's list of organizations advocating the violent overthrow of the U.S. government. As a result, ISL members could not be issued passports, which led Shachtman to sue for the group's removal from the list.[14]

In July 1955 the Justice Department held hearings on the matter. Present as expert witnesses for the ISL were left-wing anticommunists Norman Thomas, Daniel Bell, Dwight Macdonald, and Harry Fleischman, who all laughed at the notion that the ISL preached violence. To uphold its charge, the Justice Department brought in an expert witness of its own, Columbia University scholar Geroid T. Robinson. But Robinson proved to be so useless a witness that in his stead Justice's attorneys turned to Burnham. Three times Burnham refused to testify. But when the government's lawyers argued that to testify was his "patriotic duty," he gave in. "And there he was," said Shachtman, "urbane as usual, greeting me with a polite smile, which I tried my best to return with an angry and contemptuous look because that's exactly how I felt."[15]

But Burnham proved no more helpful than Robinson. He confirmed that

Lenin and Trotsky had called for the violent overthrow of the "bourgeois state," and that ISL literature contained "no explicit renunciation of the use of force and violence." But when asked by the ISL's lawyer, liberal and ADA activist Joseph L. Rauh Jr., whether he would ever lie on the government's behalf for patriotic reasons, he said he would. Then how could people know he was not lying about the ISL? Rauh triumphantly shot back.[16] In the end, Shachtman won his case and got his passport.

Burnham remembered testifying as "unpleasant," and later claimed that the government had wanted him as a witness only to get the ISL's Trotskyist roots on record. "95% of what I said," he told historian John P. Diggins in the mid-1970s, "came only because of Joe Rauh's endless cross examination…, the purpose of which, so far as I could grasp it, was to try to establish that I was a fascist and more generally a son of a bitch."

Ironically, Rauh, who later denounced Burnham as "a brazen McCarthyite who admitted he would lie," once told Shachtman that getting the ISL removed from the attorney general's list was the one mistake he had made in his career. In Rauh's eyes, Shachtman had gone bad by supporting U.S. intervention in Vietnam ("We're fighting Commies [i.e., Stalinists]," the old Trotskyist had told his scandalized attorney). Shachtman, meanwhile, did not stay mad at Burnham, but came to speak of his former friend with affection, a feeling his widow, Yetta, would echo.[17]

❖ ❖ ❖ ❖

In November 1955, after more than a year of preparation, and a few days before Burnham's fiftieth birthday, the first issue of *National Review* rolled off the presses. Buckley topped the masthead as "editor and publisher," with Burnham, Kendall, Bozell, Schlamm, and a second former *Freeman* editor, Suzanne La Follette, completing the list of senior editors. Buckley also contributed a column of political commentary called "From the Ivory Tower." Schlamm too doubled as a columnist, offering cultural criticism in a column called "Arts and Manners." Kendall wrote a column as well, "The Liberal Line," which kept track of the doings of what its author called "the Liberal Establishment" (thus introducing the British term "establishment" into American political parlance). Other columnists included Brent Bozell, with "National Trends," and Russell Kirk, whose "From the Academy" frowned on recent fashions in education. Also on hand in the first issue, as the author of a book review, was Frank S. Meyer, who would soon become an editor and write a column called "Principles and Heresies." The lead article, "Peace—with Honor," was the work of Senator William F. Knowland, a conservative Republican from California, who warned of the dangers of disarmament.

In some ways *National Review* seemed like a resurrection of the old *Freeman*: it stood for hard-line anticommunism and the free market, published many *Freeman* writers, and included among its editors two erstwhile *Freeman* editors. But unlike the *Freeman,* it also projected a Catholic aura, a reflection of the Buckley presence, the religious ties of some others among its editors,[18] and the large Irish-American contingent among its readers. What was most striking about *National Review,* however, was the number of former leftists and communists it employed, with senior editors Burnham, Schlamm, Kendall, and soon Meyer (once director of the education office of the U.S. Communist Party's Indiana-Illinois branch) heading the list.

Burnham, like his fellow editors, played a multiple role at *NR*. Besides contributing editorials, articles, reviews, and brief news items, he also served as resident expert on foreign policy and global strategy. These subjects he dealt with in a column called "The Third World War," so named, he said, because "our century's World War III" was the present global struggle between the West and Soviet communism, "not some possible conflict" of the future. Viewing the Cold War as the era's defining political reality, he found the meaning of world events in their links with that contest. Thus, commenting on a UN conference on the Middle East, he wrote, "the supposed Middle Eastern crisis is in reality a crisis in the relations between Communist Russia and the United States, between the Soviet Empire and the West, a crisis in the unfolding, irreversible struggle for the world." The "underlying and controlling question," therefore, was not what appeared on the conference's agenda, but whether Moscow was to be allowed "to establish itself" in the Middle East "and eventually take over."[19]

Burnham's commentary proceeded from his familiar premises: that the West and communism were at war, and that U.S. policy toward the Soviet bloc was hobbled by ignorance, amateurism, indecisiveness, and a tendency both liberal and generically American to lower "a moralistic, sentimental veil over the realities of power." The right way to make policy was to spurn "politics as wish," and heed history, geography, and the enduring tendencies of human nature.[20] Communists, who had created a "technology of power: rational, persistent, systematic," understood this. Accordingly, Soviet polwar campaigns were "not just a vague and formless propaganda such as we attempt," but were "conceived strategically, like any other form of genuine warfare."[21]

That American statesmen, childish and bumbling, could win out over such opponents seemed to him doubtful (though how much his doubt stemmed from neutral analysis and how much from a need to vent his frustration with U.S. policy is anybody's guess). Because of this conclusion he earned a reputation at *National Review* for unshakable pessimism. "James Burnham will see a tiny ray of hope," the magazine predicted at the end of 1955 in a tongue-in-cheek forecast of the coming year's most unlikely events.[22]

Yet Burnham also called attention to the enemy's manifold weaknesses. The USSR, he maintained, suffered not only from economic failure, a dismal standard of living, severe cultural decay, and mass discontent. It was also experiencing a slowdown in population growth, which spelled disaster for a system that demanded "ever-swelling masses of human fodder" for its army and work force. Moreover, since Stalin's death the USSR's leaders had been fighting over the succession and the issue of how to tackle the country's myriad problems. Soviet "softs" wanted greater freedom and more consumer goods, concessions to workers and peasants, and some leeway for the satellites, while "hards" insisted on loyalty to Stalin's legacy. The West had thus been handed an exceptional opportunity for action. If it worked to aggravate the strains in the Soviet system rather than to ease them in the hope of promoting "peace," the Soviet giant, standing on feet of clay, might well collapse.[23]

The Soviet threat, then, stemmed not from greater brawn but from greater political skill and determination than America's. "We overstress the USSR's strength, and understress its menace [the danger it posed because of its political flair]," Burnham liked to say.[24] To overcome the threat, the United States should not depend on nuclear weapons, for the massive retaliation strategy had no credibility, but adopt the USSR's "'indirect' strategy of multi-dimensional political warfare."[25]

Finally, Burnham's commentary reiterated, no matter how well conceived a policy might be, it would fail if it did not rest on a resolute will. In a crisis, the United States must be prepared to use force, even in violation of the sovereignty of other nations. Impatient with American timidity, Burnham dreamed of a "hard" defense of Western interests that would rank vital strategic needs above formal rights. When, for example, the possibility arose that a newly elected Icelandic government might close the U.S. air force base at Keflavik, which Washington deemed a crucial component of NATO's defenses, he imagined a simple refusal to leave. The United States might reply to an eviction notice by telling Iceland: "To protect ourselves, the nations of Western Europe, and you—whose rhetoric would not hold back the Communists a single hour—*American forces will remain in Keflavik.*" Similarly, he regretted that U.S. participation in a UN conference on the Middle East had not stopped at a peremptory message to the Middle East delegates that the United States required of their governments "a minimum number of suitable military installations" to guard the region against Soviet conquest, in return for which it would guarantee the Middle East's oil fields and strategic communications, and refrain from intervention in Middle Eastern internal affairs. "That is all. Thank you," the message would end. In short, Burnham might have summed up, the United States must find the will to cut through the smothering web of international organizations, law, and etiquette impeding its efforts to fight communism (and also stop fawning on other nations in hopes of winning their friendship). Thus, if the UN could not be made to accommodate U.S. needs, the United States would have no reason to stay in the UN—"except perhaps to sabotage it."[26]

The aim of his column, Burnham wrote, was "to note and analyze" what was "actually happening" in the world, and to explain what the consequences of different policy choices were likely to be. "I do not very often state an opinion of my own concerning what a policy 'should be' in a given conjuncture," he went on, and when he did state an opinion, he made his advocacy "explicit."[27] But in fact, he almost always wrote as an advocate, if not explicitly, then by implication, through rhetorical questions and tone. Still, he lived up to his self-description to the extent that he seldom engaged in the pulpit-pounding partisanship favored by some of his *NR* colleagues, instead maintaining an air of analytical aloofness. Sometimes, however (and more often in his unsigned editorials than in his column), his prose seethed with feeling. Such moments were most likely to occur when he was writing about what he judged to be Western cowardice or perfidy: for example abdication by the United States in the face of the enemy.[28]

But Burnham's *National Review* work encompassed much more than political commentary. At one point early on, he took a crack at reviewing movies, which led him to outline a theory of film aesthetics. "A movie should be a kind of formal pantomime," he wrote, "a cinematic *commedia dell'arte,* without any attempt at subtleties of character or idea. The joy is in the moving camera, the represented surface of the world, the visual and aural counterpoint. Don't let the movie bog down into the photographing of what is really a play or the transcription of what is really a novel; let the camera get out of doors as much as possible, so that the movie does what no other form of art can; keep the characters and plot formal, conventional, because otherwise they will turn into pretentious platitudes; in short, my ideal movie is a good Western."[29]

Nor could he resist involving himself in noneditorial matters. When the magazine needed artists, he went out to find some. He also took an interest in *NR's* distribution arrangements. And in at least one instance, he doubled as advertising manager, writing to William D. Laurie Jr. of the J. Walter Thompson ad agency to suggest that Laurie place ads for Ford Motors in *National Review.* "Actually, I have nothing to do with the business side of NR," he told Laurie, "but…I have found myself lately reflecting on the general problems of the enterprise…." In addition, he kept an eye on details such as layout, noting "the really stylish things one can do with unjustified lines." Fascinated by mechanical problems, and liking to tinker with temperamental office equipment, he even served now and then as the magazine's on-site repairman.[30]

❖ ◆ ❖ ◆

Burnham settled easily into his new career. His adjustment was aided by Buckley, who arranged *NR's* weekly editorial conference to fit his prize recruit's commuting schedule. Each Tuesday, Burnham would drive from Kent to nearby Brewster, New York, to catch the first post-rush hour train to Grand Central Station. From the station he would walk to the magazine's Murray Hill office, where his arrival would signal that the conference could begin. With Buckley presiding, Burnham would open the proceedings by reading aloud a list of topics that might be dealt with in the magazine's next issue. Then would come debate, sometimes at high volume, but Burnham would rarely enter the fray. As the storm raged around him, he would sit quietly, with a detached air, sometimes wearing what a fellow editor, J. P. McFadden, called his "little smile." Yet he would always listen attentively, less interested, some thought, in a colleague's argument than in the underlying motives that had led him to advance it. When Buckley asked for his opinion, he would speak, though "so calmly," NR editor and Dartmouth English professor Jeffrey Hart remembered, "that one never realized how powerful his presence was until it wasn't there anymore." His views, according to Buckley, tended to be "pragmatic." Hart thought he exercised "a philosophically moderating influence" on editorial policy. (For example, in hopes of finding readers outside the ranks of the McCarthy enthusiasts, he persuaded his colleagues to drop their unqualified defense of the senator.) Having expressed his opinion, he would seldom go on to argue for it, but, still wearing his little smile, would comment on what others had said, and quietly pose questions intended to provoke thought,[31] as he had once done in his classes at NYU.

Sometimes, however, he enjoyed provoking an uproar. His favorite target was the high-strung Frank Meyer, who became book editor soon after National Review began to appear. At the "agonies," quarterly gatherings at which the editors evaluated the magazine, he liked to tease Meyer by proposing that book reviews be limited to four hundred words, as in the Economist, which he thought would keep them from becoming overly ideological. Meyer, who favored long, ideologically tinged reviews, would burst out in protest, while Burnham, his little smile in place, would sit back and enjoy the fireworks. William A. Rusher, a Princeton and Harvard Law graduate who in 1957 took the overworked Buckley's place as publisher, was sure that Burnham made the proposal "merely for the fun of watching Meyer fly off the handle." But this perception did not save Rusher himself, otherwise as sharp-eyed as anyone at the magazine, from ambush by Burnham, who could also lure the publisher into exploding. "For Rusher, forewarned was not forearmed," one editor recalled. "He fell for it every time." Burnham too could blow up, however, his anger made visible by a scarlet flush across his high forehead. But fury overcame him very rarely. Buckley, who worked with him for more than two decades, saw it happen only twice.[32]

The weekly conference would end with the assignment of writing chores, after which the editors would go off to lunch together, at first in the dining room of the nearby Catawba Corporation, the Buckley family oil company, and later at Nicola Paone's, an Italian restaurant on East 34th Street. After lunch the writing would begin, continuing until early evening. Burnham usually turned out two or three one-paragraph items for the magazine's "The Week" section and as many editorials. (He did his column at home.) Writing quickly, he would draft his copy with a black ballpoint pen, then correct and type it up. After a further revision or two, he retyped the whole and the piece would be finished. (He wrote his books the same way, doing no revising until he had finished the entire first draft.) In general, he revised little, usually hitting his target on the first try and at almost exactly the prescribed length.

He did his editorial writing in a scuffed-up office overlooking East 35th Street that he shared with Buckley's sister Priscilla, a Smith graduate who came to the magazine in 1956 after working as a CIA officer in the early 1950s and then as a United Press correspondent in Paris. On top of her other chores at *NR,* Priscilla Buckley—bright, witty, and commonsensical—took on the job of restoring peace when Burnham's opinions left other editors riled. Priscilla found Burnham a perfect officemate. He was neat, quiet, and considerate, she told a visitor, and always conscious that the editors were there not to argue endlessly, but to put out the magazine.[33]

The next morning editorial writing would resume. With the afternoon deadline approaching, rather than go out to lunch the editors would have sandwiches sent in. Focusing on "fact and analysis," and making his own writing as direct and concrete as possible, Burnham would encourage his junior colleagues to follow his example. His black ballpoint pen at the ready, he would go over their copy with care, toning down emotional outbursts and removing ornate verbiage and abstractions, so that as one junior editor put it, "sesquipedalian—pardon, long and Latinate—diction became short and Anglo-Saxon."[34]

When criticizing the work of junior colleagues, he always did so with tact and even a kind of gentleness, rarely editing their copy very heavily. On his supervisory rounds, he would diffidently knock on a young editor's door and ask for permission to enter. One of the younger writers, Linda Bridges, noticed that when he wanted to look at something she had written, he would stand just outside her office, with only his well-polished black shoe visible, as if uncertain whether she would permit him to come in. Once in her office, he would approach her desk with his eyes trained shyly on the floor, and when making his comments would nervously curl his foot around the desk leg. The young people repaid his kindness—he was the only senior editor, one recalled, whom they never covertly made fun of. But he grew angry with those he thought were not really trying. When one junior editor, with the deadline near, declared himself unable to draft a paragraph on France's president Georges Pompidou and asked to be relieved of the assignment, Burnham showed no pity. "You pay your respects to M. Pompidou, and bring it to me in fifteen minutes," he coldly ordered.[35]

In the late afternoon the copy would go to the printer, whereupon all hands and any guests at the office would gather for drinks. But Burnham would normally stay only if Marcia were joining him in the city. Otherwise, he would catch the last pre–rush hour train back to Brewster, and from there drive on to Kent. On the night between the two editorial workdays, he would stay in town. If Marcia did not come in, he would phone her to chat at four o'clock and again at ten.[36]

Because Burnham spent a night each week in New York for *National Review*, in the late 1950s the magazine rented a small East Side apartment for him. A few years later he moved to a new apartment, on East 70th Street, for which the magazine again picked up the tab. When Marcia did not join him, he usually had dinner with Priscilla Buckley, often at the Budapest Café, or with William Buckley at the latter's East 73rd Street home. The next day he would wait at East 70th Street and Second Avenue for Buckley, who would pick him up in his car at a time the two OPC veterans liked to set CIA-style (for example, at 8:07, a time whose oddness made it easy to recall) for the trip downtown to the office.[37]

Burnham's colleagues, while sometimes opposing his views, greatly esteemed him. Kendall, who called him "the muscle-minded sage of Kent," joked to Hart that Burnham would never drink more than one martini at a sitting "because he would in no way impair, even for an evening, that formidable instrument inside his skull." Rusher thought Burnham "one of the most incisive analytical minds" he had ever encountered, and described him years later as "absolutely essential to the young National Review, and (next only to Buckley) responsible for its ultimate success." The Buckleys thought the world of him both as a thinker and as a friend.[38]

Yet like Burnham's Trotskyist comrades, many at *National Review* also found him a bit unsettling, sometimes because of his Machiavellian way of thinking and sometimes because of his palpable air of reserve. "Burnham was interested in the logic of power," recalled editor Joe Sobran. "His method was to look at everything in the world from the angle of its power-value. This made the moralist in me squirm, especially since he regarded even morality under the same aspect." Many people sensed that he stood slightly apart from others. At times Buckley found him unfathomable. "You could never tell whether Burnham would answer a letter or not," he once remarked. Burnham "smiled and laughed, but he was never one of the boys," observed Sobran. C. S. Simonds, a *National Review* editor in the 1970s, thought him "in no way stuffy," but rather, a man "who valued his, and respected others', social elbow room," someone "you waited for…to come to you." Editor Richard Brookhiser, who first worked for the magazine as a 1976 summer intern, sensed "something remote and withheld" in Burnham, adding, "I got the same feeling from his earliest books." Hart noticed that Burnham rarely engaged in small talk. Moreover, though Hart taught English, the well-read Burnham's major at Princeton and Oxford, Burnham never once, in all the years he worked with Hart, expressed a thought on a literary subject. Buckley's secretary, Frances Bronson, in contrast, found Burnham a highly versatile conversationalist. "He could talk about anything," she told a visitor to *NR*, "even makeup."[39]

As in his SWP days, Burnham tried to lower his shield of reserve, sensing it made others uneasy. The senior editors all called him "Jim," and he wanted the juniors to do so too, but the juniors found it difficult. "It [took] six years for most of us timidly to address him as Jim, much as we liked him," Linda Bridges remembered. "I suppose it was that air of calmly seeing through everything that made him seem like the most grown-up person we knew…." He was too shy to ask the juniors directly to call him by his nickname, and finally sent them a memo inviting them to do so.[40]

◆　◆　◆　◆

Burnham's ambitions for *National Review* were the same as the ones he had had for the *New International*. He wanted the magazine to acquire influence, to become a key voice in the national political debate, to be a publication people felt they had to read. But as time passed, he began to fear that *NR*'s tone and style might frustrate this hope. "Too many NR articles" suffered from "an academic kind of staleness," he wrote to Buckley in October 1957. Such copy was not suitable for a political weekly. A month later, in a long memorandum, he repeated this criticism, noting that people would read what was presented as "story, personality, facts, narrative, and as *felt* problem," but would not sit still for "abstract disquisitions," and disliked heavy doses of "irony, sarcasm, [and] smart aleckism."

Popularization, he insisted, need not mean vulgarization. Layout, too, needed to be livened up. There should be "more white space; more subheads; more boxes, italics, boldface…decorative devices, varied page makeup, tables, charts."

At the same time, he signaled a possible source of the readability problem: an unclear sense at NR of the magazine's identity and purpose. Would *National Review* be content to rest in a backwater, he wondered, or would it "struggle in the main channel (even if at the channel's edge)?" Would it address only people who already shared its ideas, or would it "reach out toward new layers?" Would it "express the negation of the defeated part of an older generation, or the still open perspectives of a younger?" The basic question, in sum, was "readability for whom and for what?"[41]

He saw a further problem in what he called the magazine's "Catholic" tone, which he worried would keep it from gaining political influence. "By the nature of the case," he warned Buckley, "NR has a built-in tendency to become a Catholic magazine in a parochial sense rather than a national magazine. It continues to be my understanding that you want it to be a national magazine edited by a Catholic, and not a Catholic magazine. And if that is to be the case, there must be a continuous deliberate effort against the built-in tendency. (N.B. the almost automatic way our audience becomes and stays disproportionately Catholic.)"[42]

In addition, he was unhappy with some of the magazine's columns. Kirk's education column struck him as caught in a rut, as "fighting yesterday's battles" and ignoring new issues and trends. Meyer's column was mainly acceptable in content but "frightful[ly]" written. Meyer, moreover, wrote too often about foreign affairs (Burnham's own bailiwick) but never said anything new about the subject.[43]

He also found NR's cultural section wanting, the one-time *Partisan Review* critic advised Buckley. The magazine's poetry page, for example, was a mistake.[44] "The 'cultural' poverty of the…conservative movement in general," added this former *Partisan Review* critic, "and NR (relative to what ought to be, not to other conservative manifestations, of course) specifically," stood in the way of contact with "the intellectual elites." The magazine's review section, "somehow just [did not] click." It was "too highbrow for our solid right-wingers," but also lacked appeal for college campuses. Maybe it was "too solemn, too abstract, wrong in book and topic selection, or just…too dull." NR's cultural criticism as a whole showed a philistine streak. A recent music article by William H. Chamberlain sounded "utterly stupid, banal, uninteresting, irrelevant," while a hostile article on abstract art by Buckley's brother Reid seemed "undiscerning, insensitive, uninformed, and, also, irrelevant." After all, "living art must be new, must be fresh, must be far out (from the point of view of accepted standards)." It might be, he concluded, "that the qualities that go to produce the contemporary political conservative do not, generally speaking, permit the sensitive appreciation of living art."[45]

Because of his dissatisfaction with *NR's* cultural coverage, he was at first "excited" by the arrival in 1962 of a newcomer from Canada whom he hoped would be the "theater-movies-TV-exhibitions" critic he thought the magazine needed. But the new man soon belied his hopes. "He doesn't know anything," and moreover he was "terribly un-chic," Burnham complained. "I don't mean just socially un-chic (though he is that too, of course: he usually wears sweaters in the office, and one of them in particular must have come from a Sears' shipment that got lost thirty years ago in the backwoods of Manitoba). He is un-chic about art and ideas (he couldn't wait twenty-four hours to replace that dreamy Dubuffet of Paris that Marcia put over what is now his desk with some Canadian calendar work) and people, and, well, you know how chic is."[46]

Always concerned about tone, Burnham set great store by "chic." When *National Review* introduced a food-wine-travel feature called "Gracious Living," he was quick to heap scorn on the feature's logo and title as "terrible and drawing not at all on chic." For the same reason, he kept watch on the magazine's diction, and urged "an absolute moratorium for an indefinite period on all expressions of the genus 'heh heh heh'; 'Yup'; 'Gr-r-r'; 'Ugh'; 'glug'; e tutti quanti."[47]

◆　◆　◆　◆

Burnham's paramount anxiety was that *National Review* would forfeit any chance of political influence by drifting too far from the mainstream (where he emphatically wanted it to be), becoming a right-wing equivalent of the *Socialist Appeal*. He first signaled this danger during the 1956 presidential race. When it looked as if Eisenhower, who had suffered a heart attack in 1955, might not run for a second term, Burnham urged that *NR* support Senator Knowland for the

Republican nomination, a step that would "at once give NATIONAL REVIEW a *place* in the national scene." But when Eisenhower announced that he would seek reelection, Burnham, despite his unhappiness with the president, saw no choice for *NR* but to take "American realities and the full situation into account" and endorse the Republican ticket.[48]

Some *NR* editors rejected Burnham's pragmatism. Schlamm, debating Burnham in the pages of the magazine, argued that the GOP must be "liberated from its dishonorable captivity" under the "inconsistent liberal" Eisenhower, which could be accomplished only by Eisenhower's defeat. But since he could not back the Democratic candidate (again Stevenson) either, he had decided not to vote at all. To Burnham, a ballot boycott promised only to harm conservatives, helping anticonservatives to brand them a "lunatic fringe," and cutting them off from allies unwilling to leave the GOP. If conservatives took the third-party route, he warned, they would end up in the company of "not a few plain racists masquerading as conservatives" and "all sorts of cranks and anti-Semites." Since Republicans were "*less* socialist, *less* statist" than Democrats, he would vote for them "simply as the least bad choice that reason can discover."[49]

While attending the Republican convention that summer, Burnham returned to the question of the magazine's potential influence. "It seems to me," he wrote to Buckley, that in deciding *NR*'s position on Eisenhower, "you are implicitly deciding…whether your objective is to make NR a serious (whether or not minor) force in American life, or to be content with its being essentially a literary exercise—a kind of high grade game." The day's mail, he noted, had included a sheet called *Convention News* that accused Eisenhower of surrendering to communism. If *NR* did not back Eisenhower, he advised, "it [would] be merely a fancier form of *Convention News*…. Practical politics is not just a matter of 'ideas' but also of the crowd you run with."[50]

But Buckley held back. With his editors divided, he decided only to recommend that "those who prefer Eisenhower, whom the campaign seems to have rendered preferable, vote for him, if they are convinced no other course of action holds out any practical hope."[51]

The 1956 election was not the last time Burnham tried to steer *National Review* toward the mainstream. In 1960 he returned to the charge, prompted by a plea for advice from Buckley, who had begun to wonder whether to give up journalism for a career in academe. Burnham replied at length that the magazine had to choose between two possible identities. It could hold to its present course, which pointed toward "a permanent role as a sectarian and doctrinaire organ" that would "educate conservatives rather than winning new people for conservatism," or it could become a magazine "published and edited by conservatives; written largely but not exclusively by conservatives and addressed to a literate audience extending from the Right on leftward to the point where hardened Leftist ideology cuts off the possibility of communication." The second option would mean less "plainly doctrinaire copy and wider limits of ideological tolerance," but possibly a circulation equal to that of *Harper's* and the *Atlantic Monthly.*[52]

Buckley thought Burnham's advice "superb." "You can, I think, count me among the Onward-and-Upward boys," he told Rusher. But years later he said that he had shared Burnham's view only "up to a point." His aim in founding *National Review* had been to publish "a journal of opinion, not a general circulation magazine that had an opinion" and that ran conservative articles. He had wanted to meet the need for a conservative journal.[53]

◆　◆　◆　◆

1956 was also the year of the Suez crisis and of challenges to the Soviet grip on eastern Europe, events that not only riveted Burnham's attention but also stirred his passions as perhaps no other events had since his battle with Trotsky.

Burnham looked at the Middle East not only as the "spigot of the oil that turns the wheels of Western Europe" but, more important, as "the strategic area which will probably decide the fate of the world."[54] He regarded Arab states approvingly or not according to whether their policies helped or harmed the West. Toward Israel, however, he showed a certain coolness because he viewed the country as a liberal sacred cow—a "sort of lar of the Western Left," he once called it, "of the same order…as the Spanish Republic, or picket lines." Israel's legitimacy rested squarely on the right of conquest, though perhaps also on that of "suffering." Still, all that should matter to Washington in the Middle East were the region's "strategic, economic and geopolitical realities." Yet he sometimes voiced admiration for the Jewish state. The Israelis had reached their goal "through a gigantic act of will," he wrote, and though few in number, had "through courage, resolution and political skill [virtues he ranked among the highest]…successfully taken on the entire Arab world."[55]

The event that first led Burnham to write at length about the Middle East was the 1956 Suez crisis: Egyptian strongman Gamal Abdel Nasser's nationalization of the British-owned and -operated Suez Canal; Israel's seizure, in collusion with Britain and France, of Egypt's Sinai peninsula; the Anglo-French paratroop occupation of the Canal Zone; and then their humiliating retreat at the order of the United States and the USSR. Burnham claimed that by means of Nasser (a "strutting fanatic—dictator over a country of 20,000,000 diseased and starving illiterates"), Moscow had succeeded in turning NATO's southern flank.

What upset him most, however, was what the crisis seemed to reveal about the West. The outcome had been decided not by Western material weakness, he wrote, but by "a moral collapse—a defect of will." The "sick" West, which had already fled India, Indochina, Morocco, and Ceylon, seemed incapable of "a vital reaction to this blow at its jugular." (Similarly, Britain had not been driven out of India by force, but had left voluntarily "out of some fatal feeling of guilt, no longer confident of herself or of the values and mission of her Christian civilization.") In the first phase of the Suez affair, he had hoped that the West would assert "the right of Western civilization to survive" by taking back the canal. But the West had yielded, "drugged" by the "myth of the intrinsic and necessary justice of any 'anti-colonial' struggle at any time," a myth that thought it "always just…for Indonesians to throw out the Dutch, Indians the British, Indochinese the French, dark men the white men, no matter for what purpose, nor by whom led, no matter the stage of development, nor the consequences to the local people and economy, nor the effect on world strategic relations."

The most culpable of the Western powers was the United States, which had committed the mortal sin of betraying its parent civilization while refusing aid to Hungary, which rose against communism at the peak of the Suez crisis. The United States had sided with the USSR to force Britain and France to abandon the Canal Zone, and had backed a UN resolution condemning Britain, France, and Israel. "*Over the humiliated forms of our two oldest and closest allies,*" Burnham stormed in the passionate tone he reserved for an occasional unsigned editorial, "*we clasp the hands of the murderers of the Christian heroes of Hungary,* as we run in shameless—and vain—pursuit of the 'good will' of Asia and Africa's teeming pagan multitudes."[56]

In the wake of the Suez crisis, with his tendency to overdramatize history running at full throttle, Burnham sighted a new threat to the West, portended in a visit of March 1957 to Hungary and Poland by China's premier, Chou En-lai. Chou was acting independently, he pointed out, not as "a mere agent of the Kremlin," a fact that gave his trip "a prophetic, almost an apocalyptical, dimension." The visit symbolized Asian intervention in the affairs of Europe, something that "in all history" had "never" before happened. (Had Burnham forgotten his Toynbee?) Asians believed "the great fact of the twentieth century" to be the East's "reawakening." They saw communism as "a transitory episode," a means of ending European political control ("imperialism") and destroying "Western (Christian) civilization—the civilization of white men (the Russians in due course among them)." Once they had driven the West from Asia, they would decide which Asian power—India, China, Japan, Islam—would head "the coming Asian order." These thoughts might be fantasy, he admitted, yet population trends showed that if the West accepted liberal egalitarianism, Asian world rule would become "mathematically inevitable."[57]

If intended primarily as a blast at liberalism, Burnham's warning of a danger from Asia pointed to a form of world conflict different in essence from those he had noted in the past (international class war, managerial superstate war, the Cold War), one whose deepest roots were cultural rather than economic, political, or ideological. This new idea of global struggle would henceforth surface often in his writing. So, too, would his hostility to anti-Western nationalism. To judge by the harsh language he used when discussing what was coming to be called "the Third World," the root of this hostility lay not only in his fear that Third World nationalists would open the gates to the Soviets and in his belief that Western rule meant superior government and better economic prospects for native peoples. It also lay in his indignation that populations he regarded as culturally backward, incited by self-seeking rabble-rousers and leftist ideologues, were rebelling against the tutelage of the West. He had long been writing under the influence of Halford Mackinder. Had Mackinder now been joined by Rudyard Kipling?

❖　❖　❖　❖

Even more significant in Burnham's eyes than the Suez affair was the 1956 anti-Soviet upheaval in eastern Europe. The turmoil began in Poland, where in June 1956 worker-student rioting at Poznan broke out and escalated into a siege of police and Communist Party headquarters, forcing the country's stunned communist bosses to call out the army. The rising offered just the kind of opportunity advocates of "rollback" dreamed of. Yet the Eisenhower administration, despite its 1952 campaign platform, took no action.

Burnham found the Polish explosion both exciting and depressing. The crisis showed that a liberation policy was better attuned to "Soviet realities than any policy of containment or coexistence," he argued. But it also showed that however much the administration talked of liberation, it practiced "withdrawal, coexistence, appeasement." The United States should block Soviet intervention in Poland by declaring that it would treat any Soviet military action there as "a *casus belli*." The Soviet colossus, already wobbling on feet of clay, would then have no choice but to leave the Warsaw regime to fend for itself.[58]

The USSR bought peace in Poland in October 1956 with a compromise that granted the Poles modestly liberalized rule in return for a pledge to maintain Poland's membership in the Warsaw Pact (the Soviet bloc's military alliance), the communist monopoly of power, and adherence to Moscow's line in world affairs. But only days later, mass anticommunist rioting broke out in Hungary. Faced with a new crisis, the Soviets tried to end it through a deal similar to the Polish one. But Hungary's new premier, the reformist communist Imre Nagy, wished to institute real democracy and withdraw from the Warsaw Pact. In November, Soviet armor poured into Hungary and methodically pounded the Hungarian rebels to bits.

Passionately pro-Hungarian, Burnham watched in agony. For a time, recalled Buckley, who never again saw him so angry, Burnham could not bear to be in the same room as a representative of the Soviet bloc. But he was almost as furious at the Eisenhower administration, which had failed the rebels. Should a revolt break out in a Soviet satellite, he had written in *Containment or Liberation?* the United States could not stand idly by, for such inaction would be "a final proof of the inevitability of communist world victory." Now Washington had assumed the fatal passive stance.

But much worse, he believed, America had lost its honor. Washington should have replied to the Soviet invasion of Hungary not with a UN resolution condemning the invasion, but with an ultimatum to Moscow to clear out of eastern Europe. With its leaders at odds and its western flank exposed, the USSR would have had no choice but to comply. Moreover, steps short of an ultimatum continued to be possible: the recall of the U.S. ambassador to the USSR, a boycott of the Budapest puppet regime's UN delegation, a refusal to compete in the Olympics against teams from the Soviet bloc. But the administration shrank from even these mild reactions.[59]

Overwhelmed by the heart-rending outcome of the Hungarian rising, Burnham turned the debacle into an allegory of the human condition. "Cries in the night, blood and screams, the agony of heroes and villains tore at our drugged illusions," he wrote of Hungary, "and pounded into our comfort-sodden hearts the eternal lesson that we walk in the Valley of the Shadow, that the tale of human life is not a sentimental romance but everlasting tragedy...." But he believed that the rising also taught political lessons, among them that when push came to shove the United States would not help rebellious Soviet satellites, and that GOP "roll-back" talk was just election-time rhetoric. The West, it was now clear, tacitly accepted the Soviet division of the world into two spheres: a communist-ruled "zone of peace," upon which the West would not intrude, and a noncommunist "zone of war," in which communism, operating behind such concealments as "national liberation" movements, would work to take power. In short, the Hungarian tragedy marked a turning point in the global struggle.[60]

Drawing on the lessons of Hungary, in November 1956 Burnham offered a plan under which the satellite empire might be peacefully dismantled. The puppet regimes would not survive without Soviet troops to defend them, he reasoned, so the goal must be to get Soviet troops out of eastern Europe. Since the most basic of the "Eisenhower axioms" stated that America would not "*deliberately initiate* the risk of all-out war," Washington should work for a voluntary Soviet withdrawal. Otherwise put, the West should try to "help" the Soviets carry out a retreat that Moscow might in fact secretly desire.

As bizarre as this idea might sound, he went on, Soviet leaders were divided, nervous, and aware that the USSR was overextended, so it was "by no means improbable" that they would actually be glad to withdraw—seeing the pullback as temporary—if they could do so without humiliation. Lenin, after all, had advised taking "one step backward" in order later to take "two steps forward." At the same time, to encourage eastern Europe, which feared Germany, to give up Russian protection, the German menace would have to be removed. A model agreement for achieving these ends might be the 1955 Austrian State Treaty, which provided for the withdrawal of all occupation forces from Austria and the country's reunification, neutralization, and disarmament. Thus, a settlement might be reached under which NATO and Soviet forces would be withdrawn from central and eastern Europe, Germany reunited, Germany's postwar borders with Poland and Czechoslovakia recognized by all, and the whole region disarmed and neutralized. To be sure, the West would pay a stiff price in NATO's loss of West Germany. But it would win "a chance to reconstitute Europe, and to regain control of the East European key to the Heartland."[61]

◆　◆　◆　◆

Though Burnham's "Austrian" proposal had no effect on U.S. policy, it did spark trouble at *National Review*—namely, from the volatile Willi Schlamm. Buckley's original mentor at *NR* (he once described himself as being "like a father" to Buckley), Schlamm seems to have regarded himself as the magazine's real head, or at least co-head. Buckley, for his part, at first treated Schlamm as his key associate, and when he had to be absent from the magazine he put Schlamm in charge. But before long Buckley began to weary of the overbearing Schlamm and to prefer the cool, steady Burnham, who never believed he and Buckley shared sovereign status.[62]

Hurt and resentful, Schlamm lashed out at Burnham, disguising as political disagreement a querulousness stemming from wounded pride. In November 1956, his anger vented itself in a tantrum in Buckley's office over Burnham's Austrian proposal and in a threat to resign if the magazine published the proposal. Buckley, his forebearance at an end, reacted swiftly and sharply. In a glacial note dispatched later the same day, he reminded Schlamm (and managing editor Suzanne La Follette, who had sided with Schlamm) that Burnham had been invited to join the magazine "because his essential premises are the same as my own," that he had been asked to write a column setting forth his own thoughts, "not yours or mine," on foreign affairs, and that he was entitled to use the column "to think out loud, free from censorship and, I should hope, free from sniping." "After months of deliberation, and a reservoir of patience all but exhausted," the note concluded, the time had come "to reconsider very seriously the viability of *National Review* in the light of the [Burnham-Schlamm] tensions."[63]

Burnham, though he would not yield an inch to Schlamm, was equally determined that the magazine should not founder. Two days later, he told Buckley that he would do what he could to reduce office tensions, "in particular the troubles between Willi and me."[64] Schlamm, meanwhile, was at least temporarily chastened by Buckley's rebuke.[65]

In what became known at *NR* as the "Great Debate," most of the editors opposed Burnham's plan as unrealistic. Buckley argued that even if the USSR agreed to withdraw its troops from eastern Europe, it might one day find it "irresistible" to send them back while the West's resolve to uphold the agreement "might not prove irresistible." He was therefore against the proposal "on tactical grounds." Burnham commented that "hard anti-communists" suffered from "a problem of rhetorical inertia." Associating terms such as "mutual withdrawal," "negotiation," and "neutralization" with appeasement, they preferred "to sit undisturbed inside the familiar tough rhetoric." But given the possibility of ending the Soviet occupation of eastern Europe, the familiar anticommunist "denunciation mingled with a vague and rather empty intransigence" would no longer do. (This call for fresh thinking was supported by a hard-line hero, Whittaker Chambers, whose testimony had precipitated the fall of Soviet agent Alger Hiss. "Whether we like what we see is not in point," Chambers wrote to Buckley. "To see is in point. Burnham is trying to see.")[66]

After the "Great Debate," *NR* enjoyed internal peace, but not for long. Schlamm simply could not keep his feelings in check. Burnham, taking up the problem with Buckley, chided the editor-in-chief for indulgence toward Schlamm. "You ought to stop coddling his neuroses," he said, and added that the boss had to be able to impose his authority. He also offered to resign if that would help, or have his name removed from the masthead, or at least stop attending the weekly editorial conference. But Buckley turned these offers down. Burnham's presence at *NR,* he said, was "crucial."[67]

Realizing that he must choose between Schlamm and Burnham, Buckley took action. *National Review* "as presently staffed" could not function "successfully or happily," he wrote to Schlamm on April 28. He himself saw the differences between the editors as trivial in comparison with their many areas of agreement, but "you attach a more or less total importance to [the differences]: so much so that, operationally speaking, our endeavor is being paralyzed." Hence, he now believed that Schlamm (who the year before had talked of moving to Vermont and mailing in his copy) should indeed play a smaller role at the magazine, limiting himself to his "Arts and Manners" column. "I have not discussed this letter with any editor except Brent Bozell," he added. But later that day he sent a copy to Burnham.[68]

Schlamm, however, resisted further demotion. "I no longer wish to retire to Vermont," he replied. "National Review is as much my creation and my life's central concern as it is yours." He also demanded that the editors meet to discuss his future status, and in early May they gathered at the Commodore Hotel to take up the issue. There, Schlamm went on the offensive, telling Buckley, "You can't fire me." When the meeting was over, nothing had been settled. Burnham, who was present, had dinner with Buckley afterward. "I've seen a lot in my life that is crazy," he commented, "but I've never seen anybody say you can't fire me, when you are the undisputed boss of the enterprise."[69]

The next day, Buckley informed Schlamm of the terms under which he could be "reinstated as a full time member of the office staff": no more threats to resign if he could not have his way, no more assuming that he outranked the other editors, acceptance of Buckley's full authority over *NR*. Schlamm threw in the towel.[70]

After his submission, Schlamm faded into the background. Though he worked at *National Review* for several months more, he came to the office only to write his column, rarely speaking with any of his colleagues. In August 1957 he departed on what the magazine called a year's "leave of absence," but he never returned. In the course of a long epilogue to his days at *NR,* he received generous treatment from Buckley, who let him free-lance for *NR,* and paid him an annual retainer of $2,000 until 1968 and $1,000 until 1974. Eventually Schlamm went back to Europe, settled in Germany, and became proprietor and editor-in-chief of a magazine called *Die Zeitbuehne.* He finally had a journal of his own.[71]

Schlamm's original place at *NR* was inherited by Burnham. When he himself was out of town, Buckley announced, Burnham would act as editor-in-chief every other week, with John Chamberlain spelling him during the off-week. In January 1959 Buckley deputized Burnham to serve as sole editor-in-chief during his absences. Three months later, the job of managing editor passed to Priscilla Buckley, who not only liked Burnham, but also leaned toward his conception of *NR*. With this key post in the hands of a friend and ally, Burnham achieved a status at the magazine second only to that of its proprietor and editor-in-chief.[72]

Shortly thereafter, another key position came his way. In September 1958 *National Review* had shifted to a biweekly publishing schedule. But Buckley, still wanting to publish on a weekly basis in some fashion, began every other week to put out an eight-page newsletter called the *National Review Bulletin*. At first Buckley himself wrote the *Bulletin*'s lead article. But in the 1960s, increasingly busy with other activities, such as his television interview program, *Firing Line,* he cut back on his writing for the newsletter. Burnham took his place, infusing the *Bulletin,* according to his editorial assistant Kevin Lynch, with his personal "style and tone," and making it, in Priscilla Buckley's words, "entirely his own operation."[73]

◆　◆　◆　◆

Burnham turned out to be a godsend. Buckley had originally wanted him as an editor and a columnist on foreign affairs. But Burnham soon also became Buckley's general mentor. "I would consider him the number one intellectual influence on The National Review since the day of its founding," Buckley said of Burnham after the latter's death many years later. But long before then Buckley expressed his gratitude more directly. "I think I am prepared to say," he wrote to Burnham in 1958 in reply to Burnham's condolences on Buckley's father's death, "that I am most grateful to [Buckley *père*] for making National Review possible, because by that act he made possible our association which, now that he is gone, I value second to none with any other man."[74]

# Chapter 10

# Die-Hard

T HOUGH BURNHAM'S MAIN BUSINESS at *National Review* was "The Third
World War," he sometimes touched on domestic issues. Among the most
explosive of these during the Eisenhower era was the black civil rights
struggle. Burnham and most of his *NR* colleagues sided with the segregationists,
contending that, as they put it in a 1957 editorial on black voting rights, southern whites were entitled to take the steps they deemed "necessary to prevail politically and culturally" in places where they lacked a majority, since "for the time
being" they were "the advanced race." If the majority wanted what was "socially
atavistic," the editorial went on, "then to thwart the majority may be, though
undemocratic, enlightened." For it was "more important for any community . . .
to affirm and live by civilized standards than to bow to the demands of the
numerical majority." On the same principle, the editors added, there should be
nothing sacrosanct about universal suffrage for whites.[1]

Burnham's stand on segregation stemmed from his hostility to "democratist"
ideology and big government. The school segregation issue, he maintained,
should be settled "locally—in the states and their local subdivisions, and in the
hearts of men," not by Washington, whose arguments consisted of "tanks, bayo-
nettes, [and] machine guns." The 1957 civil rights act, he charged in Burkean
tones, was "the spiritual child" of the French Revolution's "'ideological,' Utopian
and Platonic" idea of man and government, and the contrary of the "organic,

historical, traditional" outlook that shunned "wild leaps of abstract reason." "Egalitarian ideology" now had the upper hand, and as a result school integration was slowing, race relations deteriorating, and violence increasing.[2] The real villains of the piece, however, were the federal courts, especially the Supreme Court, which had usurped legislative and executive authority and the right of the people to run their schools.[3]

But the larger problem was the dizzying growth of federal power triggered by "the virus of the New Deal" and a concurrent power shift from Congress to an executive and a judiciary in thrall to the "collectivist, egalitarian and globalist course . . . charted by the Liberal Establishment." For example, much of the economy limped along under a crippling tax burden and a thickening web of regulations, while Washington made ever deeper inroads into "finance, housing, medicine, education." The proper economic role of government, according to American tradition, was "not to take over, own, or operate the economy, but to improve and expand opportunities for private enterprise."[4]

Burnham took a panoramic look at the evolution of the federal government in his next book, *Congress and the American Tradition*. Upon returning from his 1954 trip to Europe, he had intended to begin the work on communism he had postponed to write *The Web of Subversion*. But his publisher, Henry Regnery, upset by the liberal uproar over the McCarthy investigations, urged him to write on congressional investigative committees instead. Burnham, who feared that Congress might follow many twentieth-century European legislatures into "the parliamentary castration chamber," agreed to do so. But he reshaped the subject into a broader study, originally to be called *The Attack on Congress,* that would delve into the origins and history of the federal legislature and that body's relative loss of power to "a 20th century world trend toward totalitarian rule . . . and the rise of a new kind of ideological elite."[5] Armed with a $10,000 grant from the Foundation for Foreign Affairs (whose secretary was Regnery), he got to work. The research for *Congress and the American Tradition,* as he renamed the book, took almost four years and was the most wide-ranging he had ever done.[6]

The finished volume, published in 1959, turned from the topic of Burnham's four previous books, Soviet communism, to another of his long-time concerns—the evolution of American government in the twentieth century from one based on a diffusion of power toward a centralized, plebiscitarian, "Caesarist" mass "democracy." The Founding Fathers, Burnham noted, had divided sovereignty between the states and the federal government, and within the latter among three overlapping but relatively independent branches: Congress, the presidency, and the judiciary, with Congress playing the leading role. And for most of the Republic's history the legislature had indeed led. But in recent decades, the federal government had mushroomed and the presidency had replaced Congress as its primary branch. The peak moment had come with the presidency of Franklin D. Roosevelt (though the Wilson presidency had served as a "rehearsal"). Since then Congress had played "a mere junior partner" to the president, who now stood bathed in an aura of celestial light.[7]

But executive supremacy, Burnham went on to argue (recalling Trotsky's view of Stalin as a front man for the Soviet bureaucratic elite), meant the ascendancy less of the president than of the executive bureaucracy, in theory the servant of the president but in practice an autonomous power. For the occupant of the White House, standing before "the serried ranks of the managerial bureaucracy," was really "more creature than creator." Congress, now in the shadow of the executive branch, still possessed its vital power of investigation. But that power did not suffice to restore the former constitutional balance, and in any case had come under sharp attack. Congress's "final test of freedom [was] the ability—and the willingness—to say No." This it still sometimes did in minor matters, but it had not said "a big No" since 1933.[8]

Behind the growth of executive power, Burnham continued, lay the twentieth century's "permanent crisis" of economic trouble and war. But on a deeper level, the changing balance reflected a long-term trend, the managerial revolution, which meant government by executive fiat and the development of a potentially totalitarian welfare state. The change also encompassed an ideological shift, partly obscured by calling the new system "democracy." For this word was used in two quite different senses. On the one hand, it denoted what might be labeled "democratism" (which Americans called "liberalism"), a system that viewed people in the abstract, as a "mass" of equal social units whose "general will" was realized through the "typical despotism of our time," the rule of a plebiscitarian Caesar. But the word also signified "constitutional government," which was concerned more with liberty than with equality, and saw people in their concrete reality as too varied in their interests to be represented by a single leader. This kind of government worked through intermediary bodies. Congress, "the great intermediary institution" between the citizenry and a chief executive, now stood as the main safeguard of the old constitutional order against the emerging executive-bureaucratic Caesarist state.[9]

Given the current, powerful trend toward executive rule, could Congress survive in substance? Burnham wondered. Probably not, he decided with characteristic pessimism. Still, it was "nowhere decreed that men must submit to impersonal trends, however well established; and it is men who make history." But in addition to good luck (and the survival of the West "in general"), Congress's survival would require a resolve on its part to tame the bureaucracy and go beyond mere criticism of the details of policy to the formulation of policy. Above all, Congress would have to have "the will to survive."[10]

◆   ◆   ◆   ◆

*Congress and the American Tradition* may have left readers of Burnham's earlier books puzzled. Which danger to freedom did he now see as greater: Soviet communism or home-grown totalitarian "democratism"? How did he think the need to wage the Cold War, indispensable to Western survival, could be reconciled with the need to stem the growth of Caesarism, a phenomenon he attributed partly to twentieth-century wars, both hot and cold?[11] And if Caesarism was ultimately tied to the managerial revolution, would self-assertion by Congress suffice to solve the problem? Or was Burnham still prepared to tolerate Caesarism, as he had confessed himself to be when commenting on McCarthy, if it turned out to be the price of fighting communism?

Not many years later, he was faced with a further question: Did the fortunes of the presidency in the late 1960s and the 1970s invalidate his argument? For by the late 1960s the tide seemed to be turning against the White House, as opposition to the Vietnam War led many to protest what liberals now denounced as the "imperial presidency." And during the following decade, presidential power seemed to contract further and that of Congress to expand. In 1974, Congress forced Richard M. Nixon, who had recently been re-elected in a landslide, to resign, and Nixon's successors, Gerald R. Ford and Jimmy Carter, proved too weak to regain the lost ground.

Yet the future also vindicated Burnham, for Congress's legislative primacy continued to erode, in part because of presidential law-making by executive order, and in part because of liberal-activist federal judges who envisaged their function as quasi-legislative (a problem *Congress and the American Tradition* noted, but did not deal with at length). But above all, congressional power faded in the face of the ever-expanding federal bureaucracy, which Burnham had identified as the true depository of federal power. Moreover, for all their protesting against the "imperial presidency," liberals remained devoted to the executive. When they denounced presidential "abuses," they usually aimed their fire not at the executive colossus as such, but at specific policies of individual presidents they did not like. Meanwhile, the powers gathered in the White House, though sometimes challenged by Congress (as in the War Powers Act) and sometimes lying dormant, survived essentially intact.[12]

Reviewers of *Congress and the American Tradition* tended to treat it in partisan fashion. *Time,* which ran its review on its "National Affairs" page rather than in its book section, found the book "bracing." The conservative *Chicago Tribune* called it "thoughtful and often brilliant," and urged that every member of Congress read it. Yet one conservative, though largely agreeing with Burnham, did not do so unreservedly. Burnham had overlooked an important way in which Congress wielded power, Willmoore Kendall observed. A president sometimes did not send a bill to the lawmakers because of his "certain foreknowledge" that the bill would be rejected. It was in this fashion that Congress "*most* consistently [got] its way, and without anyone's noticing it."[13]

Liberal reviewers did not find the book persuasive. Paul Simon, in the *Christian Century,* praised Burnham's skill at argument, but summed up the result as "an effective presentation of a weak case." The liberal Republican *New York Herald Tribune*'s reviewer, Robert K. Carr, huffed that Burnham's "kind words for the power of congressional investigation, even when exercised by a McCarthy, seemed singularly inconsistent with a wish to defend constitutional principles and the primacy of the individual." *New York Times* reviewer Lindsay Rogers, in a tone of scornful amusement, reminded readers that Burnham's earlier prophecies had often not panned out. The *Times* review rattled Henry Regnery badly. Buckley reported him to Burnham as telling people "The New York Times has killed Jim Burnham's book," and as therefore no longer pushing it.[14]

One critical response was less easy to categorize. Writing from Italy, the poet Ezra Pound asked Regnery,

How many of yr/authors like Burnham will face ANY of the ideas which seem to me to be vital? and which, from my angle, they have been dodging for 30 years. I see Burnham refs/to Chodorov [i.e., the libertarian writer Frank Chodorov], and here is Chod. in the Richmond N. Leader, referring to that flapdoodle Keynes as an economist?? . . .

Having struggled to p 12 of Burnham, I wonder wd/ he read my notes if I make 'em?

on his bk /what I shd/ like, or in antique parlance "admire" to see wd/ be copy of Burnham's answer to Reg's enquiry (if any) as to whether Burnham wd/ answer E.P.'s comments or questions?[15]

Burnham does not appear to have replied.

◆　◆　◆　◆

His new book notwithstanding, Burnham's main subject remained the struggle for the world. Still a holdout from the 1950s bipartisan foreign policy consensus, he continued to attack Washington's performance on the global stage. U.S. foreign policy, he wrote, continued to be reactive and thus "purely defensive." One consequence was that because "major American military operations [were] invariably decided not by the exercise of our will," but in reply to thrusts by the enemy, Soviet general secretary Nikita Khrushchev had become the "effective Commander-in-Chief" of our armed forces. Moreover, the United States often passively accepted such thrusts, and so ran the risk of acquiring "*the habit of appeasement.*" American efforts to win over the Kremlin made one's heart sink. Indeed, the sight of the "see-no-evil, issue-shelving, Boy Scout Eisenhower" welcoming Khrushchev, "still encarnadined with the blood of the Hungarian Freedom Fighters," to the White House, where the Soviet boss would "walk the floors trod by Washington and Jefferson, and sleep in Lincoln's bed," induced despair. "No one ever suggested inviting Adolf Hitler to our country," Burnham noted, "not even President Franklin D. Roosevelt, who was ready for nearly anything." Nor would such fawning ultimately yield any benefits, for although an atmosphere of "*détente*" might exist for a time, it would "explode or erode away" as "the realities move[d] once again into the open."[16]

True, Secretary of State Dulles usually struck the right verbal note. Yet if Dulles's policy was an improvement over appeasement, it was still premised on containment, and therefore basically flawed. Under Dulles's version of containment, Washington never took "even the smallest initiative." As storms shook the USSR, it "stood passively by." Acheson's "loose and slippery" kind of containment had allowed the communists to take China; Dulles's "verbally inflexible" kind was letting them into Africa and the Middle East.[17]

To make things worse, Burnham charged, the basic tools of American foreign policy were poorly employed. Washington wasted foreign aid by failing to demand anything in return. "What has the United States ever got out of all the money and moral kowtowing it has lavished on India?" he asked, angry at what he saw as the hypocritical moralizing of Nehru. The principle according to which foreign aid ought to be dispensed was that "for every *quid* there should always be a balancing *quo.*" As usual, the Kremlin managed these things better. Khrushchev cut off credit to a delinquent Yugoslavia because he knew "that the way to keep gangsters like Tito in line is to knock them on the head, not lick their boots. And sure enough, Yugoslavia continued its active support of every Soviet policy, everywhere in the world."[18] Nor should the United States toady to "absurd majorities" at the United Nations in hopes of winning votes for resolutions it favored. Khrushchev was "interested not in votes but in power. If you get the power, he reasons, the votes will come in due course.[19]

Equally clumsy was the administration's handling of NATO. Discord in the alliance stemmed from the inconsistency of U.S. policy toward the Soviets. Since Washington did not seem to know whether it wanted to pursue the Cold War or make a deal with the Kremlin, why should NATO members court trouble with the Soviets by accepting American leadership? NATO's woes would persist until Washington had decided on a policy.[20]

No less hapless in Burnham's eyes were the organizations charged with waging the Cold War, foremost among them the CIA. "At a most generous estimate," he observed, the agency's record in intelligence analysis seemed "spotty." Too often, the CIA misread situations abroad, and when critical events occurred was caught by surprise. A better procedure would be to shut down the CIA's analysis branch and hire "six first-class men who know the score, give them each a comfortable, quiet office with subscriptions to the *New York Times* and the *Economist,* and forbid all committee assignments." As for polwar, the CIA's record was "cat-astrophic." But could an organization "without either strong faith or clear policy, directed by stuffed shirts and bureaucrats, staffed too often by routine clerks plus activist hired hands" be expected to do well at polwar, especially when those in charge suffered from "a defect of will as much as brains?" What was more, he added, leveling a charge that in the 1960s and 1970s would come from the Left, not only had the CIA wasted billions; it had also engaged in illegal actions in the United States. Congress, instead of letting itself be stampeded by "mystery-mon-gering" CIA men, should get this "most crucial, expensive and dangerous" body under control.[21]

He thought no better of Washington's propaganda office, the United States Information Agency. Did USIA people, he wondered, know "anything" about the USSR, communism, modern history, or beaming propaganda at foreign coun-tries? Did the United States need an official organization "to tell the world how much we admire Soviet musicians, artists, visiting firemen—and generals?" He was appalled to learn that a new USIA television series on American life was going to kick off with a show about American highways and traffic. "Is there any point in having an 'information program,'" he snapped, "if we haven't anything to say?"[22]

As for the State Department, he lamented, despite Dulles's tough talk, not much had improved since the bad old Acheson days. Run by "verbalists and intel-lectuals, not by fighters," State bent over backwards to be "sensitive" to world opinion and paid less attention to the interests of U.S. citizens than to "the sen-sibilities of Kwame Nkrumah, Fidel Castro, and Patrice Lumumba." Many State Department appeasers even seemed to think that U.S. policy's supreme concern "must be to avoid any action that might disturb, irritate or counter the Masters of the Kremlin." Yet for all its sensitivity to the feelings of foreigners, the depart-ment, judging by its feeble response when American spokesmen and symbols were attacked and insulted abroad, seemed ready to swallow any abuse that for-eigners dished out to Americans. Such conduct, among other things, fell far short of what simple manliness required.[23]

Though much preferring military men ("lions") to State Department "verbal-ists" ("foxes"), Burnham was also unhappy with the U.S. armed forces. One major defect, he argued, was the obsolete "ground-water-air division" of the military. Mostly the result of "organizational inertia," this structure promoted waste, duplication, and intraservice rivalries, and prevented the development of a rational, unified war plan. As for the individual services, the army needed to abandon its vision of "future Napoleonic campaigns on the European continent," while the navy should move beyond aircraft carriers, now "obsolescent," to nuclear submarines, and come up with a naval strategy for fighting "little wars." The navy should also junk its indoctrination program, which in typical liberal fashion mistakenly valued intellect over "moral outlook, motivation, and character." Equally foolish was the expenditure of time and money on lightly trained, short-term draftees when U.S. military needs—a nuclear deterrent and a "little war" capability—called for highly trained, professional units.

All these shortcomings reflected a more basic one, he asserted. The military *"doesn't know what it is supposed to do,"* and so does not have "a true war plan." This should come as no surprise, since "we have no national policy and *therefore* we cannot have a coherent strategic doctrine." Accordingly, the most pressing need of all was for a policy, i.e., "an organized response to the postwar technical and political world revolution."[24]

At present, however, partial improvements were possible. For example, the top command echelon of the armed forces should be reorganized through the replacement of the Joint Chiefs of Staff by a genuinely unified command, "a single General Staff" headed by a single commander and consisting of personnel who had no additional service ties.[25] In addition, the U.S. deterrent should be strengthened. Issuing a warning that would be heard often in the future, he taxed the U.S. missile program with being "too late, too small and too slow." While the USSR soared into space, the US defense behemoth lumbered along in a rut, its lead times lengthening, and its modern warfare capability eroding. As things stood, it was now possible for the U.S. missile arsenal, made vulnerable by its fixed launching sites, to be wiped out by a Soviet first strike.[26]

But above all, he asserted, the military needed a more realistic idea of the present conflict, which was being waged "through limited wars and revolts of the periphery and . . . political subversion and counter-subversion." Strategists should take note that even in the nuclear age, "stones function as weapons a good deal oftener than A bombs, and have won many more battles." Did Gandhi need strategic air power to force the British out of India? And Castro, when he set out to conquer Cuba, surely gave no thought to arming his guerrillas with nuclear weapons. In short, though the U.S. nuclear arsenal remained "essential," it should be viewed as "only a partial element of our required strategic posture."[27]

Otherwise put, in addition to a nuclear capability, the United States had to pay much more attention to alternative weapon systems, ones that involved "Blanquist cadres, crowd manipulation, guerrillas, psychological warfare, paramilitary operations, subversion, bribery, infiltration, with specialized, mobile, ranger-type units in supporting reserve—in short, political warfare."

But he was not counting as polwar such programs as "foreign aid," "truth campaigns," and "student exchange," he added. These were "Boy Scout ideas," at least as implemented by Washington. True polwar employed "agitation, propaganda, subversion, economic manipulation, incitement of riots, terror, diversionary diplomacy, sabotage, guerrilla and paramilitary actions, etc.: everything, in sum, short of the employment of the main, formal armed forces." If the United States were to wage psychological warfare, it would hammer away at ideas that caused Moscow pain, such as the USSR's status as the world's largest colonial empire. It would also increase its efforts to penetrate Soviet secrecy ("They go wild at the idea that outsiders are prying into their affairs"), and make greater use of "provocative show[s] of military force," in reply to which the Soviets never did anything but "bleat and bluster."[28]

Moreover, the current partial nuclear test ban and disarmament talks with Moscow made no sense. As desirable as lasting peace might be, the evidence of history and of human nature made it unlikely that war would ever vanish. Arms, after all, did not cause war, but rather, war, or the threat of war, caused arms. To try to eliminate war by getting rid of weapons was "to turn reality upside down."[29]

All the same, Burnham speculated, the Soviets probably did want some nuclear disarmament because for them the cost of the arms race had to be staggering and their arsenal was second-rate and outmoded. In addition, the expense of advanced weapons systems was causing restiveness among their people, who resented having to give up butter for guns. Besides, Soviet strategy did not stress all-out war but polwar, and so did not make ultra-modern weaponry its foremost aim. In fact, should full-scale war break out, the Soviets would try to turn it into an old-fashioned war, in which their quantitative superiority in conventional arms and manpower would give them the edge. Accordingly, Moscow had much to gain from a nuclear weapons ban, for nuclear disarmament really meant disarming the West.[30]

Eisenhower's decision to halt nuclear testing and seek a test ban agreement with the USSR struck Burnham as a "policy of nuclear surrender." But what upset him most was the failure of will he thought the decision implied. "Arms without will are nothing but a pile of junk," he wrote, "and this is what our vast and costly armament has become, or is fast becoming."[31] How did the two antagonists stack up against each other at present? "Communist Russia is stuck because, though she has the will and the strategic goal, she does not yet have the power," he noted in 1960. "The West is stuck because though we have and have had the power, we lack both goal and will. Which side will be the first to complete its triad?"[32]

◆    ◆    ◆    ◆

In Burnham's view, U.S. thinking on foreign policy at the close of the Eisenhower era was divided into two opposing outlooks: a "hard" view that believed the United States to be at war, and wished to win the war, and a "soft" view that believed the United States to be at peace, and wished to preserve the peace. The United States was losing the Third World War, he argued, and would go on losing it until the "hard" view gained the upper hand and brought about "a *total* change" in foreign policy and military strategy. "Nothing less than what the Russians used to call a 'purge' [would] serve, a purge of the Softs from the points of leverage."[33]

In 1952 Burnham had pinned his hopes on the Republicans, but in vain. The Eisenhower administration, he charged in 1960, in seeking "'peaceful competition'" with the Soviets, had simply repeated the error of the Democrats. Moscow was offering "peace in return for surrender," and the Eisenhower crowd, sounding eager for "peace at any price," seemed "close to accepting."[34]

Yet as the 1960 election approached, he again called upon conservatives to vote Republican, even if, as seemed likely, the candidate came from the party's Eisenhower wing. As in 1956, some of his *National Review* colleagues opposed this position. Spurning the GOP mainstream, Frank Meyer thought that the sole Republican conservatives could support was Arizona's hard-line senator, Barry M. Goldwater. Bill Rusher, longing for the day when conservatives would command the GOP, shared Meyer's view. To rally behind Vice President Richard M. Nixon, he argued, would only strengthen the party's current, unacceptable leadership.[35]

If Burnham violated a conservative taboo by urging support for whomever the GOP nominated, he compounded the offense by naming as his own choice none other than Nelson A. Rockefeller, governor of New York, a leading member of the party's liberal wing, and a villain in the eyes of *National Review* regulars. True, Burnham admitted, Rockefeller harbored New Dealish, pro-labor, welfare state opinions. But on the all-important issue of the struggle for the world, he seemed "a hard sort of man"—"harder," indeed, "than any rival of either party." Rockefeller did not mince words in criticizing the nuclear testing pause, while in his calls for better weapons, an airborne alert system, and the mass construction of bomb shelters for civilians, he showed a welcome awareness of Cold War reality. Burnham may also have known that Rockefeller was a polwar fan. All in all, Buckley once explained, Burnham saw Rockefeller as "a tough, competent anticommunist, who would be hard to outwit at a summit conference," and whose "vanity would keep him from giving in to the Soviets."[36]

But when Nixon, not Rockefeller, won the GOP nomination, Burnham glumly swung into line. "I have so little personal enthusiasm for Nixon that I may not be able to endure voting for him," he wrote to Buckley a few weeks before the election. Still, a candidate's individual characteristics mattered little, "especially in the era of bureaucratized mass societies." The Democratic nominee, Massachusetts senator John F. Kennedy, had to be defeated because his support came from "virtually all of the forces, groups, tendencies and individuals that NR is not merely against, but recognizes as its primary targets: the disintegrative leftist ideologues, including those who ruin our educational system; the most dangerous and ruthless of the trade union bureaucracy; the appeasers and collaborationists; the most extreme secularists (ironically enough! [given the attention paid to Kennedy's Catholicism]) including the most Jewish Jews; the city lumpenproletariat; the socialists, fellow-travelers and communists; and—one might add—the appeasers, socialists and collaborationists of the entire world as well as this country." The election offered "only one publicly meaningful way to declare against" such people: a vote for Nixon. "[I]f that's the way it is, then a conservative has to set his course within the frame of reality. It is the sectarian, the radical, the ideologue who leaves reality for his private dream."[37] Buckley agreed. "I hate the thought of insulating National Review from the effective political process," he wrote back, "and I do not feel that ours is a monastic function of bead-saying in isolation from the rest of the world."[38]

Since Burnham had often written scathingly of Eisenhower's policies, he may have been surprised to get a letter from Charles Percy, temporary chairman of the Republican National Convention's Resolutions Committee, asking for suggestions for the GOP's 1960 foreign policy platform. (Though Percy may only have been trying to lure grumpy right-wingers back to the GOP fold, his request nevertheless implied Republican interest in *National Review.*) In reply, Burnham sent Percy a detailed summation of his views, from his Third World War thesis to his sketch of a possible U.S. deal with Moscow, as well as an outline of his thoughts on more recent issues. Thus, with the Third World emerging as a Cold War cockpit, he advised greater and more systematic heed to the problems of Africa, Asia, and Latin America.[39]

He said nothing, however, about one of the most important occurrences of the day: the growing rift between the USSR and China. A few years earlier, he had pointed to the likelihood of a Sino-Soviet split, doubting that Mao Tse-tung, whom he had portrayed in glowing terms as vastly superior in general ability to the USSR's humdrum bosses, would submit to Soviet tutelage forever.[40] Yet now, as the Chinese-Soviet quarrel burst into the open, he questioned its genuineness. The "No. 1 current objective of Moscow's psycho-political warfare," he asserted, "is to persuade Western opinion that there exists a deep and quickly growing breach between Russia and China." This idea was meant to promote "the rest of the current communist operation," i.e., "Russo-Western *détente,* co-existence, cultural cosiness, German settlements, trade, disarmament, and so on," since it furnished "the perfect rationalization to lead even anti-Communists across the appeasement bridge." The USSR and China would not and could not "try to cut each other's throats until they [had] finished cutting ours."[41]

But if he did not mention the Sino-Soviet rift to Percy, he viewed the subject as important enough to warrant a special *National Review* supplement, of which he served as editor.[42] Eventually, he accepted the Sino-Soviet split as real. But his first, skeptical view of it was his single biggest mistake as a Cold War analyst.[43]

Finally, Burnham briefly signaled to Percy a trend that augured trouble for the future. This was the Third World population explosion, which, he commented in his column, might become the century's "controlling event." Claiming in the column to be summarizing "a remarkable paper presently circulating in certain research institutes and government agencies," he underlined the "Malthusian" conditions coming to prevail in many Third World countries and the political

instability these conditions bred. The Sino-Soviet bloc, he warned, which fed on
social turmoil and had the authoritarian will to master disorder, now seemed
"certain" to extend its power over the world's "Malthusian third." If looked at
from the perspective of the population crisis, the Cold War might be viewed as a
bi-level contest, on one level between communist and Western "systems of population management" and on the other between "individuals and groups," over
constantly shrinking amounts of food and space. For its economic survival, the
paper concluded, the United States would have to revise its Third World policy
wholesale, while to preserve its primacy in world trade, it would have to carry
out "intensive technological modernization."[44]

The population crisis never became one of Burnham's more pressing concerns. Still, in giving it serious attention,[45] he departed from his usual practice of
viewing the whole spectrum of international politics through a Cold War lens
(just as he had done in 1957, when he had pointed to an Asian political-cultural
revolt against the West, not the Cold War, as the likeliest source of future world
upheaval). The Cold War would continue to be his principal framework for interpreting world events, but it would no longer always dominate his thinking.

◆　◆　◆　◆

When John F. Kennedy replaced Eisenhower in the White House, Burnham welcomed his arrival on one count. "[I]s it not a fine thing," he exclaimed, "to have
a First Lady who goes to the National Gallery because she really likes to look at
the pictures hanging there, not to have her own picture taken; who can talk dis-
cerningly about books and plays and places; who dresses so elegantly and is so
very good looking?"[46] But otherwise there was little about Camelot he liked. To
his mind the new administration reflected the outlook of the quintessentially liberal ADA ("the egghead style" of thinking, he called it), some of whose members
held high-level posts under Kennedy. Kennedy himself, however, struck him as a
different sort of person, not a liberal ideologue, but a purveyor of crowd-pleasing
images who had brought the spirit of Madison Avenue to the Oval Office.[47]

Under the New Frontier, Burnham was soon charging, trends harmful to constitutional government were gathering steam. The White House, the Supreme
Court, and probably even the majority in Congress seemed more than ever in
thrall to a "centralizing, totalist obsession," with tragic results. Race relations,

which had begun to improve (though "far too slowly") through voluntary integration, were, with federally coerced integration, growing worse. It had become impossible "even to undertake the kind of scientific and empirical investigation that might prove objectively, once for all, whether and in what sense Negroes [were] inferior."[48]

He was also disturbed by the 1962 Supreme Court decision banning prayer in public schools. His reaction did not stem from offended piety, but from fear that the decision further weakened the constitutional order—the Court, seized by a "secularist obsession," had subordinated traditional practice to ideology. How widely, he asked, would the decision be applied? Could parents have their children say prayers in "a tax-subsidized apartment or a house with an FHA mortgage?" The Court, he contended, was endangering religious freedom. The Constitution should be amended to legalize prayer in the schools.[49]

Yet in some respects Burnham found the New Frontier engrossing. He was deeply interested, for instance, in the cool, slick-haired technocrat Robert S. McNamara, formerly head of Ford Motors and now secretary of defense. Burnham often wrote critically of McNamara, complaining that the secretary and the "whiz kids" he had gathered around him at the Pentagon relied too heavily on a computer-based, "push-button" notion of warfare. Worse, McNamara's Minuteman and Polaris missiles seemed to rest on the same flawed strategic principle as the Maginot Line. Still, McNamara had his good side: a keen mind, a refusal to curry favor, and a willingness to confront the fuddy-duddy Defense Department brass.[50]

What interested Burnham most about McNamara, however, was what he called the secretary's "historic role." McNamara's chief function, he wrote, was to insert the defense sector into America's "advanced, managerial economy" at a time of galloping technological progress. With his Harvard Business School training, corporate experience, and rationalizing activism, McNamara personified the managerial revolution. This was why he sparked not only criticism but even loathing among the mossbacks used to running the Pentagon.[51]

But, what Burnham found positively fascinating was McNamara's Apollo space program. Though an economic drain, the program would yield a huge scientific benefit, not to mention a decisive military advantage, since a space station could win the Cold War. But what really counted was that man [had] decided to move out into space. Not for any reason, for no more reason than drives men up the slopes of Everest or in a tiny boat across the Atlantic or on a scaffolding for ten years under the Sistine ceiling. The "reasons" are, really—even if they happen to be valid in their own right—rationalizations of what springs from roots deeper, and darker, than reason.

It makes no difference what the space program will cost— and of course it is going to cost double, triple, ten times as much in money as any figure anyone has so far mentioned, and very much, too, in suffering and death; not all space flights will have happy endings. It will make no difference whether anyone proves incontrovertibly that the whole program is worthless in economic, scientific, military and all other rational terms. The terrible cold and darkness, the destroying radiations, the silence and desolation and tragedy will make no difference, will only make the seduction of space more compelling.

Our souls, whose faculties can comprehend

The wondrous architecture of the world,

And measure ev'ry wandering planet's course,

Will us to wear ourselves and never rest . . .

And Marlowe's Tamburlaine will no more find sweet fruitions in a galactic than in an earthly crown.[52]

The New Frontier's foreign policy, however, seemed to Burnham as dismal as its space program seemed bright. Since World War II, he observed, U.S. foreign policy had developed as a compound of three distinct tendencies: a "Western strategy," which stressed defense of the West and took concrete form in such constructions as NATO; a "Yalta strategy," which aimed at Soviet-American collaboration and was embodied in such ventures as the nuclear disarmament talks; and a "Third World strategy," which sought friends in the former colonial sphere and found expression in foreign aid, support for decolonization, and the American commitment to the UN. From the late 1940s to the mid-1950s the Western strategy had been in the forefront. But since "the great turning point of Suez-Hungary" and Eisenhower's tacit assent to Soviet control of eastern Europe, the United States had been drifting toward the Yalta strategy. Under Kennedy the

Third World strategy had been moving up, but it was the Yalta strategy that had emerged as the "outstanding feature" of New Frontier foreign policy.[53]

Kennedy (like Eisenhower) also wobbled on the chief objective of his foreign policy. Was its highest purpose peace or victory over communism? Kennedy certainly opposed communism. But he also opposed war, and he had not made up his mind which he opposed more, i.e., had not decided which was his "one main enemy."[54]

In Burnham's eyes, the Cold War's central arena was still Europe, and within Europe, Germany. When Khrushchev threatened to transfer control over access to West Berlin to the USSR's East German puppets if the Western powers did not surrender their rights in the city, Burnham said the Soviets were bluffing. The West, however, should not meet their blackmail with mere resistance, he added, let alone give in for the sake of "peace," but launch a polwar campaign, backed by a credible show of force. If the United States adopted a "dynamic policy"—for example, "an all-out campaign" for German reunification—Moscow would not dare press its demands to the point of war. For if war broke out, it could not be sure "which way the East Germans would point their guns."[55]

In August 1961 Khrushchev resolved the Berlin crisis by authorizing East Germany to build the Berlin Wall. Washington's merely verbal protest increased Burnham's frustration. Many better responses were available, he declared, including "cumulative restrictions, boycotts, diplomatic pressures, cancellation of exchange programs, embargoes, not to speak of indirect pressures through resumption of nuclear tests, action on Cuba, and so on." The Berlin outcome, he noted that autumn, conformed to a familiar pattern. Moscow would start trouble, make demands, create tension. Next, the cry would go up to lower the tension through a "'compromise.'" Washington would dutifully agree to talks, and a settlement would be reached. "That is, we grant them half or two-thirds or nine-tenths of what they have asked, and we 'win' one-tenth. Until the next round."[56]

By the early 1960s Burnham thought it "inconceivable" that the West would oppose any Soviet advance short of a military attack. "The rhythm of this business" must at some point be broken, he wrote. If the administration did not change course, the Soviets would keep pressing forward, "and the New Frontier [would] get closer, and closer."[57]

But he doubted that the president had the will needed for the effort. In late 1961, at a University of Chicago seminar on U.S. military policy, he heard his skepticism echoed by a fellow doubter, the philosopher Leo Strauss. Asked by a third participant in the seminar, Senator Henry A. Jackson of Washington, why he thought the United States had acquiesced in the Berlin Wall, Strauss paused briefly, and then quietly answered, "Well, we are here among ourselves, and I will tell you what I really believe, though I of course have no proof and cannot have any. I believe that at Vienna [where Khrushchev and Kennedy had met in June] Khrushchev took the measure of President Kennedy, and saw that his own will was the stronger."[58] That was exactly the way it looked to Burnham.

Kennedy sometimes did well, Burnham granted, thinking of the president's 1961 announcement, in reply to a series of Soviet nuclear tests, that the United States would also resume testing, and of his June 1963 speech at the Berlin Wall. But on balance, he believed Kennedy's failures far outweighed his achievements—as, for example, the August 1963 nuclear test ban treaty with the USSR, which Burnham feared would prevent the United States from developing a more nuanced nuclear arsenal and spare the USSR an economically more burdensome arms race.

Other countries, moreover, were likely to identify the treaty with the Yalta strategy, he warned, which could only benefit neutralism. For if the United States were seen to be abandoning the West for a deal with the USSR, why should the West stay loyal to the United States? Nor had Washington driven a very hard bargain. Why had it not demanded something in return for its signature, for example, the removal of the Berlin Wall? Would that Kennedy had emulated France's president, Charles de Gaulle, who, when invited to sign the treaty, had refused with a "manly *No.*"[59]

◆　◆　◆　◆

Nonetheless, apart from the Berlin crisis and the test ban treaty, Burnham thought western Europe's prospects brilliant. On the economic plane, he noted, the region was thriving, thanks in part to the Common Market (which he called "the most promising international development, in fact, the only promising international development, of the postwar epoch"), while on the political plane, the original territory of the West seemed likely to federate and become "once again a real factor in the world equilibrium." At this juncture, he believed, new technology, growing economic opportunity, the need for a joint defense against the USSR, and a common concern with the problems of the Third World called for a further stage of Western integration, an *"Atlantic Common Market"* comprised of the United States, Britain, Canada, and the members of the European Common Market (in the early 1960s France, Italy, West Germany, Belgium, the Netherlands, and Luxembourg). This broader market could go on expanding, taking in Australia, New Zealand, South Africa, the two Rhodesias (the future Zambia and Zimbabwe), and "to the degree that their economic and political development" allowed, the Third World countries. American conservatives should give up their protectionist-isolationist traditions and welcome a global common market as "an essential part of a 'hard' line on the world conflict," a beacon of free market principles, and a body that would further the interests of U.S. trade.[60]

Still, not forsaking his characteristic pessimism completely, Burnham also noted discouraging trends in Europe, especially a growing tendency toward neutralism. Europeans now aimed at security through deals with the USSR or through self-defense, he wrote, for they believed that the United States dreaded a showdown with the Kremlin. By themselves, of course, the nations of western Europe could not achieve security against the Eurasian land mass. But an alternative existed beyond the status quo or neutralism: a revamped NATO in which the United States would give up its commanding role to become merely "first among equals."[61]

Burnham also had an economic explanation for western Europe's increasing neutralism: the consumer mentality resulting from the region's economic boom, which might therefore be judged a mixed blessing. On a 1961 trip to Italy, he and Marcia visited the town of San Sepolcro to see Piero della Francesca's *Resurrection,* to Burnham "surely one of the very greatest" of the world's paintings. As he looked at the fresco, which shows the risen Christ standing over sleeping sentries who are supposed to be guarding his tomb, an allegory took shape in his mind. What the work conveyed, "among so many other things," he decided, was "the power and wealth and luxury of Rome gone soft and sluggish, asleep instead of alert and on guard." The sleeping sentries could not see "the fierce Phoenix risen from the gathering ashes of their world." But looking again, he could see a modern allegory. "This time," he observed, "the terrible, staring form that rises above the sleeping sentries and the opened tomb . . . is the [Soviet] Anti-Christ" bringing a message "not of hope springing from the darkness, of redemption, freedom and eternal life, but of slavery and death, and a degradation much worse than death." The sentries, whom he identified with the nations of the West, were not literally asleep. Rather, it was their spirit that slumbered "in the coarse sleep of the glutton." "What if the trade with Russia gives her the machines her armies need and the profits which, skillfully funneled, nourish her Italian agents?" he imagined the sentries to be thinking. "From that trade we Italians get cheaper gasoline for our new cars and Vespas, and some of us get, in addition, pretty piles of lire. Hasn't England always lived as a nation of successful shopkeepers? What is the objection, then, to the $6 million British Trade Fair in Moscow[?]"[62]

In short, most Europeans now thought only of "food and cars, TV sets, vacations and washing machines." Nobody cared a whit about "empires, crusades, colonies, liberations, wars in distant places, justice for others, dim future threats." In going neutralist, Europeans were really saying, "We have done our part long enough and we now retire to the sidelines. . . . [W]e'll use our centuries-trained wiles to play off the giants against each other, and cultivate our rich and lovely garden."[63]

Burnham felt disdain for those who could not resist the lure of the consumer culture, even with the enemy already within the gates. He once conveyed his scorn through the thoughts he attributed to two Chinese travelers he had noticed at London's Heathrow Airport who looked, he said, as if they had come on a mission from Peking.

> They wore overcoats of drab cloth, cut with no attempt at style. Their shoes were ugly, their briefcases worn. Their faces were not the round, moonfaced Chinese stereotype, but handsome, lean and bone-showing, with tight skin. They looked around, very intelligent and very hard; and in their eyes as they . . . glance[d] now and then at the scene around them was, I could not help feeling, a cold contempt. Their eyes seemed to me to be saying: "So you soft people of the West are far enough gone to throw away your birthright for the sake of this trash!"[64]

◆ ◆ ◆ ◆

Burnham did not ignore the Cold War's non-European fronts.[65] Of these, he believed the most important to be Cuba, where Fidel Castro had come to power in 1959. At first doubtful that Castro could rightly be called a communist (Castro was not "Bolshevik" in "political style," he remarked in August 1959, but "a remarkably pure" example of "the charismatic leader"), he soon came to view the Cuban strongman as an "intolerable" tool of Soviet ambition in the Western Hemisphere, who, if he stuck to his present course, would have to be ousted. Castro presented an especially significant test of will for the United States because Cuba lay within the U.S. "strategic frontier."[66] When the Kennedy administration abandoned the anti-Castro exiles it had landed at the Bay of Pigs in 1961, it flunked the test. This boded ill for the future, Burnham warned. It was crucial that "we should *somewhere,* in *some* theater or on *some* vital issue, make a stand of unconditional firmness: that we should strike a blow against the enemy."[67]

During the period between the Bay of Pigs debacle and the 1962 Cuban missile crisis, Burnham repeatedly called upon Kennedy to topple Castro. Hence he applauded when the president, informed that the Soviets were placing intermediate range nuclear missiles in Cuba, imposed a naval blockade on the island. Curiously, however, given his readiness in 1956 for a face-off with the USSR over Poland and Hungary, he also counseled caution, writing, perhaps with Soviet missiles in mind, that in blockading Cuba, Kennedy might have confronted Moscow "a little too" directly. "The soundest strategists," he observed, "always leave *the enemy* room for retreat."[68]

But his praise for Kennedy's "hard" stance soon ceased, for in his deal with Khrushchev for removal of the missiles, the president pledged that the United States would never again invade Cuba. To Burnham, this meant renouncing the Monroe Doctrine. "Was [the hard stance], then, only an election gimmick all along?" he forlornly asked.[69]

Burnham found a second Cold War front beyond Europe in Algeria, where a native revolt for independence from France had been in progress since 1954. History, he contended, suggested that Europe could not exist "as a living, dynamic entity without North Africa." The loss of the region to the communist-backed Algerian National Liberation Front (FLN) would leave Europe "outflanked," deprived of "maneuvering and marshaling ground," close to "the point of no return—the divide beyond which the strategic road, though it may still stretch some decades into the future, leads irreversibly down."[70]

The Algerian struggle also engaged Burnham in another way: it turned him against a longtime hero, Charles de Gaulle. When de Gaulle returned to power in

1958, Burnham saluted him as towering above the era's common run of politicians ("vulgar plebeians, swollen bureaucrats, or bland robots" assembled by "the technicians of public relations"). De Gaulle, he rhapsodized, was "an authentic leader of the stern, inner-disciplined, humane and heroic kind that the egalitarian selection process of our age has sought to breed out of the human race." Africa, de Gaulle knew, was Europe's "great frontier," a continent to be "led out of its darkness, to become European, to become as did America four centuries ago a great new Europe, completing the circle of the Atlantic community." Hence his "unbreakable resolve" never to yield in Algeria.[71]

But Burnham did not know his man. For de Gaulle was ready to surrender Algeria if the effort to hold it kept him from his primary goal: a "great" France heading a European bloc able to deal with Moscow and Washington on an footing. So, when the FLN rejected his bids for compromise, he covertly turned to working out the details of France's withdrawal. This new course was sensed by the wary French settlers in Algeria, who responded to de Gaulle's "betrayal" by rebelling. In January 1960 mutinous Frenchmen raised barricades in Algiers, issuing an angry challenge to the president. But the French army, though sympathetic to the die-hards, stayed loyal to de Gaulle, and after a week of tension the barricades came down.

The "week of the barricades" put Burnham in a quandary. In spirit a die-hard himself, he could not wholly condemn the lawbreaking defenders of French Algeria. Yet as an admirer of de Gaulle, he could not wholly condemn the latter, either. His solution was simultaneously to inculpate and exculpate both. De Gaulle, he wrote, "could not yield" to the rebellious settlers, but all the same, he had "debased himself" by calling them "guilty men." As for the settlers, who had acted "to defend their homes," they could be termed "noble." Still, because of their "vain defiance" of the law they were "guilty," as de Gaulle was both justified and guilty in "rejecting and suppressing them."[72]

But by late 1960 Burnham's attachment to de Gaulle had withered. When Jacques Soustelle, one of the chief agents of the 1958 Gaullist restoration, broke with de Gaulle over Algeria, Burnham offered Soustelle advice on promoting the French Algerian cause in the United States. And learning that Soustelle was planning to visit New York, he invited him to dinner with the editors of *National Review*.[73]

When a cabal of high-ranking officers tried to overthrow de Gaulle in April

1961, only to wind up in prison or on the run, Burnham was overwhelmed by a sense of "tragedy." "The highest living embodiment of the ideal of the soldier: absolute in courage, skill, dedication, loyalty, self-sacrifice," he wrote of General Maurice Challe (supreme commander of the French forces in Algeria and one of the ringleaders of the failed coup) in an accolade of the kind he had once bestowed on de Gaulle. Officers like Challe understood Soviet aims in Algeria. They also realized that the FLN, willingly or not, would yield, as Castro had, "to the Communist embrace." And so to "save France and Europe and the Free World from a mortal danger," they had made "the most tragic decision of their lives," putting "their duty to their country, their civilization and their God above their duty to their commander-in-chief."[74]

Burnham treated the Secret Army Organization (OAS), the clandestine resistance group committed to keeping Algeria French, more warily, however. For if, as he claimed, the OAS upheld "the historical interest of France as a nation, and of the West," it also engaged in brutal acts of terror. Thus, in early 1962, as de Gaulle and the FLN completed their deal on Algerian independence, OAS killers stalked the streets of Algerian cities, randomly murdering Muslims in the hope of provoking a race war that would force the French army to return. Burnham condemned these acts, but then fled into tormented reflection that tended to blunt his condemnation. "For our own part," he agonized in 1962, "we confess with deep and troubled humility our failure to comprehend this dreadful problem of terror that has more and more become a pervasive quality of our epoch. Before the problem of terror the mind plunges into a metaphysical despair, as before those other dark dilemmas that have so long weighed on man's spirit." In contrast, he did not react to FLN terrorism with "metaphysical despair," but simply branded it "unspeakable."[75]

As for de Gaulle, Burnham wrote, he had by "self-willed obstinacy" made himself a captive of the Left and destroyed "the very meaning" of his life and career. "Isolated, half-blind, fixed in outworn political conceptions, frustrated in every major policy," he had sunk into "senile bitterness" and fallen prey to "the megalomania of the aging despot." Since by the early 1960s France had won the shooting war with the FLN, his surrender had been "needless" and hence embodied "not tragedy but pathos."

Burnham's disenchantment with de Gaulle was his worst since his break with Trotsky—and even more crushing, for he had never seen Trotsky in quite the same heroic light. But as time passed, his bitterness receded. Algeria was gone, but de Gaulle remained, his lofty self-possession, temperamental "hardness," independence of mind and will, and indifference to critics as irresistible to Burnham as ever. Though Burnham never fell back under de Gaulle's spell, he did again speak of him enthusiastically, singling him out, for example, as "almost alone" among Western statesmen in thinking on "the highest level of Grand Strategic ideas" and as an "extraordinary man, who bestrides our age of mediocrities like something rather close to a Colossus."[76]

South of Algeria lay yet another extra-European Cold War front, the vast expanse of black Africa, much of which had only recently gained independence from European rule and so become a target for Soviet penetration. In his analysis of African problems, Burnham emphasized three themes. First, that Africans, on average, were not culturally advanced enough to maintain the modern, Western-style institutions their former masters had bequeathed them. "For the most part," he asserted, "the natives are—and, who knows, may perhaps long be, perhaps prefer to be—at the stage of primitive, pre-civilized barbarism; quite simply, savagery."[77] To drive home the point, his reporting of African political violence often included references, sometimes edged with dry humor, to cannibalism. Once, denying a story that white mercenaries in the former Belgian Congo, a country writhing in anarchy in the early 1960s, had been seizing hostages, he explained that the "hostages" were in fact refugees, both black and white, who had sought out the mercenaries for protection from "the knives (and forks) of the Congolese army." He called one column on Africa "I Will Eat You."[78]

Second, he charged that Western liberals—guilt-ridden, blinkered by ideology, insisting on independence for peoples far from ready for it—were partly to blame for the chaos that often followed independence and hence for the harvest he thought Soviet policy was reaping. But he also laid some of the blame on American businessmen who lobbied for rapid decolonization because they hoped for the early removal of imperial tariffs.[79] Finally, he made much of Africa's economic potential, describing it as a rich natural endowment, still only lightly tapped, that could be properly exploited only through African-European collaboration.[80]

Yet the West, he observed, was abandoning Africa at a dizzying pace—and not because of failing strength but failing will and the ceaseless anticolonial pressure of the United States. The depth of his anger over this exodus appeared in the nightmarish picture of decolonization he drew in his column. To grasp what was happening, he wrote on one occasion, people had to rise above "ideological drivel about 'liberation,' 'fresh winds blowing,' 'awakening,' 'equality.'"

> What we see, if we are willing to look, is ourselves—us men of the West—fleeing headlong, beaten, panic-struck, fleeing as the defeated fled before Genghis, Alexander, Pompey, Caesar: fleeing in thousands, in tens and hundreds of thousands, our weapons spiked or abandoned, our homes looted, our property smashed or stolen, our women raped, our children brutalized: fleeing from Egypt, from Tunis and Morocco and the Congo, from Algeria, Kenya, Tanganyika, Uganda. Our giant warships turn and flee from the harbors; our superb warplanes flee from the great fields built by our talents and wealth; our intricate guns are pulled from their emplacements; our soldiers get their command: Retreat!

Words such as "self-determination" and "democracy" were "for most Africans" merely "ritual words without substantial content," he went on. In reality, the drive for independence was powered by racial consciousness: it was "an upsurge of black men against white men." He was especially indignant that whites in Africa had been deserted by their own people. Unlike the Israelis, who in time of trouble could turn for aid to Jews around the world, "the white, Christian, Western communities of Africa"—"the loneliest men"—received little or no outside support. Rather, because of leftist influence, they were "denounced, rejected, condemned and even actively fought by most of the Christian West."[81]

What kind of policy should the United States pursue in Africa? First, it should stop browbeating its allies into decolonizing prematurely, since haste brought social breakdown and opened the way to communism. Second, it should stop backing actions such as the UN's intervention in the Congo to block secession by the copper-rich province of Katanga, a region much more likely than the rest of the Congo to remain stable, productive, and pro-Western. Third, it should shape policy not to suit the preferences of "the Communist-Third World UN majority" but the interests of the West. Fourth, in the spirit of the Monroe

Doctrine, it should declare Africa off limits to communism, and enforce the ban with NATO air and sea power.[82]

As his writings on Africa vividly demonstrate, by the 1960s Burnham had come to loathe the United Nations (often really "half-formed pseudo-nations," he said), to his mind a hotbed of anti-Western neutralism and worse. That populous UN members such as the USSR, India, and the United States had no more voting power in the General Assembly than countries (the UN majority, he believed) less populous than Maryland incensed him. But what incensed him even more was that the United States meekly submitted to this "absurd" arrangement, and swallowed insults to boot, afraid to cross "the cannibals of the Upper Volta," for example, whose vote in the assembly it thought it might one day need. "Why in the world should any sensible person give a damn what some spokesman for cannibalistic tribes or slave-holding nomads thinks about nuclear tests?" he fumed. The UN had become a sounding board for "the immaturity, resentments, pettiness, disorderliness, idle jabber and tantrums of these cubs of the non-white, non-Christian (and while we are facing truths, let us add mostly anti-white, anti-Christian, anti-Western) Third World," yet "the grown-up powers," and mainly "the indulgent Uncle [Sam]," kept picking up the tab.[83]

What Washington should do, Burnham proposed, was regain its freedom—not by leaving the UN but by "*depoliticiz[ing]*" it, transforming the whole organization into a group of purely technical and administrative agencies dealing with such matters as sea and air transport and world health. This the United States could do simply by refusing to recognize the UN as "a decision-making body," refusing to vote or even abstain on any substantive issue and by refusing to help foot the bill for any UN political action authorized by such a vote. Because the "terrorists, savages, revolutionaries, bankrupts, demagogues, voluptuaries, and half-educated opportunists masquerading as representatives of newborn sovereign nations" who dominated the Assembly derived their leverage from U.S. support, such a boycott would render UN directives meaningless, and as a body of political consequence the UN would evaporate.[84]

◆   ◆   ◆   ◆

Was Burnham a racist? Many people would probably say yes, assuming that a person who mourned the passing of European colonial empires, described some anti-Westerners in racial terms, spoke of Africans as primitives, and was willing to tolerate U.S. racial segregation must be one. But they would answer too quickly. For if Burnham sanctioned segregation, he also considered it acceptable only as a contingent arrangement justified by historical circumstance, not as a permanent social ideal. The right goal, he agreed with liberals, was integration. The issue, to his mind, was how integration could best be achieved. Believing that the old racial order was crumbling on its own, he argued that it would be better to let it break down spontaneously, even if that took time, than to try to hasten its demise through federal coercion. Voluntary and gradual integration, he was convinced, would yield a more genuine social equality than force, and would also preserve the country's constitutional structure. Though this is certainly open to debate, it cannot simply be dismissed out of hand as racist.

When Burnham turned his eyes to the Third World, the scenes he witnessed often aroused his indignation. Much of his writing on Third World countries concerns the murderous excesses all too common in some of them and the hypocrisy indulged in by many Third World leaders, whose "Wilsonian" jargon, as he called it—"the cant about 'freedom,' 'anti-colonialism,' 'equality,' and 'self-determination'"—contrasted sharply with their often far from democratic practice.[85] Yet his hostility did not stem from racism, but from his expectation of native misrule and, above all, his anticommunism. Too often, he noted, decolonization led to neutralist and pro-Soviet regimes. When Third World politicians pursued anticommunist policies (as did, for example, Moise Tshombe, who headed secessionist Katanga and then briefly the entire Congo) he wrote of them with approval and often enthusiasm. Moreover, he believed the advancement of Western civilization to be not a product of race, but a historically based, universally attainable achievement.[86]

◆　◆　◆　◆

One further Cold War front held Burnham's attention in the early 1960s, the formerly French-ruled region of Indochina. There, in the sparsely populated, jungle-blanketed kingdom of Laos, a civil war was being fought between communists backed by the USSR and communist North Vietnam, anticommunists backed by the United States, and neutralists. The Kennedy administration, though aiding the anticommunists, did not seek their victory, but aimed instead at a neutral coalition government, with, it hoped, Soviet help. At the same time, in neighboring South Vietnam a communist revolt had broken out against the rule of the nationalist Ngo Dinh Diem. Diem, too, was receiving American aid, but there U.S. support for a neutralist solution had not yet surfaced.

Burnham, who regarded all communist offensives as merely different campaigns in a single, strategically integrated world struggle, saw the Indochinese wars as separate operations in an enterprise he called, borrowing from North Vietnam's ruler, Ho Chi Minh, "the revolution on the Mekong" (the great river that formed Indochina's primary topographical feature). What was more, he charged, if this revolution's local instigator was Ho, its supplier and ultimate director was the USSR. For the Kremlin recognized that if communism managed to master Indochina, it would be able to exert pressure on Burma and Thailand, advance more easily in Malaysia and Indonesia, outflank India, and push on into "the South Seas."[87]

To Burnham, Washington's Indochina policy seemed contradictory. In Laos it was pursuing a "soft strategy" toward a political solution, an all-party, neutralist regime, while in South Vietnam it was pursuing a "hard strategy" toward a military solution, the suppression of the communist-led rebels, the Vietcong. But "how could you make a friendly deal with the Communists in Laos—and, moreover, *force* the anti-Comunists to accept it," Burnham asked, "and do the opposite in the closely related country next door?" It was probably the Laotian half of the contradiction that revealed the true U.S. policy, he decided. For if the United States really intended to make a "serious" stand in South Vietnam, it would reverse course in Laos and, as sound strategy required, extend operations beyond South Vietnam into Laos, Cambodia, northern Thailand, North Vietnam, and even China. Otherwise, the American Marines in South Vietnam fending off "the endless hordes of faceless termites" pouring out of protected havens in North Vietnam and China would suffer "slow attrition" and eventual "suffocation under the steaming mud." (He had already issued a somewhat similar warning in *Containment or Liberation?* cautioning that "mass American land armies fighting in China, Southeast Asia and India . . . might be swamped and swallowed by Asia. The relatively minor war in Korea shows how easily and almost inadvertently this can happen.")[88] Probably, the United States would soon be pressuring Diem to name a neutralist coalition cabinet that would include the Vietcong, he predicted, in which case the current fighting in South Vietnam, which was costing American lives, was "senseless butchery."[89]

When, in early November 1963, a cabal of American-backed South Vietnamese generals abducted Diem and killed him, Burnham called the coup a dreadful error. Diem was the best man available in South Vietnam "and a damn sight better than we had any right to expect," he had written shortly before the coup. Some of the rebel generals were certainly anticommunist, he granted. Still, they had no "'social base' for an anti-Communist policy," and would be hampered by being known as the "American puppets" they in fact were. A process had begun whose outcome was easy to foresee. The new government would at once begin to fail, its leftist members would open negotiations with the Vietcong for the installation of a neutralist successor, and the latter would serve as the bridge to communist rule.[90]

◆ ◆ ◆ ◆

"Curious how things work out!" Burnham noted toward the end of 1963. De Gaulle's coup of 1958, which had seemed to guarantee French resistance to the FLN, had turned out to be the prelude to France's withdrawal from Algeria. Kennedy's hard-line naval blockade of Cuba had turned out to be the prelude to a hands-off policy toward Castro. By a similar irony, the generals' coup in Vietnam, intended to bring victory over the Vietcong, might turn out to be the prelude to the West's departure from Southeast Asia. "We hope we are wrong," he added, "but we seldom are about such matters."[91]

Burnham's premonition proved correct. The United States did pull out of Vietnam—though not until more than a decade later and a colossal escalation of the war and loss of life. But long before American TV viewers witnessed the surreal spectacle of American personnel escaping into helicopters from the roof of the U.S. Saigon embassy as North Vietnamese regulars swarmed through the streets below, Kennedy himself came to a violent end. On November 22, 1963, Burnham's fifty-eighth birthday, the president was assassinated. The widespread "sense of ineluctable tragedy" Burnham thought the murder had prompted led him to ponder a paradox he glimpsed at the heart of the communist philosophy.

> We are reminded once more that neither intelligence nor
> courage nor any techniques, programs or policies can make man

the self-sufficient master of his fate. That is the supreme illusion and ultimate heresy of Marx and Lenin, Khrushchev and Mao, and Lee Harvey Oswald. And that is why John Kennedy's death, or any death, could not be a tragedy for Khrushchev, Mao, or Oswald, but only a passing rearrangement of atoms in the eternal dialectic of matter out of which the universal Communist society, with the beginning of "truly human history," will inevitably emerge. If man creates and rules his world, it follows, by an exquisite irony, he can find no place for himself in it.[92]

# Chapter 11

# Pathologist

Burnham did not limit his criticism to American foreign policy and liberal ideology; he also occasionally directed it at the conservative movement. While praising Young Americans for Freedom (YAF), a conservative youth organization launched at the Buckley home in Sharon, Connecticut, in 1960, as "the best, the very best of the new generation," he also believed the group evidenced notable shortcomings. YAF had neither a program nor a stragegy, he told Buckley, and its statement of principles was, as *NR* contributor Gerhart Niemeyer put it, "metaphysically both false and contradictory." YAF came down to "25,000 young persons in search of a father." But were "Barry [i.e., Goldwater, YAF's choice to head the 1964 Republican ticket] and Barryism enough of a man for the role?"[1]

As this question implies, Burnham did not share conservatives' enthusiasm for the senator. Though he wrote approvingly of Goldwater, offered him advice on how to become a stronger contender for the Republican nomination, formally backed him against the incumbent president, Lyndon B. Johnson, and drew up a foreign policy agenda for a Goldwater administration,[2] his support struck some as half-hearted. Burnham still entertained "illusions about Rockefeller," remembered the fervently pro-Goldwater Rusher, who wrote of being "driven right up the tree" by a comment of Burnham's in 1964 that *NR* could, in Rusher's words, "do worse than endorse Rockefeller!" Or maybe, a fuming Rusher complained to Buckley, Burnham would go "whoring after some new false god," for example, moderate Republican Charles Percy. Buckley, however, as usual, stood by his mentor. "I rate your political knowledge and shrewdness very high indeed, and I listen intently to everything you have to say," he replied to Rusher. But "I think you would be wiser still if you permitted yourself every now and then to reflect on the fact that some very profound and shrewd political observers and philosophers have assessed James Burnham's political mind as being among the half dozen shrewdest of this century." But Buckley did not succeed in calming his exasperated colleague, who, Priscilla Buckley noted, continued to see Burnham's promotion of Rockefeller as "treasonous."[3]

Burnham also doubted that Goldwater could win the election, and in the betting at *National Review* put $120 on Johnson.[4] Nor was he upset at the prospect of a Goldwater defeat. "It would probably be unfortunate for conservatives if Goldwater should, on the off chance, be elected," he commented after the 1964 Republican convention. "It might even have been better if he had just failed to win the nomination, so that the bankruptcy of the older-line Republican leadership might have been still more thoroughly exposed and digested." For the conservative movement—which he characterized as a contradiction-riddled jumble of hard-line anticommunists, free marketeers, Gaullist-style nationalists, old-fashioned protectionists and isolationists, Burkean traditionalists, tax-protesting small businessmen, and persons hostile to beatniks and the urban underclass, linked mostly by the negative bond of antiliberalism—had not yet matured. It had neither an adequate program nor enough people qualified to staff a national administration.[5]

Unlike most of his *National Review* colleagues, Burnham approached the Goldwater campaign more as an analyst than as an advocate. "I must say," he remarked to Buckley as the 1964 primary season moved into high gear, "I would be happier if NR were trying more to understand, analyze and really report the campaign rather than to take part in it."[6] He himself acted on this advice. In March 1964 he and Marcia, with their Norwich terriers Melrose and Newport, set out on a meandering, six-week, cross-country car trip, partly because they loved to travel and partly to visit relatives, but partly also to enable Burnham to gauge political sentiment across the nation. On the way to and from Rancho de la Osa, a dude ranch in Sasabe, Arizona, not far from his brother Philip's home in Tucson, Burnham sounded the mood in cities as diverse as Memphis, Denver, and

St. Paul, talking with residents and perusing local newspapers. What he found he described as a "half-formed but growing conflict" between the Northeast and "the West-South-Southwest," which was riding a surge of population growth, economic expansion, and new money, and felt that its turn had come to run the country. Hence the Goldwater movement. But to win the White House, he pointed out, Goldwater would have to be perceived not as a regional or ideological candidate, but as a national leader with a program addressing the concerns of "the one nation."[7]

When Goldwater lost, Burnham reacted with the same detachment he had shown during the campaign. Goldwater's nomination had been "something of an accident," he wrote, more the result of "disarray" among Republican moderates than of the strength of conservatism, which in 1964 was not yet ready to govern. Still, he added, the defeat need not be a misfortune. For if Johnson could not overcome the dangers facing the country, and so made the bankruptcy of liberalism clear beyond doubt, conservative Democrats might be able to seize control of their party and make it a vehicle "even more promising" than the GOP "for a spectacular conservative advance."[8]

Soon after the election, Burnham furnished still another example of political heresy by endorsing Medicare, a Johnson "Great Society" tax-supported health insurance program for the elderly that most conservatives disliked. Burnham ordinarily frowned on Great Society ventures. He criticized Johnson's "War on Poverty" as in part a grand-scale patronage racket and in part an ideologically rooted, extraconstitutional scheme whose community councils, chosen under "class or other discriminatory criteria," were "precisely what the Russians call a 'soviet.'"[9] (Johnson himself, with his outsized personality, Caesarist aura, and, in Burnham's view, purely power-seeking motives, held a kind of fascination for him.)[10] Yet he professed himself "saddened" by a *National Review* editorial blasting Medicare, describing the attack as "a routine Pavlovian exercise: ringing the changes on a few stereotypes to start conditioned right-wing glands flowing." The problem Medicare addressed, he argued on the magazine's "Open Question" page, that of the steep medical costs burdening the elderly, rose "ineluctably" in modern society. Ideally, there might be better solutions than Medicare, but since none had been put forward, "we might as well get it through our heads that Medicare, good or bad, is here to stay." Hence, instead of inveighing against the program, conservatives should work to ensure that it would be managed as efficiently as possible. (This provoked a sharp rejoinder from fellow editor William F. Rickenbacker. "Should we urge Mr. Burnham to get it through his head that appeasement [of communism] is here to stay?" Rickenbacker shot back. "Should conservatives try to make appeasement work as well as possible?")[11]

Burnham also broke ranks with conservatives on a key defense issue. In the mid-1960s, as the question of building an antimissile barrier came to the fore, he at first opposed the idea, partly contending that the technology of the day could not achieve an antimissile defense reliable enough to justify its enormous cost, and that nothing was "more fatal for a nation than the Maginot Line style of thought." He could sanction the construction of an antimissile screen, he said, only if it were built to defend U.S. missiles or to study the potential of antimissile technology. But he suspected that the future of antimissile defense lay in a different direction—and one he thought preferable. "Orbital [rather than earth-based] weapon systems will in all probability become strategically decisive in the 1970s," he wrote in 1963. Four years later, foreseeing the "Star Wars" project pursued in the 1980s, he observed that a space-based system might someday be devised that would use lasers or a radiation shield to defend U.S. missiles and cities alike.[12]

At the end of the 1960s he swung behind the Nixon administration's Safeguard Anti-Ballistic Missile proposal, earth-based though it was, because its purpose was limited to missile launching site defense. No such system could be fully effective, he repeated. But Safeguard might suffice to deter atomic aggression by China, whose nuclear arsenal was still tiny, or some "hopped-up small nation that wanted to try a bit of nuclear blackmail," or to knock down an accidental launching. But by this time, the issue had assumed a broader meaning for him. The anti-Safeguard lobby was backed by "the whole galaxy of anti-Vietnam, disarmament, pacifist, Vietnik and generally leftist groups down to the bitter anti-American dregs," he charged, and he undoubtedly wished to see this cohort defeated.[13]

◆  ◆  ◆  ◆

Burnham's heterodoxy had been upsetting various *NR* editors almost since the magazine's founding. The irritation it provoked among these "keepers of the flame" (as Priscilla Buckley called them) was compounded by his advice that conservatives adopt a more latitudinarian stance, the better to attract recruits among liberals who had lost their faith. "To win those fellow citizens," he counseled in an address at *NR*'s tenth anniversary dinner, conservatism had to shed "the sectarian and doctrinaire clannishness that is natural enough in the early stages of every political movement," and "become more flexible, more generous, more intelligent and more humane"—advice that some in the audience found dismissive of principle. Their irritation was perhaps sharpened by his indifference to their criticism. For according to one-time *NR* editor Garry Wills, he always "treated attacks on him as beneath response."[14]

First among *National Review*'s anti-Burnham regulars, at least since the departure of Willi Schlamm, stood Frank Meyer, whose relations with Burnham Buckley summed up as "the Hundred Years War." The impassioned, chain-smoking Meyer, once described by Buckley as "the perfect ideologue," had made it his mission to unify the Right by "fusing" traditionalist and libertarian thought and anathematizing ideological nonconformists. Rarely coming to the office, Meyer worked out of his home near Woodstock, New York, keeping in touch with the outside world by means of late-night telephone calls to friends across the country. It was said that he had acquired the habit of staying up most of the night after his break with communism, fearing that party assassins, under cover of darkness, might try to kill him. A resolute man, he had acquired a New York State teacher's license so that he and his wife Elsie could school their two sons at home. When local officials tried to force the boys into public school, he stopped them cold. Meyer, one *NR* staffer noted, though a valuable editor, was a terrible "office person": argumentative, volatile, and happiest in an atmosphere of crisis.[15]

Though Meyer and Burnham's outlooks had much in common, the more orthodox and dogmatic Meyer (who, tellingly, called his column "Principles and Heresies") kept a nervous eye out for subversive action by his maverick colleague. Indeed, he even claimed that Burnham had never really left the CIA, and was now operating with instructions to report on trends among conservatives and to moderate *NR*'s more aggressive hard-line tendencies. Meyer grew especially jumpy whenever Buckley left town, fearing that Burnham would take advantage of the boss's absence to push his own, more heterodox brand of thinking. Thus, in February 1959, after Buckley had left for his annual skiing and writing stay in Switzerland, the avidly pro-Goldwater Meyer hastened to warn *NR* colleagues against what he called Burnham's "policy of pinpricks" on behalf of a Nixon (i.e.,

Eisenhower moderate) bid for the GOP nomination.[16]

But Meyer's uneasiness also had nonpolitical roots. Like Schlamm, he was bothered by Burnham's closeness to Buckley, which seems to have made him feel excluded and "anxious." To complicate matters, at Princeton, which he had entered three years after Burnham, he had once watched Burnham, by then the very image of campus success, genially presiding over a table of student bigwigs at a time when he, Meyer, unhappy at the college, was planning to drop out. He had later enrolled at Balliol, only to discover that Burnham had been there first and again won renown. "It must have seemed the work of some malicious historical imp for him to find Burnham at Bill's elbow just when Frank was trying to join the inner circle of *NR* editors," Garry Wills once mused. The idea that Burnham might come to outrank him on the magazine's masthead filled him with horror.[17]

William Rusher, too, often took the field against Burnham. Their clashes, Rusher once wrote, reflected the eternal opposition between "moralists" and "Machiavellians," between those who, like himself, believed that principles guided politics, "or ought to," and those who, like Burnham, considered "the central issue in politics" to be power, or as Burnham liked to put it, "who is to be master in the house." But the two differed as well in their conception of *National Review,* Rusher wanting a staunchly orthodox conservative journal, and Burnham a magazine of greater breadth and more moderate tone. Finally, they disagreed on a strategic issue. Rusher in the 1950s and 1960s, besides being a conservative, was also a deep-dyed Republican. Hoping for a conservative political party, he had come to see the GOP as the right framework for it. Burnham, on the other hand, was above all an anticommunist. Registered to vote as an independent, and preferring hard-line anticommunist Democrats, such as Connecticut Senator Thomas J. Dodd, to many Republican officeholders, he currently favored the Republicans only because he believed that at that point they seemed to take a harder stance on communism.[18]

In 1960 a new senior editor appeared at *National Review.* Thirty-two years old when he came to the magazine, William F. Rickenbacker was already a man of many accomplishments. A Harvard graduate who had captained the college's golf team, he was widely read in several languages, an avid flier (as befitted the son of World War I ace Eddie Rickenbacker), and a fine pianist who as a child had won first prize in the juvenile division of the National Steinway Competition.

Politically a libertarian, he caught *National Review*'s eye when he was sued by the federal government for refusing, on grounds of invasion of privacy, to fill out the 1960 census long form. Despite the efforts of *NR*'s lawyer, C. Dickerman Williams, he lost his case, and was sentenced to a $100 fine and a day's probation. In the meantime, his combative spirit and energetic prose had led Buckley, seconded by Burnham, to offer him an editorship at the magazine.[19] Rickenbacker accepted and fully lived up to their expectations. But he also became a key participant in *NR*'s office wars.

At an early point in his eight-year stay at *National Review,* Rickenbacker drew close to Rusher and Meyer. He and Rickenbacker, Rusher remembered, agreed that Burnham "needed reining in from time to time, and joined forces for that purpose," though without engaging in any "ongoing anti-Burnham collaboration." It was through Meyer, however, that Rickenbacker first collided with Burnham. Bringing copy for the magazine's next issue to the compositor one day, Rickenbacker noticed a passage in an article commissioned or written by Burnham that he thought needed editing. With the deadline looming, he telephoned Meyer (whether he first tried to reach Burnham is unclear) who gave his approval for the change, a minor correction, but one that slightly altered the piece's tone. Spotting the change, the usually cool Burnham hit the roof. Peace was soon restored, but a residual strain remained.[20]

Another instance of strain was Burnham's doing. One day at lunch, the editors fell to talking about music, and it came to light that all, as children, had taken piano lessons. This led someone to remark that Rickenbacker still practiced daily. "Jim smiled his amiable smile," Rickenbacker remembered, "and said, 'Of course the Greeks had slaves for their musicians, and Aristotle said it wasn't gentlemanly to play an instrument too well.' Then he *blushed* scarlet." Was Burnham's comment an innocent faux pas or a deliberate dig? "To this day," Rickenbacker later wrote, "I don't know the meaning of that upsurge of animal spirits," adding, "More than twenty years later, I discovered that Jim himself played the piano beautifully. One would never have known."[21]

Editorial decisions of Burnham's also fed the tension. In November 1961 Rickenbacker drafted an editorial on Kennedy's policy toward Castro that Burnham, standing in for Buckley, rejected, finding it, said Rickenbacker, "injudicious." (Rickenbacker's criticism of U.S. Cuba policy did not differ in substance from Burnham's, but it was couched in tones too vituperative for Burnham's taste.)[22] By early 1963 Rickenbacker was complaining that Burnham had turned down all his recent submissions to the *Bulletin* (in fact, only some had been rejected), and after Buckley's departure for Switzerland that year the atmosphere at editorial meetings grew stormy. On the surface, the trouble stemmed from Burnham's handling of the *Bulletin*. Priscilla Buckley gathered from a talk with Meyer that "monster suspicions" had arisen of a plan by "left-deviationist Burnham" to seize the opportunity offered by Buckley's absence to "de-gut the [*Bulletin*]; take out the message; de-ideologize it, etc." But Rickenbacker, perhaps feeling that Burnham was treating him as a novice or trying to gag him, may also have been suffering from wounded pride, for by this time, his dislike of Burnham was "so extreme," in Priscilla Buckley's words, "that even when he tries to control it he can't." If future editorial meetings resembled the last one, she wrote to her brother in early February 1963, "I think you'll be faced with an extraordinarily difficult decision upon your return."[23]

In reply, Buckley proposed that he appoint Burnham *NR*'s "executive editor" and so name him on the masthead, thereby formally establishing Burnham's supreme editorial authority. Priscilla called the idea "exactly right." But not everyone agreed. Rusher, writing at length to Buckley, urged him not to take the step. "The best medicine for what ails Bill Rickenbacker is not the promotion of Jim Burnham . . . ," he counseled, "but the firm ministrations of Frank Meyer," who had promised to talk with Rickenbacker and see that he behaved. To promote Burnham would only heat up the old Meyer–Burnham feud. Meanwhile, Rusher went on, launching a sapper attack on the powerful Burnham citadel, there was another matter that had to be borne in mind: "the aging" of Burnham, who in recent years had grown older (Burnham was now fifty-seven) "very noticeably," and whose tie with the magazine would soon necessarily loosen.[24]

Meyer, whom Buckley also informed, was so upset that he telephoned Buckley in Switzerland to contest the decision. Following up with a letter, he reported that he had had "a very serious talk" with Rickenbacker, who had agreed to stop being "provocative"—"though I think it would be unfair to say that the trouble is 100% WFR's fault," he hastened to add. "JB can be provocative himself." There was now no need, he left Buckley to surmise, for Burnham to be raised above his fellow editors on the masthead. ("The Enola Gay's billet-doux caused hardly more consternation to the citizens of Hiroshima than yours of Monday last to [Meyer]," Priscilla informed her brother. She was writing, she said, "after a) an extensive session with L. Brent [Bozell, a sometime Meyer ally against Burnham], b) an extensive session with William R[usher], c) a mammoth telephonic bout with Frank S. [Meyer], d) a nervous . . . lunch with Bill Rick in which we both drank three glasses of Chianti.")[25]

Seemingly unfazed by the tempest raging around him, but concerned, as always, with the well-being of the magazine, Burnham proposed a solution similar to the one he had offered during the Schlamm affair. Rickenbacker saw him as "his Schlamm," and was obviously unwilling to work with him, he told Priscilla. If it would help, he would stop coming to the office and instead work out of Kent, "as a sort of foreign advisor and foreign editor."[26] But again this idea found no favor with the Buckleys.

By late February, however, perhaps because of universal exhaustion, the tension began to ebb, and by March the magazine was back on a more or less even keel.[27] In early March, Burnham, in a letter to Buckley, analyzed the recent uproar. If looked at from a psychological angle, he wrote, the trouble could be attributed to Rickenbacker's emotional state. Rickenbacker was undoubtedly upset about his wife's poor health. But he also suffered from emotional instability, and had persuaded himself "that I am plotting to subvert and destroy the conservative movement and . . . him personally." True, Burnham conceded, "I have not done enough to woo Bill, but I am not much of a wooer."

If viewed from the angle of the magazine's management, he went on, the trouble could be blamed on Buckley's failure to name an "unequivocal" deputy for periods when he was out of town. At those times, signs of a vacuum of authority cropped up all over: "people coming too late to work and leaving too early; too long lunches; far too much and too long telephoning and too much yakking; chores not done on time; too much sloppiness." Someone had to be formally put in charge.

Finally, the trouble could be traced to conflict over the kind of magazine *NR* should be. He and Priscilla wanted "simply to have the best magazine in the world, assuming a general (but not too sharply defined) conservative and anticommunist point of view." Rusher, Meyer, and Rickenbacker, on the other hand, while also wanting a first-rate magazine, wanted above all "a crusade, a political party and a kind of ersatz church, and . . . want[ed] NR itself to be all these things . . . rather than a magazine-as-magazine which would have a certain aloofness from crusades, parties, and churches, even if it altogether agreed with them."[28]

By late March, Burnham seemed confident that the trouble had ended. "So far as I can judge . . . things have gone along pleasantly and well the past two weeks in the office," he wrote happily to Buckley.[29]

But it was a fragile peace, and Burnham would occasion new outbursts of wrath in the future. Rickenbacker, though keeping his hostility under tight rein, seems never to have shed his resentment of Burnham. As late as 1990 he wrote deprecatingly of his old opponent, picturing him as a man whose conduct was shaped by snobbery.[30] Trying to explain Buckley's strong attachment to Burnham, he pointed to the intellectual authority Burnham possessed in Buckley's eyes and to what he called Burnham's father-figure status for Buckley. The attachment was also tied up with religion, he asserted, for the Catholic Buckley worried about the lapsed-Catholic Burnham's soul.[31]

Once the storm had passed, Buckley decided to leave his informal deputizing arrangement in place. In the years to come, though he continued to devote much time to *National Review,* he also busied himself with many other undertakings, including: writing a syndicated column; lecturing and debating on the college circuit and elsewhere; performing Bach on the harpsicord; captaining transoceanic sailing voyages; hosting "Firing Line"; turning out many books and eventually even a spy thriller series; and in 1965 running half tongue-in-cheek as Conservative Party candidate for mayor of New York. All the while, Burnham carried on as his *NR* stand-in, still armed with no more imposing patents of authority than brief Buckley memos.

◆　◆　◆　◆

In the early 1960s, the most widely known American far-Right organization was the John Birch Society, founded in 1958 by Robert Welch, a Massachusetts candy manufacturer, and named after an American serviceman in China believed to have been killed by communists soon after World War II. It was Welch's opinion that communism, acting through a network of innocent-seeming fronts, had already gained a possibly decisive measure of power in the United States. Indeed, in a book called *The Politician,* he accused no less a personage than Dwight D. Eisenhower of being a conscious agent of the international communist conspiracy.

From the outset, Burnham viewed Welch with apprehension (though before

learning of the Birchite leader's zanier views he let the Birchites [
of *The Web of Subversion,* and blessed one of their ventures, a "Con
Summit Entanglements," which included Goldwater among its s[
Birchite magazine *American Opinion*'s "Scoreboard on Commu
which calculated the "percentage" of such influence in variou
"methodologically meaningless; and inaccurate, sometimes very inaccurate, so ̣ai
as one can pump a meaning into it," he commented to Buckley. And not only
was Birchism "ideologically hopeless." The following it drew "just doesn't seem
to have the stuff. It is made to order for Liberal attack." When Welch demanded
a U.S. withdrawal from South Vietnam, claiming that the Vietcong was only a
diversionary force fielded to tie up and exhaust American strength, Burnham
summoned serious anticommunists to shun the Birchites.[33]

Buckley, who saw his outlook and that of the Birchites as "mutually exclusive,"
needed no convincing. Soon after 1960 he banned from the *NR* masthead writers who appeared on the masthead of *American Opinion*. In February 1962,
though *National Review* numbered many Birchites among its subscribers and so
knew it was treading on dangerous ground, he made *NR*'s anti-Birchism explicit,
running a long editorial, "The Question of Robert Welch," that accused Welch
of "damaging the cause of anti-communism."[34]

Yet despite Buckley's position, the Birch question led to friction at the magazine. When Burnham, after the anti-Welch editorial, wanted to "go forward . . .
with a development of our break with [Welch]," some of his colleagues balked.
Rusher wondered whether "a widening break" was "desirable at all." He did not,
he snapped in a memo to the editors, want to declare "or have declared for me,
a widening war upon nationally-known conservative personalities for whom I
have feelings of friendship and respect." Meyer, who thought that conservatives,
if ever forced to choose between liberals and Birchites, would have to choose the
latter, sided with Rusher.[35] But Burnham prevailed. In October 1965 *NR* put out
a special issue that handed down a negative verdict not just on Welch but on the
Birch Society as a whole.[36]

◆　◆　◆　◆

Though his writing took up the greater part of his time, Burnham also continued to travel the lecture circuit. He did not, however, think much of his prowess

at the podium. "In general I am not a good 'public speaker,'" he once told Buckley. Burnham was right. As a speaker, he lacked Buckley's showmanship, Meyer's mordant intensity, Rusher's brisk assertiveness. Knowledge, logic, and clarity, not rhetorical dazzle, were his strengths, and they served him better in classrooms than before mass audiences. In a typical appearance, he would seem to be teaching a course—although in his dark suit, white shirt, and black shoes he suggested a banker or lawyer more than an academic. (Buckley and Meyer, in contrast, blended smoothly into a university atmosphere, the former, still youthful and usually slightly disheveled, conveying a 1950s undergraduate air, and the latter, in tweed jacket, plaid shirt, and knit tie, easily mistakable for a denizen of the sociology department. The lawyerly Rusher, on the other hand, at least in dress, resembled Burnham.) When delivering his lectures, which normally concerned the struggle for the world, Burnham never grew vehement, let alone shrill, but spoke in a quiet, explanatory tone. The pleasure his talks gave came from the purely intellectual satisfactions they afforded.[37]

But despite his low-keyed style, Burnham was often invited to lecture at colleges, and usually left a good impression. A talk he gave at the National War College in 1959 prompted one member of the audience to write to Buckley that the speaker had furnished "the best analysis of political warfare and political strategy that I have ever heard, and the class in general felt the same way."[38] Burnham also spoke in other than classroom settings: at a Princeton alumni forum on world politics, for example; at a "Hollywood Symposium on Freedom," which he attended with Buckley, Meyer, and Kendall; at an "Evening with National Review" in Minneapolis, with Buckley and Meyer ("450 at dinner, 1300, with a couple of hundred standing, for the yakking," he summed up the event), which included questions from local TV newsmen; at a meeting at New York's Carnegie Hall to oppose the admission of communist China to the UN.

All the while, drawing on the impressions he garnered at such gatherings, he assessed the political prospects for conservatives. The conclusions he reached were discouraging. Many people were unhappy about the course of world affairs and wanted "to do something about something," he wrote to his son Jim. But for political impact, "at least three things [were] needed: a critique; a program; an équipe (as the French call it: a 'team,' with organization)," and up until now American conservatives had only the first.[39]

◆  ◆  ◆  ◆

Burnham's main lecture topic was the Soviet threat, but he aimed his most withering fire not at communists but at liberals. As a prime example of the breed he cited Eleanor Roosevelt, in whom he claimed to find no evidence of thought, but only "*sentiment,* unguided and unrestrained by intelligence, reason, or principle." Mrs. Roosevelt "spreads a squidlike ink of directionless feeling" over "whatever subject, problem, plan or issue she touches," he observed, so that "all distinctions are blurred, all analyses fouled, and in that murk clear thought is forever impossible." Besides showing an excess of sentiment and a "wishy-washy, vague, indecisive temperament," liberals, he argued, were unable to "understand power and the uses of power." Worse, they could no longer identify anything "worth risking death for," and so "slowly, ineluctably we edge forward, as foremost among our values, biological survival (they call it peace) rather than freedom." Liberalism—or "permissive egalitarianism," in Leo Strauss's phrase—had now reached the point where it had "altogether lost touch with reality," he remarked in 1961. "Historically, I think that [liberalism] . . . ought to be, and will be, defined as 'the ideology of Western suicide.' And when you think it over, it is quite obviously suicidal, since it offers the West no objective basis on which to 'discriminate' in favor of itself as a community or enterprise: that is, no basis on which to justify historical survival." Why, he wondered in a *National Review* editorial, should anyone have been surprised when the U.S. Communist Party shut down its newspaper, the *Daily Worker?* Why carry the burden of "a big U.S. Communist setup when there are plenty of non-Communist Americans to do your work for you—and do it all the better *because* they [are] not Communists?"[40]

Burnham had never written about liberalism at length. The closest he had come were some passages in *Congress and the American Tradition* in which he had listed contrasting ideas about man and society that he had identified with liberal partisans of the presidency and conservative partisans of Congress. Such ideas, he said, constituted "syndromes," clusters of beliefs that defined liberalism and conservatism. The liberal syndrome included faith in abstract reason as the key to solving society's problems, confidence in human nature as essentially benign, apathy or hostility toward tradition, and a bias toward centralized power; the conservative included mistrust of abstract rationalist solutions, skepticism regarding the creative potential of human nature, attachment to tradition, and respect for intermediary institutions. Liberalism, based on abstract thinking and sentimentality, he viewed as no more than ideology; conservatism, based on experience, as a form of realism.[41]

Upon completing *Congress and the American Tradition,* Burnham decided to make these "syndromes" the subject of a new book. But he soon dropped this plan for a study solely of liberalism. In May 1959 he aired some preliminary reflections in three lectures he gave at the Carnegie Institute of Technology.[42] But it was not until four years later, at a seminar he led at Princeton, that he offered a detailed exposition of his major conclusion: that liberalism functioned as "the ideology of Western suicide."

Burnham's Princeton seminar originated in a conversation he had in 1961 with Princeton professor Edward T. Cone. During the chat, Cone described Princeton's Gauss Seminars in Criticism, in which a seminar leader, in six meetings, read one or more papers on a topic of his choosing, often taken from a book he was working on, and then opened the floor to criticism from an invited audience of two to three dozen persons. The program was directed by the critic R. P. Blackmur; Cone served as Blackmur's deputy. Since Burnham showed a strong interest, a few months later Blackmur and Cone invited him to lead a seminar in the 1962–63 series.[43]

Burnham at once accepted. As his topic he proposed "a general critique of 'liberalism.'" Cone seconded the opinion of a Gauss committee colleague that Burnham's letter outlining his plans was "the best" from a prospective seminar leader he had ever read. And Blackmur, Cone later said, was looking forward to "a tight, well-reasoned presentation of the reactionary point of view."[44]

Burnham pondered possible titles for his seminar, finally settling on "Liberalism as the Ideology of Western Suicide." The reading list he drew up included, among other works, John Dewey's *Liberalism and Social Action,* John Stuart Mill's *On Liberty,* Arthur Schlesinger's *The Vital Center,* and the British political thinker Michael Oakeshott's *Rationalism in Politics,* a recently published collection of Oakeshott essays, which he thought superb.[45] Asked whom he would like to be invited to the seminar, he named old friends who lived in Princeton, such as the writer William Spackman and the Wilmerdings. He also wished to have some students present.

The committee sent out additional invitations, mostly to members of the Princeton faculty. But not all of the recipients welcomed the invitations, some bristling at the thought of a notorious right-winger in their midst. "I would not take pleasure in attending . . . ," one indignant professor wrote back. "Indeed, . . . I want to register my protest against Mr. Burnham's appearance. . . ." Still, opposition to Burnham's coming "was not too serious," Cone recalled, and on February 7, 1963, at 8:30 P.M. a full audience assembled in Firestone Library's New Jersey Room for the first of the seminar's sessions.[46]

Since Gauss seminars were neither transcribed nor taped, it is impossible to know exactly what was said, but in the recollection of some who attended the atmosphere quickly turned stormy. Burnham began by giving a definition of liberalism comprising a long list of beliefs he claimed characterized liberals (e.g., human nature is rational; the possibility of social reform is unlimited). He also held up a map of the world of 1914 showing the global magnitude of Western imperial rule, and interpreted the contraction of the Western empire since that time as evidence that the West had gone into decline. In later sessions he related the decline to liberalism, to which he traced the rationalizions that cushioned the shock of the retreat. Though liberals could not solve the problems faced by the West, he argued, they were succeeding in making Western failure palatable. Hence, liberalism could be defined functionally as an ideology masking the downward trajectory of the West. This was its real, as opposed to its formal, meaning.[47]

From the outset, many at the seminar disputed Burnham's thesis. His catalogue of liberalism's typical beliefs drew much protest, and when he took out his map of the world of 1914, Lucius Wilmerding recalled, "they really roasted him." According to Cone, many in the audience, he and Blackmur included, found the presentation disappointing, judging it to be beneath Burnham's "previous intellectual level." Hoping for a critical exploration of liberal thought, they had heard instead, Cone said, "a routine right-wing polemic that set up a straw man version of liberalism to demolish." Burnham, however, did not flinch but carried on with all his usual aplomb. He later pointed to the critics as examples of the liberal mentality, noting as an instance that they had found "incomprehensible" his denial of any moral equivalence between the U.S. use of force against Castro and Castro's use of force to master Cuba.[48]

◆　◆　◆　◆

Burnham set forth his finished argument in the book-length study of liberalism he published in 1964, *Suicide of the West: An Essay on the Meaning and Destiny of Liberalism*. Primarily an analytical treatment of its subject, the book reflected the influence of his abiding intellectual masters: Aristotle, Machiavelli and the Machiavellians, Mackinder, and Toynbee, but also of the anti-ideological conservative Michael Oakeshott and, to a lesser degree, Sidney Hook.

*Suicide of the West* begins with the same reference as the seminar's to the world map of 1914 and the subsequent contraction of Western power ("like a film winding in reverse, with the West thrust backward reel by reel toward the original base from which it started its world expansion"). The many historical examples of territorial retreat and civilizational decline made it "probable," Burnham contended, that as Western power contracted geographically, the West as a civilization was decaying. Moreover, because in the early stages of the contraction—the loss of Russia in 1917 to communism—there had been no external enemy capable of overthrowing the West's global ascendancy, it must further be concluded that the causes of the retreat—"either structural changes or intellectual, moral, and spiritual factors," for example, a loss of "the will to survive"—lay within the West itself, and that the decline could therefore be likened to an act of "suicide." The question of why the West had lost its will to survive Burnham put beyond the scope of his inquiry, though he briefly speculated that the reasons might include "the decay of religion and an excess of material luxury; and . . . getting tired, worn out, as all things temporal do."[49]

Moving on to his principal subject, liberalism, the "ideological syndrome" he thought dominant in the United States since the New Deal,[50] he listed nineteen beliefs he regarded as basic to the syndrome (e.g., human nature enjoys "an indefinite potential for progressive development"; the main obstacles to progress are "ignorance and faulty social institutions"; government has a duty to guarantee everyone "food, shelter, clothing and education, and security against unemployment, illness and the problems of old age"). To these beliefs he added three "corollaries" specific to American liberalism: an "instrumentalist" approach to interpreting the Constitution, a preference for federal over state and local power, and a strong bias in favor of the presidency over Congress. Underlying the syndrome's abstract rationalism, social reformism, and historical optimism he saw a common root: a rejection of the tragic view of life central to Western thought until the Renaissance.[51]

Most liberals, Burnham wrote, like ideologues of all stripes, held their views not as "a consciously understood set of rational beliefs, but [as] a bundle of unexamined prejudices and conjoined sentiments" that helped meet their psychological needs and promoted their interests.[52] Chief among these was assuaging their feelings of guilt—an irrational guilt since liberals were not responsible for the social evils they denounced, and since liberal theory blamed such evils not on the wickedness of individuals, but on ignorance and benighted institutions. But liberalism was not only irrational, it also did harm, morally disarming its adherents before persons they considered disadvantaged and fostering "a generalized hatred" of the prosperous West.[53]

The liberal syndrome, Burnham continued, showed up in a variety of social groups. For example, in a majority of the "opinion-makers, molders and transmitters," people who might be categorized as "verbalists": faculty and administrators at the better colleges and universities; editors, publishers, and writers at the more influential newspapers, magazines, and radio and television networks; theater and movie directors; public relations men; mainstream Protestant and Jewish clergymen, as well as many Catholic bishops and priests; and personnel at tax-exempt institutions, such as nonprofit educational, philanthropic, and scientific foundations. It also thrived among government employees, especially social workers and the bureaucrats who ran the welfare state. To this list Burnham added organized labor, though in this case liberalism served mainly as a means of economic advancement, especially for the blue-collar rank and file. Minority groups (Catholics, blacks, Jews) were also often liberal, but like blue-collar workers, perhaps chiefly for reasons of self-interest. On the other hand, the syndrome did not often appear among such groups as self-employed professionals, businessmen (most notably those who personally ran their businesses), and career soldiers. Nor were farmers often liberals, except to the extent that liberalism brought them economic benefits.[54]

Whether most Americans were liberals was hard to gauge. What did seem clear was that liberalism, broadly defined, had now solidly entrenched itself as the standard "American public doctrine."[55] And this did not bode well for the future. For one thing, liberalism replaced reality with dreams, portraying human nature in a reassuringly rosy light and looking ahead to a future of infinite progress. Yet a wealth of historical evidence contradicted this outlook, while geneticists agreed that in modern society those segments of the population with "inferior genetic

assets—inferior, that is, from an intellectual, moral, and civilizing standpoint—
[were] increasing, rather rapidly, relative to those with superior assets." At the same
time, the liberal love of sentimental abstractions such as "peace" and "equality"—
and pursuit of these ideals as solutions to social problems with disregard for social
facts—made the gulf between liberalism and social reality wider. Moreover, liberalism was biased toward the negative. In the past, it had fought social abuses and
achieved notable successes. But it had proved less able to replace what it had abolished, and so appeared "better out of power than in power; better at changing
than preserving; better at destroying than building."[56]

At present, liberal government posed an especially serious danger. For the West
was confronted with three "crucial . . . challenges"—each "clearly and immediately and powerfully" jeopardizing Western survival—with which liberalism was
by nature ill-equipped to cope.[57] The first was the threat of Soviet communism.
In dealing with this problem, liberals, because of their absolutist view of civil
rights, were caught in a dilemma: either defend civil rights for those who would
use them to subvert liberal society, or restrict the civil rights of communists, and
thereby violate their own taboos. Further, liberals preferred to handle adversaries
through talk and trade-offs. This availed little against communists, whose progress
could sometimes be halted only by force. But liberals felt uncomfortable using
force, and therefore tended to use it clumsily.

Even worse, liberalism as an ideology could be diagnosed as "infected with
communism." For liberals and communists held "most of their basic axioms and
principles and many of their values and sentiments" in common: for example, an
abstract rationalist approach to social reform, a belief in the malleability of human
nature, hostility to traditional institutions and social distinctions, an identification
with science, monopolistic secularism, antinational globalism, and a commitment
to the welfare state (which communists raised to its "ultimate form," totalitarianism). Liberalism differed from communism only in that it did not carry this common program to its "logical and practical extreme." Hence, liberals found it
difficult to mount an all-out attack on communism, feeling that in doing so they
would somehow wound themselves.

Finally, to resist communism entailed a willingness to die in the struggle. But
liberalism, which scoffed at traditional reasons for self-sacrifice (family, country,
faith) as "superstitious" and "reactionary," offered no ideal of its own that people
would die for. Aside from mercenaries, saints, and neurotics, Burnham acidly

observed, no one would lay down his life "for progressive education, medicare, humanity in the abstract, the United Nations, and a ten percent rise in Social Security payments."[58]

The West faced a second challenge, Burnham went on, in the population explosion and political mobilization now rousing the Third World. Because Westerners made up only a small portion of mankind, the logic of liberal redistributionist and egalitarian ideals as applied to the Third World meant "the subjection of the West" and a sharp drop in its living standard—implications that liberals themselves preferred to ignore. These ideals, not yet fully implemented, were nonetheless at work, "like a spiritual worm, corrupting the will of the West to survive as a distinct historical entity," and smoothing its descent into "the distinctionless human mass." If it wished to survive, the West would have to abandon universalism for its preliberal conviction that its own civilization was "both different from and superior in quality to other civilizations," and find the will to reply to Third World aggression with force—imperatives from which liberals typically shrank.[59]

The third challenge, one facing the United States more than the West as a whole, was a skyrocketing crime rate, especially in the cities. A "jungle" was spreading in America, Burnham warned, a condition that civilization—always and everywhere teetering on the brink of "anarchic savagery"—could not long endure. For civilized society to last, people had to feel safe. Liberals knew this. But inhibited by guilt (criminals often came from the "disadvantaged" reaches of society), blaming crime on "social conditions" rather than criminals, and repelled by the idea of meeting it with force (rather than with education), they were unable to translate their knowledge into action.[60]

The West was retreating, Burnham repeated in the book's final chapter. In one sense liberals were responsible, for if unable to deal with communism, the Third World, and crime, they were "marvellously and specifically equipped . . . to comfort us in our afflictions; and then, by a wondrous alchemy, to transmute the dark defeats, withdrawals and catastrophes into their bright opposites: into gains, victories, advances." Thus, Western "geographical, political, demographic and strategic losses emerged as triumphs of Freedom, Equality, Progress and Virtue." Such redefining had become liberalism's major function, so that liberals, however unintentionally, were helping the West to reconcile itself to "dissolution." If liberalism were defined by function rather than formal content, it would have to be defined as "the ideology of Western suicide."[61]

◆　◆　◆　◆

Aside from *National Review*'s Edgar Ansel Mowrer, who gave *Suicide of the West* a rave review and equated Burnham with "Vico, Gibbon, Hegel, Spengler, and Toynbee" as an analyst of the decline of civilizations, few reviewers thought the book persuasive. The sociologist Andrew Hacker, writing in the *New York Herald Tribune,* credited Burnham with "real intelligence and learning," but also saw him as a man who lived in a "world of ideas," and whose "call for faith and force" maintained the tradition of Carlyle, Machiavelli, and Marx by exalting those who had "least in common with his own talents and way of life." *New York Times Book Review* critic Harvey J. Bresler, while describing Burnham's diagnosis of liberalism as often apt, rejected his claim that the West was in decline, and called his suicide thesis "respectable" but "not too strong." (More noteworthy, however, than Bresler's verdict, was the review's appearance a full six months after the book's publication and its burial on the book section's page forty-three, a sure sign that for the *Times* Burnham's stock had plummeted. The *Times* review of *The Struggle for the World* had appeared right after the book's publication on the section's front page. But in those palmy days Burnham had yet to be pigeonholed as a hard-line McCarthyite conservative.)

*Partisan Review*'s critic, the British Labour politician R. H. S. Crossman, saw in Burnham a reactionary who pined for "the era of . . . laissez-faire and White supremacy." Yet he also found virtues in the book. Not only did it strike him as "disconcertingly readable," he confessed, but Burnham was right in accusing liberals of applying double standards. A more representative liberal response was that of the *Saturday Review*'s critic, Frank Altschul, who described the book as the grumbling of a right-wing crank "in the grip of an acute obsession."[62]

Perhaps the most rancorous review was Irving Howe's. Former Trotskyist, literary and political critic, and editor of the socialist quarterly *Dissent,* Howe assaulted *Suicide of the West* in the *New York Review of Books* as a work "as puerile as a Birchite pamphlet," and expressed amazement that its author (whom he described as a combination of José Ortega y Gasset, the conservative Spanish philosopher, and Jack D. Ripper, the crazed right-wing general of Stanley Kubrick's film *Dr. Strangelove*) was not "a demented candy manufacturer" (a reference to Robert Welch), but a learned man on easy terms with Pareto and Kafka.

As Howe proceeded, his outrage grew, perhaps for reasons other than the book in question. As a teenage recruit to Trotskyism the bright, shy Howe had been dazzled, and somewhat intimidated, by the cool, reserved Burnham, then chagrined by Burnham's surprise withdrawal from Shachtman's Workers Party, and finally angered by Burnham's testimony at Shachtman's ISL hearing. These feelings may have been behind his review's denunciation of Burnham as a "Bourbon on the rocks," a "French style" reactionary, and an "'aristocratic' intellectual who makes no pretence of humaneness." Burnham had been "a cold-blooded snob" even as a Trotskyist, he self-revealingly charged, and now scorned as "weak" those who voiced "humane doubts" about his "atomic *fin du mondisme.*"[63]

But many ordinary readers praised the book. Conservatives thought it splendid. Some expressed satisfaction that liberalism had finally been "exposed," testifying to the underdog complex widespread on the Right in the mid-1960s, when liberal influence in the media and in Washington was at its peak. Leo Strauss declared the book "excellent." Starting from premises a bit different from Burnham's, he said, he himself had reached "practically the same" conclusions.[64]

Readers outside the conservative camp also sometimes approved. Thus, Irving Kristol, in 1964 an ACCF-style liberal, "thought well" of the book (though he also considered it, "like so much of [Burnham's] thinking and writing . . . too linear in its perspective"). The poet Czeslaw Milosz, whom Burnham, a decade earlier, had helped to gain admittance to the United States, and who now taught at Berkeley, where in 1964 the first great eruption of 1960s student protest took place, wrote to Burnham, "As you can guess, to be an observer of Berkeley frolics is not a very edifying experience. Your diagnosis has been confirmed by the whole 'Movement' of the young generation. I agree with you as to the transfer of guilt—though never probably one could see [*sic*] such a display as today—perhaps only among the Russian intelligentsia of the second half of the XIXth century."[65]

But despite an often enthusiastic response from readers, and for all its flashes of brilliance, *Suicide of the West* is the most uneven of Burnham's books. Centered on two subjects, the current American version of the liberal worldview and the decline of the West (a topic that in one way or another came up in all of Burnham's books), which it linked through its theory of liberalism's functional meaning, it did not deal satisfactorily with either. For example, since Burnham said nothing about the possibility of holding power without holding territory, his diagnosis of the West's imperial retreat as a symptom of general decline prompts the suspicion that he had not thought enough about this problem. Moreover, while disclaiming any wish to "refute" liberalism (he wanted only to analyze it, he claimed), he devoted most of the book to refutation. He also insisted that he did not want to stick pins into straw men.[66] Yet his singling out of certain aspects of the liberal outlook as identical with what he termed liberalism's "existential" reality (as in his comments on the supposed kinship between liberalism and communism), and his tendency to oversimplify this reality, ended up giving him a straw man as a target. As a result, his version of liberalism had no room for liberals who did not fit his model—his fellow Augustinian Reinhold Niebuhr, for example, a complex figure who could boast such sterling liberal credentials as a key role in the founding of the ADA, but whose view of the world was hardly less doleful than Burnham's.

Further, the book never resolved an annoying ambiguity. Burnham denied that liberals were to blame for the West's decline, calling liberalism a "symptom" rather than a "cause" of the decline. Yet in claiming that liberals had "helped" to bring about the decline and prevented changes in policy that might reverse it,[67] he implied that they did in fact bear much of the blame. Then, too, given his usual linking of liberalism to the managerial revolution,[68] his failure even to mention that trend is puzzling. Finally, the book's formal and real meanings diverged. For if its formal meaning was the same as its explicit content, its real meaning was Burnham's passionate urge to excoriate a worldview he loathed.

Still, the book had much to offer. For one thing, it was the first attempt at a comprehensive study—psychological and sociological as well as political and intellectual—of American liberalism in the middle of the twentieth century. For another, though it overemphasized some aspects of liberalism and virtually ignored others, focusing on what it saw as the pith of the ideology, and omitting nuance, it often hit its target squarely.[69] But what in retrospect is most striking about the book is its success as a work of prophecy. For if its image of the postwar era's liberalism was debatable, it faithfully captured the liberalism of the 1970s and 1980s.

◆  ◆  ◆  ◆

*Suicide of the West* was Burnham's eighth book (apart from the ones he had co-authored with Wheelwright and Malraux). It was also his last, though he was not yet fifty-nine when it was published. (His 1967 book, *The War We Are In: The Last Decade and the Next,* was not an original work, but a selection of his columns prefaced by introductory essays.) In February 1965 Neil McCaffrey, founder of the conservative publishing firm Arlington House, suggested that he write a book about "all the weaknesses of the UN, and how we should deal with it." But although the subject seemed right up Burnham's alley, he was not interested. Two months later, McCaffrey tried again, this time proposing a book that might be called "*The Two Americas,*" which he envisaged as "a kind of sequel" to or "elaboration" of *Suicide of the West* and which would examine the widening liberal-conservative split over such issues as religion, patriotism, and sex. But again Burnham turned him down.[70]

Henceforth, Burnham limited his writing to his *National Review* output. Why, after 1964, did he stop writing books? One friend later speculated that *Suicide of the West* did not attract the attention he had hoped it would, and that his disappointment sapped his interest in further large-scale projects.[71] Perhaps, but he had been at the grindstone for almost four decades and may simply have wished to ease up. By this time, too, his parental duties had ended. Marcie now lived in Brussels with her husband, André Willième (a Belgian with U.S. citizenship who may once have worked for the CIA and now owned a small advertising film company), and their two children, John and Anne.[72] Jim and John had followed their father to Princeton and then done a hitch in the navy. Hence, by the mid-1960s the Burnhams had regained the freedom of their first years together (now without the intrusions of teaching and Trotsky), and this may have further tempted Burnham to cut back on his work.

But it may also be that Rusher was right when he noted in 1963 that Burnham had "aged very noticeably" in recent years. At the time, Burnham's health was still good. He kept an eye on his eating and drinking, took long walks in Kent, did outdoor work on his property, and made time for golf and tennis. Once a cigarette smoker, he had given up the habit years before. His worst complaint in the early 1960s was gout (which he joked confirmed his claim to English ancestry). He dealt with this painful condition in his usual practical way, discovering all that he could about the ailment and giving up foods that provoked attacks. In 1966 and again in 1968 his doctor assessed his overall health as "good." To Buckley, Burnham appeared to be in "very good shape" into his seventies.[73]

But his aging was noticeable to some. In 1962 or 1963 his former student

Oscar Shoenfeld dropped in at *NR* in hopes of seeing him. The two had not met since 1937. Burnham greeted the erstwhile Trotskyist student leader so warmly that Shoenfeld departed glowing. But he also thought his old teacher had grown "very frail."[74] Thus, though still fit, Burnham may have experienced enough of a decline in energy as he approached his seventh decade (his sixtieth birthday plunged him into melancholy) to feel little desire to begin another book.[75]

But if Burnham now wrote less, he traveled even more. In November 1964 he and Marcia flew to Dublin for the wedding of their son Jim and his Irish fiancée, Anne Mullin. To their delight, horse-drawn carriages with high yellow wheels carried them to the wedding reception, where the guests danced jigs and, accompanied on the piano by the priest who had performed the ceremony, sang songs that an amused Burnham thought "rather bawdy." The next day the Burnhams went on to London to visit friends, including Koestler, and there bought a watercolor thought to have been painted by Ruskin. From London they crossed over to Paris and on to the vineyards of Beaune.[76]

In the spring of 1966 they returned to France for a five-week stay in a rented villa near Cannes. More than three decades had passed since Burnham's go-for-broke punting at St. Jean de Luz, but in the interval he had lost none of his zest for casino gambling. "We have dropped in to the Cannes Casino, an attractive, seductive establishment, #2, I think, after Deauville," he wrote to Buckley. "I have put a few francs on this and that, and am now trying to decide whether to get $1,000 of chips and have a fairly serious evening at chemin de fer." The play at the high stakes baccarat table fascinated him. It "has a minimum stake of 1,000 francs," he reported, "and turns over up to $25,000 or more each hand—i.e., about each half-minute."[77]

Meanwhile, an opportunity for a trip farther afield had arisen. In July 1965 he had been offered an all-expenses-paid tour of South Africa by the South African Information Service, but he had turned it down, not wanting to be charged with airing his anti-liberationist views on Africa as a mouthpiece for the Pretoria apartheid regime. "I prefer, for a number of reasons, to arrange a trip in my own time and way, and on the basis of my own resources," he had replied to his would-be hosts. But in 1966 he accepted a lecture invitation from the South African Institute of International Affairs at Witwatersrand University. The trip, scheduled to begin in November 1966, was to last for three weeks, since he wanted time to see something of this widely condemned but not much visited country. Marcia went with him, and they were joined by Priscilla Buckley, who was planning an article on South African life and politics.[78]

Burnham's lecture at the institute, "The Dialectic of American Foreign Policy," offered a quintessential sample of his thinking. U.S. foreign policy, he said, grew out of an interplay between the liberalism professed by the country's political elite and the "objective situation" of the United States in "the real world." At present, liberals normally made foreign policy, but conservatives, the realists, often applied it, and could therefore limit the damage it did to the West. But eventually one side or the other would gain the upper hand over foreign policy. If the liberals won, the result would "necessarily" be "the defeat and dissolution" of the United States and hence of the West, for liberal doctrine was at odds with "the realities of human nature, society and history." Contrary to liberal claims, men were not "rational or equal or inherently good." If the West, only a small part of mankind, renounced the use of force in its own defense, it would "self-evidently be over-run by the non-Westerners" who had not renounced force, and whom communism was working to muster against the West. U.S. policy toward South Africa, he concluded, had to be framed with these realities in mind. Political, economic, and strategic facts made it imperative for the United States to line up with South Africa, however much it might dislike Pretoria's racial policy.[79]

Burnham found his extensive travels in South Africa "fascinating," but also exhausting. Compounding his fatigue was a flareup of his gout. In mid-December the Burnhams flew to Greece for a short rest, then to Brussels to visit Marcie and her family, and finally home. Reflecting on the trip, Burnham shook his head over the South African situation. Conditions in South Africa had produced two groups of madmen, he commented: the people who thought the blacks could run the country and the people who actually did run it.[80]

The Burnhams also took many more of the long American car trips they loved. The impressions Burnham garnered along the way often led to articles for *National Review,* which, accordingly, helped to defray his travel costs.[81] In 1967, crisscrossing the country, he found the bitterness shown by moderate-to-liberal Democrats toward Lyndon Johnson over the Vietnam War stronger than he had expected. Many would seek revenge by voting for the Republican presidential nominee in 1968, he predicted, though not if the GOP gave the nod to Nixon or California's new governor, Ronald Reagan. Thus the time seemed right to nominate Rockefeller.[82]

Again in 1968, after an April visit to Mexico, he and Marcia embarked on a transcontinental tour that included a stop in San Antonio, then holding a fair to celebrate its 250th anniversary. An exhibit of thirteen rarely displayed paintings by Velasquez, El Greco, Murillo, and Goya dazzled Burnham, who pronounced each canvas "an absolute masterpiece," and the exhibit as "stunning, incomparable."[83] In September 1969, after replacing their Mercedes sedan with a Volvo station wagon (perhaps to make traveling with their Norwich terriers easier), the Burnhams set off on another cross-country journey. After a pause in the Bay Area, they headed on to Arizona for a stay at Rancho de la Osa. There, between horseback explorations of the desert, Burnham read Alexander Solzhenitsyn's *The First Circle,* a novel about Soviet scientists arrested in one of Stalin's later purges and shipped off to a combined prison and research center where they could continue their work. The book was "*marvellous* [sic]," he wrote to Buckley, especially in its portrayal of Stalin.[84]

Upon leaving Arizona, the Burnhams pushed east across desert and prairie to Fort Stockton, Texas. Here, Burnham set down some thoughts on the interstate highway network over whose myriad strands he had been coursing. These roads were "surely the greatest architectural and engineering achievement in history," he observed. "The Roman and Incaic roads and aqueducts are as close analogies as any, I suppose, though there is a sense in which the medieval cathedrals considered as a system are perhaps even closer." Still, if he was struck by the "grandeur" of the vision that had conceived the network, he also thought that "like all imperial monuments, the Interstates grow boring after a while." The great highways were "too inhuman, too inhumane, the dialectical opposite of the all-too-human [strip malls] that are an equally pervasive element in our macroscopic landscape." The technical and fiscal constraints mandating their construction in uninhabited areas also isolated them "too coldly from humans and things human."[85]

After the plains of Texas came the bayous of Louisiana, antebellum plantations, oaks dripping Spanish moss, and Cajun cooking. In Abbeville, Burnham's travel notes record, he and Marcia feasted on "Grand Isle oysters, a great-circle dozen of each . . . and the smoky-cold beer that went with them." "We are getting acquainted with the bayou country, not omitting the oysters and gumbo," he wrote to Priscilla Buckley, sounding as if ready to linger in the region indefinitely. But he promised to get home for the November 4 editorial meeting.[86]

Wherever the Burnhams went, everyone they spoke with—"neighbors at motel or café, citizens from whom we asked information, bartenders or fellow drinkers, brother-sightseers, cowboys, plantation owners, roadworkers"—gave them a cordial reception. An Alabama state trooper who pulled Marcia over for speeding did so with a graceful display of rustic chivalry, telling her, "You were driving very, very well, ma'am, but just too fast." It was not until they had returned to the crowded and rushed Northeast, at a Howard Johnson take-out counter in Metuchen, New Jersey, that they encountered surly service.

Once back home, Burnham pondered the meaning of what he had seen. The media, he noted, mesmerized by the social and cultural turmoil of the chaotic sixties, pictured the country "as splitting apart, riven by bleeding fissures and staggering under the confrontations between youth and age, dove and hawk, alienated and established, white and black." Yet if the facts behind this picture could not be denied, these same facts, viewed from a different angle, yielded a contrary picture. "Is it not astounding," he asked,

> that, *granted* all the rude facts of the raging fissures and confrontations, our country does still hold together, continues to be a manifestly *going concern?* Two hundred million citizens are somehow held together, fed and housed better, however faultily, than any citizens anywhere ever before. The economy continues to function—more spectacularly than any economy ever before. Inventions multiply, American goods, aircraft and citizens range the earth and the moon, roads and cities spread over the land, gasoline is in the pumps, there is light when the switch is turned (well, nearly always), there is a motel room at day's end for every traveler. The country shrugs off the fires of the arsonists, the crime of the cities and the riots of the youth as a great ship shrugs off the waves.[87]

# Chapter 12

# Protester

LTHOUGH BURNHAM WAS STRUCK by the underlying stability of American society, he did not dismiss "the fires of the arsonists, the crime of the cities and the riots of the youth."[1] Up until the mid-1960s, he had not paid much attention to the problem of public disorder. But then the problem began to absorb him, at first in relation to the black civil rights movement.

This movement, he asserted, showed a penchant for what he called "essentially revolutionary methods": "huge extra-legal, often bluntly illegal, mass operations—mass sitdowns, blocking of the public highways, interference in private and governmental business, deliberate provocation of mass arrests . . . [and] gigantic school boycotts." It had become clear, he argued in a piece on the Harlem rioting of 1964, that the civil rights movement, originally reformist, had been infiltrated by revolutionaries—communists, Maoists, Black Muslims, and other black nationalist groups—and "at least in some sectors" was being directed toward revolutionary ends. Supreme Court rulings, he added, were encouraging this trend, saying, "[I]f you don't like the law, if you find the law interferes with what you take to be your rights or wishes, get a mob together and break the law as you may choose. If there are enough of you, we'll change the law, and exonerate you retroactively." The trend augured serious trouble for the future, he warned. For "the line between civilization and chaos is at all times, but above all in revolutionary ages such as ours is, narrow and precarious."[2]

In the later 1960s, when violent rampages erupted in black urban neighborhoods across the country, he feared that unless something were done such outbreaks might become "part of the American way of life." His fear was not allayed by the report of the Kerner Commission, named by President Johnson to study the problem and recommend solutions. The "official" goal of "coercive, total racial integration," which the report put forward, should be replaced by one of political equality and economic opportunity for blacks, he wrote. Neither blacks nor whites seemed to want integration in the absolute sense favored by the federal government. There were "innumerable in-between gradations," and both races tended toward "one or another part-way point—not necessarily the same in every sphere of activity and every locality."[3]

The rise of the separatist black power movement confirmed him in his hunch that while most blacks probably did want "a reasonable measure of integration," many, like many whites, did not, which rendered the cause of total integration hopeless. "How can you integrate two indissoluble substances?" he asked.

Moreover, he observed, black power had a positive side. It could be taken to mean "black responsibility," and if so interpreted, pointed toward a partial solution to the racial problem. In places where blacks formed a majority, they should use the vote (guaranteed by the 1965 Voting Rights Act) to assume political control. Though he had objected in the 1930s to the communist call for an independent black homeland in the Deep South, he now thought it "conceivable" that the creation of a "non-contiguous" black nation comprising areas numerically dominated by blacks and granted "limited sovereignty" might ease racial strains. "Black nationalism may not be the most attractive imaginable prospect," he concluded, "but as an 'alternative' it is a damn sight more 'viable' than integration." Where whites formed the majority, on the other hand, they should consider voting for blacks for public office to show that blacks did not face "a solid wall of white racism at the polls."[4]

Ironically, given his sympathy for Western colonizers, he also praised the black power advocate Frantz Fanon, whose book *The Wretched of the Earth,* which celebrated Third World revolt against white imperialism, had become a major text for 1960s radicals. While admitting that the book bore the marks of an ideological tract ("exaggeration, bias, inflated rhetoric, selective indignation, cavalier treatment of inharmonious facts"), he also credited it with "insights, often embodied in wonderfully concrete observations or images, that open up compelling perspectives on complicated events."[5]

But above all, he stressed, the first concern must be public order. Action against black insurrectionists must become more professional: police and National Guard units must be better trained in riot control, the black underground must be penetrated, and the courts must treat rioters with greater severity.[6]

He was equally disturbed by another of the decade's forms of mayhem: riots and violence fomented by the campus-based "New Left." This "romantic" radicalism, he wrote, differed markedly in ideas and tone from the more stodgy Soviet kind. Leaning toward anarchism and nihilism, harboring a Luddite hostility to technology, rallying legions of "privileged and pampered" students who were now "slumming in the revolution as they went slumming a few years ago in the civil rights movement," the New Left could not in and of itself be called a "serious enterprise." Nonetheless, it posed a decidedly serious problem. Not only had it revitalized the Old Left and triggered "vast social explosions"; it had systematically violated the norms essential to democracy by resorting to violence, thus jeopardizing civilization, which, "men being what they are," did not require "very many savages within to push it over."[7]

"How democratic is the United States?" he asked in a paper rebutting the negative verdict of leftist critics. He would not claim that the country was a democracy in the civics textbook sense. But he did contend that it was "the most democratic" in the world "and probably more democratic" than any before it. Western Europe, though politically democratic, was still permeated by class consciousness. Americans, in contrast, enjoyed not only rights of all sorts, but also highly egalitarian social mores, extensive mobility, a broad range of choice, and, thanks to American business, "the chief cause or basis of America's democratic priority," the booming economy that made all this possible. "Our New Leftists wax very scornful over 'the consumer society,'" he went on. "Let us note the consumer society is the democratic society." What left-wing critics really disliked about the United States was precisely its democratic nature, which they thought "vulgar, stupid, brutal, ignorant, insensitive, prejudiced, degrading—a wasteland." They could not forgive their fellow citizens "for not making the intellectuals their leaders," and they scorned everything American from shopping habits to automobile design to TV shows. Irritated by "the complex, confused, messy, interwoven network of all [the] backward, inefficient, criss-crossing intermediary institutions" through which Americans pursued their goals, liberal pundits plumped for the rule of an enlightened Caesar, while the New Left, whose conduct was "identical to that of the young Nazis" in Weimar Germany, demanded a "participatory democracy" that would really mean "control by a self-constituted elite cadre."[8]

Liberals, he charged elsewhere, in their response to the New Left's assault on democratic society, revealed their usual "*suicidal* tendency." Guilt-ridden liberal foundations awarded grants to New Left gurus who made no secret of their hatred of American democracy. Liberal ideology legitimized rioting by attributing it to "general 'condition[s]'" such as alienation, racism, and poverty, when in fact riots were caused by rioters. Liberal authorities fell prey to a paralysis of will. Unable to deal with disorder swiftly and firmly, they made excuses for lawbreakers, claiming that the worthy ends of the radicals justified the "unfortunate" means they used to attain them. But in fact it was "methods, means, rules, procedures" rather than "abstract ends and ideals" that differentiated democratic from totalitarian behavior. When respectable liberals went on protest marches with "the Kids," what they were really doing was forming a "united front" with Maoists, communists, Trotskyists, Guevarists, anarchists, and freaks. At the same time, the ruling elite, shaped by liberalism, had lost its self-confidence. It could no longer govern, wage war, or "stand up to outlaws." But liberalism's link with the New Left went deeper. Research showed that "most" of the militants came from liberal families. Thus, liberalism had "literally" engendered the New Left and created a culture in which New Left "organisms [could] grow and multiply."[9]

Writing of the violence occasioned by the funeral of Robert F. Kennedy, Burnham remarked that something was "very wrong" with the American notion of public order. "The ideologues are perhaps right . . . in telling us how sick our nation is," he later commented. "They are the sickness." The same people preached the "will to power" that all ruling classes had to have to govern effectively. Among liberals it had become self-hatred, and this self-hatred had been "externalized as hatred of the nation that is disowning them."[10]

New Left violence was becoming "endemic," he repeatedly warned, and had to be stopped. Government existed to uphold order and to protect life and property. If it failed to act, a grass-roots reaction would engender not only a George Wallace-style third-party presidential bid, but "counter-rioting" by counterrevolutionary activists ready to battle the militants of the left.[11]

"The guerrillas have left their turfs—the campus and ghettos—and moved out into the cities," he declared in 1970 after a rash of political bombings. "The phase of urban terror has begun." Traditional policing was not geared toward coping with the problem. The time had come for harder tactics. Fighting terrorism was more like waging war than like pursuing common criminals. "In a war you don't go to court for a search warrant before breaking into an enemy installation, or presume each enemy soldier innocent until proved guilty, or grant prisoners immediate bail, or make sure that a lawyer is present before beginning an interrogation, or publish the enemy's books and provide him a public forum to conduct his psychological warfare operations and instruct his agents." But if liberal attitudes and recent court decisions on the rights of defendants prevailed, the effort to end terrorism would fail. Why were the needed steps not being taken? he asked. "No doubt we're all waiting until [Secretary of State] William Rogers or [Defense Secretary] Melvin Laird is snatched." When some radicals hijacked their first airplane, would they "demand [President] Richard Nixon in exchange for their hostages?"[12]

New Left tactics made it necessary for the Right to decide between "the traditional rules" and repressive action unrestrained by "liberal pieties" regarding means, he wrote elsewhere. It was a choice few conservatives had made, or even realized had to be made. "In both theory and practice, the American Right is underdeveloped country compared to the Left."[13]

These feelings led him to adimre the biting speeches of Vice President Spiro Agnew, whose contemptuous comments on radical protesters outraged liberals. He told Buckley:

> I have got hold of the full text of quite a number of [Agnew's]
> (or Buchanan's [Patrick J. Buchanan, then speechwriting for
> Agnew] or whoever's they are) speeches, and I must say I
> thought them pretty good: including the rhetoric; and some of
> his aphoristic sentences are at a pretty high intellectual level for
> a speech. In fact, I think Agnew's speeches are intellectually
> superior to those delivered by any other U.S. political big shots
> for many years. . . . Now there is also, no doubt, something else
> in them and in him that is harder to evaluate because it is down
> deeper, and I don't feel sure yet about estimate [*sic*] of that
> something else. Maybe it's very bad, but just possibly it's what
> the doctor ordered.[14]

Burnham reserved some of his criticism for colleagues on the Right who, attracted by the New Left's libertarian-sounding rhetoric, concluded that the Right and the New Left held some views in common. Such thinking struck him as pernicious. The true character of political movements could not be discovered in "the abstract content of . . . [their] formulas," he wrote. "*Everyone* is for Liberty, Justice, Peace and Prosperity." Reality revealed itself through action, and the New Left's actions showed that "the romantically anarchic New Left freedoms include[d] the freedom to defame, assault and imprison opponents, to deface and destroy the structures, records and artifacts of the existing social order." Conservatives, in contrast, sought above all to uphold "the inherited structure of civilization against barbarism." They wanted to improve society where possible, but regarded their primary task as preservation. Hence, their opposition to the New Left was, by definition, "strategic and total." To defend liberty, conservatives should ally themselves even with liberals (with whom they differed, at least politically if not philosophically, only on a "tactical and contingent" basis), and go to the aid of liberals under New Left attack.[15]

For Right and Left to join forces against the center meant forming what Trotsky called "an unprincipled united front," Burnham noted in reference to the Council for a Volunteer Military, an antidraft group that counted among its sponsors Karl Hess, Henry Regnery, disarmament lobbyist Sanford Gottlieb, civil rights activist James Farmer, free-market economist Milton Friedman, Norman Thomas, Frank Meyer, and YAF, and whose supporters included Barry Goldwater, Russell Kirk, and William Buckley, along with partisans of the draft-card-burning New Left. Such coalitions always proved damaging to at least one of the partners, he warned, and in this instance, it was the Right that would get hurt. Conservatives had joined for "doctrinaire, ideological reasons, reasons of 'principle' divorced from time and place," while the Left had joined for "pragmatic, strategic reasons, with its eye on . . . the specific circumstances of time and place." Hence, it was the Left that would determine "the political" nature of the council. The Left would exploit the antidraft campaign to strengthen the anti-war movement, with the ulterior motive of pulling American troops out of Vietnam. This was the real, as opposed to the formal, meaning of the council.[16]

◆   ◆   ◆   ◆

Despite his aversion to the New Left, Burnham softened his hostility when commenting on campus rebellion. While calling on college trustees to take strong and swift action against rampaging students, he also decried the college administrations that were the targets of the students. Campus protests, he commented, always included complaints about the decline of the traditional teacher-student relationship and the reduction of students to "IBM card[s]." Higher education had indeed become smothered in bureaucracy and students had been reduced to mere statistics, while teaching had sunk to "a latrine-level task assigned to graduate students, teaching fellows, and low-caste faculty members." Students were right to protest the disappearance of "humane relations between school and student, between teacher and pupil." For few human ties were of "deeper spiritual and intellectual as well as social significance" than "to sit before a true teacher."

Education was now "Big Business in a full sense," he wrote in 1967, and so naturally conformed "to the general pattern of mass-production, technologically advanced, bureaucratized modern industry." But no one knew how to fit students into the equation. Conservatives should defend "the personal and humane values" threatened by college administrations and "discriminate more carefully between [the] plus and minus elements" of campus rebellion.[17]

Burnham showed similar mixed feelings about the 1960s "counterculture," and on at least one occasion sided with "the kids" against his fellow editors. In 1970 a young conservative named Tom McSloy wrote to Buckley to complain about the magazine's disparagement of the younger generation's enthusiasms, such as rock music. "I really do like *NR*, but you can be terribly stuffy at times really," McSloy summed up. Buckley liked the letter so much that he published it and invited his colleagues to comment. Meyer did so, but with not a hint of Buckley's cordiality, peremptorily declaring the young critic out of order, and advising him that the magazine, basing itself "on principle, not on the dictates of the latest fads and fancies," existed to defend "the standards of Western civilization." Rusher's comment was similar.[18]

Burnham, however, was sympathetic. McSloy's criticism was "on the whole justified," he wrote. "It is my impression that *NR* has, relatively, a smaller audience and less influence among the young than in its earlier years. . . . Even when *NR*'s topic is something of direct concern to younger readers—and sometimes even when the text is by younger writers—there is often an older folks' perspective and a lack of empathetic projection (if I may use so barbaric a term)." Though the magazine upheld the Establishment against the radicals, it was also supposed to "criticize and satirize" the Establishment, and "stick pins into stuffed shirts." But it treated "businessmen, bureaucrats, pompous conservatives," and the Nixon administration too gently. It also showed a prissy petulance in its view not just of rock, but of contemporary art in general.[19] It should either drop its coverage of the arts completely, or be "able and willing to greet freshness, vitality, and excitement as well as serenity, elegance, and proportion."

Burnham himself tried to stay open to freshness. After reading a biography of Renoir, he recommended to Buckley what he called the "'cork theory' of human impulses," i.e., the view that, in Buckley's words, "it sometimes pays to conceive of oneself as a cork, in contrast, say, to a mooring, the better to flow, as Renoir's style did, with the currents that tease it along. . . . [T]o move along like the cork makes presumptive good sense, if you want to stay grooved in with the vibrations of modern life."[20]

But Burnham's attempts to act on this theory were not always fruitful. One evening, he and Buckley made a trip to the Fillmore East, a theater on Manhattan's lower east side known for its San Francisco-style rock concerts, which was putting on a Bach program combined with a psychedelic light show. Burnham hoped very much to enjoy the performance, but when it was over confessed disappointment. The concert, he told Buckley, had been marred by "sentimentality."[21]

The legendary August 1969 Woodstock rock festival—which packed hundreds of thousands of young people together for a dionysian weekend of music, drugs, and sex in open fields that summer downpours turned into quagmires—was seized upon by conservatives as proof that the 1960s had been a decade of moral and cultural dissolution. Burnham, on the other hand, found in the festival a welcome proof of human complexity that refuted the liberal idea of human nature. Likening Woodstock to the rites of the ancient cult of Eleusis, he saw in it "a mass ritual and mystery, a surge out of the deep and hidden springs of the spirit" whose initiates could not "be brushed off . . . as an eccentric band of weirdos or a gang of New Leftists," something that liberalism, with its shallow, rationalistic conception of man, would never be able to fathom. "Human beings," Woodstock showed, "evidently aren't going to be satisfied with guarantees of one-man, one-vote, unlimited free speech, college for all and a guaranteed income," he wrote.

But the festival also furnished grounds for irony, he added. The revelers symbolically dropped out of society and spurned the modern technological world in favor of pastoral primitivism, but with "automatic, childlike confidence" still believed that doctors would come from the despised city to heal their wounds and sickness, that helicopters made by the military-industrial complex would fly them when needed over clogged roads, that the cops would be at hand to do what only cops can do, that enough food and drink would appear to prevent any really grievous suffering."[22]

Toward those prime symbols of the counterculture, hippies, Burnham could show himself by turns stern and benign. These exotics led lives of "passive parasitism," he noted, but they were also "gentle and charming and picturesque in ways inaccessible to computer people." While the behavior of New Left militants repelled the average person, "many traces of the hippie style—in colors, dress, music, talk, methods of relaxing—rub off on the rest of us, soften and brighten our square world." Yet ironically, hippies, too, relied on "computerized" society, which created the wealth that made their unproductive lives possible.[23]

Another emblem of the counterculture, marijuana, moved him to reflection rather than ire. When YAF member Richard Cowan published an article in *National Review* urging that the drug be legalized, Burnham demurred, but amiably. Chiding Cowan for being "so all-fired solemn" (Cowan "never suggests that pot can be fun," he remarked), he agreed that the possession of a small quantity of marijuana for personal use should not be treated as a crime. All the same, he opposed early legalization. For one thing, many people would find the step offensive. For another, he found "something disturbing" in the fact that marijuana and its rituals, unlike the main drug of the West, alcohol, were of "non-western origin and tradition." But the chief reason to postpone legalization was simple prudence: at present, the drug's effects were too little known.[24]

As Burnham pondered "the riots, shootings, burnings and dissents" of the 1960s, he saw their common denominator in a "centrifugal, disintegrative impulse" that he traced to the role the United States now played in the world. Pluralistic American society, he argued, had always harbored a strong atomizing tendency, but in the past this had been held in check by its opposite: a unifying tendency rooted in common customs, beliefs, and values, and most of all in patriotic feelings that placed "prudent limits" on "dissent and divergence." But today, patriotism was fading, in line with a pattern that "usually, perhaps always," emerged when a nation-state transformed itself into an empire. For patriotism clashed with an empire's need to include "all races, colors, creeds, all gods, in its pantheon. . . ."The United States had now become an empire.The presidency had long been evolving along imperial ("Caesarist") lines, and an imperial civil service had arisen. But no new unifying force had appeared to replace the old one.The requisite intellectual class, whose role it was "to express the moral out-look that [could] sustain a sense of public duty and imperial destiny," had not yet emerged.

The United States was entangled in contradictions, he contended. "Painfully stuck, wandering between nation and empire," it found itself, in Matthew Arnold's words, "between two worlds, one dead, the other powerless to be born."[25] Could anything be done to ease the situation? Burnham did not take up this question directly, but the quasi-determinist worldview he sometimes advanced implied a negative answer.[26]

◆　◆　◆　◆

Meanwhile, U.S. foreign policy continued to strike Burnham as incoherent. In Kennedy's day, he observed in 1964, the Yalta strategy, the pursuit of a settlement with the USSR, had made headway against rival strategies, but now, under Johnson, it was becoming the only strategy.This accounted for many current U.S. problems: if Washington seemed to be seeking a deal with the Kremlin, how could it object when France courted Moscow in hopes of a deal of its own, when NATO allies traded with Cuba, when Third World countries refused to follow a pro-Western line? Meanwhile, in attributing a love of peace to the USSR, Johnson was willfully shutting his eyes to reality. Soviet conduct showed that Moscow was still bent on defeating the West. Accordingly, Soviet participation in nuclear disarmament talks was no more than a "diversionary maneuver" in the Kremlin's bid for world supremacy. The United States, as usual, was shaping its policy around abstractions—"disarmament, peace, international law"—while the USSR pursued "concrete strategic aims."[27]

Burnham found a vivid example of Johnson-administration appeasement in the U.S. reaction to the 1968 Soviet military intervention in Czechoslovakia. Afraid to irritate Moscow, neither the president nor the secretary of state nor the American ambassador to the UN would pay tribute to Czechoslovakia or con-demn its oppressors. True, in this case, in contrast to the case of Hungary, there could be no question of an ultimatum, for the Soviets now possessed a well-stocked nuclear arsenal. As for an international economic boycott against the USSR, such ventures rarely succeeded.

Still, Burnham thought, alternative steps could be taken. The time was exactly right to emphasize the fact that the USSR was a despotic imperialist power, "only a more voracious 'prisonhouse of nations'" than its tsarist predecessor. In addition, the United States could take symbolic action, such as calling the U.S. ambassador home from Moscow, suspending disarmament talks and cultural exchanges, and halting New York–Moscow commercial air traffic. The State Department had done well in cancelling an American orchestra's tour of the USSR and some other cultural events, but more was needed: for example, the exclusion of Soviet athletes from the coming Olympics. For his part, in September 1968 Burnham began a new campaign to raise money for *Kultura,* and collected almost $20,000.[28]

Despite its growing military strength, Burnham repeated through the 1960s, the USSR still suffered from internal weaknesses that more able American leaders would work to exploit. Nationalism in the Soviet empire (Czechoslovak, for example), remained one of Moscow's chronic problems. And Khrushchev's sudden removal from office in October 1964 showed once again that the Soviet regime lacked a legitimating principle, a convincing justification for its power. The United States might have used Khrushchev's fall to declare "solidarity with the subjects, not the rulers, of the Communist nations." But instead, it "almost slavishly" sought the new Soviet leaders' cooperation in the so-called "quest for peace." Moreover, as the 1966 trials of the writers Yuli Daniel and Andrei Sinyavsky made clear, the Kremlin now faced "a revolt of the intellectuals," who formed "an indispensable element" in the totalitarian system. (This revolt was "probably the most important internal Soviet development since the Moscow Trials," Burnham told Hobart Lewis of *Reader's Digest.*) Further, unlike those of Stalin's day, the victims no longer cooperated with the regime. Rather than declaring themselves guilty, they now defied their oppressors.[29]

Toward the other communist giant, China, which had just begun to acquire nuclear missiles, Burnham urged a more drastic policy. "Within two or three years," he warned in 1964, the Chinese would have an area stretching from India and Pakistan to the western Pacific within range of their missiles, which would seriously jeopardize America's position in the Far East. The best way to end the threat, perhaps for as long as a decade, would be to bomb China's nuclear reactors. True, "world opinion" would explode in anti-American protest, but "a vast sigh of relief would go up along China's entire periphery," and while the USSR might publicly denounce the strike, it would "most certainly" not aid China, and might secretly even lend the United States a hand.

Two years later, Burnham proposed another way to deal with China. The United States could give Japan a few nuclear missiles, he suggested, too few to mount an all-out attack on China, "or on anyone else," but enough to deter the Chinese from committing aggression. If critics of this idea complained of nuclear proliferation, it could be argued that there would be much less likelihood of nuclear war in the Pacific if China and Japan both had nuclear weapons than if China alone had them.

After another year and an announcement by China that it had successfully tested a long-range missile, Burnham pulled back. "What we urge, for the moment now," he wrote, "is more modest: a public and articulate confrontation of the issue of Chinese nuclear arming." But the idea of bombing China's reactors still appealed to him.

By 1969, however, he seemed less anxious about China, possibly because of the chaos produced by the "Great Proletarian Cultural Revolution" or the outbreak of frontier combat between China and the USSR. Commenting on a visit by the Australian journalist Francis James to China's nuclear installations in the remote interior province of Sinkiang, he noted that James's report pointed to "a serious Chinese intercontinental nuclear threat only a year or two" away, and supplied a clear motive for a "preventive strike by the US, the USSR, or both." But was it possible that there was really no story at all, he asked, that "James . . . figured he could get a higher price for his copy by spicing it with tall tales—like that first Western traveler to Sinkiang, Messer Marco Polo?"[30]

At this point, it was not the USSR or China but Cuba that Burnham thought posed the key test for American will. For Cuba, he noted, amounted to "an enemy beachhead *inside* our defense perimeter" and "an active center of revolutionary infection" in Latin America. He took heart when, in 1965, the Johnson administration landed Marines in the Dominican Republic to foil what it believed to be a Castroite takeover in the making. But his pleasure ebbed as it became clear that the State Department wanted a new Dominican regime based not on the anticommunist Right but on his old *bête noire,* the noncommunist

Left, which, he feared, would only reopen the way to Castro.[31]

To Burnham's mind, Washington did not act competently in dealing with communism. But the West, he conceded, did sometimes score successes. Parliamentary elections in France on the heels of that country's near-revolution of 1968 (in which student protests and the biggest general strike in French history came close to toppling de Gaulle) produced a landslide victory for the anticommunist center and Right. Voters were saying, "*We do not want a Communist revolution!*" he exulted.[32] Similarly, on a 1969 visit to Spain, he was buoyed by a talk with the country's future king, Prince Juan Carlos, who assured him that Spain would not tolerate anything like the previous year's chaos in France and would renew its defense treaty with the United States in response to the growing Soviet naval presence in the Mediterranean.[33] But if the behavior of other Western countries sometimes cheered Burnham, American policy depressed him.

A new cause for dismay was American hostility toward Greece after its armed forces seized power in 1967. To Burnham, the American attitude made no sense. Greece did not of course have "a junior Anglo-Saxon-type" democratic regime but a dictatorship, he commented upon returning from a visit there in 1968. Still, the rule of the Colonels (as the media dubbed the country's new bosses), though "no jewel," was also far from totalitarian. Rather, it resembled a Latin American dictatorship in that people who stayed out of politics were left alone. And while political detainees were sometimes subjected to torture, such abuse was a matter of "individual acts" of brutality, not the official policy of the regime.

The most important thing was that Greece occupied "a crucial strategic" place in the West's defenses. If Greece collapsed, NATO would be badly damaged, and a Soviet advance into the Mediterranean and the Middle East would be made easier. Since the Colonels were not totalitarian but "unqualifiedly anti-Communist," opposed to Soviet expansion, and eager for good relations, trade, and military cooperation with the United States, what was the point of treating them as pariahs? "If we're only willing to be cooperative with angel-nations," he concluded, "we'll have a lonely road ahead."[34]

On a month-long trip to Greece in 1971, he had found not "a fear-ridden fascist police state," he reported in a *New York Times* op-ed piece upon his return, but a country that was "cheerful, inefficient, impulsive, casually talkative, and rather anarchic." And though the regime certainly had many shortcomings, it seemed "silly to strain at the Colonels while swallowing a Mao," with whom

Washington was then seeking to improve relations.[35]

Equally wrongheaded, Burnham argued, was the American attitude toward Rhodesia, the once British-ruled African territory whose ruling minority of white settlers declared independence in 1965 rather than adopting a democratic franchise that would have shifted power to the country's black majority. The "plain courage and sweat and colonizing vision" of the settlers, Burnham wrote, quoting "a London dispatch" to the *New York Times,* had turned what had been "a region of savage tribal warfare, disease, hunger and superstition" into "a land of flourishing agriculture, mining and industrial activity." UN economic sanctions against the settlers would probably trigger violence that might "spread into a half-continental war," he warned. Hence, it would be foolish for the United States to join in a sanctions campaign, especially in partnership with such paladins of democracy as Soviet General Secretary Leonid Brezhnev, Tito, Castro, Nasser, Albanian despot Enver Hoxha, and Ethiopia's autocratic emperor, Haile Selassie. Luckily, there had been no UN in 1776 when some other British colonies had declared independence. For "that treasonous band of rebel colonies had at the time a large group of colored natives who were not recognized as part of the community, a mass of other colored who were mere chattel slaves, an assortment of voting restrictions even for whites, and a government without a shadow of a claim to legality."[36]

Why, he wondered, had the United States and other Western nations adopted a punitive policy toward white Rhodesia, especially since they did not object to undemocratic rule in countries where the rulers were not white? Liberal ideology doubtless bore some of the responsibility, but a grand strategy for economic self-defense might also play a part. For centuries the peoples of Asia and Africa had been "historically inert," while Europeans and their overseas descendants— the "whites"—had been "the historically dynamic portion of mankind," imposing their rule on the greater part of the world. Now, Asians and Africans had awakened and "moved historically on stage." The whites, who formed only a small minority of the human race and whose elite had "lost [its] nerve," thus faced a mortal challenge: how were they to preserve their privileged status? The white elite might be attempting a tacit bargain with the Third World: the whites would hand over political power to the racial majority, but ("in their own plans, at any rate") retain their hold on economic power. Accordingly, "to save its own neck" the white elite was throwing the Rhodesian settlers to the dogs.[37]

Still, for all his opposition to sanctions, neither did Burnham show much sympathy for the settlers, whose racism he decried as morally wrong and politically stupid. "Racism—white, yellow or brown," he insisted, "is in essence evil." When the settler regime held a referendum in 1969 on a new constitution mandating permanent white rule, he denounced the document as "fundamentally racist and fundamentally despotic." It would deprive blacks of any way of gaining equality, any way of becoming "fully human," except through violence.[38]

Burnham found further reason to question Washington's good sense when he pondered U.S. policy in the Middle East. Instead of approaching the Arab-Israeli conflict in the even-handed way that American interests required, the United States, he charged, was biased in favor of Israel. On the eve of the 1967 Six Day War, when Egypt blocked Israeli shipping through the Strait of Tirana, he urged Washington to take a neutral stand, the legal claims of the antagonists striking him as murky. U.S. military action to open the Strait for Israel, he warned, might turn moderate Arab governments against the United States and push them toward Nasser. The best course would be to submit the matter to the World Court. In the meantime, Israel, with U.S. help, could channel its shipping through its Mediterranean ports.[39]

When the Six Day War broke out, he interpreted the clash, "in its deeper political meaning," not simply as an Arab-Israeli contest, but as "a newly active front" in "the Middle East sector" of the struggle for the world. All the same, he continued to advise against U.S. involvement, arguing that as long as the Soviets did not intervene directly, there was "very little" the United States could do.[40] Above all, he insisted soon after the fighting had ended, Washington should shun favoritism and, despite the poor performance of the Arab armies, refrain from treating Arabs with racist contempt. "The people that carried the crescent of Islam from the Arabian Desert to the Pyrenees, to India, the isles of the South Seas and the headwaters of the Nile," he wrote, "who gave the West the symbols and concepts of the mathematics that is the core of our science and transmitted the learning of the Greeks to our Schoolmen" should not be disparaged because its soldiers had fought badly "in an episodic battle." Arabs, accusing the West of favoring Israel out of guilt over European anti-Semitism, asked why they should have to pay for crimes they had not committed—and asked "quite rightly."[41]

These counsels provoked what one *NR* staffer described as "very fevered reactions" from some readers. To supporters of Israel, they sounded like an attack on the Jewish state, and "stunned, staggered, shocked, shaken readers" protested to the magazine.[42]

As time passed, Burnham came to believe that in the end, despite Israel's superb armed forces, the Arabs, with their enormous numerical superiority, would win the Middle Eastern duel, for quality could outweigh quantity "only up to a certain point." The Middle East, he cautioned, was "one jungle American troops should stay out of."[43]

Yet for all his declared neutrality, Burnham held up Israel, not the Arab states, as the moral model he hoped Americans would follow. In a speech he drafted in 1971 for delivery by New York Senator James L. Buckley, a brother of the *National Review* Buckleys, to the American Zionist Association, he praised the Israelis as exemplars of patriotism, courage, discipline, and self-sacrifice. But above all, he observed, the Israelis had grasped an old and simple truth:

> You can't have it easy—not at any rate in this world. For the individual and for the nation, it's a tough life. You can't get through it without plenty of trouble, pain, problems, sweat, sorrows, frustrations along with the joys and happiness you may be lucky enough to harvest. This lesson . . . is one that many of the current batch of prophets has overlooked. They tell us it will be all sunshine and roses if we just follow their advice to abolish capitalism or disarm or think loving thoughts or get out of Vietnam or wear flowers or have lots of sex and smoke pot or give the peace sign. Any Israelis who ever had that sort of idea about life know by now what a delusion it is. The easy way is the way to defeat, enslavement, destruction. That is how it has been, is, and will be.

Burnham also included a thought whose logic was plain enough, but which he had never before set forth in public so explicitly: that since the Arab-Israeli conflict, whatever other meanings it had, also formed part of the struggle for the world, the United States was wise to keep up a "special relationship" with Israel. A strong and thriving Israel could pose a serious obstacle to Soviet aims in the Middle East.[44]

As for U.S. policy in Southeast Asia, Burnham wrote in 1967, if the communists took South Vietnam, the dominoes would "inevitably" start to fall, and the Pacific strategic frontier of the United States would shift east, "not at once, of course, but soon enough on the historic scale," to the American West Coast. The countries of the western Pacific would be unable to resist the pull of China, Hawaii would be reduced to a U.S. "forward outpost," and the United States would sink to the level of a "parochial power . . . under siege within [its] own inner bastion" and free to enter the western Pacific "only at the will of another."[45]

But so far, he lamented, the United States seemed no more able to pursue a coherent policy in Vietnam than anywhere else. Yet the policy choices in Vietnam were simple: "either move in with enough force to smash the Vietcong or get out." It all came down to the question: "*Have we the will to resist the advance of Communism?*" If President Johnson chose retreat, then U.S. troops should be brought home at once, for it was criminal to throw away American lives without making a serious attempt to defeat the enemy. Nor should U.S. forces be kept in South Vietnam if that country's soldiers showed themselves unwilling to fight.[46]

Johnson, whose will was being undermined by his desire to be known as the "prince-of-peace" and simultaneously as "Horatio-at-the-bridge," seemed to be angling for a deal with Hanoi that would allow the United States to withdraw without too great a loss of face.[47] But the right goal was not to disguise defeat but to achieve victory, and that would require a drastic change of strategy. The war would have to be carried to the enemy's base areas: North Vietnam, Laos, Cambodia, and maybe southern China. An air and sea blockade would have to be imposed on North Vietnam to isolate it from its Soviet and Chinese suppliers. The missile sites adjoining Hanoi and the port of Haiphong would have to be destroyed. And the North Vietnamese economy would have to be crippled by bombing industrial sites and the Red River dikes.

In addition, biological and chemical weapons should be used. North Vietnam's rice crop could be wiped out, while "an incapacitating gas" might prove ideal for ridding South Vietnamese villages of Vietcong infiltrators, since the latter could then be seized without risk to friendly locals. Nuclear devices could also be put to use, e.g., cobalt dust to create a radioactive barrier between the two Vietnams, thus cutting the Vietcong off from its northern sanctuary. To permit irrational taboos to block the use of such weapons was unpardonable. The president had no moral right to order large numbers of young Americans to war in a distant land where many would die or suffer serious wounds, yet forbid them to use the most effective weapons available. Finally, "incremental escalation" should be ended. To keep the enemy off balance and gain the strategic advantage of surprise, changes in strategy should take the form not of gradual shifts but "radical jump[s]."[48]

The risk of nuclear war or direct Soviet and Chinese intervention on the ground struck Burnham as negligible. The Soviets would not risk Moscow for Vietnam, he confidently asserted, and would find the deployment of ground forces in Southeast Asia prohibitively difficult, while China, if it tried a reprise of its Korean intervention, would have to shoulder an appalling logistical burden. A Chinese attack might be all to the good, he once observed. The West would one day have to face China anyhow, so better now, when Mao's nuclear delivery system was still incomplete.[49]

As the U.S. war machine in Vietnam ground on, chewing up men without scoring any real gains, Burnham's frustration grew. If Washington thought it impossible to thwart communist aims, had the time not come to withdraw? he asked again in 1968.[50] But given his belief that a communist victory had to be prevented, his calls to get out rather than soldier on rang hollow.

◆　◆　◆　◆

Though in his own way himself a protester against the Vietnam War, Burnham fiercely attacked the war's liberal and New Left opponents, who not only unqualifiedly condemned the intervention, but in some cases hoped the Vietcong would win. The sincere types, he charged, "marching morons—men, women, and youth 'of good will,' their addled pates stuffed with undigested humanitarian-liberal-leftist clichés swimming in idealist gravy," were only "heedless dupes" of people who won them over by calling for "peace," while really wanting communist victory in Vietnam and revolution in the United States.[51]

Nor were allegedly "hardheaded" opponents of the war—for example, the columnist Walter Lippmann and the political scientist Hans Morgenthau—right in arguing that American strategic interests were not at stake in Vietnam, that the war was "the wrong war in the wrong place." These "realists" failed to grasp the long-range consequences of a communist victory. Yet even if the realists were right, they did not understand that the national interest was at stake there simply because "we . . . have staked it." The war posed "a major test of will," he argued elsewhere. "To flunk would be to suffer a staggering defeat with immense, inescapable and cumulative global repercussions, precisely because it would prove to everyone that our will was the weaker. Maybe we didn't need to jump into the water, but now that we're in, it's either sink or swim."[52]

On one occasion, Burnham's attacks on left-wing protestors landed *National Review* in court. In a July 1962 editorial called "The Collaborators," he accused certain Old Left notables of giving "aid and comfort to the enemy," citing, among others, the Nobel Prize-winning chemist Linus Pauling, whom he called a perennial "megaphone for Soviet policy." "[Y]ear after year since time immemorial," Pauling had lent "his name, energy, voice and pen to one after another Soviet-serving enterprise," he charged. Now Pauling had signed a group letter condemning the U.S. presence in Vietnam as "imperialist aggression." To issue such statements was to justify killing Americans, so it was disgraceful that people such as Pauling were not ostracized.[53] "If our standards have so far dissolved that there is no longer *anyone* on whom we will turn our backs," he concluded, "then we as a people are ready for suicide."

Pauling responded with a million-dollar lawsuit against *National Review,* Buckley, and Rusher. The trial, which began in 1965, found Burnham eager to fight. "Pauling is, among other things, a continuous and automatic liar," he advised Buckley. If *NR* won, "we should sue LP for harassment & attempted intimidation." But as the trial proceeded, it began to disappoint him. *NR*'s lawyers "over-litigated, with dozens of motions, and appeals and applications," as if they were pleading a "standard Wall Street lawyer sort of case: big corporations, huge estates, etc.," he complained. The Pauling case was not of that kind, but "political."

Served with a subpoena, he was unhappy to discover that he was being called to testify not in the Pauling case, but in a related suit brought by Yale professor Fowler V. Harper, whom he had also named in the offending editorial. Jim was "skulking in his Kent," Priscilla Buckley told her brother, and was "making [*NR* lawyer] Dick Williams and Bill Rusher excessively nervous." In court, however, Burnham behaved with his usual aplomb. Asked by Harper's attorney how long it had taken him to write "The Collaborators," he answered, "fifteen or twenty minutes." "And how long did it take you to revise it?" the lawyer continued. "I don't need to revise," he airily replied.

In April 1966, while the Burnhams were vacationing at Cap d'Antibes, the suits were dismissed, the judge agreeing with the defense that the plaintiffs, after six weeks of trying, had not made their case. Weary of litigation, *NR* did not sue in turn. Freedom to criticize had been vindicated, and that seemed enough.[54]

◆ ◆ ◆ ◆

Meanwhile, Johnson's Vietnam policy continued to lose support. Upon returning from Cap d'Antibes, Burnham gained the impression that in his absence a significant shift of opinion against the war had occurred among "the general—the normal—population," which now seemed to be leaning toward "the verbalists." At this point, he reckoned, there was "a fair probability—perhaps as much as an even chance—" that the United States would lose. Ho Chi Minh, who had beaten the French by exploiting anti-war feeling in France rather than by mustering superior force in Vietnam, was again relying on that tactic.[55] And all the while, Johnson was unwittingly playing into Ho's hands by failing to give the war a meaningful purpose. People felt "in [their] bones" that the war, as now being fought, made no sense, and they were right. To compound the problem, this was the first war ever to appear on television, and it was being shown on "the intellectual and emotional level appropriate to TV—that is, the soap opera level."[56]

By mid-1968 Burnham was convinced that the war's end was near. The communists were winning and knew it, he wrote. Nobody in the United States was talking any more about how to defeat the enemy, but only about "*how to get out.*" In the Paris peace talks about to begin, Washington must obtain the "minimum condition for an honorable peace," he insisted—that South Vietnam, "for the next period," be spared communist rule. If it were not, the United States would be seen as reneging on its commitments. Surviving Western positions in the Far East would then soon fall, while at home "rioters, lawbreakers, vandals, revolutionaries and nihilists" would step up their assaults on a government that had shown itself weak. Yet it seemed "impossible" that the indispensable condition could be obtained, for U.S. military failure had put it politically beyond reach.[57]

But while Burnham's emotions were deeply engaged by the Vietnam War, he claimed a stance of detachment on the issue. When Dwight Macdonald (an anti-war stalwart whom Burnham mocked in his column as one of the Old Left's "arrested adolescents . . . titillated by New Left antics") declined to have dinner with him on the ground that they would only end up in a shouting match, he tried to persuade Macdonald to change his mind. "You are wrong about 'superheated politics,' so far as I am concerned," he wrote to Macdonald. "I haven't been passionate about politics for quite a while, now. I seldom do anything more than analyze. Even about the Vietnam war I have not done more than try (according to my lights) to trace out the consequences of this or that course of action. . . ."[58] But Macdonald must have been skeptical, for the dinner apparently never took place.

◆  ◆  ◆  ◆

As the 1968 elections approached, Burnham, no big fan of Richard Nixon, again proposed that the Republicans nominate Rockefeller. Knowing that Rusher, who had worked hard for Goldwater in 1964, shared his opposition to Nixon, he suggested in 1968 that they band together to put *National Review* behind a Rockefeller-Goldwater ("in that order!" a horrified Rusher recalled) "stop-Nixon" ticket. Rusher immediately rejected the proposal. Such a ticket, he later commented, would have amounted to "what Burnham himself had taught me to call an 'unprincipled' (and therefore fatally unstable) coalition." But the Rockefeller idea was close to Burnham's heart ("Jim Burnham . . . finds it so hard to force a criticism of Nelson Rockefeller through his teeth!" Rusher seethed to Buckley), and he did what little he could to keep it alive.

In April 1968 Burnham floated the name of a more recent conservative hero as a running mate for Rockefeller. "This is the way one of the coldest political analysts puts it," he wrote in a *Bulletin* article (without naming the analyst). "Nothing but a Rockefeller-Reagan ticket could stop Richard Nixon from getting the Republican nomination, and (he added in mournful recognition of reality) probably that can't." In the end, resigned to Nixon, Burnham went over to him—and again enraged Rusher, who had now come out for Reagan, by claiming at a gathering of *NR* editors that Nixon had the nomination "all wrapped up"—thus helping to make the claim come true, Rusher later contended.[59]

Burnham too was strongly attracted to Reagan, in whom he saw the model of a winning conservative candidate. Reagan accepted "the realities of practical politics," he wrote in 1966, when the former actor was running for governor of California. Reagan wanted to build a broad Republican constituency. Though avoiding the sectarianism of groups such as the John Birch Society, he did not join forces with GOP "Right-baiters," either, and though seeking the votes of Republican liberals, did not adopt their bias toward big government. Moreover, though often described as an amateur in politics, Reagan had an extraordinary gift for communication, especially on television, the "decisive medium of our era."[60]

As the '60s' political climate grew increasingly stormy, Burnham wondered whether a systemwide convulsion might not be at hand. Differences among Democrats over Vietnam and race were fracturing the once mighty Roosevelt coalition of southern whites, blue-collar workers, blacks, and liberal eggheads, he observed, and the liberals had begun to fight among themselves. If the Vietnam War were not settled before the 1968 election, the Democratic Party might break up. With the Republicans also riven along conservative-liberal lines following the regional divide between the Sun Belt and the Frost Belt, the country might be in for a major political realignment, as in 1828, 1860, and 1936.[61]

When Johnson decided not to run for a second term, leaving Vice President Hubert H. Humphrey and Senators Eugene McCarthy of Minnesota and Robert F. Kennedy of New York to battle it out for the Democratic nomination, with Governor George C. Wallace of Alabama, a segregationist Democrat, a third-party candidate, Burnham thought a Democratic breakup more likely than ever. Among the Democratic contenders, he leaned strongly toward the anti-war McCarthy—a poet and an ironist—rating him "far above average among American political figures in intelligence, learning, wit and decency." Yet he feared that McCarthy, who lacked organization, would be swallowed up by "the organizationally and ideologically experienced groups of the Marxian Left," as Henry Wallace had been in 1948, since only the left could bring him an effective campaign apparatus. The candidate he most disliked was George Wallace, whom he called "a racist-minded demagogue."[62]

But whoever won, he wrote, the country had become so divided and fractious that the new president might find it impossible to govern. The violence accompanying the Democrats' Chicago convention only deepened his anxiety. "Where indeed are we rushing," he asked, "if a city must be turned into a concentration camp in order that the nominating convention of a great political party . . . may assemble?"[63]

Nixon narrowly defeated Humphrey (with Wallace running a distant third), and once in office was able to function. Burnham regarded the new president as at heart an opportunistic politician "not solidly committed to either Right or Left," yet believed that Nixon's high-level appointees, many of whom labeled themselves "pragmatists," gave "some reason for good hope." He also believed that in light of the country's volatile condition, Nixon should foster cooperation both within the Republican Party and between Republicans and Democrats. Thus, while granting that to make Rockefeller secretary of state in hopes of winning over GOP liberals would deeply offend GOP conservatives, he assured readers that the governor could be made secretary of defense without alienating the Right. In the same spirit, he went on to suggest that Nixon make a liberal Republican, or even Hubert Humphrey, U.S. ambassador to the UN. After all, he joked, such people spoke fluent "UNese."[64]

◆　◆　◆　◆

A longtime critic of big government, Burnham did not soften his stance when Nixon entered the White House. A new federal ban on television and radio ads for cigarettes prompted him to fire a blast at "the Nursemaid State." "Are we such babies," he growled in an echo of his 1955 libertarian outburst, "No Firecrackers Allowed," "that we need a million bureaucratic nannies to wipe our noses and change our diapers?" (Still, he savored the irony that despite the ban another arm of the federal colossus, the Department of Agriculture, continued to fork out millions in subsidies to tobacco farmers.)[65]

Nor did he hesitate to oppose a stricter federal gun-control law, widely demanded after the assassinations of Martin Luther King Jr. and Robert F. Kennedy. Such a law would be utterly useless, he insisted. It would not keep guns out of the hands of criminals, but would only imperil a civil right and give birth to another regulatory "monstrosity." Some gun regulation was constitutionally proper, he conceded. No civil right could be treated as absolute. But gun laws should be the work of state and local authorities, not the federal government.[66]

When environmentalism emerged as an issue at the end of the 1960s, he wrote scornfully of the movement, seeing in it only another faddish cause giving its adherents a chance to flaunt their virtue and bureaucrats a chance to expand their power. "We've just got to find a new Cause every six months or so to keep the old adrenalin flowing," he scoffed in an *NR* editorial. "Fallout, civil rights,

Vietnam, ghettos, hunger, poverty—they've lost their kicks and something fresh must be added. Anti-pollution has got everything it takes. The Sir Galahad devotion to purity. The St. Francis dedication to the well-being of all living things. The St. George assault on dragon Big Business."[67]

In a letter of early 1970 to Buckley he outlined his views on how the magazine should deal with the subject.

> The more I think about it, the more I come to feel that NR ought not to jump whole-hog onto the ecological bandwagon. . . . [T]here are some very bad things about this whole neoconservation, anti-pollution, quality of environment crusade. Philosophically it is cockeyed. Economically and politically, it is made-to-order for statists, bureaucrats, elitists (of the kind who know what other people *ought* to want). . . . I suppose you can't be pro-pollution any more than you can be pro-war, but don't you agree that NR should keep its cool on these topics?

But despite these negative comments, he found a natural affinity between conservatism and conservation, he noted to Buckley a week after the aforementioned letter. Still, he could not reconcile himself "to merely joining in with the universal chorus. It is just too banal." He had reached "no final or dogmatic conclusion," he said, "but I find myself uneasy."[68]

"The issue is not, of course, Clean Air or Clean Water or Clean Earth," he observed in 1970. "Who can be against Cleanliness? . . . The issue might be put this way: How clean do we want our air, water and earth to be, *at what price?* The price of cleanup comes high, not merely in dollars, but in what the dollars stand for—the diversion of energy and man hours from *other* objectives, from the production or improvement of this, that and the other thing that we may also want."

By the end of 1970 he was less likely to speak disdainfully of environmentalism, but he nonetheless remained suspicious of the movement as being at least in part an expression of liberal elitism fused with the federal lust to regulate. Conservatives should take environmental problems seriously, he came to believe, but should encourage reliance on market forces to solve them.[69]

At first, Burnham approved of the Nixon administration's economic policy. Though not happy to hear the president announce, "We are all Keynesians now," he was reassured by Nixon's rejection of wage and price controls, and applauded when the administration responded to rising oil prices not by imposing a price ceiling, but by boosting supply through the removal of limits on off-shore production and imports.[70] He turned hostile, however, when, early in 1971, Nixon set up wage arbitration and monitoring panels in the construction industry, attacking the step as a "foray into price-fixing." Nor did he welcome Nixon's efforts later in the year to obtain a federal loan guarantee for the faltering Lockheed Corporation, arguing that the market should be allowed "to mete out its stern discipline to those who have played the game and lost."[71]

In August 1971, when the White House enacted a broad array of anti-inflation measures, including a comprehensive ban on wage and price increases, his anger flared. The new regulations, he contended, had "little operational thrust," and the wage and price freeze, to his mind the "sourest item in the package," would yield only "a case of severe frostbite."[72] But after a time, he shifted his protest from economic to moral grounds. "The most remarkable fact" about the plan, he wrote in 1972, was that "a nation fancying itself a republic conceived in liberty" had limply submitted to "so rude a violation of constitutional processes and the norms of a free society." Nixon ruled "by decree, not by law," he caustically noted a year later. "Up to a year ago last August, historians used to tell us that state control of the economy was the essence of the corporative state of fascism. Maybe we're all fascists now."[73]

◆  ◆  ◆  ◆

Yet for all his volleys at big government and swollen bureaucracy, this "soft Friedmanite" (as a fellow *NR* editor, the economist Alan Reynolds, called him)[74] was still willing to challenge conservative orthodoxy. In one instance his maverick streak appeared in a debate on welfare policy touched off by a 1969 *National Review* article called "Big Brother Is Dead Too." Technology, not ideology, plus "an inveterate mass-disposition to prefer the comfort of security to the loneliness of self-sufficiency," had put an end to traditional do-it-yourself individualism, argued the author, a New Zealander named Kenneth Melvin. "The planned economy, the welfare society, the benevolent bureaucracy" stemmed not from collectivist theorizing, but from "the logic of our age" and "the economics of surplus."

The birch rod of conservative principle in hand, Frank Meyer rushed forward to chastise the erring Melvin. "It is the very glory of the West, and of its Hellenic and Hebraic civilizational ancestry," Meyer intoned, "that we have always raised the standard of the person against this age-old nostalgia of mass-men for slavish security." Melvin had failed to grasp "the spirit of the West," and was hawking "an ideological myth dear to the twentieth century: the myth of social and economic determinism."[75]

Burnham, however, drew up a brief in partial defense of the article. "Welfarism" was not "a real issue," but "a pseudo-issue," he instructed Meyer in a forbearing tone. Governments had always assumed some sort of responsibility in such matters. What was different today was that under the impact of the population explosion, the end of agricultural society, and the technological revolution they had developed a broader sense of that responsibility. All modern nations were "welfarist," whatever their form of government and economy, which implied that welfarism had its roots not in any particular ideology but in "the twentieth century human condition." Freedom, moreover, could "coexist with social democracy and welfarism—in some cases, more freedoms than before, indeed, for the masses."

In calling social and economic determinism a myth, he went on, Meyer was offering an idea of freedom nearer to a New Left anarchist's than to Aristotle's. Frederick Engels came much closer to the truth when he defined freedom as "'the knowledge of necessity.'" For in fact, man's freedom was "narrowly limited by man's fate, by the human condition, by his own organism, the physical universe and the historical circumstances in which he finds himself. A man's significant choices must . . . be made within the framework of these necessities." "*Welfarism*" did not have to end in "the welfare *state* [the federal centralization of welfarism]." But no serious political position today could be based on "a simplistic anti-welfarist doctrine."[76]

On another occasion, Burnham expressed his mixed feelings more succinctly. "For some reason," he remarked after his 1969 cross-country car trip, "I was struck on this journey more than I had ever been with the ubiquity of the central government's eye and arm. Our social order is, is now, a semi-socialism. That clock is not likely to be turned back. That is the way it is, for better or worse—for better and worse, really."[77]

Burnham not only accepted but even championed federal involvement in certain other fields. He called heavy federal spending on the development of supersonic commercial aircraft (SST) of critical importance because of the SST's economic promise, military potential, and technological spin-offs. Still, the real issue, he wrote, was whether the USSR, the United States, or the Anglo-French group working on the Concorde would lead the field. And most important of all was the SST's rich symbolic meaning.

> If we bug out of the SST project, it will be the most striking symptom to date that we are bugging out as a nation, that we haven't got what it takes. It will be more striking than Vietnam. We never claimed to be so much at fighting a cockeyed kind of war in tropical jungles, but doing jobs like making lots of terrific aircraft and populating the world with them is our sort of thing. The choice has nothing to do, really, with money and priorities and ecology and the rest. All that talk is just a way of hiding. It is a matter of *will.*

When the Senate, late in 1970, voted against SST funding, he predicted that the vote would one day be considered "the most important action of the 91st Congress and very probably the most important event" of the Nixon presidency.[78] "I cannot yet believe," he wrote several months later, "that my country is so far gone that it will crawl away whining from the SST challenge."

Nor had he lost any of his enthusiasm for another costly federal undertaking: the Apollo space program. NASA was "mankind's most exciting enterprise—the test challenge for men of our epoch," he wrote in 1970, giving vent to his Promethian romanticism. The astronaut was the most recent embodiment of the American national myth, was today's equivalent of "the lone cowboy ranging on his gallant steed across the cactus-strewn desert, John Paul Jones on the bridge of his cruiser, Charles Lindbergh alone in the empty skies over the North Atlantic, Admiral Perry moving over the Arctic ice."

How marvelous it would be, he exclaimed on the eve of the Apollo moonshot, "to have launched mankind triumphantly into the new age in which all space, all worlds, the galaxy itself become man's home!" Going into space, "the ultimate frontier," was "very, very important, quite possibly more important than any other single national endeavor." For one thing, the power that controlled space would also control everything that was "less than space, including the world."

Yet the space program's ultimate importance, he observed in 1972, lay in its marking "the second fundamental change in man's relationship to the earth and to the physical universe—the cosmos." Before Copernicus, the earth had been the center of the universe, but heliocentrism had demoted it to the rank of a minor planet. Today, however, the earth's status had again been revolutionized: the planet had become (here he quoted Whittaker Chambers) "'the shore of space,' no longer man's permanent home but the starting point for his unending journey." Now man would begin to colonize other planets, "the only possible meaning of his leap into space."[79] How, then, could the country reject the space program, expensive and federally managed though it was?

Burnham also revealed his maverick streak in his criticism of the conservative press and its readers. Contending that journalists wrote "nonsense most of the time," above all when issuing warnings about the future, he included journalists on the Right. "Year after year, decade after decade," he noted, these pundits kept claiming, for example, that federal deficit spending and "welfarist extravagance" had pushed the country to the edge of bankruptcy, though experience constantly proved them wrong. But conservative readers heeded such writers anyway. What readers wanted was not "factual or predictive accuracy" but ideological fulfillment, with the resultant emotional satisfaction. "Most of what is written about these matters is a kind of pornography, and reading it, like reading pornography, is a form of intellectual masturbation. The only truths we are willing to hear about Rhodesia or China or New York City are the truths that confirm our ideological axioms. . . ."[80]

Aside from ideological bias, the media's most grievous sin was "sensationalism." In the past, the kind of materials they required were "simple, traditional and comparatively harmless ingredients like murder, sex, graft and orgies." But today they looked for "such terribly dangerous stuff as human rights, genocide, liberty, race, peace, guilt and justice," and if crises did not come along fast enough, the media invented them. "I will not argue that *NR* and my own journalistic writings are holier-than-thou exceptions," he wryly added. "Come to think of it, I guess I have been illustrating what I have been writing about."[81]

# Chapter 13

# Moralist

T HOUGH BURNHAM OBJECTED TO key features of Nixon's foreign policy, he was not unfriendly toward Nixon's most important foreign policy appointee, the owlish, gravel-voiced Henry Kissinger, for years a political scientist at Harvard and foreign policy adviser to Rockefeller, and now Nixon's national security adviser (and from 1973 his secretary of state). What first attracted Burnham to Kissinger, whom he had come to know in the 1950s when he had lectured at Kissinger's International Seminar at Harvard, was the NSC chief's dislike of Wilsonian idealism in foreign affairs. A "non-utopian" who opposed putting foreign policy at the command of ideology, Kissinger leaned toward the balance-of-power approach of such diplomatic realists as the nineteenth-century Austrian statesman Klemens von Metternich.

But Burnham also found Kissinger fascinating as a symbol. As he had once seen in the technocrat Robert McNamara the personification of the managerial revolution, so he now saw in Kissinger—"the first immigrant, the first Jew, the first PhD, and the second intellectual" (the first, presumably, being Jefferson) to serve as secretary of state—the personification of "the expanding role of the intellectual and verbalist in postindustrial cosmopolitan society" and a sign of the evolution of the United States "from parochial nation into global, imperial power."[1]

Kissinger reciprocated Burnham's interest. Perhaps hoping to soften right-wing criticism of his foreign policy, he once invited Burnham to lunch at the

State Department, where the two spent several hours closeted in the secretary's private dining room discussing world affairs. He knew that Kissinger regarded the meeting as important, Burnham said later, because not once did the phone interrupt them. A year later, Burnham received a second invitation, but turned it down, unwilling to risk losing his critical detachment.[2]

High on the list of the administration's foreign policy errors, Burnham believed, was its handling of the Vietnam problem. When Nixon, with Kissinger, continued the Johnson peace talks with Hanoi, Burnham repeated that a minimally acceptable settlement would have to guarantee South Vietnam freedom from communist rule for a period of "eight or ten years." While the South Vietnamese government could be broadened to take in neutralists, no communists could be included. Failure to gain Hanoi's assent to this stipulation, he warned, would be "a major defeat" for the United States and perhaps even "a catastrophe." A tolerable settlement would also have to provide for the departure of all North Vietnamese troops, regular and irregular, from South Vietnam, Cambodia, and Laos, as well as a phased withdrawal of all American troops. Further, North Vietnam would have to end its support for communist guerrillas in the South. But to obtain this minimum, the United States would first have to show North Vietnam by serious military action that "the era of touch-football wars" was over. On the other hand, Burnham dryly noted, Nixon could also try to win the war, either through "a quick-big-scale ('quantum') escalation to smash North Vietnam as a military force" or through "a long-term, systematic, primarily counter-insurgency" effort such as the United States had pursued in the Philippines after World War II.[3]

But Nixon seemed to want only to get out of Vietnam—a graceful withdrawal appeared to be Kissinger's cardinal aim in the peace talks—and maybe, Burnham speculated, he had no choice. Every head of government had to put domestic needs before foreign policy, and Nixon perhaps feared that to go on fighting would drive the United States to social breakdown. Moreover, as a politician operating in a democratic system, he could not endanger the GOP's, and his own, chances at the polls. Yet if the United States did get out, hiding its flight behind the smokescreen of "Vietnamization" (i.e., the shifting of the military burden to the supposedly strengthened forces of South Vietnam), it would not be able to guarantee the minimum—South Vietnam's decade of freedom from communist rule. "Does it not *therefore* follow," Burnham asked, "that [Nixon's] policy *cannot* succeed?"[4]

Seen in broader perspective, the Nixon-Kissinger Vietnam policy seemed to Burnham yet another example of the same American impulse to retreat that he saw reflected in growing isolationist sentiment, cuts in SST funding, the shrinking of the space program, the reduction of U.S. troop levels in Europe, the scrapping of hundreds of naval vessels, and the failure to resist the seizure by "rickety Latin American juntas" of mines, oil wells, and other U.S. installations that existed only because of "[American] expertise, work and money." All nations, he noted, went through "successive up and down cycles"—until "the last dip" began. If the United States had not yet reached its "end phase," there would have to be "some sort of reversal in at least one or two sectors" soon.[5]

In the spring of 1971 Burnham's spirits briefly rose. After he and Marcia had dinner with the Nixons at the White House, he wrote more approvingly of Nixon's handling of foreign affairs. Pleased by presidential statements in early 1971 warning against the temptation of isolationism, he cheered when American and South Vietnamese forces swooped into neutral Laos to deny North Vietnam a key staging area. Nixon had "abolished the idea of 'the privileged sanctuary,'" he happily announced, and given the high quality of the South Vietnamese performance in the operation, it now even seemed possible that Vietnamization would work.[6]

But Burnham's brighter mood did not last long. Nixon, it seemed, cared much more about the 1972 election than about South Vietnam. The United States had lost the war, Burnham concluded in February 1972. "I kept hoping, and then fooling myself" that Nixon would try to achieve "at least a Korean sort of stable stalemate." But what Kissinger was really negotiating at the Paris talks were the terms on which the United States would surrender—or "not so much negotiating as pleading: begging the enemy to permit us to save face."[7]

Burnham also continued to criticize anti-war protesters. Following the guilty verdict reached in the trial of Lieutenant William E. Calley (held responsible for the Mylai massacre, in which American soldiers butchered several hundred South Vietnamese villagers), he commented in a *New York Times* op-ed piece that the soldiers had no doubt done "horrible things," but that anti-war protesters, in their response to the atrocity, seemed "to be divorcing themselves from history in order to revel in an obsessed orgy of Guilt." "Horrible and obscene things happen in war, in every war; and in peace, too, and in the course of each individual's life and dying," he reminded *Times* readers. "Human existence bears no resemblance to the projections of sentimentalists and utopians. But to dwell exclusively on the horrors and obscenities is the road not to vision but to madness." If civilized people could no longer bring themselves to fight, they would "inevitably be enslaved, or destroyed by the uncivilized" who felt no such compunction. The doves, as usual, were applying a double standard, for they showed not the slightest concern about the communist murder of fifty thousand South Vietnamese civilians.[8]

When a RAND Corporation Vietnam specialist and one-time Kissinger aide named Daniel Ellsberg leaked a number of war-related classified documents (the "Pentagon Papers") to the *New York Times* and the *Washington Post,* Burnham interpreted the leak as part of a "more general campaign" to get the United States out of Vietnam and to defeat Nixon in 1972. But the leak also pointed to a broader purpose, he added: the transfer of power to the liberal "counter-government" ensconced in the federal bureaucracy. The real issue for such people was less the war than the perennial political question: who is to be "master in the house"?[9]

But protest, Burnham asserted, however important, had not been enough to prevent a U.S. victory. Rather, defeat had resulted partly from a losing strategy, but more from the administration's inability to see the war as only "one campaign or subwar" in a single world conflict. Globally, the United States had been "liquidating the cold war and pursuing détente [the policy of seeking to draw the communist states into a web of agreements based on self-interest in hopes of promoting international stability and security] with the great Communist powers at the same time that we do battle with a local Communism supplied and supported—within the United States and globally as well . . .—by those same great powers." Thus, Washington had been able neither to devise a strategy that led to victory (since such a strategy might well be incompatible with détente), nor make sense of the war to the American people (since the war, standing in contradiction to détente, made no sense).[10]

◆    ◆    ◆    ◆

Burnham often wrote of détente with deep misgivings. The 1971 U.S. approach to China, meant to create a counterweight to the USSR, had merit "up to a point," he observed. But in an age in which world politics involved not only competition among nations but also the promotion of revolution, the balance-of-power principle had to be seen in a new light. What was the point of improving relations with China if the new climate made it easier for Chinese-backed revolutionaries to harm the West? When Nixon wangled an invitation to visit Beijing, Burnham, always alert to symbolic meanings in politics, was dismayed. It was "Chamberlain who went to Munich," he recalled, "not Hitler to . . . London."[11]

Burnham found the Chinese "ant hill" both repugnant and hypnotic. "Looking at the photographs of these Mao-men, Mao-women, and Mao-children in their Mao-cities and Mao-villages, and reading the accounts of their conduct and talk," he wrote after Nixon's wooing of China had begun,

> I keep rubbing my mind's eye. This is a science-fiction world; these are robots, or what the sf writers call "humanoids," not the human beings I know as men and women. . . . Somehow these recent glimpses of China—of Maoland—have stimulated, in me at least, metaphysical rather than political or strategic reflections. They pose once more the eternal question: What is man? We should not make the mistake of assuming that there is nothing attractive in Mao's ant hill. It contains, rather, profound seductions for the disoriented psyche. The herd and swarm instincts are present in some degree in each of us. Throughout our own Western history, some of the best of us have sought salvation in the vow of poverty, chastity and obedience. For at least some of us the disgust with "consumer society" is more than the fashion of the moment. . . . This Chinese avatar of Satan is more subtle in his tempting than his predecessor who from the mountaintop offered all the riches and beauties of the world: Now he is promising the more intricate pleasure of renouncing them.[12]

Though once opposed to the admission of Mao's China to the UN, Burnham was now willing, advising the transfer to Beijing of the Taiwan-based Nationalist Chinese government's permanent Security Council seat and full diplomatic recognition. This last step, he said, should have been taken in the mid-1950s, in tune with the practice of recognizing any government that exercised genuine control over its national territory. He would even recognize North Vietnam, East

Germany, and Cuba, he went on, since recognition, when universal, signified nothing but "formal relation." Nor would recognition of China mean "betrayal" of Taiwan, he added. The only country a person could betray was his own. If national security required a reversal of alliances, then it was "not betrayal but responsible patriotism" to reverse them—and "tough luck for those who get hurt in the passage."[13]

But he remained unreservedly opposed to the expulsion of Nationalist China from the United Nations, U.S. withdrawal of recognition from the Taiwan government, and abrogation of the Taiwan–U.S. defense treaty, concessions Beijing was demanding and that he feared Nixon and Kissinger might make.[14] When the two did bow to the first demand, an angry Burnham urged Washington to learn a lesson in dignity from Beijing. Upon China's entry into the UN, he noted, after Nixon's UN ambassador, George Bush, had delivered a "fatuous little speech of welcome," the Chinese envoy, Chiao Kuan-hua, had shown that there were "still men and regimes in the world that base themselves on principle, and that scorn to hide those principles." Chiao had declared that in joining the UN, China had conceded, and would concede, nothing—that the UN and the United States had given way, not China.[15] How much more admirable, Burnham commented, were such words than those of the United States, which always revealed a longing to be loved, and habitually used the "pleading language of negotiation, disarming, joint action and détente."[16]

As for the USSR, the idea of friendship with the Soviets struck Burnham as ludicrous. Moscow's aim of world hegemony, he asserted, had not changed.[17] Yet despite this and many danger signs, the United States doggedly persisted in its errors. On the military level, it continued to depend on "super-gadgetry instead of on men, brain and will."[18] On the diplomatic level, things did not look any better. Kissinger spoke of "linkage" (linking concessions to Moscow to Soviet good behavior), but the administration, embracing the Yalta tradition, swallowed endless Soviet breaches of the spirit of détente, lest complaining bring back the Cold War. A signal instance was Washington's forebearance toward the Soviet arming of the North Vietnamese, who would not have been able to kill American soldiers without this aid. In response, Nixon at the least should cancel the 1972 Moscow summit.[19]

But the most perilous aspect of détente in Burnham's eyes was the administration's stance on arms control, which he found embodied in the 1972 Strategic

Arms Limitation Treaty (SALT). From the beginning of the SALT negotiations, he had voiced doubts about their prudence. During the 1968 election campaign, he pointed out, Nixon had insisted on U.S. nuclear "superiority" over the USSR, but now, ominously, was demanding only "sufficiency." Nixon was also ignoring "the heart of the matter": the totalitarian, amoral nature of the USSR, whose word could not be trusted. In addition, Burnham feared that American negotiators did not grasp a truth that their Soviet counterparts had always known: that disarmament negotiations were "a sophisticated phase . . . of arms competition," since limitation treaties, like increases in armaments, could lead to "differential changes in the arms equilibrium" that would transform "sufficiency" into "inferiority." Finally, he suspected Nixon of making concessions in the belief that a limitation treaty would better his chances of re-election.[20]

The SALT agreement put ceilings on the Soviet and U.S. missile arsenals that gave a noteworthy quantitative edge to the USSR. Besides accepting missile ceilings, the signers also agreed to limit their ABM systems to two: one to shield the national capital, the other to protect a single missile launching site. To Burnham, these terms threatened the United States with "disaster." "In any historic sequence," he wrote, "it is the direction of change that counts. In this matter of strategic strength there can be no mistaking the direction: [U.S.] monopoly—superiority—parity—sufficiency—inferiority." And even if the qualitative superiority of U.S. missiles were preserved, quantitative inferiority would have a harmful psychological effect. Superiority fostered "a calm and confident attitude in dealing with policy issues," while inferiority promoted ambivalence: "caution, yielding, unsureness on the one hand, and sometimes a desperate recklessness on the other."

Equally bad in his view was the ABM agreement. Technical progress might one day make a superb antimissile system feasible, he commented, but Nixon had agreed to limit ABM defense. And in return he had gained little, since the Soviet ABM system was too primitive to work. Nixon was pursuing "one-sided" détente, he concluded, and one-sided détente was functionally identical to "appeasement."[21]

Burnham then proposed an arms limitation plan of his own. History showed man to be a war-making animal, he asserted. But despite the "disharmonies" dividing the USSR and the West, no direct clash had taken place. Each was restrained by the other's missiles, which had thus turned out to be "the guardian angels of Peace." If the two sides stayed in nuclear balance this "Pax Atomica" might continue for decades. On the other hand, if either gained a first-strike capability powerful enough to prevent the other from retaliating, an "almost intolerable instability" would follow. It was crucial, therefore, that the right balance be maintained.[22] As a means of perpetuating mutual deterrence he suggested a U.S–Soviet treaty in which each side granted the other "total access to every relevant element" of its nuclear establishment—the only way, he reasoned, that full compliance with a limitation agreement could be assured. The idea might sound "absurdly utopian," he admitted. But since satellites and spy planes could be fooled, it was less utopian than the belief that communists would keep their word. What was more, if he was right, this was the only way to avoid "a very possibly catastrophic weapons development." The odds that the Kremlin would agree to total access were perhaps "1 per cent . . . or less," he acknowledged, but why should Washington not advance the proposal anyway? If the Soviets turned it down, they would damn themselves before the world and their own people as the enemy of peace. And if they proposed the idea first, "where would that leave the United States?"[23]

As for détente, in order for it to be practicable, Moscow needed to give as well as receive—and give much more than paltry concessions. But whatever pressure Washington exerted should be not merely "tactical" (directed toward short-term, partial objectives) but "strategic" (directed toward a long-term, decisive objective), i.e., the weakening of Soviet totalitarianism. Thus, in return for U.S. economic aid, the USSR should be required to "open up" by allowing free travel into and out of the Soviet bloc and the admission to Soviet territory of Western books, newspapers, magazines, television, and radio. Similarly, Washington might demand the demolition of the Berlin Wall as the price of U.S. recognition of East Germany. In short, the time had come to drive hard bargains, to try some "Yankee trading."[24]

At first glance, Burnham's feelings about détente might seem contradictory. Often, he wrote as if wholly opposed to it, picturing it as a Soviet gambit with which Nixon and Kissinger, for reasons of their own, were cooperating. But sometimes, as in his demand for "Yankee trading," he did not appear hostile to détente under any and all circumstances, but only when he found Washington too ready to accommodate Moscow. His basic belief seems to have been that détente could be pursued along either "hard" or "soft" lines, and so could either benefit or damage Western interests. If rightly conducted, it could work to undermine the USSR, just as the Soviet form worked to undermine the West.

Burnham's endorsement of "hard" détente was nothing new, as the "deal" he laid out in *The Coming Defeat of Communism* shows. All the same, by the turn of the 1970s his outlook was mellowing. The destruction rather than the mere containment of Soviet power, the liberation of the captive peoples of the Soviet bloc, the defeat of "the communist enterprise"—these remained his ultimate ends. But in place of low-intensity warfare he now stressed peaceful tactics, such as "Yankee trading."

Why this mellowing of his earlier, harder view? Had age made Burnham softer? Was he more worried about war now that the Soviets possessed a daunting nuclear arsenal? Had the Cold War's evolution into a contest in which hair-raising episodes like the Cuban missile crisis were a routine feature of world politics led him, wittingly or not, to moderate his thinking? Had the sheer persistence of the Cold War dulled the edge of his anxiety? (In 1970 he changed the name of his *NR* column from "The Third World War" to "The Protracted Conflict.")[25] Burnham's son Jim once speculated that his father may have believed that Soviet energy had run down, or come to see Beijing as a solid check on Moscow.[26] Whatever the case, Burnham seems to have judged the Soviet danger, though still significant, no longer so grave as to require a radical response.

◆　◆　◆　◆

Unhappy about Nixon's seemingly liberal drift, Burnham devoted much of his writing to criticizing the president's aberrations. But in June 1971, upon learning that Nixon was planning to visit China, he concluded that conservatives should express their displeasure not just individually but collectively. Buckley agreed, and in July 1971 gathered a dozen conservative spokesmen at his Manhattan home to draft a joint statement of opposition to administration policies. The participants included, among others, Burnham, Rusher, Meyer, Thomas S. Winter (who edited the conservative journal *Human Events*), New York Conservative Party leader J. Daniel Mahoney, and Randal C. Teague of YAF.

After long debate, the conclave drew up its indictment. Nixon's economic and social policies, found guilty of "excessive taxation and inordinate welfarism," came in for a drubbing. But the heaviest blows were reserved for the president's foreign policy. For though Nixon had so far held on in Vietnam, he had failed to react to the Soviet advance in the Mediterranean, remained silent about the perils of West Germany's *Ostpolitik,* made overtures to China without gaining anything of substance in return, and, *"above all,"* failed to repair "the deteriorated American military position in conventional and strategic arms" despite a huge weapons build-up by the Soviets.

But the twelve differed on how to respond to Nixon's straying. Some wanted to announce that they were breaking with the president. But Burnham and Buckley, unwilling to go that far, persuaded the hard-liners to adopt a less drastic course. Hence, the statement's final text declared, in words supplied by Burnham, that the group had decided "to suspend" its support of the president.[27]

When Nixon gave no sign of having noticed the conservative rebuke, and even compounded his sins by issuing his August 1971 economic decrees, the twelve took their protest a step further. Meeting again in November 1971, they voted by a majority that now included Burnham (but not, for the moment, Buckley) to put up a conservative candidate, Ohio Republican congressman John Ashbrook, against Nixon in the coming year's presidential primaries. The insurgents "believe that a lightning rod is needed to attract the real dissent among Republicans, so that Mr. Nixon can feel the shock," *National Review* announced. Ashbrook would not, however, contest the November election, it added (thereby softening the shock). He was running only to dramatize conservative "concern over the Administration's direction."[28]

To Burnham the Ashbrook venture was of great importance. The GOP had to be brought back on track, he argued, because a conservative Republican Party had become "essential to the nation's survival." No matter how many or few primary votes Ashbrook received, he told Buckley, "his running is a necessary operation, both from the point of view of an honorable portion of the conservative constituency and for the historical-moral record."[29]

The Democrats, he believed, could not be viewed as a tolerable alternative. Their nominee, Senator George McGovern of South Dakota, was the candidate not of the traditional Democratic Party (let alone of a populist movement, as liberals were claiming), but of an elite based in the Northeast and made up of "students, academics and intellectuals, foundation administrators, media . . . types"—i.e., verbalists—"plus moneymen."[30]

Like the 1964 and 1968 campaigns, the 1972 race seemed to Burnham to reflect "a general reshuffling of forces," but now he paid less attention to economic geography than to the social landscape. A month before the election, he quoted with approval Ayn Rand's observation that the McGovern candidacy was "a declaration of war on the American people by America's intellectuals." The intelligentsia, he charged, "in its defining and dominating echelons," was "a perversion." Unlike intellectuals of earlier times, who had been fully integrated into their societies and brought "reason, structure, order, grace, coherence" to its culture, today's intellectuals, condoning the "obscenities, rudeness, trashings, pornography, drugs and sexual licentiousness" of the counterculture, saw themselves as "an elite . . . outside the community and opposed to it." Ordinary citizens, who were repelled by the counterculture's "moral anarchy," recognized the link between the intelligentsia and the McGovern camp. This, rather than mere differences on policy, explained why McGovern was languishing in the polls. But the split also expressed the conflict between a death wish and a life wish: it pitted "the drop-outs (zero-minus growth, reduce the GNP, less energy output, abortion-on-demand, disarm, euthanasia, arrest technology, turn back from space, let Nature be . . . )" against "those of us who want to keep going; or, as it could be summed up, suicide v. survival."[31]

Yet throughout the campaign, Burnham also cast barbs at Nixon. Still, when his fellow *NR* editors announced that, given the sheer awfulness of the McGovern platform, *NR* preferred the re-election of Nixon, he joined in their half-hearted endorsement. In any event, Nixon and McGovern offered the only serious choices, he remarked, for to McGovern's left and Nixon's right lay the politics of the fringe.[32]

When Nixon won, Burnham warned Republicans that the Nixon majority was not the "emerging Republican majority" forecast by the political analyst Kevin Phillips, but a majority against McGovern. After all, the Democrats had kept control of Congress. Moreover, it was unlikely that the Nixon majority would endure. The GOP really was "the party of Big Business," while the Democrats were the party of the urban machines and labor, and it was hard to see "how traditional Republican businessmen [were] going to lie down peacefully, for very long, with populist-minded trade unionists, lower-middle-class ethnics and poor whites."[33] Given the GOP's uncertain future, he advised, conservatives should reflect on where they stood. The Nixon presidency had "smothered" conservatism "as a distinct doctrine and movement," so conserva-

tives should decide what, if any, role to play on the American scene as it had
evolved under Nixon.[34]

◆　◆　◆　◆

With the election behind him, Nixon could again concentrate on Vietnam. The
settlement being negotiated in Paris was not "precisely a 'defeat'" for the United
States, let alone a "surrender," Burnham commented as the peace talks moved
toward conclusion. Rather, it should be seen as a "failure," because a communist
takeover in South Vietnam meant that the United States had not achieved its purpose.[35] When the peace accord was finally signed in January 1973, Burnham
described it as "about as good as we could expect to get," since it would give
South Vietnam "a fighting chance to survive." Finding a bright spot in a mostly
gloomy picture, he wrote that if the United States had not intervened, every small
nation subjected to heavy totalitarian pressure "would have had the best of reasons to capitulate at once and get it over with." As it was, communist momentum
seemed to have been slowed.

But more often he painted the war's outcome in uniformly somber colors.
With the American retreat from Indochina, he noted a few weeks after the cease-
fire, communism would be the main power in the region. The communists would
not honor the peace agreement, and the United States would not retaliate,
Nixon's trips to Moscow and Peking having ruined the political and moral basis
for renewed intervention. "If we swallow Mao," Burnham asked, "how can we
strain at [North Vietnam's premier] Pham Van Dong?"[36]

Vietnam taught many lessons, including a moral lesson, he observed. The
teachers, by example rather than precept, were the POWs now returning from
communist captivity.

> The first POWs to be freed had been POWs for from six to
> eight years. That is, they withdrew from consumer society and
> assembled in their communes at more or less the same time as
> our counterculture people withdrew, and assembled in theirs.
> The frames of the commune life are in many respects similar: a
> minimum of machines and industrial products; no luxuries;
> simple organic and natural foods; little contact with the outside

world. . . . There were, it is true, several special features in the situation of the prisoners: Their withdrawal was not their choice,
and the oppression and injuries they suffered at the hands of the
establishment were a matter of more palpable reality . . . than the
Marcusian dialectical torments troubling the souls of the counterculture people.

Now the plain fact of the matter is that everyone . . . was
astonished at these men who emerged from that dark North
Vietnamese night to see, once more, the sun and the other stars:
at their physical and mental health, their dynamism and natu-
ralness, their positive outlook, their posture, their ebullience.

Yet there was no reason to wonder at the POWs, he went on, shifting to the
Catonian idiom he sometimes employed.

Their lives as prisoners were built on the rocks of country, family, and religion, and fashioned by courage, loyalty, and
discipline—first and above all, self-discipline. In a prison camp,
fifty pushups each morning, for seven years! You will search in
vain through all the books, manifestos, speeches, and dialogues
of the counterculture for any mention, even, of that homely
cluster—country, family, religion, courage, loyalty, discipline,
and (God Save the Mark) self-discipline.[37]

The fall of South Vietnam to the North in 1975 found Burnham unwilling to
give in. If any South Vietnamese troops wanted to go on fighting, he wrote, it
would be Washington's "minimum duty" to keep them armed and supplied. But
he also called for action far beyond this minimum. As one step in an effort to
arrest the American "global retreat," he urged the United States to send a warning to the victors that if they undertook mass killings, Hanoi and Haiphong
would be "immediately and totally atomized."[38]

The war's outcome seemed to Burnham as especially ominous in that it ran
counter to the secular trend of American history. From the colonial era to the
twentieth century, he pointed out, Americans had moved west, eventually crossing the Pacific, trading with China, opening Japan, and imposing U.S. rule on
Hawaii and the Philippines. In World War II the United States had repelled a

powerful "counterthrust eastward" by Japan, and then established a dominant military presence in East Asia, which marked the peak of its westward movement. But with the Korean stalemate, "the rising curve" had leveled off, and with the U.S. "defeat" (no longer "failure") in Vietnam, it had begun to fall. Its historical-geographical momentum having shifted into reverse, the United States was now likely to withdraw from mainland Asia and "not improbably," over a longer period of time, from the whole Asian Pacific region. But an even broader historical retreat might also lie ahead: the departure of the entire West from all of Asia.[39]

Who was to blame for the Vietnam debacle? Burnham asked. Congress, which had cut off aid to South Vietnam, and now ruled out any further intervention? But Congress had only followed the "inner logic" of the Nixon-Kissinger peace accord. Nixon and Kissinger? But they had only bowed to popular feeling. The people? But the people could express itself only through leaders and elites, and there had been no leaders and elites willing to oppose popular feeling. There were, however, blameworthy persons, never named, though their role in the tragedy was "critical and even determining." These were the rulers of the USSR—Washington's partners in détente—who had made the North Vietnamese military effort possible. Did Washington think it an "incivility" to mention them?[40]

To Burnham's dismay, Nixon continued to pursue détente in his second term. Was he attempting a USSR vs. China balance-of-power policy, Burnham mused, or did he really believe that the United States could have "genuinely friendly" relations with the communist powers? Reality argued that the latter aim could not be attained, since the Kremlin saw détente as only a tactical ploy in its pursuit of world power. Moreover, as conducted by Nixon and Kissinger, détente remained one-sided. Rather than a "hard" détente that demanded "a quid for every quo," the United States was still practicing a "soft" version that differed little from appeasement.[41]

◆　◆　◆　◆

The top story of Nixon's second term, however, was not détente, but the June 1972 break-in by agents of the Nixon re-election committee at Democratic National Committee headquarters in Washington's Watergate complex, and the president's efforts to conceal his role in this and other illegal actions. Burnham was deeply absorbed by the Watergate scandal, though upset less by the break-in and the phone-bugging scheme that lay behind it ("a venial sin," he said) than by the cover-up, whose smell, he wrote in early 1973, "even the least sensitive nose whiffs." Only the truth could get rid of "the sour, rotting quality" pervading the affair, he insisted. For the sake of the country and especially of conservatives, the administration should come clean and "purge" itself of anyone "legally or morally culpable" in the matter.[42]

In private, he criticized "the nonliberal but also nonconservative" Nixon more directly. At a February 1973 *NR* editorial meeting, "Jim allowed his present tremendous animus against Nixon to boil over," Rusher wrote to the absent Buckley, "and said at last what was really on his mind: namely, that he thinks the . . . Nixon Administration is the most outrageously secretive and Byzantine in American history, and that therefore (inferentially) the press is thoroughly justified in its present course" (accusing the White House of threatening its freedom).[43]

Not least among Burnham's reasons for anger was Nixon's invoking of executive privilege on an unprecedented scale to block the release of evidence. "[W]hat is all this Caesarist wall defending?" he asked. "The shoddy little trail of this pipsqueak Watergate business." But Watergate also caused him wry amusement. It was ironic, he observed, that Caesarist liberals, idolizers of FDR, had taken to bemoaning what they now called "the imperial presidency."[44]

Even more dismaying, he wrote, was the administration's illegal, and routine, use of federal agencies for partisan purposes. That all previous administrations had also misused public powers did not excuse Nixon, but merely underlined the importance of keeping the private and public spheres separate, for it was just this that distinguished constitutionalism from despotism. The Nixon administration, with "all the secrets, the hundred-dollar bills, . . . the spreading political paranoia that finds 'enemies' in every nook and cranny," gave off a "police state smell," he charged. The White House clearly needed "fumigating."[45]

But despite the despotic tendency he found in the administration, he thought that under Nixon the power of the presidency had declined. Nixon's agreement to Congress's cut-off of funds for war in Southeast Asia, he wrote, marked "the first major down-turn in the ascending curve of the Executive's warmaking powers" since 1940. Still, he believed that no definitive trend was visible, for in response to the 1973 Arab oil embargo, Congress had passed without protest the

National Energy Emergency Act, which authorized the president, "on his finding of an energy emergency . . . to order us to do just about anything that takes his fancy, from decreeing when, where, and how we move about to when, whether, and how we conduct our factories and stores, sail our ships, dispatch our trucks or trains, or turn on and off our furnaces and light bulbs."[46]

The media clamor over Watergate, he noted, pointed to another of the scandal's several meanings. The media, as the mouthpiece of the northeastern "Liberal Establishment in coalition with the miscellaneous Left," were pretending to a moral outrage they did not in fact feel. In the media's eyes, Watergate offered an opportunity to mount a coup, not simply to oust a hated president, but more important, to fend off "the embryonic 'new majority'" that had enabled Nixon to pulverize McGovern, and so threatened to terminate decades of liberal rule.[47]

With the October 1973 "Saturday Night Massacre" (Nixon's firing of Watergate Special Prosecutor Archibald Cox, Attorney General Eliot Richardson, and Deputy Attorney General William Ruckelshouse), Burnham's moral revulsion at the president reached its peak. The crisis could now be resolved only by Nixon's removal from office, he argued. But since impeachment was a cumbersome process, Nixon should make it unnecessary by resigning. Goldwater, who believed Nixon to be "guilty up and down the line," was the key to the problem, Burnham wrote to his son Jim. If Goldwater came out for resignation, enough conservatives would join him to isolate the president. Watergate had strengthened his own feeling that "the manner of governing" was more important than "the content," Burnham added. "Even if the U.S. is fated to be transformed into a Caesarist empire, and even if that is necessary to its survival, I still don't like Caesarism."

To make sense of Watergate, he mused, to understand how Nixon could have fallen so far so soon after his 1972 landslide victory, one had to relate his trajectory to the myth sequence in which the "supreme triumph" leads fatally to "the catastrophic fall." After the 1972 election, "the hubris that was an organic part of [Nixon's] being was fully uncorked, and necessarily provoked the gods to strike him down." Now, "everything he does goes wrong, and only sinks him further." The climax "could be either (Greek) his (symbolic) death or (Christian) his miraculous salvation." But it was hard to see how salvation was possible, "though all things are possible—since he [was] . . . guilty in so many senses."[48]

As Burnham knew, many conservatives, including several of his *NR* colleagues and probably a majority of the magazine's readers, rejected his argument that Nixon should resign. Yet some did agree, among them, Senator James L. Buckley, another conservative for whom the "Saturday Night Massacre" had been the last straw. Persuaded that Nixon had abandoned the conservative platform he had run on in 1972 and could no longer do his job effectively, that the GOP faced disaster in the coming midterm elections, and that the country would suffer great damage if the crisis dragged on, Buckley began to contemplate openly calling on the president to resign. In February 1974 he invited several people whose judgment he trusted to dinner at Washington's Lawyers' Club to sound them out on how he should proceed. One of his guests was Burnham.

The next day, Buckley asked Burnham to draft a statement for him urging Nixon to step down. Burnham agreed, and a few days later the two met in New York to go over Burnham's draft which was also reviewed by several other people. On March 19, at a press conference held in the Senate Caucus Room, Buckley read the finished text. The president, he declared, whether guilty or innocent, could no longer perform the duties of his office. Yet to impeach him would only make the crisis worse. Hence, to rescue the country from the Watergate morass and the presidency from "the death of a thousand cuts," Nixon should voluntarily quit the White House.[49]

When Nixon finally did resign in August 1974, Burnham was buoyed by the proven resilience of the constitutional order. The executive branch had grown almost powerful enough to upset the executive-legislative balance, he wrote, and signs of "civic decay" had cropped up in all too many quarters. But the nation's fundamental institutions had met the test, and after advancing for decades, the Caesarist trend had at last been halted. Watergate's outcome was "one more reason why we, as citizens, may be of good heart for our country."[50]

❖   ❖   ❖   ❖

Burnham looked forward to the presidency of Nixon's second vice president, the former Michigan congressman Gerald R. Ford. He had met Ford a decade earlier and had been favorably impressed. When Ford became vice president, succeeding Spiro Agnew (who had resigned amid charges of bribe-taking), Burnham had described him as "a first-class man, capable of whatever tasks he may be called upon to perform." In Congress, Ford had made himself an expert on military matters, Burnham now noted, and since he favored a strong defense, he was likely to approach Moscow with greater prudence and firmness than had Nixon. Burnham was also delighted by Ford's choice of Rockefeller as vice president, speculating that since Kissinger, once a Rockefeller foreign policy adviser, was going to stay on as secretary of state, the new president might be planning to put the hard-line Rockefeller on his foreign policy team. The combination of Kissinger's talent for theorizing and Rockefeller's Cold War toughness, he happily remarked, could work out well.[51]

On the plane of world affairs, Burnham observed, Ford would have to deal with a major conceptual problem. For decades, the Cold War had served as the main organizing idea behind U.S. foreign policy, giving policy coherence and continuity. Now the Cold War idea had been cast aside in favor of détente, yet no adequate replacement for the old concept had been found. Hence, Ford would have to answer the question, "What comes after the cold war?"—and do so "more intelligibly" than Nixon. He would also have to alter the operational side of policy, conducting détente with "realism and even a dash of skepticism."[52]

Burnham's enthusiasm for Ford did not last long, however, for instead of changing course, Ford stuck with Nixon's version of détente. To the disappointed Burnham this meant more appeasement. The approach was perfectly reflected, he wrote, in Ford's refusal to invite the recently exiled Russian novelist Alexander Solzhenitsyn to the White House for fear (Burnham believed) of offending the Kremlin.[53]

Under Ford there occurred what Burnham thought a particularly sorry instance of American concession-making: Washington's embrace of the 1975 Helsinki Pact. Drafted and signed by the United States, the USSR, Canada, and most of the nations of Europe, this treaty seemed to him a foolish and even perilous bestowal of bounty on the USSR in exchange for nothing. To begin with, Burnham observed, the treaty granted the USSR's long-standing desire for *de jure* recognition of its borders of 1945, and so formally abandoned millions of people to Soviet tyranny. In addition, the treaty's second section, which concerned trade and other kinds of exchange, made it easier for the Soviets to import Western goods and technology, and thus to go on increasing their military strength. Finally, its third section, which pledged the signatories to honor human rights, including freedom of movement across frontiers, left Western countries more open than ever to Soviet propaganda and espionage. But because the provision contained no enforcement machinery, it offered no means of action against Soviet violations. The United States and its allies had thus conceded much, Burnham concluded, and for pledges the Kremlin was anything but likely to keep.[54]

The United States tended to see détente as the "diplomatic equivalent of a business deal," he remarked as the pact was being signed. It expected negotiations to deliver mutual benefits: first of all, lower odds on nuclear war, then trade and various kinds of cooperation, and eventually, perhaps, friendship. Détente also served the interests of Western businessmen, who, eager for Soviet customers, found the policy "a respectable cover for their greed." Thus, "David Rockefeller and Henry Ford had more to do with the pursuit of détente than [the socialist writer] Michael Harrington and Henry Kissinger." Moscow, however, viewed détente not as a "'step toward peace'" or "a prelude to cooperation and friendship," but as "a mode of conducting the revolutionary struggle" and as "a cover for [its] fundamental strategy of aggression."[55]

But he could see no sign that the administration might change course. "The Kissinger business has become acute," he told Buckley early in 1976, "and I don't think it is going away. The root trouble seems to me to lie in the fact that the country and Henry simply do not have a coherent foreign policy. Or, more exactly: one element of Henry's policy is coherent—namely, détente—and since the rest isn't, détente dominates, and becomes in practice the only operative and continuous policy."[56]

To compound the problem, no corrective could be expected from the president. Ford was "endowed with all the forms of the Presidency," Burnham noted, but with "a considerable portion less than all its substance." His "bumbling ordinariness"—"stumbles on aircraft exits, fender-bending drives, headcolds at awkward moments, a wife who won't keep her mouth shut, slips of the tongue"—symbolically expressed his ineptitude, which certainly extended to the realm of foreign policy. Burnham was probably not puzzled when Ford, in a 1976 campaign debate with his Democratic rival, former Georgia governor Jimmy Carter, uttered what was by all odds the strangest statement ever made by a candidate in such a forum. To a question about U.S. policy toward Poland, Ford solemnly replied that the USSR held no sway over Poland and never would as long as he was president. For the next week, the media buzzed about "the gaffe," attributing it to Ford's reputedly meager intelligence. Ford had indeed blundered, Burnham wrote, but not necessarily out of run-of-the-mill stupidity. Rather, he had probably gotten muddled trying to follow a line (Don't say anything Cold War-ish about the USSR, but don't sound like an appeaser, either) that his pro-détente advisers had urged on him, but that required more verbal dexterity than he could muster.[57]

Burnham did, however, see a ray of light shining in the gloom. This was Daniel Patrick Moynihan, Democrat, former Harvard sociologist, and member, on the domestic policy side, of the Kennedy, Johnson, and Nixon administrations, who now served as U.S. ambassador to the UN. Dropping U.S. forbearance for a tough, unapologetic stance, the blunt, outspoken Moynihan sharply riposted against communist and Third World attacks on the United States, refusing to be cowed by fear of giving offense. Even when dealing with Kissinger and Ford, Burnham delightedly announced, Moynihan behaved "not as subordinate to superior but rather like a baron with his peers."[58] But Moynihan's UN stint did not last long. After only seven months, he left the job to run for the U.S. Senate— and succeeded in winning the New York seat of James L. Buckley.

Burnham was not surprised when Ford was beaten by Carter. He had predicted a Carter victory, believing that only Reagan, like Carter a Washington outsider from the Sunbelt, had had a chance of defeating the Democratic candidate, and no more than a slim chance at that. Since Ford's departure ended Kissinger's term at the State Department, the time had come, he reckoned, to fill out Kissinger's report card. The grades he gave were uneven, ranging from an A for Middle East diplomacy to an F for the settlement reached in Vietnam.[59]

◆　◆　◆　◆

Several times since the 1940s Burnham's travels had taken him to within sight of the communist world. His visits to Berlin, for example, had put him in a small Western enclave surrounded by communist territory. In 1961, after attending an Asian anticommunist conference in Manila, he had spent a day on the Nationalist Chinese island of Quemoy, a mile off the coast of China, where he had lunched with the island's commander in a man-made cave built for protection against mainland shelling.[60] But he did not set foot in a communist country until 1974.

The occasion was a sailing vacation in the Mediterranean that included a two-week visit to the coast of Yugoslavia. He likened the experience to "a first live concert after years of listening to records and radio." Yet Yugoslavia, he noted, did not belong to the Soviet bloc, the model for "standard textbook communism," and his visit was confined to the coast, which was reputed to enjoy greater freedom than the interior. On the coast, he found no sign of totalitarianism. Policemen were few, Western newspapers and magazines freely available, and American movies widely shown. The core of totalitarianism, the "qualitative and quantitative breadth" of the despotism that defined the total state, was missing. And if Yugoslavs did not appear "to be having much plain *fun*," they did not strike him as "gloomy," either. On the other hand, he observed, Yugoslavia was hardly democratic. Power lay in the hands of a single-party dictatorship that maintained tight limits on freedom of speech, among other freedoms. How, then, should the country be politically categorized?

The answer, he decided, lay in seeing that Yugoslavia, "like all contemporary states," possessed "totalitarian features," indeed, more than most countries, but not enough to merit the label "totalitarian." Yugoslavia demonstrated the possibility of non-totalist communism—a category American policymakers should keep in mind. For with communist states of the non-totalitarian kind (which might also include Poland, Czechoslovakia, and Hungary, where totalist rule had been "externally imposed and [was] at least in some measure artificial"), true détente was conceivable.[61]

Going on to consider the American practice of classifying all governments as either democratic or dictatorial, Burnham commented that reality would be better served and a more successful foreign policy achieved if this twofold division gave way to a threefold one: totalitarianism, democracy, and authoritarianism— the last a kind of government under which political freedom did not exist, but other kinds (intellectual, religious, economic, the freedom to emigrate), in varying degrees, did. If the three types of government were viewed in historical perspective, he went on, democracy seemed to be "a sport," a form of government peculiar to the West, and given current trends, perhaps unlikely to last much longer. The question, then, was not whether democracy would win out over dictatorship—his answer was no—but whether authoritarian regimes would turn totalitarian. The danger of that was greater for authoritarian governments of the Left than of the Right. For not only did left-wing authoritarianism have much in common with left-wing totalitarianism—for example, a taste for state-controlled economies—but at present, powerful leftist totalitarian states were working to spread their form of government and society, while on the Right regimes of this sort no longer existed.[62]

A year later, Burnham was given a chance to visit the very belly of the beast. The opportunity was offered by Buckley, who had conceived the whimsical notion of marking *National Review*'s twentieth anniversary by taking the editors on a tour of the USSR. Burnham was "sorely tempted," Buckley recalled, but Marcia, thinking of his CIA work, and afraid he might be hustled off to a Siberian gulag, put her foot down. Burnham bowed to her fears and stayed home. Asked why he had done so, he replied, "Well, they just might want to ask me a few questions, and I'd rather not be in a position where I might have to answer them."[63]

◆   ◆   ◆   ◆

The Burnhams continued, however, to take trips abroad, cruising on Buckley's yacht, the *Cyrano,* which they chartered several times for winter sailing in the West Indies; roaming in the Aegean; paying their first visit to Turkey (in preparation for which Burnham immersed himself in a multivolume history of Byzantium); and returning to such familiar haunts as London, Paris, Brussels, and Madrid. But Burnham's favorite kind of travel remained grand car sweeps across the United States.

At one time or another in the 1970s, treks through the American hinterland took the Burnhams as far afield as the central fissure of California's San Andreas fault, isolated Appalachian hollows, and again, Louisiana bayous. As always, Burnham paid close attention to his meals. Creole cooking he now rated "the best American food" and "at its highest levels as good as any of the world's cuisines." But he was puzzled by the South's apathy toward wine. Could it be blamed, he wondered, on the region's lack of vineyards?[64]

Despite his love of good food, Burnham stayed slim, aided by golf, tennis, walking, and outdoor work at Kent. But many of his fellow citizens, he noticed on a 1977 cross-country trip, were piling on poundage. "By direct perception, I would say that Americans are now, on average, the fattest people on earth," he commented. American fat "exuded, cascaded, ballooned, quivered, undulated in blobs and globules," made all the more visible by clothes that seemed designed "not for concealment or control but display." As if obeying recent Supreme Court rulings, American fat did not discriminate on the basis of "color, race, religion, sex, or brains," he added. But it did appear to be class-related. The operative rule seemed to be: "The richer you are, the less you eat."[65]

One of Burnham's most prized travel finds was Kentucky's State Resort Park (SRP) system, which he liked to cite as a successful example of socialism. How could SRPs be squared with free-market theory? he mused, wielding the needle he sometimes applied to free-market doctrinaires. According to the disciples of Adam Smith, such places should not be possible. Money alone could not account for the excellence of their landscape design, the high quality of their staffs, and the aesthetic superiority of their buildings and furnishings to those of competing, privately owned resorts. "Ideological generalizations" would not be adequate, he warned. "Help, please, Milton Friedman!"[66]

Travel also drew Burnham's attention to a more serious matter: the racial chasm he noticed around the country. On his 1977 and 1978 trips through the Midwest, the Southeast, and the Middle Atlantic states, he came across many black travelers, some driving expensive cars and therefore, he presumed, not poor. Yet although the Burnhams ate at all sorts of restaurants, not once did they see a black diner. Nor did they often find blacks at the motels they stayed at. Since this could no longer be traced to Jim Crow laws, it must be that blacks simply preferred to live mostly among fellow blacks, Burnham reasoned, and thus preferred "voluntary resegregation." The country might be headed for a "two-phase social structure," he conjectured, "integrated during the workday and segregated after 5 P.M." Moreover, where integration did exist it seemed "external" and "bureaucratized" rather than "of the spirit."[67]

On one occasion, discarding his tone of detached curiosity, Burnham gave a clearly approving account of the up-beat, patriotic, and antiliberal message conveyed by the nation's local bicentennial celebrations.

> No doubt it is impossible to be sure of any general interpretation of a large mass event of this sort. However, it seems plausible that the people of the nation were saying: 1) The hand-wringing, breast-beating doom-sounding intellectuals— yeah, pointy-heads, some of us call them—may be honestly expressing their own feelings, but they don't speak for us. 2) The way we are behaving and talking today is the way we like to, and we like America because a person can behave and talk like this. 3) We don't think this country is going down the drain; it's

got plenty of faults, but compare it with anyplace else . . . and you gotta believe it's the greatest.[68]

Yet when he shifted his gaze from Middle America to the West as a whole, Burnham was seized by forebodings of social and moral collapse. "All around us," he wrote in 1974, "we have been seeing unmistakable signs of the revocation of the social contract, the breakdown of the family, decay of patriotism, generalized sexual promiscuity, spread of drug, hippy, commune, and other subcultures, exotic cults, open-ended permissiveness." The West's present mixture of "affluence and softness," seemed to him almost to have invited the terrorism then jolting several Western countries.[69]

"[T]he final collapse of the West is not yet inevitable," he had written at the end of *Suicide of the West*. "[T]he report of its death would be premature. . . ." Ten years later his pessimism was less qualified. When a literary agent seeking permission to market the French translation rights for a 1975 reissue of the book asked him how he currently saw the West's prospects, he replied that the book's thesis seemed to him "as valid and as relevant now as [in 1964], and perhaps even more appropriate."[70]

The 1975 edition of the book included an "afterward" in which Burnham repeated that the West was going from defeat to defeat, but was being "reconciled" to its losses by liberalism, which turned these failures "into scenes from a Morality Play in which Equality, Justice, Peace, Internationalism, and the Environment" conquer "Greed, Racism, Pollution, Aggression, and Privilege." Liberals, he now added, seemed incapable of actions that defending a civilization could require, such as "the deliberate use of force against other human beings up to the point, sometimes, of killing them; the sacrifice of the well-being, health, or even life of others—sometimes millions of others; the violation of individual rights; the disregard of suffering, pain, and tears."

The future, then, in Burnham's view, looked ominous. "Still," he observed, sounding the faintly hopeful note on which his books often ended, "we can never be sure what human beings are going to do. The past is determined, but, for human beings, the future is free. It is too early to publish the West's obituary."[71]

But if the West was ailing, its archenemy was doing no better. In November 1977, the sixtieth anniversary of the Bolshevik revolution, Burnham assessed the health of the USSR through the November 7 diary entry of a Soviet police official he invented to serve as his mouthpiece. Surveying Soviet society, this melancholy soul complains that "graft, cheating, and venality ... have replaced the self-sacrifice, endurance, and even heroism that were not uncommon in the early years." "[M]aterialism and hooliganism" have gained the upper hand among the young, he writes, "epidemic alcoholism" rages among the peasants, and the hopeless economy survives only because Western businessmen keep rushing to its rescue.

True, the USSR's armaments are formidable, he goes on, but all the same, "we are nearly always way behind, trying to catch up." The USSR did catch up under SALT I, only to find the United States "ready with a whole new set of weapons: cruise missiles, mobile land missiles, N[eutron]-bombs." To make things worse, the USSR is caught in "a strategic vise" between China and the West, its navy lacks easy access to the open sea, and its Warsaw Pact allies are anything but reliable. In fact, on the evidence of their past behavior, not even the Russians and Ukrainians can be viewed as trustworthy. At the same time, despite outlays of billions, Soviet foreign policy is "in shambles." "Those Third World types seem to be playing us for suckers." The USSR has been shut out of India and most of the Middle East, Castro has failed to deliver the Latin American revolution he promised, efforts in Africa have gone awry, and Soviet aid to Vietnam has not brought the naval and commercial rewards expected. Further, the world communist movement, once run by Moscow, has unraveled into separate strands—Yugoslav, Eurocommunist, Chinese, ultra-leftist—most of which are also anti-Soviet. "If we are to be saved," the imaginary official ends his inventory of woe (conveying the anti-détente message that was the column's purpose), "it can only be through the enemy's stupidity, greed, and illusions."[72]

Thus, for Burnham, the greatest danger still came from within, from the West's faltering will in the face of more resolute adversaries. In the mid-1970s he found the problem starkly dramatized in a novel called *The Camp of the Saints,* the work of a French writer, Jean Raspail, that charts the swift collapse of Western civilization after hordes of destitute Indians assemble a huge fleet of rotting hulls at Calcutta and set sail for Europe to wallow in the West's abundance. Europe possesses more than enough firepower to demolish the oncoming swarm, but facing a foe comprised of hungry non-whites, cannot bring itself to pull the trigger. Instead, its will corroded by the egalitarian-universalist rhetoric of the guilt-sodden Left, it prefers suicide, and intoning sentimental liberal clichés, limply yields to the invaders (whose ranks are soon swollen by more swarms of starving Third Worlders). The United States, confronted by the masses of Latin America and an internal Third World proletariat, surrenders as well, while the USSR (also white and part of the developed world), whose sparsely populated eastern regions are coveted by an overpopulated China, is overrun by hordes invading from the East.[73]

In some ways *The Camp of the Saints* reads as *Suicide of the West* might had it been written as fiction. Burnham found the book fascinating, and spoke of it often. What may especially have seized his attention was Raspail's pungent depiction of the West's loss of will, which, smoothed over by liberal rationalizing and guilt-mongering, opens the way to apocalypse. But he did not really expect an abrupt Western collapse. "I have never gone in for doomsaying," he wrote in 1977 (probably causing some eyebrows to be raised). In all likelihood, the West would decline for "centuries, like most of its predecessors."[74]

◆   ◆   ◆   ◆

Though stressing will as the key to success in foreign policy, Burnham also expressed skepticism that a single president, however determined, could control policy to any great degree. Each occupant of the Oval Office found his options "largely determined by what [had] already been done," his column advised the incoming Jimmy Carter. Still, if "the overall direction" of policy resisted revision, the course could sometimes be shifted by "a few degrees," which might be just enough "to stay clear of the rocks."

Meanwhile, Carter faced the same conceptual void as Ford. The Cold War view of the world was considered outmoded, but no new master idea had emerged to replace it. Filling the void would now be up to Carter. If he left the job undone, U.S. policy, deprived of an analytical framework and guiding purpose, would dissolve into a jumble of *ad hoc* reactions to events.[75] Burnham himself still subscribed to the Cold War outlook. Only the United States and the USSR, he wrote, could boast "the population, territory, resources, industry, technology, location, and panoply of ultra-weapons" needed for superpower status. And because the two giants also held contrary ideas on everything from human nature to the nature of the social good, they had to see one another as adversaries.[76]

Burnham early voiced misgivings about Carter's views on policymaking. Carter's talk of rooting policy in morality, he commented after the 1976 election, showed a failure to realize that the rules binding governments and individuals were not the same. Reinhold Niebuhr, in the tradition of St. Augustine and Machiavelli, had noted this truth in his book *Moral Man and Immoral Society*. It was odd that Carter, who cited Niebuhr as a major influence on his thinking, held ideas on policy exactly the opposite of Niebuhr's. Moreover, Carter's invocations of morality, "politically meaningless but highly charged emotionally," could prove dangerous, since they ignored the truth that governments must act with prudence. But then again, Carter's moralizing probably did not rest on genuine conviction, but was merely a mixture of demagogy and sentimentality.

(In contexts other than that of policymaking, Burnham gave his blessing to Carter's calls for morality. When Carter spoke "without embarrassment of love and faith and prayer," he wrote during the campaign, the voters knew he was rejecting—as they themselves did—"the counterculture's obscenities and drugs and excesses that so many of the older leaders have condoned.")[77]

As for the specifics of Carter's foreign policy, Burnham found much to criticize. Commenting on the talks for a second SALT agreement, for instance, he accused the president of softness on the verifiability issue, charging that although the White House knew of Soviet violations of SALT I, it had done nothing, lest Moscow break off negotiations.[78] Nor was he happy with Carter's policy toward Africa, which he summed up as an effort to keep closely aligned with the continent's black rulers, whatever the consequences for personal freedom and Western security. Carter's stand on Rhodesia furnished a case in point. The settler regime, under mounting political and economic pressure, had reached a compromise with the moderate wing of the black opposition calling for universal suffrage: government by a black-white coalition headed by a black prime minister, and a small bloc of seats in parliament reserved for whites. Washington, echoing black-ruled Africa, rejected the agreement because it did not give total power to the blacks. This meant favoring "racist government founded on bloodshed and terror" over "racially integrated government founded on unrestricted democratic choice."[79]

But Burnham also found much to praise in Carter's foreign policy. Thus, he applauded Carter's criticism of the Soviet record on human rights, happy to see the USSR and other communist states "thrown . . . on the psycho-moral defensive." And if he went on to say that the president's human rights position was "mostly talk" and needed to be backed up by action—a boycott of the 1980 Moscow Olympics, for example—he also called it "good and appropriate talk" from American leaders. He was equally heartened by Carter's public support for the Soviet dissident Andrei Sakharov (so different from Ford's craven behavior toward Solzhenitsyn), by the Carter State Department's unabashed statement that the United States hoped for a decrease in communist influence in Western Europe and opposed the inclusion of communists in Western European cabinets, and by the seizure of Soviet fishing trawlers that had broken U.S. law and the arraignment of their captains in court.[80]

In the Middle East, where the main U.S. task, in Burnham's view, was to postpone "the impossible choice" between Israel and oil for as long as possible, Carter's diplomacy, he thought, deserved "a somewhat better grade" than it was getting. When Carter brokered the 1978 Camp David accords between Egypt and Israel, Burnham called the accomplishment "impressive." Since the Soviets and their Arab friends were loudly denouncing the agreement, he added, the president must have achieved something of value.[81]

Carter had also acted wisely in seeking full diplomatic relations with China, Burnham contended (though he again insisted that Washington not abandon Taiwan). The world kept changing, and governments had to "adapt sufficiently to deal with the new, painful though this [might] prove, or be stuck with outmoded and increasingly obstructive remnants from the past." Not to recognize the communist regime, which had ruled the Chinese mainland for three decades, would be "an obsolescent absurdity." Moreover, Chinese hostility to the USSR kept Moscow from concentrating its forces against the West. True, China was not a superpower, he remarked to Buckley, speaking of an article in *Commentary* by the strategist Edward Luttwak that denied China's importance as a counterweight to the USSR. Still, "a second enemy in your rear or on your flank is a major headache even if he is a minor player—and China is not all that minor." China's military strength had been underestimated before, he noted—"a generation ago by the U.S. Joint Chiefs and their field commander [i.e., MacArthur in Korea]."

Many *National Review* readers took umbrage at Burnham's support for recognition, and gave him what he called "an epistolary pounding." But Burnham stuck to his guns. His column's purpose, he replied to his critics, was "fact and analysis." He rejected all ideological theories of truth, and when his intention was advocacy he said so. Because China's change of policy was "potentially the most important development in global politics" in many a year, U.S. national interest called for "a both-Peking-and-Tapei play, not an either-or."[82]

Burnham again sided with Carter (and against most of the Right) on the emotion-laden issue of sovereignty over the Panama Canal. His willingness to give up U.S. sovereignty was not new. A decade earlier, prompted by the shut-down of the Suez Canal, he had argued that "the older imperial style" of operating such waterways no longer made sense, that in Panama, for example, a radical regime, wanting to protest U.S. sovereignty, could seize the canal or block it through acts of sabotage. The solution, however, was not a transfer of sovereignty to Panama, which was "weak, incompetent and unreliable," but to "a nonpolitical, technical" authority, vested with a multilateral guarantee, which would run all international canals.[83]

But by 1977 Burnham was willing to cede sovereignty to Panama. To do so would not make the canal any less secure, he maintained, for its security would always depend on the United States, whoever the formal sovereign happened to be. In fact, under Panamanian sovereignty security might even improve, since Panama's rulers would want to protect their biggest moneymaker. And in any case, the canal had lost the importance it had once had. Economic and strategic arguments against a transfer of sovereignty were therefore largely rationalizations or nostalgia.

But he admitted to sympathy for one anti-transfer argument. Some opponents of transfer, seeing it as the latest "humiliating" American surrender abroad, and believing that the line had to be held "somewhere, sometime, unless we're reconciled to suicide," thought the canal the best place to make the stand. But as much as he sympathized with such feelings, he wrote, he did not think the treaty the right issue for a show of firmness. To drop the treaty would only spark trouble in the Canal Zone, while to hand over sovereignty to a country as puny as Panama would be seen as "more *noblesse oblige* than capitulation." A better way to demonstrate American resolve, while at the same time gaining something of real importance, would be to reject the Chinese demand that, as the price of establishing diplomatic relations, Washington end its connection with Taiwan. Conservatives should offer Carter a deal: no opposition to the draft treaty with Panama in exchange for a pledge not to yield to China on Taiwan.[84]

Carter is "not exactly my dream prince," Burnham remarked after evaluating the president's performance for almost two years. But if Carter had weaknesses—

a soft spot for arms control treaties, an overly respectful attitude toward the UN, an energy policy that mistakenly stressed conservation over production, to name a few[85]—he also had strengths. Moreover, unlike some recent occupants of the White House, he had at least done nothing shameful—had not, for instance,

> chickened out on an invasion [the Bay of Pigs] launched by his order, thrown away to no purpose 50,000 American and a couple of million other lives by incompetent handling of a minor war, renounced a second term on the demand of rampaging students, drug-soaked hippies, and spoiled children playing revolution, brought a bungled war to an end in an ingnominious defeat christened "peace with honor," or got caught in a tangle of lies and a cheap coverup that get him booted out in disgrace while it demoralized the citizenry.[86]

Forced by failed health to retire in late 1978, Burnham could not write about Carter's last two years in the White House, and so did not record his final verdict on the Carter presidency. But of the seven presidents he had covered since the 1930s, the one he treated most amiably was Carter.

# Chapter 14

# Coming to Rest

B Y THE 1970S, WITH his thinning hair turning from gray to white and his face lined, Burnham had begun to look old. His manner, too, had changed with the passage of time. The frosty young man who had often made others feel uneasy had evolved into what a colleague at *National Review* called a "cheerful, rather grandfatherly" sort of person.[1] While still dry of tone and free of consoling illusions, he had come to suggest the proverbial kindly elder, a bit remote, perhaps, but amiable and wise.

Sometimes his wisdom took the form of practical tips. Thus, drawing on his knowledge of wine, he once told *NR* editor Linda Bridges that it was usually better to drink wine from a poor year at a great vineyard than from a great year at a poor vineyard.[2] At other times—during lunch at Paone's, at editorial conferences, in casual conversation—he might cite one observation or another from a list of ten he had compiled over the years that he believed provided a code for intelligent living. This code became known at *NR* as "Burnham's Laws." When asked if the laws were written down anywhere, he would answer, "Only in the hearts of my children." One day at lunch in the mid-1970s, his fellow editors persuaded him to recite the list. As he did so, the magazine's executive editor, Daniel Oliver, covertly copied it down, and after typing up his transcription, submitted it to a surprised Burnham for correction. Burnham made a few small changes, and then bestowed his imprimatur on the finished version, which read:

1. Everybody knows everything [i.e., no one can hide for long the truth about himself from those with whom he has an important relationship].
2. Who says A must say B.
3. Just as good, isn't.
4. You cannot invest in retrospect.
5. Wherever there is prohibition, there's a bootlegger.
6. In every project there's a Schlamm.
vii. You can't divorce yourself.
viii. Every member must pay his dues.
 ix. No excuse, sir.
10. If there's no alternative, there's no problem.

(Burnham numbered laws seven, eight, and nine with Roman numerals to set them apart from the rest, thinking them more akin to moral injunctions than the others.)[3]

Still, for all his latter-day benevolence, Burnham had lost none of his readiness to do battle with the partisans of "mush." Drawings of him heading his column in 1970 and 1971 emphasized this trait, picturing him as a curmudgeon of irate mein: face defiant, eyes accusing, lips compressed, and chin thrust pugnaciously forward. Nor did he cease to occasion storms at *National Review,* whose office experienced little détente in the 1970s. For if the death of Frank Meyer in 1972 removed a doughty adversary, and if new people at the magazine were wont to approach Burnham with deference, he could still count on lively opposition from William A. Rusher.

Rusher had never resigned himself to Burnham's ascendancy. When Buckley's absences from the office left Burnham in charge, the publisher's ancient grievances would flare up anew. In February 1973 Rusher wrote to Buckley, who as usual at that time of year had gone to Switzerland, to complain once again about Burnham's editorial control, or, as Rusher put it, to continue "the on-going discussion of what, precisely, is wrong with *National Review.*" The main problem, Rusher argued, was simply Burnham, who unfailingly turned down Rusher's ideas for "hard-hitting editorial[s] with a relatively fresh conservative proposal or angle." Indeed, Rusher went on, "pitifully few" people at *NR* were "willing or able to put a fresh, challenging and specifically conservative idea before Jim with any serious hope that it [would] receive his approval." (Buckley, however, seemed reluctant to intervene. He thanked Rusher for making his case so "eloquently," asked him to keep noting down suggestions that Burnham had rejected, and promised to tackle the problem when he got home—but then, as far as the documentary evidence shows, did not.)[4]

A new cause of discord between Burnham and Rusher was a recent arrival at *NR*, the young conservative journalist George F. Will, whom Buckley had hired to be the magazine's Washington correspondent. While Burnham held Will in high regard, Rusher thought him far too indulgent toward liberalism. "Week by week," Rusher protested in a 1975 memo to the editors, "thanks to [Will's] consistent shilling for established liberal positions, *National Review* is not only being used (and misused and abused) to further liberal objectives, but—far worse in my opinion—is being deprived of what it badly needs: a competent Washington correspondent." Yet Rusher, fatalistically, also predicted that his view of Will would not prevail, that Burnham's opinion would decide the issue.[5]

◆ ◆ ◆ ◆

If Burnham still held sway at *NR* in the 1970s, signs of his active presence there began to dwindle. By the evidence of his and Buckley's papers, he no longer contributed much to the magazine's interoffice correspondence. In 1975 he stopped coming to the office the week the *Bulletin* appeared. In September 1976, with his seventy-first birthday approaching, he announced plans to cut back further "both qualitatively and quantitatively." The time had come, he told Buckley (now the only person other than himself, he noted, who had been at *NR* from the beginning) to revise his relationship with the magazine. He would go on writing his column and the *Bulletin*'s "Abroad" section (a collection of brief foreign news items), and also contribute occasional other material so long as this fit in with the magazine's strategy. But starting in 1977 he would no longer attend the biweekly editorial conference, though he would come in when his presence could be helpful. He would also retire from *NR*'s "command echelon," and work "only as a technician and possibly, from time to time, if the command thought it relevant, as a staff consultant." It was "almost always a good idea," he added, ". . . a matter, really, of decorum . . . for old people, no matter how competent, to step outside the chain of command. If they still have useful skills or talents, there is no reason why they shouldn't exercise them. If they are asked for their opinion, it is proper for them to give it. Otherwise, a discreet silence."[6] Buckley answered with a letter paying homage to "a great teacher and . . . a great analyst," and thanking Burnham for his huge contribution over the years both to *National Review* and to his own "education and morale."[7]

Burnham may also have feared that his ability to work was declining. A few years before his semi-retirement, he had begun to ask fellow editors to double-check his copy, worried that he might have failed to catch some error.[8] A bit later he told Priscilla Buckley that his eyesight was weakening. The problem, at the time limited to the left eye, was caused by a capillary leak that was damaging the retina. Priscilla found him a magnifying glass with a built-in light, and at work he came to rely on it. By late 1977 the leakage, under treatment, had diminished, but then, abruptly, the problem worsened. In January 1978, flying home from the University of South Carolina, where he had taken part with Buckley, Ronald Reagan, Pat Buchanan, George Will, and others in a televised debate on Carter's proposed Panama Canal treaty, he suddenly lost much of the sight in his left eye, and a short time later in his right. It was virtually certain, his eye doctor told him, that he would soon go blind.[9]

Writing to Buckley a few weeks after this calamity, he described the current state of his failing eyes. He was not yet blind, he said, but, in the jargon of government forms, "'visually handicapped.'" He could still see, but the world looked "rather blurred in details." He could not drive, except perhaps in broad daylight on familiar roads with little traffic; he could not play golf, tennis, or any game that involved hitting balls; nor could he read newspapers and magazines without a magnifying glass or meet the visual demands of editing. On the other hand, he could still do his column and, "in principle," write articles and "even books"— and he could still bake bread. "[S]ince what happened results from a systemic development that is part of the aging process, the idea of a cure is somewhat like the idea of abolishing old age. This seems to be the way in which old age launched his first major assault on me."[10]

Outwardly, he faced his misfortune with stoic fortitude, and in business-like fashion readied himself for blindness. With something like enthusiasm, he described to Priscilla the steps he was taking: learning from the experience of others, gathering information about visual aids and substitutes, and putting his name on the Library of Congress's list of the visually impaired so that he could borrow library tapes and recordings free of charge. But behind his stoic mask he was consumed with rage. "[H]e really fought against 'aids'—including the tapes and records provided by the Library of Congress," Marcia later confided to Buckley.[11]

And then fate dealt him a second, much heavier blow. In early November 1978, a few weeks before his seventy-third birthday, he suffered a massive stroke. At first he seemed unlikely to survive. Marcia, in torment, called Priscilla with the news. "Nobody was ever loved the way I was loved by Jim," she sobbed. She did not know whether he should have a priest at his bedside, she said. He had never shown the least desire to return to the Church. Still, she sensed (as Priscilla recalled her words) "a certain uneasiness" in him. Priscilla phoned a priest she knew, Father John Regan of the Catholic Church in Sharon, to ask if he would come. Had Burnham expressed an interest in religion? the priest asked. No, Priscilla admitted. Father Regan came anyway, but apparently found an unresponsive patient.[12]

Though at first death seemed imminent, Burnham lived—and not only lived, but in some ways made a remarkable recovery. Within a few weeks he was speaking clearly, dressing himself, eating without help, walking easily, managing what Marcia called "all those daily things" without difficulty. "[H]e is doing everything for himself including bossing everyone else around," his daughter wrote a few months later to a friend. "His doctor says it is a real miracle." Moreover, to the puzzlement of his eye doctor, after the stroke his retinal deterioration ceased, and he was able to see adequately for the rest of his life.[13]

But Burnham's recovery, though striking, was far from total, for the stroke left his short-term memory, as Marcia put it, at "about zero." Unable to recall everyday words, he took to identifying objects by reference to their function. A glass, for instance, became a "water vessel." Marcia, who closed her real estate agency to care for him full-time, acted as his vocabulary coach. She would place several items—a book, a pen, and an ashtray, for example—on a table in front of him, and have him name them. On one occasion she asked him to identify a dollar bill. "A hundred pennies," he promptly replied. Yet his broader memory might flicker briefly into life, especially if he were summoned to perform a long familiar task.[14]

Burnham knew that his cerebral wiring had gone awry. When he had trouble thinking something through or coming up with a word he wanted, he would pause in mid-conversation, and say, "There's something wrong here." Such difficulties, Marcia suspected, caused him pain. It was hard to tell what went on inside his head, she wrote to Buckley five months after the stroke, "but I would like to give credit to the possibility that he knows most of the time that he is not 100%. Therefore, he knows that others know, and that he must, by talking with them, be a bore, a no one, a nut. How bad that is for the morale." Still, she added, a visit by their son Jim had perked him up. Jim had even managed to get him to the bridge table, "[a]nd spring is coming . . . [so] who knows?" In a letter to Sidney Hook she reaffirmed her refusal to despair, noting that although her husband's "thoughts and memory [were] in quite bad shape . . . just last night I detected a ray of sunshine—so, you never know, only hope."[15]

Life at the Burnhams' soon fell into a routine that in some ways mirrored the old one. Burnham went for walks in the woods with his shepherd Lucy, baked bread, and spent much time in the living room-study reading. But most writing was beyond him. Often he could not finish letters, forgetting what he had intended to say.[16]

His condition did not rule out long distance car trips, however, though the trips became rarer and the driving fell entirely on Marcia. In 1979 and again in 1981 the Burnhams made the trek to Tucson to visit Burnham's brother Philip and sister-in-law Monica. In the fall of 1980 they journeyed south to spend Thanksgiving in Asheville with their son John and his family. From Asheville Burnham sent Buckley a birthday card showing a tutu-clad elephant on roller skates trumpeting, "Let the good times roll!"

Such visits gave Marcia a respite from isolation. "[I]t was wonderful to have someone else around to talk to," she told Buckley after the 1979 Tucson trip. She found it hard to ascertain Burnham's mental state, she added. "It is odd how James varies. Up and down. Sometimes I think he is really nuts, other times I am not sure. . . ." But she always agonized for him. "Isn't it terrible—when you stop to think—what an awful time he has had? I get used to it, and then all of a sudden it hits me."[17]

Burnham too looked forward to seeing people, happy for breaks in what he called his "continuing sober life." Now and then, he and Marcia went into New York for dinners with friends from *National Review,* to whose social functions— a dinner for New York Conservative Party leader J. Daniel Mahoney, a party for former *NR* editor J. P. McFadden, who was now publishing the *Human Life*

*Review*—Buckley always made sure he was invited. Burnham greatly enjoyed such evenings—at which his entrance sometimes prompted an accolade—though by the next day he would usually have forgotten them.[18]

The peak evening for Burnham may have been *National Review*'s twenty-fifth anniversary dinner. There, Buckley, addressing a large audience, paid tribute to his mentor as having been "beyond any question . . . the dominant intellectual influence" at the magazine. Burnham seemed moved by Buckley's words. "For him it was a kind of milestone, I think. Really *finis*," Marcia wrote to Buckley the next day. "So far this past 2 years I have not cried a tear, but your words last night might bring them on!" Judging the dinner to be the right moment formally to end his relationship with *National Review*, Burnham decided to send Buckley his resignation the next day. But when morning came, he had forgotten the whole evening, dinner, tribute, and all.[19]

Sometimes the Burnhams themselves entertained, giving small parties to which they invited close friends. Burnham's seventy-sixth birthday occasioned a buffet dinner at which a dozen guests sipped champagne and drank toasts to the host. Buckley brought a present of twelve kinds of Austrian wine, each bottle wrapped in paper of a different color. His presents also included some video games, which he thought Burnham (who liked games but whose crippled memory prevented him from playing the traditional kind) might enjoy.[20]

Burnham's life after his stroke, while frustratingly limited—how did the former professor of aesthetics, adviser to Trotsky, theorist of the managerial revolution, author of Cold War liberation strategies, and leading conservative intellectual feel about being reduced to playing video games?—at first proceeded tranquilly. But after a time, new blows began to fall. One day while he was walking in the woods with Lucy, the old dog collapsed and died. Burnham had to carry her heavy body to the road by himself. There, he waved down a passing motorist, who took him home. But when he arrived he could not remember what had happened. Worse, in the summer of 1982 he suffered a heart attack, and although he made a good recovery, he never fully regained his earlier strength.[21]

For Marcia, daily life must have been rougher than for him. Sixty-six at the time of his stroke, she took on the job of caring for him single-handed. "If I were a writer," she once told Buckley, "I would certainly write day by day of the last 2 1/2 years—it is fascinating as well as frustrating." But fascination seems at times to have yielded to anguish. "He lets the days flow by, one like the other, perfectly happy," she reported on another occasion. "Reads the paper, but I have no real idea of what it means to him. I know there is something there waiting to be set free. . . . I cannot bear to have Jim like this." A picture of her taken at the time by Jane Wilmerding shows her looking tired and depressed.[22]

Burnham seems to have realized how heavily he depended on Marcia. One winter day when they were returning home from an outing, she could not get the car all the way up their icy, sloping driveway. While going to find a board to put under a tire, she fell on the ice and lay still for a moment in order to collect her senses. Was she all right? an anxious Burnham asked. Had she broken her hip? But "what that meant to me," she later said, "is 'Who is going to take care of me if you collapse?'"[23]

Marcia shouldered her lonely burden for almost four years. Then in August 1982, at the age of seventy, she came down with a pneumonia-like infection, and in a few days died. Her funeral was held at Kent's Congregational Church, and she was buried in the local cemetery.[24] For Burnham her death was the heaviest blow of all. "Marcia was six years younger than I, and . . . I have been trying to pull out of a severe heart attack," he wrote to Hook three weeks after the funeral. "The combination made her death before me seem especially tragic, but life and death seem, rather often, to mix up their operations. Fortunately, Marcia and I had many fine years, and it's these I must try to remember." In a letter to one of his granddaughters, he made a simple avowal of loss and grief. "It is a terrible thing about Grandma," he wrote, "and for me, as I'm sure you know, there is no real way to handle her death. But I do the best I can. . . ."

He was touched when *National Review* published an obituary. "It was a fine thing for you to do," he thanked Buckley, "and if Marcia can still read, which I will leave as an open question, I'm sure she has been having a happy time reading and re-reading it." (Still, he was miffed by the obituary's identification of his father as "a minor railroad magnate." "What does he mean, 'minor' railroad magnate?" he growled to his son Jim's wife, Anne. "It's silly to mention it, by the way," he corrected Buckley, "but in fact, I doubt that my father would be termed a 'minor' railroad magnate. I suppose that, to an eastern oriented person, anyone from the midwest or west looks that way, but in fact my father . . . moved up fast in the business world without waiting to get through college, or even into college.")[25]

◆  ◆  ◆  ◆

With Marcia's death began the final phase of Burnham's life. Her first stand-in was his daughter-in-law Anne, who came up to Kent from Washington, D.C., where her husband was working at the World Bank, to look after him until she found a full-time companion. Within a short time she had hired one, but the arrangement soon ran into trouble, for Burnham turned snappish. To make matters worse, the companion fell down on the job. Told (by whom is not clear) that Burnham could manage the short walk from his East 70th Street apartment to the Buckley home on East 73rd by himself, she let him go off one day to visit the Buckleys on his own. An hour passed before he arrived, by which time the Buckleys had grown frantic. Soon after, the companion was dismissed, and Burnham went for a sojourn at the home of Jim and Anne.

Now a new companion had to be found. This time, it was a nurse named Tessa di Nicola, an attractive, good-humored woman who seemed more like a neighbor than a companion to the elderly. She would remain with him until his death.[26]

Once back in Kent, Burnham resumed his daily routine. After breakfast, he and Tessa would drive into town to do the shopping and pick up a *New York Times* and a *Wall Street Journal,* though he would not always read them. But he did always read *National Review,* which was sent to him regularly. In the afternoon he would take a walk with his two new dogs, Tom and Dolly. He might also check on two ducks, Cheese and Quackers, he had bought to ornament his pond. Occasionally, he would bake a loaf of French bread—"the best in the world," said Tessa. As dinner drew near, he would have two vodka-and-tonics and watch the news on television, making caustic comments on the day's events. After dinner, more television, another walk with his dogs, and then bed. On the whole, Tessa thought, he seemed happy.[27]

Though his range of activity was narrow, he did not grow reclusive, but went to cocktail and dinner parties at the homes of friends in Kent, and on his eightieth birthday gave a party of his own. Buckley feared that without Marcia he would no longer visit New York. He and Priscilla were determined to get Burnham into town "at least once a month," Buckley wrote to a friend. But Burnham continued to come to the city of his own volition, accompanied sometimes by Tessa and sometimes by Marcie, who had separated from her husband

and was now living in Manhattan.[28]

On one trip to New York, for a party celebrating Sidney Hook's eightieth birthday, faces from Burnham's distant past appeared before him. One belonged to Max Shachtman's widow, Yetta, who, when she and Burnham had been Trotskyists, had felt nervous about approaching him (and now, more than four decades later, still did). She thought he looked frail, but happy to be present. Another belonged to his 1930s NYU student Norman Jacobs, who in 1950, at the Berlin launching of the Congress for Cultural Freedom, had watched him each dawn planning strategy for the coming day's session. Yet another was that of Lilian Trowbridge, who, fifty years earlier, had worked for him and Wheelwright at the *Symposium*.[29]

Though living alone, Burnham remained in close touch with his family. Now the grandfather of seven, he took pleasure in his grandchildren, whose parents brought them to visit him in Kent. At times, he would mistake a grandchild for one of his own children at a similar age. "Sit up straight, Marcie," he once admonished an otherwise named granddaughter who was slouching at the dinner table.[30]

Family visitors to Kent most often came in the summer. When the weather turned cold, it was Burnham's turn to visit. After spending Thanksgiving in Asheville with his son John, he and Tessa would move on to Pittsburgh for a stay of a month or more with Jim (who had left Washington to take a job at the Mellon Bank). In February he would head for Florida to pass two weeks at Sanibel Island with C. Dickerman Williams, *National Review*'s now-retired attorney, and then move on to Tucson to visit Philip and Monica. In mid-April, with the weather in the Northeast turning mild, he would return to Kent.

During visits, he always maintained his usual formality. In Tucson, for example, he would dress each morning in coat and tie and greet his brother with a "Good morning, Philip" and a handshake. As in Kent, he made walks a cornerstone of his day. On one visit to Tucson not even a touch of gout could persuade him to call off his walk. Though he still showed no interest in returning to the Church, he would accompany Philip and Monica to Mass on Sunday. During one stay in Tucson, he revisited a place filled with meaning for him, the Rex Ranch in nearby Amado, where almost forty years earlier he had written *The Coming Defeat of Communism*.[31]

Burnham's condition did not entirely remove him from the public eye. In

February 1983 he was awarded the Presidential Medal of Freedom by President Reagan, a prime beneficiary of the conservative movement nurtured by *National Review.* Citing him at the White House award ceremony as having "profoundly affected the way America views itself and the world," and declaring that "[f]reedom, reason, and decency" had "few greater champions in this century than James Burnham," Reagan also acknowledged a personal debt to the honoree. During his years on the mashed-potato circuit, he said, he had often turned to Burnham's writings when in need of quotations. Burnham, accompanied by his children, accepted the medal in person and with evident pleasure.[32] Through the award, the conservative phalanx he had labored hard to muster had been honored in a rite of public homage.

In December 1983, Burnham was again honored, this time as the first recipient of the Richard M. Weaver Award for Scholarly Letters. The prize, bestowed by the Ingersoll Foundation of Rockford, Illinois, on the recommendation of the conservative Rockford Institute, had been established to recognize thinkers and writers who, in their life and work, exemplified what Ingersoll's president, John Howard, called "the vision of order and virtue" underlying civilization. Burnham again collected his award in person, this time flying to a snow-dusted Chicago for the award ceremony. He was unable to deliver his acceptance speech himself, so his granddaughter Anne Lynn Willième read it for him. Called "To See the World and Man," the text struck at least one listener as "vintage Burnham," as well it should have, for it consisted of excerpts from his books, especially *The Machiavellians,* whose warning against the "straitjacket of ideology" formed its core.[33]

The Ingersoll Prize ceremony was Burnham's last public appearance. After receiving the award, he resumed his usual routine, passing the next three years quietly. But in October 1986 misfortune struck again. Marcie died in her apartment of an overdose of pills, an apparent suicide. Her body was found by her daughter, Anne Lynn, who phoned the news to Jim in Pittsburgh and Tessa in Kent. Anne Lynn's call to Kent found Burnham in the middle of a party he was giving, and since he would soon be going to bed, Tessa decided to say nothing until the next day. But in the morning, before she could talk to him, Jim called. Burnham reacted to the news quietly, saying little on the phone, but his sorrow was palpable. In the days that followed, he would sit silently in the living room-study staring out at the sear autumn scenery. Marcie's remains were brought to Kent, where she was buried next to her mother.[34]

◆   ◆   ◆   ◆

Meanwhile, Burnham's health was again deteriorating. At some point he became diabetic, and then a more deadly malady took him in its grip. In the spring of 1987, Tessa, noting that her now eighty-one-year-old charge looked less healthy than usual and had developed a chronic cough, urged him to have a full-scale physical examination. On June 3 he checked into Sharon Hospital for tests, which showed him to be suffering from cancers of the kidneys and lungs too advanced for treatment. Returning home, he had a hospital bed set up in his room, and with Tessa to nurse him, calmly awaited death. Priscilla Buckley, who visited him often, found him weaker and more "withdrawn" each time she saw him. For as long as he could, he rose to meet her. But after a while, the effort became too great, and staying seated, he would simply greet her with a smile.[35]

As Burnham's strength ebbed, his doctor, George Greiner, began to look in on him twice a day. But in addition to Dr. Greiner and Priscilla, a new visitor now appeared. This was Father O'Brien of the Catholic archdiocese of Hartford, invited on the initiative, apparently, of Tessa, who, with Priscilla and J. P. McFadden lending encouragement, persuaded her failing patient to receive the priest. Paying Burnham several visits, Father O'Brien would talk with him privately for fifteen minutes or so. (Recalling Burnham's knowledge of Thomism and love of argument, McFadden rejoiced that the priest was not an intellectual, fearing that otherwise Burnham would try to draw him away from spiritual subjects into philosophical debate.) There is no record of what was said, but in mid-July Burnham formally returned to the Church, and Father O'Brien administered the last rites.

On the morning of July 28 Tessa felt more uneasy about Burnham than usual, and phoned Dr. Greiner to come to the house early. By the time he arrived, Burnham's eyes were glazed and his breathing labored, but he did not seem to be in pain. Tessa, sitting at his bedside, held his hand. After a time, Burnham's breathing grew quieter. Then, as if drifting off to sleep, he closed his eyes and died. Dr. Greiner, who had become very attached to Burnham, was too overcome by grief to manage the deathbed chores, so these were performed by Tessa.[36]

Burnham's funeral took place four days later at Kent's Catholic Church of the Sacred Heart. Among those present at the private service was his friend Lucius Wilmerding, who had first met him at Princeton sixty-four years earlier. After the

Mass came the short trip to the cemetery, where Burnham was buried beside Marcia and Marcie. The day was windy, and dry, late-summer foliage rustled mournfully in the breeze. On August 22 a memorial service was held at the Church of Our Savior in Manhattan, not far from the offices of *National Review,* whose staff assembled to pay a last tribute to its mentor.

◆　◆　◆　◆

In a sense, Burnham's death became a public event, for it was formally noted by the White House. Burnham was "one of those principally responsible for the great intellectual odyssey of our century," President Reagan declared, "the journey away from totalitarian statism and toward the uplifting doctrines of freedom."[37]

In eulogizing Burnham as a man who had rejected totalitarianism to help lead "the great intellectual odyssey of our century"—the turn away from communism to freedom—the president (or one of his speechwriters) erred on several counts. First, Burnham cannot be called "one of those principally responsible" for this "odyssey," because no one was "principally responsible" for it. Like others who gave up Marxism-Leninism, Burnham reflected a trend that did not have leaders and followers, but participants acting as self-directed individuals. Second, Burnham had not turned away from totalitarianism, for he had never embraced it. He had resolutely opposed totalitarianism even at the peak of his Bolshevik enthusiasm. Third, Reagan implied change to be the defining act of Burnham's career. But this idea, based on Burnham's dramatic break with Trotsky and later association with the Right, is equally questionable. For Burnham's life exemplifies change much less than constancy. (His most profound change, it could be argued, the event that led to his becoming "James Burnham," was his shift not from Trotskyism to conservatism, but from literature to politics.) He himself maintained that despite his political about-face he had never forsaken the ends he had originally sought, but only the means by which he hoped to attain them—a claim that contains a considerable measure of truth.[38]

Examples of Burnham's constancy abound. For one thing, he consistently claimed that empirical reason, proceeding from verifiable fact and strictly detached from emotion and desire, offered the only possible way to arrive at truth. For another, he always believed that the human condition, while not without its satisfactions and even joys, by nature harbored an ineradicable element of tragedy. For still another, he never took an optimistic view of humanity en masse, but usually accented mankind's darker tendencies, which he deemed too deeply rooted ever to be extinguished. Moreover, no matter where he stood politically, he always believed that the main point of politics was power.

He showed an equal constancy regarding historical issues. Thus, from his Trotskyist period on, he considered the USSR to be totalitarian, expansionist, and dangerous to peace and freedom. Similarly, from the 1930s to the 1970s, he warned that presidential power had grown far beyond its intended constitutional limit and was mushrooming into what he called variously "Fascism," "Bonapartism," and (the term he finally settled on) "Caesarism." This phenomenon he believed to be connected with war and economic troubles and with what for decades he saw as the most powerful trend of the century, the process he dubbed "the managerial revolution." For an even longer time he entertained the belief that had led him to politics in the first place: that Western civilization, which he viewed as mankind's foremost, lay in mortal peril. In the 1930s he found the root of the peril in the decade's economic crash; later, in the Soviet-communist drive for global mastery, in an aroused and anti-Western Third World, and in a failure of will on the part of the West that kept it from doing what was necessary to defeat its enemies.

No less constant were his leanings in the sphere of political action. On the one hand, he always stressed the need for a journal (the *New International,* the *Socialist Appeal,* the *Freeman, National Review*) to transmit the ideas he was currently upholding. On the other, he was drawn to tiny political phalanxes (SWP, OPC, ACCF, NR) that he hoped would possess the moral resoluteness and strategic flair needed to turn larger, less coherent masses (the splintered American Left, anti-communists of different stripes, the GOP) into "united fronts" and steer them in the direction he desired. Moreover, he was always attentive to the practical demands of politics.

Burnham also displayed a constancy of emotion. He has often been described as a tough-minded realist who, seeking accurate knowledge of political reality, shunned the swamps of sentiment for the dry, hard ground of factual observation and analysis. And this was indeed the approach he tried to pursue. Yet beneath his cool surface seethed a magma of emotion that played no small part in shaping his ideas. His Pareto-like remark, "most of us try to present our point of view with a respectable overlay of rational-sounding rhetoric, but you can still hear the drumbeats throbbing underneath,"[39] certainly rings true as a comment on himself.

High on the list of his most lasting emotions was a visceral hostility to liberalism, which he denounced in his Trotskyist and conservative phases alike as "soft," "mushy," curdled by sentimental idealism, soggy with sanctimony and hypocrisy, and unable to face the stark truths of human existence—in short, as unmanly. (Only liberals who shared his tragic view of life—Reinhold Niebuhr exemplified the type—escaped his disdain, and sometimes even won his admiration.) On the other hand, always high among the virtues he most esteemed was "hardness," a stoic refusal to flee the pitiless real world into the comforting dream world of ideology.

Yet by the evidence of his attraction to commanding figures who did not seek the approval of others, his love of historical dramatics, his enchantment with such promethean enterprises as the space program, and his keen interest in the process of civilizational decline, he himself harbored a deep-seated romantic streak (which he had first revealed in some of his boyhood stories). Indeed, his romanticizing treatment of Machiavelli prompts the thought that even his realism may have grown partly from romantic roots.

His most constant emotion, however, was his attachment to his freedom. He asserted this freedom as if driven by some powerful instinct, unable to bear the thought of anyone—Soviet commissar, federal bureaucrat, meliorist liberal, or fellow conservative—pressuring him to toe somebody else's line. This insistence on going his own way, even as a member of one of his tiny phalanxes, caused his history of conflicts with his comrades-in-arms of a given moment: with most Trotskyists over unconditional support of the USSR, with the CIA over Cold War strategy, with the ACCF over McCarthy, with fellow *National Review* editors over U.S. policy in central Europe, with the Republican Right over Rockefeller, with most conservatives over ownership of the Panama Canal. At times he vented his need for freedom in tirades against big government. Yet he also accepted and even approved of big government programs if he considered them necessary for social well-being or national security. When he defended dictatorship (the Greek Colonels' regime, for example) he did so only because he saw in it a lesser evil than what he believed to be the most likely alternative: a communist regime that would not only impose a tyranny vastly more sweeping than old-fashioned strong-man rule, but would boost Moscow's chances for victory in the struggle for the world.

Burnham's heterodoxy also extended to ideas common among his more conventionally minded countrymen. Thus, in a nation generally inclined toward historical optimism, he himself showed a marked preference for visions of doom. In a nation that seamed its political discourse with democratic pieties and elevated its Founding Fathers to political sainthood, he endorsed Mosca's critique of democracy, spoke slightingly of "the abstract, sentimental rhetoric of democratic idealism," and named as the original purveyor of such rhetoric the sacrosanct Thomas Jefferson,[40] whom he seemed to think less praiseworthy than Machiavelli. In a nation that expressed hostility to imperialism, he approved of Western empire—and not only for strategic reasons, but as the best way to bring real (as opposed to merely putative) benefits to needful peoples. In an era intellectually under the thumb of liberalism, he took assertively antiliberal public stands, from "anti-anti-McCarthyism" (which led to his expulsion from the New York intelligentsia) to defending U.S. involvement in Vietnam.

Though Burnham differed in important respects from the conservative mainstream, a movement with which he did not identify until the 1950s, it could well be claimed, as *National Review* editor Richard Brookhiser has pointed out, that he was the first neoconservative. He lived his political life as an intellectual: academic, author, editor—a man who tried to influence his time as a fashioner of words, not as an office-holder. His political origins lay on the Left, specifically in the New York Trotskyist milieu. After breaking with Trotskyism, he spent more than a decade among the "New York intellectuals," the circle from which some leading neoconservatives later came. Although a dogged opponent of the Nanny State, which curbs people's freedom "for their own good" (the brunt of his complaint in "No Firecrackers Allowed"), he accepted various features of the New Deal tradition, reasoning pragmatically that modern, mobile, mass society made tax-supported, federally administered social insurance programs such as Medicare a practical necessity. And while favoring the free market, he showed no great enthusiasm for businessmen. In these views he foreshadowed neoconservatism in its early phase. His mode of argument—that of a secular and empirical-minded social scientist rather than of a deductive moralist—also resembled that of the neoconservatives, as did the low-key tone of most of his writings. Moreover, like the neoconservatives, he called for adamant resistance to the USSR and communism. Finally, though he defended tradition, his cultural sensibility was modernist.

This secular, modernist sensibility put him at odds with many fellow conservatives, often people with traditional religious beliefs and lace-curtainish cultural tastes. Indeed, despite his long tenure at *National Review,* in some ways he seemed better suited to *Partisan Review,* a magazine with which he had once been closely connected. In his youth, his Catholicism or intellectual bent or social background had sometimes made him seem out of place in his surroundings. In later years, too, he sometimes seemed out of place, though now because of his aesthetic and cultural penchants.

Burnham's thought was not free of intellectual and tonal inconsistency. For example, despite his professed espousal of a strict empiricism, he sometimes built his arguments on too narrow a foundation of fact and reached conclusions that his evidence did not warrant. Moreover, though he normally emphasized will as the key factor in politics, at times he seemed to lean more heavily toward determinism, leaving readers to wonder just where he stood on the issue. Inconsistency also marked his appraisal of the United States: often he saw the country in a glowing light, but the West as a whole in a somber one. Yet how could the United States hum with vitality and at the same time be the leader of a civilization committing suicide? Furthermore, he sometimes claimed that America was politically incompetent.

Able dialectician that he was, Burnham had no trouble reconciling these seemingly contradictory claims. Thus, he argued that will could have an impact on events, because reality, though broadly determined, still offered narrow possibilities for effective choice; and that while mainstream America had palpably retained its health, the country's liberal elite had fallen ill, and so could no longer furnish competent leadership. But it was harder to resolve inconsistencies of tone. Thus, the urgent voice of Burnham the apocalyptical editorial writer was difficult to square with the unruffled voice of Burnham the detached columnist. Nor did the Burnham whose historical pessimism, stress on will, claims of Western decadence, and emotional attraction to force made him sound like one of Europe's die-hard rightists, sit comfortably with the wry, skeptical Burnham who replied with his "little smile" to prophecies of doom that he himself, on other occasions, might utter.

Still, for all his lapses, Burnham excelled as a political analyst. A prominent participant in several of the major political movements of his day—Depression-era leftism, postwar hard-line anticommunism, the U.S. embrace of global activism, and the rise of contemporary American conservatism—he knew at first hand the world he took as his subject. Like the lens of lost ages of his Canterbury story, his wide-ranging knowledge, Augustinian sensibility, analytical prowess, synthesizing flair, and unshakable independence of mind enabled him to see and report things that others overlooked or ignored. If sometimes wrong in his view of where the world was headed, he was also often a step or two closer to the truth than his fellow pundits, who, whether liberal or conservative, tended to be blinkered by party lines. With no real counterparts among American political thinkers, he is hard to classify. But he should be ranked among the more acute interpreters of his time.

# Notes

CHAPTER ONE

1. James Burnham to William F. Buckley Jr., August 24, 1982, William F. Buckley Jr. Papers (hereafter, WFB), Sterling Memorial Library, Yale University, 1984, March addition; Mary Effie Burnham to author, May 16, 1992.

2. According to Albert Nelson Marquis, ed., *Who's Who in America, 1926–1927* (Chicago, 1926), 382, Claude Burnham was born on June 20, 1879, but James Burnham's birth certificate lists Claude's age as twenty-four, which would make 1881 the year of his birth. James B. Burnham to author, August 12, 1992. Moreover, the obituary published by *The Chicago Tribune* after Claude Burnham's death on June 22, 1928, gives his age as forty-seven, which also points to 1881 as the year of his birth. *The Chicago Tribune,* June 23, 1928. It may be that Claude Burnham gave his birth date to *Who's Who* as 1879 in order to make it appear that he was a year older rather than a year younger than his wife. The information about Claude Burnham that follows comes from his *Who's Who in America* entry; his obituary in *The Chicago Tribune* (hereafter, *CT*), June 23, 1928; his obituary in *The New York Times* (hereafter, *NYT*), June 23, 1928; James B. Burnham to author, August 12, 1992; and Suzanne Gillis Hamm to author, May 28, 1993.

3. Information about the Gillis family and Mary Mae Gillis Burnham comes from Mary Effie Burnham to author, May 16, 1992; Monica Burnham to author, June 27, 1992; John L. Gillis to author, November 9, 1992; L. P. Gillis to author, November 15, 1992; Hamm to author, May 28, 1993.

4. Colleen Browne Kilner, *Joseph Sears and His Kenilworth* (Kenilworth, Illinois: Kenilworth Historical Society, 1969) provides much information about the village.

5. Hamm to author, May 28, 1993.

6. Mr. and Mrs. John D. Hunt to James Burnham, April 24, 1947, James Burnham Papers (hereafter, JB), The Hoover Institution, Box 4.

7. James Burnham to Sidney Hook, August 19, 1946, Sidney Hook Papers (hereafter, SH), The Hoover Institution, Box 8.

8. James Burnham, "No firecrackers Allowed," *The Freeman* (hereafter, *F*) 5 (October 1955): 684.

9. Burnham to Hook, January 11, 1949, SH, Box 8; Priscilla L. Buckley to author, March 31, 1992.

10. James B. Burnham to author, June 18, 1992; Priscilla L. Buckley to author, March 31, 1992.

11. James Burnham's scholastic record, Records Office, New Trier Township High School, Winnetka, Illinois.

12. James Burnham, "Cam's Camouflage," *New Trier Echoes* (January 1920): 15.

13. Jean Paul Mandler, dean of Canterbury School, to author, June 26, 1990.

14. Records Office, Canterbury School, New Milford, Connecticut. Further information about James Burnham's life at Canterbury comes from the school newspaper, *The Tabard,* various issues, fall 1921–spring 1923.

15. James Burnham, "Riding a Morning Roundup," *The Quill* (hereafter, *Q*) 6 (December 1921): 20–23.

16. Ibid., "A New View of the Arctic," *Q* 6 (June 1922): 17–19.

17. Ibid., "Unusual Politicians," *The Canterbury Quarterly* (hereafter, *CQ*) 7 (December 1922): 9–13.

18. Ibid., "Two Men, Two Ideas, and Washington," *CQ* 7 (June 1923): 9–16.

19. Ibid., "John's Dreamy Voyage," *CQ* 7 (June 1923): 49.

20. Ibid., "The Lens of Lost Ages," *Q* 6 (March 1922): 22–23.

21. Ibid., "The Stars and the Rushing Waters," *CQ* 7 (March 1923): 14–18.

22. Ibid., "The Green, Green Hills," *CQ* 7 (June 1923): 44–47.

23. James Burnham, "Do Present Conditions in America Stimulate the Production of Literature?" *CQ* 7 (June 1923): 25–28.

24. Nelson R. Burr, *Pioneers and Princetonians: A Fiftieth Anniversary History of the Class of 1927.* (Privately printed, 1977), 9. Information about the Princeton of the 1920s from Nelson R. Burr to author, July 31, 1990.

25. Lucius Wilmerding to author, March 12, 1992; Curtin Winsor to author, February 5, 1992.

26. Burr to author, July 31, 1990.

27. Princeton University. *Princeton Bric-A-Brac* (n.p., 1926), 393.

28. Winsor to author, February 5, 1992.

29. Wilmerding to author, March 12, 1992.

30. Ibid.; Burr to author, July 31, 1990.

31. James Burnham's academic transcript. Office of the Registrar. Princeton University.

32. Burr to author, October 19, 1990; Wilmerding to author, March 12, 1992.

33. James Burnham to Sidney Schiff, September 28, 1930, Sidney Schiff Papers (hereafter, SS), The British Library. "When I first met Burnham [in 1930] he was an arrogant disciple of T. S. Eliot in all matters." Sidney Hook to Lewis S. Feuer, March 16, 1981, SH, Box 115; Sidney Hook, *Out of Step: An Unquiet Life in the Twentieth Century.* (New York: Harper and Row, 1987), 533.

34. *The Tiger* 34 (November 15, 1924): 35.

35. J. B. [*Tiger* authors signed their pieces with initials rather than full names], "Little Sister's Letter to Santy," Ibid. 34 (December 15, 1924): 40.

36. Ibid., "As Tiny Tim Remarked," Ibid. 35 (December 14, 1925): 27.

37. James Burnham, "Through a Glass Darkly," *Nassau Literary Magazine* (hereafter, *NLM*) 81 (June 1925): 99–104.

38. "J. B." (i.e., James Burnham), "Anchor," *NLM* 82 (April 1926): 291–295.

39. *Princeton Alumni Weekly* (hereafter, *PAW*) 44 (May 1944): 12–13.

40. Winsor to author, February 6, 1992; Wilmerding to author, March 12, 1992.

41. Burr to author, July 31, 1990.

42. Brand Blanshard quoted by Peter Ackroyd, *T. S. Eliot: A Life* (New York: Simon and Schuster, 1984), 59.

43. Joseph Bryan III to James Burnham, December 21, 1947, JB, Box 5.

44. *The Nassau Herald. A Record of the Class of 1927 of Princeton University.* (n.p., 1927), 64.

45. Evelyn Waugh, *A Little Learning* (London: Chapman and Hall, 1964), 167–168.

46. Anthony Powell, *Infants of the Spring* (London: Heineman, 1976), 147, 203.

47. John Jones, *Balliol College: A History, 1263–1939* (Oxford: Oxford University Press, 1988), 267–271, 273.

48. Powell, *Infants of the Spring,* 157, 159.

49. William H. McNeill, *Arnold J. Toynbee: A Life* (Oxford: Oxford University Press, 1989), 21–22.

50. Powell, *Infants of the Spring,* 146–147.

51. Evelyn Waugh, *The Diaries of Evelyn Waugh,* ed. Michael Davie (Boston: Little, Brown and Co., 1976), 320.

52. Burnham told Priscilla L. Buckley that he had given up Catholicism at Oxford. Priscilla L. Buckley to author, March 31, 1992. He told historian John P. Diggins, however, that he had left the Church "midway through college." James Burnham to John P. Diggins, June 11, 1971, notes of John P. Diggins's interview with James Burnham. My thanks to Professor Diggins for a copy of these notes. It could be that when speaking with Diggins, Burnham used the word "college" to encompass Oxford as well as Princeton.

53. James Burnham to Humphrey Ambler, n.d. but probably late 1927 or early 1928, *PAW* 28 (February 17, 1928): 534.

54. James Burnham to Charlotte Eckhart, March 7, 1928. My thanks to James B. Burnham for a copy of this letter.

55. Ibid.

56. Winsor to author, January 28, 1992.

57. Linda Bridges to author, January 8, 1992.

58. Monica Burnham to author, June 27, 1992.

59. Burnham to Schiff, February 19, 1929, SS.

60. Sidney Hook, Oral Reminiscences, SH, Box 185.

61. Philip E. Wheelwright to Sidney Hook, October 17, 1928, and March 18, 1929, SH, Box 30; Hook, *Out of Step,* 530.

62. Burnham to Schiff, February 9, 1929, March 1, 1929, July 2, 1929, SS.

63. Wheelwright to Hook, October 17, 1928, refers to Burnham, then still at Oxford, as "officially a member of the English Department; coeditor of *The Symposium*." SH, Box 30.

64. Jane Wilmerding to author, March 12, 1992.

65. Sir Ivo Elliott, ed., *The Balliol College Register (1900–1950)* (Oxford, 1953, 279; John Jones to author, March 19, 1991.

CHAPTER TWO

1. James Burnham. Application for Federal Employment, 1949, JB Box 1.
2. *The Album, 1930* (annual yearbook of New York University's Washington Square College), 75.
3. Hook, *Out of Step,* 532.
4. Wheelwright to Hook, October 18, 1931, SH, Box 30.
5. Hook, *Out of Step,* 534.
6. Norman Jacobs to author, December 27, 1990; Sidney Hook, Oral Reminiscences, SH, Box 185.
7. Hook to Feuer, March 16, 1981, SH, Box 115.
8. Akroyd, *T. S. Eliot,* 155.
9. James Burnham, "Science and Style. A Reply to Trotsky," Leon Trotsky, *In Defense of Marxism (Against the Petty-Bourgeois Opposition)* (New York: Pioneer, 1942), 194–195.
10. Hook to Feuer, March 16, 1981, SH, Box 115.
11. I have obtained information about Burnham's teaching and behavior in class from his former students Emma Cohn, Joseph Frank, Norman Jacobs, Donald Seldin, M.D., Oscar Shoenfeld, and Jeanne Wacker.
12. Joseph Frank to author, February 28, 1992.
13. Emma Cohn to author, June 16, 1992.
14. James Atlas, *Delmore Schwartz: The Life of an American Poet* (New York: Avon Books, 1977), 46.
15. Oscar Shoenfeld to author, August 20, 1990.
16. Jeanne Wacker to author, May 19, 1993.
17. Jacobs to author, December 27, 1990.
18. Burnham to Schiff, September 28, 1930, SS.
19. Ibid., May 14, 1932, SS.
20. James Burnham and Philip Wheelwright, *Introduction to Philosophical Analysis* (New York: Henry Holt and Co., 1932).
21. See, for example, George Gentry, *International Journal of Ethics* 43 (October 1932): 111; and Susan K. Langer, *Journal of Philosophy* 29 (September 1, 1932): 495–498.
22. Burnham to Schiff, May 14, 1932, SS.
23. Thus, writing to Sidney Hook about his course "Modern Irrationalism," he expressed enthusiasm: "The [course] was quite fascinating to me. There was a full registration of the very best students; and some of the discussions were, I thought, the best that I can remember from teaching experience." Burnham to Hook, January 11, 1949, SH, Box 8.
24. Lilian Trowbridge (*The Symposium's* copy editor) to Sidney Hook, June 3, 1984, SH, Box 115. Wheelwright's fretfulness was legendary.
25. Burnham to Schiff, January 2, 1930, SS; James Burnham to Lincoln Kirstein, November 17, 1929, *The Hound & Horn* Papers (hereafter, HH), Beinecke Library, Yale University; ibid., November 19, 1929, HH; James Burnham to Bernard Bandler II, November 18,

1929, HH; Burnham to Kirstein, November 19, 1932, HH. (Possibly with a later Burnham in mind, Kirstein once remembered Burnham as "very ambitious to be a political mover and shaker." He thought it "rather marvelous," he said, that "someone who wanted to be a dictator, would also be interested in art and literature." Burnham was "a monstrously clever fellow," Kirstein concluded. Lincoln Kirstein to author, July 3, 1991.

26. Burnham to Schiff, January 2, 1930; ibid., March 28, 1930; ibid., September 28, 1930, SS.

27. Ibid., November 17, 1930, SS.

28. Ibid., March 24, 1931, SS.

29. E.g., James Burnham, "Comment," *The Symposium* (hereafter, *S*) 3 (April 1932): 144.

30. Burnham to Schiff, September 28, 1930, SS.

31. James Burnham, "Progress and Tradition," *S* 1 (July 1930): 358.

32. Burnham to Schiff, May 14, 1932, SS.

33. Ibid., March 24, 1931, SS.

34. Ibid., May 23, 31, SS.

35. James Burnham, "The Wondrous Architecture of the World," *S* 2 (April 1931).

36. David Burnham, *This Our Exile* (New York: Charles Scribner's Sons, 1931), 272, 288, 299, 363–364, 416–417.

37. Burnham to Schiff, April 8, 1931, SS.

38. Ibid., March 1, 1931, SS.

39. Jane Wilmerding to author, March 12, 1993.

40. Burnham to Schiff, May 14, 1932, SS.

41. Ibid., May 14, 1932, SS.

42. *NYT,* August 29, 1990; James Burnham (unsigned), "The Week" (hereafter, TW), *National Review* (hereafter, *NR*) 4 (September 7, 1957): 195. Burnham's unsigned *National Review* editorials and short news items can be identified by way of the initialed copies of the magazine kept at the *National Review* editorial office.

43. Hook to Feuer, March 16, 1981, SH.

44. Ackroyd, *T. S. Eliot,* 41, 76, 142, 155–157, 173–174, 179.

45. The best study in English of Charles Maurras and the *Action Française* is Eugen Weber, *Action Française: Royalism and Reaction in Twentieth Century France* (Stanford, Calif.: Stanford University Press, 1962).

46. Ackroyd, *T. S. Eliot,* 41. T. S. Eliot, *For Lancelot Andrewes: Essays on Style and Order* (Garden City, N.Y.: Doubleday, Doran, 1929), vii.

47. Hook, *Out of Step,* 536. Yet, despite his embrace of Eliot's clericalism, Burnham was no more ready to abandon his critical detachment when discussing the social and cultural importance of the Church than when writing about literature. "The [medieval] Catholic synthesis had its historical chance," he commented in *The Symposium,* reviewing a volume of essays by a group of European Catholic authors. "It did not prove stable and enduring, and in fact lasted at its height an even shorter time than the Renaissance culture has lasted." Burnham, "Comment," *S* 3 (April 1932): 132.

48. Burnham and Wheelwright, *Introduction to Philosophical Analysis,* 242, 192; Burnham, "Comment: The Wondrous Architecture of the World," *S* 2 (April 1931): 166.

49. Ramon Fernandez, "Thought and Revolution, *The Symposium* 2 (January 1931).

50. Burnham to Schiff, March 1, 1931, SS.

51. Burnham, "Comment," *S* 3 (April 1932): 138, 152.

52. Sidney Hook, "Towards the Understanding of Karl Marx," *S* 2 (July 1931); Hook, *Out of Step,* 533.

53. James Burnham, review of *The History of the Russian Revolution,* I, by Leon Trotsky, *S* 3 (July 1932): 380.

54. Trotsky-Burnham exchange, *S* 3 (October 1932): 503–505.

55. Leon Trotsky to James Burnahm, December 9, 1937, Trotsky Archive (hereafter, TA), Houghton Library, Harvard University.

56. Linda Bridges, *NR* 39 (September 11, 1987): 47.

57. Burnham to Schiff, May 14, 1932, and August 15, 1932. SS.

58. Burnham to Diggins, June 11, 1971.

59. Matthew Josephson, *Infidel in the Temple: A Memoir of the Nineteen Thirties* (New York: Alfred A. Knopf, 1967), 108.

60. James Burnham, "Marxism and Esthetics," *S* 4 (January 1933): 12, 18–19, 26–29, 30.

61. Sidney Hook, *Towards the Understanding of Karl Marx: A Revolutionary Interpretation* (New York: The John Day Co., 1933), 3–8.

62. James Burnham and Philip Wheelwright, "Comment. Thirteen Propositions," *S* 4 (April 1933): 130–134; for Burnham's reply to critics of "Thirteen Propositions," *S* 4 (October 1933): 411–412.

63. Adolf A. Berle and Gardiner C. Means. *The Modern Corporation and Private Property* (New York: The Macmillan Co., 1933).

64. James Burnham, "Comment," *S* 4 (July 1933): 259, 260, 266–271.

65. Ibid., "Personal History Statement," JB, Box 1.

66. Ibid., "Comment," *S* 4 (October 1933): 413; Wilmerding to author, March 12, 1992.

67. Burnham, "Comment," *S* 4 (October 1933): 404–405, 409–410.

68. Ibid., 413; ibid. 4 (July 1933): 278–279.

69. Sidney Hook, *NR* 39 (September 11, 1987): 32.

70. Hook to Feuer, March 16, 1981, SH, Box 115.

71. Hook, *NR* 39 (September 11, 1987): 32; Burnham to Diggins, June 11, 1971.

72. James Burnham, "His Place in History," *The New Masses* 10 (January 1934): 15.

73. Hook quoted by Neil Jumonville, *Critical Crossings: The New York Intellectuals in Postwar America* (Berkeley: University of California Press, 1991), 23; Hook to Feuer, March 16, 1981, SH, Box 115.

CHAPTER THREE

1. A. J. Muste, "Sketches for an Autobiography," *The Essays of A. J. Muste,* ed. Nat Hentoff (New York, 1967) 126–127, 132, 150.

2. Muste, "An American Revolutionary Party," *Modern Monthly* 7 (January 1934) 713–718.

3. Hook, *Out of Step,* 192.

4. "Memorandum on the International Position of the AWP," Max Shachtman Papers (hereafter, MS), Tamiment Library, New York University, series I, Part E, Box 6.

5. Constance Ashton Myers, *The Prophet's Army. Trotskyists in America, 1928–1941* (Westport, Conn.: Greenwood Press 1977), 74.

6. Sidney Hook to Paul Berman, April 24, 1973, SH, Box 112.

7. Wilmerding to author, March 12, 1992.

8. James Burnham, "Their Government," *Labor Action,* March 15, 1934; April 2, 1934; May 5, 1934; June 1, 1934; July 15, 1934; September 1, 1934; November 11, 1934.

9. Jacobs to author, December 27, 1990; Seldin to author, November 28, 1990.

10. James Burnham, "Religion and Pessimism." Review of *Reflections on the End of an Era,* by Reinhold Niebuhr. *The Nation* (hereafter *N*) 139 (July 11, 1934): 50–51.

11. Jacobs to author, December 27, 1990; Hook, Oral Reminiscences, SH, Box 185; ibid., *Out of Step,* 535.

12. On the Lightner family and the early years of Marcia Lightner Burnham: James B. Burnham to author, June 18, 1992; Katherine Lightner to author, February 20, 1993 and May 25, 1993; June Boissonas to author, June 3, 1993.

13. Priscilla Buckley to author, March 31, 1992.

14. Lightner to author, February 20, 1993.

15. Hamm to author, May 28, 1993.

16. Burnham to Schiff, May 14, 1932, SS.

17. James P. Cannon, *The History of American Trotskyism: From Its Origins (1928) to the Founding of the Socialist Workers Party (1938)* (New York: Pathfinder Press, 1972), 49–50. See also Alan Wald, *The New York Intellectuals: The Rise and Decline of the Anti-Stalinist Left from the 1930s to the 1980s* (Chapel Hill: University of North Carolina Press, 1987), 168–171.

18. Wald, *The New York Intellectuals,* 173–174; Irving Howe, *A Margin of Hope: An Intellectual Biography* (New York: Harcourt Brace Jovanovich, 1982), 40; Emanuel Geltman to author, August 6, 1990.

19. Cannon, *The History of American Trotskyism,* 78–79, 86–87.

20. Ibid., 55, 132, 178.

21. Geltman to author, August 6, 1990.

22. Cannon, *The History of American Trotskyism,* 91–92; James P. Cannon, *The Struggle for a Proletarian Party,* ed. John B. Wright, 2nd ed. (New York: Pathfinder Press, 1972), 58.

23. Glotzer to author, September 20, 1990.

24. Ibid.; Max Shachtman transcript, Oral History Collection of Columbia University (hereafter, Shachtman, COHO), 327; Geltman to author, August 6, 1990; Howe, *A Margin of Hope,* 40; Irving Howe to author, June 18, 1990; Shoenfeld to author, August 20, 1990; Max Eastman, *Love and Revolution: My Journey through an Epoch* (New York, 1964), 516.

25. Howe to author, June 18, 1990; Shachtman, COHO, 321, 328–329, 332–333; Shoenfeld to author, August 20, 1990.

26. Shachtman, COHO, 330–331.

27. For Trotsky's analysis see his book *The Revolution Betrayed: What Is the Soviet Union and Where Is It Going?* trans. Max Eastman (New York: Pathfinder Press, 1970), 86–94, 112–113, 248–252, 278.

28. Cannon, *The History of American Trotskyism,* 112–113.

29. Myers, *The Prophet's Army,* 91–93.

30. Cannon, *The History of American Trotskyism,* 171.

31. Louis Budenz, *This Is My Story* (New York, 1947), 99; Hook, *Out of Step,* 202.

32. Hook to Berman, April 24, 1974, SH, box 112.

33. Trotsky to Burnham, January 31, 1934, TA; Hook, *Out of Step,* 202; Burnham to Hook, July 26, 1934; ibid., July 21, 1934, SH, box 112.

34. Hook to Berman, May 11, 1973, SH, box 112; Hook to Feuer, March 16, 1981, SH, box 115; Burnham to Hook, July 26, 1934, SH, box 112; Burnham to Hook, July 15, 1935, SH, box 8.

35. Burnham to Hook, July 21, 1934, SH, box 112.

36. Hook, *Out of Step,* 198–199; Cannon, *The History of American Trotskyism,* 178–179.

37. Hook to Berman, April 24, 1973, SH, box 112; Burnham to Hook, July 21, 1934, SH, box 112.

38. Myers, *The Prophet's Army,* 95.

39. Hook, Oral Reminiscences, SH, box 185.

40. Burnham to Diggins, June 11, 1971.

41. Cannon, *The Struggle for a Proletarian Party,* 59; Hook to Berman, April 24, 1974, SH, box 112.

42. John West (James Burnham), "Roosevelt and the New Congress," *The New International* (hereafter, *NI*) 2 (January 1935): 1–3; ibid., "The Roosevelt Security Program," *NI* 2 (March 1935): 40–43; ibid., *The New Militant* (hereafter, *NM*), November 30, 1935; ibid., January 1, 1936; ibid., "The Wagner Bill and the Working Class," *NI* 2 (October 1935), 184–185.

43. James Burnham, "Anatomy of Fascism," a review of *Fascism and Social Revolution* by R. Palme Dutt, *N* 139 (December 12, 1934): 632; John West (James Burnham), "The Bands Are Playing," *NI* 2 (July 1935): 113–116; ibid., *NM,* August 24, 1935; ibid., *War and the Workers* (n.p., 1935), 9; ibid., *NM,* March 21, 1936.

44. John West (James Burnham), *NM,* March 21, 1936; ibid., May 9, 1936; ibid., "Max Eastman's Straw Man," *NI* 2 (December 1935): 220–225.

45. James Burnham, "An American Approach." Review of *A Philosophic Approach to Communism,* by Theodore B. Brameld; *N* 137 (December 20, 1933): 712; ibid., "John Middleton Murry." Review of *The Necessity of Communism,* by John Middleton Murry, *N* 138 (June 6, 1934): 655.

46. Burnham to Hook, June 8, 1935, SH, box 132; ibid., July 15, 1935, SH, box 8; Hook to Feuer, March 16, 1981, SH, box 115.

47. Cannon, *The Struggle for a Proletarian Party,* 52.

48. Ibid., *The History of American Trotskyism,* 205, 210.

49. Ibid., 193, 195, 210; James P. Cannon to James Burnham, August 29, 1936, MS, Series I, Part G, Box 9; Myers, *The Prophet's Army,* 109.

50. Burnham to Hook, July 3, 1935; ibid., July 15, 1935, SH, box 8.

51. Burnham to Hook, July 3, 1935, SH, box 8; Geltman to author, July 26, 1990.

52. John West (James Burnham), "What Is Our Problem?" *The Workers Party Internal Bulletin,* 2 (January 1936), 3.

53. Hook to Berman, April 24, 1974, SH, box 112; Cannon, *The History of American Trotskyism,* 225–227; Harry Roskolenko, *When I Was Last on Cherry Street* (New York: Stein and Day, 1965), 168.

54. Muste, "Sketches for an Autobiography," 148–149; Hook, Oral Reminiscences, SH, box 185; Shachtman, COHO, 263. Brian Crozier, "My Pilgrimage to Kent (Connecticut) to

See James Burnham," *The New Lugano Review,* no. 11–12 (1976): 19. Some Trotskyists, including Emanuel Geltman and Joseph Carter, took the turn seriously, hoping to broaden the anti-Stalin left. Geltman to author, August 6, 1990.

55. Burnham to Hook, September 15, 1954, SH, box 8.

56. Howe, *A Margin of Hope,* 33–34.

57. Cannon, *The History of American Trotskyism,* 244–245; Myers, *The Prophet's Army,* 124.

58. James Burnham to Leon Trotsky, April 1, 1937, TA; Isaac Deutscher, *The Prophet Outcast: Trotsky: 1929–1940* (London: Oxford University Press, 1963), 371–372.

59. James T. Farrell Diary (hereafter, JTF), March 30, 1937, Van Pelt Library, University of Pennsylvania.

60. James Burnham, "His Excellency's Loyal Opposition," *The Socialist Appeal* (hereafter, *SA*) 3 (January 1937): 2.

61. James Burnham, *The People's Front: the New Betrayal* (New York: Pioneer, Circa 1937), 63.

62. James Burnham, introduction, *Why Did They Confess? A Study of the Radek-Piatakov Trial* (New York: Pioneer, 1937), 4; James Burnham to Dwight Macdonald, June 9, 1937, Dwight Macdonald Papers (hereafter, DM), Sterling Memorial Library, Yale University.

63. James Burnham, "Socialists and the Coming War," *The American Socialist Monthly,* 5 (August 1936): 24–28.

64. "Challenge" (unsigned editorial statement), *The Marxist Quarterly,* 1 (January 1937): 4; Hook to Berman, April 24, 1974, SH, box 112.

65. Geltman to author, July 26, 1990.

66. Hook, Oral Reminiscences, SH, box 185.

67. Shoenfeld to author, August 20, 1990.

68. James Burnham, *Suicide of the West: An Essay on the Meaning and Destiny of Liberalism* (New York: John Day Co., 1964), 109.

69. Bridges to author, January 18, 1992; William F. Buckley Jr. to author, January 20, 1992; Priscilla L. Buckley to author, July 24, 1992; Warren G. Fugitt to author, October 3, 1991.

70. James Burnham et al., "The Road Ahead. A Draft Program for the Socialist Party," *SA* 2 (December 15, 1936): 1–6.

71. *SA* 3 (February 1937): 13–15.

72. Ibid. 3 (March 1937): 36–39, 44.

73. Cannon, *The History of American Trotskyism,* 249.

74. Albert Glotzer, *Trotsky: Memoir and Critique* (Buffalo, New York: Prometheus, 1989), 258; Trotsky to Cannon, Shachtman, Burnham, and Weber, June 15, 1937, TA.

75. James Burnham to Albert Glotzer, June 28, 1937, Albert Glotzer Papers (Hereafter, AG), Hoover Institution, box 2.

76. James Burnham to James P. Cannon, June 15, 1937, TA.

77. Burnham to Trotsky, June 22, 1937, TA; Trotsky to Burnham, June 25, 1937, TA.

78. Cannon, *The History of American Trotskyism,* 250; M. S. Venkataramami, "Leon Trotsky's Adventure in American Radical Politics, 1935–7," *International Review of Social History* (hereafter, *IRSH*) 9, part 1 (1964): 42.

79. Venkataramami, "Leon Trotsky's Adventure in American Radical Politics," *IRSH,* 44; Howe, *A Margin of Hope,* 34–35.

CHAPTER FOUR

1. Geltman to author, August 6, 1990; Irving Panken to author, June 3, 1991; Wald, *The New York Intellectuals,* 181.

2. James Burnham, *The Managerial Revolution,* preface to the Midland Books edition (Bloomington and London: Indiana University Press), 1960), v.

3. James Burnham and Joseph Carter, "Amendment to Majority Resolution," *Internal Bulletin* (hereafter, *IB*) (November 1937): 11–14.

4. Leon Trotsky, "Not a Workers and Not a Bourgeois State?" *IB* (December 1937): 4.

5. James Burnham, "From Formula to Reality," *IB* (December 1937): 13–24.

6. Joseph Carter, "The Class Nature of the Stalinist State," *IB* (December 1937): 3–10a.

7. Leon Trotsky to James Burnham and Joseph Carter, December 15, 1937, TA.

8. Jacobs to author, December 27, 1990; Cannon, *The Struggle for a Proletarian Party,* 25–26, 138.

9. James P. Cannon and Max Shachtman, "Draft Resolution on Party Organization," MS, series I, Part G, Box 8, Folder 1.

10. James Burnham et al. "Minority Resolution," MS, Series I, Part G, Box 8, Folder 1; Burnham-Carter statement [n.d., but apparently late 1937], TA.

11. Burnham to Trotsky, December 9, 1937, TA; Trotsky to Burnham, December 1, 1937, TA.

12. Burnham to Trotsky, December 9, 1937, TA; *NI* 6 (April 1940): 76.

13. MS, Series I, Part G, Box 8, Folder 1; Roskolenko, *When I Was Last on Cherry Street,* 179.

14. Irving Howe, among others, clearly recognized this. In his autobiography, *A Margin of Hope,* he called the chapter on his years with the SWP "Life in a Sect."

15. Dwight Macdonald, *Memoirs of a Revolutionist* (New York: Meridian Books, 1958), 17.

16. James T. Farrell, "The Renegade," in *An American Dream Girl* (New York, 1950), 281–282, 288–289, 290.

17. Geltman to author, August 6, 1990; *SA,* November 5, 1938.

18. Burr to author, July 31, 1990; Winsor to author, January 21, 1992; Wilmerding to author, March 21, 1992; Sidney Schiff to David Burnham, November 10, 1937, SS. Two decades later, ex-Communist Whittaker Chambers, seeking to solve the mystery, claimed that Burnham had never really been a true believer. "To have been a Leninist [i.e., whether of the Stalinist or Trotskyist dispensation] required a commitment about reality [i.e., a total suspension of the critical faculty] in philosophy and to act at once, which I should have thought B. by temperament incapable of," he told William F. Buckley Jr. William F. Buckley Jr., *Odyssey of a Friend: Whittaker Chambers' Letters to William F. Buckley Jr., 1954–1961* (New York: G.P. Putnam's Sons, 1969), 189.

19. James Burnham, "America, I Love You," *NI* 4 (July 1938): 221.

20. James Burnham, "Their Government," *SA,* August 11, 1939.

21. "Burnham hated liberalism. He thought it was soft." Howe to author, June 18, 1990.

22. Bridges to author, January 8, 1992; Geltman to author, August 6, 1990; Glotzer to author; Nancy Macdonald to author, September 12, 1990; Yetta Shachtman to author, September 9, 1990.

23. Cannon, *The Struggle for a Proletarian Party,* 25; James Burnham to Brian Crozier, March 29, 1976, Brian Crozier Papers (hereafter, BC), The Hoover Institution.

24. Cannon, *The Struggle for a Proletarian Party,* 25, 30, 138–139.

25. Shachtman, COHO, 338–339.

26. Ibid., 338; Cannon, *The Struggle for a Proletarian Party,* 28–29.

27. Shachtman, COHO, 320, 335–336; Cannon, *The Struggle for a Proletarian Party,* 29.

28. Roskolenko, *When I Was Last on Cherry Street,* 179; Hook, *Out of Step,* 206–207; SH, Box 185.

29. Yetta Shachtman to author, September 10, 1990. In his memoirs, Sidney Hook tells a generalized version of this story. Hook, *Out of Step,* 204.

30. Jean van Heijenoort, *De Prinkipo à Coyoacan. Sept ans auprès de Trotsky* (Paris: Lettres Nouvelles Maurice Nadeau, 1978), 157.

31. Diana Trilling, *The Beginning of the Journey: The Marriage of Diana and Lionel Trilling* (New York: Harcourt Brace and Co., 1993), 302.

32. Alex Olsen to author, December 19, 1991; Shachtman, COHO, 336–338; Glotzer to author, September 20, 1991. Howe to author, June 18, 1990; JTF, January 8, 190; Shoenfeld to author, August 20, 1990.

33. Yetta Shachtman to author, September 10, 1991. Irving Kristol, *Reflections of a Neoconservative* (New York: Basic Books, 1983), 12. Shachtman, COHO, 337.

34. Howe, *A Margin of Hope,* 39; Howe to author, June 18, 1990; Geltman to author, July 26, 1990; Yetta Shachtman to author, September 10, 1990; Glotzer to author, September 20, 1990.

35. JTF, October 8, 1936; James T. Farrell, *Sam Holman* (Buffalo, N.Y.: Prometheus, 1983).

36. Olsen to author, December 19, 1992.

37. Burnham to Hook, July 15, 1935, SH, Box 8; Howe to author, June 18, 1990; Howe, *A Margin of Hope,* 55.

38. Yetta Shachtman to author, September 10, 1990; Burnham to Hook, July 15, 1935, SH, Box 8.

39. James Burnham, "Roosevelt Faces the Future," *NI* 4 (February 1938: 44; ibid., "Their Government," *SA,* November 26, 1938; February 24, 1939; March 31, 1939; April 28, 1939; May 26, 1939; June 2, 1939; June 30, 1939; July 28, 1939; September 13, 1939.

40. James Burnham, *How to Fight War: Isolation, Collective Security, Ruthless Class Struggle?* (New York: Pioneer, 1938), 1–15; ibid., "Their Government," *SA,* October 27, 1939. On at least one occasion, Burnham advocated a less apocalyptical means of keeping the United States out of war: a constitutional amendment authorizing Congress to declare war only if the step were approved in a national referendum. James Burnham, *Let the People Vote on War!* (New York: Pioneer, c. 1938–1939).

41. *SA,* October 22, 1938; ibid., February 4, 1939.

42. Burnham to Glotzer, March 8, 1939, AG, Box 2.

43. Burnham to Hook, n.d. 1938, SH, Box 8; ibid., August 2, 1938, SH, Box 8.

44. James Burnham, "Proletarian 'Grand Hotel'," a review of *The Foundry,* by Albert Halper, *N* 139 (September 12, 1934): 306; ibid., "Revolutionary Fiction," *N* 141 (October 9, 35): 416; ibid., "Incomplete Angler," a review of *To Have and Have Not,* by Ernest Hemingway, *NI* 4 (March 1938): 93; Burnham to Macdonald, June 9, 1937, DM).

45. John West (James Burnham), "Prize Novel," a review of *Marching! Marching!* by Clira Weatherwall, *NI,* 3 (February 1936): 30; James Burnham, "His Majesty's Loyal Opposition," *SA,* January 1937; James Burnham, review of *A Note on Literary Criticism,* by James T. Farrell, *American Socialist Monthly,* 5 (October 1936): 63; JTF, October 8, 1936.

46. William Phillips, *A Partisan View: Five Decades of the Literary Life* (New York: Stein and Day,

1983), 33–48.

47. Terry A. Cooney, *The Rise of the New York Intellectuals: Partisan Review and Its Circle* (Madison, Wisconsin: University of Wisconsin Press, 1986), 110.

48. Burnham to Trotsky, April 12, 1938, TA.

49. Trotsky to Burnham, April 18, 1938, TA; Leon Trotsky, "Art and Politics," *Partisan Review* (hereafter, *PR*) 5 (August–September 1938): 3–10.

50. Burnham to Hook, June 12, 1938, SH, Box 132.

51. James Burnham, "William Troy's Myths," *PR* 5 (August–September 1938): 65–68; JTF, January 22, 1940.

52. Burnham to Hook, n.d. 1938, SH, Box 8; James Burnham, "A Belated Dialectician," a review of *The Marxist Philosophy and the Sciences,* by J.B.S. Haldane, *PR* 6 (Spring 1939): 121–123.

53. Trotsky to Burnham, March 22, 1938, TA; Burnham to Diggins, June 11, 1971; ibid., "Max Eastman as Scientist," *NI* 4 (June 1938): 177–180; ibid. to Hook, June 12, 1938, SH, Box 132; ibid., "A Little Wool Pulling," *NI* (August 1938): 246–247.

54. Burnham to Hook, June 12, 1938, SH, Box 132; ibid., August 2, 1938, SH, Box 8.

55. James Burnham and Max Shachtman, "Intellectuals in Retreat. A Political Analysis of Some of the Recent Critics of Bolshevism: Sidney Hook, Max Eastman, Eugene Lyons, Ben Stolberg and Others. What Are They Doing? Where Are They Going?" *NI* 5 (January 1939): 3–22. On Burnham as principal author, Howe to author, June 18, 1990.

56. JTF, December 28, 1938, January 20, 1939, January 28, 1939, February 28, 1939, March 3, 1939; Howe to author, June 18, 1990; Geltman to author, August 6, 1990.

57. James Burnham, "On the Slogan 'For a Workers' Government,'" *IB* (August 1938): 39–42; Cannon, *The Struggle for a Proletarian Party,* 280; Myers, *The Prophet's Army,* 151.

58. Burnham to Trotsky, September 19, 1939, TA; Trotsky to Burnham, September 30, 1939, TA; Deutscher, *The Prophet Outcast,* 446, 482; Ben Sonnenberg, *Lost Property: Memoirs and Confessions of a Bad Boy* (New York: Summit, 1991), 22.

59. Cannon, *The Struggle for a Proletarian Party,* 175.

60. James Burnham, "On the Character of the War, and the Perspectives of the Fourth Internationalists," *IB* (November 6, 1939), 8–12; ibid., *SA,* August 25, 1939; ibid., September 9, 1939.

61. Cannon, *The Struggle for a Proletarian Party,* 85–86, 88; minutes, Polcom meeting of September 18, 1939, MS, series I, part G, box 8; minutes, National Committee Plenum of September 30–October 1, 1939, MS, series I, part G, box 8.

62. Leon Trotsky, "The U.S.S.R. in War," *NI* 5 (November 1939): 331, 332; ibid., "Again and Once More Again on the Nature of the U.S.S.R.," *NI,* 6 (January 1940): 13–17.

63. The Editors, "The Second World War," *NI* 5 (October 1939): 292.

64. Cannon, *The Struggle for a Proletarian Party,* 90, 114, 147, 191. Albert Glotzer, a member of the opposition, saw no social difference between the factions, but, if anything, an age difference, with the dissidents, on average, younger than the Cannon loyalists. Glotzer, *Trotsky,* 306n.

65. Minutes, Polcom meeting of October 24, 1939, MS, series I, part G, box 8; Cannon, *The Struggle for a Proletarian Party,* 14, 96.

66. Heijenoort, *De Prinkipo à Coyoacan,* 209; Cannon, *The Struggle for a Proletarian Party,* 143, 266; Myers, *The Prophet's Army,* 158; Macdonald, *Memoirs of a Revolutionist,* 18. Cannon's

enmity may also explain the disappearance of Burnham's column from *The Socialist Appeal* early in 1940, though other factors—the distraction imposed by the faction fight, for instance—might equally well have been responsible. Cannon could not have removed Burnham from *The New International* since that journal legally belonged to Shachtman.

67. Cannon, *The Struggle for a Proletarian Party,* 125.

68. Leon Trotsky, "A Petty-Bourgeois Opposition in the Socialist Workers Party," *NI* 6 (March 1940): 40; "Resolution on the Soviet-Finnish War introduced by the Minority of the Political Committee," *IB* (December 1939): 6.

69. Burnham, "Science and Style," 200; Cannon, *The Struggle for a Proletarian Party,* 119–120; Burnham, *The Managerial Revolution,* preface to the Midland Books edition, vi. See also n. 87.

70. James Burnham, "The War and Bureaucratic Conservatism," *IB* (January 1940): 3–15; Shachtman, Martin Abern, and another oppositionist, Isador Bern, also signed this article, but Burnham was its author. Myers, *The Prophet's Army,* 154; JTF, January 14, 1939.

71. Trotsky, "A Petty-Bourgeois Opposition," 35–42; Leon Trotsky, "An Open Letter to Comrade Burnham," *In Defense of Marxism,* 86, 94. In pointing to Burnham as the opposition's leader, Trotsky echoed the general view, shared by Cannon and Shachtman, and by Burnham himself. Yetta Shachtman later speculated that had it not been for Burnham's influence, her husband might not have broken with Cannon completely. Trotsky, "An Open Letter to James Burnham," *In Defense of Marxism,* 93; Cannon, *The Struggle for a Proletarian Party,* 17; Myers, *The Prophet's Army,* 164; Yetta Shachtman to author, September 10, 1990.

72. James Burnham, "Science and Style," 188, 191, 194, 202, 204, 205–206. The italics are Burnham's. The possibility that vivid prose might masquerade as logical proof had been worrying Burnham for years. He had become "almost morbidly sensitive to the dangers of relying on metaphors and emotive phrases in non-creative prose," he told Hook. Burnham to Hook, June 12, 1938, SH, Box 132.

73. MS, series I, part G, box 8; Cannon, *The Struggle for a Proletarian Party,* 174, 188; Trotsky, *In Defense of Socialism,* 157.

74. Shachtman, COHO, 317–318; Cannon, *The Struggle for a Proletarian Party,* 64–65, 173, 176, 182.

75. Cannon, *The Struggle for a Proletarian Party,* 188, 192.

76. Burr McCloskey to James Burnham, October 14, 1976, JB; Glotzer to author, September 20, 1990; Geltman to author, August 6, 1990.

77. Shachtman, COHO, 339, 341–342.

78. *SA,* April 13, 1940; ibid., April 20, 1940; Cannon, *The Struggle for a Proletarian Party,* 231–241.

79. Cannon, *The Struggle for a Proletarian Party,* 20–21.

80. Trotsky, *In Defense of Marxism,* 169, 177, 183.

81. James B. Burnham, *NR* 39 (September 11, 1987); 50–51. In a review of volume one of Isaac Deutscher's biography of Trotsky, Burnham wrote: "Trotsky, from the standpoint of an organization and 'movement,' was too angular and discontinuous. He reversed his ideas too quickly, changed too abruptly his friendships and his political alignments, too abstractly pushed his ideas beyond the range of his associates. And he deluded himself with his wonderful words. Too often (as I tried to show in a polemic against him) Trotsky mistook the metaphors and paradoxes of his own verbal style for the objective dialectic of his-

tory." Review of *The Prophet Armed: Trotsky: 1879–1921,* by Isaac Deutscher, *The Russian Review* 14 (April 1955): 151–152; Charles Lam Markmann, *The Buckleys: A Family Examined* (New York: W. Morrow, 1973), 57.

82. Shachtman, COHO, 342; Glotzer, *Trotsky,* 288–289. In a conversation of September 20, 1990, with the author, Albert Glotzer said that Burnham had resigned even before the WP's first public meeting, but had spoken at the meeting anyway, thinking that he owed it to the group.

83. James Burnham, "Letter of Resignation," May 21, 1940, TA. James T. Farrell heard that Burnham had left the WP for a further reason as well: that the "third camp" line on the war—opposition to Stalin, Hitler, and the Allies alike, and support only for world revolution—made no sense to him. JTF, May 26, 1940.

84. Panken to author, June 3, 1991; Howe, *A Margin of Hope,* 80; ibid. to author, June 18, 1990; Glotzer to author, September 20, 1990; on Dwight Macdonald's reaction, Sidney Hook, *NR* 39 (September 11, 1987): 33.

85. Shachtman, COHO, 343; Glotzer to author, September 20, 1990.

86. Burnham to Crozier, March 29, 1976, BC; Crozier, "My Pilgrimage to Kent (Connecticut)," 19. This article is drawn in part from Burnham's letter of March 29, 1976, to Crozier, but also from an interview Crozier conducted with Burnham, which the letter elucidates and supplements.

87. James Burnham, *The Machiavellians: Defenders of Freedom* (New York: The John Day Co., 1943), 5. The translation of Dante is that of Dorothy L. Sayers, *The Divine Comedy,* 1, *Hell* (New York: Penguin Books, 1949), 71.

88. James Burnham, "Lenin's Heir," *PR* 12 (1945): 61.

89. Ibid., "How Democratic Is America?" This typescript is not dated, but its contents suggest that it was written in the late 1960s, JB, Box I; Burnham to Diggins, June 11, 1971; Burnham to Crozier, March 29, 1976. "Burnham's thought, even at its most conservative, owed much to the Marxism of his youth," observes the political commentator Samuel T. Francis in his book *Power and History: The Political Thought of James Burnham* (Lanham, Maryland: University Press of America, 1984), 2. Burnham retained traces of his Trotskyist years in his speech. On his speech habits, C. H. Simonds, *NR* 39 (September 11, 1987), and Bridges to author, January 8, 1992. Long after he had left the movement, he also continued to use metaphors he had picked up from Trotsky. e.g., James Burnham, "The Protracted Conflict" (hereafter, PC), "The Italian Colonels," *NR* 23 (November 5, 1971): 1223.

90. James Burnham, Preface to the Regnery Gateway edition of *The Machiavellians* (Chicago: Henry Regnery, 1963), viii. The philosopher William Barrett, one of Burnham's colleagues at NYU, believed what he called the "sweeping character" of Burnham's thinking to be another legacy of his Marxist period. William Barrett, *The Truants: Adventures among the Intellectuals* (Garden City: Anchor-Doubleday, 1983), 87.

91. James Burnham and André Malraux, *The Case for De Gaulle* (New York: The John Day Co., 1947), 63. The italics are Burnham's.

92. Bridges to author, January 8, 1992.

CHAPTER FIVE

1. Wilmerding to author, March 12, 1992.

2. JTF, May 22, 1940.

3. E.g., James Burnham, "God Bless America," review of *The Triumph of American Capitalism,* by Louis M. Hacker, *PR* 7 (1940): 479–481; ibid., review of *The Red Decade,* by Eugene Lyons, *PR* 8 (November-December 1941): 514–515. James Burnham to William Phillips and Philip Rahv, October 5, 1943, Partisan Review Papers (hereafter, PR), Mugar Library, Boston University.

4. Burnham, "Letter of Resignation," May 22, 1940, TA.

5. James Burnham to Silva Norkela, 19 Nov. 1972, JB Box, 2. See also ibid., *The Managerial Revolution: What Is Happening in the World* (New York: The John Day Co., 1941), 7, 274.

6. Excerpts from Machajski's *The Intellectual Worker* (1904) appear in V. F. Calverton, ed. *The Making of Society: An Outline of Sociology* (New York: Modern Library, 1937), 427–436. See also Max Nomad, *Renegades and Rebels* (New York: Macmillan, 1932), 206–208.

7. Bruno Rizzi, *The Bureaucratization of the World,* trans. and ed. Adam Westoby (New York: The Free Press, 1985).

8. When he conceived his managerial theory, Burnham had not yet read Machajski. Years later, after he had he commented that the latter's ideas "indirectly...confirmed and clarified some of my own views." Nevertheless, Max Nomad, translator of portions of *The Intellectual Worker,* accused Burnham of having stolen his ideas from Machajski. But a comparison of the Machajski excerpt translated by Nomad with Burnham's theory exonerates Burnham for although the two writers deal with loosely related subjects, Burnham's ideas go far beyond a rehash of Machajski's. Burnham to Norkela, 19 Nov. 1971, JB, Box 2. Adam Westoby's introduction to Rizzi, *The Bureaucratization of the World,* 26. Rizzi also accused Burnham of plagiarism, but his charge is equally hollow. Rizzi's book had been impounded by the French authorities shortly after publication, allegedly because of its antisemitism, and hence had very few readers.

9. Trotsky, *The Revolution Betrayed,* 278.

10. Burnham named Veblen as an influence in an interview with John P. Diggins, June 11, 1971. Diggins to author, July 2, 1990. Thorsten Veblen, *The Engineers and the Price System* (New York: Viking, 1921), 125–126, 133–134. In a forward to a book on Veblen by his friend and sometime NYU colleague, Lev E. Dobriansky, Burnham noted parallels between Veblen's ideas and his own, and commented that Dobrianksy had "justifiably" linked some of Veblen's "social predictions" with the argument of *The Managerial Revolution.* Lev E. Dobriansky, *Veblenism: A New Critique* (Washington, D.C.: Public Affairs Press, 1957), v.

11. Berle and Means, *The Modern Corporation and Private Property,* 4–9; Burnham, "Comment," *S* 4 (July 1933): 259; ibid., *The Managerial Revolution,* 88–94; ibid., "What New Class?" *NR* 30 (20 Jan. 1978): 98.

12. Thurman W. Arnold, *The Folklore of Capitalism* (New Haven: Yale University Press, 1937), 38; James Burnham, "Capitalism, American Style," *PR* 4 (March 1938): 50–53. In his *Designing the Industrial State: The Intellectual Pursuit of Collectivism in America* (Chicago: Quadrangle Books, 1972), 278–279, James Gilbert claims that *The Folklore of Capitalism* "must" have suggested to Burnham some of the ideas that went into his managerial theory.

13. Lawrence Dennis, *The Coming American Fascism* (New York: Harper, 1936); Burnham to Norkela, 19 Nov. 1972, JB, Box 2.

14. Hook to Feuer, 16 Nov. 1981, SH, Box 115; Sidney Hook, "On James Burnham's *The*

*Machiavellians," Society* 25 (March–April 1988): 68.

15. In his introduction to the 1960 reprint of *The Managerial Revolution,* Burnham himself wrote that the book "was the first generalized attempt at the statement of a theory of the modern epoch that cut through the alternative of either-capitalism-or-socialism." *The Managerial Revolution,* preface to the Midland Books ed., viii. More recently, the historian Alfred D. Chandler, Jr., has written, "James Burnham...in his *Managerial Revolution* (New York, 1941) was the first to describe and analyze that phenomenon...." *The Visible Hand: The Managerial Revolution in American Business* (Cambridge, Mass.: Harvard University Press, 1977), 515n. "Burnham had a good mind, but it was the mind of a synthesizer and organizer," Sidney Hook once wrote. Hook, *Out of Step,* 536.

16. Burnham, *The Managerial Revolution,* 72–74, 77–82, 89, 118, 123–124, 135–137, 166–171, 271.

17. Ibid., 159.

18. Ibid., 257, 261.

19. Ibid., 174–176, 178–179, 225–226, 246, 264.

20. Ibid., 138.

21. Ibid., 285.

22. Ibid., 8, 183, 273, 284.

23. Hook to Feuer, 16 March 1981, SH, Box 115; Crozier, "My Pilgrimage to Kent (Connecticut)," 20.

24. *Fortune* 24 (no. 5): 100; *Time* 38 (December 15, 1941). Crozier, "My Pilgrimage to Kent (Connecticut)," 20. John P. Diggins, *Up from Communism: Conservative Odysseys in American Intellectual History* (New York: Harper and Row, 1975), 191–192; Burnham, *The Managerial Revolution,* preface to the Midland Books ed., ix; Putnam and Co. to James Burnham, Sept. 13, 1943, JB, Box 1.

25. Ralph Thompson, *NYT,* May 1, 1941; Malcolm Cowley, "Where Is the World Going?" *The New Republic* (hereafter, *TNR*) 104 (April 28, 1941): 607–608; Louis Hacker, "Capitalism Has Broken Down," *The New York Herald Tribune* (hereafter, *NYHT*), June 22, 1941; Lewis Corey, "A New Theory of Revolution," *N* 152 (26 April 1941): 505–506; Golo Mann, "False Prophets," *Decision* (hereafter, *D*), 2 (July 1941): 51–58.

26. Peter Drucker, "The Rulers of Tomorrow," *The Saturday Review of Literature* (hereafter, *SRL*) 24 (May 10, 1941): 9; Hacker described Burnham as "still bound hand and foot to Marxism." "Capitalism Has Broken Down," *NYHT,* June 22, 1941; Hans Gerth and C. Wright Mills, "A Marx for the Managers," *Ethics* (hereafter, *E*) 52 (January 1942): 200–213. A later commentator on *The Managerial Revolution,* David Spitz, also thought that the book's "Marxist" economic determinism invalidated its argument. Burnham was not enough of an empiricist, Spitz charged. He had sinned through "the fallacy of exaggeration, of extending a partial truth to a false universal" and "the fallacy of oversimplification, of treating a multidimensional problem in monistic terms." David Spitz, *Patterns of Anti-Democratic Thought,* revised ed. (New York: The Free Press, 1965), 55, 65.

27. Dwight Macdonald, "The Burnhamian Revolution," *PR* 9 (January-February 1942): 76–84; Albert Gates (Albert Glotzer), "Burnham and His Managers," *NI* 7 (July 1941): 144–148; ibid., (August 1941): 175–179; Joseph Hanson, "Burnham's `Managerial Revolution,'" *Fourth International* (hereafter, *FI*) 2 (June 1941): 157–159.

28. George Orwell, *The Collected Essays, Journalism, and Letters of George Orwell,* ed. Sonia Orwell and Ian Angus, 4 vols. (London: Secker and Warburg, 1968) 3: 74.

29. Burnham to *The Tribune,* 19 February 1944, JB, Box 1.

30. George Orwell, "James Burnham and the Managerial Revolution," *Collected Essays,* 4: 162, 172–173, 176, 178–179, 181. This piece was later reprinted under the title "James Burnham and The Managerial Revolution." Many years later, talking about his critics with fellow *National Review* editor Joseph Sobran, Burnham groped for Orwell's name, but could get no closer than "that English fellow." "Not George Orwell?" Sobran asked. "Yes, Orwell, that's the one," said Burnham. "To this day I don't know if he was pulling my leg." Joseph Sobran, *NR,* 36 (20 April 1984): 46.

31. George Orwell, *Collected Essays,* 3: 328, and 4: 8–9, in which Orwell wrote that Burnham's vision was being borne out; William Steinhoff, *George Orwell and the Origins of 1984* (Ann Arbor, Michigan: University of Michigan Press, 1975), 200–201.

32. H.G. Wells to James Burnham, August 27, 1942, JB, Box 7; Delmore Schwartz to Robert Hivnor, n.d., Robert Philips, ed., *Letters of Delmore Schwartz* (Princeton, N.J.: Ontario Review Press, 1984), 211; A.D. Lindsay to James Burnham, May 31, 1943, JB, Box 6; Bernard Baruch to James Burnham, May 1941, JB., Box 5.

33. Various readers to Burnham, various dates, JB, Box 1.

34. Indicative of Burnham's new status is his appearance in a postwar "intellectual" best-seller, David Riesman's *The Lonely Crowd,* on a list of social scientists that includes Marx, Veblen, Weber, Mosca, Michels, and Pareto. David Riesman et al. *The Lonely Crowd* (New Haven, Conn.: Yale University Press), 252.

35. *Time,* 37 (May 19, 1941): 98.

36. James Burnham, "What Future for Free Enterprise?" Town Meeting of the Air, February 5, 1942. A transcript of this public affairs radio program is available in *Town Meeting* 7 (February 9, 1942): 3–24. JB, Box 2.

37. Cf. Marx, whose view was not dissimilar: "Men make their own history, but they do not make it just as they please; they do not make it under circumstances chosen by themselves, but under circumstances directly encountered, given, and transmitted from the past. The tradition of all the dead generations weighs like a nightmare on the brain of the living." *The Eighteenth Brumaire of Louis Bonaparte, Marx and Engels: Basic Writings on Politics and Philosophy,* ed. Lewis S. Feuer (Garden City, N.Y. Anchor, 1959), 320.

38. Burnham, *The Machiavellians,* 233n.; ibid., *The Managerial Revolution,* preface to Midland Books ed., pp. vii–ix.

39. Diggins to author, 2 July 1990.

40. James Burnham to Charles Lam Markmann, 30 March 1972, JB, Box 5.

41. So thought economist John Kenneth Galbraith, not in most respects a Burnham fan. See his *The New Industrial State,* 2nd ed. (Boston: Houghton Mifflin, 1971), 115. He was "greatly indebted to *The Managerial Revolution*" for his argument in *The New Industrial State,* Galbraith told Burnham in a letter of August 6, 1971. JB, Box 6. Cf. the biographer of Burnham and columnist Samuel T. Francis, who writes, "Regardless of Burnham's errors, then, it ought to be obvious that he was essentially correct in the substance of his prophecies." "Prophet Sustained. James Burnham and the Managerial Revolution," *Chronicles* 16 (January 1992): 17.

42. In a letter of November 22, 1943, to the Municipal Court of New York explaining why he should be excused from jury duty, Burnham notes his draft classification. JB, Box 1.

43. Wilmerding to author, March 12, 1992. Washington Square College Faculty Meeting minutes, February 13, 1942. New York University Archives.

44. Burnham to Norkela, November 19, 1972, JB, Box 1.

45. Bernard C. Heyl, *New Bearings in Esthetics and Art Criticism: A Study in Semantics and Evaluation* (New Haven: Yale University Press, 1945), dedication, 50n.

46. James B. Burnham, "Father, Friend," *NR* 39 (September 11, 1987): 50.

47. Mary McGrory, "Reading and Writing," *The Washington Post* (hereafter, *WP*), February 19, 1950.

48. Robert Michels, *Political Parties: A Sociological Study of the Oligarchic Tendencies of Modern Democracy* (New York: The Free Press, 1962), 365.

49. Vilfredo Pareto, *The Mind and Society,* 4 vols. (New York: Harcourt, Brace and Co., 1935).

50. Gaetano Mosca, *The Ruling Class,* ed. and rev. Arthur Livingston, trans. Hannah D. Kahn (New York: McGraw-Hill, 1939), 196, 244, 283, 287–288, 326–327.

51. Georges Sorel, *Reflections on Violence,* trans. T. E. Hulme and J. Roth, intro. Edward A. Shils (Glencoe, Ill: The Free Press, 1950).

52. Mosca, *The Ruling Class,* 70–71.

53. Michels, *Political Parties,* 354.

54. Mosca, *The Ruling Class,* 163.

55. Ibid., 280.

56. Hook, "On James Burnham's *The Machiavellians*": 68–70; Hook to Feuer, March 16, 1938, SH, Box 115.

57. Burnham to Markmann, March 30, 1972, Box 5; Burnham, *The Machiavellians,* preface to the Regnery-Gateway ed., viii. See also Burnham to Norkela, November 19, 1972, JB, Box 2.

58. Burnham to Diggins, June 11, 1971, Diggins to author, July 2, 1990.

59. Burnham to Norkela, November 19, 1972, JB, Box 2. Burnham first mentioned Mosca's appeal for him in an article called "Is Democracy Possible?" which he published several months after *The Managerial Revolution.* James Burnham, "Is Democracy Possible?" Irving D. Talmadge, ed., *Whose Revolution? A Study in the Future Course of Liberalism in the United States* (New York: Howell, Soskin, 1941). His answer to this question was, yes, if democracy were understood to mean a political order providing personal freedom, not majority rule. See pp. 190–193, 194n., 215.

60. Burnham, *The Machiavellians,* preface to the Regnery-Gateway ed. viii.

61. Burnham, *The Machiavellians,* 74.

62. Ibid., 38, 48.

63. Ibid., 85–86, 167.

64. Ibid., 162, 238–242, 250.

65. Ibid., 259–260.

66. Ibid., 270. Just what events these words of 1942 or 1943 refer to is not clear.

67. JB, Box 2.

68. Louis M. Hacker, "Perhaps It's All in Fun," *NYHT,* May 16, 1943; John MacCormac, "Machiavelli and the Managerial Revolution," *NYT,* May 2, 1943; Reinhold Niebuhr,

"Study in Cynicism," *N* 156 (May 1, 1943): 636–638; Malcolm Cowley, "The Newest Machiavelli," *TNR* 108 (May 17, 1943): 673–674.

69. The Atlantic Bookshelf, *The Atlantic Monthly* (hereafter, *AM*) 171 (June 1943): 129; Philip Wheelwright, "Partisan and Tendencious," *Kenyon Review* (hereafter, *KR*) 6 (Winter 1944): 138–142.

70. John Chamberlain, review of *The Machiavellians*, by James Burnham, *NYT,* April 19, 1943.

71. Burnham, *The Machiavellians*, preface to the Regnery-Gateway edition, vii–viii.

72. James B. Burnham to author, June 18, 1992. People who agree that *The Machiavellians* is Burnham's most important book include former *National Review* editor Joseph Sobran, *NR* 39 (September 11, 1987): 46; the columnist and biographer of Burnham Samuel T. Francis, *Power and History,* 49; Burnham's friend, the political writer Brian Crozier, who called the book "the key to everything he wrote subsequently: the Burnham equivalent of Descartes's *Discour sur la méthode*" *NR,* 39 (September 11, 1987), 36; and Sidney Hook, "On James Burnham's *The Machiavellians*": 68.

73. Burnham, *The Machiavellians,* 265. The italics are Burnham's.

74. Ibid., 85

75. Ibid., 93–94, 245–246.

76. Barrett, *The Truants,* 89.

77. James Burnham, "The Unreconstructed Allen Tate," a review of *On the Limits of Poetry,* by Allen Tate, *PR,* 16 (February 1949); ibid., "Serious, Social, and Moral," a review of *Literature and Morality,* by James T. Farrell, *NYT,* July 13, 1947; ibid., "The Extreme and the Plausible," a review of *The Blood of Others,* by Simone de Beauvoir, and *The Plague,* by Albert Camus, *PR,* 15 (1948); ibid., "Observations on Kafka," *PR,* 14 (1947): 193–195.

## CHAPTER SIX

1. Lev E. Dobriansky to author, September 17, 1992.

2. Hook to Feuer, March 16, 1981, SH, Box 115.

3. *PR* 9 (March-April 1942): 174–176; Burnham to Macdonald, May 15, 1943, DM; JB, Box 2.

4. James Burnham, "The Sixth Turn of the Communist Screw," *PR* 11 (Summer 1944): 364–366.

5. Ibid., "Stalin and the Junkers," *The Commonweal* (hereafter, *TC*) 40 (September 15, 1944): 510–516.

6. Ibid., "Lenin's Heir," *PR* 12, n. 1 (1945): 67–68, 72.

7. Ibid., 64–65, 66–67, 68, 71, 72.

8. Ibid., 61–63; Joseph Sobran, *NR,* 39 (September 11, 1987): 46.; Diggins, *Up from Communism,* 319.

9. Burnham, "Lenin's Heir," 70, for Burnham on Macdonald's revolutionism; Dwight Macdonald, "Beat Me, Daddy," *PR* 12, n. 2 (1945): 182, 185; Orwell, "James Burnham and the Managerial Revolution," *Collected Essays* 4: 168–170; ibid., "Burnham's View of the Contemporary World Struggle," *Collected Essays* 4: 325. Regarding Macdonald's influence on Orwell, Burnham wrote: Macdonald, "who lacks either a sense of humor or of irony," had mistakenly read "Lenin's Heir" as "a song of *praise* of Stalin...Orwell took over Macdonald's interpretation, and out of this he evolved the theory that I always yielded to

the power of the moment (just how he reconciled this with the fact that I 'yielded' to Trotsky when he was an exile on Prinkipo he has never disclosed." James Burnham to Minoo Masani, July 30, 1953, JB, Box 7.

10. James Burnham, "On Eisenstein's Mea Culpa," *NL* 30 (January 4, 1947): 12. The italics are Burnham's.

11. Ibid., "The Two Republics," a review of *The Republic,* by Charles Beard, *PR,* 11 (Winter 1944): 105–106. Burnham also criticized the philosopher Mortimer J. Adler's *How to Think about War and Peace* from a historicist position; ibid., "Rules for Fishing in an Empty Sea," a review of *How to Think about War and Peace,* by Mortimer J. Adler, *PR,* 11 (Spring 1944): 204–205.

12. On Mackinder and his influence in the 1940s, see Brian W. Blouet, *Halford Mackinder: A Biography* (College Station, Texas: Texas A&M Press, 1987), 189–191, 196.

13. Toynbee explicitly rejected determinism, but the first six volumes of his work, virtually declaring the existence of laws of history, strongly implied it. On Toynbee's determinism, see Karl Loewith, *Meaning in History* (Chicago: University of Chicago Press, 1949), 13. "Rousing boys' stuff" comes from the author's wife, Wendy Anne Kelly.

14. Arnold J. Toynbee, *A Study of History,* 10 vols. (London: Oxford University Press, 1934–1954).

15. Halford J. Mackinder, "The Geographical Pivot of History," *Democratic Ideals and Reality: With Additional Papers* (New York: W.W. Norton, 1962), 243, 262–263; ibid., *Democratic Ideals and Reality,* 56, 62, 64–65, 70, 73–74, 86, 111–112, 150.

16. Halford J. Mackinder, "The Round World and the Winning of the Peace," *Democratic Ideals and Realty,* 272–273.

17. Ibid., 277; Blouet, *Halford Mackinder,* 168, 198.

18. James Burnham, "The Dialectic of American Foreign Policy," 3, typescript, n.d., but probably written in the late 1960s, JB, Box 1; Diggins, *Up from Communism,* 319.

19. Burnham to Hook, August 19, 1946, SH, Box 8.

20. Ibid., *The Struggle for the World* (New York: The John Day Co., 1947), 1, 3–4. Balkans history specialist Barbara Jelavich concedes that communists were among the leaders of the mutiny, but denies that the trouble was fomented by the EAM, attributing it instead to long-simmering discontent among anti-royalist troops." *History of the Balkans* (Cambridge: Cambridge University Press, 1983) v. 2: 281.

21. Burnham, *The Struggle for the World,* 24, 30, 35, 37, 40, 53, 55, 132, 134–135.

22. Ibid., 32, 51–52, 62, 146.

23. Ibid., 12, 59, 61, 121.

24. Ibid., 75–77, 87.

25. Ibid., 122, 127–129.

26. Ibid., 96–104.

27. Ibid., 105–110.

28. Ibid., 114–121, 135.

29. Ibid., 162, 177–180.

30. Ibid., 50–51, 181–187, 191–193, 196–198, 221.

31. Ibid., 203–209.

32. Ibid., 160, 198–199, 218, 232.

33. Ibid., 5–9, 134, 212, 215, 232. The art critic Clement Greenberg, who knew Burnham through *Partisan Review,* recalled that he had little regard for American painting and thought only European painters merited attention. Clement Greenberg to author, September 6, 1990.

34. Burnham, *The Struggle for the World.,* 10–13.

35. Ibid., 7–9, 154–155, 176, 188, 215, 233.

36. Ibid., 237–238.

37. Ibid., 239–241, 246.

38. Ibid., 223–224, 248.

39. Ibid., 147.

40. Ibid., 199.

41. Orville Prescott, *NYT,* March 17, 1947.

42. Burnham, *The Struggle for the World,* 144–145, 232.

43. Burnham, *The Struggle for the World,* 13, 35–37.

44. Ibid., 27.

45. On information from Soviet archives on Soviet atomic espionage and Soviet control of the international communist movement, see, e.g., David Holloway. *Stalin and the Bomb: The Soviet Union and Atomic Energy* (New Haven: Yale University Press, 1994); Harvey Klehr, John Earl Haynes, and Fridrikh Igorevich Firsov, *The Secret World of American Communism* (New Haven: Yale University Press, 1995); Harvey Klehr, John Earl Haynes, and Kyrill M. Anderson, *The Soviet World of American Communism* (New Haven: Yale University Press, 1998); and Richard Rhodes, *Dark Sun: The Making of the Hydrogen Bomb* (New York: Simon and Schuster, 1995).

46. Burnham, *The Struggle for the World,* 130–132. As John O'Sullivan, former editor-in-chief of *National Review,* puts it, Burnham "pared away the superficialities of any situation and dealt with its central point. . . . Occasionally, therefore, his predictions and prescriptions take on a sharpness which exiles his qualifications to the fine print." Burnham "could surely be forgiven," O'Sullivan also remarks, "for occasionally slipping into an apocalyptical style when apocalypses were occuring almost yearly." John O'Sullivan, "James Burnham and the New World Order," *NR* 42 (November 5, 1990): 39. Burnham's "thought had a simplicity achieved by shedding the irrelevancies that obsessed others, including conservatives," noted Burnham's fellow *National Review* editor Joseph Sobran on Burnham's writing, *NR* 39 (September 11, 1987): 46.

47. Burnham to Hook, August 19, 1946, SH Box 8.

48. Truman quoted by Stephen E. Ambrose, *Rise to Globalism. American Foreign Policy, 1938–1980,* second revised ed. (New York: Penguin Books, 1980), 132.

49. *The Yale Daily News* (hereafter, *YDN*), April 17, 1947.

50. Editorial, "The Truman-Burnham Parallel," *The Christian Century* (hereafter, *CC*) 64 (June 4, 1947): 702–703.

51. John Patrick Diggins, "Sidney Hook," *Grand Street* 7 (Autumn 1987): 187. Lawrence A. Smith is quoted by Justus D. Doenecke, *The Old Isolationists in the Cold War* (Lewisburg, Pa.: Bucknell University Press, 1979), 80. On communist student surveillance of Burnham's classes, see Jeanne Wacker, a noncommunist student of Burnham's, *NR* 39 (September 11, 1987): 34. On *Jimmy,* Diggins, *Up from Communism,* 325.

52. *YDN,* April 17, 1947.

53. *CC* 64 (April 9, 1947): 453; Lewis Corey, "James Burnham Rides Again," *The Antioch Review* (hereafter, *AR*) 7 (June 1947): 316; Max Lerner, "The Burnham Crusade," *Actions and Passions: Notes on the Multiple Revolution of Our Time* (New York: Simon and Schuster, 1949), 287; Harry Elmer Barnes, book review of *The Struggle for the World,* by James Burnham, *Annals of the American Academy of Political and Social Science* (hereafter, *AAAPSS* 252 (July 1947): 106.

54. Orville Prescott, review of *The Struggle for the World,* by James Burnham, *NYT,* March 17, 1947; James Reston, "Must It Be 'Their Necks or Ours'?" *NYT,* March 16, 1947; Waldemar Gurian, "James Burnham, Publicist or Poet?" *TC* 45 (April 4, 1947): 617–618; Arthur M. Schlesinger, Jr., "World War III," *N* 164 (April 5, 1947): 398–399; see also *The Times Literary Supplement* (hereafter, *TL*), May 22, 1947.

55. Orwell, "James Burnham's View of the Contemporary World Struggle," *Collected Essays* 4: 317, 319, 321, 324–325.

56. *Life* ran letters from readers on *The Struggle for the World,* and published a count of pro and con responses in its April 21, 1947, issue. For more responses, JB, Boxes 2, 4.

57. James Burnham to William Phillips, November 5, 1946, PR.

58. James Burnham to Alfred Kohlberg, May 1, 1947, Alfred Kohlberg Papers (hereafter AK), Hoover Institution, Box 22.

59. Such articles included, e.g., James Burnham, "The Belgrade 'Information Bureau,'" *NL* 30 (November 11, 1947): 9; ibid., "What Is the Purpose of the United Nations?" *AAAPSS* 252 (July 1947): 1–10; ibid., "How the United Nations Can Be Made to Work," *Reader's Digest* (hereafter, *RD*) 52 (January 1948): 81–86; ibid., "The Wallace Crusade," *PR* 15, n. 6 (1948): 701–704.

60. Burnham to Kohlberg, May 1, 1947, AK, Box 22; Dobriansky to author, September 17, 1992; JB, Box 4. Ralph de Toledano to author, April 30, 1993. Burr, *Pioneers and Princetonians,* 153; Morris A. Mayers (a member of the Class of 1927 who was present at the forum at which Burnham spoke) to author, November 19, 1990. As it happened, Truman and Toynbee, both of whom had reason to be interested in Burnham's argument, attended Princeton's 1947 graduation ceremony to receive honorary degrees. Neither, however, seems to have gone to the international affairs forum.

61. Winsor to author, January 28, 1992; Burnham to Norkela, November 19, 1972; Dr. Henry A. Kissinger's office to author, January 31, 1994; Wilmerding to author, March 12, 1992.

62. Burnham, "Personal History Statement," JB, Box 1.

63. Burnham to Hook, January 30, 1949, JB, Box 9. James Burnham, ed. *What Europe Thinks of America* (New York: John Day Co., 1953); James B. Burnham to author, June 18, 1995.

64. Burnham to Hook, December 3, 1948, and January 30, 1949, SH, Box 8.

65. United States House of Representatives. Committee on Unamerican Activities. Subcommittee on Proposed Legislation to Curb or Control the Communist Party of the United States, 80th Cong., February 1948, 381, 392, 393.

66. Iain Hamilton, *Koestler: A Biography* (New York: Macmillan, 1982), 134, 138–139, 145.

67. J. P. McFadden, once an editor at *National Review* and for many years publisher of the *Human Life Review,* speculates that Koestler may have brought Burnham and Malraux together. J. P. McFadden to author, April 22, 1993. Ralph de Toledano thinks Henry Luce may have been

the go-between. De Toledano to author, April 30, 1993. On *L'Espoir,* James Burnham, "Letter from France. Nostalgia and Strategy," *NR* 27 (November 7, 1975): 1228. On raising one another's sons, ibid., "André Malraux, RIP," *NR* 28 (December 24, 1976): 1393.

68. Burnham and Malraux, *The Case for De Gaulle,* 7–8, 8–19, 27–28, 29, 55–57, 63.

69. Burnham to Kohlberg, May 25, 1948, AK, Box 22.

70. James Burnham, *The Coming Defeat of Communism* (New York: John Day Co., 1950), 276–277; Burnham to Hook, June 12, 1947, SH, Box 8; ibid., September 15, 1948, SH, Box 8; James B. Burham, "Father, Friend," 50.

71. Burnham to Hook, December 3, 1948, SH, Box 8; Burnham to Phillips, December 3, 1948, PR; James B. Burnham, "Father, Friend," *NR,* 50.

72. Burnham to Phillips, December 3, 1948, PR; Burnham to Hook, December 3, 1948, SH, Box 8; ibid., January 11, 1949, SH, Box 8.

73. James Burnham, Application for Federal Employment, JB, Box 1; Burnham to Hook, September 15, 1948, SH, Box 8; ibid., January 11, 1949, SH, Box 8; Burnham, *The Coming Defeat of Communism,* 29, 55; Julian Amery to James Burnham, April 29, 1949, JB, Box 5.

74. Burnham to Kohlberg, October 20, 1949, AK, Box 22. Burnham, *The Coming Defeat of Communism,* 3–7, 9, 12, 18, 20, 21–27, 98.

75. Ibid., 23–24, 30–34, 100, 272.

76. Ibid., 12, 76–91, 95, 104–106, 136–138, 140–141, 141–144, 147–148.

77. Ibid., 166, 177, 182, 195, 199, 201–203, 207, 211, 217–219, 230–231; 233, 240–244, 246–247.

78. Ibid., 108–111, 113–116, 123, 124, 130–133, 178–179, 232.

79. Ibid., 131, 143, 274–276. The italics are Burnham's.

80. Ibid., 153–155, 159–164.

81. Ibid., 19, 275.

82. Hook, *NR,* 39 (September 11, 1987): 33; Burnham, *The Coming Defeat of Communism,* 274, 276–278.

83. Burnham, *The Coming Defeat of Communism,* 276.

84. On businessmen, ibid., 253–257, 266–268, 270. On labor, ibid., 79–80.

85. Ibid., 252.

86. Ibid., 277; Burnham to Hook, December 3, 1948, and January 11, 1949, SH, Box 8.

87. For Burnham's defense of his record as a prophet, see Harvey Breit, "Talk with James Burnham," *NYT,* February 26, 1950. Charles J. Rolo, review of *The Coming Defeat of Communism,* by James Burnham, *A* 15 (March 1950): 176: Arthur Krock to George F. Kennan, December 29, 1949, JB, Box 6. For a sample of reviews, see Harry W. Baehr, "Mr. Burnham Suggests an Offensive," *NYHT,* February 19, 1950 (mostly favorable); Waldemar Gurian, *TC* 51 (March 17, 1950): 610–612 (mostly favorable); George S. Pettee, *The American Political Science Review* (hereafter, *APSR*) 44 (September 1950): 748–751 (mostly favorable); Louis Fischer, "Offensive Political-Subversive War," *SRL* 33 (February 25, 1950): 11–12 (mostly unfavorable); James Reston, "A Charter for Taming the Russians," *NYT,* February 19, 1950 (mostly unfavorable); David Spitz, "Burnham's War on the Soviets," *TNR* 122 (March 20, 1950): 18–19 (highly unfavorable). David Carpenter, "James Burnham's Fantastic but Dangerous Anti-Soviet Tirade," *The Daily Worker* (hereafter, *DW*), March 1, 1950 (utterly damning).

88. Letters from William C. Bullitt, H. V. Kaltenborn et al. to James Burnham, JB, Box 2; Shachtman, COHO, 344.

89. Max Eastman to James Burnham, July 15, 1950, JB, Box 6; Paul Palmer to Max Eastman, August 16, 1950, JB, Box 6. Chapters of *The Coming Defeat of Communism* published in modified form in magazines include: James Burnham, "Our Spineless Foreign Policy," *The American Mercury* (hereafter, *AM*) 70 (January 1950): 3–13; ibid., "What Can We Expect of Europe?" *AM* 70 (February 1950): 131–142; ibid., "The Nature of Modern War," *TC* 51 (February 10, 1950): 480–483; and ibid., *NYHT. This Week,* February 19, 1950. See also ibid., "What Is the Purpose of the United Nations?" *AAAPSS* 252 (July 1947): 1–10, and ibid., "How the United Nations Can Be Made to Work," *RD* 52 (January 1948): 81–86.

90. Burnham's papers contain a clipping of the article "Burnham vs. Kennan," but neither the name of the paper nor the date of the article is given. The paper is probably *The Washington Post*. Townsend Hoopes, *The Devil and John Foster Dulles* (Boston: Little, Brown, and Co., 1973), 118; Diggins, *Up from Communism,* 12, 386; George H. Nash, *The Conservative Intellectual Movement in America* (New York: Basic Books, 1976), 91, 97; Sidney Blumenthal, "The Conservative Crackup," *Foreign Policy,* no. 69 (Winter 1987–1988): 169. Breit, "Talk with James Burnham," *NYT,* February 26, 1950.

91. James Burnham, "Art and Man's Fate," *F* 4 (November 30, 1953): 171.

CHAPTER SEVEN

1. Burnham to Hook, January 11, 1949, SH, Box 8.

2. James B. Burnham to author, June 18, 1992; Joseph Bryan III, to James Burnham, December 12, 1947, JB Box 5.

3. Bryan to Burnham, n.d. 1949, JB, Box 5.

4. William M. Leary, ed. *The Central Intelligence Agency: History and Documents* (University, Alabama: University of Alabama Press, 1984), 131–133.

5. For information on Frank Wisner, see Edward Colby, *Honorable Men: My Life in the CIA* (New York: Simon and Schuster, 1978); Burton Hersh, *The Old Boys: The American Elite and the Origins of the CIA* (New York: Charles Scribner's Sons, 1992); G. J. A. O'Toole, *The Encyclopedia of American Intelligence and Espionage* (New York, 1988); and Thomas Powers, *The Man Who Kept the Secrets: Richard Helms and the CIA* (New York: Alfred A. Knopf, 1979).

6. Colby, *Honorable Men,* 77, 80, 87; Hersh, *The Old Boys,* 229; Powers, *The Man Who Kept the Secrets,* 37, 39, 48–49.

7. Fugitt to author, October 3, 1991; Gregory Treverton, *Covert Action: The Limits of Intervention in the Postwar World* (New York: Basic Books, 1987), 40; John Ranelagh, *The Agency: The Rise and Decline of the CIA* (New York: Simon and Schuster, 1986), 218.

8. E. Howard Hunt, *Undercover: Memoirs of an American Secret Agent* (New York: Berkeley, 1974), 67–68; Powers, *The Man Who Kept the Secrets,* 39–40; Christopher Simpson, *Blowback: America's Recruitment of Nazis and Its Effects on the Cold War* (New York: Weidenfeld and Nicolson, 1988), 171–174; Ranelagh, *The Agency,* 226; Colby, *Honorable Men,* 82–84. On the Albanian operation, Hersh, *The Old Boys,* 271; Simpson, *Blowback,* 124; Powers, *The Man Who Kept the Secrets,* 44–47; Jelavich, *History of the Balkans,* 2: 378–379.

9. Bryan to Burnham, n.d. (but written between January and March) 1949, JB, Box 5.

10. Bryan to Burnham, June 30, 1949; Frederick W. Williams to James Burnham, July 21, 1949; Bryan to Burnham, August 2, 1949, JB, Box 5.

11. Warren G. Fugitt thought Burnham "impatient" and eager for action, and speculated that he had grown dissatisfied with merely writing against communism and wanted to pursue his anticommunist effort more directly. Fugitt confirmed Burnham's admiration for Czapski as a cultivated, anticommunist man of action. Fugitt to author, October 3, 1991. Talking with Burnham soon after the latter's 1948 meeting with Malraux, William Barrett concluded that Burnham "dreamed of some such independent intellectual position of power as [Malraux] commanded." Barrett, *The Truants,* 86.

12. On moral seriousness: Burnham refused, for example, any involvement with organizations that did not exclude loyal citizens of communist countries, JB, Box 10. "Emergency" seems to be the word Burnham used to describe the situation he thought the United States faced when he wrote to NYU's Dean Thomas Clark Pollock in 1949 to request further leave. In a letter of 1951 to Burnham, in which he referred to Burnham's request, Pollock recalled that Burnham had cited an "emergency" as the reason for the request. Dean Thomas Pollock to James Burnham, January 23, 1951, JB, Box 1.

13. James Burnham file. Department of Justice. An FBI memorandum (whose addressee and date are illegible) states that the FBI has not investigated Burnham, but that another agency has done so.

14. Application for Federal Employment. Personal History Statement, JB, Box 1.

15. See note 10.

16. Pollock to Burnham, January 23, 1951, JB, Box 1.

17. Breit, "Talk with James Burnham," *NYT,* February 26, 1950; James Reston, "A Charter for Taming the Russians," *NYT,* February 19, 1950; James B. Burnham to author, June 18, 1992. For "Hamburn," see, e.g., International Association for Cultural Freedom Papers (hereafter, IACF), Series II, Box 48, Regenstein Library, University of Chicago. For "Hambley," see James Burnham, unsigned, unaddressed OPC memorandum, September 17, 1950, on travel expenses, JB, Box 11. Warren G. Fugitt remembers "Hambley." Fugitt to author, October 3, 1991.

18. Hunt, *Undercover,* 66.

19. James Burnham to DeWitt Wallace, undated but probably 1950 or 1951. JB, Box 2. Hunt, *Undercover,* 69; James Burnham unsigned, unaddressed OPC memoranda, November 16, 1949, November 22, 1949, December 12, 1950; ibid., unsigned memorandum to Joseph Bryan III, November 1, 1950, JB, Box 11. James B. Burnham to author, June 18, 1992.

20. Fugitt to author, October 3, 1991. James Burnham to Dr. Arthur Arzt, April 11, 1950; ibid. to Arzt, June 13, 1950; Arzt to Burnham, June 22, 1950; ibid. to Burnham, November 7, 1950; Burnham to Arzt, February 28, 1951, JB, Box 5; ibid., unsigned, to John Baker, September 15, 1950, JB, Box 11; ibid. to Czapski, April 10, 1950; ibid., May 22, 1950. See also an undated memorandum by Burnham headed "A Breach of Security," which records that in the spring of 1950 the OPC began subsidizing *Kultura,* and that this relationship was to be kept secret. JB, Box 9. On *The New Leader,* James Burnham, unsigned, unaddressed OPC memoranda, November 21, 1949, January 12, 1950, February 20, 1950, JB, Box 11.

21. James Burnham to Vladimir Gorachek of Possev, May 22, 1951; Possev to Burnham, June 2, 1951; Eugene Romanov to James Burnham, October 20, 1951, JB, Box 2; James Burnham to Chou Hsiang-kuang, August 15, 1951; ibid., December 6, 1951, JB, Box 6.

22. James Burnham, "The Development of the Anti-Communist Exile and Resistance Movements," typescript, n.d., ibid., "The Russian 'Solidarist Movement' (NTS) and Its Program Announced in 'Look' Magazine of Oct. 26, 1948," typescript, n.d.; ibid. to V. Poremsky, April 25, 1952, JB, Box 2; ibid., "The Strategy of the Politburo and the Problem of American Counter Strategy," typescript, October 1950, JB, Box 11. The italics are Burnham's. Dobriansky to author, September 17, 1992.

23. Mary McGrory, "Reading and Writing," *Washington Post* (hereafter, *WP*) February 19, 1950; Jozéf Czapski to James Burnham, June 1, 1950, JB, Box 9. Raymond Aron, *Mémoires* (Paris: Julliard, 1983) 1: 335; James Burnham, unsigned, unaddressed OPC memorandum on Raymond Aron, JB, Box 11; James B. Burnham, "Father, Friend," *NR* 39 (September 11, 1987): 50.

24. James Burnham to Arthur Koestler, September 14, 1950, JB, Box 6; Dobriansky to author, September 17, 1992. Burnham's writings include, e.g., "Forrestal and National Security," *NL* 34 (November 26, 1951): 20–21; ibid., contribution to the symposium "Our Country and Our Culture," *PR* 19 (1952): 289–291; ibid., "The Humanities and the Law," *New York University Law Review* 27 (January 1952): 67–69; ibid., "The Philosophy of Communism," *Naval War College Review* (March 1952): 57–79; ibid., "The People at the Polls," *AM* 75 (August 1952): 104–107; ibid., "How Long Will the Cold War Last?" *Banking* (September 1952): 35ff.; ibid., "An Examination of Gaylord Babbitt," *NYT,* March 15, 1953; ibid., "What Will Happen to the Jews behind the Iron Curtain?" *The National Jewish Monthly* 67 (April 1953): 288ff.

25. Marcia Burnham to François Bondy, October 1, 1950, IACF, series II, Box 48; Dobriansky to author, September 17, 1992.

26. In one such case, the British poet Stephen Spender, a communist in the mid-1930s, fell afoul of the McCarran Act. Irving Kristol, then coeditor with Spender of the recently founded journal *Encounter,* turned to Burnham for help. Irving Kristol to James Burnham, January 8, 1953, JB, Box 8. Spender did get into the United States, though whether a push by Burnham did the trick is hard to say. On Czeslaw Milosz, James Burnham to Francis Hand, November 26, 1951, JB, Box 11; ibid. to Charles Sternberg of the International Rescue and Relief Committee, February 16, 1953. My thanks to Charles Sternberg for a copy of this letter. On using McCarthy against McCarran, Fugitt to author, October 3, 1991.

27. James Burnham, unsigned, unaddressed OPC memorandum, February 15, 1951, JB, Box 11; Warren G. Fugitt to James Burnham, March 23, 1983, JB, Box 9; Fugitt to author, October 3, 1991.

28. Hook, *Out of Step,* 384–395; Nicolas Nabokov, *Bagazh: Memoirs of a Russian Cosmoplitan* (New York: Athenaeum, 1975), 236–238.

29. On Melvin Lasky and Michael Josselson, see Alexander Bloom, *Prodigal Sons: The New York Intellectuals and Their World* (New York: Oxford University Press, 1986), 261–262; Gary Dorrien, *The Neoconservative Mind: Politics, Culture, and the War of Ideology* (Philadelphia: Temple University Press, 1993), 79–80; Peter Coleman, *The Liberal Conspiracy: The Congress for Cultural Freedom and the Mind of Postwar Europe* (New York: The Free Press, 1989), 40–41.

30. Josselson quoted in Coleman, *The Liberal Conspiracy,* 6.

31. Hook, *Out of Step,* 397. Hook remembered Rousset's event as "The International Day of Resistance against War and Fascism"; on Burnham as "too anti-Communist," Coleman, *The Liberal Conspiracy,* 7; for Hook's statement to the press, *NYT,* April 21, 1949.

32. Coleman, *The Liberal Conspiracy,* 7, 15–16; Hook, *Out of Step,* 432.

33. Melvin Lasky to James Burnham, January 24, 1950; "Hook Report on Paris April 30th Congress," November 15, 1949, JB, Box 11; Fugitt to author, October 3, 1991. For Burnham as source of funds, see, e.g., receipt dated June 9, 1959 and signed by Arnold Beichman reading, "Received from James Burnham Five Hundred (500) dollars for Congress for Cultural Freedom," JB, Box 8; Hook on Burnham as "eminence grise," SH, Box 185.

34. James Burnham to François Bondy, February 8, 1951, JB, Box 8; ibid. to Koestler, April 10, 1950, JB, Box 6.

35. Burnham quoted in Koestler's diary, Hamilton, *Koestler,* 177; on conference planning, undated (but probably May 4, 1950) memorandum by Aron, Burnham, and Koestler, JB, Box 8.

36. Mamaine Koestler, *Living with Koestler: Mamaine Koestler's Letters 1945–1951,* ed. Cecilia Goodman (New York, 1985), 137–138.

37. James Burnham, unsigned, unaddressed OPC memborandum, May 17, 1950, JB, Box 11.

38. James Burnham to Arno Siedel, August 11, 1950, JB, Box 5.

39. Hook, *Out of Step,* 432–434; Arthur Koestler, *The Trail of the Dinosaur* (London: Macmillan, 1970), 112; Papers of the American Committee for Cultural Freedom (hereafter ACCF), Tamiment Library, New York University, Box 1; Coleman, *The Liberal Conspiracy,* 21; Jacobs to author, December 27, 1990; Mamaine Koestler, *Living with Koestler,* 142. On Irving Brown, Hersh, *The Old Boys,* 238–239, 444.

40. James Burnham, "Rhetoric and Peace," *PR* 17 (1950): 861–871. The italics are Burnham's. James Burnham to Julian Amery, May 26, 1950, JB, Box 6.

41. Jacobs (who also passes on Hook's comment) to author, December 27, 1990.

42. James Burnham to Philip Rahv, October 4, 1950, PR; Burnham quoted in Hamilton, *Koestler,* 197.

43. For the Manifesto, Koestler, *The Trail of the Dinosaur,* 112–115; Mamaine Koestler, *Living with Koestler,* 145.

44. James Burnham, "Work to Be Done" undated memorandum, JB, Box 8; François Bondy's notes on a talk between Burnham, Koestler, et al. July 18, 1950, at Fontaine-le-Port (i.e., Verte Rive), IACF, Series II, Box 2. For Czapski's idea, see Lasky's notes on the Congress, IACF, Series III, Box 1; Mamaine Koestler, *Living with Koestler,* 148, 151.

45. James Burnham, unsigned, unaddressed OPC memorandum on July 21, 1950, talk with Charles de Gaulle, August 16, 1950, JB, Box 11.

46. Unsigned letter (perhaps from François Bondy) to James Burnham, October 24, 1950, on the Brussels meeting, IACF, Series II, Box 48; Burnham to Bondy, October 27, 1950, ibid.; on denouncing the Partisans for Peace conference, CCF press release, November 23, 1950, ACCF, Box 1; on Czapski's project, IACF, Series III, Box 1a; Coleman, *The Liberal Conspiracy,* 50–51.

47. James Burnham, unsigned, unaddressed OPC memorandum, August 16, 1950, JB, Box 11;

ibid. quoted in Hamilton, *Koestler,* 199–220; James Burnham to German Arceniegas, September 14, 1950, JB, Box 8; ibid. to Sylvain Troeder, February 7, 1951, JB, Box 7.

48. Coleman, *The Liberal Conspiracy,* 46–47, 220; Cf. William Phillips: the CIA circa 1950 "was an elitist outfit, staffed largely by academics, and...[with] a strong liberal-leftish wing. In fact, it was this wing that initiated the creation of the Congress and its journals," believing that only leftists could offer effective resistance to communism. "Comment. 'The Liberal Conspiracy,'" *PR* 57 (Winter 1990): 9. Thomas W. Braden, "I'm Glad the CIA Is 'Immoral,'" *The Saturday Evening Post* 240 (May 20, 1967): 10–14.

49. Burnham to Beichman, October 26, 1950, JB, Box 8.

50. Nicolas Nabokov to James Burnham, January 21, 1951, JB, Box 8. In his memoirs, Hook says that by early 1951 he had heard, "like almost everyone else, that in some way the CIA was involved in funding the congress. Everyone mentioned it, even though no one had any hard evidence." After a time, he goes on, he had "no doubt" of CIA financing, "but I was never privy to the amount or to the mechanism of its operation." Hook, *Out of Step,* 450–451; James Burnham, OPC memorandum of July 4, 1951, JB, Box 11.

51. On the Fairfield Foundation, ACCF, Box 6; on Fleishman's denials, Stephen Spender, *The Thirties and After: Poetry, Politics, People 1933–1975* (London: Macmillan, 1978), 163.

52. Pollock to Burnham, January 23, 1951, JB, Box 1; James Burnham to Dean Thomas Pollock, May 1, 1953, JB, Box 1.

53. Louis Dobos-Gibarti to James Burnham, November 2, 1950, JB, Box 6.

54. James Burnham to Daniel Apert of the CCF's International Executive Committee staff, January 19, 1951, JB, Box 5; James Burnham to Denis de Rougemont, January 29, 1951, JB, Box 8; James Burnham to Nicolas Nabokov, January 30, 1951, JB, Box 8.

55. Koestler to Burnham, August 1950, JB, Box 6; Coleman, *The Liberal Conspiracy,* 33–34. Koestler to Burnham, January 29, 1951, JB, Box 8; Burnham to Koestler, February 8, 1951, JB, Box 8. Ibid., unsigned, unaddressed OPC memorandum "Arthur Koestler," May 31, 1951, JB, Box 11. On Koestler's abrasive personality: Hook once remarked that Koestler could not recite the multiplication tables without driving someone into a rage. Coleman, *The Liberal Conspiracy,* 33–34. Nor was Koestler much drawn to Hook. "I really have nothing against him except that he gets on my nerves," he told Burnham, adding, "which is my fault, not his." Koestler to Burnham, October 15, 1949, JB, Box 6.

56. James Burnham, unsigned memorandum, January 22, 1951, JB, Box 8; Burnham to Bondy, February 6, 1951, Box 8; Bondy to Burnham, February 16, 1951, JB, Box 8; Denis de Rougemont to James Burnham, February 24, 1951, Box 6; Burnham to Bondy, February 26, 1951, JB, Box 8.

57. Burnham to Nabokov, June 1, 1951, IACF, Series II, Box 48; Nabokov to Burnham, June 6, 1951, JB, Box 8.

58. Nabokov to Burnham, June 27, 1951, JB, Box 8; Burnham to Nabokov, June 16, 1951, IACF, Series II, Box 48; ibid., July 10, 1951, JB, Box 8; James Burnham, unsigned, unaddressed OPC memorandum headed "An International Arts Festival," June 4, 1951, JB, Box 11.

59. James Burnham, unsigned, unaddressed OPC memorandum headed "PARIS ARTS FESTIVAL," October 31, 1951, JB, Box 11; ibid., unsigned, unaddressed OPC memorandum on the funding of the Arts Festival, August 15, 1951, JB, Box 11; ibid., unsigned, unaddressed OPC memorandum headed "Transfer of Money to PARIS ARTS FESTIVAL,"

December 10, 1951, JB, Box 11; ibid., unsigned, unaddressed OPC memorandum headed "American Committee for Cultural Freedom," October 29, 1951, JB, Box 11.

60. Minoo Masani. *Against the Tide* (New Delhi:Vikas, 1981), 53, 60–61.

61. Burnham to Masani, January 10, 1951, JB, Box 7; ibid. to Koestler, February 8, 1951, JB, Box 6; ibid., unsigned, unaddressed OPC memorandum concerning the January 31, 1951, meeting of the executive committee of the American Committee for Cultural Freedom, JB, Box 11; Indian Congress for Cultural Freedom to James Burnham, JB, Box 8; James Burnham, unsigned, unaddressed OPC memorandum, January 12, 1951, JB, Box 11; Fugitt to author, October 3, 1991.

62. James Burnham's address to the Indian Congress of Cultural Freedom, Bombay, March 28–31, 1951, JB, Box 2.

63. On Auden, Fugitt to author, October 7, 1991.

64. James Burnham, "Parakeets and Parchesi: An Indian Memorandum," *PR* 18 (1951): 560.

65. Burnham to the International Secretariat of the Congress for Cultural Freedom, June 1, 1951, JB, Box 8.

66. Burnham, "Parakeets and Parchesi," 559–561.

67. Ibid., "A Yankee at Nehru's Court," *F* 4 (March 8, 1954): 425.

68. J. R. D. Tata to James Burnham, January 5, 1952, JB, Box 7; the editors, *Thought,* November 2, 1951, IACF, Series II, Box 48; Arthur Schlesinger, Jr., to James Burnham, October 5, 1951, JB, Box 7.

69. Hook, *Out of Step,* 420–423.

70. Ibid., 425–426; on Fairfield Foundation contributions, Sidney Hook to John F. Dailey, Jr., a member of Fairfield's board of directors, June 25, 1952, ACCF, Box 6; for Pearl Kluger's lists of expenses to Burnham, JB, Box 8. See also James Burnham, unsigned, unaddressed OPC memorandum, July 26, 1951, on the ACCF's financial situation, JB, Box 11. In his memoirs, Hook says that rumors identifying Fairfield as a CIA money conduit led him to raise the issue in 1955 with its chairman, Julius Fleischmann, only to have Fleischmann reply that the ACCF could avoid embarrassment quite easily: all it had to do was refuse any money from the foundation. This the ACCF eventually did. *Out of Step,* 426. According to historian Mary S. McAuliffe, the ACCF got no money from the Fairfield Foundation until 1955. Mary McAuliffe, *Crisis on the Left: Cold War Politics and American Liberals, 1947–1954* Amherst, Mass. (University of Massachusetts Press, 1978), 121. But Hook's letter of June 26, 1952, to John F. Dailey, Jr., cited above, suggests otherwise. On the ACCF's "elegant office," Jeanne Wacker, then an NYU graduate student and a secretary at the ACCF office, to author, May 19, 1993.

71. Burnham to Hook, October 20, 1950, JB, Box 6. Examples of Burnham's recommendations to Hook et al. can be found in JB, Box 8. In a letter of May 23, 1991, to the author, Daniel Bell, who was an active member of the ACCF, wrote that Burnham "was not at all involved in the activities of the American Committee." Bell may be remembering Burnham's virtual withdrawal in 1952, a prelude to his resignation from the ACCF in 1954.

72. Minutes, ACCF Executive Committee Meeting, June 6, 1951, ACCF, Box 7; on Mishima, Burnham memorandum of December 12, 1951, JB, Box 8.

73. Burnham to Czapski, March 5, 1951, JB, Box 9; ibid. to Nabokov, June 1, 1951, IACF,

Series II, Box 48; ibid., June 15, 1951, IACF, Series II, Box 48; ibid. To Czapski, July 9, 1951, JB, Box 9.

74. *NYT,* July 23, 1951.

75. James Burnham to Levering Tyson, August 17, 1951, JB, Box 9.

76. Ibid., unsigned, unaddressed OPC memorandum, November 29, 1951, JB, Box 11.

77. James Burnham to Adolf A. Berle, January 23, 1952; ibid., February 8, 1952, JB, Box 9. The italics are Burnham's. Ibid. to Czapski, February 12, 1952, JB, Box 9.

78. Ibid. to Tyson, February 27, 1951, JB, Box 9.

79. C. D. Jackson to Levering Tyson, September 20, 1951, JB, Box 9.

80. Minutes of the annual meeting of the Assembly of the Association of the Free Europe University in Exile ("College de l'Europe Libre") (apparent date, 1951), IACF, Series II, Box 29; James Burnham, "How Democratic Is America?" (typescript, n.d., but probably from the late 1960s), 11–12, JB, Box 1.

81. James Burnham, "The Third World War [Burnham's *NR* column—hereafter, "TWW"]," *NR* 2 (May 30, 1956): 12; ibid., *Containment or Liberation?* (The John Day Co., 1953), 197.

82. James Burnham, "Democracy, Oligarchy, and Freedom" (typescript of a lecture delivered at the Aspen Institute July 15, 1952), JB, Box 3. Cf. Alexis de Tocqueville, *Democracy in America,* ed, J. P. Mayer, trans. George Lawrence (New York: Harper Collins, 1988); 690–695.

83. On polwar as "the best way" to defeat communism, Burnham typescript, untitled, n.d., but probably 1950 or 1951, JB, Box 2. Ibid., "Can the United States Conduct Effective Political Warfare Against the Soviet Union?" typescript, n.d., but probably 1953, 5–9, JB, Box 2. The italics are Burnham's.

84. Ibid., *Containment or Liberation?,* 35, 41, 43, 47–48, 251.

85. Ibid., 83–84, 111–112, 128–132, 138–139, 252. The italics are Burnham's.

86. Ibid., 147–152, 183, 220–228.

87. Ibid., 122–123, 251.

88. Ibid., 186–188, 191–192, 196.

89. Ibid., 201–202.

90. Ibid., 202–203, 208.

91. Ibid., 203–206.

92. Ibid., 213–214.

93. Ibid., 179, 254.

94. Burnham rightly called himself an "ardent crusader" in the cause of political warfare. James Burnham to Paul Palmer, July 6, 1951, JB, Box 2.

95. *Foreign Affairs* (hereafter, *FA*) 31 (July 1953): 675; Robert Strausz-Hupé, review of *Containment or Liberation?* by James Burnham, *AAAPSS* 288 (July 1953): 154–156; see also William Henry Chamberlain, review of *Containment or Liberation?* by James Burnham, *Chicago Sunday Tribune Magazine of Books* (hereafter, *CST*), March 1, 1953.

96. William H. Hessler, "The Oversimplifications of James Burnham," *The Reporter* (hereafter, *R*) 8 (March 31, 1953): 37; Richard H. Rovere, review of *Containment or Liberation?* by James Burnham, *United Nations World* (hereafter, *UNW*) 7 (May 1953): 48. For other adverse reactions, see Gordon A. Craig, "A Program by Mr. Burnham," *NYHT,* March 1, 1953, and Charles Rolo, review of *Containment or Liberation?* by James Burnham, *A* 191 (April 1953): 82–84.

97. Readers' letters on *Containment or Liberation?* JB, Box 3. Charles de Gaulle to James Burnham, June 19, 1953, ibid., Box 6; Martin Walker, *The Cold War: A History* (New York: Henry Holt and Co., 1995), 102.

98. George F. Kennan, *Memoirs* (Boston: Little, Brown, 1972) 2: 100.

99. James Burnham to James B. Burnham, November 19, 1961. My thanks to James B. Burnham for a copy of this letter.

100. Ibid.

101. Ibid., February 19, 1966. My thanks to James B. Burnham for a copy of this letter.

102. Burnham, *Suicide of the West,* 260.

103. Ludwell Lee Montague, *General Walter Bedell Smith as Director of Central Intelligence, October 1950–February 1953* (University Park, Penn.: The Pennsylvania State University Press, 1992), 204, 213.

## Chapter Eight

1. Karl Hess to author, May 27, 1993.

2. Ralph de Toledano to author, May [n.d.] 1993. See also Ralph Robert Toledano, "Professor Burnham, Mafioso Costello, and Me," *Chronicles* 18 (October 1944): 44–45.

3. Toledano to author, May [n.d.] 1993.

4. Burnham to Czapski, April 8, 1952, JB, Box 8; Earl Latham, *The Communist Controversy in Washington: From the New Deal to McCarthy* (Cambridge, Mass.: Harvard University Press, 1966), 296–316; O'Neill, *A Better World,* 269; Nash, *The Conservative Intellectual Movement in America,* 107. James Burnham to Peter Ehlers, March 30, 1950, JB, Box 8; James B. Burnham to author, June 18, 1992.

5. James Burnham to Nathaniel Weyl, May 12, 1966, JB, Box 7.

6. James Burnham, "How the IPR Helped Stalin Seize China," *F* 2 (June 1955): 647–653.

7. Ibid. to Ehlers, March 30, 1950, JB, Box 8.

8. Ibid., "Editor Meets Senator," *F* 3 (June 15, 1953): 661–662.

9. Ibid. to Christopher Emmet, July 17, 1954, Christoper Emmet Papers (hereafter, CE), The Hoover Institution, 65.

10. Burnham to Hook, August 18, 1954, SH, Box 142. The italics are Burnham's.

11. Hook, *Out of Step,* 422.

12. E.g., the ACCF meeting of March 1, 1952, which debated McCarthyism. IACF, series II, Box 29; on the Waldorf forum, Hook, *Out of Step,* 427, and O'Neill, *A Better World,* 298.

13. James Burnham, typescript, March 30, 1952, JB, Box 1.

14. Minutes, ACCF executive committee Meeting of April 12, 1952, ACCF, Box 7.

15. Burnham, "Can the United States Conduct Effective Political Warfare against the Soviet Union?" 7; John B. Judis, *Grand Illusion: Critics and Champions of the American Century* (New York: Farrar, Strauss & Giroux, 1992), 171.

16. James Burnham, "The Case against Adlai Stevenson," *AM* 75 (October 1952): 12, 16–19.

17. Arthur Schlesinger, Jr., to Sidney Hook, October 1, 1952, SH, Box 53; Hook to Burnham, October 6, 1952, JB, Box 3; James Burnham [n.d.] to *AM,* JB, Box JB, Box 3.

18. Arthur Schlesinger, Jr., letter to *AM* 75 (December 1952): 64; Burnham's reply to Schlesinger, ibid., 65–65.

19. Arthur Schlesinger, Jr., "Middle-Aged Man with a Horn," *TNR* 128 (March 16, 1953): 16.

20. Irving Kristol to Arthur S. Schlesinger, Jr., January 1, 1953, ACCF, Box 4; Minutes, ACCF executive committee meeting of May 5, 1953, ACCF, Box 7.

21. Miles Copeland, *NR* 39 (September 11, 1987): 37; Fugitt to author, October 3, 1991.

22. James Burnham, "After Stalin What?" *F* 3 (March 23, 1953): 439–440.

23. Ibid., "Positive Political Warfare," a review of *The Ultimate Political Weapon,* by Oleg Anisimov, *F* 3 (May 18, 1953): 604–605.

24. Burnham to James B. Burnham, November 19, 1961. The italics are James Burnham's.

25. Powers, *The Man Who Kept the Secrets,* 45–46, Mickelson, *America's Other Voice,* 85–86. James Burnham, "Was Bohlen a Blunder?" *F* 3 (May 4, 1953): 551–554; Jeffrey Hart (long one of Burnham's fellow editors at *National Review*) to author, July 8, 1992; James Burnham memorandum to Howard Phillips on "Bureaucracy," December 13, 1949, JB, Box 11; ibid. to Joseph Bryan III, December 19, 1949, JB, Box 11.

26. Fugitt to author, October 3, 1991.

27. Hersh, *The Old Boys,* 326; Powers, *The Man Who Kept the Secrets,* 63.

28. John B. Judis, *William F. Buckley, Jr.: Patron Saint of the Conservatives* (New York: Simon and Schuster, 1988), 123.

29. Burnham to Pollock, May 1, 1953, JB, Box 1.

30. E. Howard Hunt to James Burnham, May 15, 1962, JB, Box 6. As things turned out, Burnham's resignation from the CIA did not mean an end to all contact with the Agency. He had made friends there as well as enemies, and stayed in touch with some of the former long after he left Washington. This may explain why in the future he sometimes possessed information that would have been at best difficult to obtain from other sources. Priscilla L. Buckley to author, March 31, 1992.

31. James Burnham to Francis P. McGuire, January 27, 1964, JB, Box 1. On the mas, Lucius and Jane Wilmerding to author, March 12, 1992; Priscilla L. Buckley to author, March 31, 1992; Lightner to author, May 25, 1993; Mary Effie Burnham to author, May 16, 1992; James B. Burnham to author, June 18, 1992; Crozier, "My Pilgrimage to Kent," 18.

32. Priscilla L. Buckley, *NR* 39 (September 11, 1987): 54; James B. Burnham, *NR* 39 (September 11, 1987): 51; author's observations during a 1992 visit to the Burnham house.

33. Bridges to author, January 8, 1992; Priscilla L. Buckley to author, March 31, 1992; WFB, Box 105; James Burnham, "TWW. Oh Hateful Love, Oh Loving Hate," *NR* 18 (April 19, 1966): 353; Lightner to author, May 25, 1993; Lucius and Jane Wilmerding to author, March 12, 1992.

34. Mary Effie Burnham to author, May 16, 1992; James B. Burnham, *NR* 39 (September 11, 1987): 51.

35. Priscilla L. Buckley to author, March 31, 1992; Mary Effie Burnham to author, May 16, 1992; James B. Burnham to author, June 18, 1992; Lightner to author, May 25, 1993; Burnham to Buckley, March 14, 1976, WFB, Box 105.

36. Bridges to author, January 8, 1992; Christopher Buckley, "Happy Birthday to Us," *NR* 22 (December 5, 1975): 1373; Burnham to Buckley, March 14, 1976, WFB, Box 105; Mary Effie Burnham to author, May 16, 1992; Crozier, "My Pilgrimage to Kent," 18.

37. Priscilla L. Buckley to author, July 24, 1992; Bridges to author, January 8, 1992; Mary Effie Burnham to author, May 16, 1992; Philip Roth to author, December 3, 1991; Jane Wilmerding to author, March 12, 1992.

38. Bridges to author, January 8, 1992.

39. Hook to Feuer, March 16, 1981, SH, Box 115; Burnham to Hook, August 18, 1954, SH, 142; ibid., September 15, 1954.

40. Burnham, ed. *What Europe Thinks of America,* viii.

41. James Burnham to the editors of *Partisan Review,* September 25, 1953, JB, Box 1; *PR* 20 (1953): 716–717. The italics are Burnham's.

42. James Burnham, Introduction to *The Secret War for the A-Bomb,* by Medgar Evans (Chicago: Regnery, 1953), xi–xii.

43. Edward A. Shils, "Conspiratorial Hallucinations," *The Bulletin of the Atomic Scientists* 10 (February 1954): 53–54.

44. Daniel Bell to Sidney Hook, November 23, 1953, ACCF, Box 3.

45. James Burnham to Sol Stein, December 8, 1953, ACCF, Box 14. The italics are Burnham's.

46. Minutes. ACCF executive committee meeting of December 12, 1953, ACCF, Box 7; Bell to Hook, November 23, 1953, ACCF, Box 3; David Riesman to Sol Stein, December 15, 1953, ACCF, Box 14; ibid., December 17, 1953. ACCF, Box 14; Sol Stein to David Riesman, December 23, 1953, ACCF, Box 14; Hook, *Out of Step,* 428–429.

47. James Burnham to Richard J. Walsh, September 6, 1953; ibid. to Benjamin Mandel, September 9, 1953, JB, Box 3.

48. James Burnham, *The Web of Subversion: Underground Networks in the U.S. Government* (New York: The John Day Co., 1954), acknowledgments. Paul Palmer to James Burnham, September 21, 1953, JB, Box 3.

49. Burnham, *The Web of Subversion,* 15–18, 29, 222.

50. Ibid., 169.

51. Ibid., 79–80, 110.

52. Ibid., 211, 220–221.

53. Ibid., 212, 218–219, 221.

54. Ibid., 222–227.

55. Ibid., 227–236. The italics are Burnham's.

56. "Dark Suspicion: Red A-Bombs inside the U.S.," *Newsweek* 43 (March 15, 1954): 110; Willard Edwards, "The Deadly Entanglements of Espionage and Subversion," *CST,* March 14, 1954; Erwin D. Canham, "Not Too Well Concealed and Not Too Clever," *NYT,* March 21, 1954; *NYT,* July 1, 1954.

57. Arthur M. Schlesinger, Jr., "Freedom's Enemies," *SR* 36 (March 20, 1954): 16–17; Robert Gorham Davis, "A Machiavellian Views Subversion," *NL* 37 (May 10, 1954): 17–18; James Burnham, letter to *NL,* 37 (July 26, 1954): 29.

58. James Burnham, "Letter from Spain," *F* 4 (March 22, 1954): 455, 456; ibid., "Letter from Spain: Smiles for Americans," *F* 4 (April 19, 1954): 529, 530; ibid., "Bureaucracy in Spain," *F* 4 (May 31, 1954): 629.

59. James Burnham to Henry Regnery, June 21, 1954, Henry Regnery Papers (hereafter HR), Hoover Institution, Box 11; ibid., February 14, 1955, HR, Box 11; Henry Regnery to James Burnham, June 2, 1954, HR, Box 11.

60. James Burnham, "Do Europeans Really Hate Us?" *This Week, NYHT,* August 29, 1954, 7, 31–32; ibid., "Letter from France: Food, Sports, Tourists," *F* 4 (June 28, 1954): 707–708.

61. Burnham to Eastman, March 14, 1955, Max Eastman Papers (hereafter, ME), Lily Library, Indiana University.

62. Burnham to Hook, July 8, 1954, SH, Box 8.

63. James Burnham to Robert Gorham Davis, September 15, 1954, ACCF, Box 3; Burnham to Regnery, February 14, 1955, HR, Box 11; Burnham to Eastman, September 28, 1954, ME; ibid., March 14, 1955, ME.

64. *NYT,* November 16, 1954.

65. James Burnham, "Tribunes of the People," *F* 5 (February 1955): 309–311; Ibid., "Tribunes of the People" (condensed version), *RD* 66 (February 1955): 59–64; Burnham to Regnery, February 14, 1955, HR, Box 11.

66. Ibid., "TWW. Re-legitimation," *NR* 3 (June 1, 1957): 518.

67. "Casualty" is William Barret's word. *The Truants,* 85; Burnham to Rahv and Phillips, July 24, 1954, PR.

68. Barrett, *The Truants,* 85–86; Rahv quoted in ibid., 195. cf. Lionel Trilling: "In the United States at this time [the early 1950s] liberalism is not only the dominant but even the sole intellectual tradition." *The Liberal Imagination* (Garden City, N.Y.: Doubleday, 1953), vii. In 1953 Burnham described one form of the kind of banishment he was soon to experience. "In our land also there is an *official* history, or what amounts almost to that," he wrote in October 1954. "Historians who deviate too far from its norm are not exiled or shot, but they seldom taste the grants of the great Foundations, nor do they sit in the endowed Chairs of the major universities. To them the State Department does not easily open its doors or files. Their road to a publisher is rocky, and in the leading book sections, though physically still immune, they will be spiritually drawn and quartered." "Rewriting History," *F* 4 (October 5, 1953): 27.

69. Diana Trilling to author, December 14, 1990.

70. Joseph Sobran, *NR* 39 (September 11, 1987): 47.

71. Crozier, "My Pilgrimage to Kent," 20; Burnham to Crozier, April 15, 1976, BC.

72. Nash, *The Conservative Intellectual Movement,* 118; Barrett, *The Truants,* 86.

73. Regnery to Burnham, April 7, 1953, HR; James Burnham, review of *A Program for Conservatives,* by Russell Kirk, *AAAPSS* 298 (March 1955): 216.

74. James Burnham [unsigned], "The Week" (hereafter, *TW*), *NR* 1 (March 28, 1956): 4.

75. Burnham, "No Firecrackers Allowed," 684–686. William F. Buckley Jr. to author, May 11, 1992.

76. James B. Burnham, *NR* 39 (September 11, 1987): 51; William F. Buckley Jr., "On the Right [hereafter, OTR]. Why Not ID?" *NR* 47 (August 28, 1995): 55.

77. James Burnham, "Observations on Kafka," *PR* 14 (1947): 193; ibid. [unsigned], "Pablo Picasso, RIP," *NR* 25 (April 4, 1973): 456.

78. Burnham, *The Coming Defeat of Communism,* 110.

79. Ibid., *The Case for De Gaulle,* 13.

80. Ibid., *The Coming Defeat of Communism,* 267.

81. Ibid. to Buckley, October 23, 1957, WFB, Box 2. The italics are Burnham's. John Judis, "Apocalypse Now and Then," *TNR* 197 (August 31, 1987): 35; Burnham to Crozier,

March 29, 1976, BC. The italics are Burnham's.

82. Russell Kirk to Kevin Smant, February 25, 1990. My thanks to Professor Smant, a biographer of Burnham, for providing me with a copy of this letter. F. Reid Buckley to James Burnham, April 7, 1969, JB, Box 3. "Actually, the major portion of my writing is morally neutral," Burnham told Buckley family biographer Charles Lam Markmann. Burnham to Markmann, March 30, 1972, JB, Box 5; see also Craig Schiller, *The (Guilty) Conscience of a Conservative* (New Rochelle, N.Y.: Arlington House, 1978), 67; and [unsigned], "James Burnham Celebrated," *NR* 35 (March 18, 1983): 300.

83. James Burnham, "The Protracted Conflict" (the new name Burnham gave his *National Review* column, which he had first called "The Third World War"; hereafter PC), "Panama or Taiwan?" *NR* 29 (September 16, 1977): 1043.

84. Cf. Samuel T. Francis, *NR* 39 (September 11, 1987), 38–39, see also Paul Gottfried and Thomas Fleming, *The Conservative Movement* (Boston, 1988), 69; Gary Dorrien, *The Neoconservative Mind: Politics, Culture, and the War of Ideology* (Philadelphia: Temple University Press, 1993), 15, 63; "the first of the neocons," Burnham's *NR* colleague Richard Brookhiser once called him. *NR* 49 (January 27, 1997): 20.

85. Burnham, *The Coming Defeat of Communism*, 169; Nash, *The Conservative Intellectual Movement in America*, 141–142.

86. Burnham to Eastman, June 2, 1953, ME; Burnham to Regnery, May 19, 1953, HR, Box 11.

87. Burnham to Regnery, June 21, 1954, HR, Box 11; Burnham to Hook, August 18, 1954, Box 142.

88. Regnery to Burnham, August 3, 1954, HR, Box 11; Burnham to Regnery, August 10, 1954, HR, Box 11.

## CHAPTER NINE

1. Buckley to author, January 20, 1992; James Burnham to James V. Selzer, JB, Box 5.

2. Hunt, *Undercover*, 77.

3. Buckley to Burnham, n.d. (but probably 1957), JB, Box 5.

4. John Chamberlain, *A Life with the Printed Word* (Chicago: Regnery-Gateway, 1982), 67, 90–91, 141.

5. Ibid., 145–147.

6. Buckley to author, January 20, 1992.

7. William F. Buckley Jr., "Notes and Asides," *NR* (March 3, 1992): 20.

8. Burnham to Buckley, November 27, 1954, WFB, Box 1.

9. Garry Wills, *Confessions of a Conservative* (Garden City, New York: Doubleday, 1979), 35.

10. Burnham to Buckley, November 27, 1954, WFB, Box 1; ibid. to Buckley, May 17, 1955, WFB, Box 1; ibid. to Buckley, July 5, 1955, Box 1; *NYT*, October 14, 1955.

11. Burnham to Buckley, January 3, 1955, WFB, Box 1; the Orlando Committee to James Burnham, November 11, 1954, JB, Box 8; Burnham to Buckley, July 30, 1955, WFB, Box 1; ibid. to Buckley, May 30, 1955, WFB, Box 1; ibid. to Buckley, July 5, 1955, WFB, Box 1; ibid. to Buckley, July 27, 1955, WFB, Box 1; Buckley to author, January 20, 1992.

12. Burnham to Buckley, September 23, 1954, WFB, Box 1; ibid. to Buckley, November 29,

1954, WFB, Box 1.

13. Ibid. to Buckley, September 18, 1955, WFB, Box 1.

14. *NYT,* June 24, 1955; ibid., July 17, 1955; Glotzer to author, September 20, 1990.

15. *NYT,* June 24, 1955; ibid., July 17, 1955; Shachtman, COHO, 345–346; Albert to author, September 20, 1990; Burnham, *Personal History Statement,* JB, Box 1.

16. Department of Justice, *In the Matter of the Designation of Workers Party, Independent Socialist League, Socialist Youth League Pursuant to Executive Order Number 10450: Proposed Findings of Fact,* 27–29; Glotzer to author, September 20, 1990.

17. Joseph L. Rauh, Jr., to author, June 18, 1991; James Burnham to John P. Diggins, October 24, n.d. (but probably 1975), John P. Diggins Folder (hereafter, JPD) containing letters to Diggins from James Burnham and Sidney Hook, The Hoover Institution; John P. Diggins to James Burnham, September 7, 1975, JB, Box 8; Yetta Shachtman to author, September 10, 1990.

18. Curiously, many *National Review* editors, among them Willmoore Kendall, Russell Kirk, L. Brent Bozell, Jeffrey Hart, and Frank Meyer, were converts to Catholicism.

19. *NR* 1 (November 19, 1955): 6; James Burnham, "PC: The Second Generation," *NR* 15 (April 21, 1970): 400; Ibid., "TWW: Mideastern Irrelevancies," *NR* 6 (August 30, 1958): 156.

20. James Burnham, "Laid on the Line," *NR* 8 (January 2, 1960): 17.

21. Ibid., "TWW: The Main Line," *NR* 7 (November 7, 1959): 452; ibid., "TWW: Is Fidel Castro a Communist?" *NR* 7 (August 15, 1959): 268; ibid. (unsigned), "Trials of the UN," *National Review Bulletin* (hereafter, *NRB*) 12 (May 29, 1962): 4.

22. *NR* 1 (December 28, 1955): back cover. "At times, Burnham seemed to take pleasure in staring into the abyss, so much so that readers accused him of admiring his enemies," wrote *NR*'s Richard Brookhiser in 1985. Brookhiser, "James Burnham, a Hard Man to Snooker," *NR* 37 (December 31, 1985): 62.

23. James Burnham (unsigned), "Which End of the Telescope," *NR* 3 (February 2, 1957): 100–101; ibid. (unsigned), "The Cradle and the Grave," *NR* 3 (March 2, 1957): 197–198; ibid., "TWW: When Thieves Fall Out," *NR* 2 (October 20, 1956): 17; ibid. (unsigned), "Keep the Pot Boiling," *NR* 4 (July 20, 1957): 76–77; ibid. (unsigned), "The Will to Be Deceived," *NR* 1 (April 4, 1956): 6; ibid., "TWW" (untitled), *NR* 1 (April 11, 1956): 24.

24. Buckley to author, May 11, 1992.

25. James Burnham, "TWW: Strategy at Dead Center," *NR* 2 (June 27, 1956): 7; ibid., "TWW: Maginot Line of the Air?" *NR* 2 (July 11, 1956): 15.

26. James Burnham (unsigned), "A Dream," *NR* 2 (July 11, 1956): 5. The italics are Burnham's. Ibid., "TWW: Mideastern Irrelevancies," *NR* 7 (August 30, 1958): 156; ibid., "The United States, the United Nations, and Africa," in Frank S. Meyer, *The African Nettle: Dilemmas of an Emerging Continent* (New York: John Day, 1965), 253.

27. James Burnham, *The War We Are In* (Arlington House: New Rochelle, N.Y., 1981), 15, 107. ibid., "PC. No Entangling Alliances," *NR* 30 (September 15, 1978): 1132.

28. Ibid., (unsigned), "Abstractions Kill the West," *NR* 2 (December 8, 1956): 6–7.

29. Ibid., "A Movie for Grownups," a review of the film *The Red and the Black, NR* 6 (May 28, 1958): 20–21.

30. William F. Buckley Jr., memorandum to the editors of *National Review* summarizing a

recent editorial conference, May 19, 1960, WFB, Box 10; Judis, *William F. Buckley,* 124; on distribution, unsigned *National Review* memorandum of July 11, 1961, WFB, Box 14; James Burnham to William D. Laurie, December 31, 1965, JB, Box 10; Burnham to Buckley, March 6, 1970, WFB, Box 165; Bridges to author, January 8, 1992.

31. Bridges to author, January 8, 1992; Buckley to author, January 20, 1992; William F. Buckley Jr., *NR* 39 (September 11, 1987): 32; Priscilla L. Buckley, *NR* 39 September 11, 1987): 52; Jeffrey Hart, *NR* 39 (September 11, 1987): 43; Jeffrey Hart to author, July 8, 1992; McFadden to author, April 22, 1993.

32. Priscilla L. Buckley, *NR* 39 (September 11, 1987): 53; Hart to author, July 8, 1992; Bridges to author, January 8, 1992; William A. Rusher to author, June 25, 1992; Buckley to author, January 20, 1992.

33. Bridges to author, January 8, 1992; James Burnham to Jerzy Giedroyc, August 29, 1952, JB, Box 9; Priscilla L. Buckley to author, March 31, 1992; Priscilla L. Buckley, *NR* 39 (September 11, 1987): 52; Judis, "Apolcalypse Now and Then," 35.

34. C. H. Simonds, *NR* 39 (September 11, 1987): 45; Brookhiser, "James Burnham: A Hard Man to Snooker," 62–63; "Notes and Asides," *NR* 49 (January 27, 1997): 20; Hart, *NR* 39 (September 11, 1987): 43.

35. Bridges to author, January 8, 1992; Priscilla L. Buckley, *NR* 39 (September 11, 1987): 52; C. H. Simonds, NR 39 (September 11, 1987): 45. Burnham always insisted on getting down to work without postponements or excuses. "The only way to write a book is to write it," Arthur Koestler once told a young writer. "This sounds like Hemingway, but it was actually James Burnham who once said it to me." Arthur Koestler and Cynthia Koestler, *Stranger on the Square,* ed. Harold Harris (New York: Random House, 1984), 90.

36. Bridges to author, January 8, 1992; Priscilla L. Buckley, *NR* 39 (September 11, 1987): 52.

37. Bridges to author, January 8, 1992.

38. Priscilla L. Buckley, *NR* 39 (September 11, 1987): 52; Willmoore Kendall quoted in Henry Regnery, *Memoirs of a Dissident Publisher* (New York: Harcourt, Brace, Jovanovich, 1979), 186; Hart, *NR* 39 (September 11, 1987): 43; Rusher to author, June 25, 1992; William R. Rusher to Kevin J. Smant, May 15, 1990. My thanks to Professor Smant for a copy of this letter.

39. Sobran, *NR* 39 (September 11, 1987): 46; *NR* 34 (September 1982): 1068; William F. Buckley Jr., *Overdrive* (Garden City, New York: Doubleday and Co., 1983), 232; ibid. to author, January 20, 1992; C.H. Simonds, *NR* 39 (September 11, 1987): 45; Richard Brookhiser, "Back to the Scratchpad," *The Intercollegiate Review* 29 (Fall 1993): 38–39; Hart, *NR* 39 (September 11, 1987): 44; Hart to author, July 8, 1992; Frances Bronson to author, January 20, 1992.

40. Linda Bridges, *NR* 39 (September 11, 1987): 47; Kevin Lynch, *NR* 39 (September 11, 1987): 49.

41. Burnham to Buckley, October 10, 1957, WFB, Box 2; ibid., memorandum on readability, November 24, 1957, WFB, Box 2. See also James Burnham to William F. Buckley Jr. and Priscilla L. Buckley, n.d., on *National Review*'s articles policy, JB, Box 10.

42. Burnham to Buckley, July 20, 1963, WFB, Box 26.

43. Ibid. to Buckley, n.d. (but probably 1961), on *NR*'s columns, JB, Box 10.

44. Burnham to Buckley, n.d. (but probably 1961) on *NR*'s columns, JB, Box 10.

45. Ibid. to Buckley, March 17, 1962, WFB, Box 20; ibid. to Buckley, April 4, 1959, WFB, Box 8.

46. Ibid. to Buckley, n.d. (but probably 1961), on *NR*'s columns, JB, Box 10; ibid. to Buckley, March 11, 1962, WFB, Box 20.

47. Ibid. to Buckley, December 27, 1966, WFB, Box 39. William F. Buckley Jr., *NR* 39 (September 11, 1987): 32; Burnham to Buckley, October 12, 1963, WFB, Box 26.

48. Burnham to Buckley, August 25, 1956, WFB, Box 2.

49. James Burnham and William S. Schlamm, "Should Conservatives Vote for Eisenhower-Nixon?" *NR* 2 (October 20, 1956): 12–14. The italics are Burnham's.

50. Burnham to Buckley, August 25, 1956, WFB, Box 2.

51. Ibid., October 4, 1956, WFB, Box 2. The italics are Burnham's; William F. Buckley Jr., "Reflections on Election Eve," *NR* 2 (November 3, 1956): 7.

52. Burnham to Buckley, February 7, 1960, WFB, Box 10; Burnham's memorandum to Buckley on *National Review*'s "strategic development" (undated, but probably May or June 1960), JB, Box 10; Gerhart Niemeyer's analysis of *National Review*, 1958, JB, Box 10.

53. William F. Buckley Jr. to William A. Rusher, June 21, 1960, WFB, Box 10; Buckley to author, January 20, 1992, May 11, 1992.

54. James Burnham, "TWW: As the Geographer Sees It," *NR* 1 (November 26, 1955): 20; ibid. (unsigned), "Stumbling Toward the Summit," *NR* 6 (August 16, 1958): 124–125.

55. Ibid., "Three Years of Tension," book review of *Violent Truce,* by Commander E.T. Hutchinson, USNR, *NR* 2 (August 11, 1956): 19; ibid. (unsigned), "Not Too Fast," *NR* 19 (June 13, 1967): 621; ibid. (unsigned), "Wings for Nasser?" *NR* 3 (March 16, 1957): 250; ibid. (unsigned), "Doves, Hawks, and Morality," *NR* 19 (July 11, 1967): 723; ibid. (unsigned), "Are Big Nations Always Bad?" *NR* 2 (October 20, 1956): 7; ibid. (unsigned), "Israel and the Elections," *NR* 1 (February 15, 1956): 5; ibid., "TWW: Fulcrum for a Lever," *NR* 10 (June 3, 1961): 344ff.; ibid., "TWW: The Loneliest Men," *NR* 8 (March 12, 1960): 164.

56. James Burnham (unsigned), "New Hero of the Left," *NR* 2 (September 22, 1956): 5; ibid. (unsigned), "Earthquake at Suez," *NR* 2 (August 11, 1956): 4–5; ibid. (unsigned), "Formula for Blackmail," *NR* 2 (October 27, 1956): 5–6; ibid. (unsigned), "The Shadow of Suez," *NR* 2 (August 18, 1956): 4–5; ibid. (unsigned), "The Cost of Dishonor," *NR* 2 (September 29, 1956): 4; ibid. (unsigned), "Abstractions Kill the West," *NR* 2 (December 8, 1956): 6. The italics are Burnham's.

57. James Burnham, "TWW: Signs and Portents," *NR* 3 (March 23, 1957): 284.

58. James Burnham (unsigned), "End of the Masquerade," *NR* 2 (July 18, 1956): 5; ibid. (unsigned), "The Kremlin and the Poles," *NR* 2 (November 3, 1956): 5; ibid., "The Problem of No. 1," *NR* 2 (October 13, 1956): 9–13.

59. Buckley to author, January 20, 1992; James Burnham (unsigned), "Double Standard," *NR* 2 (November 24, 1956): 5–6; ibid., "TWW: The Dialectics of Capitalist Suicide," *NR* 2 (December 1, 1956): 11; ibid. (unsigned), "Platonic Sorrow?" *NR* 2 (December 22, 1956): 4.

60. Ibid. (unsigned), "Are You There?" *NR* 2 (November 10, 1956): 5. ibid., *The War We Are In,* 15–16.

61. Ibid. (unsigned), "Next Stage in Eastern Europe," *NR* 2 (November 10, 1956): 6–7; ibid., "TWW: Adenauer's Move," *NR* 2 (November 17, 1956): 10; ibid., "TWW: Sighting the Target," *NR* 2 (December 29, 1956): 12. On the most basic Eisenhower axiom, ibid., "TWW: Definitions and Distinctions," *NR* 3 (March 9, 1957): 239. The italics are Burnham's.

62. Chamberlain, *A Life with the Printed Word,* 146; William F. Buckley Jr., memorandum to "Members of the Staff," June 15, 1956, WFB, Box 2.

63. William F. Buckley Jr. to William S. Schlamm and Suzanne La Follette, November 7, 1956. WFB, Box 2.

64. Burnham to Buckley, November 9, 1956, WFB, Box 2.

65. Buckley to Schlamm, December 26, 1956, WFB, Box 2.

66. William S. Schlamm, "Neutralization: What Next?" *NR* 3 (January 26, 1957): 81–82; L. Brent Bozell, "Mr. Burnham's Missing Sanctions," *NR* 3 (February 9, 1957): 127–129; Frank S. Meyer, "'New Ideas' or Old Truth," *NR* 3 (February 2, 1957): 107–108; Ralph de Toledano, letter to *NR* 3 (February 9, 1957); William F. Buckley Jr., "Neutralization: Liberal Assumptions," *NR* 3 (February 23, 1957): 178; James Burnham, "Liberation: What Next?" *NR* 3 (January 19, 1957): 61, 62, 71. The "concealed Communist" charge is quoted in Whittaker Chambers, *Odyssey of a Friend: Whittaker Chambers' Letters to William F. Buckley, Jr., 1954–1961* (New York: Putnam, 1970), 188, n. 56; for Chambers's endorsement, ibid., 190.

67. Burnham to Buckley, April 10, 1957, WFB, Box 2; Buckley to Burnham, n.d. (but probably April 11, 1957), JB, Box 2.

68. Buckley to Schlamm, April 28, 1957, WFB, Box 65; for the copy and note, JB, Box 5.

69. William S. Schlamm to William F. Buckley Jr., May 1, 1957, WFB, Box 65; Judis, *William F. Buckley,* 155–156; Buckley to Schlamm, May 2, 1957, Schlamm to Buckley, May 2, 1957, WFB, Box 65.

70. Buckley to Schlamm, May 2, 1957, WFB, Box 65; Schlamm to Buckley, May 2, 1957, WFB, Box 65.

71. Schlamm to Buckley, July 24, 1957, WFB, Box 65; William F. Buckley Jr. to Rose Flynn, December 9, 1968, WFB 50; ibid., August 1, 1974, WFB, Box 167; Chamberlain, *A Life with the Printed Word,* 146.

72. Buckley to La Follette, September 9, 1957, WFB, Box 2; Buckley to the Editors, January 8, 1959.

73. Buckley to author, January 20, 1992; Priscilla L. Buckley to author, March 31, 1992; Kevin Lynch, *NR* 39 (September 11, 1987): 49.

74. Buckley quoted in Burnham's *New York Times* obituary, *NYT,* July 30, 1987; William F. Buckley Jr., *NR* 39 (September 11, 1987): 32. McFadden to author, April 22, 1993; Buckley to Burnham, n.d. (but probably October 1958), JB, Box 5.

CHAPTER TEN

1. The Editors, "Why the South Must Prevail," *NR* 4 (August 24, 1957): 148–149. Alone among the editors, Brent Bozell rejected the majority position. L. Brent Bozell, "The Open Question," *NR* 4 (September 7, 1957): 209.

2. James Burnham (unsigned), "Segregation and Democracy," *NR* 1 (January 25, 1956): 5; ibid. (unsigned), "The Tank as Educator," *NR* 2 (September 22, 1956): 6; ibid. (unsigned), "Utopia and Civil Rights," *NR* 4 (August 3, 1957): 127–128; ibid. (unsigned), "The Court Views Its Handiwork," *NR* 4 (September 21, 1957): 245; ibid. (unsigned), "The Court Reaps Its Whirlwind," *NR* 6 (October 25, 1958): 262; ibid. (unsigned), "TW," paragraph on Mrs. Lee Lorch, *NR* 4 (October 19, 1957): 340.

3. Ibid. (unsigned), "Logical Steps Forward," *NR* 3 (April 6, 1957): 323–324; ibid. (unsigned), "Earl Warren: Ideologue," *NR* 2 (July 4, 1956): 5–6; ibid., "Why Not Investigate the Court," *NR* 4 (July 20, 1957): 83–85. But a few years later, when some conservatives called for the impeachment of Earl Warren, Burnham called the idea "silly." Ibid. (unsigned), "A Provocative Pair," *NR* 15 (December 17, 1963): 514.

4. Ibid. (unsigned), "Has Congress Abdicated?" *NR* 4 (June 29, 1957): 5; ibid. (unsigned), "The Number One Cartel," *NR* 1 (December 7, 1955): 5–6; ibid. (unsigned), "Who's Kidding Whom?" *NR* 3 (March 2, 1957): 199; ibid. (unsigned), "Something for Nothing?" *NR* 3 (June 1, 1957): 514; ibid. (unsigned), "Haloes over Miami," *NR* 3 (February 16, 1957): 148; ibid. (unsigned), "Three Bows to Mr. Meany," *NR* 2 (May 23, 1956): 7; ibid., *Congress and the American Tradition* (Chicago: Henry Regnery Co., 1959), 86.

5. Regnery to Burnham, August 3, 1954, HR, Box 11; Henry Regnery, *Memoirs of a Dissident Publisher* (New York: Harcourt, Brace, Jovanovich, 1979), 176; James Burnham (unsigned), "Has Congress Abdicated?" *NR* 4 (June 29, 1957): 6; Burnham to Regnery, March 30, 1955, HR, Box 11; ibid., May 12, 1955, HR, Box 11.

6. Burnham to Regnery, June 3, 1955, HR, Box 11.

7. Burnham, *Congress and the American Tradition*, 16–17, 38, 54, 57, 92, 108–109, 128–129, 255, 309.

8. Ibid., 137–138, 148, 159, 161, 174–175, 221, 240, 259, 278, 298.

9. Ibid., 175, 277, 281, 288–299, 301, 320, 321–322, 332, 333, 335–337, 340.

10. Ibid., 278, 337–338, 345–350.

11. Thus Burnham supported the U.S. military effort in Korea, as a necessary response to Soviet expansionism. But in *Congress and the American Tradition* he cited Truman's involvement of the United States in that war without a declaration of war by Congress as an example of the drift toward Caesarism. *Congress and the American Tradition*, 149.

12. In his 1996 State of the Union message, President Clinton announced (not credibly, some critics thought) that the era of "big government" was "over." But cabinet, congressional, and media liberals gave no sign of welcoming this news.

13. "The U.S. Congress. Is It a Victim of Democratism?" *Time* 73 (May 25, 1959): 15; Williard Edwards, "Atrophy on Capitol Hill," *CST*, June 28, 1959; Willmoore Kendall, *Willmoore Kendall Contra Mundum* (New Rochelle, N.Y.: Arlington House, 1971), 210–211.

14. Paul Simon, "The Survival of Congress," *The Christian Century* 76 (November 11, 1959): 1314; Robert K. Carr, "A Conservative's Argument for a Stronger Congress," *NYHT*, August 30, 1959; Lindsay Rogers, "Is Capitol Hill Losing Its Rightful Powers?" *NYT*, May 31, 1959; James Burnham's letter protesting Rogers' review and Rogers' reply, *NYT*, July 26, 1959; Buckley to Burnham, September 1, 1959, WFB, Box 8.

15. Ezra Pound to Henry Regnery, July 12, 1959, JB, Box 7.

16. James Burnham (unsigned), "General Khrushchev, USA," *NR* 6 (September 13, 1958): 173; ibid. (unsigned), "They Got Strauss," *NR* 6 (June 21, 1958): the italics are Burnham's. Ibid. (unsigned), "Day of No Return," *NR* 4 (November 9, 1957): 412; ibid. (unsigned), "The End of the Affair?" *NR* 5 (March 15, 1958): 245; ibid. (unsigned), "Mr. Eisenhower Falls to the Summit," *NR* 7 (August 15, 1959) 263, 265; ibid. (unsigned), "Triumphal March," *NR* 7 (September 12, 1959): 319.

17. Ibid. (unsigned), "On the Brink," *NR* 1 (February 1, 1956): 4; ibid. (unsigned), "Mr.

Dulles on Red China," *NR* 4 (July 13, 1957): 52–53; ibid. (unsigned), "Mr. Dulles Nods," *NR* 1 (March 14, 1956): 6; ibid. (unsigned), "The World and Mr. Dulles," *NR* 6 (February 28, 1959): 542; ibid., "TWW: The Dulles Record: An Appraisal," *NR* 7 (May 9, 1959): 44.

18. Ibid. (unsigned), "*We* Should Swoon for *Her?*" *NR* 2 (December 29, 1956): 5; ibid., "TWW: Pangs of Friendship," *NR* 1 (January 25, 1956): 21; ibid. (unsigned), "TW," *NR* 5 (June 14, 1958): 555–556.

19. Ibid. (unsigned), "How Fares the UN?" *NR* 1 (January 11, 1956): 5; ibid. (unsigned), "Meditations on a UN Fortnight," *NR* 9 (October 8, 1960): 199–200.

20. Ibid., "NATO on Its Birthday," *NR* 6 (April 11, 1959): 639; ibid. (unsigned), "The NATO Crisis," *NR* 8 (January 2, 1960): 6–7.

21. Ibid. (unsigned), "Watching the Watchers," *NR* 1 (February 1, 1956): 5–6; ibid. (unsigned), "CIA Flops Again," *NR* 2 (September 15, 1956): 6; ibid., "TWW: Too Much and Too Many," *NR* 6 (February 14, 1959): 520–522; Who Makes History?" *NR* 23 (November 19, 1971): 1286. Ibid., "The Case of the Missing U-2," *NR* 8 (May 21, 1960): 322–324; ibid. (unsigned), "Whose Secret," *NR* 1 (May 2, 1956): 8.

22. Ibid. (unsigned), "What Tune for the Voice?" *NR* 1 (January 4, 1956): 5.

23. Ibid., "TWW: Nuclear Madness," *NR* 6 (September 13, 1958): 179; ibid. (unsigned), "State, Couchant, As Usual," *NR* 9 (August 27, 1960): 103; ibid. (unsigned), "Post-Summit Parenthesis," *NR* 8 (June 4, 1960): 350; ibid., "TWW: Mr. Nixon's Bitter Harvest," *NR* 5 (May 31, 1958): 516; ibid., "TWW: To This Challenge, What Response?" *NR* 8 (July 2, 1960): 419.

24. Ibid., "TWW: The Lions Are Ousting the Foxes," *NR* 6 (November 8, 1958): 304; ibid., "TWW: The Changing Nature of War," *NR* 3 (April 20, 1957): 375; ibid., "TWW: Nuclear Facts and Pre-Nuclear Ideas," *NR* 3 (May 4, 1957): 424; ibid., "TWW: Lessons of Strike Back," *NR* 4 (October 19, 1957): 344; ibid., "TWW: Some Relevant Proposals," *NR* 3 (May 18, 1957); 471; ibid., "TWW: Reorganizing the Pentagon," *NR* 5 (April 19, 1958): 370. (The italics are Burnham's).

25. Ibid., "TWW: Some Relevant Proposals," *NR* 3 (May 18, 1957): 471; ibid. (unsigned), "Fresh Meat for Old Salts," *NR* 9 (December 17, 1960): 368.

26. Ibid. (unsigned), "Release Them from Their Cages," *NR* 8 (February 13, 1960): 94–95; ibid. (unsigned), "New Helmsman, Same Course," *NR* 7 (December 19, 1959) 543–544.

27. Ibid., "TWW: Are High-Yield Nuclear Weapons Obsolescent?" *NR* 6 (January 17, 1959): 452; ibid., "TWW: The Undecisive Weapon," *NR* 7 (July 4, 1959): 176; ibid., "TWW: Sticks and Stones Break Our Bones," *NR* 9 (September 10, 1960): 140; ibid. (unsigned), "The End of Massive Retaliation?" *NR* 7 (November 21, 1959): 480; ibid., "Horns of the Nuclear Dilemma," book review of *Nuclear Weapons and Foreign Policy,* by Henry A. Kissinger, *NR* 4 (August 31, 1957): 187–188.

28. Ibid. (unsigned), "The End of Massive Retaliation?" *NR* 7 (November 21, 1959): 480; ibid. (unsigned), "Oman Repeats a Lesson," *NR* 4 (August 31, 1957): 173; ibid., "TWW: Sticks and Stones Break Our Bones," *NR* 9 (September 10, 1960): 140; ibid., "TWW: What Targets for Polwar?" *NR* 9 (December 3, 1960): 340.

29. Ibid., "TWW: Is Disarmament Possible?" *NR* 8 (January 30, 1960): 67; ibid., "TWW: The Disarmament Industry," *NR* 4 (July 13, 1957): 59; ibid., "TWW: Summit This Summer?"

*NR* 5 (March 22, 1958): 274; ibid. (unsigned), "The Mindless Way," *NR* 8 (March 26, 1960): 189; ibid. (unsigned), "Communists Don't Negotiate," *NR* 7 (May 23, 1959): 69; ibid. (unsigned), "The Agenda Was Adopted Eighteenth Months Ago," *NR* 7 (June 6, 1959): 103.

30. Ibid. (unsigned), "How Sincere Was Khrushchev?" *NR* 7 (October 24, 1959): 413–414; ibid., "TWW: Who Wants Disarmament?" *NR* 5 (April 5, 1958): 321; ibid. (unsigned), "The Moon Is Up," *NR* 4 (October 19, 1957): 341; ibid., "TWW: Dialectic Doubled and Redoubled," *NR* 4 (December 28, 1957): 584; ibid., "TWW: Why Moscow Wants to Stop Nuclear Tests," *NR* 6 (July 19, 1958): 86.

31. Ibid., "TWW: Who Wants Disarmament?" *NR* 5 (April 5, 1958): 321; ibid., "TWW: Is Disarmament Possible?" *NR* 8 (January 30, 1960): 67; ibid. (unsigned), "A Test for Mr. Nixon," *NR* 9 (July 30, 1960): 38; ibid. (unsigned), "Needed: An Armament Conference," *NRB* 8 (April 16, 1960): 4.

32. Ibid., "TWW: What Price Arms," *NR* 5 (January 25, 1958): 80; ibid., "TWW: Notes on the Soviet Exhibition," *NR* 7 (August 1, 1959); 286; ibid., "TWW: What Happened to the Summit?" *NR* 8 (June 4, 1960): 356.

33. Ibid., "TWW: Softs, Hards, and American Strategy," *NR* 9 (December 7, 1960): 374. The italics are Burnham's.

34. Ibid., "TWW: To This Challenge, What Response?" *NR* 8 (July 2, 1960): 419; ibid., "TWW: What Kind of War?" *NR* 8 (April 9, 1960): 228; ibid., "TWW: The Quiet Kremlin," *NR* 2 (October 6, 1956): 14.

35. Frank Meyer memorandum to the editors of *National Review,* May 10, 1960, WFB, Box 10; Rusher to Buckley, October 10, 1960, WFB, Box 10.

36. James Burnham (unsigned), "What Is Rockefeller Up To?" *NR* 9 (July 30, 1960): 40; On Rockefeller's enthusiasm for polwar, Powers, *The Man Who Kept the Secrets,* 47; William F. Buckley Jr. to author, January 20, 1992.

37. Burnham to Buckley, October 9, 1960, WFB, Box 10.

38. Buckley to Burnham, October 11, 1960, WFB, Box 10.

39. James Burnham to Charles H. Percy, July 16, 1960. "Suggestions on foreign policy proposals for Republican Platform of 1960." JB, Box 7. The italics are Burnham's. Ibid., "TWW: After-Effects of Hungary," *NR* 4 (September 7, 1957): 204.

40. E.g., "Judged by individual qualities and accomplishments, Mao is today, and by far, the greatest exemplar of world communism," Burnham wrote in April 1956. "TWW: The Long Silence of Mao," *NR* 1 (April 18, 1956): 14.

41. Ibid., "TWW: The Main Line," *NR* 7 (November 7, 1959): 452.

42. James Burnham to Eugene Lyons, July 21, 1960, JB, Box 2; James Burnham, ed. "Bear and Dragon. What Is the Relation between Moscow and Peking?" supplement to *NR* 9 (November 5, 1960).

43. Burnham did not assign the Soviets a perfect score in the polwar contest. They too sometimes slipped up, he admitted. See, e.g. (unsigned), "TW," paragraph on the communist-run 8th World Youth Festival for Peace and Freedom, *NRB* 13 (September 4, 1962): 2.

44. Ibid., "TWW: Too Many, Too Soon," *NR* 9 (August 27, 1960): 107.

45. See, for example, ibid. (unsigned), "Crowded Darkness," *NR* 12 (May 22, 1962): 354–355.

46. Ibid., "TWW: Needed: A Blow," *NR* 10 (April 22, 1961): 248.

47. Ibid., "Does the ADA Run the New Frontier?" *NR* 14 (May 7, 1963): 355–364; ibid. (unsigned), "You Can't Make a Policy without Breaking Eggheads," *NR* 14 (February 26, 1963): 141–143; ibid. (unsigned), *NRB* 12 (April 3, 1962): 1.

48. James Burnham (unsigned), *NRB* 13 (October 16, 1962): 1; Burnham to James B. Burnham, October 15, 1961. My thanks to James B. Burnham for a copy of this letter.

49. James Burnham (unsigned), "God Save This Honorable Court," *NR* 13 (July 17, 1962): 10–12; ibid. (unsigned), "Thou Shalt Not Pray," *NR* 13 (July 31, 1962): 52.

50. Ibid., "TWW: The Polaris Line," *NR* 17 (February 9, 1965): 104; ibid., "TWW: The McNamara Line," *NR* 17 (February 9, 1965): 104; ibid. (unsigned), "Operation Bulldozer," *NR* 15 (December 31, 1963): 555–556; ibid., "TWW: The McNamara Legacy," *NR* 20 (April 9, 1968): 334. Defending McNamara was also enjoyable, Burnham told his son Jim, because "there is a certain amount of fun in shocking NR readers." Burnham to James B. Burnham, August 25, 1967. My thanks to James B. Burnham for a copy of this letter.

51. Ibid., "Why Do They Hate Robert Strange McNamara?" *NR* 18 (November 15, 1966): 1152–1161. Reader response, most of it negative, to this article was "one of the most monumental in our history," *National Review* reported. *NR* 19 (February 21, 1967): 169.

52. Ibid., "TWW: Wandering Planet's Course," *NR* 13 (August 28, 1962): 135.

53. Ibid., "TWW: The Foreign Policy of the Kennedy Administration," *NR* 15 (December 17, 1963): 522; ibid. to James B. Burnham, October 15, 1961.

54. Ibid., "TWW: On the Horns of Our Dilemma," *NR* 11 (October 21, 1961): 265.

55. Ibid. (unsigned), "The German Question: West," *NR* 6 (November 24, 1958): 326; ibid., "TWW: Watch Out for That Back Door," *NR* 8 (April 25, 1959): 12; ibid., "TWW: The Problem That Isn't There," *NR* 11 (July 29, 1961): 46.

56. Ibid. (unsigned), "Bankruptcy in Berlin," *NR* 11 (August 26, 1961): 112; ibid. (unsigned), "In Vino Veritas?" *NR* 11 (October 7, 1961): 222.

57. Ibid. (unsigned), "Closer and Closer," *NR* 11 (September 9, 1961): 149.

58. Burnham to James B. Burnham, October 2, 1961. My thanks to James B. Burnham for a copy of this letter.

59. Ibid. (unsigned), "Playing the Numbers," *NR* 14 March 26, 1963): 220–221; ibid. (unsigned), "He Who Says No," *NR* 15 (August 13, 1963): 88; ibid., "TWW: Who Is Conning Whom?" *NR* 15 (August 13, 1963): 101; ibid., "TWW: Questions Begging," *NR* 15 (August 27, 1963): 148; ibid. (unsigned), *NRB* 15 (August 20, 1963): 1; ibid., "TWW: The Yalta Strategy," *NR* 15 (September 24, 1963): 273.

60. Ibid., "TWW: West Europe: New Challenger," *NR* 6 (April 11, 1959): 643; ibid., "TWW: Future of the Common Market," *NR* 7 (September 26, 1959): 356; ibid., "TWW: Toward the Atlantic Common Market," *NR* 11 (November 18, 1961): 332. The italics are Burnham's. Ibid., "TWW: Common Market Dialectic," *NR* 13 (October 9, 1962): 262; ibid., "TWW: Conservatives and the Common Market," *NR* 11 (December 16, 1961): 409.

61. Ibid., *The War We Are In,* 173; ibid., "TWW: How Europe Sees It," *NR* 14 (June 4, 1963): 451; ibid., "TWW: Who Will Defend Europe?" *NR* 14 (March 12, 1963): 190; ibid. (unsigned), "The Land-Sea Split," *NRB* 14 (February 5, 1963): 3.

62. Ibid., "TWW: Sleeping Sentries," *NR* 10 (June 17, 1961): 377.

63. Ibid., "TWW: Depoliticization in Europe," *NR* 16 (December 15, 1964): 1096; ibid.,

"TWW: It's Your Ball, Chum," *NR* 18 (May 17, 1966): 457.

64. Ibid., "TWW: Depoliticization in Europe," *NR* 16 (December 15, 1964): 1096.

65. Ibid. (unsigned), "Stalemate Breaking Up?" *NR* 9 (December 31, 1960): 399.

66. Ibid. (unsigned), "Castro and the Communists," *NR* 6 (February 14, 1959): 510; ibid., "TWW: Is Fidel Castro a Communist?" *NR* 7 (August 15, 1959): 268; ibid. (unsigned), "Intervention: Eventually—Why Not Now?" *NR* 8 (April 23, 1960): 253–254.

67. Ibid., "TWW: Need: A Blow," *NR* 10 (April 22, 1961): 248. The italics are Burnham's.

68. Ibid. (unsigned), "Has Cuba Defeated Us?" *NR* 13 (September 25, 1962): 217–218; ibid. (unsigned), "Fire the Softs on Cuba!" *NRB* 13 (November 27, 1962): 2–3; ibid., "TWW: Is Cuba a Threat?" *NR* 13 (October 23, 1962): 306; ibid. (unsigned), "Action Stations?" *NR* 13 (November 6, 1962): 340–341. The italics are Burnham's.

69. Ibid. (unsigned), "Footnotes on Cuba," *NR* 13 (November 20, 1962): 380; ibid. (unsigned), "From the Jaws of Victory," *NR* 13 (December 4, 1962): 420.

70. Ibid., "TWW: The Strangling of the Cities," *NR* 12 (June 5, 1962): 406; ibid. (unsigned), "FLN in the School of Mao," *NR* 9 (July 16, 1960): 9–10.

71. James Burnham (unsigned), "A Look at the Leader," *NRB* 8 (April 30, 1960): 2–3; ibid. (unsigned), "Charles the Difficult," *NR* 7 (August 1, 1959): 232.

72. Ibid. (unsigned), "No Villains. No Hero," *NR* 8 (February 13, 1960): 96.

73. James Burnham to Jacques Soustelle, October 21, 1960, JB, Box 7.

74. James Burnham (unsigned), "Charles de Gaulle: Prisoner," *NR* 10 (May 6, 1961): 270–271.

75. Ibid., "TWW: La Triste France," *NR* 12 (February 27, 1962): 128; ibid., "TWW: France Is the Fulcrum," *NR* 12 (July 3, 1962): 476; ibid. (unsigned), "The Secret Army Terror," *NR* 12 (June 5, 1962): 395; cf. ibid. (unsigned), "The Melouza Massacre," *NR* 3 (June 15, 1957): 564.

76. Ibid. (unsigned), "Charles de Gaulle: Prisoner," *NR* 10 (May 6, 1961): 270–271; ibid., "TWW: Varus, Varus, Where Are My Legions?" *NR* 11 (October 17, 1961): 226; ibid. (unsigned), "The Pathetic Charles de Gaulle," *NRB* 12 (April 3, 1962): 2–3; ibid., "TWW: Put Up Or Shut Up, *NR* 16 (February 25, 1964): 150; ibid. (unsigned), "C'est Moi, de Gaulle," *NR* 16 (February 11, 1964): 97.

77. Ibid., *The War We Are In,* 19; ibid. (unsigned), "No Light on the Dark," *NR* 3 (April 20, 1957): 370; ibid., "TWW: What Is Ahead for Black Africa?" *NR* 9 (October 22, 1960): 240.

78. Ibid. (unsigned), "Jungle Taking Over," *NR* 11 (December 2, 1961): 366–367; ibid. (unsigned), "Grand Guignol," *NR* 9 (August 27, 1960): 101; ibid., "TWW: At the Crack of Khrushchev's Whip," *NR* 9 (November 5, 1960): 272; ibid., "TWW: Who Are the Mercenaries?" *NR* 19 (September 5, 1967): 959; ibid., "TWW: I Will Eat You," *NR* 16 (January 28, 1964): 60.

79. Ibid. (unsigned), "Let's Play Congo Roulette," *NRB* 8 (January 9, 1960): 3–4; ibid., "The United States, the United Nations, and Africa," Meyer, *The African Nettle,* 265.

80. Ibid., "TWW: The African Shambles," *NR* 10 (January 28, 1961): 45.

81. Ibid., *The War We Are In,* 19; ibid., "TWW: The African Shambles," *NR* 10 (January 28, 1961): 45; ibid., "TWW: The Loneliest Men," *NR* 8 (March 12, 1960): 164.

82. Ibid., "TWW: What Is Ahead for Black Africa?" *NR* 9 (October 22, 1960): 240; ibid. (unsigned), "Rx Africa: the Kennedy Doctrine," *NR* 10 (March 25, 1961): 170–171; ibid. (unsigned), *NRB* 14 (January 22, 1963): 1; ibid., "The United States, the United Nations,

and Africa," Meyer, *The African Nettle,* 250, 253; ibid. (unsigned), "The Secret Everyone Knows," *NR* 10 (April 22, 1961): 241.

83. Ibid., "Dialectic of American Foreign Policy" (a speech Burnham gave in South Africa in 1966), JB, Box 1; ibid., "TWW: Emancipation Proclamation," *NR* 13 (November 6, 1962): 348. In fact, the USSR had three votes in the General Assembly, those of Russia, the Ukraine, and Belorussia. Ibid. (unsigned), "Let's Get Not Going!" *NR* 9 (November 5, 1960): 268; ibid., "TWW: Ideology and Common Sense," *NR* 9 (October 8, 1960): 208; ibid. (unsigned), "U Thant Gets the Job," *NR* 13 (December 18, 1962): 463.

84. Ibid., "TWW: The Arithmetic of the United Nations," *NR* 8 (February 13, 1960): 99. The italics are Burnham's. Ibid., "TWW: The UN Chicken Home to Roost," *NR* 16 (February 11, 1964): 106; ibid., "TWW: What to Do about the UN," *NR* 12 (April 24, 1962): 284; ibid., "TWW: Why Do We Take It?" *NR* 17 (January 12, 1965): 20; ibid., "TWW: Emanicpation Proclamation," *NR* 13 (November 6, 1962): 348.

85. Ibid. (unsigned), "A Myth Dissolves," *NR* 17 (November 16, 1965): 1016–1017; ibid. (unsigned), "Let's Play Congo Roulette," *NRB* 8 (January 9, 1960): 4.

86. Ibid., "TWW: What Is Ahead for Black Africa?" *NR* 9 (October 22, 1960): 240.

87. Ibid., "TWW: The Revolution on the Mekong," *NR* 15 (November 19, 1963): 436.

88. Ibid., "TWW: The Southeast Asia Contradiction," *NR* 12 (March 13, 1962): 163; ibid. (unsigned), "TW," *NR* 12 (June 5, 1962): 393–394; ibid., "TWW: The Yalta Strategy," *NR* 15 (September 24, 1963): 237. The italics are Burnham's. On the danger awaiting U.S. ground forces in Asia, ibid., *Containment or Liberation?* 110.

89. One aspect of the Kennedy policy pleased Burnham: the development of methods for fighting guerrillas (Green Beret units, for example) of the kind that he himself had been urging for a decade. James Burnham (unsigned), "Take Off the Wraps," *NRB* 12 (May 1, 1962): 4.

90. James Burnham, "TWW: What Chance in Vietnam?" *NR* 15 (October 8, 1963): 304; ibid., "TWW: The Revolution on the Mekong," *NR* 15 (November 19, 1963): 436.

91. Ibid. (unsigned), "Once Again: No Win," *NR* 15 (December 3, 1963): 469.

92. Ibid. (unsigned), *NRB* 15 (December 10, 1963): 1.

CHAPTER ELEVEN

1. James Burnham to Sen. Thomas J. Dodd, February 18, 1962, JB, Box 6; ibid. to Buckley, March 17, 1962, WFB, Box 20.

2. Ibid. (unsigned), "The Dialogue Begins," *NR* 16 (January 28, 1964): 51; ibid., "TWW: Keep on the Premises," *NR* 12 (May 8, 1962): 324; ibid. (unsigned), "Bell for Round One," *NR* 16 (February 11, 1964): 94–95; ibid. (unsigned), "Some Proposals to a Goldwater Administration Concerning Foreign Affairs," *NR* 16 (July 14, 1964): 589–593.

3. Rusher to author, June 25, 1992; Rusher to Buckley, April 13, 1964, WFB, Box 30; Buckley to Rusher, April 14, 1964, WFB, Box 30; Priscilla L. Buckley to author, March 31, 1992.

4. Rusher to author, June 25, 1992; James Burnham (unsigned), "What New Hampshire Said," *NR* 16 (March 24, 1964): 219–220; ibid., "A Landslide View," *NR* 16 (April 21, 1964): 317–318; Priscilla L. Buckley to author, March 31, 1992. Buckley to the editors, January 8, 1964, WFB, Box 30.

5. James Burnham, "Goldwater as Omen," typescript, n.d., but probably written in August 1964, and possibly intended for publication in Britain, JB, Box 4.

6. Burnham to Buckley, February 27, 1964, WFB, Box 30.

7. Marcia Burnham to William F. Buckley Jr., February 22, 1964, WFB, Box 29; Burnham to Buckley, April 4, 1964, WFB, Box 30; ibid., "Bread, Butter and Abstractions," NR 16 (May 5, 1964): 350; ibid., "A Landslide View," NR 16 (April 21, 1964): 317–318.

8. James Burnham, "TWW: Must Conservatives Be Republicans?" NR 16 (December 1, 1964): 1052. "I am registered as an independent, and have no particular brief for the Republican Party," Burnham told a Connecticut newspaper in September 1964. "I write as a political analyst, not a partisan." WFB, Box 29.

9. Ibid. (unsigned), "Course for the Opposition," NR 19 (January 24, 1967): 69; ibid. (unsigned), "All Power to the Soviets," NR 17 (June 15, 1965) 494.

10. Ibid. (unsigned), "TW," NRB 17 (August 3, 1965): 2; ibid. (unsigned), NRB 20 (January 9, 1968): 1.

11. Ibid., "Rhetoric and Medicare," NR 17 (August 24, 1965): 720; William F. Rickenbacker, "Medicare and Mr. Burnham," NR 17 (October 5, 1965): 877.

12. James Burnham, "TWW: Why Not an Anti-Missile Missile?" NR 18 (June 14, 1966): 567; ibid., "TWW: The AMS Campaign," NR 19 (March 3, 1967): 238; ibid., "TWW: The Battle for Aerospace," NR 15 (October 22, 1963): 346; ibid., "TWW: Who Rules Aerospace..." NR 19 (November 28, 1967): 1317.

13. Ibid. (unsigned), "The Reluctant Leader," NR 21 (May 20, 1969): 477; ibid. (unsigned), "Everyman His Own Missile-Master," NR 21 (August 12, 1969): 791; ibid. (unsigned), "TW," NRB 21 (July 19, 1969): 105; ibid., "Load Your Missiles, Men," NR 21 (May 6, 1969): 427.

14. Priscilla L. Buckley to author, March 31, 1992; James B. Burnham to author, June 18, 1992; Tenth Anniversary Issue, NR 17 (November 30, 1965): 1123; Wills, Confessions of a Conservative, 11.

15. Buckley to author, May 11, 1992; Priscilla L. Buckley to author, March 31, 1992; Bridges to author, January 8, 1992.

16. Wills, Confessions of a Conservative, 46; William F. Rickenbacker to Kevin J. Smant, June 20, 1990. My thanks to Prof. Smant for a copy of this letter. Rusher to Buckley, January 24, 1959, WFB, Box 8; ibid., February 8, 1959, WFB, Box 8.

17. "Anxious" is Priscilla Buckley's word to describe Meyer's state of mind. Priscilla L. Buckley to author, March 31, 1992. Wills, Confessions of a Conservative, 46.

18. Rusher to author, June 25, 1992; Rusher to Smant, June 15, 1990. My thanks to Prof. Smant for a copy of this letter. Priscilla L. Buckley to author, March 31, 1992.

19. William F. Buckley Jr., Introduction to William F. Rickenbacker, The Fourth House: Collected Essays (New York: Walker and Co., 1971): xii–xiii.

20. Rusher to author, June 25, 1992; Priscilla L. Buckley to author, March 31, 1992; Bridges to author, January 8, 1992.

21. William F. Rickenbacker to Kevin J. Smant, May 3, 1990. The italics are Rickenbacker's. My thanks to Prof. Smant for a copy of this letter.

22. Rickenbacker used the word "injudicious" in his letter of May 3, 1990, to Kevin J. Smant. He later published the piece, "Castro Has Triumphed," in his collection of short political

pieces, *The Fourth House,* 19–21.

23. Priscilla Buckley to William F. Buckley Jr., February 7, 1963, WFB, Box 26.

24. Ibid., February 15, 1963, WFB, Box 26; Burnham to Buckley, March 3, 1963, WFB, Box 26; Rusher to Buckley, February 13, 1963, WFB, Box 26; ibid., February 19, 1963, WFB, Box 26.

25. Frank S. Meyer to William F. Buckley Jr., February 21, 1963, WFB, Box 26; Priscilla L. Buckley to Buckley, February 18, 1963, WFB, Box 26.

26. Priscilla L. Buckley to Buckley, February 7, 1963, Box 26.

27. Rickenbacker to Smant, May 3, 1990.

28. Burnham to Buckley, March 3, 1963, WFB, Box 26.

29. Ibid., March 23, 1963, WFB, Box 26.

30. "It must not be overlooked," Rickenbacker wrote to Kevin J. Smant, "that Jim married an heiress to the Pillsbury fortune [?] and was always concerned with the niceties of social standing, salon manners, unexceptionable opinions [!!], decorous dress and so on. He had raised Hell as a Trotskyite and now wanted to be accepted in the right circles. [In the 1950s and '60s, working at *National Review* was anything but a ticket to 'the right circles.'] He and Marcia lived in fashionable exurban Kent [hardly fashionable during their first decades there], and raised Norwich terriers [Burnham's dog was a German shepherd], pronounced, of course, Norritch." Rickenbacker to Smant, May 3, 1990.

31. Rickenbacker to Smant, May 3, 1990; ibid., June 20, 1990.

32. James Burnham (unsigned), "Stay Off the Summit," *NR* 7 (June 20, 1959): 133; Diggins, *Up from Communism,* 329.

33. Burnham to Buckley, July 19, 1958, WFB, Box 5; ibid. to James B. Burnham, November 19, 1961. My thanks to James B. Burnham for a copy of this letter. Burnham to Buckley, July 20, 1963, WFB, Box 26; ibid., "TWW: Get Us Out!" *NR* 17 (October 19, 1965): 927.

34. Rusher to Smant, May 15, 1990; Buckley to Schlamm, January 2, 1962, WFB, Box 65; William F. Buckley Jr., "In Search of Anti-Semitism," *NR* 43 (December 30, 1991): 37; The Editors, "The Question of Robert Welch," *NR* 12 (February 13, 1962): 84.

35. William A. Rusher to William F. Buckley Jr., James Burnham, William F. Rickenbacker, and Priscilla Buckley, January 30, 1962, WFB, Box 20; Frank S. Meyer to William F. Buckley Jr., James Burnham, William F. Rickenbacker, William A. Rusher, Priscilla L. Buckley, February 4, 1962. On choosing between liberalism and Birchism, Frank S. Meyer to author, c. 1961.

36. The Editors, "The John Birch Society and the Conservative Movement," *NR* 17 (October 19, 1965): 914–929 Record of the *National Review* editors meeting of August 25, 1965, WFB 35.

37. Burnham to Buckley, September 19, 1959, WFB, Box 8. The description of Burnham's lecturing is based on the author's recollection of a Burnham appearance at the University of Wisconsin in the early 1960s. The descriptions of Meyer, Buckley, and Rusher are also based on his recollections.

38. William F. Buckley Jr. to Marcia Burnham, December 15, 1959, WFB, Box 7.

39. James Burnham to James B. Burnham, October 15, 1961. The italics are James Burnham's.

40. Ibid., "A Too Sentimental Journey," *F* 3 (August 24, 1953): 855; ibid., *Containment or Liberation?* 171; on liberalism's failure to understand power, undated note in JB, Box 4; ibid. (unsigned), "Now You See It," *NR* 12 (April 10, 1962): 236; ibid. to James B. Burnham, October 15, 1961; ibid. (unsigned), "No Coals to Newcastle," *NR* 5 (January 25, 1958):

78. The italics are Burnham's.

41. Ibid., *Congress and the American Tradition,* 28–30, 60–61, 89–90, 118–123.

42. Regnery to Burnham, May 18, 1960, JB, Box 7. Maurice Falk Lecture Series announcement, JB, Box 4.

43. Edward T. Cone to author, March 24, 1992; Edward T. Cone to James Burnham, January 12, 1962, Gauss Seminar Records, Princeton University Archives (hereafter, GSR).

44. James Burnham to Edward T. Cone, January 20, 1962, GSR; Cone to Burnham, January 24, 1962, GSR; Cone to author, March 24, 1992.

45. For the seminar titles Burnham considered and the program and reading list for his seminar, JB, Box 4.

46. James Burnham to Cornelia N. Borgerhoff, Gauss Seminar secretary, January 18, 1963, GS; Erich [no last name is given, but probably Erich Kahler] to R. P. Blackmur, January 30, 1963, GSR; see also Burnham to Cone, January 11, 1963, GSR; [illegible] to R.P. Blackmur, February 27, 1963, GSR; Cone to author, March 24, 1992.

47. Cone to author, March 24, 1992; Burnham, *Suicide of the West,* 43; Wilmerding to author, March 12, 1992.

48. Wilmerding to author, March 12, 1992; Burnham, *Suicide of the West,* 185 n.; Cone to author, March 24, 1992.

49. Burnham, *Suicide of the West,* 14–17, 22, 24, 301.

50. Ibid., 44, 67.

51. Ibid., 51, 97–98, 118. 125–130, 185.

52. Ibid., 132, 145, 155.

53. Ibid., 190, 193, 196–197, 200–201.

54. Ibid., 32, 239–247.

55. Ibid., 31–32.

56. Ibid., 134–136, 228, 278–280, 281–283.

57. Ibid., 283.

58. Ibid., 140, 205, 217–218, 248, 288–291, 293. The italics are Burnham's.

59. Ibid., 287–288.

60. Ibid., 202–203, 284–286, 292–293.

61. Ibid., 297–305.

62. Edgar Ansel Mowrer, "The Will to Survive?" *NR* 16 (April 21, 1964): 321–323; Andrew Hacker, "Is Democracy Fatal in Large Doses?" *NYHT,* May 17, 1964; Harvey J. Bresler, "Seen from the Right," *NYT,* October 4, 1964; R. H. S. Crossman, "Radicals on the Right," *PR* 31 (Fall 1964): 559–564; Frank Altschul, "Time and the Political Tide," *SR* 47 (April 25, 1964): 36ff.

63. Irving Howe, "Bourbon on the Rocks," *New York Review of Books* (hereafter, *NYRB*) 2 (May 14, 1964): 12–13. Howe was the only ex-Trotskyist the author spoke with who showed hostility to Burnham.

64. For Burnham's fan mail, see JB, Box 4. *Suicide of the West* "became the gospel of conservative prophecy in the sixties," Burnham's first biographer, John P. Diggins, wrote in *Up from Communism,* 451. Leo Strauss to the John Day Co., March 10, 1964, JB, Box 7.

65. Irving Kristol to author, April 19, 1993; Czeslaw Milosz to James Burnham, undated, JB, Box 10.

66. Burnham, *Suicide of the West,* 132, 146. For caricature, see, for example, Burnham's summation of Walt W. Rostow's "stages of growth" thesis. Ibid., 304–305.

67. Ibid., 300–301.

68. E.g., ibid., *Congress and the American Tradition,* 298, 320.

69. Ibid., 111–118.

70. Neil McCaffrey to James Burnham, February 12, 1965, JB, Box 6; ibid., April 13, 1965, JB, Box 6.

71. Smant, *How Great the Triumph,* 117.

72. On Marcie Burnham, Joan Gates (Joseph Bryan's daughter and a friend of Marcie Burnham's) to author, November 28, 1990; Jane Wilmerding to author, March 12, 1992; James Burnham to Frank Shakespeare, May 1, 1969, JB, Box 4; André Willième to James Burnham, March 4, 1975, JB, Box 5.

73. Priscilla L. Buckley to author, March 31, 1992; Richard Brookhiser to author, July 13, 1998; Buckley to author, January 20, 1992; Burnham to James B. Burnham, October 15, 1961. Theodore W. Oppel, M.D., to James Burnham, July 20, 1964, JB, Box 1; ibid., December 1, 1968, JB, Box 1.

74. Schoenfeld to author, August 20, 1990.

75. Marcia Burnham to Gertrude [no last name is given], October 1965, WFB, Box 34

76. Burnham to Buckley, November 10, 1964, WFB, 29; for the water color, JB, Box 1.

77. JB, Box 1; Burnham to Buckley, April 16, 1966, WFB, Box 38.

78. H. L. Buurman, acting director of the Information Service of South Africa, to James Burnham, July 20, 1965, JB 8; James Burnham to H. L. Buurman, July 30, 1965, JB Box 8; James Burnham to the South African Institute of International Affairs, January 9, 1966, JB, Box 8.

79. James Burnham, "The Dialectic of American Foreign Policy," typescript, n.d. JB, Box 1.

80. Burnham to Buckley, November 26, 1966, WFB, Box 38; Priscilla L. Buckley, "South Africa: An Unsentimental Journey," *NR* 19 (January 10, 1967): 18–25; James Burnham, "TWW: The View from Outside," *NR* 19 (February 7, 1967): 128; John L. Burnham to author, July 30, 1995.

81. For one such trip to enable him to "get material for articles and editorials for NR,...do general background research, especially on political trends and public opinion,...[and] make contacts useful for NR, etc.," the magazine agreed to pay him 10¢ per mile for driving costs and $25.00 per diem for food and lodging. Buckley to Burnham, September 17, 1969, WFB, Box 61. James Burnham, "Notes by the Way. Tapping the Grass Roots," *NR* 19 (October 3, 1967): 1063.

82. James Burnham to James B. Burnham, August 25, 1967. My thanks to James B. Burnham for a copy of this letter. Burnham, "Notes by the Way," *NR* 19 (October 3, 1967): 1063–1064.

83. James Burnham, "TWW: Empire and Emperor," *NR* 20 (May 7, 1968): 443; ibid., "World's Fair with a Latin Beat," *NR* 20 (July 30, 1968): 761.

84. James Burnham, "Travels with Melrose. Notes from the Road," *NR* 21 (December 2, 1969): 1210–1211; Burnham to Buckley, October 1969, WFB, Box 61. The italics are Burnham's.

85. James Burnham, "Travels with Melrose. More Notes from the Road," *NR* 21 (December

16, 1969): 1269–1270.

86. Ibid., 1270; Burnham to Priscilla Buckley, October 28, 1969, WFB, Box 59.

87. Burnham, "Travels with Melrose. More Notes from the Road," *NR* 21 (December 16, 1969): 1270–1271. The italics are Burnham's.

Chapter Twelve

1. Burnham, "Travels with Melrose. More Notes from the Road," *NR* 21 (December 16, 1969): 1270–1271.

2. Ibid. (unsigned), *NRB* 16 (February 18, 1964): 1; ibid. (unsigned), "Equality Is a Two-Way Street," *NR* 16 (August 25, 1964): 710; ibid. (unsigned), "Civil Disobedience: An Imprimatur," *NR* 16 (December 29, 1964): 1135; ibid. (unsigned), "The Thin Blue Line," *NR* 16 (August 11, 1964): 679.

3. Ibid., "TWW: In the Camp of the Enemy," *NR* 18 (September 6, 1966): 876; ibid. (unsigned), "The Permanent Insurrection," *NR* 19 (August 8, 1967): 835, 837; ibid. (unsigned), *NRB* 20 (March 19, 1968): 40.

4. Ibid. (unsigned), "What Price Integration?" *NR* 19 (August 22, 1967): 887–888; ibid., "Travels with Melrose. More Notes from the Road," *NR* 21 (December 16, 1969): 1271; ibid., "PC: The Black Nation," *NR* 22 (October 20, 1970): 1102; ibid. (unsigned), *NRB* 18 (May 24, 1966): 1.

5. Ibid., "PC: Are American Blacks Natives?" *NR* 23 (February 9, 1971): 133.

6. Ibid. (unsigned), "The Permanent Insurrection," *NR* 19 (August 8, 1967): 835–837.

7. Ibid., "TWW: In the Camp of the Enemy," *NR* 18 (September 6, 1966): 876; ibid., "TWW: Prometheus Unbound," *NR* 20 (June 4, 1968): 539ff.; ibid., "TWW: The New Left and the Old," *NR* 20 (July 2, 1968): 645. On New Left efforts to undermine democracy and the danger terrorists posed to civilization, ibid., "TWW: Can Democracy Work?" *NR* 19 (May 16, 1967): 510; ibid. (unsigned), *NRB* 23 (May 11, 1971): 1; ibid., "PC: Party to Movement," *NR* 22 (September 22, 1970): 993.

8. Ibid., "How Democratic Is the United States?" JB, Box 1.

9. Ibid., "TWW: Sock It to Us, Herbert," *NR* 20 (November 19, 1968),: 1158. The italic's are Burnham's. Ibid.., "TWW: The Right to Riot," *NR* 20 (October 8, 1968): 1000; ibid., "TWW: The Pueblo Syndrome," *NR* 21 (May 20, 1969): 480; ibid. (unsigned), *NRB* 20 (May 28, 1968): 81; ibid., "PC: Barbarians at the Gates," *NR* 23 (May 18, 1971): 523; ibid., "Travels with Melrose. More Notes from the Road.," *NR* 21 (December 16, 1969): 1271; ibid., Afterward, *Suicide of the West* (New Rochelle, New York: Arlington House, 1975), 314.

10. Ibid. (unsigned), "Anything Goes," *NR* 20 (June 18, 1968): 592–593; ibid. (unsigned), *NRB* 20 (June 25, 1968): 97; ibid., "PC: Mandate Running Out," *NR* 22 (September 8, 1970): 937.

11. Ibid., "TW. The Right to Riot," *NR* 20 (October 8, 1968): 1000; ibid. (unsigned), "File and Forget," *NR* 21 (December 30, 1969): 1308.

12. Ibid. (unsigned), *NRB* 22 (March 31, 1970): 41; ibid. (unsigned), *NRB* 22 (September 1, 1970): 129; ibid., "PC: Parallel Power," *NR* 22 (November 3, 1970): 1153; ibid. (unsigned), "How to Stop Hijacking," *NR* 22 (September 22, 1970): 986.

13. Ibid., "Notes on Authority, Morality, and Power," *NR* 22 (December 1, 1970): 1289. This

article is Burnham's contribution to a *National Review* symposium called "After Liberalism, What?"

14. Burnham to Buckley, March 3, 1970, WFB, Box 165.

15. Ibid., "TWW: The New Left and the Right," *NR* 20 (July 16, 1968): 690. The italics are Burnham's.

16. James Burnham, "TWW: The Antidraft Movement," *NR* 19 (June 13, 1970): 629; Frank S. Meyer, "PH," *NR* 19 (July 11, 1967): 749.

17. James Burnham (unsigned), "Who Shall Be Master in the House?" *NR* 21 (May 6, 1969): 423–424; ibid. (unsigned), *NRB.* (May 14, 1968): 73; ibid. (unsigned), "Students, Teachers, Bureaucrats," *NR* 17 (March 23, 1965): 228–230; ibid., "Notes by the Way," *NR* 19 (October 17, 1967): 1138.

18. Tom McSloy letter in "Notes and Asides," *NR* 22 (April 7, 1970): 347–348, with an introductory note by William F. Buckley Jr.; Frank S. Meyer, *NR* 22 (April 7, 1970): 348–349; William A. Rusher, *NR* 22 (April 7, 1970): 351.

19. James Burnham, *NR* 22 (April 7, 1970): 350–351.

20. William F. Buckley Jr., *Cruising Speed* (New York: Bantam Books, 1972): 119.

21. Ibid., 41. Buckley to author, May 11, 1992.

22. James Burnham (unsigned), *NRB* 21 (September 2, 1969): 129.

23. Ibid., "TWW: Their Morals and Ours," *NR* 21 (August 13, 1969): 793.

24. Richard Cowan, "American Conservatives Should Revise Their Position on Marijuana," *NR* 24 (December 8, 1972): 1344–1346; James Burnham, "What's the Rush?" *NR* 24 (December 8, 1972): 1346–1348.

25. James Burnham, "TWW: Empire and Emperor," *NR* 20 (May 7, 1968): 443.

26. Ibid., "PC: Accounting for Tastes," *NR* 25 (March 30, 1973): 358; ibid., *Suicide of the West,* 254. For Burnham's quasi-determinism, see also, e.g., "[T]he established momentum of these bureaucratized mammoths is so formidable that few leaders, for all their bombast, really affect matters much one way or the other. Leviathan pretty much goes his own predestined way." Ibid. (unsigned), *NRB* 24 (January 28, 1972): 9.

27. Ibid., "TWW: Does Johnson Have a Foreign Policy?" *NR* 16 (March 10, 1964): 190; ibid. (unsigned), *NRB* 16 (February 4, 1964): 1; ibid. (unsigned), *NRB* 17 (January 19, 165): 1; ibid. (unsigned), *NRB* 19 (July 4, 1967): 1; ibid. (unsigned), "Not Right Now, Please," *NR* 19 (February 21, 1967): 180; ibid. (unsigned), "Non-Proliferation Gambit out of Moscow" *NR* 18 (Narch 22, 1966): 255.

28. Ibid. (unsigned), *NRB* 20 (August 6, 1968): 121; ibid., "TWW: Prisonhouse of Nations," *NR* 20 (September 10, 1968): 897; ibid. (unsigned), "For the Honor of the Games," *NR* 20 (September 24, 1968): 949; On *Kultura,* ibid. (unsigned), "They Will Not Be Silenced," *NR* 20 (September 24, 1968): 949–950. Burnham's fund appeal letter of October 10, 1968, can be found in JB, Box 9.

29. Ibid., "TWW: Their NLFs and Ours," *NR* 21 (April 8, 1969): 323; ibid. (unsigned), "Under the Knout," *NR* 20 (September 10, 1968): 893; ibid., "TWW: Notes on the Khrushchev Ouster," *NR* 16 (November 3, 1964): 952; ibid. (unsigned), *NRB* 18 (March 1, 1966): 1; ibid. to Hobart Lewis, May 22, 1966, JB, Box 9; ibid., "TWW: The More It Changes...," *NR* 21 (August 26, 1969): 845.

30. Ibid. (unsigned), "A Positive Proposal," *NR* 16 (December 1, 1964): 1045; Burnham

repeated the proposal six weeks later in a second editorial, entitled "Should We Bomb Red China's Bomb?" *NR* 17 (January 12, 1965): 8–9; ibid. (unsigned), "Should We Give Japan Some Bombs?" *NR* 17 (October 19, 1965): 910; ibid. (unsigned), "What to Do about Peking's Missile," *NR* 18 (November 15, 1966): 1144–1145; Ibid. (unsigned), "Writhing Dragon," *NR* 19 (January 24, 1967): 70–72; ibid. (unsigned), "A Puzzlement," *NR* 20 (July 30, 1968): 736; ibid., "TWW: Incredible, Yes. True?" *NR* 21 (July 15, 1969): 687.

31. Ibid., "TWW: Cuba in 1964," *NR* 16 (January 14, 1964): 16; The italics are Burnham's. Ibid. (unsigned), "Spawns of Castro," *NR* 17 (May 18, 1965): 405; ibid. (unsigned), *NRB* 17 (June 18, 1965): 1; ibid., "TWW: By Which People?" *NR* 17 (October 5, 1965): 864.

32. Ibid. (unsigned), "TW," *NR* 20 (July 16, 1968): 683. The italics are Burnham's.

33. Ibid., memorandum of a conversation of January 22, 1969, with Prince Juan Carlos, JB, Box 4.

34. Ibid., "What Are We Asking For?" *NR* 20 (October 22, 1968): 1062–1064; ibid., "TWW: Torture and the Colonels," *NR* 20 (December 31, 1968): 1313; ibid. (unsigned), "What to Do with the Colonels?" *NR* 21 (December 30, 1969): 1304.

35. Ibid., "The Greek Colonels as Bogeymen," *NYT,* November 30, 1971.

36. Ibid. (unsigned), *NRB* 17 (October 26, 1965): 1; ibid. (unsigned), "Fire Burn, Cauldron Bubble," *NR* 17 (November 30, 1965): 1062–1063; ibid. (unsigned), *NRB* 17 (December 21, 1965): 1.

37. Ibid., "TWW: Global Apartheid?" *NR* 18 (October 18, 1966): 1037; ibid., "TWW: Do Sanctions Work?" *NR* 19 (November 14, 1967): 1254.

38. Ibid. (unsigned), "Fire Burn, Cauldron Bubble," *NR* 17 (November 30, 1965): 1063; ibid. (unsigned), "Closing the Doors," *NR* 21 (June 17, 1969): 578.

39. Ibid. (unsigned), "Not Too Fast," *NR* 19 (June 13, 1967): 621–622.

40. Ibid. (unsigned), *NRB* 19 (June 20, 1967): 1.

41. Ibid., "TWW: The Battle and the War," *NR* 19 (June 27, 1967): 680.

42. *NR* staffer D[orothy] R[ea] to the Editors, July 27, 1967, WFB, Box 43.

43. Ibid., "TWW: Our Next Vietnam?" *NR* 21 (October 7, 1969): 1002; ibid., "PC: Stripped Down," *NR* 22 (July 28, 1970): 778. The italics are Burnham's.

44. Ibid., "What Americans Can Learn from Israel." Typescript of a speech dated April 1971 for delivery by Senator James L. Buckley to the American Zionist Association. JB, Box 5.

45. Ibid. (unsigned), *NRB* 19 (June 20, 1967): 1. The italics are Burnham's. Ibid., "TWW: Crumbling Line," *NR* 16 (June 16, 1964): 493; ibid., "TWW: The Chinese Bomb," *NR* 16 (October 20, 1964): 910.

46. Ibid. (unsigned), "What's a Little War between Friends?" *NR* 17 (September 7, 1965): 756–758; ibid., "TWW: The Perils of Under-Simplification," *NR* 16 (September 8, 1964): 766; ibid. (unsigned), *NRB* 17 (March 16, 1965): 1. The italics are Burnham's. Ibid. (unsigned), "TW," *NR* 16 (November 17, 1964): 998; ibid., "Some Proposals," *NR* 16 (July 14, 1964): 592.

47. Ibid., "TWW: Can the President Square the Circle?" *NR* 18 (February 8, 1966): 106; ibid., "TWW: What Price Liberalism?" *NR* 17 (June 1, 1965): 456; ibid. (unsigned), "A Problem of Communication," *NR* 17 (February 23, 1965): 136–137; ibid., "TWW: How Serious Is the President?" *NR* 17 (May 18, 1965): 412.

48. Ibid. (unsigned), "Vietnamese Schizophrenia," *NR* 16 (March 10, 1964): 186; ibid., "TWW: Bell for the Next Round," *NR* 17 (July 13, 1965): 583; ibid. (unsigned), "Close

to His Vest," *NR* 17 (August 10, 1965): 680; ibid., "TWW: Knots of Our Own Tying," *NR* 17 (September 7, 1965): 762; ibid., "TWW: Conventional Nuclear Weapons," *NR* 16 (September 22, 1964): 808; ibid. (unsigned), "Vietnam Potpourri," *NR* 18 (January 25, 1966): 56–57; ibid., "TWW: What Is the President Waiting For?" *NR* 18 (June 28, 1966): 613; ibid., "TWW: General Gavin's Trilemma," *NR* 18 (February 22, 1966): 151; James Burnham to James B. Burnham, February 19, 1966. My thanks to James B. Burnham for a copy of this letter.

49. Ibid., "TWW: What is the President Waiting For?" *NR* 18 (June 28, 1966): 613; ibid., "McNamara's Non-War," *NR* 19 (September 19, 1967): 1013.

50. Ibid., "TWW: Time for Some Answers," *NR* 20 (March 26, 1968): 282.

51. Ibid. (unsigned), "Public Opinion and Vietnam," *NR* 17 (August 10, 1965): 678; ibid., "TWW: Gulliver and the Vietniks," *NR* 17 (December 28, 1965): 1188; ibid., "TWW: Whose Peace?" *NR* 17 (June 29, 1965): 541.

52. Ibid. (unsigned), *NRB* 18 (March 29, 1966): 1; ibid., "TWW: The Weakest Front," *NR* 17 (June 15, 1965): 499.

53. Ibid. (unsigned), "The Collaborators," *NR* 13 (July 17, 1962): 8–10. The italics are Burnham's. Ibid. (unsigned), "Linus Pauling v. *National Review*," *NR* 17 (November 2, 1965): 962.

54. Burnham to Buckley, April 7, 1966, WFB, Box 38; ibid. to James B. Burnham, February 19, 1966; Priscilla Buckley to Buckley, March 15, 1966, WFB, Box 39; James B. Burnham to author, June 18, 1992; the Editors, *NR* 18 (May 3, 1966): 403.

55. Ibid., "TWW: Ground Slipping," *NR* 18 (May 31, 1966): 509; ibid., "TWW: Hanoi's Special Weapons System," *NR* 18 (August 9, 1966): 765; ibid. to James B. Burnham, February 19, 1966.

56. Ibid. (unsigned), "The Winding Line of LBJ," *NR* 18 (March 22, 1966): 250–252; ibid. (unsigned), *NRB* 19 (May 23, 1967): 1; ibid. (unsigned), *NRB* 19 (October 24, 1967): 1; ibid., "TWW: The War in Studio 7," *NR* 20 (February 27, 1968): 179.

57. Ibid., "TWW: An Honorable Peace," *NR* 20 (August 13, 1968): 792. The italics are Burnham's. Ibid., "TWW: Just Shut Your Eyes," *NR* 20 (May 21, 1968): 487.

58. Ibid., "TWW: The New Left and the Old," *NR* 20 (July 2, 1968): 645; Burnham to Macdonald, n.d., DM.

59. Rusher to author, June 25, 1992; Rusher to Buckley, February 15, 1968, WFB, Box 50; James Burnham (unsigned), *NRB* 20 (April 2, 1968): 50.

60. James Burnham (unsigned), *NRB* 18 (June 21, 1966): 1; ibid. (unsigned), *NRB* 20 (August 20, 1968): 1.

61. Ibid. (unsigned), *NRB* 19 (January 31, 1967): 1; ibid. (unsigned), *NRB* 19 (March 28, 1967): 1; ibid. (unsigned), "Crrrack!" *NR* 17 (November 30, 1965): 1062; ibid., "For the Editors," *NR* 17 (November 30, 1965): 1123.

62. Ibid. (unsigned), *NRB* 20 (April 2, 1968): 49; ibid. (unsigned), "The Fate of McCarthyism," *NR* 19 (December 26, 1967): 1416–1417; ibid. (unsigned), "Wallace Insurance," *NR* 20 (July 30, 1968): 733.

63. Ibid. (unsigned), "Wallace Insurance," *NR* 20 (July 30, 1968): 732–733; ibid. (unsigned), *NRB* 20 (August 20, 1968): 129; ibid. (unsigned), "The Unhappy Warrior," *NR* 20 (September 10, 1968): 889.

64. Ibid. (unsigned), "What Is Nixon's Policy?" *NR* 21 (February 25, 1969): 159; ibid. (unsigned), *NRB* 20 (December 24, 1968): 201; ibid. (unsigned), *NRB* 20 (November 26, 1968): 185.

65. James Burnham (unsigned), *NRB* 23 (January 19, 1971): 1.

66. Ibid., "How Guilty Are Guns?" *NR* 20 (July 2, 1968): 640–641.

67. Ibid. (unsigned), *NRB* 22 (January 20, 1970): 1.

68. Burnham to Buckley, February 6, 1970, WFB, Box 165. The italics are Burnham's. Ibid. to Buckley, February 13, 1970, WFB, Box 165; Buckley to Burnham, February 26, 1970, WFB, Box 165.

69. James Burnham (unsigned), "The Antipollution Squeeze," *NR* 22 (November 3, 1970): 1150; ibid. (unsigned), *NRB* 22 (October 27, 1970): 161; Burnham to Buckley, March 6, 1970, WFB, Box 165.

70. Ibid. (unsigned), "Are the Elephant and the Donkey Twins?" *NR* 23 (March 23, 1971): 303; ibid. (unsigned), "Applied Economics I," *NR* 22 (December 29, 1970): 1383–1384.

71. Ibid. (unsigned), "Pass the Barrel of Worms, Please," *NR* 23 (April 20, 1971): 413–414; ibid. (unsigned), "Do Losers Have to Pay Up?" *NR* 23 (June 29, 1971): 686–687.

72. Ibid. (unsigned), *NRB* 23 (August 31, 1971): 129; ibid., "PC: The More Things Change...," *NR* 23 (September 10, 1971): 977; ibid. (unsigned): "There's Also the Risk of Frostbite, Mr. President," *NR* 23 (September 10, 1971): 969–970; ibid. (unsigned), "An NEP of a Different Color," *NR* 23 (September 24, 1971): 1043.

73. Ibid. (unsigned), *NRB* 24 (January 14, 1972): 1; ibid. (unsigned), *NRB* 24 (November 3, 1972): 169.

74. Alan Reynolds to author, November 19, 1992. The reference is to free market economist Milton Friedman.

75. Kenneth Melvin, "Big Brother Is Dead Too," *NR* 21 (February 11, 1969): 116–118; Frank S. Meyer, "PH: Brave New World," *NR* 21 (February 25, 1969): 180.

76. James Burnham, "The Open Question. The Welfare Non-Issue," *NR* 21 (March 11, 1969): 222. The italics are Burnham's.

77. Burnham, "Travels with Melrose. More Notes from the Road," *NR* 21 (December 16, 1969): 1269. The italics are Burnham's.

78. Ibid., "TWW: What the SST Means," *NR* 22 (February 24, 1970): 194; ibid., "PC: To Fly or Not to Fly?" *NR* 22 (June 30, 1970): 666. The italics are Burnham's. Ibid. (unsigned), *NRB* 22 (December 22, 1970): 193; ibid., "PC: SST: Dead or Phoenix?" *NR* 23 (April 6, 1971): 361.

79. Burnham, "TWW: What the SST Means," *NR* 22 (February 24, 1970), 194; ibid. (unsigned), "Moon Men and Moon Robots," *NR* 23 (February 23, 1971): 184; ibid. (unsigned), *NRB* 21 (July 22, 1969): 105; ibid. (unsigned), "Zond Calling," *NR* 20 (October 8, 1968): 993–994; ibid. (unsigned), *NRB* 24 (December 29, 1972): 201.

80. Ibid., "TWW: Pollycassandra," *NR* 18 (July 26, 1966): 720.

81. Ibid., "PC: Who Makes History?" *NR* 23 (November 19, 1971): 1286.

## Chapter Thirteen

1. James Burnham (unsigned), "Secretary Dr. Kissinger," *NR* 25 (September 14, 1973): 983; ibid., "PC: The Kissinger Style," *NR* 26 (February 15, 1974): 191; ibid. (unsigned), *NRB*

26 (July 26, 1974): 105.

2. James B. Burnham to author, June 18, 1992.

3. James Burnham (unsigned), "Heavy, Heavy, Over His Head," *NR* 20 (December 31, 1968): 1306–1307; ibid. (unsigned), "What Now in Vietnam?" *NR* 21 (May 6, 1969): 418–421; ibid. (unsigned), "The Sands Are Running," *NR* 21 (July 29, 1969): 737.

4. Ibid., "TWW: Richard de Nixon, Gaullist?" *NR* 21 (April 22, 1969): 382; ibid., "PC: Stripped Down," *NR* 22 (July 28, 1970): 778. The italics are Burnham's. Ibid., "TWW: Heavy Grows the Crown," *NR* 22 (April 7, 1970): 353.

5. Ibid., "PC: The Great Retreat," *NR* 22 (December 15, 1970): 1339.

6. Buckley to Marcia Burnham, February 12, 1971, WFB, Box 165; James Burnham (unsigned), *NRB* 23 (March 30, 1971): 41; ibid. (unsigned), *NRB* 23 (March 2, 1971): 25; ibid. (unsigned), "The Situation along Route 9," *NRB* 23 (March 23, 1971): 298.

7. James Burnham, "PC: I'll Tell You a Secret," *NR* 24 (February 18, 1972): 144.

8. Ibid., "A War Distorted," *NYT,* April 5, 1971.

9. Ibid. (unsigned), "I Have in My Hand a Photostatic Copy of . . .," *NR* 23 (June 29, 1971): 686; ibid. (unsigned), *NRB* 23 (July 6, 1971): 97; ibid. (unsigned), "The Counter-Government and the Pentagon Papers," *NR* 23 (July 13, 1971): 740–741.

10. James Burnham, "PC: Is It All Over in Vietnam?" *NR* 24 (April 28, 1972): 449; ibid., "PC: I'll Tell You a Secret," *NR* 24 (February 18, 1972): 144.

11. Ibid. (unsigned), "The Twain Shall Meet," *NR* 23 (August 10, 1971): 845–847; ibid., "PC: Whose Serve?" *NR* 23 (May 4, 1971): 469.

12. Ibid., "PC: The Ant Hill," *NR* 23 (June 1, 1971): 580.

13. Ibid. (unsigned), "Close to Zero on Peiping," *NR* 11 (July 14, 1961): 6–7; ibid., "PC: How to Solve the China Problem," *NR* 23 (June 29, 1971): 693; ibid., "PC: The Question of Timing," *NR* 23 (December 17, 1971): 1401; ibid., "PC: Omelette à la Richard Nixon," *NR* 24 (March 17, 1972): 279.

14. Ibid., "PC: How to Solve the China Problem," *NR* 23 (June 19, 1971): 693; ibid. (unsigned), *NRB* 23 (August 17, 1971): 121; ibid. "PC: What Quid for What Quo?" *NR* 24 (March 3, 1972): 210.

15. Ibid. (unsigned), "China's UN Debut," *NR* 23 (December 3, 1971): 1336.

16. Ibid (unsigned), *NRB* 21 (March 4, 1969): 25.

17. James Burnham, "PC: The Heart of the Matter," *NR* 24 (June 23, 1972): 684; ibid., "PC: The Right to Leave," *NR* 23 (March 23, 1971): 306.

18. Ibid., "TWW: The Pueblo Syndrome," *NR* 21 (May 20, 1969): 480; ibid. (unsigned), *NRB* 23 (December 10, 1971): 185.

19. Ibid. (unsigned), "Cancel Those Reservations, Please," *NR* 24 (April 28, 1972): 441; ibid. (unsigned), *NRB* 24 (May 5, 1972): 65.

20. Ibid., "TWW: Games Nations Play," *NR* 21 (December 2, 1969): 1219; ibid. (unsigned), *NRB* 21 (April 1, 1969): 41; ibid., "PC: SALT on Whose Tail?" *NR* 24 (July 21, 1972): 788; ibid. (unsigned), *NRB* 23 (June 8, 1971): 81.

21. Ibid. (unsigned), "Bitter SALT," *NR* 26 (May 10, 1974): 515–516; ibid. (unsigned), *NRB,* 26 (June 16, 1972): 89; ibid., "PC: "Underkill?" *NR* 26 (July 7, 1972): 733. The italics are Burnham's. Ibid., "PC: Estimate of the Strategic Situation," *NR* 24 (October 26, 1973): 1172.

22. Ibid., "PC: Men Will Be Men," *NR* 23 (December 23, 1971): 1458; ibid., "PC: Pax

Atomica," *NR* 22 (July 14, 1970): 729; ibid., "TWW: Strike Three and Out," *NR* 21 (June 3, 1969): 551ff.

23. Ibid., "TWW: Strike Three and Out," *NR* 21 (June 3, 1969): 551ff.; ibid., "TWW: To Guard the Guards," *NR* (June 17, 1969): 583.

24. Ibid., "PC: Why Not Some Yankee Trading," *NR* 24 (September 15, 1972): 998; ibid., "PC: Doing Business with the Kremlin," *NR* 24 (November 24, 1972): 1292.

25. Ibid., "PC: The Second Generation," *NR* 22 (April 21, 1970): 400.

26. James B. Burnham to author, June 18, 1992; Craig Schiller notes Burnham's evolution on the Cold War in his memoir, *The (Guilty) Conscience of a Conservative* (New Rochelle, New York: Arlington House, 1978): 24–25.

27. Buckley to author, May 11, 1992; Judis, *William F. Buckley,* 329–330; Nash, *The Conservative Intellectual Movement in America,* 337; James Burnham et al., "A Declaration," *NR* 23 (August 10, 1971): 842. The italics are in the text. *NYT,* July 29, 1971.

28. The Editors, "In Re New Hampshire," *NR* 23 (December 31, 1971): 1449.

29. James Burnham, "The Ashbrook Candidacy," *NR* 24 (January 21, 1972): 21. Burnham wrote this editorial as a joint statement by the editors. Burnham to Buckley, February 7, 1972, WFB, Box 166.

30. James Burnham (unsigned), "Is McGovern a Populist?" *NR* 24 (July 7, 1972): 725.

31. Ibid. (unsigned), *NRB* 24 (October 6, 1972): 153; ibid., "Selective, Yes. Humanism, Maybe," *NR* 24 (May 12, 1972): 516.

32. Ibid., "PC: Vietnamization: Where Now?" *NR* 24 (September 29, 1972): 1078. Burnham also published this column as a *New York Times* op-ed piece under the title "Vietnam Policy: Who's on First?" *NYT,* September 25, 1972; the Editors, "Nixon-Agnew in 1972," *NR* 24 (September 1, 1972): 934; Smant, *How Great the Triumph,* 142; James Burnham (unsigned), *NRB* 24 (August 11, 1972): 121.

33. James Burnham, "View from the Mountain: Micro- v. Macro-Politics," *NR* 24 (September 1, 1972): 943; ibid. (unsigned), "A New Majority?" *NR* 24 (November 24, 1972): 1284–1286.

34. Ibid. (unsigned), "What Next?" *NR* 24 (November 24, 1972): 1287.

35. Ibid., "PC: Victory, Stalemate, Failure, Defeat?" *NR* 24 (December 22, 1972): 1394; ibid. (unsigned), "Penultimate Round?" *NR* 25 (January 5, 1973): 14; ibid., "PC: Drawing on His Last Reserves," *NR* 25 (January 19, 1973): 82.

36. Ibid. (unsigned), "TW." *NR* 25 (February 2, 1973): 128; ibid. (unsigned), *NRB* 25 (February 9, 1973): 9; ibid., "PC: Under Northern Eyes," *NR* 25 (March 3, 1973): 303.

37. Ibid. (unsigned), *NRB* 25 (March 9, 1973): 25.

38. Ibid. (unsigned), *NRB* 27 (January 24, 1975): 1; ibid. (unsigned), "Welcome," *NR* 27 (May 9, 1975): 490; ibid. (unsigned), "Next Round," *NR* 27 (April 25, 1975): 432–433.

39. Ibid., "PC: Go East, Old Man," *NR* 27 (January 31, 1975): 96; ibid., "PC: Reflections on Defeat," *NR* 27 (May 23, 1975): 549.

40. Ibid., "PC: It's All Your Fault," *NR* 27 (April 25, 1975): 441.

41. Ibid. (unsigned), "Richard at the Summit," *NR* 25 (July 6, 1973): 720; ibid. (unsigned), *NRB* 25 (September 21, 1973): 173; ibid., "Special Report: Communism or Communisms?" *NR* 26 (July 19, 1974): 814; ibid., "PC: Whatever Happened to Horsetrading?" *NR* 25 (August 31, 1973): 935; ibid. (unsigned), "Detente (Deletions)," *NR*

26 (August 2, 1974): 857; ibid. (unsigned), *NRB* 26 (July 12, 1974): 97.

42. Ibid. (unsigned), "Meditations on Watergate," *NR* 25 (February 2, 1973): 131–132.

43. Ibid. (unsigned), *NRB* 25 (February 23, 1973): 17; Rusher to Buckley, February 21, 1973, WFB, Box 166; James Burnham (unsigned), *NRB* 25 (April 6, 1973): 41.

44. James Burnham (unsigned), *NRB* 25 (January 26, 1973): 1.

45. Ibid. (unsigned), "A Line Must Be Drawn Somewhere," *NR* 25 (July 20, 1973): 770.

46. Ibid. (unsigned), *NRB* 25 (July 27, 1973): 105; ibid. (unsigned), *NRB* 25 (December 14, 1973): 185.

47. Ibid. (unsigned), *NRB* 25 (June 29, 1973): 89; ibid. (unsigned), *NRB* 27 (December 25, 1975): 193.

48. Ibid. (unsigned), "Where Do We Go from Here?" *NR* 25 (November 9, 1973): 1221; Burnham to James B. Burnham, November 8, 1973. My thanks to James B. Burnham for a copy of this letter.

49. Burnham to James B. Burnham, November 8, 1973; James L. Buckley, *If Men Were Angels: A View from the Senate* (New York: G.P. Putnam, 1975), 56–61; The [James L.] Buckley-Burnham statement, "Why Richard Nixon Should Resign the Presidency," also appeared in *NR* 26 (April 12, 1974): 413–415.

50. Ibid. (unsigned), "The Dimensions of Watergate," *NR* 26 (August 30, 1974): 967; ibid. (unsigned), *NRB* 26 (August 23, 1974): 121; ibid. (unsigned), *NRB* 26 (September 6, 1974): 129.

51. Burnham to James B. Burnham, November 8, 1973; ibid. (unsigned), *NRB* 25 (December 28, 1973): 193; ibid. (unsigned), "A Ford Foreign Policy," *NR* 26 (August 30, 1974): 959; Hart, *NR* 39 (September 11, 1987): 44; James Burnham (unsigned), *NRB* 26 (September 6, 1974): 129.

52. Ibid. (unsigned), "A Ford Foreign Policy," *NR* 26 (August 30, 1974): 959–960.

53. Ibid. (unsigned), *NRB* 27 (May 2, 1975): 57; ibid. (unsigned), *NRB* 27 (July 25, 1975): 105.

54. Ibid. (unsigned), "The Spirit of Helsinki," *NR* 27, 1975): 812–813; ibid. (unsigned), *NRB* 27 (July 11, 1975): 97; ibid., "PC: The Logic of Detente," *NR* 27 (August 15, 1975): 873; ibid., "Letter from France. Nostalgia and Strategy," *NR* 27 (November 7, 1975): 1229.

55. Ibid., "PC: The Dialectics of Detente," *NR* 27 (August 29, 1975): 928; ibid., "PC: The Detente Party," *NR* 29 (March 18, 1977): 318.

56. Burnham to Buckley, March 14, 1976, WFB, Box 105.

57. Ibid. (unsigned), *NRB* 28 (February 27, 1976): 17. ibid. (unsigned), *NRB* 27 (November 14, 1975): 169; ibid., "PC: What the Gaffe Said," *NR* 28 (November 26, 1976): 1283.

58. Ibid. (unsigned), *NRB* 28 (February 27, 1976): 17.

59. Ibid. (unsigned), *NRB* 28 (July 16, 1976): 97; ibid., review of *Henry Kissinger: The Anguish of Power,* by John G. Stoessinger, *NR* 29 (February 18, 1977): 221.

60. James Burnham, "TWW: Fulcrum for a Lever," *NR* 10 (June 3, 1961): 344ff.; ibid., *The War We Are In,* 130.

61. Ibid., "Communism Dalmatian Style," *NR* 26 (July 5, 1974): 755–757. The italics are Burnham's. Ibid., "Special Report: Communism or Communisms?" *NR* 26 (July 19, 1974): 813–814.

62. Ibid., "PC: The Alternatives to Democracy," *NR* 26 (October 25, 1974): 1223; ibid., "PC:

Distinctions within Distinctions," *NR* 27 (January 17, 1975): 27. Much of Burnham's argument in these columns anticipates the thesis advanced five years later by Jeane Kirkpatrick in her widely read article "Dictatorships and Double Standards," *Commentary* 68 (November 1979): 34–45.

63. William F. Buckley Jr. to author, May 11, 1992; Linda Bridges, *NR* 39 (September 11, 1987): 47.

64. James Burnham, "Special Report: Southern Perspectives," *NR* 26 (February 1, 1974): 131–132; ibid., "Notes from the Road. Carterland Impressions," *NR* 29 (April 15, 1977): 431–432.

65. Ibid., "Notes from the Road. Impressions by the Way," *NR* 29 (October 14, 1977): 1178.

66. Ibid., "Notes from the Road. Socialism with a Southern Face," *NR* 29 (September 30, 1977): 1102.

67. Ibid., "Notes from the Road. Carterland Impressions," *NR* 29 (April 15, 1977): 432; ibid., "Notes from the Road. An Autumn Miscellany," *NR* 30 (November 10, 1978): 1421.

68. Ibid. (unsigned), *NRB* 28 (July 30, 1976): 105.

69. Ibid., "PC: Roots of Terrorism," *NR* 26 (March 15, 1974): 311.

70. Ibid., *Suicide of the West,* 305–306; ibid. to Michelle Lapautre, February 2, 1976, JB, Box 4.

71. Ibid., Afterward, *Suicide of the West,* 1975 ed., 315–320.

72. Ibid., "PC: Through the Mirror," *NR* 29 (November 11, 1977): 1288.

73. Jean Raspail, *Le camp des saints* (Paris: Robert Laffont, 1973).

74. Hart to author, July 8, 1992; James Burnham, "Notes from the Road. Sorry Can't Make It," *NR* 29 (April 1, 1977): 377ff.; ibid., "PC: Not Serious," *NR* 29 (May 13, 1977): 540.

75. Ibid., "PC: Jimmy Carter Meets the World," *NR* 29 (January 21, 1977): 82; ibid, "Year-End Review. Jimmy Meets the World," *NR* 30 (February 3, 1978): 149.

76. Ibid. (unsigned), "Education of a President," *NR* 30 (June 23, 1978): 760–761.

77. Ibid., "Politics and Morality," *NR* 28 (November 11, 1976): 1226; see also ibid., "PC: Do-Good as Foreign Policy," *NR* 29 (January 7, 1977): 23; ibid. (unsigned), *NRB* 28 (June 4, 1976): 73.

78. Ibid., "PC: Salt – Verifiability = 0," *NR* 30 (January 6, 1978): 22; ibid. (unsigned), "Unsalted," *NR* 29 (October 14, 1977): 1158; ibid., "PC: Carter's Mideast Gamble," *NR* 30 (October 27, 1978): 1332.

79. Ibid. (unsigned), "Maybe a Surprise Ahead," *NR* 30 (April 14, 1978): 450–451; ibid. (unsigned), *NRB* 30 (July 28, 1978): 105; ibid., "PC: Watch Out! Here We Come!" *NR* 29 (June 10, 1977): 659.

80. Ibid., "Year-End Review. Jimmy Meets the World," *NR* 30 (February 3, 1978): 150; ibid., "PC: Tit for Tat," *NR* 30 (August 4, 1978): 943; ibid., "Morals, Arms, and Liberals," *NR* 29 (February 18, 1977): 194–195; ibid. (unsigned), "Ahoy, Comrades," *NR* 29 (April 29, 1977): 480–481.

81. Ibid., "PC: Which Mideast Problem?" *NR* 29 (December 23, 1977): 1480; ibid., "PC: A Separate Peace?" *NR* 30 (January 20, 1978): 81; ibid. (unsigned), *NRB* 30 (October 6, 1978): 145.

82. Ibid., "PC: Breaching the Great Wall," *NR* 30 (June 23, 1978): 768; ibid., "PC: Growing Pains," *NR* 30 (July 7, 1978): 823; Burnham to Buckley, July 2, 1978, WFB, Box 168; ibid., "PC: No Entangling Alliances," *NR* 30 (September 15, 1978): 1132.

83. Ibid. (unsigned), "Rough Sailing Ahead," *NR* 19 (July 11, 1967): 724–726; ibid., "TWW: The Rights of Large Nations," *NR* 19 (July 11, 1967): 730.

84. Ibid. (unsigned), "Treaties Can't Shoot," *NR* 29 (September 16, 1977): 1036; ibid., "PC: Panama or Taiwan?" *NR* 29 (September 16, 1977): 1043; ibid., "PC: The Canal: Interim Notes," *NR* 29 (November 25, 1977): 1354.

85. Ibid., "PC: Not Serious," *NR* 29 (May 13, 1977): 540.

86. Ibid., "PC: The President and the Bomb," *NR* 30 (May 12, 1978): 579.

## CHAPTER FOURTEEN

1. Bridges, *NR* 39 (September 11, 1987): 47.

2. Bridges to author, January 8, 1992.

3. Bridges, *NR* 39 (September 11, 1987): 48; James B. Burnham, *NR* 39 (September 11, 1987): 51.

4. Rusher to Buckley, February 21, 1973, WFB, Box 166; Buckley to Rusher, March 6, 1973, WFB, Box 166.

5. William A. Rusher to the Editors, March 27, 1975, WFB, Box 167; Judis, *William F. Buckley,* 349; Rusher to Buckley, April 10, 1975, WFB, Box 167.

6. Burnham to Buckley, September 5, 1976, JB, Box 5.

7. Buckley to Burnham [n.d., but probably late 1976], JB, Box 5; Priscilla L. Buckley, *NR* 39 (September 11, 1987): 53.

8. Hart to author, July 8, 1992.

9. Ibid.; Burnham to Buckley, March 7, 1978, WFB, Box 105; Priscilla L. Buckley, *NR* 39 (September 11, 1987): 53; Buckley, *Overdrive,* 233.

10. Burnham to Buckley, March 7, 1978, WFB, Box 168.

11. Ibid.; Priscilla L. Buckley, *NR* 39 (September 11, 1987): 54; Marcia Burnham to Buckley, December 17, 1978, WFB, Box 105.

12. George Greiner, M.D., "Medical Summary—James Burnham," January 3, 1983. My thanks to Tessa di Nicola for a copy of this report. Buckley, *Overdrive,* 234; Priscilla L. Buckley to author, March 31, 1992.

13. Greiner, "Medical Summary"; Marcia Burnham to Buckley, December 26, 1978, WFB, Box 105; Marcia Willième to Patricia Buckley (Mrs. William F. Buckley Jr.), n.d., but probably August 1979, WFB, 1981 January addition; Buckley, *Overdrive,* 233; Priscilla L. Buckley, *NR* 39 (September 11, 1987): 54.

14. Marcia Burnham to Buckley, December 26, 1978, WFB, Box 105; Mary Effie Burnham to author, May 16, 1992; Bridges to author, January 8, 1992; Priscilla L. Buckley to author, March 31, 1992.

15. Mary Effie Burnham to author, May 16, 1992; Marcia Burnham to Buckley, April 16, 1979, WFB, 1981 January edition; James B. Burnham to William F. Buckley Jr., August 24, 1979, WFB, 1981 January addition; Marcia Burnham to Sidney Hook, n.d., SHP, Box 8.

16. Marcia Burnham to Buckley, December 17, 1978, WFB, Box 105.

17. Mary Effie Burnham to author, May 16, 1992; Marcia Burnham to Buckley, March 8, 1979, WFB, 1981 January addition; Burnham to Buckley, November 22, 1980, WFB, 1982 September addition; Buckley to Burnham, February 18, 1981, WFB, 1983 October addi-

tion; James B. Burnham to Buckley, February 11, 1981, WFB, 1983 October addition.

18. James Burnham to Patricia Buckley, June 24, 1979, WFB, 1981 January addition; Priscilla L. Buckley, NR 39 (September 11, 1987): 54; Marcia Burnham to Buckley, May 7, 1981, WFB, 1983 October addition.

19. William F. Buckley Jr. NR 39 (September 11, 11987): 31; Marcia Burnham to Buckley, December 6, 1980, WFB, 1982 September addition; Buckley, Overdrive, 233.

20. Buckley, Overdrive, 184–185, 224, 233–234; Burnham to Buckley, December 5, 1981, WFB, 1984 March addition.

21. Marcia Willième to William F. Buckley Jr., November 13 [no year, but probably 1979], WFB, 1981 January addition.

22. Marcia Burnham to Buckley, March 8, 1981, WFB, 1983 October addition; ibid., December 26, 1978, WFB, Box 105. My thanks to Jane Wilmerding for showing me the photograph referred to.

23. Marcia Burnham to Buckley, December 26, 1978, WFB, Box 105.

24. Mary Effie Burnham to author, May 16, 1992; Bridges to author, January 8, 1992.

25. Burnham to Hook, August 30, 1982, SH, Box 8; Burnham in a letter to a granddaughter quoted by James B. Burnham, NR 39 (September 11, 1987): 51; Burnham to Buckley, August 24, 1982, WFB, 1984 March addition; James B. Burnham to Buckley, August 27, 1982, WFB, 1984 March addition.

26. Tessa di Nicola to author, May 18, 1992; Marcia Willième to James Burnham, January 24, 1983, JB, Box 5; William F. Buckley Jr. to Philip Burnham, December 9, 1982, WFB, 1984 March addition.

27. Di Nicola to author, May 18, 1992; Mary Effie Burnham to author, May 16, 1992.

28. Di Nicola to author, May 18, 1992; Buckley to Philip Burnham, December 9, 1982, WFB, 1984 March addition.

29. Yetta Shachtman to author, September 10, 1990; Norman Jacobs to author, December 27, 1990; Lilian Trowbridge to Sidney Hook, June 3, 1984, SH, Box 115.

30. Di Nicola to author, May 18, 1992; James B. Burnham, NR 39 (September 11, 1987): 51.

31. Burr to author, July 31, 1990; Di Nicola to author, May 18, 1992; Monica Burnham to author, June 27, 1992.

32. James Burnham's Medal of Freedom Citation, NR 39 (September 11, 1987): 53; Priscilla L. Buckley, "Medal of Freedom," NR 35 (April 1, 1983): 378–379; Trowbridge to Hook, June 3, 1984, SH, Box 115.

33. NYT, September 28, 1983; John Coyne, "Burnham and Borges," NR 36 (January 27, 1984): 44–46; James Burnham, "To See the World and Man," Chronicles of Culture 8 (April 1984): 4–5.

34. Di Nicola to author, May 18, 1992; Bridges to author, January 8, 1992; Priscilla L. Buckley to author, March 31, 1992; Mary Efle Burnham to author, May 16, 1992.

35. Di Nicola to author, May 18, 1992; Roger W. Moore, M.D., Sharon Hospital, "Discharge Summary for James Burnham," June 23, 1987. My thanks to Tessa di Nicola for a copy of this report; Priscilla L. Buckley, NR 39 (September 11, 1987): 54.

36. Priscilla L. Buckley to author, March 31, 1992; J. P. McFadden to author, April 22, 1993; Di Nicola to author, May 18, 1992.

37. NYT, July 30, 1987.

38. Bridges, *NR* 39 (September 11, 1987): 48. Speaking of the title of John P. Diggins's book *Up from Communism,* part of which concerned Burnham's political evolution, Burnham told Diggins that he had "always been anti-Communist Party," and that "perhaps there wasn't quite as much change as suggested by a simple communism to anti-communism dichotomy." Burnham to Diggins, October 24 (no year, but probably 1975), JPD.

39. Burnham, "PC. Panama or Taiwan?" *NR* 29 (September 16, 1977): 1043.

40. Ibid., *The Struggle for the World,* 10.

# *Index*

## A

Abern, Martin, 385n

Ackroyd, Peter, 375–77n

Ad Hoc Committee for Intellectual
  Freedom, 157

Adler, Mortimer, J., 392n

Africa, 262–63

Agnew, Spiro, 301

Algerian National Liberation Front (FLN),
  259–60

Altschul, Frank, 420n

Ambler, Humphrey, 375n

Ambrose, Stephen E., 393n

American Committee for Cultural
  Freedom (ACCF), 170–71, 188–89,
  191, 202

American Committee for the Defense of
  Leon Trotsky, 56

American Labor Party (ALP), 55

American Workers Party (AWP), 39,
  41–42; merger with CLA, 50–51

Americans for Democratic Action (ADA),
  190

Americans for Intellectual Freedom (AIF),
  158

Amery, Julian, 395n, 399n

Anderson, Kyrill M., 393n

Anisimov, F., 404n

antimissle defense, 272

Apert, Daniel, 400n

Apollo space program, 323–24

Arceniegas, German, 400n

Arnold, Thurman W., 93, 387n

Arzt, Arthur, 397n

Ashbrook, John, 334

*Atlantic Common Market,* 256

Atlas, James, 376n, 385n

## B

Baher, Harry W., 395n

Baker, John, 397n

Balliol College, Oxford, 15–16

Barnes, Harry Elmer, 394n

Barret, William, 386n, 397n, 406n

Baruch, Bernard, 389n

Bay of Pigs, 259

Beard, Charles, 392n

Beichman, 399–400n

Bell, Daniel, 401n, 405n

Berle, Adolf A., 378n, 387n, 402n

Berlin Wall, 255

Berman, Paul, 379n

Bern, Isador, 385n

Blackmur, R. P., 420n

Blansard, Brand, 375n

Bloom, Alexander, 398n

Blouet, Brian W., 392n

Blumenthal, Sidney, 396n

Boissonas, June, 379n

Bolshevism, 78

Bombay conference, the, 168

Bonapartism, 109

Bondy, François, 398–400n

Borgerhoff, Cornelia N., 420n

Bozell, L. Brent, 212, 408n, 411n

Braden, Thomas W., 400n

Brameld, Theodore B., 380n

Bresler, Harvey J., 420n

Bridges, Linda, 375n, 378n, 381n, 386n, 404–405n, 409n, 418n, 430–433n

Bronson, Frances, 409n

Brookhiser, Richard, 407–409n, 421n

Bryan III, Joseph, 13, 149, 151, 375n, 396n, 397n

Buckley, Christopher, 404n

Buckley, F. Reid, 407n

Buckley, James L., 341, 424n

Buckley, Priscilla, 223, 236, 374–75n, 379n, 381n, 404n, 409n, 411n, 417–419n, 421–422n, 425n, 431–432n

Buckley, William F. Buckley, Jr., 210–15, 235–37, 270, 276, 278–79, 373–74n, 381–82n, 404n, 406–408n, 410–411n, 414n, 417n, 419n, 421n, 423n, 427–432n

Budenz, Louis, 379n

Bulletin of the Atomic Scientists, 196

Bullitt, William C., 396n

Burnham, Claude, 1–3, 17, 373n

Burnham, David, 30, 377n, 382n

Burnham, James, 3, 244, 291, 297, 373–84n, 386–417n, 419–23n, 425–31n, 433n; on Africa, 262–63; on Algeria, 259; on arms limitation plan, 331; articles on Trotsky, 82; on Asia, 228, 231; Austrian proposal, 234; on Bolshevism, 78; break with Marxism, 86; and cancer, 366; at the Canterbury School, 5–6; on Caesarism, 174; on Carter, 351; and the CIA, 192, 245; on the civil rights movement, 297; and

communism, 38–39, 117–18, 123; on Congress, 241–42; and the Congress for Cultural Freedom, 159, 161–62, 165–66; conservatism, 205; constancy of, 367–69; on containment, 175; and cross-country travel, 138; on Cuba, 258; death of, 366–67; on a defensive policy, 124; eyesight of, 358; on education, 303; on Eisenhower, 228; on environmentalism, 319–20; first published work of, 4; on the Free Europe University, 172–73; and Hungary, 232–33; on India, 169; on Indochina, 265–66; as John West, 51; lectures of, 280; on liberalism, 281–85, 287; and libertarianism, 206; life at Balliol College, Oxford, 16–18; life at Princeton, 10, 14; and literary criticism, 75; and the Machiavellians, 107; and Marxism, 33–34, 36, 38, 52; on McCarthy, 186–88; on Medicare, 271; on the Middle East, 229; at National Review, 218, 220–21, 357; on NATO, 245; on neutralism, 257; and the New Deal, 73, 95; and the New International, 76–77; on the New Left, 299–301; at NYU, 21, 26; on an offensive policy, 124–25; and the OPC, 151–53; on Panama, 353; and Partisan Review, 76–77; on polwar, 174, 248; and the Presidential Medal of Freedom, 365; resignation from the ACCF, 202; resignation from NYU, 164; resignation from Partisan Review, 195; and the Richard M. Weaver Award for Scholarly Letters, 365; school writings of, 6–8; on segregation, 239; seminar at Princeton, 282–83; on Sino-Soviet split, 251; and the Socialist Party, 61–62; ; social life of, 68; on the space program, 253, 323; on Stalin, 57, 116, 118; strategy to end Soviet threat, 140–43; stroke of, 359; and the Symposium writings, 9, 27–28; his teaching, 23–25; and "Their Government" column, 43; travels of, 292–94; on Trotskyism, 88; and Ukraine, 155; on the United Nations,

264; on the United States, 126–27, 143–44; on the U.S. armed forces, 246–47; on U.S. foreign policy, 244–45, 254; on the United States Information Agency, 246; on the USSR, 64, 80, 115, 348–49; on Robert Welch, 278; on the West, 230, 348; during World War II, 104

Burnham, James B., 403–04n, 415n, 425n, 427–28n, 431–32n

Burnham, John L., 421n

Burnham, Marcia , 45–46, 69, 194, 359–61, 379n, 398n, 417n, 421n, 427n, 431–32n; death of, 362

Burnham, Mary Effie, 373n, 431–32n

Burnham, Mary Mae Gillis, 2, 373n

Burnham, Monica, 373n, 375n, 432n

Burnham, Philip, 432n

Burnham, Samuel T., 391n

Burnham's Laws, 355–56

Burr, Nelson R., 374–75n, 382n, 394, 432n

Buurman, H. L., 421n

## C

Caesarism, 174

Calverton, V. F., 387n

*Camp of the Saints, The,* 349–50

Camus, Albert, 391n

Canham, Erwin, D., 405n

Cannon, James Patrick, 47, 49, 61, 69, 73, 79, 81, 84, 379–85n

Carpenter, David, 395n

Carr, Robert K., 412n

Carter, Jimmy, 343–44, 350–54; foreign policy of, 351

Carter, Joe, 63, 381–82n; on the USSR, 63

Castro, Fidel, 259

Central Intelligence Agency (CIA), 149–50, 192, 245–46

centralism, 65

Chamberlain, John, 391n, 407n, 411n

Chamberlain, William Henry, 402n

Chambers, Whittaker, 382n, 411n

Chandler, Alfred D., Jr., 388n

China, 307–08, 328–30

*Christian Century,* 131

civil rights movement, 297

Cohn, Emma, 376n

Colby, Edward, 396n

Coleman, Peter, 398–400n

*Coming American Fascism, The,* 93

*Coming Defeat of Communism, The,* 140, 143, 145, 154; reviews of, 140, 143, 145

Common Market, 256

communism, 38–39

Communist League of America (CLA); aim of, 47–48, 50; merger with AWP, 50–52

Cone, Edward T., 282–83, 420n

*Congress and the American Tradition,* 240, 242; reviews of, 243

Congress for Cultural Freedom (CCF), 157, 159–61, 163; Indian branch of, 168–69

*Containment or Liberation?,* 175, 177, 179–80; reviews of, 178

Cooney, Terry A., 384n

Copeland, Miles, 404n

Corey, Lewis, 388n

Costello, Frank, 183–84

Cowan, Richard, 423n

Cowley, Malcom, 388n, 391n

Craig, Gordon A., 402n

Crossman, R. H. S., 420n

Crozier, Brian, 380n, 382n, 386n, 388n, 391n, 404n, 406n

Cuba, 258, 308

Cultural and Scientific Conference for World Peace, 157

Czapski, Józef, 134–35, 397–99n, 401–03n

Czechoslovakia, Soviet military intervention in, 306

## D

Dailey, John F., Jr., 401n

Davie, Michael, 375n

Davis, Robert Gorham, 405–06n

de Beauvoir, Simone, 391n

de Gaulle, Charles, 162, 259–62, 399n, 403n, 416n,

de Rougemont, Denis, 400n

de Tocqueville, Alexis, 402n
de Toledano, Ralph, 183–84, 394–95n,
    403n, 411n
della Francesca, Piero, 257
Democratic Ideals and Reality: A Study in the
    Politics of Reconstruction, 120
Dennis, Lawrence, 402n
détente, 328, 330, 332–33, 338, 342–43
Dewey, John, 56
di Nicola, Tessa, 363, 431–32n
Diem, Ngo Dinh, 266-267
Diggins, John P., 375n, 378n, 380n, 384n,
    386–88n, 390–93n, 396n, 408n,
    419–20n, 433n
Dobos–Gibarti, Louis, 400n
Dobriansky, Lev E., 387n, 391n, 394n,
    398n
Dodd, Martha, 32
Dodd, Thomas J., Sen., 417n
Doenecke, Justus, 393n
Dorrien, Gary, 398n
Dorrien, Gary, 407n
Drucker, Peter, 388n
Dutt, R. Palme, 380n


E


Eaton's Ranch, 4
Eckhart, Charlotte, 375n
Edwards, Williard, 405n, 412n
Ehlers, Peter, 403n
Eliot, T. S., 33
Elliott, Sir Ivo, 376n
Emmet, Christopher, 403n
Engineers and the Price System, The, 93
Evans, Medford, 195
Evans, Medgar, 405n


F


Falk, Maurice, 420n
Farrell, James T., 67, 381–83n, 386n, 391n
Fernandez, Ramon, 377n
Feuer, Lewis, S, 374n, 376–78n, 380n,
    387–89n, 390–91n, 405n
Firsov, Fridrikh Igorevich, 392n

Fischer, Louis, 395n
Fleming, Thomas, 407n
Flint, F. Cudworth, 11
Flynn, Rose, 411n
Folklore of Capitalism, The, 93
Ford, Gerald R., 341–43
Francis, Samuel T., 386n, 389n, 407n
Frank, Joseph, 376n
Free Europe University in Exile, 171–72
Freedom Manifesto, 165
freedom, 322
Freeman, 209–10
Freishman, Julius, 400–01n
Friedman, Joseph. See Carter, Joe
Friedman, Milton, 426n
Fugitt, Warren, G., 381n, 397–99n, 401n,
    404n


G


Galbraith, John Kenneth, 389n
Geltman, Emanuel, 379–83n, 385n
Gentry, George, 376n
George, Lawrence, 93, 387n
Gerth, Hans, 388n
Gilbert, James, 387n
Gillis, Finley, 2
Gillis, John L., 373n
Gillis, L. P., 373n
Gillis, Mary Mae. See Burnham, Mary
    Mae Gillis
Glotzer, Albert, 379n, 381–84n, 386n,
    388n, 408n
God and Man at Yale, 212
Goldwater, Barry M., 249, 269–71
Goodman, Cecilia, 399n
Gorachek, Vladimir, 398n
Gottfried, Paul, 407n
Greece, 309
Greenberg, Clement, 392n
Greiner, George, 431n


H


Hacker, Andrew, 420n
Hacker, Louis M., 387–88n, 390n

Haldane, J. B. S., 384n
Hamilton, Iain, 394n, 399n
Hamm, Suzanne Gillis, 373n, 379n
Hand, Francis, 398n
Hanson, Joseph, 388n
Harris, Harold, 409n
Hart, Jeffrey, 404n, 408–09n, 431n
Haynes John Earl, 392–93n
Heijenoort, Jean van, 383–84n
Helsinki Pact, 342
Hentoff Nat, 378n
Hersh, Burton, 396n, 399n, 404n
Hess, Karl, 183, 403n
Hessler, William H., 402n
Heyl, Bernard C., 390n
Hivnor, Robert, 389n
Holloway, David, 392n
Hook, Sidney, 157, 159, 374n–76n,
    378–81n, 383–88n, 390–95n,
    399–401n, 403n, 405–08n, 431–32n
Howe, Irving, 288–89, 379n, 381–83n,
    420n
Hsiang-kuang, Chou, 398n
Hulme, T.E., 390n
Humphrey, Hubert H., 318
Hungary, 232
Hunt, E. Howard, 396–97n, 404n, 407n
Hunt, John D., 373n


**I**

imperialism, 81
Independent Socialist league (ISL), 216
Indochina, 265–66
Institute of Pacific Relations (IPR),
    184–85
"Intellectuals in Retreat," 78–79
Internal Security Act, 155
International Day of Resistance to
    Dictatorship and War, 159
*Introduction to Philosophical Analysis,* 27, 33
Israel, 311–12

**J**

Jackson, C. D., 402n
Jacobs, Norman, 65, 376n, 379n, 382n,
    399n, 432n
Jelavich, Barbara, 392n, 396n
John Birch Society, 278
Jones, John, 375n–76n
Josephson, Matthew, 378n
Josselson, Michael, 158, 398–99n
Jovanovich, Harcourt Brace, 379n
Judis, John B., 403–04n, 406n
Jumonville, Neil, 378n


**K**

Kahn, Hannah D., 390n
Kaltenborn, H.V., 396n
Kelly, Wendy Anne, 392n
Kendall, Willmoore, 212, 408–09n, 412n
Kennan, George F., 395n, 403n
Kennedy, John F., 250, 252, 256
Kentucky's State Resort Park (SRP) sys-
    tem, 347
Kerner Commission, 298
Kilner, Colleen Browne, 373n
Kirk, Russell, 205, 406–08n
Kirkpatrick, Jeane, 430n
Kissinger, Henry A., Dr., 325–26, 394n
Klehr, Harvey, 392n
Kluger, Pearl, 401n
Koestler, Arthur, 135–36, 165–66, 394n,
    398–401n, 409n
Koestler, Cynthia, 409n
Koestler, Mamaine, 399n
Kohlberg, Albred, 394–95n
Kristol, Irving, 383n, 398n, 404n, 420n
Krock, Arthur., 395n


**L**

La Follette, Suzanne, 411n
Langer, Susan K., 376n
Lasky, Melvin, 158–59, 398–99n
Latham, Earl, 403n

Laurie, William D., 409n
Leary, William M., 396n
Lerner, Max, 394n
liberalism, 281, 286
Lightner, Katherine, 379n, 404n
Lightner, Marcia, See Burnham, Marcia
Lindsay, A. D., 389n
Livingston, Arthur, 390n
Loewith, Karl, 392n
Luce, Henry, 394n
Lynch, Kevin, 409n, 411n
Lyons, Eugene, 384n, 386n, 414n


## M


MacCormac, John, 390n
Macdonald, Dwight, 381–83n, 386n, 388n,
    391n, 425n
Macdonald, Nancy, 382n
Machajski, Waclaw, 92, 387n
Machiavellians, The, 105–06, 108–09,
    112–13; reviews of, 110–11
Mackinder, Halford, 119–21, 392n
Malraux, André, 136, 386n, 394–95n, 397n
managerial revolution, the, 92, 95, 97 98,
    103–04, 112–13
Managerial Revolution: What Is Happening in
    the World, The, 94; readers of, 99;
    reviews of, 97–98
managerialism, 95
Mandel, Benjamin, 405n
Mandler, Jean Paul, 374n
Mann, Gogo, 388n
Markmann, Charles Lam, 386n, 389n,
    390n, 407n
Marquis, Albert Nelson, 373n
Marxism, 33, 38, 77
Masani, Minoo, 392n, 400n
"Masterpieces of the Twentieth Century,"
    167
Maurras, Charles, 33, 377
Mayer, J. P., 402n
Mayers, Morris A., 394n
McAuliffe, Mary S., 401n
McCaffrey, Neil, 421n
McCarthy and His Enemies, 212
McCarthy, Joseph R., 185–86, 203

McCloskey, Burr, 385n
McFadden, J.P., 394n, 411n, 432n
McGovern, George, 334–35
McGrory, Mary, 390n, 398n,
McGuire, Francis P., 404n
McNamara, Robert S., 253
McNeill, William H., 375n
McSloy, Tom, 303, 423n
Means, Gardiner C., 378n, 387n
media, on the Watergate scandal, 340
Medicare, 271
Melvin, Kenneth, 321–22, 426n
Meyer, Frank S., 218, 222, 249, 273–76,
    279, 321–22, 408n, 411–12n, 414n,
    416–17n, 419n, 423n, 426n
Michels, Robert, 105, 108, 389–90n
Mills, C. Wright, 388n
Milosz, Czeslaw, 398n, 420n
Modern Corporation and Private Property, The,
    37, 93
Montague, Ludwell Lee, 403n
Mosca, Gaetano, 105–06, 108, 389–90n
Mowrer, Edgar Ansel, 420n
Moynihan, Daniel Patrick, 344
Murry, Middleton, 380n
Muste, A. J., 41, 378n
Myers, Constance Ashton, 378–80n, 384n


## N


Nabokov, Nicolas, 398–401n
Nash, George H., 396n, 406n
Nassau Literary Magazine, 12
National Committee for a Free Europe
    (NCFE), 171
National Review Bulletin, 237
National Review, 214, 217–18, 225; and the
    "Great Debate," 235; lawsuit against,
    315; twenty-fifth anniversary of, 361
National Security Council (NSC), 149
NATO (North Atlantic Treaty
    Organization), 137, 245
New International, 76–77
New Left, 299, 302
New Trier Echoes, 4
Niebuhr, Reinhold, 44, 351, 379n, 390n
Niemeyer, Gerhart, 410n

Nixon, Richard M., 250, 317, 319, 325–27, 333–36, 338–41; resignation of, 341
Nomad, Max, 387n
Norkela, Silva, 387n, 390n, 394n

## O

Office of Policy Coordination (OPC), 149–51, 163–64
Office of Strategic Services (OSS), 121
Olsen, Alex, 383n
Oppel, Theodore, W., 421n
Orwell , George, 132, 389n, 391n; on *The Managerial Revolution,* 98–99
O'Sullivan, John, 393n
O'Toole, G. J. A., 396n

## P

Palmer, Paul, 396n, 402n, 405n
Panama, issue of sovereignty, 353
Panken, Irving, 382n, 386n
Pareto, Vilfredo, 105, 108, 389n
*Partisan Review,* 76–77, 195
Patero, Vilfredo, 390n
Pauling, Linus, 315
Percy, Charles, 251, 414n
Pettee, George S., 395n
Philips, Robert, 389n
Phillips, Howard, 404n
Phillips, William, 383n, 387n, 394n, 400n, 406n
Poland, 232
Pollock, Dean Thomas, 400n, 404n
Pollock, Thomas Clark, 397n, 400n
polwar, 174, 176–77, 248
Pound, Ezra, 243, 412n
Powell, Anthony, 375n
Powers, Thomas, 396n, 404n
POWs, 336–37
Prescott, Orville, 392n, 394n
*Princeton Tiger,* 12
Princeton, 9

## Q

*Quill,* 6–7

## R

Rabinowitch, Eugene, 196–97
Rahv, Philip, 387n, 399n, 406n
Ranelagh, John, 396n
Rauh, Joseph L. Jr., 408n
Reagan, Ronald, 317–18, 365, 367
Regnery, Henry, 209, 213, 386n, 405–07n, 409n, 412n, 420n
Reston, James, 394–95n, 397n
*Resurrection,* 257
Reynolds, Alan, 426n
Rhodes, Richard, 393n
Rhodesia, 310
Rickenbacker, William F., 274–78, 417n, 419n
Riesman, David, 389n, 405n
Rizzi, Bruno, 92, 387n
Rockefeller, Nelson A., 250, 317, 342
Rolo, Charles J., 395n, 402n
Romanov, Eugene, 398n
Roosevelt, Eleanor, 281
Roskolenko, Harry, 380n, 382n
Rostow, Walt, W., 421n
Roth, J., 390n
Roth, Philip, 405n
Rousset, David, 159, 399n
Rovere, Richard H., 402n
Rusher, William A., 222, 274–76, 279, 356–57, 409–10n, 414n, 417–19n, 423n, 429n, 431n

## S

Safeguard anti-ballistic missile proposal, 272
Sayers, Dorothy L., 386n
Schiff, Sidney, 374–77n, 379n, 382n
Schiller, Craig, 407n
Schlamm, William S., 213–14, 234–36, 410–11n

Schlesinger, Arthur M., Jr., 189–91, 394n, 401n, 403–05n

Schwartz, Delmore, 389n

Secret Army Organization (OAS), 261

Secret War for the A-Bomb, The, 195–96

Seldin, Donald, 376n, 379n

Selzer, James V., 407n

Shachtman, Max, 47, 73, 146, 216, 378–86n, 396n, 408n

Shachtman, Yetta, 382–83n, 385n, 432n

Shakespeare, Frank, 421n

Shils, Edward A., 390n, 405n

Shoenfield, Oscar, 58, 376n, 379n, 381n

Siedel, Arno, 399n

Simonds, C.H, 386n, 409n

Simpson, Christopher, 396n

Six Day War, 311

Skirstein, Lincoln, 376–77n

Smant, Kevin, 407n, 409n, 418–19n

Smith, Lawrence A., 393n

Sobran, Joseph, 389n, 391n, 393n, 406n, 409n

Socialist Party (SP), 54–55, 60

Socialist Workers Party (SWP), American Section of the Fourth International, The, 66; split of, 85

Sonnenberg, Ben, 384n

Sorel, Georges, 106, 390n

Soustelle, Jacques, 260, 416n

Spender, Stephen, 398n, 400n

Spitz, David, 388n, 395n

Stalin, Joseph, 116

Stein, Sol, 405n

Steinhoff, William, 389n

Stern, Alfred K., 32

Sternberg, Charles, 398n

Stevenson, Adlai, E., 189–90

Stolberg, Ben, 384n

Strategic Arms Limitation Treaty (SALT), 331

Strausz-Hupé, Robert, 402n

Struggle for the World, The, 121–22, 128–30; reviews of, 131–32

Study of History, A, 120

Suez crisis, 230

Suicide of the West, 180, 284, 348; reviews of, 288–90

supersonic commercial aircraft (SST), 323

Symposium, 18, 44

**T**

Tata, J. R. D., 401n

Tate, Allen, 391n

This Our Exile, 30–31

Thompson, Ralph, 388n

Toynbee, Arnold, 119–20, 392n, 394n

Treverton, Gregory, 396n

Trilling, Diana, 383n, 406n

Trilling, Lionel, 406n

Troeder, Sylvain, 400n

Trotsky, Leon, 34–35, 49, 56, 61, 67, 79, 376n, 378–82n, 385–86n, 392n; articles on Burnham, 82–83; on the USSR, 64, 80

Trowbridge, Lilian, 376n, 432n

Truman doctrine, 131, 137

Truman, Harry, 394n

Tyson, Levering, 402n

**U**

Ukraine, 155

United Nations, 264

USSR, the, 64; the political nature of, 63

**V**

Veblen, Thorstein, 93, 387n, 389n

Venkataramami, M. S., 381n

Vietnam, 313–14, 316, 326–27, 336–38

**W**

Wacker, Jeanne, 376n, 393n, 401n

Waldorf Conference. See Cultural and Scientific Conference for World Peace

Walk, Alan, 379n

Walsh, Richard J., 405n

Warren, Earl, 412n

Watergate scandal, 339–40

Waugh, Evelyn, 375n

Weatherwall, Clira, 383n

Web of Subversion: Underground Networks in

*the U.S. Government, The,* 198–99; reviews of, 200

Weber, Eugen, 377n, 381n, 389n

Welch, Robert, 278–79

Wells, H. G., 389n

West, John, 380n, 383n

Westoby, Adam, 387n

Weyl, Nathaniel, 403n

*What Europe Thinks of America,* 195

Wheelwright, Philip E., 11, 22–23, 26, 375–76n, 378n, 391n

Will, George F., 357

Williams, Frederick, W., 397n

Willième, André, 421n

Willième, Marcia, 431–32n

Wills, Garry, 407n

Wilmerding, Jane, 375n, 377n, 379n, 382n, 386n, 390n, 394n, 404–05n, 420–21n, 432n

Wilmerding, Lucius, 374n, 404n

Winsor, Curtin, 374n, 382n, 394n

Wisner, Frank, 150–51, 396n

Woodstock, 304

Workers Party of the United States (WPUS), 51, 53–54

Workers Party (WP), 85

World War II, 104

**Y**

Young Americans for Freedom (YAF), 269

Yugoslavia, 344–45